Eastern Europe

Fodor's Travel Publications, Inc.
New York & London

ISBN 0-679-01618–X

Fodor's Eastern Europe

Editor: Richard Moore
Area Editors: Victoria Clark, George Hamilton, Sylvie Nickels, Witek Radwanski
Contributors: Robert Brown, Leslie Gardiner, George Maddocks, George Schöpflin
Drawings: Lorraine Calaora
Maps: C.W. Bacon, Jeremy Ford, Alex Murphy, Brian Stimpson, Swanston Graphics, Bryan Woodfield
Cover Photograph: Michael Spring

Cover Design: Vignelli Associates

MANUFACTURED IN THE UNITED STATES OF AMERICA
10 9 8 7 6 5 4 3 2 1

CONTENTS

PLANNING YOUR TRIP

How to Go, 11; Tours, 12; When to Go, 13; Travel Documents, 13; Insurance, 14; Money, 15; What to Take, 15; Student and Youth Travel, 16; Handicapped Travel, 16; Utilities, 16; Photography, 17; Getting to Eastern Europe, 17; Arriving in Eastern Europe, 23; Getting Around Eastern Europe, 23; Leaving Eastern Europe, 26.

BULGARIA

CZECHOSLOVAKIA

EAST GERMANY

CONTENTS

HUNGARY

POLAND

ROMANIA

FOREWORD

There are not all that many voyages of genuine discovery left to be made in the course of taking a vacation. It is all the more exciting, then, to find a region that lies just beyond our own everyday life, touching it at many points; a region that was once an integral part of the Europe we know, part of its culture, thought, art and way of life, and yet never completely so; a region that for centuries lay halfway between the Occident and the Orient, sharing in the fascinations of both while preserving its own deeply ingrained character. This region we have called Eastern Europe and it includes Bulgaria, Czechoslovakia, Hungary, Poland, East Germany, and Romania, an area that stretched from the old Europe down into the Balkans.

The very nature of its isolation from the Western world over the last few decades has meant that Eastern Europe has preserved many of the qualities of charm and tradition that materialism and a more frenzied pace of life have to a large extent made things of the past in Western Europe. But, as we say elsewhere in this book, this sundering of Europe is a very recent phenomenon when looked at from the point of view of history. What are four decades of separation when they have been preceded by two thousand years and more of close correspondence? During those long, vibrant centuries Eastern Europe accumulated an enormously rich cultural heritage which can be seen today not only in the great Baroque cities, but also in the churches, monasteries and castles that rise proudly throughout the countryside.

And what a countryside! The huge area covered by this book contains some of the most lovely and spectacular natural features anywhere on earth. Mountain ranges that thrust skyward between Poland and Czechoslovakia, providing summer outings and winter sports to rival anything in Switzerland; spas and beaches to delight everyone from a rheumatic sufferer to the most active skin diver; river trips through ancient landscapes, with spacious meadows for camping.

A visit to Eastern Europe is not only fascinating for its discovery of the works of art and nature, rich and varied though those are, it can also be fascinating for its revelation of the people and their way of life, especially if such a journey can take in more than one country and thus provide the chance to compare life in neighboring lands.

And, while we are on the subject of "meeting the people," some of our readers have asked us about rumors that conversations with visitors to Eastern Europe are reported to the authorities. The situation varies widely across the six countries we cover, in this regard as in all others. In Romania there is a very strict law that all contacts with non-Romanians must be reported, and that applies as much to contacts with Soviet citizens as it does to contacts with Americans. In Bulgaria and Czechoslovakia contact with foreigners is actively discouraged. In East Germany, Hungary, and Poland there are very few problems, the position being virtually as it is in the West. Courtesy and commonsense should rule in this situation—avoid politics if you possibly can, and have nothing whatever to do with the black market.

* * *

We have been greatly assisted in our revision of this book by many people, both here and in the six countries concerned. We would like to thank especially: Mr. A. Atanasov of the State Committee for Tourism in Bulgaria and his staff, and Mr. L. Hadjistoyanov, Director of the Bulgarian National Tourist Office and his staff in London; Mr. Václav Dvořák, Director of Foreign Tourism of Čedok in Prague and his staff, and Mr. Miloslav Holub, Director of Čedok, the Czechoslovakia Travel Bureau, in London and his staff; Mr.Gabor Tarr, the Managing Director of Danube Travel, the London representative of IBUSZ, the official Hungarian Travel Bureau, for his valuable interest and assistance over a number of years; the Corvina Press in Budapest and its excellent publications for much valuable information and in particular Mr. László Boros, former Editor-in-Chief of Corvina, for his constant help and interest; the staff of Polorbis in London; Mr. Nicolae Paduraru of the Ministry of Tourism in Bucharest and the Director of the Romanian National Tourist Office in London, for their support.

We would like to make it very clear that any opinions expressed in this book are those of the editors and can in no way be attributed to any of the above mentioned people, for whose courtesy and kindness we are deeply grateful.

* * *

While every care has been taken to assure the accuracy of the information in this guide, the passage of time will always bring change, and consequently the publisher cannot accept responsibility for errors that may occur.

All prices and opening times quoted in this guide are based on information available to us at press time. Hours and admission fees may change, however, and the prudent traveler will avoid inconvenience by calling ahead.

Fodor's wants to hear about your travel experiences, both pleasant and unpleasant. When a hotel or restaurant fails to live up to its billing, let us know and we will investigate the complaint and revise our entries where the facts warrant it.

Send your letters to the editors of Fodor's Travel Publications, 201 East 50th Street, New York, NY 10022, or to Fodor's Travel Publications, 30–32 Bedford Square, London WC1B 3SG, England.

INTRODUCING

EASTERN EUROPE

Similarities and Differences

by
GEORGE SCHÖPFLIN

George Schöpflin is a specialist writer on East European affairs who teaches East European politics at the London School of Economics and the School of Slavonic and East European Studies. He visits the area regularly and has published widely on East European topics.

The first and in many ways rather obvious point that has to be understood about Eastern Europe is that despite all the myths that have attached themselves to the countries of the area, it is a part of Europe. But it is Europe with a difference. To look at, many of the cities of Poland or Czechoslovakia or Hungary look remarkably like cities in Austria or Germany. The people, too, at first sight seem to be very similar to their Western neighbors. Their concerns are alike, their hopes for a reasonable life, with an ample supply of consumer goods and ways of spending their free time would be recognizable to people in other parts of Europe. The differences lie under the surface. They may even remain there all the time and not trouble the casual visitor.

1

But sometimes they emerge to startle the unwary by some unexpected response. A sensitivity may be aroused through some quite innocent remark, a community's pride may be challenged and it may take a good bit of tact to smooth things over again. Or the visitor may find himself or herself wondering about the East Europeans' ignorance or very partial knowledge about something which might be a commonplace at home. Perhaps the most important of these underlying differences is how the East Europeans see themselves in relation to the West. This is a complex process and varies in time and place. But in general, especially among the young, there is a sense of inferiority, of lagging behind, of something close to a belief in a kind of mythical West which just does not exist—it is too good to be true—but towards which the East Europeans aspire. In this sense, they feel they have missed out on something.

One sociological survey taken in an East European country showed that people's "ideal" country was Sweden, the Sweden of a high standard of living, social tranquillity and democracy. But they were largely uninterested in the fact that the Swedes work much harder than most East Europeans and that the "Swedish myth" contains as much legend as reality. This sense of cultural, scientific and intellectual inferiority in Eastern Europe is coupled with something that can come close to arrogance—the idea that certain things about the world are known only to East Europeans, that East Europeans have a special mission in the world to make the benighted West aware of this. The role of Russia and the reality of Soviet power—as the East Europeans see this power—is nowadays the central such belief. But there are others. The Poles, for one, hold firmly to notions of honor that most Westerners reject as hopelessly old fashioned, straight out of 19th century romances.

Eastern Myths, Western Myths

Then, there are also the myths that Westerners live by. Two are significant. One is that Eastern Europe is different, romantic or just completely remote. Neville Chamberlain's comment about Czechoslovakia in 1938 is still applied by some people—"a far away country of which we know nothing"—even if that comment contained as much wishful thinking as truth. Images of Dracula, of mysterious people doing mysterious things, even of "the noble savage" still lurking in some mountainous corner, reinforced by the idea of East Europeans speaking obscure and unpronounceable languages remain widespread.

The other, more important myth, is the one about communism. Those who have never been to a communist country tend to imagine it as a place where sullen workers and peasants are dragooned to work in barbed wire encampments by armed guards. There are counter-myths held by a few Marxists, wearing a bit thin these days perhaps, of a socialist paradise, where there is equality, social justice and order imposed by an all-wise state. Both these pictures are myths. The Western visitor first going to Budapest or Prague or Warsaw will wonder where on earth he or she ever got these ideas from in the first place.

Once again, the differences will emerge later. Usually these become evident when the Western visitor has his or her first dealing with the endless and often troublesome bureaucracy that seems to surround every transaction in Eastern Europe. The "three-queue system" is as good an example of this as any. You first queue up to choose what it is you want to buy.

Having chosen, you receive a slip of paper and queue at the cashier's to pay. Then, when the cashier has stamped the receipt, you queue again to collect your purchase. Slowly this system, which is so heavy on time and energy, is being ousted by self-service stores. But a brush with bureaucracy, at this level anyway, is no bad experience for Westerners. It gives them an insight into what the locals have to live with every day of their lives.

Communism and Reality

There are more serious restraints which spring from the system that calls itself "communist" or "socialist," neither a particularly accurate term since they imply that the political and economic systems of Eastern Europe have something in common with the utopia, the paradise on earth, sketched by Marx over a hundred years ago. They may be headed in this direction, but as they themselves would admit, there is a long way to go. The central truth of these systems is that the state believes that it knows better than the individual and the presumption generally is loaded against the citizen in favor of the government. Starting from this, the political organization calling itself "communist party" or "workers' party" holds the levers of power and the leaders, the real rulers, operate these levers in such a way as to ensure that they go on doing so. They do this partly because they enjoy exercising power—which politician, East or West, does not?—and partly too because they are certain that they are entitled to do so. This would not be undesirable in itself. The problem is that there are virtually no ways short of a major upheaval to challenge this, to call the system to account, to hold the leaders responsible for their stewardship. The old political cry from America, "throw the rascals out," becomes a cry in the wilderness in Eastern Europe, because attempts to eject rulers have resulted in the Soviet Union marching in and putting the rulers back in office.

The communist revolution in Eastern Europe—and like it or not, it was a revolution in that it completely changed some (though not all) of the political system and political habits of East Europeans—did begin or continue the process of modernizing the countries of the area. That it did not do so either very efficiently or in line with the traditions of Eastern Europe is another matter. But much of the infrastructure that makes a country "modern"—an administrative system covering the entire country, an effective system of education for all, universal literacy, a health system, communications, press, radio and television and a degree of social mobility—were brought to Eastern Europe during this communist revolution. Much of what is modern in the area, then, was brought in since the communists have run these countries. There is subsidized transport (still amazingly cheap), housing, a health service, subsidized holidays for many workers, a social welfare net and no unemployment. Because these countries are poorer than most of the West, the welfare provision may not be as striking as their Western counterparts offer, but they are real enough. And generally in Eastern Europe the crime problem is not as acute as in the West—the streets are by and large safe.

But because the revolution was, in fact, assisted from outside and in an alien way, quite a bit of the way in which it works tends to be against the grain of tradition rather than with it. This can sometimes make it difficult for people as a whole to identify with the system and accept it in full. Too often, East Europeans believe that the political system is more suited to the Soviet Union than to them.

This, then, brings one to what is the bottom line in East European politics—the wishes of Moscow. It is evident enough that flouting the Kremlin's will leads to trouble, but discovering what that will actually *is* at any given moment is another matter. In Stalin's day, these things were crystal clear. The Soviet pattern was applied to Eastern Europe in an unprecedented wave of imposed uniformity. But things have moved on since then. Gradually, over the last thirty years, the Soviet Union has acquiesced in Eastern Europe becoming more East European. Poles are often enough allowed to do things in their own Polish way in many areas. East Germany is as recognizably German as it is communist. And so on.

Where the Kremlin Fits In

The Kremlin seems to be caught in a real dilemma over what to do about Eastern Europe. Until the late 1980s, when Mikhail Gorbachev launched his program of reforms, the general view in Moscow was that if an Eastern European country was allowed to follow its local, domestic wishes and aspirations, Soviet interests would be quickly harmed. Many people in the Soviet Union still believe this. The reformers have adopted another approach. This is based on the idea that if the Soviet pattern is applied too rigidly, the East Europeans will become restive thus ruling the country concerned becomes potentially more costly.

The solution in the past has been a mixture of making concessions and then tightening up, when it appeared as if the invisible line might be breached. But under Gorbachev what the Kremlin wants has become more complex. The reforms, which have come to be known by their Russian names of *glasnost* (openness) and *perestroika* (restructuring), are not to be forced on Eastern Europe. On the other hand, the East Europeans are being encouraged to change their political and economic systems, in order to make them more efficient. They appear to have a fair amount of leeway for this. This produces uncertainty in Eastern Europe about what can be done and what cannot, but it's certainly preferable to the relentless and mindless rigidities of Stalin's time.

The problem at another level is that the East Europeans really do have rich and varied traditions of their own, which are very different from those of the Soviet Union, not to speak of Imperial Russia. In one superficial respect only is there a similarity. Just as the Soviet Union is the descendant of an empire, so is Eastern Europe—actually, of four empires. These were the Russian, which ruled much of Poland until 1917; the German, Western Poland was German until the end of the First World War; the Ottoman, which was only ejected from the last of its Balkan possessions in 1912; and the Austro-Hungarian, which ruled over the rest.

Poles—Catholics and Survivors

Each of these empires left its mark on the people it ruled, both negatively and positively. Poles, say, reacted against Russian rule in the 19th century and at the same time subtly adopted certain cultural patterns that are more Russian than anything else. It is a commonplace that today Poland is the most fervently Roman Catholic country in Europe and that the process of industrialization has not been accompanied by the growth of secularization that is evident in, for example, Spain and Italy. At the same time, Polish Catholicism is not quite as straightforward as may be assumed from a visit to, say, the Mariacki church in Cracow, which is as crowded as any in Poland on a Sunday. Polish Catholicism combines an equal respect for religious dogma and the individual conscience, which can allow Poles to choose where there is a conflict between the two without excessive agonizing.

In politics, the Poles have made it very clear—not least through their attachment to Solidarity during 1980–81—that ideally they would like a political system that would reflect their wishes and hopes for a more equal and open society than the communist one they are saddled with. But few people in Poland have the choice today and they have to make the best of what they do have. So they tend to live in two worlds. There is the unavoidable one of the daily round, of a declining or stagnant standard of living in the 1980s, of living with the rule of General Jaruzelski's part military, part bureaucratic regime. At the same time, there is another world of a half private sense of solidarity, of real comradeships and friendships, all backed up by the Church. In this half private world, there is a separate cultural life, with its own rules and regulations, which don't apply to the public one. To give one example—pilfering from one's place of work is so commonplace as to be the expected thing, but stealing from a private individual is theft, subject to the most stringent moral condemnation. In the same way, what the authorities say is treated with scepticism; rumor is trusted as a personal source of information and, therefore, as genuine. In the 1980s, then, Poles have developed their own strategies for coping with a situation which is not of their own devising or wishes.

Czechoslovakia—Normalization and Normality

If the Poles strike one as having come through this experience with much of their morale and spirit and liveliness intact, the Czechs look very different. Czechoslovakia had its equivalent of Poland's Solidarity in the Prague Spring of 1968, an attempt to graft democracy and socialism onto each other, which threatened to be so successful that the Soviet Union intervened militarily, flanked by four of its allies. The Prague Spring was actually the culmination of a several year old extraordinary cultural ferment, which looked to change the whole of society to a much more attractive shape politically and economically. The price paid for this was very high. Czechoslovakia was duly returned to what a normal system should look like in Moscow's eyes, hence the process was called "normalization." This "normalized" system is still in place. The Czechs may not like it, but they have learned to live with it by getting as much out of it as they can.

The cities today may look a little shabby and worn, though much of the countryside is as beautiful as ever and many of the historic smaller towns have been elegantly restored. Prague itself continues to undergo extensive, impressive restoration work. But the people have tended to turn in on themselves, to stay out of politics, maybe to wait for better times than exist currently. There is a kind of sluggishness about the country, especially the Western lands of Bohemia and Moravia, that can look a bit low-key to the Western visitor. It is all the more striking for those who remember either the heady days of 1968 or the even more remote inter-war republic, which was a haven of reasonable, efficient and tolerant politics, until it came under attack from Nazi Germany in 1938, and then from communist pressure ten years later. Very little of the change encouraged by Moscow was visible as the 1980s were coming to an end.

Slovakia, the eastern third of the country, has done better out of normal-ization than the Czechs, not least because before 1968 the Slovaks' main concern was to gain greater autonomy for themselves from Prague. The Slovaks speak a language which is different from Czech, though they un-derstand each other without much effort, and they have a rather different cultural tradition. Formerly, the Slovaks—who had been through a sepa-rate historical development—were the poor relations of a country, which was only set up in its present form in 1918. Normalization has seen to it that Slovakia is well on its way to catching up with the richer Czech lands and the grey blanket of cultural uniformity has sat more lightly on the Slovaks than on the Czechs in the last decade or so.

East Germany—Communist and German

East Germany is a kind of a paradox in many ways. For a start, if com-munism really does have deep historical roots anywhere, these should be in Germany, seeing that Marx was a German. And East Germans make no bones about this. Under communist rule, East Germany—the German Democratic Republic—has established itself both as German and as com-munist. Oddly, in some ways it has also preserved more of the traditional Germany than the West German state, which has changed enormously in the last four decades. Yet the East Germans have major successes to chalk up. They rebuilt a war-shattered country and have made it into a big industrial power. It runs in a reasonably effective way and regards itself as an example to be followed elsewhere. In truth, the East German recipe works because of the particular traditions, skills and organization of its people.

The G.D.R. is a new state, founded only in 1949 as a result of a trade-off between the occupying powers. It took a while to settle down—in 1953 it was the scene of a major upheaval when workers protested against harder conditions—but it gradually became a going concern. Its origins have left their mark and the East Germans often seem anxious to be ac-cepted as a fully-fledged country. Their extraordinary efforts in making themselves a major sporting power are partly about this—to put the coun-try on the map. This has been a success story.

The 1970s also saw the G.D.R. coming to terms with its German ante-cedents. Way back in the 1950s, Prussia was regarded by East German ideologists as a seed-bed of militarism and Nazism, but these attitudes soft-ened in the 1970s and aspects of Prussia were gradually accepted. So, now-adays, the G.D.R. regards Frederick the Great and Otto von Bismarck as among its ancestors. Prussian discipline and Marxist welfare seem to be the clearest characteristics of the G.D.R. In the 1980s, the GDR was still going strong as the industrial powerhouse of communist Europe. This gave the leadership the self-confidence to ignore Gorbachev's reforms and the pursue a specifically German policy of better relations with West Ger-many coupled with discipline at home.

Hungary—Making the Best of It

The Hungarians had an anti-Habsburg revolution in 1848–49, but ended up looking remarkably like a kind of neo-Habsburg state after the First World War, with a bit of bureaucratic sloth, genteel corruption mixed with a measure of respect for political pluralism. They had another revolution in 1956 and have again ended up looking like the least undesirable version of a Soviet-type system in the 1980s. There is a contradiction here. Many people outside Hungary, in Eastern as well as in Western Europe, regard it with envy and awe, principally because the Hungarians have managed to get away with so much and to have applied the system with so much flexibility. The Hungarians themselves don't see it all quite like this. They do believe that they are better off than their neighbors—the regime encourages this belief tacitly as a way of promoting complacency—but they also have to work extremely hard for the privilege. A majority of Hungarians will do two jobs: they have to, to make ends meet. A few streets in central Budapest really do have the flashy elegance of Paris or London, but few Hungarians will actually be able to afford the prices in the fashionable boutiques.

Ironically, the ultimate foundation for this was the revolution of 1956, which so shook both rulers and ruled that they tacitly agreed that a compromise of sorts was needed in order to prevent anything as devastating happening again. The terms of this compromise were never, of course, spelled out in so many words and they can be changed by the rulers without consulting the ruled. One of its features is that Hungarians are encouraged to make money instead of politics—power is the privilege of the political elite and no one else. In the 1980s, as Hungary's economic position deteriorated, they have to work ever harder to stay in the same place and they have become obsessed with this, almost to the exclusion of anything else. It has resulted in a growing irritability and a rising curve of stress related illnesses. In no other country were *glasnost* and *perestroika* embraced with more enthusiasm, for these new policies were seen as the best way out of the country's difficulties as the 1980s were coming to an end. There seems to be more electricity in the atmosphere, than say, in Prague. That is, if the impenetrable mysteries of the Hungarian language are put to one side.

Romania—Making the Worst of It

Romania enjoyed the reputation of being the maverick of Eastern Europe for a while in the 1970s. President Ceauşescu pursued a foreign policy that seemed to place independence from the Soviet Union at a premium. Eventually this turned out to be a pipedream and one for which the Romanians have had to pay a terrible price economically. The foreign policy successes were used by the leadership to try and push through a massive industrialization. When this ran aground in the early 1980s, Romania was saddled with a huge foreign debt and next to nothing with which to pay it off. The result was an acute squeeze on consumption, that has sent Romanian living standards tumbling downwards.

Romania was a poor country even before the war and had a well deserved reputation for having the most elaborate corruptibility in Eastern Europe. What made and still makes this particularly galling is that the country is rich in natural resources and its people are highly talented, but it has suffered misrule by a self-seeking elite, whether communist or not. The popular response is the one learned under the Ottoman empire—to pretend to acquiesce and to hope that the regime will go away, like bad weather. Where the communist system is worse than its predecessors is that it is more efficient in the way in which it uses power, but from the standpoint of the man in the street, there may otherwise be little to choose.

Bucharest, which saw itself as the Paris of the East before the war, still has the trappings of a faded elegance—but even this is being eroded both by poverty and by the bulldozer, destroying part of the historic city to build a massive administrative district. The Romanians are proud of being Latins. They claim that their language is descended from the Roman legions that occupied the area nearly two millennia ago—but in the 1980s they needed all their Latin *esprit de joie* to get through a uniquely difficult period of their history.

Bulgaria—Equality and Market Gardens

Bulgaria has an unfair reputation of being the nearest thing to a Soviet clone in Eastern Europe, of being Moscow's most loyal ally, of being the one country that will always do the Soviets' bidding. This underrates the Bulgarians' own abilities and traditions. While they are certainly well disposed towards the Russians, whom they regard as their liberators from Turkish rule in the 19th century, they have quite genuine traditions of their own, both communist and non-communist. In religion and language, they are not unlike the Russians, being Orthodox and Slav, but they developed a culture separate from that of Russia and lacking the Russians' imperial ambitions.

Before the war, for all the incompetence of its rulers, Bulgaria was a surprisingly egalitarian place. Secondly, it had a well deserved reputation for efficiency in agriculture. Both these traditions have resurfaced in different forms. Communist rule, while not liberal by any stretch of the imagination, has provided Bulgarians with a respectable standard of living, and the huge income disparities that one finds in the Soviet Union, say, have no place in Bulgaria. Much of the country's prosperity is based on a reasonably efficiently managed agriculture—as was once remarked, "the Bulgarians have been market gardeners to somebody's empire for two thousand years; why should things change under communism?"

On the Ground

Later on in this book you will find practical pointers to behavior while traveling in Eastern Europe—camera etiquette, avoiding currency deals, trying not to become involved in traffic accidents. You may find that a certain amount of patience will come in handy, as you meet situations which local citizens have long learned to accept philosophically, such as arbitrary changes of program, unexpected closure of restaurants, monuments or museums closed for restoration, or even whole towns wreathed in scaffolding. But here, as a final note, it is enough to stress the warmth and welcome, on a personal level, that you will find. Away from the major resorts and cities, you will meet people who want to show you their homes and offer hospitality. You will find a real curiosity about the West and an equally genuine enthusiasm which can lead to worthwhile exchanges of views. There will be many things over which you will find agreement and your disagreements will almost certainly be in unexpected areas. You may choose to go to Eastern Europe for the scenery—mountains, lakes or forests—or for the people. It will certainly be different from what you anticipated.

PLANNING YOUR TRIP

PLANNING YOUR TRIP

HOW TO GO. Travel to Eastern Europe is by no means the uncertain, complex affair it once was, and all the Eastern bloc countries are extremely eager to attract Western visitors. Nearly all foreign travel to Eastern Europe is organized by the State National Tourist Offices, which essentially means taking a group or package tour, or at least taking advantage of the prepaid voucher system. Though there are certainly no obstacles placed in the way of the independent traveler and anyone is free to travel at will within any given country, you will find that essential services such as hotels, restaurants, filling stations and the like, do not compare with those in the West. So if you have not made reservations in advance or bought vouchers before leaving, trying to find a hotel or restaurant, especially off the beaten track, can be both time-consuming and frustrating and you are liable to waste a good deal of time and money.

The first and most important step to take in planning your trip, is to contact the office of the National Tourist Office of the country you want to visit, or one of the many travel agents officially accredited by them (these include many of the major and a good number of the lesser travel agents). They will supply details of the many hundreds of trips and deals on offer. For the independent traveler, these include a variety of freelance arrangements, some details of which are given under each country. Similarly, visas, as well as many of the other important regulations that must be complied with, can also be arranged. One of the other major advantages of prepaid services such as these is that they overcome the necessity of changing a minimum amount of foreign currency for every day of your stay (this is usually around $15 per person per day), a regulation that is strictly enforced in every Eastern European country except Bulgaria and Hungary.

The names and addresses of the State National Tourist Offices are:
In the U.S.:
Bulgaria, Balkan Holidays (authorized agent), 161 East 86th St., New York, NY 10028 (tel. 212–722–7626).
Czechoslovakia, Čedok, 10 East 40th St., New York, NY 10016 (tel. 212–689–9720).
East Germany, see *East Germany* chapter.
Hungary, (IBUSZ), 630 Fifth Ave., Suite 2455, New York, NY 10111 (tel. 212–582–7412).
Poland, Orbis, 500 Fifth Ave., New York, NY 10110 (tel. 212–391–0844).
Romania, Romanian National Tourist Office, 573 Third Ave., New York, NY 10016 (tel. 212–697–6971).

In the U.K.:
Bulgaria, Bulgarian National Tourist Office, 18 Princes St., London W1R 7RE (tel. 01–499–6988).
Czechoslovakia, Čedok, 17–18 Old Bond St., London W1X 3DA (tel. 01–629–6058).
East Germany, Berolina Travel (agents of the Reisebüro der D.D.R.), 22 Conduit St., London W1R 9TD (tel. 01–629–1664).
Hungary, Danube Travel Ltd (agents of IBUSZ), 6 Conduit St., London W1R 9TG (tel. 01–493–0263).
Poland, Orbis, 82 Mortimer St., London W1N 7DE (tel. 01–636–2217).
Romania, Romanian National Tourist Office, 29 Thurloe Pl., London SW7 2HP (tel. 01–584–8090).

For further details of travel to Eastern European countries, see *Facts at Your Fingertips* for the particular country you are interested in. Details of hotels and restaurants, as well as of prices, are also in the *Facts at Your Fingertips* sections.

TOURS. "Grand tours" of Eastern Europe, those 12–20 day sweeps through the region, are scarcely less numerous than their West European counterparts. A few of the possibilities are listed here; in-depth tours of individual countries are outlined in the chapters describing those countries. (All details are for 1988, so check for up-to-the-minute information).

From the U.S.:

Globus-Gateway/Cosmos offers a 16-day escorted skip through Germany (East and West), Poland, Czechoslovakia, Hungary, and Austria, entitled "Central and Eastern Europe," for $1,185–$1,215 (land cost only).

For those with slightly more luxurious tastes, *Travcoa* offers its 22-day "Classics of Eastern Europe," which begins in Warsaw, stops over in Leningrad and Moscow, and then moves on to Prague, Budapest, Bucharest, Sofia (Bulgaria) and ends in Dubrovnik (Yugoslavia), all for around $3,795 (land costs only).

A similar program, "Best of Eastern Europe," offers roughly the same itinerary, with slightly extended stays in the Soviet Union and Yugoslavia. *Hemphill Harris* puts it out; land costs for this 26-day tour begin at $1,995.

Argosy Tours, a division of Salen Linblad Cruising, has a 1,600-km. (1,000-mile) journey down the Danube from Vienna to the Black Sea port of Constanta, in Romania, aboard the MS *Rousse.* The eastbound route begins in Austria and follows the river through Hungary, Czechoslovakia, Yugoslavia, Bulgaria and Romania, with shore excursions in Wachau, Budapest, Belgrade and Bucharest. The westbound route is exactly the same, in reverse. The entire itinerary runs 12 days, 7 of which are aboard the ship, and includes three nights in Vienna. The tour costs from $1,585, excluding airfares.

ETS Tours offers various city packages, which shuffle Vienna, Budapest, Prague, Warsaw, and Bucharest in various combinations.

Orbis, the Polish national tourist organization, sponsors "Poland and the Heart of Europe," which stops in Yugoslavia, Hungary, Poland, East Germany, Czechoslovakia, and Austria. Land costs are around $1,300

Tour Operators:

Argosy Tours, 133 East 55th St., New York, NY 10022 (tel. 212–751–2300).

Globus-Gateway/Cosmos, 95–25 Queens Blvd., Rego Park, NY 11374 (tel. 718–268–1700).

ETS Tours, 5 Penn Plaza, New York, NY 10001 (tel. 800–346–6314; in NY, 212–563–0780).

Hemphill Harris Travel Corp., 16000 Ventura Blvd., Encino, CA 91436 (tel. 818–906–8086).

Litoral Travel, 124 E. 40th St., Suite 403, New York, NY 10016 (tel. 212–986–4210).

Love Holidays, 15315 Magnolia Blvd., Ste. 110, Sherman Oaks, CA 91403 (tel. 800–456–5683; 818–501–6868).

Maupintour, 15151 St. Andrews Dr., Lawrence, KS 66046 (tel. 255–4266).

Orbis, Polish Travel Bureau, Inc., 500 Fifth Ave., New York, NY 10110 (tel. 212–391–0844).

Pan Am Holidays, Pan Am Bldg., New York, NY 10016 (tel. 800–THE–TOUR).

Travcoa, 4000 MacArthur Blvd., Ste. 650E, Newport Beach, CA 92660 (tel. 714–476–2800).

From the U.K.:

Cosmos offer a coach holiday "Central and East European Capitals" which takes 14 days and goes through Belgium and Germany before entering Eastern Europe. The cost is £374–399 plus a charge for visas. They also offer a flight plus coach holiday for 15 days, "Balkan Adventure," which travels from Yugoslavia to Sofia, the Valley of Roses, Bucharest, back to Yugoslavia. Cost is £455, including flights.

Wallace Arnold offer a multi country coach tour that takes in Salzburg, Vienna, Budapest and Sopron, with France, Belgium, and Germany en route—14 days, three of them in Hungary, from £439. Their "Bohemian Forests" tour takes 12 days, seven of them in Czechoslovakia. Their affiliate company, *Overland,* has an "Eastern Carousel," 14 days from £529, covering East Berlin, Prague, Cracow, and Budapest.

Peltours are specialists for the independent traveler to Eastern Europe, and will help you put together your own itinerary, pursuing your own particular interests and hobbies.

Tour Operators:
Cosmos, Tourama House, 17 Homesdale Rd., Bromley, Kent BR2 9LX (tel. 01–464–3400).

Peltours, Mappin House, 4 Winsley St., London W1N 7AR (tel. 01–637–4373).

Progressive Tours, 12 Porchester Pl., London W2 2BS (tel. 01–262–1676).

Wallace Arnold, (Continental Dept.), Gelderd Rd., Leeds LS12 6DH, West Yorkshire (tel. 0532–636456).

WHEN TO GO. The summer season in Eastern Europe lasts from May through September, or October on the Black Sea coast. The peak months are July and August, when the Black Sea and Lake Balaton resorts, in particular, are crowded with visitors from abroad and neighboring countries.

There is a thriving winter sports season lasting, in some centers, from November to May. The peak months are usually December to March. Winter is also a good time to visit the capitals, which offer a lively variety of cultural events. We give full details in *Facts at Your Fingertips* for each country.

TRAVEL DOCUMENTS. Visas. In addition to a valid passport (details of how to apply for a passport are given below), all Western visitors to Eastern Europe will require a visa for every country they intend visiting, with some exceptions in the case of Bulgaria. We give details of the specific requirements for visa applications in the *Facts at Your Fingertips* sections for individual countries. In most cases it is advisable or essential to obtain your visas prior to departure, and wise to apply for them some weeks before your intended departure date as the process can sometimes be rather slow. Consulates and many travel agents can arrange visas. If your itinerary involves crossing from one country to another and back again, check whether you need more than one visa for that country. Transit visas are also required if you plan only to travel through an Eastern European country.

Passports. American Citizens. Major post offices and many county courthouses process passport applications, as do U.S. Passport Agency offices in various cities. Addresses and phone numbers are available under governmental listings in the white or blue pages of local telephone directories. Renewals can be handled by mail (form DSP-82) provided that your previous passport is not more than 12 years old. You will need 1) Proof of citizenship, such as a birth certificate; 2) two recent, identical photographs two inches square, in either black and white or color, on non-glossy paper; 3) $35 for the passport itself plus a $7 processing fee if you are applying in person (no processing fee when applying by mail) for those 18 years and older, or if you are under 18, $20 for the passport plus a $7 processing fee if you are applying in person (again, no extra fee when applying by mail). Adult passports are valid for 10 years, others for five years; 4) proof of identity that includes a photo and signature such as a driver's license, previous passport, any governmental ID card, or a copy of an income tax return. When you receive your passport, write down its number, date and place of issue separately. The loss of a valid passport should be reported immediately to the local police and the U.S. Dept. of State, 1425 K. St., NW, Washington, DC 20524. If your passport is lost or stolen while abroad, report it immediately to the local authorities and apply for a replacement at the nearest U.S. Embassy or consular office.

Canadian Citizens. Canadian citizens apply in person to regional passport offices, post offices or by mail to Bureau of Passports, Complexe Guy Favreau, 200 Dorchester West, Montreal, Quebec H2Z 1X4 (514–283–2152). A $25 fee, two photographs, a guarantor and evidence of citizenship are required. Canadian passports are valid for five years and are non-renewable.

British Citizens. You should apply on forms obtainable from your travel agency or local main post office. The application should be sent to the Passport Office for your area (as indicated on the form). The regional passport offices are located in London, Liverpool, Peterborough, Belfast, Glasgow, and Newport (Gwent). The application must be countersigned by your bank manager, or a solicitor, barrister, doctor, clergyman or Justice of the Peace who knows you. Enclose two photos and a fee of £15.

Health Certificates. These are not required to visit any East European country.

INSURANCE. The different varieties of travel insurance cover everything from health and accident costs, to lost baggage and trip cancellation. Insurance is available from many sources, however, and many travelers unwittingly end up with duplicate coverage. Before purchasing separate travel insurance of any kind, be sure to check your regular policies carefully. At the same time make sure you don't neglect some eventuality which could end up costing a small fortune.

Your travel agent is a good source of information on travel insurance. She or he should have an idea of the insurance demands of different destinations; moreover, several of the travel insurance companies retail exclusively through travel agents. The American Society of Travel Agents endorses the *Travel Guard* plan, issued by The Insurance Company of North America. Travel Guard offers an insurance package that includes coverage for sickness, injury or death, lost baggage, and interruption or cancellation of your trip. Lost baggage coverage will also cover unauthorized use of your credit cards, while trip cancellation or interruption coverage will reimburse you for additional costs incurred due to a sudden halt (or failed start) to your trip. The Travel Guard Gold program has three plans: advance purchase, for trips up to 30 days ($19); super advance purchase, for trips up to 45 days ($39); and comprehensive, for trips up to 180 days (8% of the cost of travel). Optional features with the Travel Guard Gold program include cancellation and supplemental CDW (collision damage waiver) coverage. For more information, talk to your travel agent, or Travel Guard, 1100 Center Point Dr., Stevens Point, WI 54481 (tel. 800–826–1300).

The *Travelers Companies* has a "Travel Insurance Pak," also sold through travel agents. It is broken down into three parts: Travel Accident Coverage (sickness, injury, or death), Baggage Loss, and Trip Cancellation. Any one of the three parts can be bought separately. Again, your travel agent should have full details, or you can get in touch with the Travelers Companies, Ticket and Travel, One Tower Square, Hartford, CT 06183 (tel. 800–243–3174).

If an accident occurs, paying for medical care may be a less urgent problem than finding it. Several companies offer emergency medical assistance along with insurance. *Access America* offers travel insurance and the assistance of a 24-hour hotline in Washington DC that can direct distressed travelers to a nearby source of aid. They maintain contact with a worldwide network of doctors, hospitals and pharmacies, offer medical evacuation services (a particular problem if you're hurt in an out-of-the-way spot), on-site cash provision services (if it's needed to pay for medical care), legal assistance, and help with lost documents and ticket replacement. Access America offers its services through travel agents and AAA. Costs range from $5 to $10 a day. For more information, Access America, 600 Third Avenue, Box 807, New York, NY 10163 (tel. 800–851–2800).

Other organizations that offer similar assistance are:
Travel Assistance International, Europ Assistance Worldwide Services Inc., 1333 F St. N.W., Washington DC 20004 (tel. 800–821–2828), the American arm of Europ Assistance, offers comprehensive medical and personal emergency services.

Carefree Travel Insurance, c/o ARM Coverage, Inc., 120 Mineola Blvd., Box 310, Mineola, NY 11510 underwritten by the Hartford Accident and Indemnity Co., offers a comprehensive benefits package that includes trip cancellation and interruption, medical, and accidental death/dismemberment coverage, as well as medical, legal and economic assistance. Trip cancellation and interruption insurance can be purchased separately. Call 800–654–2424 for additional information.

International SOS Assistance, Inc., Box 11568, Philadelphia, PA 19116 (tel. 800–523–8930).

IAMAT (International Association for Medical Assistance to Travelers), 417 Center St., Lewiston, NY 14092 (tel. 716–754–4883); 188 Nicklin Rd., Guelph, Ontario N1H 7L5 (tel. 519–836–0102).

In Britain, *Europ Assistance Ltd* is highly recommended and offers considerable help to its members. Multilingual personnel staff a 24-hour, 365-days-a-year telephone service, which brings the aid of a network of medical advisers to assist in any emergency. Special medical insurance is available for a moderate sum. Further information, plus details of their excellent insurance scheme for motorists, from 252 High St, Croydon, Surrey CR0 1NF (tel. 01–680–1234). Some degree of medical care is available to U.K. citizens in all Eastern European countries (see Leaflet SA30 from the D.H.S.S.).

MONEY. There are a number of points to be aware of concerning money and financial transactions in Eastern Europe. The first is that unless you have prepaid services of some kind (for example, if you are on a package tour or have reservations for hotels made and paid for in advance or have vouchers for hotels, restaurants, campsites, etc.) you will be required to buy a minimum amount of local currency (usually around $15 per person) for every day of your stay in all Eastern European countries except Bulgaria and Hungary. You must therefore be able to prove on entering the country that you have at least this minimum amount of foreign currency. Bulgaria and (if you have prepaid a Čedok tour) Czechoslovakia offer very much more favorable rates of exchange than the official rates. All main frontier posts and points of entry have official bureaux de change, as do most major hotels and tourist shops.

Any amount of foreign currency may be imported into any Eastern European country and any left unspent may be exported, provided the original amount was declared on arrival; but no local currencies may be exported or imported. This also applies even if you are returning to one of the countries in the region after visiting another. Major credit cards are accepted in most principal tourist resort hotels, restaurants and tourist shops, as are traveler's checks.

Finally, be very wary of the thriving black market in currency exchange. You may be offered a rate of exchange several times better than the official one. But penalties for dealing in this black market are severe and unpleasant. The inside of any gaol is pretty nasty; the inside of an Eastern European gaol is very nasty.

WHAT TO TAKE. The first principle is to travel light. Airline baggage restrictions vary, but most American and major European carriers allow two checked bags, one no larger than 62″ overall, the other no larger than 55″ overall (and neither more than 70 lbs.) and one piece of carryon luggage, no more than 45″ overall. Several of the East European carriers, however, have stricter rules, limiting your baggage's *total* weight to 44 lbs. Check before you go. Penalties for excess baggage are very severe. But in any case, do not take more than you can carry yourself; it's a lifesaver in places where porters are thin on the ground. In practice, this means more or less everywhere these days.

It's a good idea to pack the bulk of your things in one large bag and put everything you need for overnight, or for two or three nights, in another smaller one so that you don't have to pack and repack at every stop. Motorists should limit luggage to what can be locked into the trunk or boot of your car.

Clothing. Informal dress is quite acceptable for Eastern Europe, though the smarter hotels and restaurants expect men to wear a tie for dinner. Pack lightweight clothes for summer visits, but take along a cardigan or sweater for cooler nights, also a raincoat. If traveling in winter you'll need thick woolens, heavy overcoats and boots or heavy shoes. Don't forget to leave some room in your suitcase for souvenirs and presents to bring back home.

Medicines and Toiletries. Take all the medicines, cosmetics and toiletries you think you'll need. Most items can be bought in Eastern Europe, but some are difficult to find. If you wear glasses or contact lenses, take the prescription.

STUDENT AND YOUTH TRAVEL. From America. Students considering travel to Hungary might want to write the *Youth Express Travel Office* there (Semmelweis ut #4, 1051 Budapest, Hungary). It has full information on opportunities for student travel in that country. Poland offers special discount vouchers ($7) to travelers with the international student ID, and to those without one, but still under 35. The vouchers are good for a room and breakfast. For more information, get in touch with Orbis.

From Britain. Government-subsidized exchange visits for young working people are arranged every year to Romania. For details of this and visits to other Eastern European countries, contact the 'East Europe Interchange', *Educational Interchange Council,* 43 Russell Square, London WC1. Booklets and directories of summer jobs, voluntary work and adventure travel abroad are also published by *Vacation-Work Publications,* 9 Park End St, Oxford OX1 1HJ.

HANDICAPPED TRAVEL. Facilities for the handicapped traveler in Eastern Europe are extremely limited, to say the least. Those in wheelchairs in particular are liable to find few if any special facilities in hotels, public transport or places of interest. Where they do exist, they are skimpy at best. In Poland, for example, there are wheelchairs available at all airports and most trains have specially designated seats for the handicapped. Hungary has a *Society for Rehabilitation* at PO Box 1, H-1528, Budapest 123, and there is also a 12-page guide listing hotels in Hungary with facilities for the handicapped. But this is published in German only and is not available outside Hungary and Austria. Sadly, this is largely the extent of special facilities for handicapped people in Eastern Europe. You are also likely to find that the attitude of many officials toward handicapped travelers can be unhelpful, not to put too fine a point on it.

If you do plan to visit Eastern Europe, there are resources to help you plan. *Access to the World: A Travel Guide for the Handicapped* by Louise Weiss is an outstanding book, covering all aspects of travel for those with medical problems. Published by Henry Holt & Co. ($16.95), the book can be ordered from *Facts on File,* 460 Park Ave. South, New York, NY 10016. The *Travel Information Service* at Moss Rehabilitation Center, 12th St. and Tabor Rd., Philadelphia, PA 19141 (tel. 215-329-5715), can answer many inquiries concerning travel to specific countries and cities. So can the *Society for the Advancement of Travel for the Handicapped* (SATH), 26 Court St., Penthouse Suite, Brooklyn, NY 11242 (tel. 718-858-5483). Send a SASE for their list of tour operators who specialize in travel for the handicapped.

In Britain contact the *RADAR* (Royal Association for Disability and Rehabilitation), 25 Mortimer St., London W1 (tel. 01-637-5400). The *Air Transport Users Committee,* 129 Kingsway, London WC2, publish a useful booklet for handicapped passengers entitled *Care in the Air,* free of charge.

UTILITIES. It is worth remembering that erratic plumbing and temperamental electric wiring have been traditional problems throughout Eastern Europe, and remain so despite much new building. There is little you will be able to do about it—you might find that even a change of hotel room only brings you a new set of little problems! Bath and wash basin plugs are often missing, so we recommend taking a universal one. You'll probably also be glad of a small supply of tissues or toilet paper when away from your hotel.

Most parts of Eastern Europe use 220 volt alternating current, though some older establishments, particularly in Romania, still use 110 volt, AC. A transformer can be attached to all kinds of electrical appliances you may take with you, but it will be satisfactory only where the appliance has no timing mechanism. The reason for this is that the current is 50 cycle instead of 60 cycle; an electric clock, for example, would run so slowly as to be worthless. Since there may be local variations you should always inquire in advance. Also note that most plugs are a different fit from both British and American plugs.

PHOTOGRAPHY. Throughout Eastern Europe, it is forbidden to take photographs at frontiers or at military, industrial and transport installations (including trains and rail stations). There is a special international sign on roads where photography is forbidden—a camera in a red circle with a red line through the camera. Otherwise you can snap away when and where you like.

In some countries it can be difficult to obtain supplies of Western makes of film, though the foreign, or hard, currency shops usually stock a limited range. It's advisable to take your full limit of film with you.

Getting to Eastern Europe

FROM NORTH AMERICA

BY AIR. There are still very limited direct services available from North America to Eastern Europe. It is often easiest to fly to Europe first, and pick up one of the numerous flights available there. Pan Am currently flies to Budapest (Hungary), Warsaw and Cracow (Poland), and Bucharest (Romania).

Service to Poland is available on *Lot Airlines* (500 Fifth Ave., New York, NY 10110, tel. 212–869–1074), which flies from New York, Montreal and Toronto to Warsaw. Lot also arranges inexpensive charter flights to Warsaw from Chicago, Detroit, and Los Angeles. *Czechoslovak Airlines* (CSA) (545 Fifth Ave., New York, NY 10017, tel. 212–682–5833) flies twice weekly to Prague from New York and Montreal. The Romanian carrier *Tarom Airlines* (200 E. 38th St., New York, NY 10016, tel. 212–687–6013) flies twice weekly to Bucharest from New York, with a stop in Vienna.

Fares. Given the many ways one might put together a flight to Eastern Europe (and the different costs one might incur), the best thing to do is consult a travel agent, who should be able to arrange the best itinerary at the lowest cost. Sample roundtrip fares as of mid-1988 were:

NY–Bucharest: No First Class; Economy $1,270; APEX $949.

NY–Prague: No First Class; Business Class $1,450; APEX $623–$783.

NY–Warsaw: Economy $1,682; Excursion $1,132 (minimum and maximum stay requirements); APEX $766.

BY SEA. *Polish Ocean Lines* (POL) has withdrawn its passenger ship, the *Stephan Batory,* from service and at the time of writing (mid-1988) there was no news of a replacement. However, there is still a chance a vessel may be found for 1989. POL also operate passenger-carrying freighters, but these have very limited accommodations available. Details from Gdynia American Shipping Lines, 39 Broadway, 14th Floor, New York, NY 10006 (tel. 212–952–1280). in the U.K. from Gdynia America Shipping Lines,238 City Rd., London EC1 (tel. 01–251–3389).

FROM WESTERN EUROPE

BY AIR. The two "halves" of Europe have a very good network of air links uniting them though flights are not as frequent as between West European destinations. Any good travel agent will be able to advise on the best services to suit your requirements. The national carriers of all the East European countries have services to most Western European capitals and main cities, some non-stop, the remainder through services. Similarly, the national carriers of most West European countries have frequent services to East Europe. Unfortunately there are fewer low-cost tickets to Eastern Europe than to destinations in Western Europe as the bulk of travelers go either on charter flights or by rail. But the best is an APEX ticket; from London, these cost approximately £130 to Prague, £230 to Warsaw, £213 to Budapest and £280 to Sofia.

BY TRAIN. There are good train links between Western and Eastern Europe, several of which have connecting services from London. If you intend traveling around Eastern Europe by train once you arrive, it is always best to work out your basic itinerary and buy tickets before you leave. This will save many difficulties—standing in line, language problems and the need to pay supplements for fast/express trains.

For planning the itinerary the Thomas Cook European Timetable is essential reading. It contains details of all the international train services from Western Europe to the East, details of the main internal services, and information on the more important river ferries. Because the rail schedules in Europe differ greatly between summer and winter it is essential to get a copy which covers the period of the proposed visit. In the U.S. it can be obtained by mail from *Forsyth Travel Library,* 9154 West 57th St., PO Box 2975, Dept. T.C.T., Shawnee Mission, Kansas 66201. In the U.K. over the counter at any branch of Thomas Cook, or by post from *Thomas Cook Ltd,* PO Box 36, Peterborough PE3 6SB. Always reserve seats and couchettes or other accommodations on trains well in advance. Reservations are in any case obligatory on many express trains within Eastern Europe. Details are available from travel agents and State National Tourist Offices.

Young people who wish to travel extensively in Europe by rail should buy an Inter Rail Card; this entitles those under-26 to unlimited 2nd class travel for one calendar month in 19 European countries and 50% on some cross-channel ferries and on Hoverspeed hovercraft services, plus 50% off travel in the country in which the pass is bought. It covers both Hungary and Romania. Its current cost in the U.K. is around £140.

For older people, a "Rail Europ Senior" pass is valid for Hungary and most West European countries (including the U.K.) to those who already hold a local senior citizens' pass; it entitles the holder to reductions of from 30% to 50% on the railways of 17 European countries as well as a 30% reduction on Sealink cross-Channel ferries and Hoverspeed hovercraft. This card costs £5 in the U.K.

Note: Neither of the two passes described above is available to Americans, though American students who have been resident for 6 months in the U.K. are allowed to purchase the Inter Rail Card. As the Eurail pass does not apply to the Eastern European countries, rail travel for the majority of Americans will have to be at full rate. However rail fares in Eastern Europe are much lower than in the West.

To Bulgaria. There is only one through train from the West to Bulgaria; this is the *Istanbul Express,* which runs daily through the year from Munich and Venice to Sofia, though at different times in winter and summer. In summer it leaves Munich at 17.34 and Venice at 16.56, the two branches of the train joining at Belgrade; it arrives at Sofia at 19.23 on the second day. From both Munich and Venice there are sleepers as far as Belgrade; after that, second class couchettes only. There are no restaurant or buffet car facilities. Between Venice and Belgrade, the train is known as the *Venezia Express.*

To Czechoslovakia. There are no through services from the Channel ports to Czechoslovakia and passengers are advised to travel by one of the following trains.

From Paris, there is a good service; this is the *Paris-Praha Express* (known in Czechoslovakia as the *Zapadní Express*). The train leaves the Gare de l'Est in Paris at 23.00 and travels via Frankfurt and Nürnberg, arriving at Prague (Main Station) at 17.53 the following day. There are through second class couchettes to Prague and on certain days (except in high summer) there is a first and second class sleeper as far as Frankfurt (arrival 07.29). A buffet car runs between Frankfurt and Prague.

From Cologne, the *Donau Kurier* provides the first link in a daylight service to Prague. Departure from Cologne (Hauptbahnhof) is at 07.58, arriving at Nürnberg at 12.43 where you board a train with through coaches to Prague (Main Station), arriving at 21.55.

To East Germany. There are numerous train routes to East Germany, and trips are easy to arrange. Again, it is easiest to fix up your trip via one of the officially-sanctioned operators or through a travel agent, but independent travel is perfectly feasible. If you do go independently, it is wise to get your visa before you leave. In theory it is possible to get a visa at the border, but in practice this is generally a courtesy offered mainly to business travelers headed for the Leipzig Fair. In order to get a visa at the border, you must have prepaid hotel or camping vouchers. Transit visas can be issued at the border, but you must have a visa for the next country you plan to visit, if a visa is needed.

The most convenient train to Berlin for visitors from the U.K. is that from the Hook of Holland, connecting with the overnight ferry from Harwich. The *Ost-West Express* from Ostend, with train and jetfoil connections from London (Victoria) also provides a convenient overnight service for Berlin.

Virtually all major West German cities have good through connections to East Germany and there are also direct train connections from other West European cities, including Vienna, Brussels and Paris.

To Hungary. There are four all-year through services from the West to Budapest, plus a fifth in the summer. The most famous is the *Orient Express,* though do not confuse this with the privately-owned and highly luxurious *Venice-Simplon Orient Express. This* Orient Express is that made famous by many novelists and which originally continued on to Istanbul (today it peters out at Bucharest). However, its route is still of interest. It leaves the Gare de l'Est at Paris at 23.15, giving a daytime run through Bavaria and Austria (very dramatic), arriving at Budapest (East Station) at 20.18 the following evening. This train comprises first and second class through day-cars from Paris to Budapest, first and second class sleepers and couchettes from Paris to Salzburg. There are restaurant car services from Stuttgart to Vienna, and from Vienna to Budapest. During the summer (June through Oct.) there is a second train, the *Rapide Paris-Wien* (known as the *Rosen Kavalier* from Munich to Vienna), which leaves Paris Est at 21.20. This train carries first and second class sleepers from Paris to Vienna.

The *Oostende-Wien Express* provides a useful all-year service from Ostend to Budapest. There is a connecting train leaving London (Victoria) at 0.9.00 for Dover and Ostend. In summer you can leave Victoria at 11.30 if you take the fast Jetfoil service. The train runs via Brussels and Cologne to Vienna (West) where it arrives at 09.04 in good time to change to the Wiener Walzer which leaves at 09.30 (see below) for Budapest. Light refreshments are available from Ostend to Frankfurt and a buffet car caters for breakfast from Passau onwards. Reservation on this train is obligatory.

The *Wiener Walzer* connects Basle and Budapest, running via Zurich, Salzburg and Vienna. Departure from Basle (SBB) is at 20.27 and arrival in the Hungarian capital is at 13.20 the following day. There are sleepers and couchettes as far as Vienna and a restaurant car from Salzburg to Budapest. Here, too, reservation is compulsory.

Finally, there is a through train from Rome. It leaves Rome at 22.55 and arrives in Budapest at 22.45 the following day, having traveled via Venice, Ljubljana and Zagreb. There are first and second class sleeping cars and day cars from Rome to Budapest, but no restaurant or buffet car; lengthy stops at Venice and Zagreb allow time for a visit to the station buffet, however.

To Poland. Warsaw is well-served by through trains from the West, and a wide choice of starting points is available. There are trains from the Hook of Holland,

Ostend, Paris, Cologne, Frankfurt and Basle. The best services to use from Britain
are those from the Hook, Ostend and Paris.

The train from the Hook is called the *Hook-Warszawa Express.* It runs daily in
the summer and three times a week in the winter. There is a connecting service
from London (Liverpool Street) which leaves at 9.45 (09.20 on Sundays) for Harwich, from where there is a ferry service to the Hook. This connects with the *Hook-
Warszawa Express,* which leaves at 19.59 and arrives at Warsaw (Central Station)
at 15.40 the next day. There are first and second class sleepers throughout and,
in the summer, couchettes as far as Berlin. A Polish buffet car joins the train at
Berlin (Hbf), reached at 06.17. In winter the sleepers run on three days a week only.
The summer timings have been given here. Winter timings are very different: the
train leaves the Hook at the same time but does not reach Warsaw until 17.50.

The service from Ostend is called the *Ost-West Express* and is similarly convenient. There is a connecting service from London (Victoria), which leaves at 09.00
and connects with the Sealink ferry from Dover. However, from May to September,
it is possible to leave Victoria at 11.30 and, by making use of the P&O Europe-
an/RTM Jetfoil, arrive in Ostend at 16.00 in good time to catch the *Ost-West Express,* which leaves at 17.08 (in winter it leaves at 17.08). The train runs overnight
to Berlin and arrives at Warsaw (Central Station) at 18.34 the next day. There are
first and second class sleeping cars for the whole trip and second class couchettes
as far as Berlin. There is a Polish buffet car from Berlin (Hbf). Reservation is obligatory on this train.

There are also through sleeping cars and couchettes on the train leaving Paris
(Nord) at 17.44 for Warsaw, where it arrives at the Central Station at 17.50; also
buffet car.

From West Germany there is a through train, the *Leningrad Express,* which
leaves Cologne at 13.12; it runs via Hannover and Berlin and arrives at Warsaw
(Central Station) at 7.40 the following day. There is an East German (Mitropa)
buffet car as far as Berlin and second class couchettes from Hannover to Warsaw.

From Switzerland, there is a through train from Bern to Warsaw, leaving at
15.51, calling at Basle (S.B.B. Station depart 17.33) and arriving at Warsaw (Central
Station) at 17.50 the following day. This has first and second class sleepers and second class couchettes for the night journey.

To Romania. Two of the international trains mentioned in the section on Hungary continue on to Bucharest: the *Orient Express* and the *Wiener Walzer,* the latter
in summer only. The *Orient Express* leaves Budapest at 21.00 (on day two of its
journey) to give a lunchtime arrival at 12.20 (day three). Romanian sleeping cars,
both first and second class, are attached at Budapest on two days a week and second
class couchettes every day, while a Romanian restaurant car provides sustenance.
The *Wiener Walzer* leaves Budapest (East) at 15.10 and arrives at Bucharest at
08.10 next morning; it has a first class sleeper, second class couchettes and a restaurant car. This train runs in summer only.

BY CAR. Travel into Eastern Europe by car is still something of an adventure.
Road conditions are not really comparable to those in Western Europe; filling stations, for example, are far and few between while facilities for dealing with break-
downs are naturally pretty scarce. Good preparation is therefore very important.
It is a good idea to get in touch with one of the motoring organizations or the State
National Tourist Office of the country concerned before you go. They are important
sources of information.

Only Hungary now requires drivers to have an International Driving License,
but it is advisable to have one just the same. They are obtainable from motoring
organizations. In the U.S., try the American Automobile Association, 8111 Gate-
house Rd., Falls Church, VA 22042 (tel. 703–222–6000). In the U.K., both the AA,
Fanum House, Basingstoke, Hants RG21 2EA (or any of their regional offices) and
the RAC, 49 Pall Mall, London SW1Y 5JG (or any of their regional offices) can
supply you with an International Driving License. There is a small fee.

Similarly, the Green Card, which gives full insurance cover abroad, is not strictly necessary, but it would be foolish not to have one. If you don't have one you may anyway be obliged to purchase alternative insurance. They are also good for Western Europe, but are not required in Western Europe for citizens of EEC countries. They are readily available from insurance companies and cost from £5. In the case of a rented car, the rental agency will arrange it for you. Ensure that it is valid for the countries you wish to visit (and signed by yourself). For a rental car you will also need written confirmation of your permission to use the vehicle and a copy of the vehicle registration document. This last is also required if you take your own car.

Apart from your visa for the country you plan to visit, check the requirements for transit visas for any Eastern European countries you may travel through.

Vouchers for gasoline purchased in hard currency are essential for Bulgaria, Poland and Romania, and available (but not essential) for Czechoslovakia. You can buy them at the frontier before entering the country. In the case of Czechoslovakia, you can also buy them before you leave. But in all cases, check with the State National Tourist Offices as the situation concerning vouchers is in constant flux. It is also possible that they will be reintroduced for Hungary.

Good road atlases to buy are the *AA Road Book of Europe* (which covers all the countries concerned except Northern Romania) and Hallwag's *Europa* which covers the whole area. These are available from any large map bookshop, where you can also buy individual country maps. Specific information on road routes and conditions can be obtained from the continental operations departments of your motoring organization.

Note that quite a number of frontier crossings between the socialist countries are only open to the nationals of these countries. Do not, therefore, be tempted by a less obvious crossing point without making sure first that you are entitled to use it, for you will only run the risk of being turned back. That said, it is worth avoiding major crossing points at the height of summer with their attendant queues. A slightly longer route is often rewarded by much lighter traffic and sometimes less spoilt scenery.

FERRIES FROM THE U.K. The following are the main ferry crossings that most conveniently connect with the principal highways through Western Europe: Felixstowe-Zeebrugge (Belgium): P&O European Ferries; Sheerness-Vlissingen (Holland): Olau; Ramsgate-Dunkerque (France): Sally-Viking; Dover-Zeebrugge (Belgium): P&O European Ferries; Dover-Ostend (Belgium): P&O European Ferries; Dover-Calais (France): Sealink British Ferries and P&O European Ferries; Dover-Boulogne (France): P&O European Ferries; Folkestone-Boulogne (France): Sealink British Ferries. There are also Hoverspeed services for both cars and passengers between Dover and Calais and Dover and Boulogne.

ACCESS ROUTES. Bulgaria. Bulgaria is usually approached via West Germany, Austria and Yugoslavia, particularly by motorists in transit to Turkey. There are also border crossings from Romania and Greece.

From Romania—(E85/E83) Bucharest-Sofia; (E87) Black Sea coast road, Constanta-Varna. From Yugoslavia—(E770) Skopje-Sofia; (E80) Niš-Sofia. From Greece—(E79) Thessaloniki-Sofia. From Turkey—(E80) Istanbul-Sofia.

Czechoslovakia. The three principal routes are via West Germany, East Germany or Austria. From West Germany—(E12) Nürnberg-Plzeň. From East Germany (transit crossings only—not stopping or staying in Berlin West or East)—Leipzig or Berlin to (E15) Dresden-Prague. From Austria—(E14) Linz-České Budějovice-Prague; (E7) Vienna-Brno; (9) Vienna-Bratislava (A4 highway when completed).

East Germany. In addition to the points of entry from West Berlin, there are ten highway borders (West German highway number/West German town/East

German town): B104/Lübeck-Schlutup/Selmsdorf; A24/Gudow/Zarrentin; B5/ Lauenberg/Horst; B71/Bergen (Dumme)/Salzwedel; A2/Helmstedt/Marienborn; B247/Duderstadt/Worbis; Herleshausen/Wartha; B19/Eubenhausen/ Meiningen; B4/Rottenbach/Eisfeld; A9/Rudolphstein/Hirschberg. Your travel agent will be able to give you further details.

Hungary. The main entry point to Hungary is via Austria and the Vienna-Budapest highway. From Austria—(E5) Vienna-Budapest; (16) Vienna-Sopron; (65, 307, 8, 84) Graz-(Lake Balaton)-(E96/M7) Budapest. From Yugoslavia (E96) Zagreb-(Lake Balaton)-Budapest; (E5) Belgrade-Novi Sad-Szeged-Budapest.

Poland. Poland is best reached through East Germany or Czechoslovakia. From East Germany (E8) Berlin bypass-Frankfurt an der Oder-Poznań-Warsaw; (E8, E15/E22) Berlin bypass-Wrocław. From Czechoslovakia (E14) Prague-Wrocław; (E12) Prague-Wrocław; (E7) Brno-Cracow; (E16) Vienna-Bratislava-Cracow.

Romania. The most direct route to Romania is via West Germany, Austria and Hungary. From Hungary, travel via Budapest-Oradea (E15/E15A)-Bucharest. From Yugoslavia, travel via Belgrade-(E94)-Dobreta/Turnu Severin-Craiova-Bucharest.

BY BUS. The reliable operators have grouped together under the banner of National Express-Eurolines. Services run from London Victoria Coach Station to relatively few destinations in Eastern Europe. Berlin has three services a week during the summer, return fare around £86. There is a service to Poland, but the dates of operation tend to vary! The sole route is to Poznań, Warsaw, Wrocław, Katowice and Cracow—check for dates—and the trip takes three days. Return fare to any destination around £140. There is a weekly service to Zagreb in Yugoslavia. This also takes three days, return fare around £120. Details of all these services can be obtained from the operators: National Express-Eurolines, The Coach Travel Center, 13 Regent St., London SW1Y 4LR (tel. 01–730 0202)—or from any National Express coach station. *Note:* It is essential that you obtain visas for *all* the countries through which the bus travels. Also don't forget to take some spending money in local currency for buying refreshments en route.

BY BOAT. The only all year round direct sailing from the U.K. to Eastern Europe is the freighter service which alternates its calls between London (Tilbury) and Middlesbrough (Teeside) and sails to Gdynia on the Baltic coast of Poland, via the Kiel Canal. Passenger accommodations are limited. For details, contact Gdynia America Shipping Lines, 238 City Rd., London EC1. In North America, contact Gdynia American Shipping Lines, 39 Broadway, 14th Floor, New York, NY 10006.

Several companies run cruises along the Danube; these usually start at Passau in West Germany or Vienna in Austria. Peter Dielmann have recently introduced a cruise program (7 days) from Passau to Budapest and return, which is truly for the discerning in search of luxury and service. English spoken by all staff. Prices include all meals, accommodations and flight from London. Details from Peter Dielmann, Victoria Plaza, 111 Buckingham Palace Rd., London SW1W 0SP. Alternatively, try one of the cruises by Soviet Danube Lines which run from Passau calling at Vienna, Budapest, Belgrade, Ruse, and Giurgiu before entering the Soviet port of Izmail. There you change to an ocean-going vessel for a cruise to Istanbul calling at Yalta on the return run. On the upstream journey calls are made at Ruse, Nikopol, Tekija, Belgrade, Novisad, Budapest, Vienna, and Linz. The full round trip from Passau lasts 20 days and costs from 25,854 to 41,156 Austrian Schillings depending on class. There are several departures from April to September. Details from CTC Lines, 1 Regent St., London, SW1Y 4NN, or direct from Soviet Danube Shipping Agency, Freudenauer Hafenstrasse 8, A-1020 Vienna, Austria. More recently the Bulgarians have entered the Danube cruise market from Passau to Ruse with two fine modern ships. Details from the Bulgarian National Tourist Office.

The Romanians also now operate cruises from Vienna to Cernavodă, with bus connections to Black Sea resorts; details from the Romanian National Tourist Office.

From April to October there is a regular hydrofoil service from Vienna to Budapest (daily on weekdays, additional service on Mondays and Thursday in peak season), taking about 4½ hours. Single fare is around 800 Austrian Schillings. There is also a daily service (excluding Mondays) from April to mid-October between Vienna and Bratislava, which takes an hour. Timings are suitable for a day trip. Return fare is around 500 Austrian Schillings including port taxes and visa charges.

Arriving in Eastern Europe

BORDERS. A number of readers have reported long delays and/or abrupt treatment at border crossings, especially by road. Immigration officers in most countries are a law unto themselves and there is little to be done but to remain firm and courteous, and report unreasonable behavior to local representatives and the embassy concerned.

Getting Around Eastern Europe

BY PLANE. The state-owned airlines in Eastern Europe operate an extensive network of services within the region and, other than in Hungary, within their own countries. All the capitals are linked by services at least twice daily. Most services are by jets (generally TU 124s and 134s, more or less like DC9s and Boeing 727s). Some services, however, are still operated by four engined turbo-prop Ilyushin 18 aircraft while Tarom, the Romanian airline, flies British designed BAC 1–11s (twin jet). On some longer routes such as Prague to Bucharest the larger four engined Ilyushin 62 jet is used. Flights are usually all one class, although you will sometimes find that a special section has been marked off for VIPs.

In addition to the capital linking routes there are services connecting main cities in neighboring countries, for example Cracow (Poland) and Bratislava (Czechoslovakia).

BY TRAIN. The railways of Eastern Europe are all state-owned and are mainly standard gauge (although the broad Russian gauge penetrates into part of Czechoslovakia), with some narrow gauge services. Traction is electric or diesel, with the former rapidly expanding. There are still a few steam trains left in operation.

Standards have improved in the last few years although on the whole they are far short of what is acceptable in the West. Trains are very busy and it is rare to find one running less than full or almost so. The design of carriages is similar to that in Western Europe (often they are indistinguishable, although the decor is more severe) and some of the crack expresses are quite luxurious.

All the countries operate their own dining, buffet and refreshment services. Always busy, they tend to open and close at the whims of the staff. Sleeping cars and couchettes for internal travel are directly operated by the railways, other than in Poland where they are operated by Orbis. Through sleeping cars from the U.S.S.R. are all Soviet owned and operated. Couchette cars are second class only.

Full timetables for individual countries aren't easy to come by. Berolina Travel, the East German State travel organization, will send the East German railway timetable. The timetables for Czechoslovakia, Hungary and Poland are available from BAS Overseas Publications, 48–50 Sheen Lane, London SW14 8LP.

Buying a ticket for internal travel within each country is comparatively easy though always time-consuming. Never leave it to the last minute. For international travel (unless you have already obtained your ticket outside Eastern Europe) it is not so easy. It is highly advisable to enlist the help of the nearest office of the State Tourist Organization. In most cases they will be able to issue the ticket or at least obtain it for you.

In those cities where there are several stations—Warsaw, Prague and Budapest are the best examples—be quite certain which station your train leaves from or arrives at. It is not always as logical as it might seem.

While as we have said trains are always busy in Eastern Europe we do recommend that you use them at least for part of your travel. You will almost certainly find that your fellow travelers are more than ready to enter into conversation—a rarity at airports.

BY CAR. The main roads of Eastern Europe are built to a fairly high standard in tarmac or concrete. There are now quite substantial stretches of highway on main routes and a lot of road rebuilding work is being carried out. Some information on where the worst of the delays caused by roadworks occur is available from British motoring organizations. Off the main roads, and throughout much of Romania, surfacing may be poor and care should be taken to avoid vehicle damage.

Particular road dangers to be wary of are—extremely slippy conditions on tarmac after light rain; sudden drastic changes in camber; the many slow agricultural vehicles (some animal drawn); the poor lighting of trucks, bikes and farm carts at night; and wandering livestock in rural areas. In towns the major public transport is by trams—treat them warily as they have the right of way over cars in many situations, people get off and on in the middle of the street (they have absolute priority) and at road junctions they can cut in unexpectedly from the left.

Gas stations are fewer than in the West, sited at intervals of about 30 miles (48 km) along main routes and on the outskirts of large towns. Very few stations are open after 9.30 P.M. At least two grades of petrol are sold in all countries—usually 90–93 octane (regular) and 96–98 octane (super). Hungary is unusual in that Western brands of fuel are available—Shell, BP and Agip. The supply of gas to filling stations is by no means regular, so that there are sometimes long lines and considerable delays. Try to keep your tank topped up. Tourists nearly always require Super for their Western-built cars, and some Eastern bloc countries will not sell anything else.

Note that in Bulgaria, Poland and Romania, gasoline is only available to visitors in exchange for vouchers pre-paid in hard currency. Details are given in Facts at Your Fingertips for each country.

Also note that in East Germany a highway toll is charged, payable in West German currency. It is M.5 for up to 200 km., M.15 for up to 300 km., M.20 for up to 400 km. and M.25 for up to 500 km.

Rules of the road. In all countries of Eastern Europe traffic police have the power to make on-the-spot fines for minor motoring offences. In more serious cases the state can order the vehicle to be impounded and a cash deposit may be levied against future legal costs. After an accident, even a minor one, ensure that the police are called, summon medical assistance if necessary and remain with your vehicle if at all possible. In all countries it is necessary to inform the nearest office of the state's vehicle insurance company as soon as possible after an accident.

Throughout Eastern Europe it is prohibited to drink and drive—there is no fixed permitted alcohol level and heavy penalties can be imposed (prison terms are not unusual) on any driver proven to have taken alcohol.

Main road speed limits vary from 80 kph to 100 kph (50 mph to 62 mph) and up to 120 kph (72 mph) on the few stretches of motorways; these are advised by conventional speed limit signs. In towns speed limits are 50 to 60 kph (31 mph to 37 mph). Precise speed limit details are available from your automobile club. In Bulgaria main road parking is limited to lay-bys designated by 'P'; in Hungary only on the right-hand side; in Czechoslovakia it is forbidden on main roads.

On most main routes traffic has priority over sideroad traffic, but on anything other than the main international routes, unless otherwise indicated, traffic emerging from the right has priority. At roundabouts traffic entering has priority over traffic on the roundabout—except in Poland where the reverse of this system is operated, but in Eastern European countries nothing, but nothing, should be taken for granted by visiting motorists. The wearing of seat belts is compulsory.

In Bulgaria, border police have the power to inspect vehicles and insist that any repair work they deem necessary be carried out before the vehicle can enter the country. It is as well to recognize that crossing the frontiers of a communist country, even when all goes well, can be a very long business. For this reason it is essential that all your papers should be in order and that you can produce them instantly when requested. Border guards take their work very seriously and it is advisable to take them seriously, too.

Road signs in all the countries are the same international types used in Western Europe with a few local variations. In all countries, except Bulgaria, main route signposting is in Roman characters. In Bulgaria there are a few dual-language signs on major tourist routes, but away from these the majority of signposts have Cyrillic characters. For reference to Western maps you will have to translate the destinations into Roman characters (use the conversion alphabet given on page 81).

For roadside assistance, help with any legal problems after accidents and tourist information, contact the following head offices of the automobile clubs in the relevant country.

Bulgaria. *Union of Bulgarian Motorists* (SBA), 6 Sveta Sofia St., Sofia (tel. 878801). Emergency service, tel. 146 in main town areas.

Czechoslovakia. *Autoturist,* Na Rybničku 16, Prague 2 (tel. 203355). Emergency service in Prague, tel. 154 (motorists), 155 (ambulance), 158 (police).

East Germany. There is no national organization, but on the autobahns emergency phones will connect you with the nearest service station.

Hungary. *Magyar Autóklub* (MAK), Rómer Flóris Utca 4/a, Budapest II (tel. 666–404); emergency service 260–668.

Poland. *Polski Zwiazek Motorowy* (PZM), ul. Krucza 14, Warsaw (tel. 296252). Ring local offices for breakdown service.

Romania. *Automobil Clubul Roman* (ACR), Strada Cihovschi 2, Bucharest 1 (tel. 123456 in Bucharest, 12345 elsewhere in Romania). Local office telephone numbers for breakdown emergencies are shown on road signs.

Car Hire. Both major Western car rental companies, *Avis* and *Hertz,* can make advanced bookings on rental cars in the Eastern bloc countries. Bookings are made through the normal international reservations system with associate companies in the particular country. Fly-drive packages ex-U.K. are available in most of the countries concerned. See *Facts at your Fingertips* for each country.

You can hire cars within Eastern Europe from major hotel reception desks or through the tourist offices.

Conversion Tables. One of the most confusing experiences for many motorists is their first encounter with the metric system, used all over Europe.

The following quick conversion tables may help speed you on your way.

Kilometers into Miles

This simple chart will help you to convert to both miles and kilometers. If you want to convert from miles into kilometers read from the center column to the right, if from kilometers into miles, from the center column to the left. Example: 5 miles = 8.0 kilometers, 5 kilometers = 3.1 miles.

Miles		Kilometers	Miles		Kilometers
0.6	1	1.6	37.3	60	96.6
1.2	2	3.2	43.5	70	112.3
1.9	3	4.8	49.7	80	128.7
2.5	4	6.3	55.9	90	144.8
3.1	5	8.0	62.1	100	160.9
3.7	6	9.6	124.3	200	321.9
4.3	7	11.3	186.4	300	482.8
5.0	8	12.9	248.5	400	643.7
5.6	9	14.5	310.7	500	804.7

Miles		Kilometers	Miles		Kilometers
6.2	10	16.1	372.8	600	965.6
12.4	20	32.2	434.9	700	1,126.5
18.6	30	48.3	497.1	800	1,287.5
24.8	40	64.4	559.2	900	1,448.4
31.0	50	80.5	621.4	1,000	1,609.3

Tire Pressure Converter

Pounds per Square Inch	16	18	20	22	24	26	28	30	32
Kilogrammes per Square Centimeter	1.12	1.26	1.40	1.54	1.68	1.82	1.96	2.10	2.24

Gallons into Liters

U.S.		Imperial (British)	
Gallon	Liters	Gallon	Liters
1	3.78	1	4.54
2	7.57	2	9.09
3	11.36	3	13.63
4	15.14	4	18.18
5	18.93	5	22.73
6	22.71	6	27.27
7	26.50	7	31.82
8	30.28	8	36.36
9	34.07	9	40.91
10	37.85	10	45.46

There are 5 Imperial (British) gallons to 6 U.S. gallons.

Leaving Eastern Europe

CUSTOMS ON RETURNING HOME. U.S. Residents may bring in $400 worth of foreign merchandise as gifts or for personal use without having to pay duty, provided they have been out of the country more than 48 hours and provided they have not claimed a similar exemption within the previous 30 days. Every member of a family is entitled to the same exemption, regardless of age, and the exemptions can be pooled. For the next $1,000 worth of goods, inspectors will assess a flat 10% duty based on the price actually paid, so it is a good idea to keep your receipts.

Included in the $400 allowance for travelers over the age of 21 are one liter of alcohol, 100 cigars (non-Cuban) and 200 cigarettes. Any amount in excess of those limits will be taxed at the port of entry, and may additionally be taxed in the traveler's home state. Only one bottle of perfume trademarked in the U.S. may be brought in. However, there is no duty on antiques or art over 100 years old—though you may be called upon to provide verification of the item's age. Write to U.S. Customs Service, Box 7407, Washington, DC 20044, for information regarding importation of automobiles and/or motorcycles. You may not bring home meats, fruits, plants, soil or other agricultural items.

Gifts valued at under $50 may be mailed to friends or relatives at home, but not more than one per day (of receipt) to any one addressee. These gifts must not include perfumes costing more than $5, tobacco or liquor.

If you are traveling with such foreign made articles as cameras, watches or binoculars that were purchased at home, it is best either to carry the receipt for them with you or to register them with U.S. Customs prior to departing. This will save much time (and potential aggravation) upon your return.

Canadian Residents may, after 7 days out of the country and upon written declaration, claim an exemption of $300 in Canadian funds a year plus an allowance of 40 ounces of liquor, 50 cigars, 200 cigarettes and 2 lb of tobacco. Personal gifts should be mailed as 'Unsolicited gifts, value under $40'. For further details, ask for the Canadian Customs brochure, *I Declare.*

British Residents, except those under the age of 17 years, may import duty-free from *any* country the following: 200 cigarettes or 100 cigarillos or 50 cigars or 250 grams of tobacco; 1 liter of alcoholic drinks over 22% volume or 2 liters of alcoholic drinks not over 22% fortified, sparkling or still wine, plus 2 liters of still table wine. Also 50 grams of perfume, ¼ liter of toilet water and £32 worth of other normally dutiable goods.

Returning from any EEC country, you may, instead of the above exemptions, bring in the following, provided they were *not* bought in a duty-free shop: 300 cigarettes or 150 cigarillos or 75 cigars or 400 grams of tobacco; 1½ liters of alcoholic drinks over 22% volume or 3 liters of alcoholic drinks not over 22% or fortified, sparkling or still wines, plus 5 liters of still table wine; 75 grams of perfume and ⅜ liter of toilet water and £250 worth of other normally dutiable goods.

BULGARIA

BULGARIA—FACTS AT YOUR FINGERTIPS

HOW TO GO. The main tourist authority in Bulgaria is the Bulgarian Association for Tourism and Recreation under whose umbrella come such separate organizations as Balkantourist, which is principally concerned with foreign travelers. The Association also runs the Bulgarian National Tourist Offices overseas. These do not organize tours to Bulgaria themselves (this can only be done by travel agents officially accredited by Balkantourist, which includes many of the major operators), but they will be able to advise on all aspects of travel to and within the country. And indeed within Bulgaria, they own and operate a growing chain of hotels and restaurants and arrange tours of all kinds as well as being responsible for currency exchange.

The addresses of the Bulgarian National Tourist Office are:

In the U.S., Balkan Holidays, 161 East 86th St., New York, NY 10028 (tel. 212–722–1110).
In the U.K., 18 Princes St., London W1R 7RE (tel. 01–499–6988).

Balkantourist also run offices handling reservations and dispensing information in all towns and resorts.

Of special interest to independent travelers is the Bureau of Tourist Information and Reservations in Sofia which is a central agency for all accommodations and travel reservations. Its two offices can be found at the Palace of Culture, off Vitoša Blvd., and 35 Eksarh Josif St., near Lenin Square.

TOURS. The least expensive and simplest way to visit Bulgaria is on prepaid package tours which are available for groups and individuals. Thus independent travelers can also benefit from advantageous hotel rates, while still retaining freedom of movement through the systems of currency or meal vouchers (see "Money" and "Restaurants" below) which have been devised to provide more flexibility.

In 1988 the cost of a two-week holiday (ex-London) in a popular Black Sea resort, at the height of the season, was from £275 to £550 depending on the category of accommodations. This includes a return flight, half board, and an allocation of meal vouchers enabling visitors to eat at other Balkantourist hotels and restaurants (which means most of them). Prices drop by up to one-third for off-season holidays, when other extras, such as a free evening of folklore entertainment, and some free sports amenities, are often provided. Reductions for children of two to 12 years can be 25–50%, and from 13 to 16 years 20–25% when sharing accommodations with adults. Families with small children are particularly well catered for in terms of child-minding services and entertainments for the young.

Other possibilities include the combination of a week on the coast with a week touring by coach throughout the country. Danube cruises all the way upstream from the Bulgarian river port of Ruse to Vienna are combined with short stays in Vienna, Sofia and a Black Sea resort. In winter, skiing packages are arranged and, throughout the low season, weekend trips to Sofia and other short-duration arrangements are available.

Among less conventional arrangements are those devoted specially to Bulgarian culture and history, monastery tours, a cookery and wine-tasting tour, and attractive itineraries traveling by horse-drawn caravan. For groups, pottery, woodcarving, carpet weaving, folk dancing and embroidery courses are also featured, and sporting holidays include hunting, riding and fishing. Arrangements can be made by Balkantourist to cater for any special interest or study group; for example, those devoted to agriculture or different branches of industry. Excursions of one or more

31

days in length are organized from main towns and resorts, ranging from local sight-seeing to trips to Greece, Turkey, Romania or even Moscow or Leningrad.

Those who do not wish to be tied by prearranged itineraries can book a Freelance Holiday (return flight and currency voucher), enabling them to plan from day to day, though naturally at the height of the season they run the risk of finding hotels fully booked. Similarly, they can prepay the hire of a self-drive car.

The major tour operators are:

In the U.S., *Balkan Holidays USA Ltd.,* 161 E. 86th St., New York, NY 10028 (tel. 212–722–1110). *Litoral Travel,* 249 E. 77th St., New York, NY 10021 (tel. 212–535–7746).

In the U.K., *Balkan Holidays Ltd.,* Sofia House, 19 Conduit St., London W1R 9TD (tel. 01–493–8612). *Enterprise,* P.O. Box 100, 17–27 High St., Hounslow, Middlesex TW3 1TB (tel. 01–370–4545). *Global,* 26 Elmfield Rd., Bromley, Kent BR1 1LR (tel. 01–464–6666). *Intasun,* Cromwell Ave., Bromley, Kent BR2 9AQ (tel. 01–290–1900).

VISAS. The following do not require visas: 1) tourists traveling on a package tour by charter flight or in groups of six or more by scheduled transport, unless they plan an overnight trip (other than Balkantourist excursion) away from the tour arrangements; 2) married couples with or without children or single parents with one or more children, providing they pay a minimum of two overnights at Balkantourist offices at the border. Otherwise apply to the Bulgarian Embassy for visas which, at press time cost, in the U.K.: single transit (valid 30 hours) £6; double transit £10; tourist entry £10. No visas are issued at the border checkpoints, but you can extend your stay by obtaining permission from the country's passport services.

American travelers should apply for their visas at least two to three weeks before departure to the Embassy of the People's Republic of Bulgaria, 1621 22nd St. NW, Washington DC 20008. They should submit the following: a valid passport, visa application, one passport-size photo, a self-addressed envelope with $4 for postage and handling, plus $15, the visa fee at press time.

MONEY. Unlike some other East European countries, Bulgaria imposes no minimum daily expenditure obligations.

The unit of currency is the lev (plural leva), divided into 100 stotinki. There are notes of 1, 2, 5, 10 and 20 leva; coins of 1, 2, 5, 10, 20 and 50 stotinki, and 1, 2 and 5 leva. The rate of exchange at the time of writing (mid-1988) was approximately 0.95 lev to the U.S. dollar and 1.50 to the pound sterling.

You may import any amount of foreign currency, including traveler's checks, and exchange it at branches of the Bulgarian State Bank, Balkantourist hotels and offices, airports and all border posts. If possible, always exchange it through a Balkantourist office which will add a generous currency bonus, providing you have paid a minimum of two nights' hotel accommodations.

Both the import and export of Bulgarian currency is forbidden; unspent leva *must* be exchanged at frontier posts on departure *before* going through passport control, using official exchange slips to show the leva were legally purchased. There is an active black market in foreign currency but there are very heavy penalties should you be caught in such illegal transactions (you are also likely to be cheated).

Credit Cards. Major credit cards such as American Express, Diners Club, MasterCard (Access, Eurocard), Visa and so on, are accepted in larger stores, hotels and restaurants.

COSTS. Costs in Bulgaria, as in most East European countries, are generally low, and it is eminently possible to have a very reasonably-priced holiday here. The generous currency bonus (see *Money*) is an additional advantage. As in the case of other East European countries, Bulgaria is best geared to prepaid arrangements, though these can be very flexible, as outlined in *Tours.* However, prepaid vouchers, for all their advantages, are valid only for accommodations and restaurants listed by Balkantourist and their varied services. Establishments run by other agencies can also offer good—at times even better—value. If you are prepared to take the rough with the smooth and exercise patience, you may well be rewarded by experiencing areas not on the usual tourist circuits and by a closer contact with the Bulgarian people. On the whole though, most people prefer to play safe and take advantage of the increasingly varied opportunities offered by Balkantourist.

Sample Costs. Theater or opera seat from 1.20 to 6.0 leva (more for international performances); museum entrance 0.20–0.90 leva; coffee in moderate restaurant 1–2 leva; bottle of wine in moderate restaurant from 4 leva; trip on a tram, trolley, or bus 6 stotinki.

MEDICAL INSURANCE. Bulgaria has a reciprocal health arrangement with the U.K. and British visitors are recommended to carry their National Health Medical Card. Charges are normally made only for any medicines prescribed. Other nationals are advised to have medical insurance, though emergency treatment is usually free. In Sofia, there is a Clinic for Foreign Citizens at Mladost 1, 1 Evgeni Pavolvski St. (tel. 75361).

CLIMATE. Very warm, but not unpleasant even in summer when Black Sea resorts benefit from breezes and, inland, one can cool off in the mountains. Coastal areas get 2,240 hours of sunshine per year, nearly 30% more than southern England. Cold, crisp winters give good snow conditions for skiing in mountain resorts.
The Black Sea coast has a rather long season, from late May to October. It's at its warmest and liveliest in July and August, but there is much to be said for the more temperate and less crowded months of spring and autumn. The coast is rather dry throughout the year, inland the wettest months are March/April. If you choose May or early June you will witness the fabulous harvesting of blooms in the Valley of the Roses (providing you are prepared to get up early). April/May are good times for fruit blossom, October for Fall colors. The main skiing season is January through March, and this is also the time when Sofia is enjoying a lively season of cultural events. Main festivities are listed below.

Average afternoon daily temperatures in degrees Fahrenheit and centigrade:

Sofia	Jan.	Feb.	Mar.	Apr.	May	June	July	Aug.	Sept.	Oct.	Nov.	Dec.
F°	34	39	51	62	70	76	82	82	74	63	50	37
C°	1	4	11	17	21	24	28	28	23	17	10	3

SPECIAL EVENTS. Balkantourist can give the latest information, but the following are the most important annual festivals:
Local traditional events are particularly lively along the Black Sea coast throughout the summer and in the towns and villages around Christmas and New Year. The most important among them are Trifon Zaresan, the vinegrowers' festival, **February** 14; Martenitzas, the Festival of Spring, **March** 1; Lararouvane, Slavic festival of youth and marriagable girls, **April** 1; Labor Day, **May** 1; St. George's Day, May 6; and The Day of Bulgarian Culture, May 24. The International Sofia Weeks of Music run for four weeks during May and **June,** and in the first half of June the Festival of Roses is celebrated with parades and carnivals at Karlovo and Kazanluk. The International Book Fair at Sofia and the Golden Orpheus International Pop Festival (alternate years, even numbers) at Sunny Beach also fall in June.
In **June and July** the Summer International Festival of Music is held in Varna and Golden Sands; the International Ballet Contest in Varna (every two years); and Song and Dance Festivals at Golden Sands. In late **August** the International Folklore Festival flourishes at Bourgas and Sunny Beach. In **September** there is an International Arts Festival at Plovdiv (the second city), which also fills its hotels in May

and September with delegates to the two International Trade Fairs. In **November** Pleven hosts the Katya Popova Laureate Days International Festival.

National Holidays. Jan. 1; May 1 and 2 (Labor Day); May 24 (Day of Bulgarian Culture); Sept. 9 and 10 (Liberation Days); Nov. 7 (October Revolution Day).

CUSTOMS. You may import duty free into Bulgaria 250 grs. of tobacco products, plus one liter of spirits and two liters of wine. It's advisable to declare valuable items such as cameras, tape recorders, etc. in order to facilitate re-exportation when leaving the country. Articles up to the value of 50 leva may be exported but items of great historic or cultural value and works of art are, of course, prohibited. Foreign currency purchases may be freely exported. Customs and currency inspection tend to be casual. For currency regulations, see "Money."

LANGUAGE. Bulgarian is a Slav language, closely allied to Russian and written in the Cyrillic alphabet. Though the Latin alphabet is increasingly common in tourist spots it is highly advisable, especially for independent travelers, to learn the Cyrillic letters, if only to identify *PECTOPAHT* as "restaurant," to be able to read road signs away from the main routes and to find museums. As yet very little tourist literature is available in English away from the main cities and Black Sea resorts. English is spoken and understood fairly widely. It is important to remember that in Bulgaria, a nod of the head means "no" and a shake of the head, "yes."

There is also the problem of spelling in the Latin alphabet, which varies considerably from one source to another. Most official maps use a system of accents, and this is the form we have adopted throughout these chapters. However, many tourist publications employ a phonetic spelling and the following may help in identifying (and pronouncing) places, hotel names, dishes etc. spelt by this method: Borovec–Borovets; Caravec–Tsaravets; Družba–Drouzhba; Nesebâr–Nessebur; Slânčev Brjag–Slunchev Bryag; Šipka–Shipka; Târnovo–Turnovo; Vitoša–Vitosha; Zlatni Pjasâci–Zlatni Pyassutsi.

A detailed transcription of the Cyrillic alphabet is given under *Tourist Vocabulary.*

HOTELS. Hotels in Bulgaria are divided according to the international one- to five-star system. These correspond more or less exactly to our grading of Bulgarian hotels in the listings that follow as five-star Deluxe (L), four-star Expensive (E), three-star Moderate (M) and two- or one-star Inexpensive (I). In addition to these official gradings, there are about a dozen in the first two categories that are classified as Interhotels. In theory, this means that they conform to international standards expected of hotels of this type. In practise however, this is by no means always the case.

A high proportion of hotels date from the 1960s and 1970s and, aware of some of their shortcomings, the Bulgarians' present policy is to concentrate on the improvement of existing hotels rather than the building of new ones (with some exceptions as shown in our hotel lists). As elsewhere in Eastern Europe, one of the most common faults is erratic plumbing.

Most of the hotels used by Western visitors are owned by Balkantourist. In some of the coastal resorts there are sprawling modern complexes each consisting of several hotels of different categories, often with their own shops, hairdressers and entertainment facilities. The general impression can be rather clinical, but what they lack in local character, they make up for in convenience.

Other hotels are run by the municipal authorities or by organizations catering for particular categories of visitor, usually in groups only. Examples are the establishments operated by Šipka for motorists, Orbita for young people, Pirin for hikers and Cooptourist for Cooperative farmers.

Two people in a double room with half board can expect to pay:

	Sofia	Elsewhere
Deluxe (L)	over $115	over $90

Expensive (E)	$70–$115	$50–$90
Moderate (M)	$50–$70	$35–$50
Inexpensive (I)	$25–$50	$20–$35

Note that prices in Black Sea resorts are usually at the upper end of these ranges for the high season, but reductions of 25–40% apply in the low season. There are also substantial reductions for children (see "Tours" above).

Self-Catering

This is a growth industry in Bulgaria. Major new complexes tastefully built with foreign cooperation at Dyuni and Elinité on the Black Sea coast offer a wide range of amenities. Elsewhere, picturesque cottages in the "museum town" of Koprivštica and the fishing port of Sozopol are on offer, as well as individually-styled bungalows of a former artists' colony called Zora (Dawn) on the Black Sea near Slânčev Brjag (Sunny Beach). The typical self-catering cottage has basic sleeping, bathing and snack-food facilities (boil a kettle but not cook a meal) and vouchers for meals in local restaurants are included in the deal. An English-speaking manager is always on hand. Arrange with Balkantourist, New York or London. All-in rates for 1988, ex-London were £189–£305 per head (if four in a party) for 14 days full board in a villa, depending on the grade of the villa and the season. Prices for apartments are lower.

Private Accommodations

These have increased enormously in recent years and offer an excellent opportunity to experience Bulgaria from a different angle, as well as inexpensively. There are now 150,000 beds available, about three-quarters of them on the coast. Balkantourist can make the arrangements for you. Costs per person in the top of three categories are: bed and breakfast for two, from about $12 in Sofia, from $10 elsewhere.

Hostels

These provide clean though basic accommodations for those on a tight budget. Check with Orbita, 45A Stambolijski St. in Sofia.

Camping

There are over 100 campsites throughout the country many of them near the Black Sea beaches. These are classified as three-, two-, and one-star, and in the top two categories will have hot and cold water, showers, electricity, grocery stores and restaurants. A map showing their location is available from Balkantourist. Those on the coast and in the winter resorts of Borovec and Pamporovo have attractive bungalows for hire.

RESTAURANTS. One of the best ways to eat in Bulgaria is to take advantage of the excellent prepaid voucher scheme under which you can eat in a variety of different restaurants even if you have booked for full board in a particular hotel. These meal vouchers are issued on arrival in Bulgaria, the number of them varying according to the category of accommodations booked. They are valid in all Balkantourist restaurants throughout the country. They also have the advantage of allowing you to eat modestly on one occasion and gorge on another; or pay the difference and gorge every time. Unfortunately, in those inexpensive restaurants and cafeterias run by municipal authorities, vouchers are not valid. Unspent vouchers cannot be exchanged for currency on departure.

The standard varies considerably, but has improved a great deal in recent years, though there is still a tendency to serve food lukewarm. The standard in the smaller folk-style restaurants is often better than in the main tourist hotels. An increasing number of these attractive establishments have been opened, not only in resorts, but in towns and villages along the way. Frequently there is folkloric music, and sometimes dancing. Evening meals in hotels are invariably accompanied by music and, in the Balkans, they like their music *loud*. If you are among those who don't, it can be an endurance test!

Prices are very reasonable, and in the establishments listed in the following pages you can estimate as follows: Expensive (E) 15–20 leva, Moderate (M) 10–15 leva, Inexpensive (I) 5–10 leva; all exclusive of strong drinks and per person.

TIPPING. Officially this is discouraged, but is nevertheless acceptable—10% is safe.

MAIL. Letters and postcards cost 45 stotinki to the U.K., 60 stotinki to North America; but check before mailing.

TIME. Bulgaria is seven hours ahead of Eastern Standard Time and two hours ahead of Greenwich Mean Time.

CLOSING TIMES. Stores keep about the same hours as their counterparts in America and Britain. Most open between 8 and 10, and close between 5 and 7, Monday through Friday, or 12–2 on Saturday. Quite often shops may close for several hours in the middle of the day, staying open later in the evening, especially in summer. Some stores operate non-stop throughout the day in main centers. Museums are usually open 8 to 6.30, but are often closed Monday or Tuesday. Check locally.

SHOPPING. The State commercial organization *Corecom* runs a network of shops in which Bulgarian and imported articles are sold for hard currency only, at favorable prices. There is a branch in most main hotels. Some of the attractive local items to look out for are replicas of antique jewelry, leatherwork, woodcarving, embroidery, metalwork, and copies of some of the beautiful old icons and medieval frescoes.

SPAS. Bulgaria has well over 500 mineral springs and some 130 spas. There are major spas at the following places: Velingrad, in the Rhodope Mountains, Kjustendil, in western Bulgaria, Sandanski, in the foothills of the Pirin Mountains, Hisarya, on the southern slopes of the Sredna Gora Mountains. There are also a number of spas on the Black Sea coast. Cost of treatment is very low by Western standards—more expensive on the Black Sea coast. Spa packages at Sandanski and on the Black Sea coast are now marketed ex-U.K.

SPORTS. Facilities for waterskiing, sailing and windsurfing exist in the Black Sea coastal resorts, along with tennis and mini-golf and possibilities for horse riding and cycling. Fishing and hunting tours are organized by Balkantourist who can make all the necessary arrangements regarding permits, guides, equipment and accommodations. Game includes various species of deer, wild boar, pheasant, duck and, on occasions, bear and wild goat. Birdwatching holidays can be arranged and walking tours are marketed ex-U.K.

WINTER SPORTS. In recent years, Bulgarian winter sports resorts have begun to make their impact on Western markets, the main centers being Vitoša just beside Sofia, Pamporovo south of Plovdiv, and Borovec south-east of Sofia in the Rila Mountains. Costs compare very favorably with those of Western resorts, but don't expect the variety and sophistication of après-ski or the same choice of ski runs that you would find in the established Alpine centers. Information on current winter sports tours can be had from the Balkantourist offices.

MONASTERIES. There are a large number of monasteries in Bulgaria, some of which made a vital contribution to keeping the nation's cultural identity alive during the dark centuries of Turkish rule. Their secluded positions, often deep in the mountains and difficult to reach, largely protected them from the destruction that took place elsewhere. Nevertheless, battles and fires took their toll and many of the original buildings were rebuilt in the early decades of the 19th century, bequeathing their own testimonial to the vitality and talents of the National Revival movement. Older buildings and treasures that have survived are also to be found in these beautiful places. The best-known are those of Rila in the heart of the Rila Mountains south of Sofia; Bačkovo, in the Rhodopes south of Plovdiv; Trojan in the central Balkan Range; Drjanovo, in the Balkan Range between Veliko Târnovo and Gabrovo; Rožen, near Melnik in the southwest corner of Bulgaria; and Preobraženski near Veliko Târnovo. An excellent booklet describing these is available from Balkantourist. Entrance is free but some ask a small charge for visiting museum collections.

GETTING AROUND BULGARIA. By Air. The state airline *Balkan Bulgarian Airlines* (often known as *Balkanair*) have two internal routes linking Sofia the capital with Burgas and Varna on the Black Sea coast. Flight times are between about 50 minutes (by turbo-prop) and 35 minutes (by jet). There are several services each way daily. Other domestic air links from Sofia are to Gorna Orjahovica, Ruse, Silistra, Târgovište and Vidin. Overbooking is not unusual; best book through Balkantourist offices.

By Train. Buy tickets in advance at a railway ticket office—there is one in each of the major centers—and avoid long lines at the station. Trains are very busy—seat reservations are obligatory on expresses. All medium and long distance trains have 1st- and 2nd-class carriages and limited buffet services; overnight trains between Sofia and Black Sea resorts have 1st- and 2nd-class sleeping cars and bunk beds. From Sofia there are five main routes—to Varna and to Burgas on the Black Sea coast; to Plovdiv and on to the Turkish border; to Dragoman and the Yugoslav border; and to Kulata and the Greek border. Large sections of the main line are electrified—plans to electrify the rest are under way.

By Boat. In addition to the cruise vessels (see page 22) there are hydrofoil services along the Bulgarian stretch of the Danube linking a number of towns. From Vidin to Calafat there is a vehicle ferry linking Bulgaria with Romania. Summer hydrofoil and boat services operate along the Black Sea coast.

By Car. If you do not have a Green Card you will need to obtain a Blue Card (insurance you can obtain at the frontier checkpoint). Traffic drives on the right, and the usual continental rules of the road should be observed. Do not sound horn after dark and avoid using it at all in towns. Speed limits are 60 kph (37 mph) in built-up areas, 80 kph (50 mph) elsewhere except on motorways where it is 120 kph (80 mph). The limit for cars towing caravans is 10–20 kph (6–12 mph) less. The law concerning drinking and driving is very strict—no alcohol allowed at all. You are now also required to carry a first-aid kit in the vehicle.

At border points, be prepared for a delay while your documents are deciphered and duly stamped. A large-scale motorway construction program has begun which will eventually link all main towns on a circular route. Completed stretches include Kalotina (Yugoslav border)–Sofia and Sofia–Plovdiv. Motorways are free of charge. Otherwise main roads are good, though some stretches of through routes are narrow for the weight of traffic they have to carry. The number of gasoline stations on such main roads is reasonable; elsewhere they may be few and far between. You will find them marked on the motoring map issued free by Balkantourist. Bring a spare parts kit with you.

Note: gasoline in Bulgaria can only be purchased with vouchers bought with hard currency in advance from Šipka Tourist agency offices at the border, in cities and resorts, and Balkantourist roadside facilities. In case of trouble, dial 146.

A new Rent-a-Car organization has been set up with offices in several main centers. Independent self-drive holidays can be prebooked through Balkantourist agents abroad. There are also fly-drive arrangements.

INTRODUCING BULGARIA

Until relatively recently, few foreign tourists visited Bulgaria. Its people, tucked away in the heart of the Balkan peninsula, were considered rather mysterious. What did we know of them? That, in the 19th century, they were the victims of some terrible atrocities; that they produced bass singers and champion weight-lifters; that they also produced a perfume oil called attar of roses and an expensive tobacco, Balkan Sobranie—that was about all.

We know them better now. Since the early 1960s tourism has been Bulgaria's chief industry. More than six million vacationers visit Bulgaria annually, most of them from the West. A splendid coastline on the Black Sea, a lovely hinterland of forested ridges, lakes and swift rivers, burgeoning winter sports resorts, picturesque monasteries and old towns, a diverse flora and fauna, a rich colorful folklore and a settled climate—all these features proclaim a land made for tourists. And, although Bulgaria is the Soviet Union's most faithful client and supporter, she is in some ways the most westernized of Eastern bloc countries, with simplified passport and visa formalities, sophisticated hotels, self-catering cottages and an amazingly open and tolerant attitude to the foibles (and, sadly, the patronizing condescension) of her Western guests.

Turmoil of History

Some say the Danube basin, between Bulgaria and Romania, was the cradle of the human race. The Bulgarians go along with that. Archeological finds have demonstrated the presence of a settled, artistic people as far back as 6000 B.C. The extensive building programs of the post-war regime have turned up evidence in pots, wall-paintings and sculptures of prehistoric cultural dynasties—generations of farming and shepherd folk who developed the characteristic "sampler" patterns in black, red and green which today decorate the craftworks and fabrics in the folk-art shops of Sofia.

Those early inhabitants were Thracians, often mentioned in Greek mythology (Orpheus was one of them). But they were absorbed by Alexander the Great and his armies. Then came the Romans, to establish the great crossroads cities of Serdica (Sofia) and Trimontium (Plovdiv), to uncover warm springs which are still in use and to push their northern frontier to the Danube. All Bulgaria's river ports had Roman names: Vidin was Bonnonia, Silistra was Durostorum.

The vacuum left by the departing Romans in 395 A.D. was gradually filled by invading Slavs, the chief ethnic component in Bulgaria's population today; but it was a rival race, of Turkish origin, which appointed the first real king, Khan Asparukh, in 681. Despite the attempts of Byzantine emperors to break up the emergent kingdom, it hung together, adopted Christianity, and launched a monastic tradition which flowered brilliantly around 865, when the brother-monks Cyril and Methodius created the first Slav alphabet. (Hence the term "Cyrillic" for the script used in most Slav countries now.)

Scholars speak of this church-inspired golden age as the Bulgarian Renaissance, and indeed, Old Bulgarian survived as an ecclesiastical language from that very early time—a powerful missionary tool.

Turkish Domination

The Byzantines eventually conquered the country. Through the 12th century Bulgaria was at the mercy of the Crusaders (vicious freebooters, not at all the saints in armor that legend portrays). The nation found another champion, Ivan Assen II, a clever ambitious leader, who secured her independence and removed the capital from Preslav on the plains (it had its 1,000th birthday in 1981) to Veliko Târnovo above the mountain gorges. But in 1393 this most attractive and romantically-sited of Bulgarian cities fell to the Turks. They maintained an iron grip on the country for the next five centuries. For Bulgaria, history stood still; but surreptitiously, in fortified monasteries which were also citadels of refuge for a cowering population, notable works of art and literature were produced.

Uprisings against the Turks grew more frequent as the influence of this cultural revival began to be felt at home and abroad. Two prominent revolutionaries were Vassil Levsky (1837–1873) and Hristo Botev (1848–1876). They died violently and young, but you cannot avoid being reminded of them in the names of Bulgaria's streets, lakes and mountains. The most promising revolt, the so-called "April Uprising," took place in 1876 at Koprivštica, now a mountain resort of brightly-painted cottages. It was savagely crushed—this was the year of the "Bulgarian atrocities" which shocked the civilized world.

Next year the Russians accomplished Bulgaria's revolution for her by going to war with Turkey. Fierce battles occurred at Pleven and on the Šipka Pass, as grandiose monuments testify. From that short war dates Bulgaria's eternal gratitude to the Russian people. It is one of the Warsaw Pact countries which preserves in her capital city a monument to monarchy: Alexander II, a 19th-century Russian tsar.

Into the 20th Century

In 1879 a German princeling, Alexander of Battenberg, was elected to the throne in Sofia by the European powers. (Germans were favored for the new states then forming in Europe, because it was considered that Germany could never be a threat to European peace.) A disenchanted Alexander abdicated after seven years and Ferdinand of Saxe-Coburg replaced him. He lost favor (and some territory) by opportunistically joining in the second Balkan War of 1913 and then backing the loser in World War I, 1914–1918. Faced with mounting rebellion, he also abdicated and his son Boris took over.

A revolutionary ideology found expression in the power struggles at the top. A military dictatorship in 1923 stamped out Europe's first anti-fascist rising (Ernest Hemingway wrote passionately in defense of the "peasants' revolt") but one of its leaders, Georgi Dimitrov, lived to become First Secretary of socialist Bulgaria after 1945. He died in 1949 and lies in a white mausoleum in central Sofia. He is regarded as the father of his nation.

The Russian armies once again drove out an occupying power in 1944 (this time it was Hitler's Germany, with which the hapless Boris had had to ally himself). Boris left the country, the socialist state was proclaimed and the nation's history since then has been of fairly rapid industrialization—advanced engineering, science and technology, electronics and shipbuilding. Within the past few years first-class motorways have been constructed and custom-built resorts set up for tourism.

Yet in large part Bulgaria remains a simple, peasant society, a land of farmers and shepherds. You can still buy the tobacco and the soft fruits of the "salad-bowl of Europe"—the difference is that they are more stylishly packaged. You can still see the weight-lifters training (along with the national football squad) at the health resort of Berkovica. You can still buy attar of roses, or "rose oil" as it is called—if you have the dollars. "Roses are our golden currency," says the schoolhouse sign in a Valley-of-Roses village. It is an understatement, for the price of attar, ounce for ounce, has gone way above the price of gold on the international market.

The Cultural Heritage

"Even though he lives nobly, man must die and another take his place"—the 9th-century inscription is freely translated because it is written in a language imperfectly understood. It comes from a memorial pillar at Târnovo and is perhaps the first poetic line in Bulgarian literature.

We have already noted that Bulgaria's language and literature were born in misery and turmoil; that Cyril and Methodius invented an alphabet and gave modern Bulgarian its written shape; and that, under Turkish domination, the great monastic fortresses sheltered whole communities and through writings and teachings helped develop a national spirit. The most influential monk was Païssi of Hilendar who in 1762 produced the *History of the Slav-Bulgarians*. Unable to print or distribute it, he wandered through the countryside, reading it to his enslaved compatriots. He gave expression to a dream of nationhood.

Païssi's successors were the 19th-century educationists, the writers of historical and theological textbooks. In 1844 Konstantin Fotinov published the first Bulgarian periodical *Ljuboslovie* ("Love of Speech") and two years later Ivan Bogorov launched the first newspaper, *Bulgarski Orel* ("Bulgarian Eagle"). Soon afterwards came Hristo Botev (1848–1876), the poet and revolutionary, and then the first (and still most famous) novel *Under the Yoke,* by Ivan Vazov (1850–1921).

When Bulgaria recovered her nationhood in 1908 her literature was marked by less political fervor and more pointed satire. Of authors of that period available in English translation, Elin Pelin (1878–1949) and Yordan Yovkov (1884–1937) are the most readable.

The present-day Bulgarian is highly literate. First-time visitors always comment on the number of smart bookshops in the cities and, while much of the reading material is heavy political economy, you will also find (if you can decipher the Cyrillic titles) all the world's great literature. (A fat, dirty, gypsy woman was recently observed in the train, eating lentils by the handful and equally eagerly devouring a thick book—it was Dickens's *Bleak House.*) At the bookshops you will also find modern Bulgarian literature in English or German translation—mostly collections of short stories, that being the popular literary form. They contain more witty or sly criticism of "the way we live now" than an innocent Westerner would think possible in a society where all publishing is state-controlled. Look out for the works of short-story and play writer Yordan Radičkov (born 1929; *Gunpowder Primer, Attempt at Flying*); novelist Pavel Vežinov (died 1984; *At Night with the White Horses*); and novelist Dimiter Dimov (*Damned Souls, Tobacco*).

The Plastic Arts

Bulgaria's first artists were inspired by religious ideals. Her contributions to world pictorial art are icons, murals and miniatures from the monastic schools. Many are of crudely allegorical character—local curators nonetheless seem inordinately proud of them. Genuine icons of the best period (14th–15th centuries) are displayed in the crypt of the Alexander Nevski cathedral in Sofia and there is a mixed bag of venerable and not-so-venerable icons on display at the Rila monastery, a popular tourist venue.

Bulgarian painting, isolated from European influences, has not advanced much. The modern painters, with admirable technique, mainly go in for representational landscapes and studies of agricultural life. Picture exhibitions attract sizeable crowds, however, and the summer *plein-air* (out-of-doors) competitions arouse enthusiasm. Among a handful of unashamedly *avant-garde* artists, Nikolai Masterov (born 1941) is prominent.

Sculpture of the monumental commemorative kind is very much alive, as the shortest city tour will reveal; but there has been no continuing sculptural tradition. Those who have toured the Soviet Union will easily identify the inspiration for all that stern symbolism in granite.

The domestic crafts, involving wood, clay, metal and textiles, on the other hand, have a distinguished history. Many a preserved "museum house" (mostly rich merchants' houses on which local decorative talents were employed) is a treasury of imaginative skillful works by rural craftsmen of old, from carpet-weavers and rug-makers to wood-carvers and fresco-painters. The splendor and variety of country costumes, too, hint at a strong aesthetic sense as well as painstaking needlework.

Traditional pottery is vaguely Turkish in decoration, but of idiosyncratic shape and form. White, yellow and green are favored colors, with geometric, floral or bird designs combed or incised on the pot.

Architectural relics survive from the Thracian period (a world-renowned warrior's tomb at Kazanlâk), from ancient Greece (at Nesebâr on the Black Sea coast), from the Roman empire (notably Plovdiv) and from the Slav dynasties (Pliska, Preslav, Bojana, Madura). Bulgaria's architectural glory is undoubtedly her dozen or so monasteries—Rila, Bačkovo, Preobraženski, Trojan, Drjanovo and others. Their situations, hanging from high crags or rising from deep gorges, enhance their beauty.

Recent large-scale building works, like the tower-block hotels of Sofia, Plovdiv and the seaside resorts, generally turn out to have been designed by the French, Belgians or Japanese. But the ziggurat-like seafront hotels of Albena, the latest vacationland, were a native design, considered sensational by some.

Spirit of Orpheus

Bulgaria, land of roses, is also the land of song. The spirit of Orpheus the Thracian lives on. All large towns have their opera theaters and symphony orchestras. Singers whom they have given the world (and consequently rarely seen in Bulgaria) include Boris Hristov (Christoff), Nikolai Ghiaurov, Elena Nikolai and Raina Kabaivanska. It is estimated that one million music performances take place annually and are seen by 160 million people—not bad for a nation whose population is nine million.

Alternate years in June, Sunny Beach plays host to the "Golden Orpheus" pop festival; two weeks later the "Decade of Symphonic Music" is held. International folk ensembles meet every year in August at Bourgas. Sofia has its "Music Weeks" in May; Varna a big choir festival and a chamber music festival in May and June. A world ballet competition is held in the Varna opera theater every three years. The Children's Symphony Orchestra and Bulgarian Children's Choir are well worth hearing—they tour the country, appear on radio and television and make records.

Stage and Screen

No great impact has been made on the world by Bulgaria's theater or cinema. The theater was virtually unknown 100 years ago, the "seventh art" (as Bulgarians call the cinema) is barely 40 years old. Every town and village has its drama group, but you are more likely to see the perennial foreign favorites—Ibsen, Molière, Shakespeare—than a homegrown play. Most respected abroad of modern playwrights are Dragomir Assenov (*Gold Backing*), Stanislav Stratiev (*Suede Jacket*) and Konstantin Pavlov (*Easter Wine*).

In mime, shadow-play and puppetry the Bulgarians are supreme. The Central Puppet Theater of Sofia is much in demand at festivals abroad—using hands and fingers only, they present quite long works with tremendous zest and expertise. You may find them playing at the Ivan Vazov theater in Sofia.

The state organization produces several movies every year, mostly cartoons and travelogues, which have won prizes at film festivals abroad. Full-length features tend now to move away from the "socialist realism" of the past and to deal with social and environmental themes—the drift to the towns (*A Tree without Roots, Peasant on a Bicycle*); consumerism (*Villa Zone*); and growing up (*The Pool, Boomerang, Sun Stroke*).

One director who has gained international renown is Binka Željazkova. Her work usually carries a moral message. *Last Word* (1977) and *Great*

Night Bath (1981) deal with women's place in modern society; they may still be seen in Bulgaria's cinemas.

BULGARIAN FOOD AND DRINK

The Home of Yogurt

Bulgarian food can be very good indeed, its wines light and inexpensive, its world-famous fruits and vegetables delicious. Balkan cooking—which you will also find with various national and local variations in neighboring Yugoslavia, Greece and Romania—relies heavily on lamb or pork, potatoes, peppers, egg-plant, tomatoes, onions, carrots, and quite a few spices.

The many attractive folk restaurants make a point of serving national dishes and local specialties, and they are well worth seeking out, as too many hotel menus still place too much emphasis on "international" dishes. If the word "Picnic" appears in a restaurant name, incidentally, it simply means you will be eating *al fresco*.

Starters and Salads

In all folk restaurants and some others, you'll find a small dish of *čubrica* on your table: a tasty herbal salt mixture in which you dip pieces of bread, or use to sprinkle on cheese. The bread itself is likely to be a tasty small warm loaf (*pitka*) varying in flavor according to whether or not the dough has been mixed with yogurt and soda, with eggs and oil, or with white cheese. Soups are generally very good: for example, the so-called Monastery Soup, which is made of well-soaked dried beans, and a variety of vegetables; and the nourishing *škembe čurba* (a variety of meats and spices cooked in milk). Delicious, as well as refreshing, is *tarator,* a cold soup of finely chopped cucumber, ground walnuts, sour milk, dill and a dash of sunflower oil.

Salads provide a preface or accompaniment to almost any meal, one of the most popular, *šopska* salad, being a combination of tomato, cucumber, sweet pepper, onion and grated white sheep's cheese.

Main Courses

It won't be long before you're offered *kebapčeta*—very tasty grilled minced meat rolls, usually veal or pork with lots of spice. *Gjuveč* is a kind of hotpot containing an astonishing variety of vegetables, including potatoes. Preferably, but not necessarily, it should have meat, and the real thing is cooked and served in an earthenware dish. *Kavarma* is another variation on this theme, with plenty of pork pieces, mushrooms, and vegetables. In the case of *drusan kebab,* pork pieces are first grilled on a skewer and then finished off in a hot oven in a covered earthenware pot with onions, mushrooms, tomatoes and herbs. *Pile paprikaš,* chicken in a rich sauce of tomatoes and peppers, can be delicious; alternatively a similar sauce can be used with fish.

Liver, rice and herbs are the basic ingredients of *drob sarma,* but it's given a new dimension with a topping of yogurt beaten with egg and flour and baked for a few minutes to form a kind of crust. *Agneški drebulijki* is grilled liver, kidneys and other lamb variety meats, which tastes better than it might sound. *Mešana skara* is a Bulgarian version of mixed grill. *Sarmi* are cabbage leaves stuffed with meat; various other leaves and vegetables like vine, peppers and egg-plant, can be treated in the same way with very tasty results. *Imama bajalda* is a delicious cold vegetarian dish made from egg-plant stuffed with finely chopped onions, carrots, celery, and tomatoes. *Sirene po šopski* is a tasty baked cheese dish.

Yogurt and Sweeter Things

Bulgaria, of course, is *the* place for yogurt, for this is its original home. It's called *kiselo mleko* here and if you get the real thick, creamy home-made version, yogurt will never taste the same again anywhere else. It is partly to do with the milk—which should be sheep's—and the way it is fermented with a well-disposed bacteria whose name *Lactobacillus bulgaricus* confirms its national origins.

From spring through fall, the nicest way to round off a meal is with fresh fruit. Bulgarian fruits are in a class by themselves—and cheap. The first cherries and strawberries appear in May, reaching their peak in June and July, along with orange-red apricots and raspberries. Apples, pears and peaches are in abundance from June through October. Water and musk melons last from July to September, and plums and rich, amber-colored grapes can be enjoyed from July through October.

Many of these fruits are incorporated into rich creamy cakes, as are the walnuts which proliferate in the Bulgarian countryside. As in other parts of the Balkans subjected to long periods of Ottoman rule, sweet sticky delicacies like *baklava,* dripping with syrup, often turn up among the list of desserts. You'll find plenty of *lokum* (Turkish delight) in the shops, too.

What to Drink

When it comes to stronger drinks, *the* national pick-me-up is *slivova,* plum or grape brandy. A typical Bulgarian meal invariably starts with a glass of *slivova* and one of the best brands is *Trojanska slivova,* which comes from the Trojan region. As an alternative you can try *mastika,* with an aniseed base; you add a little water to taste, which makes it go milky. Vodka is also popular. The most famous Bulgarian liqueur is the one made from rose petals in the beautiful Valley of Roses.

The choice of pleasant wines is considerable. Look out for the reasonably dry white *Trakia Pinot Chardonnay, Trakia Blanc de Blanc,* or *Songurlarski Misket.* Dry reds are *Trakia Cabernet Sauvignon, Gumza* or *Mavrud.* If you prefer semi-dry, there's *Manastirska Izba* (white), or sweet, *Manastirsko Šušukane* (red).

A great variety of non-alcoholic drinks is available, including Coca-Cola. Best of all are the excellent bottled soft drinks from 100 percent natural fruit juices—ask for *sok* (juice) or *nektar* (which is much thicker). These are readily available in stores, but unfortunately, not often in hotels and restaurants. Mineral waters include the well-known ones from Gorna Banja and Hisar, and there are also fruit-flavored varieties.

Coffee, served in small cups in Turkish style, is thick and strong, but in some places is being superseded by *espresso,* which can be even stronger. Tea is usually drunk without milk, but with a slice of lemon.

SOFIA

City Beneath the Mountains

Two of Sofia's trump cards are its location and its climate. Situated at about 550 meters (1,800 feet) pretty well in the center of the Balkan Peninsular, it lies on the high Sofia Plain ringed by mountain ranges of varying proximity: the Balkan range to the north, Ljulin Mountains to the west, Mount Vitoša to the southwest and part of the Sredna Gora Mountains to the southeast. Mount Vitoša is in fact on the city's doorstep, providing a marvelous natural playground for its inhabitants at all seasons. The city's setting contributes to summers that are relatively cool for these latitudes, and crisp winters, which provide excellent skiing.

The first general impression one gets of the city itself is neither of great age nor of great beauty, though in fact it is extremely old and has some delightful corners both above and below ground. The first thing to remember is that just about a century ago, it was a rather down-at-heel Oriental town, capital of the Turkish province of Rumelia. At that time, it had 3,000 houses and 15,000 inhabitants, living in narrow twisting streets punctuated by mosques and little churches, crouching half underground, for their roofs were not allowed to reach higher than a man on horseback. Two of the mosques and one or two of the churches remain, but otherwise most of central Sofia today has its origins in the first town plans drawn up in 1880 and later, and it was in the process of creating this new European capital that a number of sites of great antiquity were uncovered.

The area has been inhabited for about 5,000 years, but the first people about whom anything is known is the Thracian tribe of Serdi who gave Sofia its first name, Serdica. Then as now, it was on one of the main routes between east and west, and suffered regular harassment as a result. The Romans made it into the splendid capital of the province of Thracia and it seems to have been much favored by Constantine the Great. In A.D. 447 it was destroyed by the Huns under Attila, to be rebuilt in the 6th century by Justinian, who also added the Church of St. Sofia.

In Byzantine times, the city was known as Triadica ("between the mountains"); the Slavs changed it to Sredec ("in the center"), and by the end of the 14th century it had become Sofia. In the meantime, it had been subjected to pillage and attack by Pechenegs, Magyars, Serbs, Crusaders, and even in the Second Bulgarian Kingdom never retrieved its former importance. During the five centuries of Turkish rule however, Sofia was a major economic and cultural center within the Empire, until the 19th century, when there was a sharp decline in population.

Today, the streets are broad, the traffic light (though not as light as it used to be) and there are spacious green parks and open-air cafes in which to join the people of Sofia in relaxation on warm summer days. The main sights of the city can be seen in a couple of days, and another day at least should be allowed for Mount Vitoša. But if you are interested in Bulgarian culture, you will want to stay longer, for there are a number of museums devoted to various aspects of the subject, and musical performances are of a high standard.

Exploring Sofia—Looking South

Most of the city's main sights are centrally situated and can easily be visited on foot. We suggest you take Lenin Square as the hub, for most places can be found in relation to this.

The south side of the square is dominated by 19th-century Sveta Nedelja Church and behind it you enter Vitoša Boulevard, with the heights of Mount Vitoša rising straight ahead of you. Take very special note of the imposing first building on your right, formerly the Courts of Justice and now housing the National History Museum. If you only have time to visit one monument in Sofia, make sure it is this one.

This, and the Art and History Museum in Varna, exhibit some of the most exciting early finds in Europe, excavated from the Varna necropolis which dates from the 4th millennium B.C. There is only a token selection of these in Sofia but they are quite stunning and, overall, the National History Museum collections are vast, featuring amazing and priceless Thracian treasures (including the nine-piece set of vessels of the Panagjurište Gold Treasure, until recently in Plovdiv), Roman mosaics and artefacts, and every period of Bulgarian workmanship and art. Some of the earliest of the latter are elaborate enamelled jewelry from the First Bulgarian Kingdom, inscribed columns from the 8th–10th centuries recording events of the times, and big collections of religious art, safeguarded by the monasteries during Ottoman rule.

Back on Vitoša Boulevard, you'll find the northern part of this thoroughfare has been turned into a pedestrian precinct with all kinds of small shops and eating places, and in a few blocks you will come to a large modern building set in pleasant gardens, dominated by a modern sculpture commemorating the 1,300th anniversary of Bulgaria's nationhood. The building is the Ljudmila Živkova National Palace of Culture, housing a big complex of congress halls for international conventions and a wide variety of cultural activities. Its underpass built on several levels features discos, bowling alley, shops and restaurants.

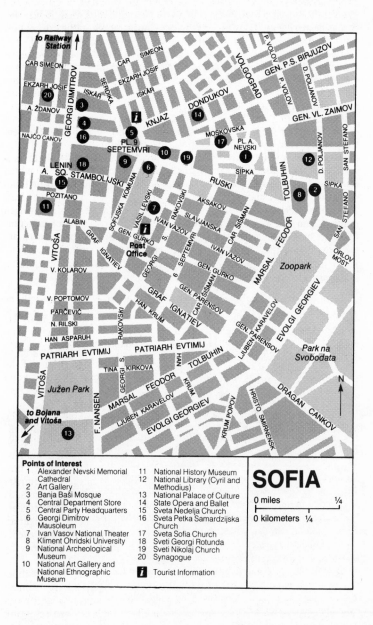

Points of Interest

1 Alexander Nevski Memorial Cathedral
2 Art Gallery
3 Banja Baši Mosque
4 Central Department Store
5 Central Party Headquarters
6 Georgi Dimitrov Mausoleum
7 Ivan Vasov National Theater
8 Kliment Ohridski University
9 National Archeological Museum
10 National Art Gallery and National Ethnographic Museum
11 National History Museum
12 National Library (Cyril and Methodius)
13 National Palace of Culture
14 State Opera and Ballet
15 Sveta Nedelja Church
16 Sveta Petka Samardzijska Church
17 Sveta Sofia Church
18 Sveti Georgi Rotunda
19 Sveti Nikolaj Church
20 Synagogue

i Tourist Information

SOFIA

0 miles ¼

0 kilometers ¼

A little further south begin the great green acres of Južen Park, partly well-arranged formal gardens, but mainly an extensive area of woods criss-crossed by a network of paths. The park will eventually be extended to link with the most impressive of Sofia's playgrounds, Mount Vitoša, a range of mountains rising out of the city's southern outskirts. With its highest point—Černi Vrăh—reaching over 2,290 meters (7,500 feet), this is a wonderful natural playground for any city to have and, winter or summer, the citizens of Sofia make the most of it.

Mainly East

On the west side of Lenin Square, you'll see the monument to Lenin and, opposite, steps lead down to an underpass which provides a very pleasant oasis in the middle of the city bustle. Here you'll find an open-air cafe, some shops, and the charming little church of Sveta Petka Samardzijska. It dates from the 14th century and is particularly notable for the frescoes discovered during its restoration.

There is another peaceful spot and a church that dates back a full millennium more only a stone's throw away. This is the rotunda of Sveti Georgi which crouches in the courtyard of one of Sofia's most newly restored and grand hotels, the Sheraton Sofia Balkan on the southeast side of Lenin Square. Originally built in the 4th century as a Roman temple, it was destroyed by the Huns, rebuilt by Justinian and turned into a mosque by the Turks. Recent restoration has revealed frescoes from the 11th–15th centuries, but it is not yet open to the public.

From Lenin Square, head east now towards the Communist Party Headquarters building. Right in front of it another underpass leads you back nearly 2,000 years—to the Serdica of Roman times. Here you will find quite substantial chunks of Roman walls, a stretch of Roman paved street and a collection of stone blocks and carvings.

The Communist Party building is at the junction of Dondukov Boulevard and Deveti Septemvri Square. Facing the latter on your right, with its entrance on parallel Alexander Stambolijski Boulevard, is the National Archeological Museum housed in the former Bujuk or Great Mosque, a fascinating quadrangular building from the 15th century. Its most important collections have been transferred to the National History Museum. In the next block is the Georgi Dimitrov Mausoleum containing the embalmed body of this revered Bulgarian revolutionary leader, who died in Moscow in 1949. A changing of the guard ceremony takes place before it every hour on the hour. Across the road is the National Art Gallery in the former Royal Palace and next to that, the ornate Russian church of St. Nikolaj (St. Nicholas), built 1912–14.

At this point you enter Ruski Boulevard on which is the building of the National Assembly. Before it is the Monument to the Liberators, dominated by the equestrian statue of Tsar Alexander II of Russia. Beyond the National Assembly, one of the city's most distinctive edifices stands beneath its glittering domes: the Alexander Nevski Memorial Church. It is named after Alexander II's patron saint, a 13th-century Prince of Novgorod. This church was built in the early years of this century as a token of the gratitude of the Bulgarian people for Russian help in gaining their independence from Turkey. Its elaborate and ornate interior incorporates the work of many Russian and East European artists. Don't miss the museum in the crypt if you are interested in icons; it is an exceptionally fine collection. Nor should you miss any opportunity to attend a religious service here, for several members of the choir are also members of the National Opera and the singing is superb.

The church and its adjoining square are on the site of a great Roman necropolis, the highest point of the city. But the most notable church in Sofia lies just across the square to the west. St. Sofia, in whose honor the city was renamed in the 14th century, dates back to the early 6th century and has just undergone restoration. It was converted into a mosque in the 16th century, and was then partially destroyed by earthquakes, before being restored to its original form. Lacking the ornamentation of its modern neighbor, the great age and simplicity of this three-nave church in mellow red brick are impressive. It is built in the form of a symmetrical cross beneath a central dome, typical of the basilicas of Asia Minor; but there are also Romanesque features in the rounded arches of the vaulting. Traces of two older churches have been found in the course of excavations, and a mosaic from the second of these (5th-century) still survives. Just outside St. Sofia, a monument to the Unknown Soldier was unveiled in 1981.

Returning to Ruski Boulevard, you'll soon come to Park na Svobodata (Freedom Park), with its lake and fountains, woods and lawns. One of several green areas near the city center, it also has sports and entertainments facilities including an open-air theater and the vast Vasil Levski Sports Stadium.

Finally, back on Lenin Square you should take a brief look north at Georgi Dimitrov Boulevard which eventually leads to the main railway station. The large building on the right is the Central Department Store if you want to browse round one of Sofia's biggest shops; it's recently had a major facelift. Just beyond it is Banja Baši Mosque, one of the few major buildings left by the Turks. It dates from the 16th century, but is not open to visitors. Just across the boulevard from here you'll find the Central Market Hall, a good place to meet Sofia's housewives about their daily shopping. Behind it is a very large synagogue. The big public mineral baths are also near the mosque, a reminder of the presence in and around Sofia of many hot and cold health-giving mineral springs.

In the Environs

The most interesting or attractive places are to be found on the south side of the city in the general direction of Mount Vitoša or actually on the mountains. Undoubtedly the most notable is Bojana, only about 10 km. (six miles) from the city center, and the site of one of Bulgaria's most precious monuments. This is the little church of Bojana which dates from the Middle Ages and contains some exquisite frescoes, painted between the 11th–13th centuries. Alas, it has been closed for many years for restoration; however, there is now a replica in the vicinity, so that copies of the outstanding frescoes can be viewed by visitors without risk of damage to the originals.

In the beechwoods above the nearby village of Dragalevci is Dragalevci Monastery, its 14th-century church still surviving and decorated with 15th- and 17th-century frescoes. A chairlift from Dragalevci and a new cable car from Simeonovo take you up to the resort complex of Aleko on the northeastern slopes of Vitoša, also accessible by a good road. From near here another chairlift takes you to the top of Malak Rezen beneath Černi Vrâh; there are many marked walking and ski trails.

On the northwestern slopes, reached by road and cable car from Knjaževo, is the Kopitoto Hotel with a fabulous view over the city. A network of marked trails probe into many parts of the massif, including Zlatnite Mostove (Golden Bridges), with its foaming mountain waters. This can be reached by road; there is a pleasant restaurant.

Another charming destination about ten km. (six miles) from the center at the foot of Mount Vitoša is a monument dedicated to peace and the children of the world. It consists of a collection of bells of every imaginable size and shape from 89 different countries and there are usually plenty of children of all ages around trying out their various tones.

PRACTICAL INFORMATION FOR SOFIA

TOURIST INFORMATION. The head office of Balkantourist is 1 Vitoša Boulevard and there are offices in all main hotels.

WHEN TO COME. Spring is the time for blossom in the surrounding countryside; summer for the hottest weather, usually tempered by the city's altitude. Winter has the double advantage of being the best season for cultural programs and for the skiing, which is right on Sofia's doorstep. Music lovers should note the Sofia Music Weeks, end May to end June.

GETTING AROUND SOFIA. By Train, Bus and Trolley. Work has begun on a new metro system, but for the moment you can use trams, buses and trolleys. It's best to buy your tickets in advance from special kiosks by the streetcar stop. Each costs six stotinki and you must punch it in a machine after boarding the vehicle (watch how other people do it).

By Taxi. Taxis are inexpensive, but rather scarce; quickest is to order one from your hotel, or keep a watch out for a taxi stand.

Car Hire. Available through Balkantourist and hotel reception desks.

HOTELS. All hotels listed below have restaurants unless otherwise stated; some have rooms in more than one category. All are open year round. Should you arrive in Sofia without reservations, the following accommodations offices can help: Interhotels Central Office, 4 Sveta Sofia St. (Interhotels only); Balkantourist, 37 Dondukov Blvd. (hotels other than Interhotels, plus private accommodations; open 7 A.M.–10.30 P.M.); Bureau of Tourist Information and Reservations, 35 Eksarh Josif St. (near Lenin Square) and Palace of Culture (off Vitoša Blvd.)—both deal with all forms of accommodations; Central Rail Station.

Deluxe

Novotel Europa, 131 Georgi Dimitrov Blvd. Interhotel, 600 rooms. One of the French Novotel chain; near rail station and not too far from center.

Sheraton Sofia Hotel Balkan, Lenin Sq. Interhotel, 163 rooms, four restaurants, nightclub, health club, top facilities. Formerly the Grand Hotel Balkan and now completely renovated; in the very heart of the city.

Vitoša-New Otani, 100 Anton Ivanov Blvd. Interhotel, 454 rooms, various restaurants (including Japanese), nightclub, casino, indoor pool, sauna, health center. Japanese-designed, on the south side of the city, near Južen Park.

Expensive

Grand Hotel Sofia, Narodno Sobranie Sq. Interhotel, 172 rooms, nightclub, folk tavern. Very central.

Park Hotel Moskva, 25 Nezabravka St. Interhotel, 390 rooms, several restaurants (including Russian), nightclub, folk tavern. In parkland setting, but not central.

Rodina, 4 Ruski-Pametnik. 536 rooms, nightclub, indoor pool, sauna, sports hall. Sofia's newest high-rise hotel, a short distance from center on road to southwest.

Moderate

Bulgaria, 4 Ruski Blvd. 72 rooms. Old-fashioned; very central, but quiet.

Hemus, 31 Georgi Traikov Blvd. 240 rooms, nightclub, folk tavern. Near Vitoša-New Otani.

Serdika, 2 General Zaimov St. 140 rooms. With Old Berlin–style restaurant serving German specialties. Central.

Slavjanska Beseda, 127 Rakovski St. 110 rooms, no restaurant. Central.

Inexpensive

Pliska, 87 Lenin Blvd. 205 rooms. Some distance from center, near Freedom Park.

Slavia, 2 Sofijski Geroi. 75 rooms. Some distance from center to the southwest.

Sofia Environs

At Aleko on the northeastern slopes of Mount Vitoša, 25 km. (15 miles) from the city and reached by road or cable car from the suburb of Simeonovo:

Prostor (M), 100 rooms, nightclub, indoor pool, sauna.

Štastliveca (I), 70 rooms, folk tavern.

On Vitoša's northwestern slopes, a few hundred yards from the top station of another cable car, is **Kopitoto** (I), 15 rooms.

MOTELS AND CAMPSITES. Božur (M), 80 rooms. 17 km. (11 miles) southeast of Sofia on E80. Part of rest area with gas station and shops.

Iztok (M), 80 rooms. 16 km. (ten miles) southeast of Sofia on E80.

Gorubljane (I), 28 rooms. Ten km. (six miles) southeast of Sofia on E80.

Sofia-West (M), 18 km. (11 miles) northwest of Sofia on E80. Part of rest area with gas station and shops.

Černija Kos. Campsite 13 km. (eight miles) from city between Vitoša and Ljulin mountains. Chalets for hire, good restaurant.

Ivaniane. Campsite near Bankja spa, west of city. Chalets for hire.

Vrana. Campsite off the E80. Best facilities. Chalets for hire.

RESTAURANTS. In addition to the hotel restaurants, there is a growing number of eating places concentrating on local specialties, often with an attractive folkloric setting.

Expensive

Berlin, 2 General Zaimov St. Bulgarian and German food; in Serdika Hotel.

Budapest, 145 G.S. Rakovski St. Hungarian food and music.

Crystal, 10 Aksakov St. Restaurant-tavern.

Havana, 27 Vitoša Blvd.

Krim, 2 Dobrudja St. Russian food, summer garden.

Rubin, 4 Lenin Sq. Can also be (M). Eating complex in city center, with snack bar for the budget minded, and elegant restaurant serving Bulgarian and international food.

Moderate

Bojansko Hanche, about ten km. (six miles) from center, near historic Bojana church; folkloric program, national specialties.

Černata Kotka, about 13 km. (eight miles) southeast of city on E80; folk music.

Gorubljane, attached to motel about ten km. (six miles) out to southeast on E80; folk program.

Koprivštica, 3 Vitoša Blvd; folk music.

Ropotamo, 73 Lenin Blvd.

Strandjata, 19 Lenin Sq; folk music.

Šumako, ten km. (six miles) south of center on Simeonovo-Bistrica road; folk music.

Tirolska Srešta, 94 Vitoša Blvd.

Vietnamese Restaurant, 1 G. Kirkov St. Atmosphere and specialties appropriate to its name.

Vodeničarski Mehani, incorporating three old mills, at foot of Mount Vitoša above Dragalevci district; folkloric show, national specialties.

Zlatna Ribka, about 24 km. (15 miles) south of city on road to Borovec; folk music.

Zlatnite Mostove, on Mount Vitoša, about 19 km. (12 miles) from city; mountain style, live music in evenings.

MUSEUMS. Monday is usually, but not invariably, the day of closure, so it's best to check. The following are the main museums and galleries of general interest:

Art Gallery, 6 Šipka St. Exhibitions of Bulgarian and foreign artists.

Bojana Church National Museum, about ten km. (six miles) from the city center. Currently closed but a replica has been built in the vicinity so that copies of the outstanding frescos may be viewed.

Crypt of Alexander Nevski Memorial Church. A stunning display of icons and other religious works. Try to hear the superb choir. Crypt open 10.30–6.30, closed Tues.

Ethnographical Museum, 9 Septemvri Sq. Displaying folk art, particularly costumes, from every region of the country. Housed in the former royal palace. Open 10.30–6.30, closed Tues.

Georgi Dimitrov Mausoleum, 9 Septemvri Sq. Here lies the embalmed body of Bulgaria's revered leader. A museum devoted to his life is at 66 Opulčenska St.

National Archeological Museum, 2 Alexander Stambolijski Blvd. Changing exhibitions of Bulgarian and foreign treasures. Open 10–5, closed Mon. and Tues.

National Art Gallery, 9 Septemvri Sq. Bulgarian art from medieval times to the present. Housed in the former royal palace. Open 10.30–6.30, closed Tues.

National History Museum, 2 Vitoša Blvd. An absolute "must." Recently opened in former Courts of Justice, with exhibits ranging from prehistory to 1878. Includes a token selection of the priceless gold objects from the Varna necropolis (4th millennium B.C.), the Penagyurishte Gold Treasure (nine-piece set of magnificent gold vessels, 4th–3rd centuries B.C.), Roman mosaics and artefacts, and early Bulgarian art. Open 10.30–6.30, 2–6.30 on Fri., closed Mon.

OPERA, CONCERTS AND THEATER. The standard of opera is high in Bulgaria as is that of the folkloric performances, notably the excellent National Folk Ensemble. The standard of concerts is also high. The following are the main theaters and venues.

Bulgaria Hall, 1 Aksakov St. Regular concerts by leading Bulgarian and foreign orchestras and soloists.

Central Puppet Theater, 14 Gurko St. Puppet performances are very popular and of high standard.

Ivan Vazov National Theater, 5 Levski St, the country's largest.

Open-air Summer Theater, Freedom Park.

People's Army Theater, 98 Rakovski St.

State Opera House, entrance from 1 Janko Zabunov St. Over the years the company has produced some international singers. Production standards are solid, if old-fashioned.

Stefan Makedonski Musical Theater, 4 Volgograd Blvd.

It is also well worth attending an Orthodox Church service, which can be both a musical and moving experience. The choir of the Alexander Nevski Memorial Church is exceptional.

NIGHTLIFE. Nightlife is not Sofia's strongest feature, though many restaurants have live bands, and the atmosphere generally is quite lively. Those who need their nightclub ration will find a nightclub with floor show at the *Vitoša-New Otani Hotel,* the *Moskva Park Hotel,* and the *Grand Hotel Sofia.* There is also a disco in the *Novotel Hotel.* The *National Palace of Culture Ljudmila Zivkova,* reached along Vitoša Blvd., includes nightclub, disco and bowling alley; another disco is in the underpass at the junction of Bulgaria Blvd. and Emil Markov St. Gamblers might try their luck at the *Vitoša-New Otani Casino.*

SHOPPING. There is a good selection of arts and crafts at the shop of the *Union of Bulgarian Artists,* 6 Ruski Blvd., and a range of souvenirs at *Sredec,* 7 Legue St; *Souvenir Store,* 7 Stambolijski Blvd.; *Prizma Store,* 2 Ruski Blvd. If you are interested in furs or leather, try one of the following—4 Slavjanska St., 7 Car Kalojan St., or 2 Ruski Blvd. For recordings of Bulgarian folk and other music, go to *Maestro Atanassov,* 8 Ruski Blvd. *Mineralsouvenir,* 10 Ruski Blvd., has unusual mementos, jewelry, watches, and ornaments made of marble, other stones, silver, and gold.

All kinds of foodstuffs are on sale at the *Central Market Hall,* 25 Georgi Dimitrov Blvd., where you'll be able to choose from some of Bulgaria's excellent fruit and vegetable preserves as well as local wines and spirits. Latest shopping center is in the subway of the modern *Palace of Culture,* selling fashion and leather goods, plus all forms of handicrafts. There are also three souvenir shops in the underpass at Sv. Petka Samardzijska church. The pedestrian precinct in Vitoša Boulevard features many new small shops.

Other countries' department stores are always interesting to browse through and the main newly renovated *Central Department Store* is at 2 Georgi Dimitrov Blvd.

SIGHTSEEING. Balkantourist can arrange a wide selection of tours by car or minibus. These include sightseeing in Sofia by day and night, folklore evenings and day trips to Rila Monastery, Koprivštica, the Valley of Roses, the mountain resort of Borovec, and Plovdiv. Longer trips available as well.

USEFUL ADDRESSES. Embassies. *American,* 1 Stambolijski Blvd. (tel. 884801/02/03); *British,* 65 Blvd. Tolbuhin (tel. 885361/878325).

Travel Arrangements. *Balkantourist,* 1 Vitoša Blvd. (head office), 37 Dondukov Blvd. (for all accommodations other than Interhotels) (tel. 884430); Balkantourist also have offices in all main hotels. *Interhotels Central Office,* 4 Sveta Sofia St. *Bureau of Tourist Information and Reservations,* 35 Eksarh Josif St. (near Lenin Sq.) and Palace of Culture (off Vitoša Blvd.). *Balkan Bulgarian Airlines,* 12 Narodno Sobranije Sq., (domestic services) 10 Sofiska Komuna St. *Rila International Railway Bureau,* 5 Gurko St. *Domestic Railway Bureau,* 23 G. Dimitrov Blvd. *Šipka Agency* (Union of Bulgarian Motorists), 6 Sveta Sofia St. *Orbita Bureau for Youth International Excursions,* 45A Stambolijski Blvd. *Pirin Tourist Bureau* (Union of Bulgarian Hikers), 30 Alexander Stambolijski Blvd. *Cooptourist Tourist Bureau* (Central Cooperative Union), 99 Rakovski St. *Balkanautoservice* (hard currency only) for automobile repairs, 239 Botevgradsko Shausse Blvd.

Emergency Telephone. Motorists 146, Ambulance 150, Fire 160, Police 166; for information on all-night pharmacies 178.

INLAND BULGARIA

Peaks versus Plains

Even a quick look at a relief map shows that Bulgaria falls quite readily
into clearly defined topographical compartments, following more or less
horizontal lines. In the north, the Danube forms the border and its plains
soon merge to the south with the foothills of the Balkan Range of mountains, whose presence has played such an important part in Bulgarian history; they are marked as 'Stara Planina' (meaning 'old mountains') on
most relief maps. Parallel with these are the lower heights of the Sredna
Gora Mountains, with the famous Valley of Roses running between the
two ranges. South of the Sredna Gora lies the fertile Thracian Plain, setting for Bulgaria's second-largest city, Plovdiv. The southwest and south
of the country is largely made up of a series of mountain groups: Rila,
Pirin and the Rhodopes.

The three main routes linking Sofia with the Black Sea coast follow these
three main latitudinal divisions: the northernmost passing through the ancient capital of Veliko Târnovo in the northern hills of the Balkan Range;
the central one through the Valley of Roses; and the southern one through
Plovdiv and the Thracian Plain. The central one can easily be combined
with either of the other two for variety on a circular tour. It joins forces
in any case with the southern route at Sliven. But if it is Bulgaria's past
that particularly intrigues you, you'd do well to include the northern route
for, in addition to Veliko Târnovo, two even older capitals lie just off your
way: Pliska and Preslav.

Danube to Balkan Range

Whether you are heading from Sofia to the Danube or the Black Sea coast, the road through the Iskar Gorge is recommended even though, for the latter destination, it will add to your mileage. Through this gorge, the Iskar river can claim to be the only Bulgarian waterway cutting across the Balkan Range to flow into the Danube. The most attractive section is the 67 km. (42 miles) to the north of Kurilo, near which are the curious Kutino Earth Pyramids. About 40 km. (25 miles) north of Kurilo are the precipitous rocks of Lakatnik, from which the more intrepid enjoy dangling from ropes. There are also some caves in the area. The Sofia-Ruse railway follows the Iskar for most of the way to Pleven and provides some spectacular stretches.

The Bulgarian banks of the Danube are little visited by Western tourists, but several places on or near them should be mentioned. In the northwesternmost corner of Bulgaria, Belogradčik is another place known for the extravagance of its red sandstone formations; Romans and Turks incorporated them in their fortifications and, from these, there are splendid views across the Danube plain and over the extraordinary sculptures of this petrified forest of rocks. The area offers scope for energetic rambling in remarkable scenery whose twisted shapes have given rise to a host of legends. Some kilometers away are the caves of Magura, among Bulgaria's biggest, whose most important features are the primitive paintings created in bat guano by its Early Bronze Age inhabitants. Birds and animals are depicted along with hunting scenes and dancing ladies.

Bulgaria's section of the Danube is 472 km. (nearly 300 miles) long and lavish in its complexities of islands and marshes. As part of the northern boundary of the Roman empire, its importance both strategically and as a thoroughfare goes back into the dim mists of prehistory. Fortifications punctuate its passage, starting in the west with the medieval ones of Vidin. Here, the Citadel of Baba Vida is the most impressive in Bulgaria from that period. With its massive walls and towers rising almost out of the Danube, it is well worth visiting, and it is a fitting setting for an annual Shakespeare Festival. In the vicinity two historic buildings have been adapted as places of entertainment: the old Turkish Post Office is now a cafe and disco and a Venetian warehouse has been transformed into a night club.

Most of the others have vanished or been reduced to ruins. There is not a great deal to see unless you would like to take to the water on board one of the regular hydrofoils that link the riverside communities. One of these is Kozloduj where the shipping station is three or four km. west of the modern town. Beside the shipping station is a memorial to the poet and one of the great leaders of the anti-Turk uprisings, Hristo Botev. His name is spelled out in trees on the hill above. One of the most interesting sites lies a little inland from the mouth of the Iskar river, near the village of Gigen. Here are the substantial remains of the major Roman city of Oescus, in whose large palace a superb mosaic was discovered. This fortified town once stood at a major crossroads, and during the fourth century a massive bridge spanned the Danube at this point. There is a substantial Turkish element in this Danube area, and they are even in the majority in some towns such as Nikopol, which has a dishevelled charm and a colorful small market by a very ancient church.

The two most interesting towns are Švistov and Ruse, the latter also offering the only road connection across the Danube from Bulgaria to Romania, although there is a ferry from Vidin. Švistov produced several major Bulgarian artists and writers, including Aleko Konstantinov to whom a museum is devoted. Ruse is Bulgaria's fourth city and rather new in appearance, though it stands on the site of the Roman fortress of Sexaginta Prista and was a bustling Oriental town in the 17th and 18th centuries. It's a lively town and port, with pleasant riverside walks. Several good museums include the house of Baba Tonka, who sheltered anti-Turk revolutionaries; the history museum; and the transport museum in the old railroad station. The Pantheon is a memorial to the revolutionaries in which an eternal flame burns, watched over by a team of young people.

The Leventa restaurant, housed in an 18th-century fortification on a hill overlooking the town, is made up of a series of attractive rooms whose decor represents the folkloric traditions of the eight countries through which the Danube runs.

A notable, if off-beat, excursion from Ruse is to follow the Rusenki Lom and Černy Lom rivers south to Červen, though you'll need a rugged vehicle for this particular route (about 30 km./20 miles). Apart from its scenic beauty, the gorge shelters a number of little-known 13th- and 14th-century rock churches and monasteries. The most famous is the cave church of Ivanovo and this can be reached by a path and steps high above the old village of Ivanovo at the northernmost end of the gorge, nearest to Ruse. At Červen, which is also more easily accessible by modern roads, the ruins of a medieval fortress crown a rocky ridge above a loop of the Černy Lom river.

The Thracian tomb of Sveštari (3rd century B.C.) is another recent and highly significant discovery, about 50 km. (30 miles) east of Ruse and near Kubrat. The style and composition of its remarkable decoration are very similar to those of the Kazanlâk tomb, described later.

Silistra, further east along the Danube from Ruse, stands on the site of yet another Roman fortress. Beyond it the Danube turns away into Romania. There is an outstandingly good nature reserve in nearby Lake Srebarna; in fact all along these Danube waters there is fascination in store for bird enthusiasts.

Southeast from Ruse the E70 crosses part of the little-visited northeast corner of Bulgaria to Šumen. On the way it passes through Razgrad, an industrial town built on the site of a Thracian settlement, later fortified by the Romans. They called it Arbitus and its extensive remains, together with the museum attached to them, are well worth visiting on the outskirts of the modern town. If you're not pressed for time, head 20 km. (12 miles) north to the village of Topčii whose traditional architecture and rural culture have led it to become a so-called Ethnographic Complex; don't be discouraged by this daunting title, for the place is charming.

The road south from Ruse is the main E85/E83 to Sofia, the new capital, and via E85/E771 to Veliko Târnovo, the old. The former passes through the main town of Bulgaria's Danubian Plain: Pleven, with the usual long history but modern appearance. The Ottomans made it an important fortress, and it held out for five months against the Russians in 1877. A panorama museum commemorates these epic battles, as well as an imposing Mausoleum to the Fallen.

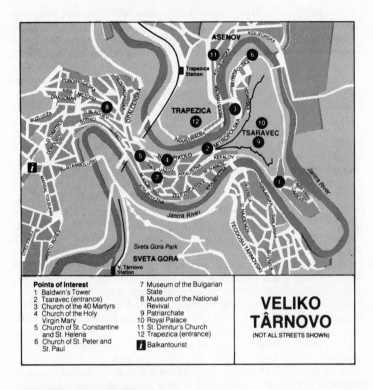

Points of Interest
1 Baldwin's Tower
2 Tsaravec (entrance)
3 Church of the 40 Martyrs
4 Church of the Holy Virgin Mary
5 Church of St. Constantine and St. Helena
6 Church of St. Peter and St. Paul
7 Museum of the Bulgarian State
8 Museum of the National Revival
9 Patriarchate
10 Royal Palace
11 St. Dimitur's Church
12 Trapezica (entrance)
i Balkantourist

VELIKO TÂRNOVO
(NOT ALL STREETS SHOWN)

Early Cradles of Culture

On the whole though, it would be more rewarding to take the route via Veliko Târnovo, which is the most attractively sited of all Bulgaria's larger towns. It literally seems to spill down the hillside to converge on the river Jantra. Main roads from the four points of the compass twist through the mountains to meet at Veliko Târnovo.

Your best move is to find a vantage point above the town, drink in the view and pick out the landmarks. Thus you can see how the river pursues extravagant contortions through it, dividing it into three main hilly peninsulas. The oldest part is Tsaravec, so-called because it was the area where the tsar or king and the patriarch had their palaces. Thick walls, gates, towers and battlements surrounded it in those days and, as it is almost completely contained within a wild loop in the river, the only means of access is by a drawbridge. This fascinating area, including the Patriarchate and the royal palace, is under restoration, with paths and stairways for easier viewing of the extensive ruins. The ways are steep, but the setting is splendid, and you should allow at least an hour or two for this. One of the most prominent features is the tower known as Baldwin's Tower, because according to tradition, it was here that Baldwin of Flanders, Crusader leader and briefly the Latin Emperor of Constantinople, was imprisoned and died after being captured in the Battle of Adrianople in 1205.

Another of the peninsulas, Trapezica, was also fortified and it was here that the boyars or noblemen had their palaces and family chapels. The ruins of nearly a score of these can still be seen. The third peninsula is the wooded Sveta Gora on which there is a camp site, motel and restaurant offering a really splendid view over the town.

On either side of the river between the steep slopes of Tsaravec and Trapezica lies the medieval district of Asenov, or rather, what remains of it.

The year 1393 is important in Bulgarian history. That was the year that Veliko Târnovo fell to the Ottomans, and the year which marked the beginning of nearly half a millennium of lost liberty. Veliko Târnovo, captured after a long siege, was more or less razed to the ground, as well as damaged by subsequent attacks and an earthquake in 1913 so that what can be seen of the medieval city today is mainly restored ruins and scattered foundations. Three churches from that period, all in the Asenov district, or craftsmen's quarter, are "musts;" although it is quite a long way from the center. One is the Church of St. Dimitur, marking the place where the brothers Peter and Asen proclaimed the liberation of Bulgaria from Byzantine domination and thereby launched the Second Bulgarian Kingdom in 1185. Repeatedly damaged over the centuries, it has now been restored. Then there is the Church of the Forty Martyrs built in the 13th century, subsequently used as a mosque, and with two interesting inscribed columns; one commemorates a victory over the Byzantines in 1230 and the other, very much older, of Khan Omortag from the 9th century contains the pious hope "May it please God that he live a hundred years." Thirdly, there is the church of SS. Peter and Paul from the 13th and 14th centuries, which suffered much damage in the 1913 earthquake, but has very well preserved 14th-century frescoes.

Later, during Ottoman rule, the newer "older" city of the Varuša district grew up the slopes of Orlovec Hill to the west, the houses stacked steeply above each other. It is here you will find many fine surviving or restored examples of the National Revival period along little thoroughfares such as Gurko Street and Samovodska Čaršija (featuring a handicrafts center in Rakovski Street). One of the greatest exponents of this style was the self-taught master builder Nikola Fičev (known as Koljo Fičeto) and among his finest buildings is Nikoli Han, now a museum devoted to that National Revival Period. The style of these houses, with their red-tiled roofs and jutting upper stories, adds enormously to the charm of this city and a stroll through the steep, narrow streets of the old districts will be amply rewarded. An elegant church from this period is St. Constantine and St. Helena, designed by Fičev. Another of this prolific artist's buildings is the imposing Konak, scene of major historical events and recently restored to house the Museum of the Bulgarian State and Târnovo Constitution, one of the country's most important historical museums. During the centuries of Turkish rule, incidentally, Veliko Târnovo was by no means quiescent. There were a number of uprisings and the city is dotted with monuments to these courageous if ill-fated bids for freedom.

One could spend a lot of time in this area which has cradled the nation's culture over so many centuries. One of the sights that should not be missed is Preobrženski Monastery, the most interesting of the 11 monasteries in the area, superbly situated at the foot of limestone cliffs, looking out across a deep valley. It lies just over five km. (three miles) to the northwest, and was founded in the 14th century—although rebuilt in the 19th—the tower of the main monastery church being another of Nikola Fičev's designs, (he was responsible for the splendid iconostasis). The frescoes include a couple of rare portraits by the leading painter of the National Revival period, Zahari Zograf, and the one above the door of the inner church bears his signature. There is also a massive picture of the *Last Judgment.*

The village of Arbanasi is another of the local sights a few miles northeast of Veliko Târnovo. Founded in the 16th century it flourished economically in the 17th and 18th centuries. The style of its great fortress-like stone houses, hidden away behind high walls, is like nothing else in Bulgaria, and the interiors reveal some beautifully carved ceilings, doors and shutters. Five churches and two monasteries, with a remarkable collection of 17th–19th century iconostasis gates, also survive in this enigmatic village, remote from the doings of the 20th century. Yet another worthwhile trip is 18 km. (11 miles) north of Veliko Târnovo to the ruins of the Roman city of Nicopolis ad Istrum.

One area that does not easily fit into any circular itinerary, but which could be visited on a detour from either the main E771 to Varna or E772 to Burgas is Kotel, situated roughly mid-way between the two roads northeast of Sliven. Kotel is particularly known for its carpet workshops, and some attractive houses survive in what remains of the older quarter. Better still is the small town of Žeravna a few miles away, its huddle of old wooden houses now carefully restored and some offering delightful accommodations for visitors.

The E771 also links Veliko Târnovo with Šumen, the nearest town to one of the most important areas in terms of Bulgaria's early history, still relatively little known to Western visitors. Nowadays, Šumen is mainly an industrial center, albeit with a well-developed taste for cultural activities. The first National Theater was established here in 1856, and it is the birthplace of several literary figures. The 18th-century Tombul Mosque is the largest and finest in Bulgaria.

About 20 km. (12 miles) southwest of Šumen are the ruins of Preslav, which has the distinction of being Bulgaria's second capital from 893 to 972, in the distant Golden Age of the First Kingdom. John the Exarch, living in those times, described "tall palaces and churches with countless tones, woodwork and painting, lined on the inside with marble and copper, silver and gold . . . " The Turks made a pretty good job of destroying it down to its foundations, some of which can still be seen widely scattered over three square miles of the undulating countryside. Restoration work has been carried out on the fortress walls, palace buildings, and a round church whose interior mosaics and gilded cupola make it a unique example of early Bulgarian architecture. Of special interest in the Archeological Museum here are marble columns and chunks of sculptured stonework inlaid with colored stone fragments, and silver and gold decorations.

The Horseman of Madara

A few miles east of Šumen at the junction with a minor road to Madara, you will see a copy of the famous Horseman of Madara. To see the original and much else, you must continue the few miles to the village of Madara and its backdrop of cliffs. Here there are remarkable remains from a whole tangle of cultures, going back to prehistoric times, the earliest from the third millennium B.C.

The famous Horseman of Madara itself was created by an unknown 8th-century chiseler high up on the cliff and continues to confound the experts. You can view it from a natural platform above the village, reached by 200 steps (binoculars will be helpful). It depicts a horseman now established as Tervel—one of the earliest Bulgarian kings—slaying a lion with a lance and closely followed by a dog. There are some inscriptions in Greek, the earliest surviving examples of Bulgarian writing. The cliff face is also pitted with what were once the cells of a monastery. As you reach the top of the steps you will see footpaths leading off in both directions. If you follow the one to the right, in a few hundred yards you will come to the Small and Large Caves, in which have been found traces of habitation from pre-historic to medieval times. Nearby there is a medieval rock chapel. A foot-path to the left of the steps leads to the foundations of a 9th- and 10th-century royal palace on the hillside, and eventually round the back of the cliffs to the plateau on the top. Here is the once great fortress of Madara. It probably dates from the 5th century, with later alterations, and was in use until its destruction by the Turks. The view from up here extends far over the valley and Balkan Range. Not far from the fortress are the remains of a Roman villa. At the foot of the steps, near the coach park, is a museum. Just to the east of the present village of Madara are the remains of a considerable Roman villa. Small wonder that Madara became known as the 'Bulgarian Troy.'

Pre-dating Preslav by two centuries was Bulgaria's first capital of all. You will find the well-organized remains of Pliska set in cornfields east of the Madara turning and a few miles to the north of the main road (about 24 km./15 miles northeast of şumen). Spread out over several square miles of the plain, the foundations of a triple line of fortifications as well as traces of the palace, temples and feudal residences have been uncovered. They are thought to date mainly from the reign of Omortag in the 9th century, although the earliest constructions are probably from the late 7th century. The second line of fortifications is being substantially reconstructed, as are the royal palace and nearby basilica. The museum has a lapidarium and various tools, trinkets and vessels on display. These are less sophisticated than those found at Preslav, the site to which the capital was moved after its conversion to Christianity as a result of its better natural defenses and the presence around Pliska of pagan tribes.

About 25 km. (15 miles) from Pliska, recent discoveries associated with the 9th–10th century monastery of Čerkvišteto on the Provadijska river have resulted in a remarkable collection of early Greek and Bulgarian inscriptions and drawings. Such discoveries are constantly expanding knowledge of the early cultures that flourished in these remote areas of the Balkans.

To the Valley of Roses

The main road south of Veliko Târnovo to Gabrovo winds attractively through limestone country, at times quite ravine-like in character. About half way you pass Drjanovo Monastery, huddled down in a hollow just below the road and scene of another desperate shoot-out with the Turks in 1876. A short distance north of Gabrovo, a minor road leads to the pretty village of Boženci. Several score of its fine National Revival houses, now restored, are witness to its former importance as a trading and crafts center, and the rural setting is idyllic, especially if you can avoid coinciding with an influx of tourist buses.

Gabrovo is a major industrial center on the upper reaches of the Jantra river. Indeed, it is known as the Pittsburgh of Bulgaria, although its backdrop of the Balkan Mountain Range gives it a certain scenic edge over its U.S. rival; in fact the town is twinned with Aberdeen in Scotland. Gabrovo's inhabitants are famous for their sense of humor, to such an extent that the town features a House of Humor, with a collection of over 110,000 humorous items from all over the world. A festival of comedy and humor is held here every year. The main square, the old bridges and the river banks are pleasant enough, but a place not to be missed is the museum-park of Etur, five miles (eight km.) away. It is a living museum delightfully set in a mountain valley, its original houses grouped along a stream whose waters are used to power all kinds of activities from grinding corn to turning a roasting spit. Not only the architectural styles of the National Revival period are to be seen here, but also the way of life, arts and crafts, for each building is devoted to some end product: bakery, coppersmith, cobbler, potter, blacksmith, weaver, wood turner and so on. Some of the products can be bought. It is worth a detour. Seventeen km. (11 miles) east of Gabrovo the small town of Trjavna was once the center of a flourishing school of icon-painting and woodcarving. It still has some lovely National Revival houses with fine wood carvings.

South of Gabrovo, the road continues into the Balkan Range to cross the Šipka Pass before dropping down on to the Valley of Roses. The defense of the Pass was the reason for yet another epic battle in the Russo-Turkish war and a mighty monument, approached by a flight of steps, commemorates those who fell here in 1877. These monuments to battles and uprisings are very much part of any journey through Bulgaria; visitors who may begin to weary of them should remember that without the events that they commemorate Bulgaria would simply not exist. Some of the fiercest battles of all were fought against this mountain backdrop, so don't be surprised if you arrive in the village of Šipka to find it milling with Soviet tourists. For here, 20 years after the war was won, a large memorial church was built, honoring the 200,000 Russian soldiers and Bulgarian volunteers who perished here. The church is very colorful and ornate, and was designed by the same architect as the Nevski Memorial Church in Sofia. Its bells were cast in metal which came from bullets used in battle against the Turks.

We are now approaching the famous Valley of Roses, funneling between the Balkan Range and the hills of Sredna Gora. The rose-growing area extends along the valley floor from Kazanlâk in the east to Klisura in the west, linked by one of the through routes between Sofia and the Black Sea. But if it is the roses and their harvesting that you are interested in, you should come in May or early June—and be prepared to get up early, as the rose pickers must be. The picking is done between dawn and about 8 A.M., for the good reason that once the sun gets too high in the sky the rose petals lose up to 50 per cent of their oil. Since between 3,000 and 6,000 kilos of rose petals are needed to make one liter of rose oil, a minor army of nimble-fingered pickers is at work while most tourists are still asleep. This fragrant harvest is then fed into giant copper vats; the precious attar is extracted still leaving a fragrant and useful residue of rosewater. In addition to the famous attar of roses, the blooms also contribute to the making of liqueurs, sweetmeats, jam—and medicines especially useful in treating skin complaints.

The production of attar of roses was begun in the 1830s under the Turks, who have always been partial to sweet smells and sweet flavors, and it is the oldest industry in Bulgaria. The Museum of Rose Production at Kazanlâk traces its history and preserves some of the early tools and equipment used. Though unfortunately it lacks any explanatory text in English, it is fairly easy to pick up a general idea of what went on. Incidentally, the valley grows things other than roses—notably fruit crops, lavender, sunflowers, and vines, which add their own attractive blooms and fruit to the scene in due season.

The other great sight of Kazanlâk, which otherwise has rather an industrial character nowadays, is a Thracian Tomb. The original is closed to the public for its better protection, but an exact replica has been constructed near it, so you can get an accurate idea of one of Bulgaria's most impressive single monuments, demonstrating the high level of artistic taste of those original inhabitants of the land. The tomb dates from the 3rd or 4th century B.C. and was the last resting place of a local chieftain. The inner wall surfaces of the corridor and small domed burial chamber are decorated with frescoes depicting a scene from the burial feast, warriors on foot and on horseback, and a chariot race. They are finely drawn and full of movement.

West of Kazanlâk, the road heads up the valley past the artificial waters created by Georgi Dimitrov Dam which drown the ruins of the ancient Thracian capital of Seuthopolis. The valley narrows as you proceed west, and soon after passing through the little town of Kalofer you cross a watershed and come to the upper end of the Valley of Roses; including Karlovo, Sopot, and Klisura.

Artists and Revolutionaries

Kalofer has some picturesque corners and is revered as the birthplace of Bulgaria's great poet and revolutionary Hristo Botev to whom there is a monument and a museum. Karlovo also offers a monument and museum to one of its sons, another great revolutionary, Vasil Levski, while in Sopot you can see the small underground church where he used to disguise himself as a nun to foil his Turkish pursuers. Both towns have some attractive National Revival houses, one of Sopot's being the home (now museum) of the most translated Bulgarian writer of those revolutionary times, Ivan Vasov. A road from Karlovo leads south over 26 km. (16 miles) to Hisarja, one of the best equipped of all Bulgaria's spas. Good use was made of its mineral sources by the Thracians and, even more, by the Romans who built an elaborate water system to feed their splendid baths. Part of the 4th-century walls are well preserved and there are remains of very early Christian basilicas.

At the village of Karnare, between Sopot and Klisura, a sinuous road leads north over the Balkan range to the attractive town of Trojan and, a few kilometers away, Trojan monastery nestling in the heart of the mountains, the third largest in Bulgaria. This can also be approached from the north, from the main Sofia–Veliko Târnovo road, but the road out of the Valley of Roses has the merit of providing wonderful views, not only over the valley and the Sredna Gora range, but beyond this to the rugged profiles of the Rhodopes. Trojan Monastery church, like so many others, was rebuilt in the 19th century, but it is extremely picturesque and its icons, wood carvings, and frescoes are fine examples of National Revival art. Zahari Zograf is among the artists.

Klisura huddles near the head of the valley and beyond it the road climbs up and over the Koznica Pass. Soon after this a minor road leads south in a few kilometers to one of Bulgaria's showpiece villages, Ko-

privština. Once again you see a veritable living museum of National Revival architecture, but this time adapted to a setting of mountain pastures
and pine forests, at about 915 meters (3,000 ft.) in the Sredna Gora range.
Many of the houses are museums and can be visited, several of them belonging to poets and artists. There are courtyards behind studded wooden
gates, broad verandahs and overhanging eaves, and nothing much has
changed since the revolutionaries met in the pharmacy here to lay their
plans for a free Bulgaria. The first shots of the tragic April uprising of
1876 were fired here and naturally there is a museum to tell you about
this landmark in Bulgaria's history. This is a place of pilgrimage for many
Bulgarians who come here to do honor to the first Bulgarian town briefly
to taste freedom before the bloodbath of subsequent events, and it is also
an increasingly popular destination for Western visitors who have heard
of its picturesque houses and beautiful location.

South Bulgaria—the Road to Turkey

Two main traffic arteries bore through the southern half of Bulgaria.
One of them is the new A1 Motorway gradually replacing the old E80
southeast from Sofia to Turkey and already completed as far as Plovdiv.
Basically it follows the Marica river through the Thracian Plain. The sec-
ond main road is the E79 mostly following the river Struma which eventu-
ally empties itself into the northern Aegean as the Greek river Strymon.
This road is your route for the mountains of Rila (the highest in southeast
Europe) and Pirin.

Let's take the A1/E80 first. Recreating history sometimes needs a fair
dose of imagination and this will probably be the case when you find yourself part of a stream of tourist traffic and long-distance trucks heading in
the general direction of Istanbul. However, it is worth exercising your
imaginative talents a little to remember that you are following one of the
oldest strategic routes in history. The Thracians and Macedonians, the
Romans and Byzantines, the Slavs, Bulgarians, Crusaders and Turks, all
passed this way and the pity of it is that they were all so successful in destroying what went before. A few traces remain, but nothing really worth
leaving the motorway for, except perhaps the Church of the Holy Virgin
at Pazardzik with its gloriously carved iconostasis. Since it was built during the period of Ottoman rule, you may be struck by its unusual size,
which is accounted for by a nice story. It was decreed that the church
must be no larger than the size of a sheepskin. The townspeople, however,
had other ideas and during the night diligently cut a sheepskin into the
tiniest strips. When placed end to end, these enclosed a considerable
area—certainly much larger than that intended by the authorities. But
they were allowed to get away with it.

Plovdiv

As Bulgaria's second-largest city, a major industrial center and site of
two of the most important trade fairs in the Balkans each Spring and Fall,
it might seem unlikely that Plovdiv would have much in the way of character. But it has much to offer from its extreme antiquity. Here stood the
Pulpudeva of the Thracians, the Philippopolis of Philip II of Macedonia,
the Trimontium of the Romans and the Filibé of the Turks. Here, too,
was the scene of terrible slaughter after the 1876 uprising against the
Turks.

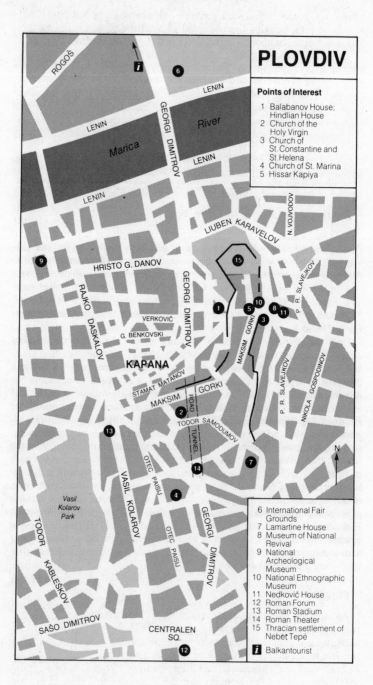

PLOVDIV

Points of Interest

1 Balabanov House;
  Hindlian House
2 Church of the
  Holy Virgin
3 Church of
  St. Constantine and
  St. Helena
4 Church of St. Marina
5 Hissar Kapiya

6 International Fair
  Grounds
7 Lamartine House
8 Museum of National
  Revival
9 National
  Archeological
  Museum
10 National Ethnographic
  Museum
11 Nedković House
12 Roman Forum
13 Roman Stadium
14 Roman Theater
15 Thracian settlement of
  Nebet Tepé

i Balkantourist

The situation on several hills on the banks of the Marica river was one of the attractions, as noted by the French writer and poet Lamartine when he traveled this way in 1833, for this is a truly commanding position from which to control the Thracian Plain. The old part of the town scrambles over the hillier southern side of the river and, on one of the three eminences that made up the Roman town of Trimontium, you will find Thracian foundations upon which Roman walls were superimposed. A fine Roman amphitheater, discovered in recent years, has now been restored and is one of the city's major sights, not only for its ancient stonework but also for its expansive views over the city and surroundings. It provides a memorable setting for drama and opera performances.

The amphitheater stands above the southern entrance to a modern road tunnel that burrows under this hilly oldest district of Plovdiv. As you walk through its narrow twisting cobbled streets, you will pass innumerable examples of buildings from the famed National Revival period which, in essence, marked a kind of Bulgarian Renaissance. Indeed, it was in Plovdiv that this style first made its impact. As a new sense of national identity developed in the late 18th and 19th centuries, some of its more affluent citizens—with the benefit of education and sometimes foreign travel—began to build in a style that incorporated various ancient elements of Bulgarian culture, fused with ideas imported from abroad. To accord with the narrowness of the streets, these houses were built on a narrower base, their upper stories jutting out and sometimes all but meeting over the smaller alleys. Many of them have now been restored and, with their color-washed facades and distinctive style, make a most charming effect. In time, the style spread to other parts of the country, but was adapted according to terrain and local tradition.

The true Plovdiv style (curvaceous roof and colonnaded central portion balanced on either side by matching wings) is quite distinctive and an excellent example of it is the House of Arghir Kouyoumidjioglu (the Goldsmith), now the National Ethnographic Museum. It stands just above the ancient gateway of Hissar Kapiya, part of the Byzantine and medieval fortifications of which there are further remnants nearby. Below the gateway, another fine National Revival building is Georgiadi's House containing the Museum of the National Revival Period, and the steep narrow street of Strumna which leads down from here is lined with workshops and boutiques in various recently restored houses, some reached through little courtyards.

Several more fine old houses can be visited and you should seek out at least Balabanov's House and Hindlian's House, both sharing the same peaceful courtyard. The second, which features a Turkish bath, is original both in construction and furnishings, and must provide a beautiful setting for the concerts held here in September. The Lamartine House, in which the famous French writer stayed, is another striking building, not far from the Roman amphitheater.

The old shopping and commercial part of town lies immediately west below the district just described. Its main artery is Vasil Kolarov street, a pedestrian precinct. Close to the northern end of this is the Kapana district currently undergoing restoration to become an attractive nucleus of small shops and restaurants in traditional style. Actually beneath the northern end of Vasil Kolarov Street you will see the remains of part of a Roman stadium. At its southern end, Vasil Kolarov street opens out on to what was once the Roman forum, now Centralen Square, with a park on one side—and the main Post Office on the other. A number of Roman foundations and columns are to be seen here, and excavations are still in progress.

Two 15th-century mosques and a handsome clock tower are Ottoman legacies to note. The three most interesting churches—St. Constantine and St. Helena, St. Marina, and the Church of the Holy Virgin—are all from the 19th century, but again contain good examples of National Revival art.

For a sight of one of Plovdiv's most famous treasures, the nine-piece set of vessels in magnificently worked pure gold known as the Panagjurište Gold Treasure, you must go to the National Archeological Museum, though what you will see is a replica, for the original has been whisked off to Sofia. It dates from the 4th–3rd century B.C. and is quite stunning. In total contrast is the modern and very moving Common Grave Memorial Center, completed in 1978 on the western outskirts of the city to commemorate 100 years of liberation from Turkish rule. Scenes from those and more recent events in Bulgaria's fight against oppression have been graphically created in granite and iron, and they can hardly fail to move you.

Beyond Plovdiv

The road east from Plovdiv leads across the Thracian Plain via the E772 through Stara Zagora and Sliven to the coast, mostly following the foothills of the Balkan Range. These are pleasant rolling landscapes of cornfields, fruit trees and, as you approach the coast, increasingly extensive vineyards. Just east of Plovdiv, the E80 heads southeast for Turkey, crossing the border beyond Svilengrad whose 16th-century bridge still carries the heavy traffic between Europe and the Middle East. A domed Thracian tomb at Mezek, six km. (over three miles) to the southwest, is of special interest, and west of Mezek lies the well-preserved medieval fortress of Neutsikon.

The roads south of Plovdiv take you right into the Rhodope Mountains. The transition is abrupt. One minute you are crossing the Thracian Plain towards the barrier of mountains, the next—immediately beyond the tobacco and wine center of Asenovgrad—you enter the magnificent Čepelarska River gorge burrowing deep into the precipitous heights. Near the entrance to the gorge a side road leads very soon right up to the medieval ruins of Asenov fortress and the Church of the Virgin of Petrič. They virtually seem to be suspended over the valley, a spectacular sight when viewed from the main road that passes beneath, and even more so if you climb the steep steps to this eyrie (not recommended for those suffering from vertigo). The fortress was built to protect this main trading route from Byzantium and, as you head deeper into the mountains, you may well marvel at the conditions that must have prevailed before the building of a modern highway.

A few miles further on and in a similarly magnificent setting, a road to the left leads shortly to the second-oldest, second-largest—and one of the finest—of Bulgaria's monasteries: that of Bačkovo. It was founded in 1083 and the oldest surviving part is the Church of the Trinity, about 300 meters east of the main complex. It is currently closed for restoration but contains an ossuary from those earliest times and 12th–14th-century frescoes. The monastery was abandoned when the Turks came, but the monks

returned in the 17th century and much of what you see dates from then
or later, with the exception of the smaller Church of the Archangels (walls
from 12th–13th centuries). Of particular interest is the fresco by Zograf
on an exterior wall of the Refectory. It depicts a religious procession carrying an icon from 1311 and shows the monastery complex as it was at the
time he painted it in 1843. The icon itself is on view in the early 17th-
century Church of the Virgin, largest of the three churches within the
monastery walls. National Revival art is also well represented in the small
19th-century Church of St. Nicholas (usually closed), entirely decorated
by Zograf.

The Rhodopes are dotted with spas and one of them, about 48 km. (30
miles) further, is also a winter sports center whose reputation has spread
far beyond Bulgaria's boundaries. This is Pamporovo, about 80 km. (50
miles) south of Plovdiv at an altitude of 1,600 meters (5,250 ft.). It's a
lovely setting in summer too, even if you are perfectly healthy. Guided
walks are arranged in summer and, indeed, walkers and climbers will be
in their element, though they should note that, for the moment, the many
mountain chalets dotted about these beautiful landscapes are not open to
independent foreign visitors. Pamporovo has been a mountain resort for
some 50 years, but the present developments mainly date from the 1960s
onwards.

If you follow minor roads west of Pamporovo, you will eventually join
up with itineraries described in the following sections. Even if you do not
go so far, try at least to visit the very picturesque village of Široka Lâka,
a few kilometers to the west of Pamporovo, where fine examples of the
picturesque Rhodope form of National Revival architecture, adapted to
the steep terrain, can be seen.

South Bulgaria—On and Off the Road to Greece

To the west of the Rhodopes are the two fine mountain groups which
fill most of the southwest corner of Bulgaria: Pirin bordering on to northern Greece and to the north of it, Rila, which gives its name to Bulgaria's
most famous monastery.

The E79, which provides speedy access to them from Sofia, curves
round Vitoša mountain on its way south and soon enters a rolling agricultural countryside, rich in orchards and misty with their blossoms in spring.
Indeed, in the hilly Struma valley to the west of here along E770, the town
of Kjustendil is the heart of a major fruit-growing area. It has had the
usual chequered history, stretching back as far as the Thracians. The Romans, notably the Emperor Trajan, made good use of the warm mineral
springs, which have now made this a popular thermal resort.

A detour to Kjustendil is only suggested if you have plenty of time.
Today it is mainly of modern aspect, but in the old center there is a historic
group of monuments worthy of attention. Head for Hristo Smirnenski
street and you will find the quite substantial foundations of the Roman
temple and bath of Asklepion. Beside it are some old Turkish baths, still
in use, and the 16th-century mosque of Ahmed Bey now housing the District Museum, while across the road is 15th-century Pirgov's Tower, part
of the feudal fortifications. Half a mile up the hill from the center, the 13th-
century Church of St. George is undergoing much-needed restoration.

You can return east to E79 from Kjustendil by minor roads following
the Struma river which, close to Nevestino, is spanned by a beautiful five-
arch bridge from the 15th century, bearing an inscription in Turkish.

The Struma soon joins the E79 all the way to the Greek border. The whole of this area is important tobacco-growing country, with the seedlings protected under long rows of cloches in spring before being planted out in the fields painstakingly by hand about May. The mature tobacco has to be picked in the very early hours of the morning before the sun gets up, and harvesting begins in July. From then on, you will see vast quantities of the "pernicious weed" drying on wooden racks along the roadside and in every village. Wine is another major local product.

It is more likely that you will have remained on the E79 from Sofia and passed through Stanke Dimitrov, a few miles east of which is the spa of Sapareva Banja, which has the distinction of producing the hottest and most sulphurous mineral water in Bulgaria (over 100°C/212°F). More to the point, the road to it continues along the northern edge of the magnificent Rila Mountains to Samokov and Borovec, the country's oldest and most famous mountain resort.

In fact you can reach both Samokov and Borovec more directly (71 km./44 miles) from Sofia via the upper Iskar gorge and lake. On the way you pass Pančarevo, a small lake with sports facilities, while lake Iskar (also offering water sports) is the largest in Bulgaria. In Samokov there is a rather charming mosque, rebuilt in the late 18th century in National Revival style; rather like a private house with a minaret tacked on. Above all, however, this small town was a major center for the dissemination of National Revival art. The Samokov school of painting, for example, is of great importance in Bulgarian art history. It was founded by Hristo Dimitrov, whose son Zahari Zograf was one of its most gifted exponents; his works embellish monasteries and churches throughout the country. The Samokov master woodcarvers acquired a considerable reputation; the iconostasis in the monastery church of Rila is among their creations, as is the splendid one in the Church of the Virgin in Samokov.

Borovec is at an altitude of about 1,300 meters (4,300 ft.) on the northern slopes of the Rila Mountains. Prince Ferdinand built three palaces and a hunting lodge here at the turn of the century, and these were subsequently followed by the villas of nobles and high officials, now mainly trade union holiday homes. Together with the hotels they are scattered about the deep pine forests that clothe these mountain slopes. It is an excellent walking center and has now become well known in the West as a reasonably priced winter sports resort. This is the most convenient point for the ascent of Mount Musala (2,925 meters/9,596 ft.), the highest in the Balkan peninsula.

To reach the Rila Monastery you must continue further south on E79, turning off for the village of Kočerinovo. The Rila Mountains soar into the sky ahead of you, making a really splendid backdrop to the tobacco fields and pasture-land that surround this village, which is also known for its prodigious population of storks, their nests adorning most of the village roofs. The approach to the monastery is through a steep, forested valley; watched over by its encirclement of mountains, it is easy to understand how the founders of Rila found the peace and beauty they sought for their spiritual pursuits, and also how, remote from the ravages of power struggles, it remained a stronghold of Bulgarian art and learning during the dark centuries of Ottoman rule.

The group of buildings, fortress-like in their compactness, stands at 1,147 meters (3,760 ft.). The monastery was founded in the 10th century by Ivan of Rila or Rilski. After damage by avalanche and fire, it was rebuilt on its present site in the 14th century by Hrelju, a feudal overlord, who also built a church and a tower. Alas, the centuries took their toll. Rila may have been largely spared the onslaught of weapons, but it did not escape that ubiquitous destroyer of so many ancient buildings, fire. On several occasions the silent mountains witnessed the depredations of the flames and, in 1833, the greatest of them all destroyed virtually everything. A notable exception was the tower that Hrelju built, which stands today, its rugged stonework contrasting with the arcaded elegance of the great complex that surrounds it. The money for the reconstruction of the monastery was collected from all over the country, coinciding with the potent impulses of the National Revival movement of which it is such a grand example. The foremost masters of the Samokov, Bansko and Debar schools of painting and woodcarving are represented in the monastery church, including the brothers Zahari and Dimitur Zograf. The sarcophagus containing the embalmed body of Ivan of Rila can also be seen in the main church of the monastery. Early on, a printing press was established at Rila by the monks and the monastery library houses 16,000 volumes, many of great value, though at present it is open only to specialists.

Much of the rest of the complex, however, has been turned into a museum featuring old icons, frescoes, Hrelju's 14th-century throne and tombstone, some ancient manuscripts, and a collection of objects in gold and silver. The monk's cells have been turned into guest rooms.

There are 14 small churches and chapels in the surroundings of the monastery with wall paintings from the 15th and 17th centuries. One of them is the little Church of St Luke, four km. (nearly three miles) east of the present monastery, close to the simple monastic cell first established by Ivan of Rila. Rila Monastery is also an excellent starting point for a number of climbs to peaks 2,592–2,745 meters (8,500–9,000 ft.) high.

Peaceful Backwaters

Continuing south on E79 along the Struma valley you pass through the industrial town of Blagoevgrad which is also the home of an outstanding folkloric group, the Pirin State Ensemble, winners of many international awards. Soon the Pirin mountains replace those of Rila on your left. You won't find many tourist hordes around here, but there are certainly places to see on the way to the Greek border, as well as some very fine scenery. One is the spa of Sandanski, just off the main road, said to be the birthplace of the legendary Roman gladiator Spartacus whose statue greets you on the approaches to town. The healing properties of its mineral springs have been in use since earliest times and these, allied with the town's excellent climate, have proved very effective in modern times, especially with respiratory disorders and degenerative diseases of the joints. Its well-equipped new Hydro complex features excellent treatment, sports and entertainment facilities, and it is now undoubtedly Bulgaria's top inland spa for Western visitors.

The little town of Melnik is a few miles east of the main road down towards the Greek border. Once famous for its silk factory and still famous for its wines, its original total of 14,000 inhabitants has shrunk to 370, and it can now claim to be Bulgaria's smallest town. Set amid eroded sandstone cliffs, it is also one of its most picturesque. Once a fortress, then a feudal capital, later a major trade center, Melnik suffered badly in the Balkan Wars. Recently, however, the unique style and great beauty of its surviving houses—many dating from the 18th and 19th centuries—have earned it well-deserved attention from artists and discerning visitors. Though only 116 of its former 3,600 buildings remain, they are almost all delightful and several are open to visitors. One of them, Pašov's House, is the District Museum.

Melnik is now included on quite a few tourist circuits though, as always, the best time to be there is before or after the tourist buses have come or gone. You could ensure this by staying overnight in private accommodations or in the one hotel.

About eight km. (five miles) further east into the increasingly bizarre sandstone landscapes of these mountains lies the restored Rožen Monastery. Be warned, it's a stiff uphill walk of about a mile to reach it from road's end at the hamlet of Rožen, but the monastery itself and the views from the grassy plateau on which it stands are well worth the effort. Originally from the 14th century but subsequently rebuilt and completely restored in 1982, the outer walls of the monastery are as solid as a fortress. Within their protection, the church dates from 1600 with exterior frescoes repainted in 1732, dominated by the usual Day of Judgment scenes. It also harbors a magnificent iconostasis and, unusual for an Orthodox church, two small stained glass windows from 1715. But, above all, it is the utter peace and the beauty of the setting which leave the most lasting impression.

Minor but good roads lead east from E79 over the Pirin Mountains, eventually into the neighboring ranges of the Rhodopes. One of them brings you through Bansko, beautifully situated in a wide bowl surrounded by the Rila, Pirin and Rhodope peaks. Once famous for its school of painting and woodcarving, it still has a considerable number of National Revival houses and a church (1835) of unusual size for its period. One of Bansko's greatest sons was the monk and historian Païssi of Hilendar.

South of Bansko, another minor road follows the Mesta valley. Enthusiasts for things Roman should seek out the substantial ruins of Nicopolis ad Nestum, currently being excavated about seven km. (four miles) east of Goce Delčev. You'll need to enquire locally as it is reached by a side road.

PRACTICAL INFORMATION FOR

INLAND BULGARIA

TOURIST INFORMATION. There is a Balkantourist office in most towns and resorts. Main ones are: **Blagoevgrad,** 2 G. Nikolov Str.; **Gabrovo,** 2 Opulčenska Str.; **Kjustendil,** 39 D. Kaljashki Str.; **Pleven,** 10 Canko Cerkovski St.; **Plovdiv,** 34 Moskva Blvd.; **Ruse,** 45D Blagoev St.; **Stara Zagora,** 5 Lenin Blvd.; **Veliko Târnovo,** 2 Vasil Levski St.; and **Vidin,** 4 Dondukov Str.

WHEN TO COME. Late spring, summer and early autumn are the best times for these landscapes combining plains and mountains, remembering that summers can be very warm in the valleys and plains. There is much lovely spring blossom and, in the famous Valley of Roses, May and early June are the peak times for the harvesting of millions of blooms. Bulgaria's increasing winter sports amenities are attracting growing numbers to the mountains from January through March.

GETTING AROUND. Ideally by self-drive car. Otherwise, there is a selection of organized tours. Rail or bus services between them cover all parts of the country, if you can sort out the timetables. Hydrofoils link communities along the Danube.

HOTELS AND RESTAURANTS. The establishments listed below are classified according to price. Unless otherwise stated, all have restaurants and are open year-round. Private accommodations are available in many places through Balkantourist offices.

Asenovgrad. *Asenovec* (I), 148 rooms, nightclub. Pleasant open-air restaurant south of town where road branches right for Asenov fortress.

Bansko. *Pirin* (I), 63 rooms.

Blagoevgrad. *Alen Mak* (M), 160 rooms, good folk tavern.

Borovec. *Bor* (M), 48 rooms, folk tavern. *Breza* (M), 34 rooms. *Ela* (M), new, folk tavern. *Musala* (M), 98 rooms. *Rila* (M), major French-designed complex. 2,000 beds in hotel and studio flats. *Edelweiss* (I), 80 rooms.
Also available are 25 chalet-type villas, in woodland, with 2 bedrooms each, plus kitchen and dining room (M).

Gabrovo. *Balkan* (M), 200 rooms, folk tavern. *Jantra* (I), 200 rooms. *Etur* (I), inn at village museum, 8 km. (5 miles) from town.
Restaurant. *Strano-Priemnicata* (M). Attractive folk style.

Hisarja. *Balneosanatoria Augusta* (M), 80 rooms, spa facilities.
Restaurant. *Slaveev Dol,* folk style.

Karlovo. *Rozova Dolina* (I), 54 rooms.

Kazanlâk. *Kazanlâk* (I), 200 rooms, nightclub, roof-top bar, tavern, indoor pool, sports hall. *Roza* (I), 80 rooms. *Zornica* (I), 50 rooms, disco.
Three km. (two miles) north, the *Krunska Kourija* complex features a motel, restaurant, campsite.

Koprivštica. *Koprivštica* (I), 30 rooms. Rooms also available in some of the beautiful, restored old houses—*Sapoundiev, Mavroudiev,* and *Hadji Gencho* houses, with a total of 16 rooms between them (I). Several attractive folk restaurants include *Djado Liben* inn.

Kotel. *Kotel* (I), 30 rooms. Accommodations available in attractive restored houses in nearby village of *Žeravna,* a National Revival tourist complex also featuring folk restaurants.

Kjustendil. *Velbužd* (E), 145 rooms, nightclub, sports hall. New. *Pautalija* (M), 60 rooms, folk tavern.

Melnik. *Melnik* (I), 34 rooms, folk tavern. Fine views. Private accommodations also available in some of the beautiful old houses.

Pamporovo. Several of the hotels stand in a row sharing similar fine views of forested mountains. All have discos. *Mourgavec* (M), 75 rooms, 9th-floor cafe. *Perelik* (M), newest and best, 230 rooms, folk tavern, indoor pool, sports hall. *Orfeus* (I), 78 rooms. Folk tavern; short walk from resort center. *Panorama* (I), 75 rooms, three km. (two miles) from center. *Prespa* (I), 80 rooms, recently renovated. *Rožen* (I), 90 rooms, recently renovated. *Snežanka* (I), 41 rooms. The oldest, built in 1961.
Also accommodations in *Malina* (M), 30 chalets near ski lift terminal, three km. (two miles) from center.

Restaurants. *Čevermeto* (M), folk restaurant in style of Rhodope dairy in resort center. *Malina* (M), near above chalets, in style of local dwelling. *Vodenicata* (M), seven km. (four miles), folk restaurant in old water mill.

Pleven. *Pleven* (M), 200 rooms, several restaurants, disco. *Rosto na Don* (I), complex in city center, 109 rooms, restaurants, nightclub.

Restaurants. *Karadjeikata* (Water Mill) (M), folk style, large open-air section, traditional dishes. *Pešterata* (M), adapted from natural cave. *Srebrostroui* (M), out of town, but free transport provided.

Plovdiv. Bulgaria's second city. *Novotel Plovdiv* (L), 2 Zlatju Boyadjiev St. Interhotel with 322 rooms, nightclub, folk tavern, indoor and open-air pools, sports hall. Modern, near fair grounds and across river from city center. *Trimontium* (E), 2 Kapitan Raičo St. Interhotel with 163 rooms, folk tavern. Built in early 1950s, large rooms, comfortable. Good central position for old town, by Centralen Square. *Leningrad* (M), 97 Moskva Blvd. 370 rooms; nightclub, indoor pool. Modern highrise on north side of river, some distance from center. *Marica* (M), 5 Georgi Dimitrov St., 171 rooms. Modern, near Novotel. *Bulgaria* (I), 13 Patriarch Evtimii St., 78 rooms. Central for old town. *Leipzig* (I), 70 Ruski Blvd., 135 rooms. Not so central.

Restaurants. *Pldin* (E), attractive folk restaurant in old town. *Alafrangues* (M), also in charming folk style in old town. *Rhetora* (M), coffee bar in beautifully restored old house near Roman amphitheater in old town. *Riton* (M), Zelezarka St. in Kapana district of old town. *Trakijski Stan* (M), another pleasant folk restaurant in old town. *Zlatnijt Elen* (Golden Stag) (M), in Hotel Bulgaria, game specialties.

Preslav. *Preslav* (I), 44 rooms, folk tavern.

Rila. *Rila* (M), 110 rooms. Near the famous monastery in the Rila Mountains.

Ruse. Largest port on the Danube. *Riga* (M), Interhotel with 180 rooms, restaurant, nightclub. On the riverside. *Dunav* (I), Interhotel, 82 rooms, disco.

Sandanski. *Hydro* (E), fine new Austrian-built hotel, 293 rooms, nightclub, bowling alley, indoor and open-air pools, sports facilities—best in the country—for those undertaking spa treatment. Specially-designed rooms with dust-repellent flooring; well-equipped for children.

Smoljan. Main town in Rhodope mountains. *Smoljan* (M), 169 rooms, pool.

Šumen. *Madara* (M), 100 rooms. Recently renovated. The *Bezistena* complex in converted, ancient Turkish building includes traditional restaurant.

Restaurant. *Peti Kilometer* (M), on main road on outskirts of town. Good value.

Sliven. *Sliven* (I), 150 rooms.

Restaurant. *Deboja* (M), adapted from former caravanserai and storehouse; disco.

Sopot. *Sopot* (I), 42 rooms.

Stara Zagora. *Vereja* (M), 239 rooms, restaurant, nightclub. Central.

Svilengrad. *Svilena complex* (I), 100 rooms, folk tavern.

Veliko Târnovo. Former capital and museum city in the mountains. *Veliko Târnovo* (E), Interhotel with 195 rooms, disco, indoor pool, sports hall. *Yantra* (M), 60 rooms. Both have stunning views across river to Tsaravec. *Etâr* (I), 80 rooms.

Restaurants. *Boljarska Izba* (M), Dimiter Blagoev St., *Hadji Minčo* (M), Poborničeski Sq., *Vinarna Tavern* (M), 1 Gurko St.

Vidin. *Bononia* (I), 50 rooms, restaurant. *Rovno* (I), 145 rooms, restaurant.

Vraca. *Hemus* (I), 90 rooms, restaurant.

THE BLACK SEA COAST

Space to Spare

The Black Sea coast has been known to traders and invaders since the earliest days of recorded history, and more recent finds by means of underwater archeology have probed even further back in time, with the discovery of over 200 stone anchors from the 2nd to early 1st millennium B.C. Thracians, Greeks and Romans were here, leaving their traces all along the coast; and the Vikings, who had reached the Black Sea a little further north via the river Dnieper, must have seen the self-same beaches from their vessels bound for Constantinople. The Bulgarians, Byzantines, and Ottoman Turks tussled over possession of the ports of this strategic strip. Exquisite churches were built in the name of less worldly conquests. Finally tourism arrived, a large, ever-growing, eminently peaceful kind of new invasion.

There is no denying that it is all very new. In the days before World War II those who found their way to these beaches were the adventurous or the privileged few. The latter would have had their own property here, since except in the ports there were no hotels. The great white modern buildings that you see now would have been as alien to the local people as the private villas of the rich. In those days too, the coast was also infested with snakes, although thankfully they are no longer a hazard. The problem was solved, so the story goes, by importing an army of hedgehogs which devoured them before being sold off themselves as pets!

From the point of view of sun, sand and scenery, the coast is well served. The resorts of Slânčev Brjag (Sunny Beach), and Zlatni Pjasâci (Golden Sands), are both well named. When it comes to beaches this is an ideal family coast, and visually it lacks the flatness of neighboring Romania, for here the last hills of the Balkan Range and Strandja Mountains stretch down to the sea.

The Northern Section

If you come via Romania from the north, you soon meet the mountains, and come to Šabla. Don't turn off for the coast here or you will find yourself in Bulgaria's only oil fields. A little to the south, the small resort of Rusalka sits by the sea beneath the hills. The rocky peninsula of Cape Kaliakra, just to the south of it, has perpendicular cliffs pierced by caves and was made into a formidable stronghold in medieval times. The cape is also the home of Bulgaria's only colony of seals.

Back on the main road, Kavarna is the first small town in Bulgaria followed, a few miles later, by Balčik. Before the Second World War, this was still part of Romania and a fashionable resort. In the 1920s, Romania's Queen Marie built herself a summer villa here, its gardens sharply terraced into the natural cliffs. These are now beautiful botanical gardens open to visitors who may wander through the labyrinth of paths and steps, past fountains and waterfalls and stone crosses of great antiquity from different parts of the Mediterranean. The grounds are dotted with curious little buildings in which Oriental and Western elements are combined, including a small Byzantine-style church. Just above the seashore, near the largest of the buildings which incorporates a minaret, you find the marble seat on which the Queen is said to have spent many hours looking out to sea. Elsewhere in Balčik, the villas that were once the holiday homes of the Romanian aristocracy provide a recreational setting for Bulgaria's writers, artists, scientists, and various trade unions and institutes. About 35 km. (21 miles) inland from Balčik, restoration work on the old core of the modern town of Tolbuhin is recreating a charming complex of National Revival houses, shops, and cafes.

Only a few miles down the coast is the first and newest of the coast's modern resorts. This is Albena, and very modern it is, too, its pyramidical architectural styles recreating the National Revival style of the 18th and 19th centuries with a futuristic injection of the 1970s and '80s. Fine beaches are caught between the curving hillsides. It's a young resort and has definite youth appeal, with plenty of sports and a lively summer program of entertainment. The Cultural and Information Center near the entrance to the resort is a modern establishment offering concerts, lectures, exhibitions, disco nights, children's events. It also arranges meetings between visitors of different nationalities.

Famous Zlatni Pjasâci (Golden Sands) comes next, with three km. (two miles) of sands backed by wooded slopes—and a plethora of hotels of every shape and size. There are all the usual sports and entertainment facilities, and a Cultural Information Center similar to the one at Albena, but an "extra" here is provided by the natural warm water mineral springs which feed the public swimming pools, and contribute to some of the many forms of therapy available at the resort's well-equipped medical centers.

Inland, and only four km. (over two miles) from Golden Sands, Aladja Rock Monastery, one of Bulgaria's oldest, has been chipped out of the limestone cliffs that rise from steep and beautiful woods. Its origins are obscure, though coins and pottery finds from the 5th–6th centuries show that the area was in use in early Byzantine times, probably as poor dwellings or as a refuge from barbarian attack. The existing complex of monastic cells and church built into the cliff face on several levels and now made accessible by sturdy iron stairways, probably dates from the 13th–14th centuries. Some surviving traces of frescoes have been restored.

Only eight km. (five miles) from Golden Sands, Družba (meaning Friendship) is Bulgaria's oldest Black Sea resort, which began developing in the late 1940s. This is another place blessed with beneficial mineral springs and there is rather a nice story about their accidental discovery. In 1947 a search for oil was in hand on the principle that, since neighboring Romania was well endowed with the stuff, there seemed every good reason to anticipate sources here too. Instead of striking oil, they struck clear, natural warm mineral water. Not a great deal of attention was paid to it for some years until some Austrians, who had been making good use of it, spoke enthusiastically of the beneficial effects it was having on their rheumatism and announced that it was making their hair grow!

Družba is the smallest and cosiest of the modern resorts, its amenities dotted about a wooded park by a series of sandy coves. It can also claim to have the most luxurious hotel on the coast, the Grand Hotel Varna which opened in 1977 and was constructed by a Swedish company.

Apart from its elegance, the Varna has some very sophisticated balnealogical equipment and can offer all kinds of hydrotherapy under medical supervision. As a resort, Družba benefits from the proximity of Golden Sands and its amenities while retaining its own calm and intimate character.

Varna

Only a few miles south of Družba you come to Bulgaria's third-largest city and major port: Varna, whose modern appearance belies its great age. Recent finds in the area include copper and superbly worked gold objects—perhaps the oldest in the world—dating back to around 3600 B.C. or 1,000 years older than anything comparable elsewhere. Later, as far back as the 12th century B.C., a Thracian tribe of farmers and shepherds had their dwellings around the nearby lakes. Greek colonists from Asia Minor founded the city in the 6th-century B.C. and called it Odessos. Later it became a major trading center in this part of the Roman Empire. By 681 A.D., it was Varna—and Bulgarian.

Varna's medieval heyday came during the Second Bulgarian Kingdom in the 13th and 14th centuries and, if you give your imagination a polish, you might visualize the ships of those days setting off for Constantinople, Genoa, Venice and Ragusa (now Dubrovnik). In 1389, the city was captured by the Turks and for five centuries was a major Ottoman stronghold against periodical attack by Christian armies. In contrast, during the Crimean War, Turkey's allies—including Britain—had their headquarters here for a while.

Under the Turks trade flourished once more, and Varna's importance as a modern port was foreshadowed in 1866, when they opened the first railway of their still extensive empire linking Varna with Ruse on the Danube. It only needs a quick glance at the map of Europe to see the importance of this link between the Black Sea and central and western Europe. Today its airport is a major gateway to the coast for countless holidaymakers. It is also a traffic hub for road connections inland and along the coast, and is linked by hydrofoil or boat services to most coastal towns and resorts.

Present-day Varna has mainly been built since the turn of the century and most of its interesting historical items are contained in museums. The latest is the splendid new Museum of Art and History, housed in a late 19th-century building at 41 Dimitar Blagoev Blvd. This is one of the great if lesser known museums of Europe and simply must not be missed by anyone with a curiosity about our ancient ancestors or an appreciation for the magnificent treasures they created. Texts in English are as yet sadly lacking, but guides are available.

Most spectacular of the exhibits in terms of antiquity are the finds from the Varna necropolis (4th millennium B.C.), originally discovered by chance in 1972 by one of the excavators digging a canal, and likely to be under investigation by archeologists for many more years to come. The finds, including gold and copper objects which are arguably the oldest of their kind in the world, come from extensive graves in many layers, a few of which have been carefully recreated to show the skeletal remains, just as they were discovered, with their gold or shell adornments, weapons and other artefacts. Nearby cases display other finds such as gold death masks, copper instruments, and some of the many gold plates representing animal figures indicating the importance of livestock breeding at the time. Other sections of the museum display superb treasures from Thracian, Greek and Roman times (6th century B.C. to 6th century A.D.), including the following (an entirely subjective selection from this treasurehouse): an exquisite gold statuette of the winged goddess of victory Nike, its amazing detail revealed by a well-placed magnifying glass; a series of three magnificent caskets—respectively of gold encrusted with precious stones, silver, and marble (5th century A.D.); a ceramic baptismal font of astonishing complexity (5th century A.D.); highly recognizable surgical and dental instruments in bronze (3rd century A.D.); a 7th century canoe dredged from Varna lake. Another section of the museum is devoted to a fine collection of icons.

Among Varna's other major sights are the Roman Thermae, the very substantial remains of public baths dating from the 2nd–3rd centuries A.D. from the Roman city of Odessos. The different sections—antechambers, dressing rooms, rest rooms, and various cold, warm and hot baths with their corresponding heating systems—can be clearly distinguished among the tumbled stonework with the help of an excellent small guidebook in English available on the spot. Not far from these Thermae, Druzki Street, one of the older little streets of Varna, has been restored and is lined with restaurants, taverns and coffee houses.

Of the modern city, the most pleasant area is around the verdant Marine Gardens from which you get fine views over the whole Bay of Varna. The gardens also contain a rather good aquarium devoted to the flora and fauna of the Black Sea and, not far away, the Naval Museum, which will appeal if you'd like to know more about the early days of navigation on both the Danube and the Black Sea. Finally, Varna is the main center for cultural and congressional activities along the coast, and there is good music and opera, especially during the annual 'Varna Summer' international music festival. Every two years an international ballet competition is also held here.

West of the city lies Varna Lake, linked by a canal to the sea, and in the same direction, 16 km. (ten miles) along the road to Sofia is a fascinating curiosity aptly named Pobiti Kamuni (the Stone Forest). The first to ponder about this strange place was a British Officer by name of Captain

Spratt, stationed in the area during the Crimean War, and well he might have wondered at these scattered groups of round stone trunks up to five meters (17 ft.) high, and up to three meters (10 ft.) thick. They are thought to be a kind of maritime stalagmite formed on the ancient sea bed when this was the bottom of the Lutsian Sea.

South of Varna

The stretch of coast immediately south of Varna has not yet been developed except for campsites and small tourist complexes mainly catering for domestic tourism. There are splendid views of the city from the bridge that carries the main road southwards out of Varna. The road curves inland initially, winding through the wooded hills that form one of the three terminal arms of the Balkan range, and crossing the Kamčija river. A minor road leads to the mouth of this, and the fine adjoining beaches, which are now in the early stages of a major development program. The banks of this estuary, with its several arms, are almost tropical in their lushness, rich in flora and bird life. Ancient trees, some of them submerged in the water, weave dense curtains of foliage, reeds crowd the banks and water lilies drift on the surface. Boat trips are sometimes arranged and give the best opportunity to appreciate fully the jungle-like profusion of the area.

The main road returns towards the sea just before Obzor, a small resort, popular among the Bulgarians, founded by the Greeks and still displaying the fragments of a Roman Temple of Jupiter. There are ruins of a Roman and a medieval Bulgarian fortress in the vicinity. Then the road crosses the bulge of Cape Emine before descending on to one of the most famous of all Bulgaria's resorts.

Slânčev Brjag (Sunny Beach) is the resort par excellence for families. It has wide, safe beaches, amenities with every kind of youngster appeal and, not forgetting the parents, offers various baby-sitting and child-minding services. The resort is spread out over a wide area, so those who are addicted to popping in and out of the sea at frequent intervals should make sure of a hotel with a beach-side location. There are plenty enough of these, as well as beach-side restaurants. Despite its size and popularity, the layout of Sunny Beach leaves no impression of crowding; hotels are well spaced out and there are plenty of gardens and green spaces. If your taste runs to the old and quaint, this is not a resort for you—nor indeed are any of the others. You would do better to find rooms in one of the small fishing towns.

An Ancient Trading Center

Sunny Beach does, however, have the advantage of being very close to Nesebâr and it would be hard to find anything older and more interesting than this. Indeed, in terms of interest it is *the* sight of the Bulgarian coast. Clustered on a rocky peninsula just south of Sunny Beach and reached by a narrow causeway, this picture postcard of a place is peppered with ancient churches, of which the oldest is from the 5th century and the "newest" from the 17th century. Greek colonists founded it as a trading center 25 centuries ago. They called it Mesembria and thus it was known throughout successive empires—notably by the Romans under whom it became a backwater on the fringes of the empire, and the Byzantines who built the first of its churches and turned it into a fortified outpost of their Black Sea possessions. It was finally incorporated into Bulgarian territory by the redoubtable Khan Krum in 812. Happily, after falling to the Turks in 1453, Nesebâr was granted a number of privileges, and allowed to keep its churches.

What the coastal resorts lack in antiquity, old Nesebâr more than makes up for. You won't find any blocks of concrete and glass here, but houses mainly in the National Revival style huddled along the narrow cobbled streets and punctuated by the ancient churches in various stages of preservation. These can be divided into four groups. The earliest from the 5th and 6th centuries are the Old Metropolitan Church and the larger so-called Basilica on the Seashore. A second group dates from the 10th or 11th centuries and includes the rather well-preserved St. John the Baptist and St. Stephen's Church, also known as the New Metropolitan Church, in which there are some particularly good frescoes. The largest group dates from the 13th and 14th centuries and is characterized by cream-colored stone interspersed with layers and decoration in slim red brick—a typical artistic style of that period of Bulgarian–Byzantine architecture which reached its peak here in Nesebâr. The five best churches in this group are those of the Pantokrator, St. John Aliturgetos (the best of all), Archangels Michael and Gabriel, and St. Paraskeva. The final group of less interest is from Ottoman times, the 16th and 17th centuries.

Inevitably, this is a popular sightseeing destination. The highrise buildings of modern tourism prod the sky just across the water and excursion buses come in droves from all along the coast at the height of the season. To see it at its best then, you want to be there early in the morning or, better still, rent a room in the old town.

Bulgaria's Salt Center

The next town, Pomorie, similarly clusters on a point and it, too, was founded very early as a Greek colony, Anhialo, which became a serious threat to neighboring Mesembria. Under the Romans it fared rather better and prospered as the administrative center of the area. In contrast to present-day Nesebâr, it has little visual appeal, but it does have some extremely effective mud which is extracted from the adjoining lake for the relief of arthritis and sciatica. The local balneosanatorium is one of the largest in Bulgaria. Pomorie is also the center of a major wine-growing area (try the white *dimjat*) but, most important of all, it's the center for the nation's salt production. The local salt pans may be of interest to bird watchers, as indeed will be other salt-water stretches along this coast.

On the main road near Pomorie and 19 km. (11 miles) before Burgas, look out for a sign on the right indicating another notable ancient monument. Beneath a grassy mound, a Thracian–Roman tomb dates from the 3rd–4th centuries A.D.: a remarkable mushroom-shaped construction supported by a hollow central column.

Burgas comes next—Bulgaria's second main port on the Black Sea and the largest town on this southern section. The main specialties of this busy place are oil refineries and fast-growing industries of many kinds, and its chief assets for the visitor are the very pleasant Maritime Park and extensive beach just below it.

Little-Known Treasures

Bulgaria's southernmost section of Black Sea coast is, as yet, little developed though there are plenty of camping sites and private lodgings available. Well on the way to being discovered is the fishing port of Sozopol, on a small cape about 32 km. (20 miles) south of Burgas. Indeed, it is very picturesque with its old houses in the National Revival style and no modern architecture allowed to intrude. It's a popular haunt for Bulgarian and, increasingly, foreign writers and artists; private and self-catering accommodations are available for visitors. This was the ancient Apollonia, oldest of all the Greek colonies founded in 610 B.C. and a great rival to Mesembria (Nesebâr). A huge statue of Apollo was erected in honor of the sun god in 460 B.C. Unlike Mesembria, Apollonia put up a fight against Rome and got sacked for its pains in A.D. 72. Apollo's splendid statue was part of the booty—to see it, you must go to the Capitol in Rome.

Further south still, you approach the hills of Bulgaria's southern boundary range, the Stranja Mountains, that slip across the border into Turkey. The coast has remained almost unexploited, despite its beautiful sandy bays, but things are changing—the first sign is the new and extensive holiday development of Djuni, just ten km. (six miles) south of Sozopol. The Ropotamo river flows down to the sea only a few miles further and has some of the same jungle-like qualities of the Kamčija already mentioned, though on a smaller and less impressive scale. Boat trips are, however, more regularly available through its leafy waters, beginning near the bridge which carries the main road.

Beyond, the coast continues in a series of rocky cliffs and sandy coves as yet untouched by mass tourism, though there are campsites and some holiday homes and the big Georgi Dimitrov international youth center of Primorsko. Near the small fishing and commercial town of Mičurin, the main road turns inland to cross the hills into Turkey. A minor road continues along the coast to service a handful of communities such as Ahtopol, Bulgaria's picturesque southernmost town, and finally the village of Rezovo, across the little Rezovo river.

PRACTICAL INFORMATION FOR
THE BLACK SEA COAST

TOURIST INFORMATION. There is a Balkantourist office in most towns and resorts. Main ones include **Burgas:** 2 Purvi Mai St. and **Varna:** 3 Musala St. (main office), 3 Lenin Blvd. (private accommodations).

WHEN TO COME. In summer for the liveliest entertainments program and cultural events; spring and autumn for less crowds. Many hotels close in winter, but prices are very reasonable in those that don't. It can be very hot in high summer; winters are relatively mild and dry.

GETTING AROUND. Frequent bus services operate all along the coast and are very inexpensive. It's advisable to get your tickets in advance. In addition there is a regular service by hydrofoil linking Varna–Nesebâr–Burgas–Sozopol, and a regular boat service between Varna–Družba–Golden Sands–Albena–Balčik. Numerous excursions are arranged from all resorts. Note the boat trips organized on the Ropotamo and, less regularly, Kamčija rivers. The hire of bicycles and self-drive cars is readily available. Indeed, the use of cycles is popular for moving about within rather widespread resorts such as Sunny Beach and Golden Sands, both of which also operate a system of regular public transport on small open road-"trains."

HOTELS AND RESTAURANTS. An ambitious hotel construction program has equipped the main resorts with comfortable modern facilities. As specified in the following lists, some hotels stay open year-round, offering substantial reductions in winter. Otherwise they are usually open from May to Oct. Private accommodations and self-catering villas and apartments are also available through Balkantourist.

The coastal resorts cater admirably for families, with excellent discounts for children. Since there is a large number of hotels in each resort, the following is only a selection. Older hotels are progressively being renovated, and there is an increasing emphasis on self-catering complexes.

Albena. Youngest and northernmost resort. *Dobrudja* (E), 270 rooms, indoor and open-air pools, modern medical center. The resort's tallest, newest and best-equipped hotel, with a touch of imagination in the high-rise design; a short walk from beach. Open year-round.

Dobrotica (M), 140 rooms. Near beach. *Dorostor* (M), 130 rooms. Near beach. *Gergana* (M), 260 rooms. On beach at south end of resort. *Karvuna* (M), 114 rooms. Short walk from beach. *Orlov* (M), 110 rooms. Near beach. *Slavjanka* (M), 140 rooms. Best value in this price range. Short walk from beach.

Bratislava (I), 190 rooms, tennis, disco. Short walk from beach. *Praga* (I), 220 rooms, no restaurant. Short walk from beach.

Restaurants. *Arabella* (E) on board a frigate at north end of beach, with dancing into early hours. *Gorski Car* (E), nightclub with floor show. In woods near resort center.

Orehite (Walnut Trees) (M), open-air, with folk show, fire dancing. *Slavianski Kt* (M), folk restaurant with specialty dishes including spiced and peppered stew; folk show. Near Gorski Car. *Starobulgarski Stan* (M), in traditional style, game specialties, folk show. Near Gorski Car.

Balčik. *Beljat Brjag* motoring complex by beach, 6 km. (3½ miles) north of town. Includes two motels, restaurants, open-air disco.

Burgas. *Bulgaria* (E), Interhotel, 196 rooms, nightclub, restaurants include pleasant winter garden. High-rise hotel in city center. Open year round. *Primorec* (I), 93 rooms, nightclub. By Maritime Park. Open year-round.

Restaurant. *Starata Gemia* (Old Boat). Fish specialties. By central beach.

Djuni. Brand new Austrian-built holiday complex on undeveloped coast ten km. (six miles) south of Sozopol on or above north end of long sandy bay backed by dunes. Very nicely designed and divided into three sections, it features a hotel and varied selection of self-catering villas and apartments, with restaurants, bars, shops and wide range of sports and entertainment facilities. Nearby is a protected nature reserve.

Družba. Oldest and cosiest of the resorts, set in woods and round sandy coves. *Grand Hotel Varna* (L), Interhotel, 325 rooms, nightclub, indoor and open-air pools, sports hall, tennis, bowling alley, treatment facilities. Swedish-built and the best on the coast. Near beach. Open year-round.

Čaika (M), 96 rooms, no restaurant. At north end of resort, standing back above beach. *Rubin* (I), 130 rooms, no restaurant. Near beach at south end of resort. Several other hotels are being restored. Oldest and among the cheapest is *Roza* (I), 120 rooms, no restaurant, no rooms with shower. Basic, but quiet, attractive position above beach.

Restaurants. *Bulgarska Svatba* (M), folk style with show on outskirts of resort. *Černomorec* (M), recently reconstructed, next to hotel Roza. Disco and nightclub. *Manastirska Izba* (I), in resort center, with terrace.

Slânčev Brjag (Sunny Beach). Particularly well-equipped for children, the resort consists of a number of tourist complexes, each with several hotels, restaurants, shops and other amenities. *Burgas* (M), 250 rooms, indoor and open-air pools, sports hall. By beach at southern end of resort. Open year-round. *Glarus* (M), 220 rooms. By beach at north end of resort. *Globus* (M), 100 rooms, indoor pool, sports hall. Probably the best. By beach, near resort center. Open year-round. *Kuban* (M), 216 rooms. In resort center, short stroll from beach. Open year-round.

Čaika (I), 36 rooms, near beach and center. *Nesebâr* (I), 160 rooms. Near the Burgas. *Sirena* (I), 60 rooms. *Venera* (I), 50 rooms. Near center, short stroll from beach.

The fine Finnish-built self-catering complex of *Elenite* lies 10 km. (six miles) to the north, with restaurants, shops, and wide range of sports and entertainment facilities. Closer to the resort is the cottage-colony of *Zora* with 54 small villas.

Restaurants include *Bčvata* and *Viatrna Melnica* (above the resort); *Hanska Šatra* (about five km./three miles up in the hills) with a folk and variety program; *Picnic* (about 13 km./eight miles north) with fire dancing and barbecue: all (M).

Čučura is (I). Restaurants with taverns are *Neptune, Strandja* and *Lazur* (on the beach), all (I). Several other beach-side restaurants include *Ribarska Hiza* (fish), and *Rusalka* and *Zlatna Jabalka,* both with disco.

Varna. Historic Black Sea port. *Černo More* (E), Interhotel, 230 rooms, nightclub. Near center and Marine Gardens. Open year-round. *Odessa* (I), 90 rooms. Overlooks Marine Gardens. Open year-round.

Restaurants. In recently restored old Druzki Street, *Starata Kušta* (the Old House) and *Galerata* are two of several restaurants and bars in this new catering complex featuring national specialties in an old-time Varna atmosphere.

Zlatni Pjasâci (Golden Sands). Resort and year-round spa with wide-ranging facilities in undulating woods. *Ambassador* (E), 130 rooms, indoor and open-air pools, medical center. Recently renovated. Set in woods not far from beach. Open year-round. *Astoria* (E), 70 rooms, nightclub. Near beach. *International* (E), 210 rooms, indoor pool, medical center. Near beach in resort center. Open year-round.

Metropol (M), 100 rooms, no restaurant but 10th-floor bar with good views. Near beach. *Morsko Oko* (M), 90 rooms. Near beach towards north end of resort. *Rodina* (M), 125 rooms, no restaurant. Near beach in resort center. *Šipka* (M), 130 rooms, nightclub. In woods towards south end of resort, about one km. (½-mile) from beach.

Diana (I), 140 rooms, no restaurant. Wooded setting some distance from beach. *Gdansk, Pliska* and *Veliko Târnovo* (all I), three pyramid-style hotels, next to each other in the woods near Šipka Hotel, no restaurants, but each with pastry shop and disco.

Restaurants. *Košarata* (Sheepfold) (M), on outskirts of resort; various mutton specialties including one cooked in earthenware jug. Open year-round, with folk show. *Meča Poljana* (M), in wooded hills above resort, is one of a group of four open-air restaurants and has the best floor show. *Trifon Zarezan* (M), good folk restaurant on road to Družba. *Vodenicata* (Water Mill) (M), arranged round mill and mill stream, open-air and indoor, noted for freshly baked cheese pastries and charcoal-grilled poultry. Open year-round.

Kukeri, in a woodland about five km. (three miles) from resort center, is a bar and disco.

SPORTS FACILITIES. In addition to sea bathing, a number of hotels have swimming pools as indicated. Tennis, mini-golf, horse riding, cycling, waterskiing, windsurfing, sailing and water parachuting can be enjoyed at all the resorts. Instruction in sailing, waterskiing and windsurfing is available at Albena, Golden Sands and Sunny Beach; in underwater sports at Golden Sands; and in tennis at Družba and Golden Sands. Several campsites also have water sports facilities, and some windsurfing schools.

TOURIST VOCABULARY

Unlike the tourist vocabularies for the other countries in this book, we have not included a column giving the phrases in original Bulgarian. This is because Bulgarian *(bulgarski)* is written in *Cyrillic,* an alphabet almost identical to that used in Russia, and we felt that it was better to give phrases intended for immediate use in their most assimilable form.

However, since you will see Cyrillic written in Bulgaria, here is the alphabet with the approximate equivalent in the Roman alphabet for each letter, with its pronunciation. On most maps and town plans you will find the Latin form uses the system of accents shown below, but much of the tourist literature, as well as hotels, restaurants, etc., employs phonetic spelling (as indicated in brackets after each letter).

А а	A (a)	as in father			Р р	R (r)	as in rod
Б б	B (b)	„ „	brother		С с	S (s)	„ „	sod
В в	V (v)	„ „	vodka		Т т	T (t)	„ „	too
Г г	G (g)	„ „	go		У у	U (u)	„ „	room
Д д	D (d)	„ „	do		Ф ф	F (f)	„ „	fa !
Е е	E (e)	„ „	let		Х х	H (gh)	„ „	hot
Ж ж	Ž (zh)	„ „	pleasure		Ц ц	C (ts)	„ „	lots
З з	Z (z)	„ „	zero		Ч ч	Č (tch)	„ „	church
И и	I (i)	„ „	if		Ш ш	Š (sh)	„ „	shoe
Й й	J (y)	„ „	year		Щ щ	Št (sht)	„ „	ashtray
К к	K (k)	„ „	keg		Ъ ъ	Â (û)	„ „	turnip
Л л	L (l)	„ „	lad		Ю ю	Yu(yu)	„ „	you
М м	M(m)	„ „	map		Я я	Ya (ya)	„ „	yard
Н н	N(n)	„ „	no		ь	j (y) with another		
О о	O(o)	„ „	orb		letter indicates soft sound eg.		
П п	P (p)	„ „	pop		Н ь	Nj (ny) as in news		

Two points about the pronunciations below—the stressed syllables have been set in italic type; the 'a' is the same as the vowel in 'but'.

USEFUL EXPRESSIONS

Hello, how do you do	*do*bar den
Good morning	dobr*o* outro
Good evening	*do*bar *ve*cher
Goodnight	*le*ka nosht
Goodbye	dovizh*da*ne
Please	*mo*lya
Thank you	blagodary*a*
Thank you very much	*mno*go
Yes	da
No	ne
You're welcome	ny*a*ma zasht*o*
Excuse me	iz*vi*nete
Come in!	*vle*ste
I'm sorry	sazhaly*a*vam
My name is . . .	*ka*zvam se . . .
Do you speak English?	gov*o*rite li angl*i*yski?

I don't speak Bulgarian	ne govorya bulgarski
I don't understand	ne razbiram
Please speak slowly	molya, govorete bavno
Please write it down	molya vi se, napishete go
Where is . . . ?	kade e . . . ?
What is this place called?	kak se kazva tova myasto?
Please show me	molya vi se, pokazhete mi
I would like . . .	bikh zhelal (a woman says bikh zhelala)
How much does it cost?	kolko struva?

ARRIVAL

Passport check	pasporten kontrol
Your passport, please	molya, vashiya pasport
I am with the group	az sam s grupata
Customs	mitnitsa
Anything to declare?	neshto za deklarirane?
Nothing to declare	nishto za deklarirane
Baggage claim	bagazhna sluzhba
This suitcase is mine	tozi kufar e moy
A porter	nosach
Transportation	
to the bus	na aftobusa
to a taxi	taksito
to the Hotel . . . , please	molya, do hotel . . .

MONEY

Money	pari
The currency exchange office	bankata
Do you have change for this?	mozhete li da razvalite tova?
May I pay	mozhe li da se plashta
with a traveler's check?	s chek?
with a voucher?	s-talon?
with this credit card?	s tazi kreditna karta?
I would like to change some traveler's checks	bih zhelal (zhelala) da smenya nyakolko cheka

THE HOTEL

A hotel	hotel
I have a reservation	imam rezervirana staya
A room with a bath	staya banya
a shower	dush
a toilet	toalet
hot running water	topla voda
What floor is it on?	na koy etazhe?
ground floor	parter
second floor	parvi etazh
The elevator	asansyora
Have the baggage sent up, please	molya vi se, ispratete mi gore bagazha
The key to number . . . , please	klyucha na staya nomer . . .
Please call me at seven o'clock	sabudete me sedem chasa
Have the baggage brought down	donesete mi dolu bagazha
The check	smetkata
A tip	bakshish

THE RESTAURANT

A restaurant	restorant
Waiter!	kelner
Waitress!	gospozhitse
The menu	kartata, menyuto
I would like to order this	bih zhelal (zhelala) da poracham tova
Some more . . . , please	oshte malko
That's enough	stiga
The check, please	smetkata
Breakfast	zakuska
Lunch	obed
Dinner	vecherya
Bread	hlyab
Butter	maslo
Jam	marmalad
Salt	sol
Pepper	piper
Mustard	gorchitsa
Sauce, gravy	sos
Vinegar	otset
Oil	olio
Bottle	butilka
Wine	vino
Red, white wine	cherveno, byalo vino
Beer	bira
Water	voda
Mineral water	mineralna voda
Milk	mlyako
Coffee, with milk	kafe s mlyako
Turkish	tursko kafe
Tea (with lemon)	chay (s limon)
Chocolate	shokolat
Sugar	zahar
Spirits	rakiya, slivova (plum brandy)

MAIL

A letter	pismo
A postcard	poshtenska kartichka
An envelope	plik
A mailbox	poshtenska kutiya
The post office	poshtata
A stamp	marka
By airmail	vazdushna poshta
How much does it cost	kolko struva
to send a letter	da se prati
a letter (a postcard) airmail to United States (Great Britain, Canada)?	pismo (poshtenska kartichka) vazdushna poshta za saedinenite shtati (velikobritaniya, kanada)?
to send a telegram, cable?	da se prati telegrama?

LOCATIONS

. . . Street	ulitsa

. . . Avenue	bulevard
. . . Square	ploshtat
The airport	letishteto
A bank	banka
The beach	plazha
The bridge	mosta
The castle	zamaka
The cathedral	katedralata
The church	cherkvata
The coffee house, cafe	kafeneto
The garden	gradinata
The hospital	bolnitsata
The movies, cinema	kinoto
a movie	film
The museum	muzeya
A nightclub	bar
The palace	dvoretsa
The park	parka
The station	garata
The theater	teatara
a play	piesa
The travel bureau	turistichesko buiro
The university	universiteta

TRAVEL

Arrival	pristigane
Departure	zaminavane

The airplane	samolet
I want to reconfirm a reservation on flight number . . . for . . .	iskam da potvardya rezerviranoto myasto za . . .
Where is the check-in?	kade e kontrola?
I am checking in for . . .	otivam za . . .
Fasten your seat belt	zakopchaite kolana

The railroad	zhepe liniya
The train	vlaka
From what track does the train to . . . leave?	ot koi peron zaminava vlakat za . . . ?
Which way is the dining car?	na koya posoka e vagon-restorantat?

streetcar	aftobus, tramvai
this bus go to . . . ?	otiva li tozi aftobus do . . . ?
trolley bus	troleibus
I want to get off at . . . Street	iskam da sleza na . . . ulitsa
at the next stop	na sledvashtata spirka

Taxi	taksi
I (we) would like to go to . . . , please	molya, iskam da otida (iskame da otidem) na . . .
Stop at . . .	sprete na . . .
Stop here	sprete tuk

NUMBERS

1	edin		3	tri
2	dva		4	chetiri

5	pet	30	triiset
6	shest	40	chet*i*riset
7	s*e*dem	50	pedes*e*t
8	*o*sem	60	sh*e*yset
9	d*e*vet	70	sedemdes*e*t
10	d*e*set	80	osemdes*e*t
11	edinayset	90	devetdes*e*t
12	dvan*a*yset	100	sto
13	trin*a*yset	200	dv*e*sta
14	chetirin*a*yset	300	tr*i*sta
15	petn*a*yset	400	chetiristotin
16	shesn*a*yset	500	petstotin
17	sedemn*a*yset	600	sh*e*stostotin
18	osemn*a*yset	700	s*e*demstotin
19	devetn*a*yset	800	*o*semstotin
20	dv*a*yset	900	d*e*vetstotin
25	dv*a*yset i pet	1,000	hily*a*da

DAYS OF THE WEEK

Sunday	ned*e*lya
Monday	poned*e*lnik
Tuesday	ft*o*rnik
Wednesday	sry*a*da
Thursday	chetvartak
Friday	p*e*tak
Saturday	sabota

CZECHOSLOVAKIA

CZECHOSLOVAKIA—FACTS AT YOUR FINGERTIPS

HOW TO GO. Nearly all foreign travel to Czechoslovakia is handled by Čedok, the Czechoslovak Travel Bureau, or the many travel agents accredited by them. Unlike the State Travel Offices of other European countries, you may actually book tours to Czechoslovakia via Čedok or their agents, a list of which is available from Čedok offices; they include a lot of the major agents in both the U.K. and the U.S.

Within Czechoslovakia, Čedok owns and operates many hotels, organizes tours of all kinds, can arrange tickets for all types of transport, make reservations for cultural events, provide guides; in short, arrange more or less anything from a stay in a spa to a hunting trip.

As well as the many offices they have within Czechoslovakia Čedok has a number of offices overseas. Their addresses include:

In the U.S., 10 East 40th St., New York, NY 10016 (tel. 212–689–9720).

In the U.K., 17–18 Old Bond St., London W1X 4RB (tel. 01–629–6058).

In addition to Čedok, a number of other travel organizations operate in particular spheres, but they are mainly geared to group travel and do not normally cater for individuals, except insofar as accommodations may be available in their establishments for independent travelers who happen to chance upon them when they are not fully booked. The following are some principal organizations:

Balnea caters exclusively for those following spa treatments and their companions, and runs a considerable number of sanatoria, some of them very modern and with highly sophisticated equipment. Many are in very beautiful settings. Balnea is concerned with those in Bohemia and Moravia, and its counterpart, *Slovakoterma,* is concerned with those in Slovakia. Reservations at these sanatoria can be made through Čedok offices abroad.

CKM (Youth Travel Bureau) deals essentially with youth groups, runs its own hotels, youth centers, camps, and rents other accommodations for such groups. A few of their larger and more modern hotels will accept any independent traveler if they have room, but in other cases a small percentage of the accommodations are reserved only for holders of International Youth Hostels Federation or student cards.

Sport-Turist, as its name suggests, concentrates on all kinds of sporting holidays, again for groups only.

Rekrea (Czech Union of Consumer Cooperatives) and *Tatratour,* its counterpart in Slovakia, collaborate with some overseas tour operators or will accept independent travelers if they have accommodations to spare; but their main focus is holiday or study tours for groups.

TOURS. Čedok offers over a dozen inexpensive half-day sightseeing tours exploring for instance "Prague by Night," "Pearls of Czech Gothic Art," and "Beauty Spots of Southern Bohemia," among others. Seven- and 14-day tours of the country range from $410 to $943, covering transport from Prague, accommodations, most meals, and sightseeing.

Other Čedok tours marketed overseas include wine tours, spa holidays, and a widening range of motoring tours (with your own or rented car), based on one or more centers and offering a considerable degree of flexibility. The latter provide excellent opportunities to see a lot of the country with the secure knowledge that all your accommodations have been prebooked.

For groups there is a varied selection of special interest tours. In the U.S., other companies include: *Health and Pleasure Tours Inc.,* offering a week-long stay in Prague for $1,232, including airfare (though little in the way of guided touring is involved) and *ETS Tours Inc.,* offering a similar package. Their addresses are:

ETS Tours Inc., 5 Penn Plaza, New York, NY 10001 (tel. 800–346–6314); in NY (tel. 212–563–0780).

Health and Pleasure Tours, Inc., 165 W. 46th St., New York, NY 10036 (tel. 212–586–1775).

From the U.K., sample costs for Čedok tours are: a seven-night stay in Prague with half-board in a 3-star hotel, return flight, in high season is from £359. A 15-day Grand Tour, with return flight, mostly half-board in 3- and 4-star hotels, transport and entrance fees, is £399. A pleasantly flexible three-night arrangement costing £179–£199 ex-London (according to season and departure date), covers return flight to Prague, a voucher to a local value of £30 towards the cost of accommodations and meals, and a half-day's sightseeing. This arrangement can be extended at a cost of £11 per day, providing that it is booked prior to departure. Private accommodations in Prague and the High Tatras are now also available through Čedok.

VISAS. Nationals of almost all countries, except those of the eastern bloc, require visas. These are obtainable from Czechoslovak consulates (allow several weeks). In the U.K., Čedok will process your visa for £14 if you've booked an inclusive Čedok tour; otherwise the charge at press time is £20 (plus £3 service charge if obtained through Čedok). In the U.S. the cost is $16 and you should apply to the Czechoslovak Embassy, 3900 Linnean Avenue NW, Washington, DC 20008. In Canada, apply to the Czechoslovak Embassy, 50 Rideau Terrace, Ottowa, Ontario K1M 2A1, or the Consulate General of Czechoslovakia, 1305 Pine Ave., West Montreal, Quebec, H3G 1B2. Apart from a valid passport and the completed application form, you will need two passport-size photos. Visas—good for five months from the date of issue—are not issued at points of entry (though the situation is under review); they can be extended once you are in Czechoslovakia. Some time in 1989, visas will be obtainable at certain border crossings with West Germany and Austria.

If you plan to stay with relatives or friends in Czechoslovakia,you must apply for your visa from a Czechoslovak embassy and must register with the police within 48 hours of writing.

MONEY. There is an obligatory minimum daily exchange requirement (currently 30 Deutschmarks per day or its equivalent in other foreign currencies) for the number of days for which your visa is valid. This does not, however, apply if the requirement is already covered by prepaid arrangements.

The unit of currency in Czechoslovakia is the crown or Koruna (Kčs.) divided into 100 hellers or halér. There are coins of 10, 20 and 50 hellers, and 1, 2 and 5 Kčs.; and notes of 10, 20, 50, 100, 500 and 1,000 Kčs.

The tourist rate of exchange at the time of writing (mid-1988) was about 8.50 Kčs. to the U.S. dollar and about 15 Kčs. to the pound sterling. In addition to these rates, if you take most Čedok package arrangements you will be entitled to a 36% bonus by exchanging your traveler's checks or special currency voucher (which you buy from Čedok before departure) at Čedok exchange offices, any Čedok hotel, or at a Balnea hotel or sanatorium; currency acquired at this special rate may not be reconverted to foreign currency.

You may import any amount of foreign currency into Czechoslovakia and export the balance provided the original amount was registered on arrival. The import and export of Czechoslovakian currency is not allowed. It is therefore important that all exchanges should be noted on your visa form as only surplus Korunas from such exchanges can be refunded to you in hard currency at your departure. Even then there can be communication problems. Traveler's checks and major credit cards may be used to exchange currency and are accepted in the better hotels.

COSTS. Despite recent increases, costs in Czechoslovakia are low by West European standards. This is especially true of meals, local transport and entertainment, so however you choose to visit the country, it should be possible to have a vacation for significantly less than in the West. The most convenient way is to prebook arrangements for a package or independent holiday through Čedok, the Czechoslovak Travel Bureau, or one of their accredited agencies. In both cases you avoid the necessity of having to comply with the minimum daily exchange regulations, as well as circumvent the problems caused by the acute shortage of accommodations. Another advantage of a Čedok package arrangement (other than the Economy Tour or Car Hire), is that you will be entitled to a currency bonus (see *Money*). That said, if you are prepared to forego the currency bonus and take a chance on finding accommodations, there are many hotels and restaurants that do not feature on Čedok's lists, offering good, and in some cases better, value for money. Further guidance is given in the following pages.

All prices quoted are those of mid-1988.

Sample Costs. Cinema seat from 10 Kčs. (special showings up to 30 Kčs.); good theater seat 40–100 Kčs.; bottle of good Moravian wine 20–40 Kčs. (in a store), 60–80 Kčs. (in a good restaurant); glass Scotch whisky 35–50 Kčs.; glass slivovice 12.50 Kčs.; 20 cigarettes (best local) 14 Kčs., imported 30 Kčs. (more in hotel kiosks and bars); ice cream cone 1.40–2.60 Kčs.

MEDICAL INSURANCE. This is strongly advised for all travelers to Czechoslovakia. Visitors from the U.K. benefit from a reciprocal agreement which insures a degree of free medical treatment, but they too are advised to take out medical insurance.

CLIMATE. Czechoslovakia enjoys the extremes of a Continental climate: warm summers and cold winters, so conditions are ideal for outdoor activities appropriate to these seasons. May is a delightful month for fruit trees in blossom along almost every roadside, and blazing yellow rape fields. This is also the time of the famous Prague Spring Music Festival. The fall offers the rewards of beautiful coloring in the many extensive woods. Since much of Czechoslovakia's fascination is historical, architectural and cultural, it can be enjoyed at any time. Though some monuments, especially castles, are closed in winter, this is a particularly lively time culturally in the cities.

Average afternoon temperatures in degrees Fahrenheit and centigrade:

Prague	Jan.	Feb.	Mar.	Apr.	May	June	July	Aug.	Sept.	Oct.	Nov.	Dec.
F°	34	38	45	55	65	72	74	73	65	54	41	34
C°	1	3	7	13	18	22	23	23	18	12	5	1

SPECIAL EVENTS. One of the world's great gymnastic events, Spartakiada, takes places every 5 years; the next is in 1990. Principal annual events are as follows. **April,** International Trade Fair of Consumer Goods, Brno; **April/May,** Flora Olomouc, flower show, Olomouc; **May,** Prague Spring Music Festival; Dvořák Music Festival, Příbram; Summer Theater in Castle grounds, Karlštejn and Konopiště (through August); **June,** Bratislava International Song Festival; Kmochův Kolín Festival of Brass Music, Kolín; Východná Folk Art Festival; Strážnice Folk Art Festival; **June–August,** Bratislava Culture Summer; **July,** International Puppet Festival, Chrudim; Karlovy Vary International Film Festival (biennial); **August,** Chopin Festival, Mariánské Lázně; International Festival of Dance, Telč; Brno Grand Prix Motor Rally; Chod Festival (folklore), Domažlice; Flora Olomouc, flower show, Olomouc; **September,** Dvořák Festival, Karlovy Vary; Znojmo Wine Festival; Brno International Music Festival, Brno (into October); Bratislava International Music Festival (into October); International Engineering Trade Fair, Brno; Hop Festival, Žatec; **October,** Pardubice Grand Steeplechase.

National Holidays. The principal national and religious holidays are Jan. 1; Easter Monday; May 1 (Labor Day); May 9 (Liberation Day); Dec. 25/26.

CUSTOMS. Valuable items should be declared to facilitate re-exportation when leaving the country. You may import duty-free into Czechoslovakia 250 cigarettes or the equivalent in tobacco; plus one liter of spirits and two liters of wine (for those over 18 only); plus ½ liter of perfume. See *Money* for currency regulations.

You are also permitted to import duty-free up to 1,000 Kčs. worth of gifts and souvenirs. Clothing may be left duty-free. Purchases up to 1,000 Kčs. may be freely exported. More valuable items, including articles from Tuzex (state-run stores that accept hard-currency only), may be exported duty-free, provided you have the bills. Note that certain items (including cut glass, porcelain and sports goods) bought with local currency are subject to 100% duty and should be accompanied by an export permit.

LANGUAGE. Czech and Slovak, both Slavic national tongues, are very similar. In Bohemia and Moravia, Czech is spoken by the Czechs and in Slovakia, Slovak. There are a lot of Hungarians in Slovakia and Poles in the northeast border regions who retain their national languages. Of western languages, German and, increasingly, English are the most readily understood and widely spoken. You might find a German phrasebook very useful.

HOTELS. The official classification of hotels is changing to the international star system, although it will be some time before it completely supersedes the earlier method (Deluxe, A*, B*, B, C, etc.). These ratings correspond closely to our gradings as follows: Deluxe or 5-star (L); A* or 4-star (E); B* or 3-star (M); and B or 2-star (I). There are also C hotels, usually with cold water only available, and a very few have been included as indicated, where accommodations are limited. For indications of hotel prices see the table below. Many hotels have rooms in more than one category; most have all or some rooms with private baths or showers.

Older hotels are gradually being renovated to good effect, and it is quite possible that some of those listed in these pages will be undergoing this process at the time of your visit and either be temporarily closed or have improved their amenities. The best of these have great style and character. It is better, however, not to expect the same standards of facilities and services as in equivalent categories in Western countries. That said, prices compare very favorably with those of Western hotels.

Hotels are operated by various organizations, of which the most important from the tourist's point of view is Čedok. These are known as Interhotels and described as such in our hotel lists. It cannot be emphasized too strongly that there is an acute shortage of accommodations in Czechoslovakia in the peak seasons and you will be very wise to prebook if you want to be sure of good accommodations. On the other hand, if you are prepared to take your chance and dispense with the advantage of the currency bonus in exchange for greater freedom of movement, you are almost certain to find a room of some kind, especially among the less publicized non-Čedok hotels, some of which offer excellent value. Čedok handle reservations for some non-Čedok hotels. Note that (except in Interhotels where hard currency only is accepted) you can pay for your accommodations in Kčs. providing you have evidence that these have been legitimately acquired (currency transactions will be shown on your visa form). This ruling is sometimes incorrectly interpreted by hotel receptionists who may ask you to pay in foreign currency.

Two people in a double room with bath or shower will pay approximately:

	Prague	Elsewhere
Deluxe (5-stars)	$150–200	$100–120
Expensive (4-stars)	$100–150	$80–100
Moderate (3-stars)	$66–100	$55–80
Inexpensive (2-stars)	$55–66	$40–55

Prices at the upper end of the scale apply to the high season. Additionally, there is an overlap in these price scales as hotels in main towns and some tourist centers can be more expensive than establishments in a higher category in other places. Our classifications therefore indicate standard as well as cost. These prices include half board, except for 5-star (L) establishments which are for accommodations and breakfast only. Note that the charge for having a bath if you do not book a room with private facilities can be astonishingly high—from 10–60 Kčs., depending on category and location.

Self-Catering

Self-catering costs are from $6–12.50 per person daily in cottages or bungalows. These are usually attached to motels or autocamps.

Private Accommodations

Private accommodations are now available through Čedok and Pragotur in Prague and Čedok in the High Tatras.

Youth Hostels

These do not exist in the western sense, but in summer CKM (Youth Travel Service) operate or rent accommodations in various premises throughout the country and a percentage of these are at the disposal of independent foreign students or holders of International Youth Hostels Federation cards as listed in the IYHF handbook. These include student colleges in Prague, Bratislava and Brno available as youth accommodations in summer; ask for *kolej* in Czech and *internat* in Slovak. It's best to check the latest situation with CKM.

Camping

Camping vouchers for selected sites run by the motoring organization Autotourist may be available through Čedok in the U.K. A free, detailed booklet of maps and sites throughout the country, which are run by a number of organizations, is obtainable from Čedok. The range is from $1.50–2.00 per person per day in own tent or caravan, according to site category, plus a small charge per car, tent or caravan in the better sites. These will have all the regular facilities.

RESTAURANTS. The selection of restaurants is very wide, and there are some particularly attractive wine cellars *(vinárna)* and suitably down-to-earth beer taverns *(pivnice)* in some of which you can get snacks or even full meals, and in all of which you will find the Czechoslovaks indulging in their favorite pastime of talking. The self-service snack bar is an increasingly popular amenity in main towns and there is a scattering of small coffee bars where you can also eat at reasonable prices. Eating out is popular and it is wise to make reservations whenever possible; also check opening times, for many places close for part or all of the weekend.

We have divided restaurants in our listings into three categories: Expensive (E), Moderate (M) and Inexpensive (I). Prices per person in Prague, excluding drinks, for Expensive restaurants are from 100 Kčs., for Moderate restaurants 50–100 Kčs. and for Inexpensive restaurants under 50 Kčs. Outside Prague, prices are 25–50% lower.

On group tours, *table d'hôte* meals are included in the price on a full- or half-board basis. In the case of Čedok's regular weekend and one-week breaks to Prague, and in all cases of independent hotel arrangements, meal coupons are provided on arrival at hotel reception. These can be used in all Čedok hotels and restaurants in the city or area, but the value of unused coupons cannot be refunded.

We suggest that you always check the total on your bill carefully to make sure that the figure is correct.

TIPPING. In popular restaurants, it is normal to round up the bill by a few Kčs. In better restaurants add at least 10%. In restaurants, theaters and other public places there is usually a 0.40–1 Kčs. cloakroom charge for leaving your coat and it is normal to give a little extra. For taxis add 5 Kčs. to the fare; for hairdressers 5–10 Kčs. Give airport porters 3–5 Kčs. additional to the fixed rate. You won't find any rail porters. In theaters, round up cost of program to nearest Kč. Foreign currency or Tuzex vouchers would certainly (though unofficially) be welcomed by anyone rendering you special service.

MAIL AND TELEPHONES. An airmail letter costs from 6 Kčs., postcard 5 Kčs. to the U.S.; 4 Kčs. for letters and 3 Kčs. for postcards to European countries. There is a 24-hour service at the main post office in Prague, Jindřišská Ulice 24, Nové Město.

In public phone booths insert a 1 Kčs. piece and dial (local calls). Special international pay booths in central Prague will take 5 Kčs., but your best bet is to go to the main post office (see above) where you pay after your call according to duration. Long distance calls to most of the country, and internationally, are now automatic.

TIME. Czechoslovakia is six hours ahead of Eastern Standard and Daylight Times and one hour ahead of British Standard and Summer Times.

CLOSING TIMES. Shops generally open from 9–6, Mondays through Fridays (larger shops 9–8 on Thursdays), some closing on Saturdays, others open until noon and department stores until 4. Food stores open at 6 A.M. Banks are open 8–14, Monday through Friday. Museums, art galleries, and similar places of interest usually open from 9 or 10 to 4 or 5 and close on Mondays. Some museums and other monuments, especially castles, are open only in summer. Čedok can advise. It is also important to note that in recent years a considerable amount of restoration work has been in progress on buildings of historic interest, and it is possible that some places mentioned in these pages may be closed for some months or longer, though where known, this has been indicated. Again Čedok can provide the latest information.

SHOPPING. For tourists in Czechoslovakia, shopping tends to center upon Tuzex where only hard currency or its equivalent in Tuzex coupons is accepted. The Tuzex head office is at Rytířská 19, Prague 1, and it has branches all over Prague, including in some main hotels, as well as all over the country, in large towns, spas, and resorts. In the larger shops you can buy all kinds of imported goods from the West, including liquor, cigarettes, and everything from tools to transistor radios; you will also find some of the best national souvenirs, such as Bohemian glass and crystal, peasant pottery, porcelain, wooden toys and folk carvings, charming corn-husk figurines, hand-embroidered clothing, and food items. Tuzex coupons will make a welcome gift to Czech friends or anyone who has been particularly helpful. An up-to-date list of Tuzex outlets can be obtained from the head office of Čedok.

In addition, there are a number of excellent shops specializing in glass and crystal, and various associations of Czechoslovak artists and craftsmen run their own retail outlets. In these you pay in local currency (but note the warning under *Customs*) and some of their addresses are given under *Shopping* for Prague. Here, too, you will find the addresses of some of the main department stores where you can buy inexpensively the kind of everyday articles you may need. Other good buys are records of excellent quality, charming folk toys, and an amazing range of costume jewelry.

In the provinces, look out for handmade pottery (at Kolovce and Strážnice in particular); folk ceramics in eastern Slovakia; china ornaments and geyserstone carvings at Karlovy Vary; delicate lace and needle embroidery in many Moravian towns; wood carvings from Spišská Belá; blood-red garnets and semi-precious stones from Bohemia.

SPAS. The spas of Czechoslovakia are famous. Many an ailing, aristocratic body has sought treatment or relaxation at one of them, most notably at Karlovy Vary and Mariánské Lázně in the days when they were known as Karlsbad and Marienbad. The medical facilities are excellent. In some spas, a few of the older hotels have been renovated, and modern and sophisticated sanatoria have been built. The location of many is very beautiful, making them holiday resorts in their own right, as well as spas. All this, combined with a long-established tradition of caring for the sick has given the Czechoslovak spas a well-deserved reputation abroad. Western visitors are coming in increasing numbers, many of them appreciating the reasonable prices attached to these services and the emphasis that is put on health rather than high fashion. The spas may not be as chic as some of their western counterparts, but the suffering will find all the priorities are in the right direction, while their healthier companions will find plenty of amenities for entertainment, sports and sightseeing activities.

Altogether there are 56 spas and health resorts, about two-thirds of them in Bohemia and Moravia where the organization Balnea coordinates all the necessary services, and one-third in Slovakia, where the organization Slovakoterma is responsible. Both cooperate with Čedok and their agencies abroad.

An example of prices for a three-week arrangement ex-London, covering return flight, first-class accommodations in a double room with bath, medical examination and full medical care, full board with dietary meals where necessary and spa treatment according to doctor's prescription, is £1,199 in Piešťany, £1,099 in Karlovy Vary. Prices in some other spas are lower and, in all cases, accompanying adults without treatment pay less.

SPORTS. Though conditions in Czechoslovakia are excellent for a number of sports, arrangements mainly cater for groups. Those with their own equipment and prepared to make their own way, however, will usually find local sports clubs extremely willing to advise and assist if approached on the spot. The appropriate addresses can be obtained through Čedok.

Facilities for a variety of water sports, including windsurfing and waterskiing, have been created in a number of the artificial lakes. Fast rivers provide excellent canoeing, for example, the Lužnice and Ohře rivers in western Bohemia, the Hornád in Slovakia; or one of the country's principal rivers: the Labe (Elbe) and Vltava in Bohemia, the Morava and Dyje (Thaya) in Moravia, and the Dunaj (Danube), Váh and Hron in Slovakia. Walkers will find a very good network of marked trails in all mountain areas, and can obtain detailed local maps on the spot in most cases. Walking tours are arranged ex-U.K. by *Ramblers Holidays,* 13 Longcroft House, Fretherne Road, Welwyn Garden City, Herts. AL8 6PQ.

Two other activities for which good facilities exist for foreign visitors are hunting and fishing. Čedok can arrange for permits and appropriate accommodations. For groups, a wide range of activity holidays is available.

WINTER SPORTS. There are first class skiing conditions in many parts of the country and a developing range of amenities with which to enjoy them. The best-equipped resorts at present are Špindlerův Mlýn in the Krkonoše (Giant Mountains) of northeast Bohemia, and Štrbské Pleso, Starý Smokovec and Tatranská Lomnica in the High Tatras range of Slovakia. These all offer ski lifts, ski instruction, and hire of equipment as well as good accommodations and some *après-ski* life. Winter sports tours are arranged by Čedok through some overseas agencies, but it is best to check for the latest details.

GETTING AROUND CZECHOSLOVAKIA. By Air. Although not a large country, Czechoslovakia has a remarkably good internal air service linking Prague with eight centers including Brno, Bratislava, Poprad (for the High Tatras) and the health resorts of Karlovy Vary and Piešťany. Reservations can be made through Čedok or ČSA (Czechoslovak Airlines). Flights are by jet or turbo-prop aircraft. Prague's airport (Ruzyně) is about twelve miles from the city center with regular bus connections in addition to taxis.

By Train. There is an extensive rail network throughout the whole country. Eurail and other concessionary tariffs do not apply in Czechoslovakia except on the Czechoslovak section of certain international rail routes. As with other Eastern European countries, trains are always busy and fares low in comparison to Western

Europe, though a supplement is payable on almost all express trains. (If you have already purchased your ticket outside Czechoslovakia this does not apply.) Long distance trains carry restaurant or buffet services and overnight trains connecting main centers have sleeping cars and second class couchettes.

By Bus. Czechoslovakia has an extensive bus system. However, much of this is complementary to the railway, although in some cases (eg. Prague to Karlovy Vary, the health resort in Bohemia) it is in direct competition with the rail network. Fares are usually higher than by rail. Buses are always busy and on long distance routes you should reserve seats wherever possible. Čedok is helpful in doing this.

By Car. A varied series of motoring tours is now available, with your own or a rented car, through Čedok (those with your own car entitle you to the currency bonus). You may prefer the greater adventure of a less planned itinerary, but note the comments under *Hotels*. Czechs drive on the right and the usual continental rules of the road are observed, except that a right turn is permitted on a red light if accompanied by a green arrow. There are speed limits of 110 kph (70 mph) on motorways, 90 kph (55 mph) on other open roads and 60 kph (40 mph) in built-up areas. Watch where motorway regulations begin as it is not always obvious, and if towing a caravan, never exceed 80 kph (50 mph). Seat belts are compulsory and drinking is absolutely prohibited.

The very center of Prague is closed to private cars and parking in central areas is limited to a few specially reserved parking lots. Other than in such lots, you risk having your car towed away and retrieval is expensive. In short, a car is a liability. Elsewhere there are few problems.

Information on the documents you will need if you're taking your own car into the country is given on *page 20*. You can purchase non-refundable gasoline coupons (92 and 96 octane) entitling you to about a 20% reduction from Čedok in London, from Živnostenska Banka, 104–106 Leadenhall Street, EC3 4AA, or from the Tuzex Information Center, Rytířská 19, in Prague, or at border crossings. It's best to purchase coupons in advance, to avoid tiresome waits, but if you are entitled to the currency bonus (see *Money*), they offer no real benefit. For diesel you must have coupons—not available in this case from Čedok, though they can provide a list of the limited number of gasoline stations which sell it.

In the case of accident or repair problems, get in touch with *Autotourist,* Na Rybnícku 16, Prague 2 (tel. 203355) who operate a patrol service on main roads, can provide motoring information of all kinds, and operate auto-camps throughout the country. Carry a spare parts kit with you. The emergency number for motorists is 154.

A number of main European (E) through routes cross Czechoslovakia. They include E50 (West Germany) – Rozvadov – Plzeň – Prague – Jihlava – Brno – Trenčín – Prešov – Košice; E55 (East Germany) – Cínovec – Teplice – Prague – Tábor – C. Budějovice – Dol. Dvořiště – (Austria); E65 (Poland) – Harrachov – Turnov – M1. Boleslav – Prague – Jihlava – Brno Breclav – Bratislava – (Austria/Hungary); E75 (Poland) – C. Těšín – Žilina – Trenčín - Piešťany – Bratislava – (Austria/Hungary). Main roads are usually maintained in good condition; secondary roads are reasonable.

Car Hire. Self-drive cars may be hired through *Avis* and *Pragocar* at Ruzyně airport and Štěpánská 42, Prague 1, or pre-booked through Čedok and some of its overseas partners in all towns and resorts.

INTRODUCING
CZECHOSLOVAKIA

Shakespeare has been declared ignorant for setting a scene of *The Winter's Tale* on the "seacoast of Bohemia." That old kingdom was completely landlocked, as is Czechoslovakia today, but there were times when Bohemia was an expansionist power, with territory all over the "lands of the Holy Crown," reaching to the Adriatic in what is now Yugoslavia. There were other periods when the proud kingdom shrank almost to vanishing point. It was ever the Bohemians' fate to live cheek by jowl with rapacious neighbors. In modern Czechoslovakia, some may be dissatisfied with her position as a Soviet satellite country; but none can deny that the alignments of 1945 have brought peace to her frontiers for the longest period in history.

This heartland of old Bohemia is centrally situated in Europe. Prague, the capital, is equidistant from the North Sea, the Baltic and the Adriatic, and important trans-continental routes pass through it. Though smaller than the state of Pennsylvania, with a population of 15 million, Czechoslovakia is ringed and intersected by formidable pine-forested mountain ranges and, if rolled out flat, would probably cover half Europe.

She is really three countries: Bohemia, capital Prague, in the west; Moravia, chief town Brno ("Burrno") in the middle; and Slovakia, capital Bratislava, in the east. Politically, the Czechoslovak Republic consists of two federal states, the Czech Republic and the Slovak Republic; and, to the annoyance of the notoriously prickly Slovaks, the national capital is Prague.

Although the land has no sea, it is exceptionally well-watered. In the countryside you are hardly ever out of sight of a lake—some are big enough to have ocean-worthy motor vessels and ferryboats on them. Mineral springs abound. Builders of new apartment blocks complain that wherever they put down a drill, hot water comes up. The hilly regions give birth to innumerable fast-flowing torrents. Slovakia has a share in a 50-mile stretch of the Danube, but the river chiefly associated with the country is the Vltava ("Vool-tava"), river of Prague, which ends up in Germany as the Elbe. Thus Czechoslovakia is the watershed of Europe. On several high plateaux adjacent snowfields melt into the North Sea and the Black Sea respectively.

Few love their country more passionately than the Czechs and Slovaks. They express it physically: they are a great nation for the woods and fields, lakes and rivers, country cottages, picnics and outdoor athletics. Keeping fit is a national obsession. Summer weekends see the exit roads from cities crammed with little automobiles, all carrying tents and canoes; in winter, skis. Not surprisingly, the nation performs brilliantly in Olympics sports, notably canoe slalom, rowing and downhill skiing. At the highest level she contributes champions out of all proportion to her numbers—older fans will recall the long-distance runner Emil Zátopek, and everyone knows Mandlikova, Navratilova and Lendl.

Bohemia Down the Ages

From earliest times, the country was occupied by gypsyish wandering tribes of mainly Celtic origin. ("Bohemian" is still synonymous with "free spirit.") Rome's influence was never strong and before the Roman empire broke up, around 450 A.D., Bohemia had received her first permanent settlers. They were Slavs, the same people who took over most of Russia and the Balkan peninsula.

The first sovereign state, grandiloquently called the Greater Moravian Empire, was established in the time of Charlemagne, about 800 A.D. By that date much of the country had been Christianized and in 880 the ecclesiastics made the historic decision to adhere to the Roman, rather than the Orthodox, brand of Catholicism. This decision gave Bohemia her Latin alphabet, instead of the Cyrillic, and ensured that she would look west, politically and culturally, rather than east. But internal squabbles weakened her and the area now known as Slovakia fell under the influence of her southern neighbor, Hungary; while for 300 years the rest of Bohemia had to suffer the incursions and maneuverings of *its* neighbors, a loose alliance of Germanic states.

To this era belongs the short and stormy reign of Václav, defender of the faith, assassinated and canonized as Saint Václav, a name Latinized as "Wenceslas." Today he sits astride his iron horse in Prague's Wenceslas Square and shakes his lance at the traffic. He is the "good king Wenceslas" of the Christmas carol—a song written by a 19th-century English clergyman, having no base in Czech history or legend.

It was one of his successors, Otakar II (reigned 1253–1278) who expanded Bohemia's dominions and aroused dreams of empire on the shores of the Adriatic. In the end he lost more than he gained, but within three generations a more successful ruler, Charles IV, had really put Bohemia on the map.

From the tangled web of *mitteleuropaïsche* politics, Charles eventually emerged as nothing less than Holy Roman Emperor (1355). The market town of Prague was suddenly elevated to capital city of all western Europe. Bohemia entered upon her golden age of commerce and power. The capital is today a picturesque confusion of architectural styles but its hallmark, the "Bohemian Gothic" of St Vitus's cathedral, dates from Charles IV's reign. He also founded Carlsbad, Marienbad and Franzensbad and made that western corner of Bohemia the spa capital of Europe.

Reformation and Counter-Reformation

Towards the end of the Middle Ages, the country entered a long period of religious wars and was torn apart. They began after the reformist crusades of Jan Hus (John Huss), burnt as a heretic in 1415. Reformation and counter-Reformation, Protestant versus Catholic, split court and country, especially after the crown passed to a Habsburg dynasty and Bohemia joined Slovakia under Hungarian (Catholic) rule. The intense recatholicization of a nation which had been sliding towards Protestantism sparked off the incident of 1618 which crops up in many a school examination paper: the Defenestration of Prague. You can still see the garbage tip under Hradčany palace walls on which the imperial counsellors landed when Prague's Protestant court officials threw them out of the window. Indirectly the incident led to the Thirty Years War which involved most of Europe.

The battle of the White Mountain (1620) confirmed Habsburg domination. The native-born aristocracy virtually disappeared, to be replaced by foreigners who inspired the Czechs' hereditary dislike of Hungarians. By 1749, under the Austro-Hungarian empress Maria Theresa, Slovakia was ruled from Budapest (Hungary) and Bohemia and Moravia from Vienna (Austria). The official language was German.

Birth of a Nation

Flickerings of national aspirations grew gradually into a steady flame. Bicker as they might among themselves, the Czechs and Slovaks never forgot their glorious past. Pressure from within failed to achieve much; and the popular uprising of 1848, the year of revolutions all over Europe, was squashed by Austro-Hungarian troops. The first real bid for nationhood occurred at the beginning of the 20th century, when Tomáš Masaryk founded his Realist Party and gained seats in the Imperial parliament on a home-rule ticket. Masaryk (he married an American girl, Charlotte Garrigue) got his big chance at the outbreak of World War I in 1914. From Paris he organized the Czechoslovak National Council and the Czechoslovak (military) Legion and in 1919, with President Wilson's support, the Allies granted the heirs of Václav, Otakar and Charles IV their independence.

Czechoslovakia now appeared for the first time on the map of Europe. Partly industrialized (the Baťa shoe and Škoda armaments firms were leaders in automation) and with an advanced social-security system, the country flourished despite inevitable domestic wrangles. All was brought to an end when Hitler laid claim to the German-oriented inhabitants of the Sudetenland in 1938—one of his celebrated "last territorial demands in Europe." To buy time in the face of approaching war, Czechoslovakia's guarantors, France and Britain, sacrificed her.

Under German occupation the country suffered conscription, forced labor and the persecution of Jews. As a reprisal for the assassination of

Reichsprotektor Heydrich in Prague in 1942, every inhabitant of a village was either shot or sent to a concentration camp. The galleries and memorial gardens of this place, Lidice, are now among Czechoslovakia's mandatory tourist sites.

During World War II the Slovaks conducted a determined partisan campaign in their mountains and many Czechs found their way to Britain to fight against Nazism. The Soviet armies liberated the country and the first post-war government, headed by Dr Beneš, pre-war President and colleague of Masaryk, contained a socialist majority. In 1948 the hard-line Communist Klement Gottwald ousted Beneš. Since his time, dissidents have made several bids for political freedom, notably in the "Prague Spring" of 1968, when Alexander Dubček, a Slovak, became First Secretary of the Communist Party and introduced liberalizing measures. But after eight months the armed might of the Warsaw Pact brought Czechoslovakia to heel.

Under Dubček's successors the nation has accepted state control in most areas of public and private life. For the Czechs and Slovaks, bowing to *force majeure* is nothing new. Living in a beautiful and interesting little country, enjoying increasing material prosperity, better health and improving contact with the West, they may reflect that things might have turned out worse.

The Cultural Heritage

Nothing memorable or influential appeared in the Czech or Slovak languages (which differ almost as do Swedish and Norwegian) until the statesman Tomáš Masaryk produced his political history, *The Making of a State,* earlier this century. But the novelists and playwrights who sprang from nowhere at the same time are known and revered throughout the world: the profound and enigmatic writer Franz Kafka (*The Trial, The Castle, America* and other novels); Karel Čapek, who invented the word "robot" (*R.U.R., The Insect Play* and other works of a comic imagination); and Jaroslav Hašek, creator of the immortal *Good Soldier Schweik* (the uncomplaining, downtrodden man who always manages to survive—in some respects a personification of the typical Czech). The regime, curiously, has made a pet of Hašek; all tourists visit the Švejk tavern (*U Kalicha*) in Prague, though they may find it disappointing nowadays. Of Kafka and Čapek, with their dangerous symbolism, it is tolerant but not enthusiastic.

Among living writers the conventionally patriotic and safe novelist Bohumil Říha is the darling of the masses. His *Wide Open Land* and *Dr Meluzin* are available in English translation. A few authors are popular abroad not for their literary accomplishments but for the fact that in 1977 they signed Charter 77, a manifesto of human rights.

Provided they do not overtly attack the system, Czech and Slovak writers have considerable latitude to indulge a characteristic fondness for sly satire. Ladislav Mňačko, a Slovak, published in 1967 the novel *A Taste of Power,* hinting that power can corrupt both capitalists and Communists; Bohumil Hrabal's *The Pearls* shows that crime and prostitution can flourish even in socialist societies; and Jan Očenášek, in *Citizen Brych* and *Lovers in the Year One,* discusses the problems of people bewildered by the times in which they live. Václav Havel's exposures of totalitarian bureaucracy's absurdities have made such plays as *The Memorandum* popular in the West.

Poetry, too, has moved on from the "socialist humanism" of the 1950s into more obscure and experimental areas. František Hrubín and Ivan Skála are two prominent contemporary poets.

Cartoon and children's books published by the 50-odd state, trade union and literary society organizations have gained prizes abroad.

There is a museum of Czech literature in the former Strahov monastery in Prague.

"Every Czech a Musician"

The old saying still holds true. Observe the music-and-dance festivals, the brass band competitions and the country weddings where teenage Vendulkas and Marinkas do not scorn to stamp out the dances in their (or more likely their grandmothers') swirling skirts and dazzlingly embroidered bodices—just like a Czech folk opera. This nation has loved and composed great music, too, ever since Mozart's time—*Don Giovanni* was premiered in Prague. It is astonishing that so small a country should have produced, in the space of 50 years, such towering figures as Smetana, Dvořák, Janáček and Martinů. Those composers are honored with museums in Prague, Brno and Bratislava and with incessant performances of their works—especially Smetana, whose operas on Czech legendary subjects and symphonic poems redolent of the Bohemian countryside stimulated the rising nationalism of the 1880s.

Great native singers arose then and afterwards, of whom Emmy Destin was perhaps the best-loved abroad; and great virtuosi, of whom Josef Suk the violinist, founder of the Czech String Quartet, is the latest example.

The National Theater in Prague, opened again in refurbished splendor in 1984, is a remarkable complex of concert halls and playhouses centered on the building where, 100 years earlier, a wildly enthusiastic audience first heard Smetana's *Má Vlast* ("My Country"). The great Prague Spring Festival, from the second week in May, has its headquarters here. There are big music festivals too in Bratislava, Brno, Ostrava and Karlovy Vary; and many summer concerts out of doors.

Jazz and rock are popular, and not frowned on—jazz composers enjoy much prestige.

Pictorial Arts

The household names are those veterans of the national revival who, under French impressionist inspiration, made their names at the turn of this century and went on painting until quite recently: Vincenc Beneš (1883–1979), Vilém Novák (1886–1977) and Jan Zrzavý (1890–1977). To some extent they still stand in the light of younger and more original talents, but the "anti-impressionist" Václav Rabas, the versatile Jiří Trnka (also a famous puppet playwright) and the sculptor Jan Štursa have built reputations in Eastern Europe; while Josef Palaček (born 1932) has long been a master of book design and illustration, especially of children's books.

Stage and Screen

Fantasy, psychological depth and a touch of irreverent satire are what theater and cinema audiences expect. Czechoslovakia's 84 permanent theaters cover a repertoire of classics old and new, from Molière to G.B. Shaw and from Euripides to Brecht. Puppetry, mime and ballet perpetuate the older traditions, while the notorious "little theaters"—Viola, Rokoko, Ypsilon, Naïve, Black and others, chiefly in Prague—have provoked imitations the world over. The *Laterna Magica* show, labeled daringly *avant-garde,* is really for tourist consumption, but remains effective enough for all that.

The Český Krumlov theater, in the town of that name on the upper Vltava, is said to be the oldest in Europe.

The movie has always been regarded as an original art-form to which the Czechoslovaks instinctively respond. The outstanding living director, Miloš Forman (*Ragtime, One Flew Over the Cuckoo's Nest*), works mainly in Hollywood but recently made his extremely successful film *Amadeus* in Prague. A great movie still popular with film clubs is *Closely Observed Trains,* an adaptation of a Bohumil Hrabal novel.

Film festivals held annually at Mariánské Lázně and Karlovy Vary attract movies, actors, actresses and critics from many lands.

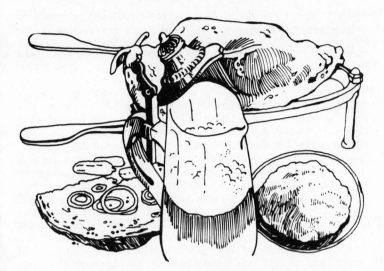

CZECHOSLOVAK
FOOD AND DRINK

Pork, Game and Beer

Czech and Slovak cooking is living witness to the country's position as the crossroads of Europe. The Slav influence from the East brought the sour cream, vinegar, and sour vegetables, such as pickles. The goulash came from Hungary, the schnitzels from Vienna and the roast goose with sauerkraut and dumplings are German imports. The diet tends to be heavy, but the preparation of food is a tradition with Czechs and you will find eating out, especially in Prague, a thoroughly enjoyable gastronomic experience. Typical and often very attractive eating or drinking places throughout the country are *vinárna* (wine cellars) and *pivnice* (beer taverns) or, in Slovakia, the folk-style *koliba*.

Starters

King of the cold table is the regal Prague ham, which sets a standard for hams everywhere. The range of *hors d'oeuvres* is good, from eggs with caviar and smoked meats to Russian crabmeat in mayonnaise, and there is an excellent variety of salads in which pickles in an enormous number of guises are a recurrent theme. Herrings and sardines are other regular *hors d'oeuvres* items. When it comes to cheeses, some of the most interesting come from Slovakia and are made from sheep's milk.

Meat and Fish Dishes

The true Czech loves are pork, game, and goose. *The* Czech meal is roast or smoked pork with sauerkraut and dumplings; roast goose or duck similarly adorned are close seconds. Being a land where the art of conservation dates from the Middle Ages, the country abounds in game so hare, venison, and game birds are fairly common in season. Fish occupies a rather small place in the national cuisine; but the lakes of South Bohemia yield the Czech national fish, carp, served traditionally on Christmas Eve in several variations. The streams of Slovakia produce good trout.

Among other major meat dishes are variations on exotic stews. The goulash in Slovakia is particularly delicious, excellently seasoned with sweet paprika and slightly sharper than its Czech counterpart. *Svíčková* combines pieces of beef with spices and vegetables, braised in the oven and served with a cream sauce. Tasty sauces or rich thick gravy are a feature of many meat dishes, but don't look for an accompaniment of fresh green vegetables. The best you may do is pickled tomatoes or cucumbers, and canned peas and carrots. Fresh vegetables, particularly in winter, are extremely rare, and aside from tomatoes and cabbage, the Czech restaurants don't seem to know how to prepare them. An exception will be some of the most delicious-tasting mushrooms you have ever had. For some reason, these flourish in the Czechoslovakian fields and forests and a favorite weekend pastime is to take a trip out from the city to gather this delectable harvest.

The Ubiquitous Dumpling

Soups are another excellent feature, often with small dumplings floating in them. The soups come in all varieties and some of them are veritable meals in their own right. One of the most popular is *bramboračka* (made with potatoes), but you will also frequently encounter a thin meat *bouillon* containing small pieces of meat and macaroni. The dumplings, which come with so many dishes and help you to mop up that excellent gravy, also come in many varieties. The basic Czech recipe is a mixture of slightly-dried bread cubes bound together with eggs, milk and flour; in Slovakia they are likely to be made from potato, flour, water and salt dropped into hot water then rolled in fat. Called *halušky,* they are probably eaten with *bryndza,* cream cheese made from ewe's milk. There are also sweet dumplings, stuffed with plums or other types of fruit.

For a quick, cheap snack, look out for kiosks selling *bramborák,* grated potato with egg, flour and seasoning, fried in oil, and very tasty.

Pancakes and Pastries

The Czechs are not lacking a sweet tooth either, so on the whole it is best to put aside your diet altogether. From apple strudels and mouth-watering pancakes filled with jam or fruit or soaked in chocolate sauce, you can pass on to the many different pastries and cakes, made from chocolate, almonds, or other nuts, and delectable combinations of eggs and flour. All are topped with cream icings and finished off with swirls of whipped cream. Incidentally, although Czechoslovakia produces an abundance of fruit herself, the imported varieties—citrus fruits, bananas and so on—are rarely to be seen.

What to Drink

A typical Czech meal needs something to wash it down. The favorite Czech drink is beer, and in recent years its popularity has spread in Slovakia, which otherwise is a wine-drinking region. In addition to the world-famous *Pilsen Urquell,* there is the *Budvar* beer from České Budějovice, and a number of ale houses produce their own brew. The town of České Budějovice was, incidentally, originally called Budweis and should you get to this fine historic town in South Bohemia, you may hear some colorful views expressed concerning Budweiser—Budvar's American near-namesake!

Slovakia is the main wine-growing area, but there are some excellent Moravian reds. Bohemia's best wine comes from around Mělník. *Slivovice* or plum brandy is the national strong drink, the most famous brands coming from Moravia. Coffee is widely drunk, usually served in the so-called Turkish (unfiltered) style, without milk, and can be a bit gritty.

PRAGUE

The Golden City

Poets and artists, royalty and commoners down through the ages have praised the regal beauty of the capital of Czechoslovakia. Prague, like Rome, is built on seven hills and it spans the Vltava River (so graphically portrayed in music in Bedřich Smetana's tone poems *Má Vlast*). Few other cities in Europe possess a lovelier combination of varied architecture from many centuries, interspersed with fine parks and gardens. Through it all threads the winding river spanned by 16 bridges, and from the surrounding slopes are any number of magnificent views.

The visitor knows that history has been here a long time. Legend has it that The Princess Libuše, the prophetess of Czech tradition, stood on a rocky precipice overlooking the Vltava. Transfigured with inspiration she stretched forth her hands and cried, "I see a great city, whose glory will touch the stars. The town you will build here shall be called Praha (threshold). Honor and praise shall be given to it, and it shall be renowned throughout the world." She then dispatched her white horse to fetch her a consort and, when he returned with a certain Přemysl, a robust farmer, this rather unlikely pair founded the Přemyslide dynasty. So Prague came into being on the site where Slav tribes used to ford the river at its most shallow point, and where Charles Bridge stands today. Two fortresses, Vyšehrad and Hradčany, were built on the heights above the river. Traces of romanesque Prague can still be seen in the Church of St. George at Hradčany and elsewhere, but the wooden houses of the common people have long since been destroyed.

Prague took the shape we know today during the 13th and 14th centuries. Much of the Gothic splendor of the city can be attributed to Charles IV, King of Bohemia and Moravia and Holy Roman Emperor, who made Prague the seat of his empire. During his reign (1346–1378), Charles University and Nové Město (the New Town) were founded, and Charles Bridge and other architectural monuments built.

The 15th century saw Prague torn by the religious and nationalist conflict of the Hussite Wars. For over 20 years, the Czech nation, noble and peasant alike, fought and defeated seven crusades mounted against them by the Holy Roman Empire and the Pope. The Czechs became known as the scourge of Europe and the word 'Bohemian' evoked the devil.

But the fighting was a tragedy for Prague. Trade could not flourish in the war-torn land and the ancient trading routes between the Baltic and the Danube were rerouted through German territory, never to return to Prague. The Czechs were eventually driven to defeat. Habsburg oppression caused the nation to rise once again in 1618, touching off the Thirty Years' War, which decimated the population of Central Europe. With the harsh reimposition of Habsburg rule after the defeat of the Czech nobility at the battle of White Mountain in 1620, Prague started to recover—albeit at a price. The favorite nobles of the Habsburgs confiscated the rich and fertile estates of the Bohemian aristocrats, and with the wealth acquired from their new lands, glorified their power in Baroque monuments. Baroque was also the medium of the Jesuit movement of the counter reformation, which nowhere was more militant than in Bohemia. Thus, Prague was transformed by palaces and churches and made beautiful by landscaped, terraced gardens. The city also became a musical capital. Mozart walked her streets, claiming that no one but the Praguers understood him well.

With the coming of long-desired independence in 1918, Prague became the capital of the newly-formed Czechoslovak republic. During the interwar period she was a commercial center for Central Europe while retaining her cultural primacy. Fortunately, Prague suffered little from the bombings of the Second World War. The city, which was liberated by its citizens between the 5th and the 8th May, 1945, was practically unscathed.

Nevertheless, long periods of neglect took their toll and in due course a huge program was launched to clean, restore and refurbish historic buildings and whole districts of the older part of the city. By now an enormous amount has been achieved. Restoration of the Castle and Lesser Town area is now largely completed; the third and final Metro line is ready. Attention is now focused on the Old Town.

Exploring Prague

Prague, perhaps even more than other cities, is best seen on foot. But if you are going to spend only a day or so, the fastest way to see as many highlights as possible is to take one of the bus tours arranged by Čedok. If you are going to stay several days, your best move is to familiarize yourself with the map and the main districts of Prague, get an idea of the public transport system (you can buy a map with all the routes marked), and put on your walking shoes. You could start off by going to the top of one of the higher buildings, such as the Powder Tower or Intercontinental Hotel, to sort out all the towers and spires and the layout of the city.

There are four districts of Prague which are your main concern. (1) Hradčany (the Castle area), the crowning glory of the city's skyline,

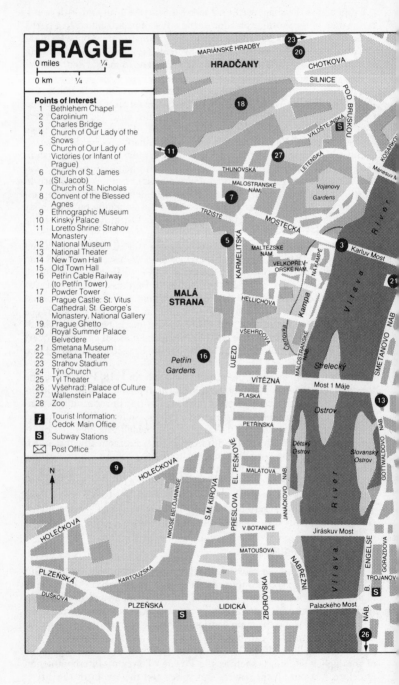

PRAGUE

0 miles   ¼

0 km   ¼

Points of Interest

1 Bethlehem Chapel
2 Carolinium
3 Charles Bridge
4 Church of Our Lady of the
   Snows
5 Church of Our Lady of
   Victories (or Infant of
   Prague)
6 Church of St. James
   (St. Jacob)
7 Church of St. Nicholas
8 Convent of the Blessed
   Agnes
9 Ethnographic Museum
10 Kinský Palace
11 Loretto Shrine: Strahov
   Monastery
12 National Museum
13 National Theater
14 New Town Hall
15 Old Town Hall
16 Petřin Cable Railway
   (to Petřin Tower)
17 Powder Tower
18 Prague Castle: St. Vitus
   Cathedral, St. George's
   Monastery, National Gallery
19 Prague Ghetto
20 Royal Summer Palace
   Belvedere
21 Smetana Museum
22 Smetana Theater
23 Strahov Stadium
24 Týn Church
25 Tyl Theater
26 Vyšehrad: Palace of Culture
27 Wallenstein Palace
28 Zoo

i Tourist Information:
   Čedok Main Office

S Subway Stations

✉ Post Office

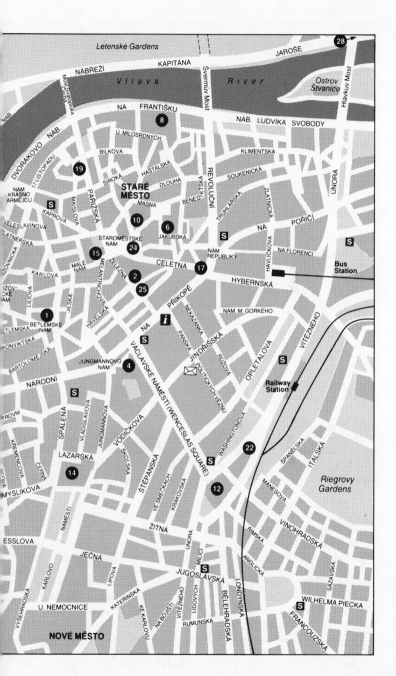

perched above the River Vltava; (2) Malá Strana (Lesser Town) linking Hradčany with the river and Charles Bridge; (3) Staré Město (Old Town) across the river; and (4) Nové Město (New Town, founded in the 14th century!), an extension of the Old Town.

If you have a car, note that the center of the city is closed to private traffic, unless you are accommodated there. There is a comprehensive network of trams and buses, and the new subway system is clean, modern and very efficient. One of the stations, Gottwaldova, is worth traveling to for its panoramic view alone.

Since Wenceslas Square is probably the best-known landmark in Prague and you are likely to be staying in or near it, we may as well start off here. The first thing to note is that Václavské Náměstí is not a square at all, but a long, broad boulevard, sloping down from the National Museum to what was once the moat around the Old Town. The "square" itself is closed to private cars and has subway stations at either end, with access to them also from the middle. The moat, which linked with the river at each end, is now occupied by the streets of Národní, 28 rijna and Na příkopě (at the moat), and Revoluční. Part of this historic artery adjoining Wenceslas Square is now a pedestrian precinct and, along or near it, you will find many of the city's tourist services and best shops. Once you have crossed to the other side of it, you are in Staré Město, the Old Town.

Staré Město (Old Town)

This is the area on which restoration programs are currently focused, so expect to encounter the paraphernalia that goes with it. In fact, the splendid buildings of Staré Město are far too numerous to mention them all; the most important are described, but you can hardly avoid making your own discoveries, whether it be some graceful piece of Gothic vaulting, or some exuberant piece of Baroque carving. The best advice is to walk always with your eyes up, not down, and to probe into the tiniest alleys and the smallest courtyards.

At one end of Na Příkopě is a splendid remnant of the old fortifications, the Powder Tower, originally built by Matěj Rejsek in 1475 but rebuilt in neo-Gothic in the 19th century. Once you have passed beneath it, or taken any of the other streets into the Old Town, you will very soon come to its hub, Staroměstské Náměstí (Old Town Square). The obvious choice is to turn under the Powder Tower into Celetná street, where you'll find yourself on the old Royal Route once followed by coronation processions through Old Town Square, Karlova, across Charles Bridge and up to the Castle. The fine buildings along this route are being splendidly restored, and Celetná street itself is now most attractive, as well as being a pedestrian precinct. An alternative from na Příkopě would be to follow Železná street on which the Carolinium and Tyl Theater stand next to each other. The Carolinium is the original Charles University building, founded in 1348 though much restored, and it was at the Tyl Theater (now being restored) that the first performance of Mozart's *Don Giovanni* was given in 1787, only four years after the building was completed.

Old Town Square, together with the adjoining Malé Náměstí (Little Square), is a delight. In the center is the statue (1915) of John Huss, or Jan Hus, whose humanistic teachings have made him both a religious and national symbol to the Czechs. In one corner is the famous 15th-century astronomical clock at the Old Town Hall, beneath which crowds gather every hour to watch Christ and the 12 Apostles show themselves at two little windows above the clock face. Then the skeleton figure of Death standing below tolls the bell on the hour.

The Old Town Hall was actually founded in 1338, built out of the proceeds of the wine tax, and rebuilt in late-Gothic style in 1470. The Nazis destroyed part of later additions in the Second World War, but the Gothic chapel, the tower and the splendid old Council Chamber remain. Opposite the Town Hall, the Týn Church is one of the gems of Prague Gothic to which later times have added an extravaganza of interior Baroque decoration (closed for restoration). Near it is the rococo Kinský Palace.

If you take Pařížská or Maislova street out of Old Town Square, you will very soon be in the old Jewish Quarter, whose ancient buildings now comprise the State Jewish Museum. The Prague Ghetto is one of the oldest in Europe, dating back at least to the 10th century. By the 17th century, it had become a focal point for Hebrew culture in Central Europe. With the abrogation of the segregationist laws against the Jews after 1848, the Ghetto's autonomous existence ceased.

Built about 1270, the Old-New Synagogue, still used for worship, is one of Prague's best examples of early Gothic, its wealth of sculptural decoration foreshadowing the naturalism of High Gothic. The Old Jewish Town Hall was restored in the 18th century, and is in the same building as the High Synagogue in which is displayed a fine collection of Torah mantles and silver. The richest display, however, is in the Maisel Synagogue with magnificent examples of all the artefacts used in worship—Torah wrappers and mantles, silver pointers, breast plates and spice boxes; superb candlesticks (the eight-branched Hanukkah and the seven-branched Menora); and Levite washing sets. The Jewish State Museum contains an intensely moving collection of drawings and paintings by children in concentration camps. The appalling war-time chapter in the story of Prague Jewry is told in the ancient Pinkas Synagogue (currently closed for restoration), in which over 77,000 names are inscribed in rows on the interior walls— names of Jewish men, women and children from Bohemia and Moravia who were liquidated by the Nazis.

The last astonishing sight of this district is the Old Jewish Cemetery, which seems unbelievably old and unbelievably crowded; it is both. With space restricted, graves were superimposed on each other—over 12,000 in a dozen layers—and the ancient tombstones lean and joggle against each other in the resulting subsidence. The oldest preserved tomb dates from 1439; burials continued here until 1787, when a new cemetery was built elsewhere. Probably the most visited tomb is that of scholar Rabbi Löw who died in 1609 and was the creator of the mythical and magical being Golem. Even today scraps of paper bearing prayers and requests are stuffed into a crack in the tomb in which, it is said, many Jews hid their valuables before they were transported to concentration camps.

The cemetery makes up one corner of Náměstí Krasnoarmějců on which is also the elegant late 19th-century House of Artists, concert hall and home of the Czech Philharmonic. There is a splendid view from one angle of this square across the river to Hradčany. Another square with a splendid view across the river is Křižovnické Náměstí (Square of the Knights of the Cross), with the marvels of Charles Bridge in the foreground. From this square there is access to the huge complex of the Klementinum (1653–1722), which was originally a Jesuit College and now houses a major part of the State Libraries. The square, which is considered one of the finest in Central Europe, is bounded by the 16th-century church of St. Salvador, the Baroque church of St. Frances (also known as the Church of the Crusaders), and the Gothic Old Town Bridge Tower (1357) dominating one end of Charles Bridge. The Smetana Museum is also near here. Tapes of the great composer's music are played, and there are fine views of his beloved city and river from the museum's windows.

Only a short walk away on Betlémské Náměstí is the most revered of all the Hussite monuments in Prague, the Bethlehem Chapel. It was here that John Huss preached from 1402 until he left Prague to be martyred in 1415. The chapel was founded in 1391, later demolished and painstakingly rebuilt in its original form in the early 1950s. Its completion was marked by a massive attendance of the citizens of Prague who packed the church and the square outside in an atmosphere charged with emotion. Inside, note the wooden threshold of the pulpit, which John Huss used to cross on his way to preach over 500 years ago, and one of the walls bearing an original inscription of his teachings. The floor of the present building is several meters higher than the original and beneath the whole of this area is a labyrinth of structures going right back to Celtic times, although not normally open to the public.

Finally, another major sight in the northern part of the Old Town, not far from the Intercontinental Hotel, is the beautifully restored 13th-century Monastery of the Blessed Agnes, the church and rooms off its old cloisters now containing a fine exhibition of 19th-century Czech art.

Charles Bridge and Malá Strana (Lesser Town)

Now it's time to follow the historic royal trail across Charles Bridge and the Vltava to the Lesser Town. The bridge itself was commissioned by Charles IV in 1357; its architect, Peter Parler of Grund, was then only 27 years old. Today it has been faithfully restored and measures 660 yards (603 meters) between the towers at either end. The wealth of statuary was mainly added in the 18th and 19th centuries, 26 of the 30 between 1706 and 1714. A few have been replaced, either by copies or later works, but most remain as powerful examples of the vitality of Prague Baroque. Opinion generally concedes first place in artistic merit to the group around Saint Luitgarda (Matthias Braun, 1710), the 12th statue on the left as you go from the Old Town. The best loved is that of Saint John of Mathy, Felix, and Ivan with the Turk by F. M. Brokoff (1714), the 14th on the left.

As you approach Malá Strana, you cross the island of Kampa and Čertovka (Devil's Brook), the little arm of the Vltava that divides the Kampa from Malá Strana. This peaceful island with its old houses was the home of Vladimir Holan, one of Czechoslovakia's greatest modern poets.

Malá Strana is a most picturesque quarter of the city, full of winding streets, impressive palaces, fine churches, little taverns, and old houses with ornamental signs. The district developed rapidly from the middle of the 13th century, though a great part of it was destroyed in the disastrous fire of 1541. The wide spaces that were left were gradually filled by the Renaissance and Baroque palaces of the nobility, many of them today adapted as foreign embassies, museums or government departments. One of the grandest is the Valdštejn or Wallenstein Palace (1623–30), in whose riding school is an art gallery. Its spacious gardens sometimes provide a noble setting for open-air concerts.

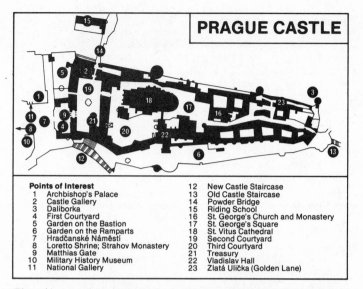

PRAGUE CASTLE

Points of Interest

1	Archbishop's Palace	12	New Castle Staircase
2	Castle Gallery	13	Old Castle Staircase
3	Daliborka	14	Powder Bridge
4	First Courtyard	15	Riding School
5	Garden on the Bastion	16	St. George's Church and Monastery
6	Garden on the Ramparts	17	St. George's Square
7	Hradčanské Náměstí	18	St. Vitus Cathedral
8	Loretto Shrine; Strahov Monastery	19	Second Courtyard
9	Matthias Gate	20	Third Courtyard
10	Military History Museum	21	Treasury
11	National Gallery	22	Vladislav Hall
		23	Zlatá Ulička (Golden Lane)

The main way through Malá Strana is along Mostecká (Bridge Street), a continuation of Charles Bridge. Wander off to the left and you are in a maze of small streets around charming Maltézské Náměstí (Maltese Square) and Velkopřevorské Náměstí, both bounded by 17th- and 18th-century former palaces. Now head for Karmelitská street and the very early Baroque Church of Our Lady of Victories (1611–1654), also known as the Church of the Infant of Prague (Pražskeho Jezulátko) because of its small but famous figurine of the Infant Jesus. This Spanish Renaissance wax effigy was the gift of Polyxena Lobkowitz in 1628, and today boasts a wardrobe of 45 different costumes, which are changed according to the Christian calendar. Miraculous powers associated with the Infant started a vogue of replicas in churches all over the world.

Very close by and reached through the entrance of 25 Karmelitská are Vrtba gardens, steeply terraced, fragrant with flowers in summer, and dotted with Baroque statues—some of them by Matthias Braun. This charming oasis created in 1720 is little known to Prague's visitors and offers not only a wondrous calm but fine views of the roofs and spires of the city.

Also in this area are the Petřín Gardens, part of the extensive parkland dominating this part of town. They contain the delightful collections of the Ethnographical Museum and Petřín Tower, the 60-meter (197-ft.) copy of the Eiffel Tower, built in 1891, a good place to check out the city's layout. It can now be reached by funicular, the lower station being near Most 1 máje (1st May Bridge).

The heart of the Malá Strana is Malostranské Náměstí (Lesser Town Square), dominated by the most splendid of Prague's Baroque churches, that of St. Nicholas, yet another creation associated with the Dienzenhofers, father and son, who were responsible for so much of Baroque Bohemia.

Hradčany (the Castle Area)

You can approach the Castle on foot either through the heart of the Lesser Town or by taking the steps which lead from near Malostranská subway station up through the Gardens under the Castle. The whole district grew from Hradčanské Náměstí, the great Castle Square, rebuilt and expanded after the fire of 1541. On this square you will find the Baroque Archbishop's Palace, and a passage leading to the entrance to the Šternberk Palace, with its magnificent art collections of the National Gallery. Also on this square is the Schwarzenberg (formerly Lobkovic) Palace from the 16th century with its distinctive graffito decoration, restored in 1957. Today it houses the interesting Museum of Military History in whose courtyards tournaments are quite often held.

Hradčanské Náměstí (Castle Square) is the culminating point, in more ways than one, of your Prague sightseeing tour. The Přemyslide rulers moved here from their original seat a few miles upstream at Vyšehrad, and by the 12th century there was an extended stone castle. After damage by fire, it was reconstructed into an imperial palace for Karel (Charles) IV. Matthias of Arras and Peter Parler are two names closely associated with both castle and cathedral.

Charles' son, Václav (Wenceslas) IV, preferred to live in the Old Town, and it was under the Jagellonian king, Vladislav, in the late 15th century that significant building work was resumed, including the great Vladislav Hall. The fire of 1541 did extensive damage, but reconstruction and expansion continued and, under Rudolf II, the castle became a center for the arts and sciences. Further damage was wrought by the troops of Frederick the Great in 1757 and, over the centuries of Habsburg rule, many choice items were dispatched to Vienna. Indeed, the later Habsburgs made infrequent use of the castle, though its Baroque overlays date mainly from the reign of Maria Theresa, as does the present main gateway. You will be told which of the Castle's magnificent rooms are open to the public and should not in any case miss the grandiose Vladislav Hall. Tournaments were also held here, hence the broad "equestrian" staircase leading to it.

St. Vitus Cathedral and its towering spires rise out of the Third Courtyard. Remains of earlier churches from the 10th and 11th centuries can be seen beneath the Cathedral, but interrupted by the Hussite wars, the fire of 1541, the Turkish wars, and general lack of interest on the part of some rulers, the present building spans nearly six centuries, from 1344–1929. Thus it is a blending of Gothic and neo-Gothic, the original work of Matthias of Arras and Peter Parler, finally completed in the late 19th and early 20th centuries.

The main body of the church is soaring Gothic, the oldest parts being in the eastern half, around the high altar, with 11 of the cathedral's 19 chapels. They include the Chapel of St. Václav, its walls studded with semi-precious stones, containing the tomb and relics of the great Wenceslas. The tombs of the two architects, Matthias of Arras and Peter Parler, are in the Valdštejn Chapel. Two of the Přemyslide kings are buried in the Šternberg but the main 16th-century Royal Mausoleum is in the center of the Cathedral before the high altar and, in the crypt below, lie the remains of both great and lesser Bohemian kings.

Some of the truly fabulous Bohemian crown jewels (including the St. Wenceslas crown to which Charles IV added a thorn, supposedly from

Christ's crown of thorns) are rarely on display; but there is a rich treasury in the Chapel of the Holy Rood in the Second Courtyard. The Cathedral's brilliant stained glass is modern.

Also reached from the Second Courtyard is the Castle Picture Gallery, displaying the very fine former collections of Rudolf II. The paintings originally belonged to Charles I of England, and were thought lost for 200 years, until they were found by chance in an abandoned storeroom in 1962. Restoration work, criticized by some as being too thorough, has brought these works by Rubens, Titian, Tintoretto and others, back to life. From this courtyard, too, you have access to the Powder Bridge with the Old Riding School beyond it, where temporary art exhibitions are held. This is also the way to the Royal Gardens, not open to the public, so to reach the best Renaissance building in Prague in the eastern part of the gardens, you must approach it from Mariánské hradby street. This is the Royal Summer Residence, or Belvedere, now another National Gallery exhibition venue, with its trim gardens and "singing fountain." Not too far away to the northeast, incidentally, is the huge Strahov stadium (180,000 seats) and its associated cluster of sports amenities, venue for the outstanding gymnastics event Spartakiada every five years.

Across the square behind the Cathedral rise the towers of St. George's Church and Monastery, the earliest Romanesque complex still in use today and now housing a superb collection of early and Baroque Bohemian art. Beyond it, in Jiřská street, the Lobkovic Palace now houses a splendid historical exhibition covering the period from the Přemyslides to 1948. Parallel to Jiřská street, and north of it you come to Zlatá Ulička (Golden Lane), a most picturesque huddle of tiny houses built into the Castle walls in 1541, occupied over the centuries by many craftsmen including the royal goldsmiths. Kafka once lived here. At the end of the lane, Daliborka, the castle keep, contains some sinister dungeons and is named after its first occupant, the knight Dalibor of Kozojed. Immediately west of the Castle is the district known as New World (Nový Svět), with narrow streets, good restaurants and arts and crafts studios.

Whatever you do, don't leave the Castle area without strolling through the Gardens on the Ramparts. The views over the river and city are spectacular. At their best in May, with chestnut, laburnum and lilac blossom, they extend along the ridge to the east. Similar views may be savored over a drink or meal in one of the restaurants in Letenské Sady Park or Petřín Gardens.

From the Castle it is a short walk to Loretánské Náměstí, which is dominated by two imposing Baroque buildings, the Černín Palace and the Loretto shrine and church. This takes its name from the Italian town to which, according to tradition, the Holy House of Nazareth, scene of the Annunciation, was miraculously transported in the 13th century to save it from the infidel. This version of it was donated by a Czech noblewoman in 1626, subsequently enlarged and provided with its Baroque facade by the younger Dienzenhofer. The Loretto has a beautiful carillon from 1694, and a fabulous treasury of precious items whose crowning glory is the "Sun of Prague," a glittering monstrance set with 6,222 diamonds. Loretánské Náměstí, incidentally, offers the novel opportunity to have your shoes repaired while you relax over refreshments at U Ševce Matouše (At the Cobblers).

A short distance to the south, you come to another religious foundation, the Strahov monastery, originating from the 12th century, rebuilt in the

16th to 18th centuries. It became known for its splendid collection of manuscripts and incunabula and so, fittingly, it is now in use as a Memorial to National Literature. From here there is a splendid walk along a promenade below Strahov, passing first through fruit trees and then woods in the parks below Petřín Tower. It offers unusual and glorious views over Prague, and from it you can descend from various points back through the Lesser Town to Charles Bridge or, farther on, to the Bridge of 1st May and the National Theater.

Nové Město (New Town)

Nové Město is, on the whole, where all the action is—most of the main museums, theaters, concert halls, hotels, commercial and office blocks, and the main shops. In the early 14th century a scattering of villages and hamlets existed in the countryside outside the walls of the Old Town. In the 1340s Charles IV founded the New Town that would weld them into a new district of his prospering and expanding city. Most of the grand plans died with him and what you see today is largely 19th and 20th century Prague, but dotted among it are not a few buildings, especially churches, that still echo that Golden Age.

Most of them have been built, restored, and rebuilt again, and the most striking impression imparted by Nové Město is the neo-Renaissance of the great buildings that went up at the end of the 19th and early 20th centuries. One such building is the National Museum dominating the scene from the top of sloping Václavské Náměstí (Wenceslas Square). This broad boulevard gets its name from the equestrian statue of that romantic and ill-fated ruler, who it is said will awake to lead his people again in their time of greatest need.

The area south of the National Museum is peppered with churches founded at the time of Charles IV, though much altered since. A place you should seek out is one of K. I. Dienzenhofer's most charming secular buildings, a summer residence called Villa Amerika (1712–1720) on Ke Karlovu street, now housing the Antonín Dvořák Museum. This is another pleasant setting for summer concerts.

Very near is another building with a quite different cultural association—the inn of U Kalicha on Na Bojišti street, on the site of the one-time haunt of writer Jaroslav Hašek and his immortal Good Soldier Švejk (Schweik). Various items commemorate this anti-hero, but you may find the place disappointing.

If you go west from here, you will come to Karlovo Náměstí (Charles Square), the former hub of Charles IV's New Town. There is a lovely Baroque arch (another of Dienzenhofer's creations), and one of the buildings has become known as Faust's house, due to a succession of owners who dabbled in the occult sciences. These included the English alchemist Edward Kelly, who lived here in the late 16th century. The oldest building on the square is the New Town Hall, on the north side, dating from 1367, rebuilt in 1561, and where the Hussite revolution began.

North of Charles Square, Jungmannova street will bring you to the little square of the same name. Here, the Church of Our Lady of the Snows has the highest nave and the largest altar of all Prague's churches, and was one of the first in which Hussite services were held.

You are now only a stone's throw from Václavské Náměstí, and just round the corner from Národní Street. If you turn left down the latter, you will come to the river and the neo-Renaissance splendors of the National Theater, magnificently restored over recent years. Performances here are usually booked up months ahead, but if you get the opportunity don't miss it—it will be a glittering experience. Adjoining it to form the three other sides of a piazza is a modern complex of buildings; the ugly mushroom-like structure houses an excellent, more intimate theater with some very advanced technical equipment, while the others contain restaurants and offices.

The island to the south is Slovanský Ostrov, Slavonic Island, with a park and another neo-Renaissance building still used for concerts and exhibitions.

Vysehrad and Other Sights

There are still a few major sights that do not fit so easily into a particular area slot. One of these is Vyšehrad where the story of Prague first began, a couple of miles upstream from the National Theater and the boundaries of the Old Town. It stands on the top of an almost sheer rock face rising from the river bank, through which a tunnel has been built to accommodate the road. The early Přemyslides had their royal seat here. Under Charles IV a new castle was built and fortifications to link it with the New Town. The castle was destroyed by the Hussites and little remains except quite extensive fortification walls. Among the later or restored buildings up here are the Church of SS. Peter and Paul and the 11th-century Rotunda of St. Martin, but, perhaps most important, is the old cemetery. This is the last resting place for some of Czechoslovakia's leading writers, musicians and artists, among them Smetana, Božena Němcová and Karel Čapek. To the east, next to the scenic subway station of Gottwaldova, is the striking Palace of Culture, opened in 1981, with concert halls and restaurants. A massive viaduct spans the valley carrying the main road and Metro.

On the opposite bank of the Vltava is the Prague 5 district where, on Mozartova street, you will find lovely, peaceful Bertramka, the villa in which Mozart stayed on his visits to Prague. It belonged then to the Dušek family and is now the Mozart Museum—a most evocative place where you can listen to his music as you wander through the rooms, restored as far as possible to their original form.

Further out in Prague 6 district are the delightful park and palace of Hvězda. This unusual star-shaped Renaissance building serves as a museum to the tragic Battle of White Mountain which took place in the vicinity.

Kafka's grave is in the Modern Jewish Cemetery out at Žižkov, reached by the Metro.

PRACTICAL INFORMATION FOR PRAGUE

TOURIST INFORMATION. *Čedok,* Na příkopě 18, Prague 1 and (for their Department of Accommodation Services) round the corner at Panská 5. *Pragotur,* U Obecního domu, Prague 1.

In addition to the offices of Čedok and Pragotur, there is the *Prague Information Service* at Na příkopě 20, Prague 1. Ask them for a copy of *This Month in Prague*—a misnomer as it is published infrequently, but things don't change too much and it lists all the hotels, restaurants, major sights, places of entertainment and sports facilities.

WHEN TO COME. A year-round city, Prague is loveliest in the spring, when its trees are blossoming and its parks and palaces resound with concerts and chamber music. The International Prague Spring Festival (May 12 to June 4) is the music lover's delight, attracting some of the world's outstanding soloists, ensembles and orchestras. Open-air concerts are a feature of summer too—a time when there are also good opportunities for water sports on the nearby lakes. There are plenty of cultural activities in winter.

GETTING AROUND PRAGUE. Tickets costing 1 Kč. are valid on all forms of the city's public transport system: metro (subway), trams and buses. Note that each piece of luggage also requires a ticket. From some subway stations you can get a day ticket for 8 Kčs. that is valid for unlimited use on all public transport.

By Subway. Prague's three modern subway lines are easy to use, well-designed, spotlessly clean and provide the simplest and fastest means of transport. Most new maps of Prague mark the routes. Tickets can be obtained from machines in the stations, and then should be canceled by another machine as you enter the route to the trains. Tickets have a 90-minute limit.

By Tram and Bus. Prior to boarding, buy your ticket (you would be well-advised to get several) available from news-stands, tobacco shops, some stores or hotels. Each ticket entitles you to one ride and must be punched or validated as you board—just watch how the other passengers do it.

By Taxi. Taxis are inexpensive, but can be difficult to get. They are best ordered from a hotel.

By Boat. Regular pleasure boat trips are of varying duration; the furthest is to Slapy Dam (37 km./23 miles).

Car Hire. This can be arranged through *Pragocar* at Ruzyně airport and Štěpánska 42, Prague 1; or through Čedok.

HOTELS. All hotels are classified as outlined in *Facts at Your Fingertips*. In most hotels which are 3-star or more, you can expect to find an exchange bureau, one or more bars, and hairdresser and barber services on or near the premises; all have restaurants unless otherwise stated, and a good proportion of rooms with bath or shower, again unless otherwise stated. Note the comment regarding the charge for baths in *Facts at Your Fingertips*. Though it is unwise to generalize, you may find that, as in many countries, some front-desk clerks lack charm; others will take great trouble to be helpful.

Prague's hotels get very full indeed and if, unwisely, you have not prebooked, go to Čedok's Department for Accommodation Services at Panská 5, Prague 1 who also have some private accommodations. Private as well as less expensive hotel accommodations are also handled by Pragotur, U Obecního domu, Prague 1, near the Powder Tower. Private accommodations are mostly on modern housing estates in the suburbs with easy access to the center by public transport; reservations must be for a minimum of three days.

Note that Deluxe listings are all 5-star hotels whose tariffs cover bed and breakfast only. In all other cases you get half board for your money.

Deluxe

Alcron, Štěpánska 40, Prague 1. Central, off Wenceslas Square, and an old favorite, with good restaurant. 150 rooms and suites. Interhotel.

Esplanade, Washingtonova 19, Prague 1. Central, elegant, facing park near National Museum. 65 rooms and suites; famous Est Bar nightclub. Interhotel.

Intercontinental, náměstí Curieových, Prague 1. One of the American chain; splendid position on bank of river in Old Town, and the most expensive. Over 400 rooms and suites, saunas, health club; ground-floor restaurant (M) and elegant top-floor Zlatá Praha restaurant (E) with superb view; also top-floor nightclub. Interhotel.

Jalta, Václavské náměsti 45, Prague 1. Very central, a bit shabby but comfortable; popular bar and restaurant. Nearly 90 rooms and suites; nightclub. Interhotel.

Expensive

Forum, Štětkova ul., Prague 4. Prague's latest high-rise, opened 1988 near ancient Vyšehrad castle. 531 rooms, saunas, pool, bowling alleys, minigolf, well-equipped gymnasium, nightclub, roulette. Interhotel.

Panorama, Milevská 7, Prague 4. 430 rooms and suites; folk-style wine cellar, nightclub, bar, pool, saunas, solarium, splendid views from upper floors. Near Vyšehrad Castle and subway station for quick access to center. Interhotel.

U Tří Pštrosů (Three Ostriches), Dražického náměstí 12, Prague 1. Magically located at Malá Strana end of Charles Bridge; 17th-century atmosphere and one of the most sought-after places in town. 18 rooms and suites.

Moderate

Europa, Václavské Náměstí 29, Prague 1. Very central, recently renovated *art nouveau* style. Over 100 rooms, some (I).

International, náměstí Družby 1, Prague 6. Not central, known to some as the Russian Ritz for its architectural pretensions. 375 rooms and suites; Interhotel. Prices (E) in high season.

Olympik, Invalidovna, Prague 8. Modern, but not central. Over 300 rooms; nightclub. Interhotel.

Paříž, U Obecního domu, Prague 7. Very central Old Town location near Powder Tower; tastefully renovated in *art nouveau* style. 86 rooms. Interhotel.

Parkhotel, Veletržní 20, Prague 7. Fairly new, but not central. Over 200 rooms; nightclub. Interhotel.

Splendid, Ovenecká 33, Prague 7. Quiet location near Strahov Stadium and Zoo. 45 rooms. Interhotel.

Zlatá Husa, Václavské náměstí 7, Prague 1. Very central, recently renovated. 87 rooms. Service erratic; popular disco. Prices (E) in high season. Interhotel.

Three botels anchored along the Vltava River are popular despite cramped quarters, all (M): **Amirál,** Hořejší, Prague 5; **Albatros,** Nábřeží L. Svobody, Prague 1; **Racek,** Dvorecká louky, Prague 4. All have discos, so choose your cabin carefully!

Inexpensive

Central, Rybná 8, Prague 1. Very central Old Town location. Over 100 rooms, Popular local rendezvous, could be noisy.

Centrum, Na poříčí 31, Prague 1. Fairly central. 60 rooms.

Olympik II-Garni, Invalidovna, Prague 8. Opposite Olympik. 275 rooms; guests use Olympik's restaurant. Interhotel.

RESTAURANTS. Prague has a very wide selection of eating places. Look out for some of the characteristic ones, usually with a folkloric decor and regional specialties; also *vinárny* (wine cellars), which may have full restaurant service or simply serve snacks, but often in a cosy atmosphere; and *pivnice* (beer taverns) mostly offering inexpensive plain food and excellent beer, sometimes their own brew, in a more earthly and usually crowded setting. Quite a few places close for part or all of the weekend, or on one or two evenings of the week, and in many, advance reservations are advisable, so check first. All establishments are officially graded 1st, 2nd, or 3rd-class (although a 2nd-class wine cellar is much classier—and more expensive—than a 2nd-class beer tavern). In summer, cafe tables are often placed outside, but many establishments are in cellars, down lanes or in courtyards, or behind barely recognizable doors. Persist and ask—the obscure ones are often the best finds. There has been a welcome increase in coffee houses and snack bars offering inexpensive refreshments. Watch restaurant checks for possible mistakes.

Staré Město (Old Town)

U Červeného kola (E), Anežka. Near entrance to Agnes Monastery.

Klášterní (E), Národni 8. Good wine restaurant in former Ursuline convent; emphasis on Czech home cooking.

Opera Grill (M), Divadelní 24. One of the most stylish small restaurants in town (antique Meissen candelabra), featuring Czech specialties.

Rotisserie (M), Mikulanská 6. Excellent kitchen, always crowded for lunch.

U Zlatého Hada (M), Karlova 18. Prague's first coffee house dating from the early 18th century. Ideal for snacks, coffee, resting (no hustle). Popular with students. Modern decor.

U Zlatého Jelena (M), Celetná 11. Magnificent restored wine vaults. Popular with the young set. Service can be offhand.

U Zlaté Konvice (M), Melantrichova 20. Unusual underground Gothic labyrinth with tables set among huge wine barrels. Cold food only.

Železné Dveře (M), Michalská. Popular, specializes in Moravian wines.

U Medvídků (I), Na Perštýně 7. South Bohemian and old Czech specialties in noisy, jolly atmosphere.

U Rudolfa II (I), Maislova 5. Very small, intimate, excellent food.

U Zlatého Tygra (I), Husova 17. A favorite with not-so-young beer connoisseurs; typical no-frills Prague pub.

Malá Strana (Lesser Town)

U Malířů (E), Maltézské náměstí 11. Picturesque wine tavern, popular with the artist set.

U Mecenáše (E), Malostranské nám. 10. Wine restaurant in medieval setting; elegant, especially in back room.

Valdštejnská Hospoda (M), Tomášska 16. Pleasant, restful atmosphere; next to Wallenstein Palace.

Lobkovická Vinárna (E), Vlašská 17. Wine restaurant with aristocratic origins. Specializes in fine Mělník wines.

Nebozízek (E), at the halfway station on the funicular to Petřín Tower. Splendid views.

U Bonaparta (I), Nerudova 29. 16th century, in lovely old part of town. Wine restaurant with relaxed Bohemian atmosphere.

U Sv. Tomáše (I), Letenská 12. Founded by Augustinian monks in the 14th century; serves super 12° dark ale in ancient-style rooms; plain honest food.

Hradčany (Castle Area)

U Labutí (E), Hradčanské nám. 11. Exclusive dining in tastefully remodeled stables.

U Zlaté Hrušky (E), Nový Svět 3. Restored to its 18th-century period style.

Espreso Kajetánka (M), Kajetanské zahrady. Just under the castle ramparts, gorgeous view.

U Černého Vola (M), Loretánské nám. 1.

U Lorety (M), Loretánské nám. 8. Next to Baroque church of same name with its carillon bells, an agreeable spot.

U Zlaté Uličky Grill Bar (M), U Daliborky 8. Snack-bar grill in castle grounds; erratic opening hours.

Vikárka (M), Vikářská 6. In Prague Castle.

Nové Město (New Town)

Čínská Restaurace (E), Vodičkova 19. Chinese decor and authentic recipes with emphasis on Canton and Szechwan regions. Good, but pricey.

Indická Restaurace (E), Štěpánská. Indian food is a rarity here, so you must pay the price, but the menu is good.

Slovanský Dům (M–I), Na příkopě 22. Several restaurants and bars serving Czech food and snacks; central, handy and usually elbow room.

U Fleků (M), Křemencova 11. Most famous of all Prague's beer taverns, brewing its own 13° caramel-dark beer. Several rooms include particularly good Knights Hall and gardens with evening entertainment. Convivial.

U Kalicha (M), na Bojišti 12, Prague. Associations with the Good Soldier Švejk (*Schweik*); disappointing.

U Pastýřky-koliba (M), Bělehradská 15. Folk-style decor and Slovak specialties, worth the two-tram stop trek from the center.

U Pinkasů (I), Jungmannovo náměstí 15. Good draught beer and goulash are the specialties here.

You can eat for very reasonable cost in the restaurants of the department stores. For a quick snack at rock-bottom prices, go to the **Koruna** self-service complex, very handy at the bottom of Václavské náměstí, near the corner with Na příkopě. It's stand-up eating, except in the bar where you can also get coffee; but the range covers everything from soup and hot dishes to salads and sticky pastries. Other central snack bars are **Blaník** and **Družba** on Wenceslas Square, and another next to the Alcron hotel. You can get good quick snacks at the **Moskva** in Na příkopě.

An all-night snack bar operates in **Slovanský Dům** restaurant.

Farther Afield

Chalupa (M), in Club Motel, ten km. (six miles) south of town. Farmhouse atmosphere and country cooking.

Maxmilianka Koliba (M), in small town of Roztoky north of city. Attractive decor, good food, worth the ride.

HISTORICAL MONUMENTS. Prague has been and is undergoing a massive program of restoration, resulting in the closure of some buildings to the public. It is always wise to check on the latest situation with Čedok or the Prague Information Service—the focus is currently on Staré Město (Old Town). Of the buildings that have been described in this chapter, the most common opening hours are 9 or 10 to 4 or 5, but times vary according to season, and some may close in winter. Admittance into the churches is free; elsewhere there is a small fee (usually around 3–5 Kčs.).

MUSEUMS. Prague's many museums contain noteworthy collections of every description. The following is a list of some of the most interesting ones.

Antonín Dvořák Museum, Ke Karlovu 20, Prague 2.

Bedřich Smetana Museum, Novotného lávka, Staré Město, Prague 1. Mainly musical scores and documents associated with this great composer. Tapes of his compositions are played, and there are fine views over the river to Hradčany from the museum windows.

Bertramka, Mozartova 169, Prague 5. The delightful villa in which Mozart stayed on his visits to Prague. Tapes of his music are played and concerts are sometimes held here.

History Exhibition, in the Lobkovic Palace, Jiřská Street, Prague Castle. Fine new collection covering the period from the Přemyslides to 1948.

Lenin Museum, Hybernská 7, Nové Město, Prague 1.

Military Historical Museum, Hradčanské nám. 2, Hradčany, Prague 1. Housed in part of the former Schwarzenberg Palace. Exhibits of European arms up to World War I. Medieval jousting tournaments staged here in summer.

Museum of Applied Arts, 17 Listopadu, Staré Město, Prague 1. There is also a huge glass collection.

Musical Instruments Museum, Lázeňská 2, Malá Strana, Prague 1. A charming collection.

National Museum, Václavské nám. 68, Nové Město, Prague 1. Specializes in prehistoric, historic, natural science, zoological and numismatic departments. Its mineralogical collection is world famous.

Strahov Library Museum of National Literature, Strahov Courtyard, Hradčany, Prague 1. Beautifully preserved ancient manuscripts and bibles exhibited in former monastery, but viewing of magnificent rooms restricted to prevent damage.

State Jewish Museum, Jáchymova 3, Staré Město, Prague 1. Spread over several buildings, has a large collection of temple furnishings. Specializes in the history and customs of the Jewish community in Bohemia and Moravia. Also a remarkable ancient cemetery. The Pinkas Synagogue is closed for restoration.

ART GALLERIES AND EXHIBITION HALLS. Prague has a traditional appreciation of the graphic arts. State galleries are often housed in beautiful palaces, and there are dozens of small galleries offering works for sale by contemporary Czechoslovak artists. Check the latest situation with the Prague Information Service.

Château Zbraslav, originally a Cistercian monastery, 12 km. (7½ miles) south of Prague. Collection of 19th- and 20th-century Czech sculpture.

Kinský Palace, Staroměstské nám. 12, Staré Město, Prague 1. Collection of graphic art.

The National Gallery has the following collections. **Convent of the Blessed Agnes,** Anežská ulice, Old Town. Restored 13th-century convent housing superb collection of 19th-century Czech art. **Šternberk Palace,** Hradčanské nám. 15, Hradčany, Prague 1. A splendid collection of European art including all the main schools and the works of such masters as Canaletto, Goya, Ribera, El Greco, the two Brueghels, Rubens, Dürer and most of the French Impressionists. Well worth it. **St. George's Monastery,** Castle precincts, Prague 1. Beautifully restored to house an outstanding collection of Old Bohemian art from the 13th century onwards. The first floor concentrates on Bohemian Baroque art from the early 17th to the late 18th centuries.

In addition, the National Gallery has exhibition halls in the **Royal Summer House (Belvedere)** (under restoration), Chotkovy sady; and in the **Wallenstein Riding School,** Valdštejnská 2, Malá Strana, all Prague 1.

Prague Castle Gallery, Hradčany, Prague 1. Situated on the northern side of the second courtyard.

OPERA, CONCERTS, THEATER. A monthly program of events is available from the Prague Information Service. Prague has a sophisticated musical and cultural tradition, but performances are usually booked up well ahead. Note that for the Czechs such occasions are for dressing up. The Prague Spring Music Festival from mid-May–early June is one of the great events on the European calendar. Čedok's office at Bilkova is the main ticket agency for foreigners, but there's a wider choice through Sluna, Pasáž Cerna Rúzě, off na Příkopě. Tickets are the cheapest from box offices.

Opera and Ballet. Opera especially is outstanding. Opera and ballet performances are held at the three following theaters: the *National Theater* at Narodní 2, has reopened after major restoration of this magnificently decorated 19th-century building, while the adjoining ultramodern building linked to it houses a second, more intimate stage—this is now one of the grand theaters of Europe. The *Smetana Theater,* Vitězného února 8, is another splendid restoration job. The historic *Tyl Theater,* Železná 11, is currently closed for renovation.

Theater. One place where you won't need to know the language is *Divadlo na Zábradli* (Theater on the Balustrade), Anenské nám. 5. This is the home of the famous Black Theater when it is (rather rarely) in Prague; it is very difficult to get tickets, but if you're lucky you will find this skillful and imaginative company an unforgettable experience. This theater is also the venue for the very talented mime Fialka. Finally here, too, you can see performances of the famous chanson singer Hegerová. *Laterna Magika* (Magic Lantern), Národní 40. Very popular with foreign visitors, this is an extravaganza combining live actors, mime and very advanced cine techniques; also performances at the **Palace of Culture** (see below).

Concerts. These are held at the *House of Artists,* Dvořák Hall, Krasnoarmějců nám. and *Smetana Hall* (not to be confused with the Smetana Theater), nám. Republiky 5, an extravaganza of turn-of-the-century design. The new *Palace of Culture* (Metro Gottwalda—two stops from Muzeum) seats about 2,000 comfortably in the large hall. Good inexpensive restaurant with a fine view. The Czech Philharmonic is first rate, as is the Smetana Quartet. There are literally dozens of talented ensembles and performers, and you can hardly go wrong. Sunday afternoon music sessions are held in a hall of the *National Museum,* where one sits on steps of the grand staircase, and in the rooms of the *National Gallery,* thereby making the experience a visual treat as well. *Bertramka,* Mozartova 169, the lovely villa where Mozart used to stay, is a lovely setting for the music of Mozart and his contemporaries. Not to be missed are the marvelous organ recitals in the magnificently appropriate settings of *St. James'* (Old Town), *U Křížovníků* (near Charles Bridge) and *St. Nicholas* (Lesser Town). Military bands are very popular and there are rousing open-air concerts including on the terraces of the *Castle Gardens* in summer.

Puppet shows. These are brought to a high art form at the *Špejbl and Hurvínek Theater,* Římská 45, which provides a unique opportunity to observe the actual skills of puppet manipulation on stage. Note also the *Jiří Wolker Theater,* Dlouhá třída. The *Central Puppet Theater* performs at Loutka, nám. M. Gorkého 28.

NIGHTLIFE. Western-style nightlife is not one of Prague's specialties, but there are a number of bars with dancing, of which some also have cabaret: *Night Club,* Intercontinental Hotel; *Est Bar,* Hotel Esplanade; *Jalta Club,* Hotel Jalta; *Embassy,* Hotel Ambassador; *Park-Club,* Hotel Park; *Gruzia,* Na příkopě 29; *Lucerna,* Štěpánská 61. All (E). The best are *Varieté Praha,* an entertainment center with a more moderate nightclub, and the *Alhambra,* recently renovated, with a three-part floor show with dancers, clowns and mime outfits plus a movie presentation. *The International Hotel* puts on special programs, especially in the season. There are several discos nowadays, including on the three botels *Amirál, Albatros* and *Racek.* The best known and the most crowded is at the *Zlata Husa* hotel.

SHOPPING. *Tuzex,* the government chain, has a network of shops throughout the country where you can purchase quality goods of foreign and local production for Tuzex vouchers or directly in exchange for hard currency. Prices can be advantageous.

For the latest information on Tuzex outlets try Rytířská 11, Prague 1.

The following are addresses of some of the best local currency shops specializing in various wares. **Antiques:** Václavské nám. 60, Prague 1; Uhelný trh 6, Prague 1; Nerudova, Prague 2.

Jewelry: Na příkopě 12, Prague 1; Staroměstské nám. 6, Prague 1.

Glass and porcelain: Malé nám. 6, Prague 1 (modern Bor glass); Pařížská 2, Prague 1 (traditional Bohemian glass); Na Kampě, under Charles Bridge, Prague 1 (traditional pottery); Keramo, Melantrichova, Prague 1 (traditional pottery).

Objets d'art, paintings, prints: Dílo shops at 28 Října 6, Prague 1, Vodičkova 32, Prague 2 and Bruselská 5, Prague 4; Mánes, Gottwaldovo nábř. 250, Prague 1; Výtvarná řemesla, Křižovnické nám. 2, Prague 1.

Folk art: Krásná jizba—ULUV, Národní tř. 36, Prague 1; UVA, Na příkopě 25, Prague 1; Česká jizba, Karlova 12, Prague 1; Slovenská jizba, Václavské nám. 40, Prague 1; Umělecká Řemesla, Rytířská 12, Prague 1.

For inexpensive shopping and general interest, try *department stores* such as Bílá Labuť, Na poříčí 23; Družba, Václavské nám. 21; Kotva, nám. Republiky 8—all Prague 1.

SIGHTSEEING. A good choice of guided bus tours is arranged regularly by Čedok, with English-speaking guides provided. There are city sightseeing tours by day and by night, and trips out into the surrounding countryside, ranging from wine-tasting in Mělník to various one-day tours of different parts of Bohemia. Longer arrangements include a five-day itinerary in Bohemia and a 12-day Grand Tour of Czechoslovakia. A wide range of special interest tours is available for groups.

USEFUL ADDRESSES (see also Tourist Information, page 115). **Embassies.** *British,* Malá Strana, Thunovská 14; *American,* Malá Strana, Tržiště 15; *Canadian,* Mickiewiczova 6.

Travel Organizations. *Balnea* (for spas in Bohemia and Moravia), Pařížská 11, Prague 1. *Youth Travel Bureau (CKM),* Žitná 12, Prague 2 and Jindřišska 28, Prague 1. *Autoturist* (information), Ječna 40, Prague 2; (assistance), Limuzská, Malešice, Prague 10. *Rekrea* (Cooperative Travel Office for Bohemia and Moravia), Revoluční 13, Prague.

Transport. *ČSA* (Československé Aerolinie), Nové Město, Kotva Building, Revoluční 4 (tickets); Vltava Building, Revoluční 25 (terminal). *British Airways,* Nové Město, Štěpánská 63. *Railways,* Main Rail Station at Hlavni nádraží, near Wenceslas Square. *Buses,* Central Bus Station at Na Florenci, near the main rail station. All in Prague.

Emergency telephone 154 (motorists); 155 (first aid); 158 (police). Catering especially for foreigners, for payment in hard currency only, is Fakultní poliklinika, Karlovo náměstí 32, Prague 2, with English-speaking doctors on call from 8 A.M. to 4 P.M. There is an all-night drug store at Na příkopě 7, Prague 1.

BOHEMIA

A Stormy Heart

Bohemia should be approached with caution. So many rulers and noble families of greater or lesser stature have built so many castles, palaces, and churches, that there is a grave risk of seeing too much and remembering very little at all. In the following pages a selection of the more important and attractive sites has been made, to which you can add your own discoveries according to the time available.

Broadly speaking, you head north or northeast of Prague for the grandest scenery, and south or southwest for the historic-cultural sights. Naturally, this is a very general guideline and, in fact, you can be sure of a good deal of history and a lot of fine scenery whichever way you go. Since many places can be visited on half- or full-day trips out of Prague, we shall deal first with the highlights of central Bohemia.

Central Bohemia

Starting in the south we come to the first of many castles encircling the capital: Zbraslav, less than 12 km. (over seven miles) away. It was founded by Václav II as a Cistercian monastery and burial place for the Czech kings, but what you see now is an 18th-century château, which now houses the National Gallery's excellent collection of modern Czech sculpture. There are valuable paintings by Škréta and Brandl in the adjoining St. James Church.

One of the most pleasant areas within easy reach of Prague combines natural beauty and human technology. A series of dams has been built on the Vltava river, trapping its waters into a chain of sinuous lakes between wooded hills, thus forming a marvelous recreation area, notably round the leisure center of Nová Rabyně. No waterskiing or motor boats are allowed, but the waters become alive with sailing boats, windsurfers, canoes and kayaks, and there are any number of pleasant walks in the surrounding woods. You can reach this area either by road or, in summer, by boat from Prague.

The best-known castle south of the city is that of Konopiště, originally built in the 13th century, but rebuilt and restored many times. This was (literally) the happy hunting ground of Archduke Ferdinand (his assassination in Sarajevo, Yugoslavia, in 1914 sparked off World War I), whose somewhat overdeveloped passion for bloodsports claimed 300,000 victims. In the Weapons Hall you'll find one of the best collections of arms from the 16th to 18th centuries in Europe.

The castle of Český Šternberk to the east was also founded in the 13th century and much restored. It has a particularly striking location on a promontory overlooking the Sázava Valley, and you can pass it on the way to the next major destination, which is also one of the most important of all near Prague and to its southeast: Kutná Hora.

The fame of the town dates back to the 13th century when silver deposits were found here, transforming the little village into a royal town almost overnight. A Royal Mint was established to make the Prague groschen, which became the medieval counterpart to the British pound sterling of the 19th century. The coin was designed and struck by Florentine craftsmen invited to Kutná Hora, where the mint built especially for them is still known as Vlašský dvůr, the Italian Court. The town's prosperity reached its peak during the 14th to 15th centuries.

The town has a lovely main square and many attractive Baroque houses with Gothic details, but the two main sights are Vlašský dvůr itself and St. Barbara's Cathedral. Vlašský dvůr has a superb main hall with painted ceiling, a coin museum (in which in summer you can watch small silvery 'groschen' being struck and buy replicas), and some exquisitely carved wooden triptychs in the chapel. St. Barbara's is a lovely Cathedral in late Gothic style, built by the lords of Kutná Hora to rival St. Vitus Cathedral in Prague. Many interesting details include the 15th-century frescoes in the Smíšek chapel, featuring the Queen of Sheba and the Crucifixion; the statue of a miner in apron and smock, from about 1700, in the nave; and the Mintners' Chapel, with 15th-century frescoes showing the mintners at work.

East of Prague, Poděbrady is one of Bohemia's leading spas, with plenty of sports and cultural activities; it was also the birthplace of Jiří (George) of Poděbrady, in 1420, the Hussite king of Bohemia. Almost due north of the capital, Mělník is well worth visiting for the splendid castle standing high above the confluence of the rivers Vltava and Labe (Elbe), and the vineyards which clothe the slopes for miles around. From here comes the famous Ludmila white wine, named after the mother-in-law of King Wenceslas' mother (who, incidentally, had her murdered). The castle has some very good Renaissance and Baroque sections, and houses a wine restaurant.

Southwest of here, Veltrusy castle is particularly notable for its beautifully landscaped park and, nearby, the rather austere Renaissance Nelahozeves castle broods over the village of the same name. The house of its most famous son—Antonín Dvořák—is now a museum; but more important is the splendid collection of the Dvořák Museum at Zlonice, about 15 km. away—don't miss it.

A few miles northwest of Prague is the village of Lidice, where one of the great abominations of World War II was perpetrated on June 9th 1942. Following the assassination of Reinhard Heydrich, the ruthless Nazi Protector of Bohemia and Moravia, Lidice was selected for reprisals. The village was razed to the ground, its population executed or deported, mostly to die in concentration camps. A new village has been built, but old Lidice remains as a poignant memorial, now garnished with rose bushes sent from all over the world.

About an hour's drive west of Prague is the Castle of Křivoklát, a favorite hunting ground of Czech rulers from time immemorial. The present building dates from the end of the 15th century, with 19th-century alterations; but the castle's great feature is its wonderful woodland setting. From here you can drive via the Berounka river valley to Koněprusy, and the largest underground Karst grottoes in Bohemia. They are really only of interest to cave enthusiasts and rather difficult to find (look out for signs marked *"jeskyně"* meaning caves), but their situation is attractive and they were certainly inhabited in prehistoric times. In the 15th century, they also provided a hidey-hole for forgers of counterfeit Hussite money.

Following the Berounka river, you reach the castle of Karlštejn, an impressive pile perched high above the valley. It was built by Charles IV (restored in the 19th century) as a magnificent repository for his crown jewels and the holy relics of which he was such an avid collector. Alas, the crown jewels are no longer there and the stunning Chapel of the Holy Cross in which they were once kept has been closed indefinitely because of pollution from sightseeing hordes and sheer wanton damage caused by some visitors. It has now been restored so should it reopen, don't miss it. Its 128 Gothic panel and wall paintings by Master Theodorik, and walls encrusted with over 2,000 gems, make it a visual feast.

Southern Bohemia

This is the right direction to head for charming old towns, Hussite history, and gentle, lake-strewn, wooded countryside, gradually rising to the substantial heights of the Šumava mountains along the West German border.

Tábor, 88 km. (55 miles) south of Prague, is the first place to go, founded by the Hussites in 1420, near the castle of Kozí Hrádek where their leader had spent the last years of his life. Its founders were convinced that the Czech nation was chosen by God to destroy the temporal power of the church and state, and usher in a New Jerusalem. The people called themselves Táborites after their town, and adopted a patriarchal constitution.

Tábor is a very different town today, but the old part is well worth seeing, with its twisting streets built to prevent the enemy gaining easy access to the center. On Žižka Square is the Táborite church and the Town Hall from 1520 containing a museum to Hussitism. Note the invention of one of its greatest leaders, Jan Žižka—an armored wagon, forerunner of the modern tank. Beneath the museum is a labyrinth of tunnels and cellars used by the Táborites as both living quarters and as links with the outer defenses of the town.

South Bohemia is strewn with old towns and villages of which part or all have been declared urban reservations because of their architectural value. Some restoration work has been done, much more is still to be done, but the basic shapes and structures are there, evidence of a prosperity that began to burgeon in that distant golden era of Charles IV, and sometimes even earlier. In most cases, their focal point is the main square, usually bounded by arcaded houses that show an infinity of variations on Gothic, Renaissance and Baroque themes. One such town is Jindřichův Hradec, which also has a landmark of a castle terraced above the Nežárka river on one side and reflected in a lake on the other. About 15 km. (nine miles) away, the deep pink Renaissance castle of Červená Lhota is another South Bohemian gem.

About halfway between here and the South Bohemian capital of České Budějovice is the small town of Třeboň, another architectural jewel still partially surrounded by 16th-century walls. Třeboň has a severe castle with an interesting museum, and is also a spa, but above all it is the heart of pond and fish country. There are literally hundreds of ponds in South Bohemia, created by aristocratic and ecclesiastic landlords in the 14th to 16th centuries, partly to drain the land and partly to provide fish farms for breeding the highly-prized carp, which is a major delicacy of Czech gastronomy. The Rožmberk family peppered the countryside with both castles and ponds, many of which qualify as lakes and the largest of which bears their name just north of Třeboň.

The main sight of České Budějovice is the massive main Žižka Square (you will find there are an awful lot of Žižka Squares in this South Bohemian Hussite country), said to be one of the largest in Europe and certainly one of the most handsome, with arcades all the way round and a fine Baroque fountain with a statue of Samson in the middle; this was once the town's only water supply. A few miles to the north, Hluboká is an attractive little place in more pond country with a castle that may look curiously familiar; it is in fact a mini replica of Windsor Castle. The adjacent riding academy houses the Mikuláš Aleš South Bohemian Gallery, featuring a fine collection of Gothic art.

České Budějovice is on the Vltava river, and we strongly recommend you follow this capricious waterway upstream, first due south then pursuing a twisting curve to the northwest to its birthplace in the Šumava mountains on the border with West Germany. On the way you will come to Český Krumlov, once the main seat of the Rožmberks and one of the most delectable old towns of all—or it will be once the current massive program of much-needed restoration is completed. The setting is enchanting with the Vltava snaking through the town, which is stacked steeply on either side of it. Flights of steps link various levels and twisting narrow lanes converge on the arcaded Old Town Square. Inevitably there is yet another Rožmberk castle, well worth visiting for its collections, its 18th-century theater (one of the oldest in Europe) and the adjoining Masquerade Hall with extraordinary life-like murals. The town also has an open-air theater with revolving auditorium.

South of Český Krumlov, the Vltava scurries along between steep wooded hills. Soon after the small town of Rožmberk (and, you've guessed it, another castle), the valley sharply changes direction and before long you come to a great dam behind which the trapped river has swollen into the twisting elongated lake of Lipno. This, too, has become a popular recreation area and, though it suffers from a shortage of good hotels, it is peppered with campsites, many with chalets to rent. There are good water-sports facilities, too, including waterskiing and windsurfing, and the surroundings offer good walking.

From here a recommended route back to Prague is via Prachatice, once on the Golden Trail along which salt was brought from the Bavarian mines to Bohemia as early as the 9th century. It's a beautiful old town, its main square partly arcaded and lined with fine Gothic or Renaissance buildings, some of their facades lavishly decorated with scenes from medieval times or the Hussite wars. Husinec, a pretty village five km. (three miles) to the north, was the birthplace of John Huss; the house is now a museum. Further north still is Písek whose seven-arched stone bridge over the Otava river is even older than Charles Bridge in Prague and is similarly adorned with statues from the 18th century. An interesting event each June in this area is the Schweik Walk, which follows the route taken by that unwilling Good Soldier whose admirers now come from far and wide to participate in it. Zvíkov Castle stands a few miles to the north of Písek above the confluence of the Otava and Vltava rivers, now swollen to lake-size proportions by the dams downstream. From here northwards, these man-made lakes stretch almost continuously to within a few miles of Prague. Orlík Castle is magnificently placed beside them.

If you are not in a hurry to return to Prague from Prachatice, we strongly advise a wander west into the Šumava area described in the next section.

Liquid Assets

As a region, West Bohemia has a lot of particularly "liquid" assets; notably the mineral springs that feed some of the world's oldest and best-known spas, and the beer which flows from the breweries of Plzeň (Pilsen) to the furthest corners of the earth.

The story goes that around 1347, Charles IV stumbled by chance upon the spring of Vřídlo during a hunting expedition; or rather his dog did for, as the harried stag turned suddenly in a last-ditch stand, the poor hound fell into boiling water and was scalded. Charles investigated the matter and, familiar with health cures in Italy, ordered baths to be established here in the village of Vary. Thus was Karlovy Vary (Karlsbad) born. It reached its heyday during the 19th century when kings, princes, and dukes came from all over Europe and, in their wake, the fashionable sets of the day. The colonnades, baths, pensions, sanatoria, and luxurious hotels date from this period, though new ones of course have been built.

The colonnades, punctuated by the health-giving springs, follow the curve of the little Teplá river through the resort beneath the wooded hills. This is the place to stroll, sip the waters in traditional-shaped cups, nibble rich Karlovy Vary wafers *(oplatky)* and, finally, sample the water from the "13th spring", a liqueur called Becherovka made from Karlovy Vary water and herbs.

Both Karlovy Vary and Mariánské Lázně (Marienbad) have a cultural life to entertain everyone, and they have the two best golf courses in the country, as well as excellent opportunities for pleasant walks. Mariánské Lázně is younger, and its waters have quite different and more varied properties than those of Karlovy Vary. It is also more spacious, though smaller, with its lovely parks and homogeneous architecture. Indeed this was the spa much favored by Britain's Edward VII but, from all accounts, he did not waste too much time on strict diets or rigorous treatment.

The third well-known spa in West Bohemia is Františkovy Lázně (Franzensbad), five km. (three miles) from which is the SOOS Nature Reserve, an extraordinary area of marshland, moor, volcanic mud and thermal springs, providing a haven for rare flora and birds. But the place that really revolutionized medical science is Jáchymov, north of Karlovy Vary. This originally made its living from mining silver ore and here were struck the famous Maria Theresa "thalers," from which the American dollar derives its name. The silver was exhausted, and the town might have died, if the Austrian government of that time had not sent to a certain M. and Mme. Curie two railway cars of local pitchblende (uranium ore) to help in their research. From this, in 1898, they isolated two new miracle elements. One they named polonium after Mme. Curie's native Poland; the other they called radium. The mining of uranium ore for the production of radium was started in 1908. The mining of the ore for the uranium itself was a post-World War II development.

All roads from the west lead through Plzeň, with some dignified architecture from Gothic and later times in and near the main Republic Square. There is good beer in the restaurant beside the brewery.

To the southeast and south of Plzeň lies the rather lesser-known (to Western visitors) area of Šumava on the border with West Germany, a lovely region of wooded mountains, gorgeous little towns, and a folklore of its own. Part of it is the region of the Chods, for centuries traditionally the guardians of Bohemia's frontiers for which they were granted special privileges. Domažlice is the main town of the area and very charming it is, too, (though lacking good hotels) with some original fortifications and a lovely arcaded square. The castle houses a Chod Museum, and there is another one, Kozinův Statek, in a restored manor at Újezd, five km. (three miles) to the west. Chod folklore is particularly interesting and very much alive, the dancing especially contagious with its accompaniment of the local version of Scottish bagpipes. Pottery, painting, embroidery, painted Easter eggs, and distinctive local costumes are other Chod specialties.

Chod culture is limited to the Domažlice area, but the Šumava mountains (highest point Boubín, 1,362 meters/4,467 ft.) follow the frontier more or less from here southeast to Lipno, described earlier. A network of narrow but well-surfaced roads burrow along the upper reaches of rivers such as the Otava and Vltava, with plenty of campsites along the way. One of the best-known resorts is Železná Ruda, right on the border, but there is a number of pleasant hotels dotted about the wooded heights, such as at Srní and Zadov, offering skiing facilities in winter and good walking in summer. Some of the towns are attractive too, such as Sušice on the Otava, and villages like Kvilda on the Vltava.

Charming and Rural

The most spectacular scenery in all Bohemia is undoubtedly in the northeast, in the Krkonoše (Giant Mountains) bordering Poland. Not only is the scenery beautiful, but the local architecture is refreshingly rural, the steep-roofed timber houses painted in warm colors that look just right against sunlit pinewoods or snowy pastures. Excellent winter and summer maps of the area can be bought locally, marking ski or walking trails.

A town to note for a refreshment stop on the way to this fine region is Jičín, which has a lovely arcaded square and remains of medieval fortifications. It's traditionally associated with Rumcajs, a kind of 17th-century Robin Hood, around whom many a tale is woven. The Giant Mountains were known long before the days of vacationing. Through its mountain passes the Protestant exiles fled across the frontier to escape persecution. To assist the fugitives on their way, a "bouda" or wooden hut was built in Bílá Louka (the White Meadow) in 1620. In memory many hostels and hotels are called "bouda" today.

The principal resorts are Harrachov (fast developing with many new recreation facilities), Pec pod Sněžkou, Jánské Lázně (another spa) and Špindlerův Mlýn, this last being the most sophisticated in its accommodations and facilities. It is attractively placed astride the rippling river Labe (Elbe), here in its early formative stages. A good trip is to take a bus from Špindlerův Mlýn via Jánské Lázně to Pec pod Sněžkou, there embark on the two-stage chair lift to the top of Sněžka (highest at 1,611 meters (5,290 ft.) and right on the Polish border), then walk the 11 km. (seven miles) down, eventually through deep, silent pinewoods, to Špindlerův Mlýn again.

The source of the Labe also springs from the heights near the Polish border. From Harrachov, walkers can reach it by a marked trail (about ten km./six miles); from Špindlerův Mlýn you can get within two km. (over a mile) by road.

Vrchlabí is a quaint town of leaning old wooden houses. Of the other towns in East Bohemia, little Nové Město nad Metují is one of the most remarkable Renaissance monuments in Central Europe with its one arcaded square and its exquisite Renaissance castle. Litomyšl in the foothills of the Bohemian-Moravian highlands is another worthy little place, its main square considered to be one of the most beautiful in the country. It has, of course, a castle and, close to it, a Baroque brewery notable for being the birthplace of Bedřich Smetana in 1824. East Bohemia's capital is Hradec Králové, which combines old and new architecture rather well. Its red brick Cathedral of the Holy Ghost on the main square (where most of the historic monuments are) is early Gothic.

Traveling west from the Giant Mountains you come to the Lusation range (Lužické Hory). To the south of them lies the heart of Bohemia's famous glass-making industry. Its most important center is Nový Bor, whose crystal tableware, painted glass and chandeliers have graced the halls of Europe's greatest crowns and princes. Other major centers are Železný Brod (cut and engraved glass) and Jablonec (glass jewelry). All have museums.

Two areas of unusual natural interest are the Bohemian Paradise (Český Raj, main town Turnov) and Bohemian Switzerland (Děčínské Stěny, best visited from Děčín). Both are remarkable for their ravines and strangely eroded rock formations of Cretaceous sandstone. These areas—and especially the latter—are really walking and scrambling country, but those less energetic may take boat trips through some of the gorges of the Kamenice river from Hřensko in Bohemian Switzerland, right on the East German border.

Two other places should be mentioned for very different reasons. One is Teplice, Czechoslovakia's oldest spa, near the East German border. The other is Litoměřice, a beautiful old town on the Labe (Elbe) river whose art gallery makes a special feature of naïve paintings. Near here is Terezín where the Nazi concentration camp of Teresienstadt is now left as a poignant memorial to the countless numbers who did not survive its horrors. It is yet another reminder of how Bohemia has paid the price for being the stormy heart of Europe.

PRACTICAL INFORMATION FOR BOHEMIA

TOURIST INFORMATION. Most towns and resorts have a Čedok office. The principal ones for the region are as follows: **České Budějovice,** Hroznova 21; **Česky Krumlov,** Gottwaldov náměstí; **Domažlice,** náměstí Míru 129; **Hradec Králové,** Leninova třída 63; **Karlovy Vary,** Tržiště 23; **Kladno,** nám. Revoluce 4/5; **Liberec,** Revoluční 66; **Mariánské Lázně,** Odborářů 48; **Mladá Boleslav,** třída Lidových milicí; **Plzeň,** Prešovská 10; **Tábor,** Tř. 9 května 1282; **Trutnov,** Gottwaldovo nám. 120/21; **Ústi nad Labem,** Hrnčířská 9/3; **Vrchlabí,** Leninova 148.

WHEN TO COME. Spring (especially lovely for fruit blossom), summer and early fall are all good times for touring and sightseeing. January through March is the season for the Giant Mountains (Krkonoše) resorts. Note that some monuments, especially castles, close in winter. Spa treatment is available year round.

GETTING AROUND BOHEMIA. Čedok have various tours. Touring by car gives the greatest freedom. Rail and bus connections between them cover the region and are inexpensive, if you can sort out the timetables.

HOTELS AND RESTAURANTS. Please note the comments regarding classification in *Facts at Your Fingertips.* Those listed have a restaurant and all or a good proportion of rooms with bath or shower unless otherwise stated.

České Budějovice. *Gomel* (E), 180 rooms, nightclub. A short walk from main square. Interhotel. *Zvon* (E), 50 rooms, some (I). *Slunce* (I), 30 rooms, very few private baths. Old fashioned but friendly. Interhotel.

Český Krumlov. (M), 33 rooms, some (I); historic building on lovely square in heart of Old Town. Interhotel. *Růže* (M), 16 rooms, some (I), and due for expansion; in attractively restored old building in Old Town. No restaurant, but evening snack bar. *Vyšehrad* (I), 48 rooms; on edge of Old Town with fine views.

Domažlice. *Chodský Hotel* (I), 20 rooms. *Družba* (I), 44 rooms, short walk from main square.

Františkovy Lázně. *Bajkal* (M), 46 rooms. *Slovan* (M), 23 rooms. Built in 1870, recently modernized. Interhotel.

Harrachov. *Hubertus* (M), 17 rooms (some I); near resort center. Interhotel. *Junior* (M), 71 rooms, disco, pool; accommodations available if not fully booked by youth groups in this modern CKM sports center above resort, near new ski lift.

Hluboká. *Parkhotel* (I), 50 rooms. Lake-side situation. Interhotel.

Hradec Králové. *Černigov* (E), 230 rooms. Interhotel. *Alessandria* (M), 97 rooms. Interhotel. *Bystrica* (M), 87 rooms, some (I).

Jablonec. *Corso* (I), 37 rooms, some (M). *Praha* (I), 17 rooms. *Zlatý Lev* (I), 15 rooms, a few (M).

Jánské Lázně. *Horský Hotel* (M), 45 rooms, a few with bath. Interhotel. *Praha* (I), 19 rooms without bath. Interhotel.

Jičín. Restaurant. *U Rumcajse* (I), tavern style, two km. (over a mile) out on the Liberec road.

Jindřichův Hradec. *Grand* (I), 26 rooms without bath. *Vajgar* (I), 30 rooms, a few with shower, no restaurant.

Karlovy Vary. *Grand Hotel Moskva* (L), 170 rooms, some (M), several restaurants and taverns, nightclub, sports facilities. Patronized by glittering list of the famous, and features splendid early 18th-century hall, Slavnostní sál. Interhotel. *Parkhotel* (E), 110 rooms, some (M). Two restaurants including oriental; nightclub. Interhotel. *Motel* (E), on outskirts of spa. Interhotel. *Adria* (M), 40 rooms. *Alice* (M), 186 beds. Modern hotel run by CKM. *Central* (M), 70 rooms. Renovated but with traditional atmosphere and excellent location. Interhotel.
Sevastopol-Horník (I), 85 rooms, a few (M). Interhotel.
The *Terminal Spa Sanatorium,* with 533 rooms, is very central, modern and extremely well equipped for those following treatment and their companions. Its fine open-air thermal pools are available to everyone.

Karlštejn. Restaurants. *U Elišky* (I). On main road below castle. Simple, good value. *U Karla IV* (I). More traditional style.

Konopiště. *Motel* (M), 40 rooms, attractive forest setting near castle, mini-golf, riding facilities. Interhotel. *Myslivna* (M), 30 rooms. In castle grounds.

Kutná Hora. *Mědínek* (M), 90 rooms, some (I).

Litomyšl. *Dalibor* (I), 68 rooms, new, on main road about half a mile from center. Interhotel.

Mariánské Lázně. *Golf* (L), 30 rooms, newly renovated, one of the best in the country, pool, sports facilities; excellent restaurant, by the golf course, a little out of town. Interhotel. *Palace Hotel Praha* (E), 45 rooms, some (M), plus annexes, nightclub. Elegant building dating from 1875. Interhotel.
Esplanade (M), 60 rooms, some (I), woodland setting about a mile from town. Interhotel. *Excelsior* (M), 70 rooms, good service, central. Traditional style, renovated. Interhotel. *Krakonoš* (M), 57 rooms. Manor-style hotel run by CKM.
Corso (I), 28 rooms, some (M), central. Interhotel. *Cristal* (I), 93 rooms, a few (M), central. Interhotel.

Mělník. *Ludmila* (M), 70 rooms. Restaurant in the castle.

Nové Město Nad Metují *Metuj* (I), 50 rooms without bath.

Nový Bor. *Grand* (I), 35 rooms without bath.

Pardubice. *Labe* (E), 210 rooms, new, near main street. Interhotel.

Pec Pod Sněžkou. *Horizont* (E), modern high-rise, 126 rooms, some (M), excellent facilities including wine tavern and Havana snack bar. Interhotel. *Kovárna* (M), restaurant and disco, attractive decor.

Písek. *Otava* (I), 37 rooms, some (M). Historic building with frescos. Interhotel.

Plzeň. *Ural* (E), 85 rooms. *Continental* (M), 50 rooms. Built in 1895, recently renovated, central. Interhotel. *Slovan* (I), 116 rooms, a few (M). Built in 1891, modernized. Interhotel.

Poděbrady. (M), 17 rooms, some (I). *Praha* (M), 16 rooms, some (I).

Prachatice. *Národní Dům* (I), 14 rooms, a few (M).
Restaurant. *Zlatá Stezka,* tavern style.

Slapy. *Nová Rabyně* (I), 50 rooms without bath. Good location by lake.

Špindlerův Mlýn *Montana* (E), 65 rooms, wine cellar and folk tavern, modern and on the outskirts of resort. Interhotel. *Savoy* (E), 53 rooms, including annexe, some (M); more traditional but renovated and in resort center. *Praha* (M), some (I) rooms, newly renovated. Interhotel. *Alpský* (M), 23 rooms, some (I). Traditional style in Sv. Petr above resort. Interhotel.

Labská Bouda (M), 57 rooms, some (I), very modern, is by the source of the Labe river in fine mountain setting some miles from resort. Interhotel.

Restaurants. *Krkonošká Chalupa* (M), folk style, next to Montana hotel; *Labužník* (M), nightclub next to Savoy Hotel; *Myslivna* (M), hunting chalet style on resort outskirts; *Budvarka* (I), near bridge, simple, good value.

Srní. *Šumava* (M), 33 rooms, some (I). Mountain setting.

Sušice. *Fialka* (I), 34 rooms, a few with shower. Recently renovated, on main square.

Tábor. *Palcát* (M), 68 rooms, the best; a short walk from main square. *Slavie* (M), recently renovated, opposite railway station.

Třeboň. *Svět* (I), 50 rooms, some with shower, on lake shore; sandy beach. Interhotel.

Vrchlabí. *Krakonoš* (I), 18 rooms, recently renovated.

Zadov. *Churáňov* (I), 50 rooms. Fine mountainside location.

Zelezná Ruda. *Javor* (M), 36 rooms. In resort center.

Zelezný Brod. *Cristal* (M), 45 rooms, some (I). Interhotel.

MORAVIA

Forests and Furnaces

Moravia is separated from Bohemia by the Bohemian–Moravian highlands, and from Slovakia by the Little and White Carpathian mountains. In the north is the industrial and coal-rich area that was once part of the historically much-disputed region of Silesia. Central Moravia is a series of valleys watered by the Morava River and its tributaries, opening into Austria in the south.

The Moravians will still energetically argue that temperamentally they are quite different from the Czechs of Bohemia. Indeed, within Moravia there are a number of quite distinct groups whose separate ethnic development is reflected in dialect, costume and folk culture. So it is perhaps not surprising that Czechoslovakia's most colorful annual folkloric event occurs on Moravian soil; at Strážnice, near the southeastern border with Slovakia.

Moravia produces most of the country's best wines, offers some very fine grottoes, lovely river valleys, and one or two mountain areas of note. It can also claim to be the earliest nucleus of the future Czechoslovak state.

South Moravia and the Approach to Brno

Brno is Czechoslovakia's third-largest city and the capital of Moravia. If you have been exploring South Bohemia your approach is fortuitously through one of Czechoslovakia's prettiest towns: Telč whose long rectangular square, almost surrounded by arcades, will be the delight of any architectural historian. On the lowest levels are beautifully-vaulted Gothic halls, then some Renaissance floors and, last but not least, Baroque gables, the whole complex gleaming in white and pastel tones. Overlooking the square, part of the original battlements adjoin a high watchtower from which trigger-happy photographers will be in their element snapping splendid perspectives of the arcaded square. At the other end is the impressive Gothic-Renaissance castle and its landscaped gardens. Baroque statuary is another feature of this astonishing little town. The surrounding countryside is lovely, too.

Eastwards towards Brno, Třebíč is a pleasant highland town with the Romanesque-Gothic Church of St. Procopius retaining its character and a lovely Gothic entrance despite later reconstructions. The town is especially known for its production of Christmas cribs.

An alternative route to Brno from Telč would be the more devious one south through Znojmo, on the threshold of the great Moravian wine-growing region. Despite its industrial appearance, Znojmo has retained sections of medieval ramparts, and a variety of monuments. The most important is the 11th-century rotunda of St. Catherine near the castle displaying a rare cycle of frescoes (restored) from which you can see what various members of the Přemyslide dynasty looked like, at least to a contemporary artist. While you are here, it is well worth following the upstream meanderings of the river Dyje. These will bring you to the artificial lake of Vranov, a popular holiday area overlooked by a very fine Baroque castle near its eastern end.

The whole vineyard area adjoining Znojmo echoes its long associations with the Liechtenstein family who started cultivating the grape almost as soon as they arrived here in medieval times. They also dotted the scene with castles. One of these, which they subsequently sold to the Dietrich-steins, is at Mikulov near the Austrian border and you should certainly seek it out. The castle, restyled in Baroque, houses a hotel, a wine restaurant, wine cellars, and a museum; remarkable is a wine cask made in 1643 with a capacity of over 22,000 gallons!

Valtice, to the southeast of Mikulov, has another Liechtenstein castle (now largely Baroque) with 365 windows, painted ceilings, and much exuberantly ornate woodwork. Between here and yet another Liechtenstein pile at Lednice to the northwest, this family of avid builders peppered the pleasant countryside with neo-Classical temples and follies in the 19th century. The grounds of Lednice even boast a minaret and, just by this very fine stately home, there are massive greenhouses full of exotic flora.

So man has moulded and made his marks on the countryside over the centuries, unaware and probably uncaring that very, very much longer ago his early ancestors had done just the same. Near Dolní Věstonice in the Pavlov hills, only a few miles from Mikulov, one of the most exciting excavation sites revealed, in 1950, traces of a settlement, graves, and a load of ivory and mammoth bones left by hunters over 20,000 years ago. Some of the first ceramics in the world were discovered here, too, among them a most curvaceous female figurine of ash and clay, which has become known as the Věstonice Venus. The original is at Brno, but you can see replicas of her and much else of archeological interest in the excellent museum at Dolní Věstonice.

Another feature of this region of South Moravia are the wine-producing villages, each with its nearby but separate community of privately owned *sklepy,* such as that of the village of Prušánsky. A *sklep* is a wine cellar in which each family matures and stores its own wine, and many of these little buildings are charmingly constructed and decorated with folk motifs. At weekends you are likely to find members of the family congregated here and often very willing to let you sample their wares—and perhaps even sell you a bottle or two.

If your approach to Brno is from East Bohemia, your route will take you right through the Bohemia-Moravian Highlands via Žďár, near the source of the Sázava river and a starting point for trips into the northern part of the Bohemian-Moravian Highlands. The castle at Žďár houses a particularly fine Book Museum, tracing the development of writing and printing from earliest times.

A somewhat circuitous route from Žďár would bring you most pleasantly down the lovely Svratka River, starting with Vír artificial lake, and proceeding via Pernštejn Castle and the old mining town of Tišnov. Pernštejn Castle, perched on a rocky headland above the Svratka River looks every inch the fortress it was, and is one of the best-preserved late medieval structures in Moravia. The residential palace within it, with a stunning late Gothic facade, is of particular interest.

Brno

No one would claim this industrial metropolis is Czechoslovakia's most beautiful city but, as visitors to its regular international trade fairs will know, there is more to it than initially meets the eye. Two of its sights, however, cannot fail to meet the eye very rapidly. One is Špilberk Castle sitting up on its hill and which was only finally subdued by Napoleon, after which it was turned from a fortress into a prison. Its dungeons and torture chambers are its macabre main sights, having witnessed horrors from the time of the Habsburgs to the Nazis, and it is a relief to escape to the pleasant restaurant and enjoy open-air refreshments-with-a-view in summer. The other hill-top sight is the Cathedral of Saints Peter and Paul on Petrov hill. Its Gothic look dates from the early 20th century and there is some good interior Baroque.

Around these two monuments is the old part of town. You can follow steps down from the cathedral to the market place (nám. 25 února), whose stalls are set up around the Baroque Parnassus Fountain.

The Dietrichstein Palace, now the Moravian Museum, is on one side of the square, its courts decorated with Renaissance arcades. The museum possesses a good art gallery and, in a separate building, exhibits of Moravian folk art and ceramics. The Old Town Hall in the same square is worth seeing for its exquisite Gothic stone portal. Both these buildings have recently been restored. Another, if macabre, "must" very close to the market place is the Capuchin Monastery in whose crypt and underground halls is displayed an impressive collection of mummified bodies of nobles and monks, preserved by air circulating through a system of vents and chimneys since the late 17th and 18th centuries. Of the original 200 bodies, 41 survive. The busy hub of Brno is Freedom Square (Naměstí Svobody), which has one or two fine Renaissance and Baroque buildings, one of which is the interesting Ethnographic Museum. A short distance away is one of the best Gothic buildings in Brno, the Church of St. James, with a splendidly austere simplicity and a tower 91 meters (300 ft.) high. If you prefer Baroque, the Jesuit Church of Jesuitská has some memorable statuary and restored paintings. After which you can refresh yourself in one of the cafes in the pleasant gardens off Rooseveltova street. On Malinovsky

Square, the modern Janáček Opera House is a tribute to that composer's close association with Brno. His *Sinfonietta* is dedicated to the city. Don't miss an opportunity to attend a concert here.

On the outskirts of the town, the Exhibition Grounds themselves have some eye-catching modern architecture and are open all the year.

Border Country

Only a few miles or so to the east of Brno lies the site of one of the great battlefields of European history: Slavkov, better known to us as Austerlitz, where the armies of Napoleon met and defeated the combined forces of Austrian Emperor Francis I and Russian Alexander I. If you happen to have Tolstoy's *War and Peace* handy, you will find no better account of it. Scattered about the wide rolling agricultural landscapes are a museum, a landscaped garden, and the memorial chapel of the impressive Cairn of Peace and, in the town of Slavkov itself, the Baroque château houses more memorabilia from the battle—well worth visiting.

Further east still you reach the Morava valley, with its many links with the days of the Great Moravian Empire of the 9th century. Remains from those and earlier days have been found on the outskirts of Uherské Hradiště and near Břeclav, but the most extensive are about five km. (three miles) from Mikulčice, a few miles south of Hodonín where remains (6th to 10th centuries) of defenses, a fortress, palace, 12 churches and many graves have been uncovered, some containing jewelry, weapons, coins and crucifixes. Because of the nature of the soil, in most cases only the outline of buildings is marked, but the more substantial remains of one of the churches and surrounding graves have been protected within a building, and attached to the site is a fine museum with many artefacts that have been uncovered during the excavations which will continue for many more years to come. The whole provides a well-planned natural archeological museum.

Northeast of Hodonín in this border country with Slovakia, known as Moravian Slovakia, you will find Strážnice, where the top annual folklore festival is held each summer. The Institute of Folk Art has its museum in Strážnice Castle, which was most recently reconstructed around 1850. Near the town is a growing open-air museum of dwellings and workshops.

If it's scenic tourism you want, however, you should head north from Brno up the Svitava valley and into the Moravský Kras. This Moravian Karst is an area of limestone formations, underground stalactite caves, rivers, and tunnels. The most interesting part is near Blansko and includes Kateřinská jeskyně (Catherine Cave), Punkevní jeskyně (Punkva Caves), and the celebrated Macocha abyss, the deepest drop (over 138 meters/400 ft.) of the Karst. Several of these caves can be visited, the most impressive probably being those of Punkva; in this case, the tour also brings you into the depths of the Macocha abyss and includes a boat trip along an underground river. There's an excellent small restaurant near the lip of the abyss, though this is some miles by road from the entrance to the Punkva caves themselves.

Northern Moravia

Industry and agriculture are two major themes of North Moravia. Here, near the northern border with Poland, lie the rich coalfields of former southern Silesia, which gave impetus to the major mining towns of Opava and Ostrava, Czechoslovakia's fourth-largest city. Historically Opava is particularly important as the one-time capital of Silesia.

To the southwest of them lies Olomouc. It sprawls in the middle of the great granary of the Haná Plain, only about an hour's drive northeast of Brno, a region of formerly rich farmers that has produced its own folklore. To get a better idea of this fertile countryside, however, you would do better to take a route via Kroměřiž still in South Moravia. Much of it was destroyed during the Thirty Years' War, but subsequent reconstruction—mainly Baroque—has left it with a main square splendidly bounded by patrician houses and a great palace, with an elegant English park and a splendid art collection.

Olomouc, despite its industry, retains its historic core from its days as the Moravian capital. The Town Hall has very attractive Renaissance features, although the present clock is modern. The best Gothic building is the Church of St. Maurice, whose colossal Baroque organ is said to have 2,311 pipes, should you not feel like counting them. The town is famous for its superb flower exhibitions, held annually.

You now have the choice of North Moravia's two main mountain ranges: the Hrubý Jeseník to the northwest and the Moravskoslezské Beskydy (Moravian-Silesian Beskydy) to the east. The former certainly offer tempting walking country, with plenty of marked trails, mountain chalets and inns, and a number of pleasant little spas. The Beskydy have a wilder, more primeval quality.

The composer Leoš Janáček was born in the village of Hukvaldy. Only a few miles away, Příbor produced its own famous son, Sigmund Freud, two years later in 1856. Štramberk is a charming little town of largely timbered houses. Much larger, Nový Jičín's arcaded square and mainly Renaissance and Baroque architecture are attractive.

The Beskydy Mountains and the neighboring Javorníky roughly form the boundaries of Valašsko (Wallachia). This is the domain of the wooden cottage and the wooden church, and the valleys and hills are dotted with them. Valašské Meziříčí is the main gateway. If you haven't time to go further, go at least to the open-air museum at nearby Rožnov pod Radhoštěm with its splendid collection of folk architecture and folk activities. In summer you can watch many traditional skills being practised by craftsmen in authentic surroundings. From here it's only a short drive to the hill resort of Pustevny for fine views of the Beskydy and attractive local-style accommodations and restaurant. If you have more time, follow the Bečva valley from which you can branch off for the village of Velké Karlovice on another branch of the Bečva and where there are good examples of Wallachian houses. You can rejoin the main road to cross the forested ridge of the Javorníky Mountains into Slovakia.

PRACTICAL INFORMATION FOR MORAVIA

TOURIST INFORMATION. Most towns and resorts have a Čedok office. The principal ones for the region are as follows: **Brno,** Divadelní 3; **Gottwaldov,** Kvítkova 80; **Olomouc,** nám. Míru 2; **Ostrava,** Dimitrovova 9.

WHEN TO COME. The seasons are the same as for Bohemia, though the early fall has the added advantages of vintage time in some of the country's best wine-producing regions, and is also the time for one of Brno's major international trade fairs.

GETTING AROUND MORAVIA. Čedok arrange sightseeing in and from Brno, and Moravia is included in more general tours of Czechoslovakia. Most people combine Moravia with Bohemia, and the same comments apply as for Bohemia.

HOTELS AND RESTAURANTS. Please note the comments regarding classification in *Facts at Your Fingertips*. Hotels listed below have a restaurant and all or a good proportion of rooms have bath or shower unless otherwise stated.

Brno. *Continental* (E), Leninova 20, a little away from center, 180 rooms, nightclub. Interhotel. *Grand* (E), Tř. 1 máje 18/20, 110 rooms, recently renovated, near railway station; several restaurants including Asian. Interhotel. *International* (E), Husova 16, 290 rooms, modern, central; Interhotel. *Voroněž* (E), Křížkovskeho 47, 380 rooms, congress hall, nightclub, pool, sauna, modern and adjacent to the exhibition grounds on outskirts of town; Interhotel. Next door is the modern *Voroněž 2* (E), 110 rooms, with new attractive Moravian-style restaurant and tavern. Interhotel.

Slovan (M), Lidická 23, 110 rooms, some (I), nightclub. Interhotel. *Metropol* (M), Dornychova 5, 53 rooms, some (M), near railway station, old fashioned; Interhotel.

Restaurants. *U Královny Elišky* (E), a restored ancient wine cellar in former cloister with fireplace grill; *Hradní Vinárna* (M), wine restaurant in Castle Špilberk, good atmosphere, folk band; *M Club* (M), small, pleasant with attractive wine cellar section, below Cathedral on way to market place; *Myslivna* (M), in outskirts, good views of city; *Motorest 9 křížů* (I), excellent value on main road 25 km. (16 miles) west of city.

Gottwaldov. *Moskva* (E), 235 rooms, modern, good amenities, central; Interhotel. *Družba* (M), 73 rooms, in the outskirts; Interhotel.

Restaurant. *Valašská koliba* (M), folk style, short stroll from Moskva hotel.

Hodonín. *Grand* (I), 26 rooms without bath.

Kroměříž. *Haná* (I), 60 rooms, some (M).

Mikulov. *Zámecká Vinárna* (I), 12 rooms without bath; part of castle.

Nový Jičin. *Praha* (M), 21 rooms, some (I).

Olomouc. *Flora* (M), 170 rooms, newest; Interhotel. *Národní Dům* (M), 65 rooms, some (I); traditional but renovated; Interhotel. *Palác* (M), 48 rooms, half (I); Interhotel.

Ostrava. *Imperial* (E), 130 rooms, some (M); restaurant features regional specialties; Interhotel. *Atom* (M), 57 rooms. *Palace* (M), over 200 rooms, some (I); several restaurants. Interhotel.

Příbor. *Letka* (I), 40 rooms, some (M).

Rožnov. *Tesla* (M), modern, adequate; Interhotel. Good restaurant at *Motorest Horal* (M), near modern autocamp with chalets for rent.

Strážnice. *Strážnice* (M), 52 rooms, new, quiet family atmosphere, Moravian specialties; Interhotel. *Černy Orel* (I), 11 rooms.

Šumperk. *Grand* (M), 57 rooms.

Telč. *Černý Orel* (M), 23 rooms, newly renovated.

Tišnov. *Květnice* (I), 21 rooms, a few (M).

Třebič. Recent (M) hotel, 40 rooms. *Zlatý Kříž* (I), 23 rooms, some (M).

Uherské Hradiště. *Grand* (M), 34 rooms, some (I). *Morava* (I), 56 rooms without bath.

Valašské Meziříčí. *Apollo* (M), 66 rooms.

Velké Karlovice. *Razula* (M), 40 rooms.

Znojmo. *Družba* (M), 68 rooms. *Dukla* (M), 110 rooms. *Znojmo* (I), 26 rooms without bath.

Ždár. *Bílý Lev* (M), 40 rooms. *Tálský Mlýn* (M), 19 rooms.

SLOVAKIA

Mountains and Medieval Castles

The predominant ethnic group of this second half of the Czechoslovak federated state is of course Slovak, but there are important minorities of Hungarians along the southern borders and a number of Ukrainians in the east. Geographically, Slovakia is separated from Moravia in the west by the White Carpathians and river Morava. It has a rich folklore and great contrasts of scenery, including some of the most spectacular in Europe. In the south are the fertile plains of the Danube and its tributaries—a major Czechoslovakian granary—but these give way to hills and mountains, rising sometimes quite suddenly from the plains, in the north. They reach their greatest height (2,655 meters/8,710 ft.) in the High Tatras.

Although they speak a language closely related to Czech, there is a strong force of Slovak nationalism and, indeed, the two Slav groups developed quite separately. Though united in the 9th century as part of the Great Moravian Empire, a century later the Slovaks were conquered by the Magyars and remained under Hungarian or Habsburg rule until 1918. Following the Tartar invasions in the 13th century, many Saxons were invited to re-settle the land and develop the economy, including the rich mineral resources. In the 15th and 16th centuries, Romanian shepherds migrated from Wallachia through the Carpathians into Slovakia, and the merging of these varied ethnic groups with the resident Slavs bequeathed upon the region a rich folk culture and some unique forms of architecture, especially in the east.

146

Bratislava

Bratislava is the second-largest city of Czechoslovakia and capital of Slovakia. Its history goes back to Celtic and Roman times. The Slavs settled here in the 5th century under their leader Břetislav, but the city came under the rule of Hungary who called it Pozsony. Its many German-speaking settlers called it Pressburg and only in 1918 did it regain its Slavic name. It lies on the Danube close to the frontiers of Austria and Hungary and thus its three names reflect the racial confusion of this meeting place of cultures.

After the capture of Buda by the Turks, Bratislava became the capital of Hungary in 1536 and many monarchs were crowned in the Cathedral of St. Martin. A university was founded here in 1467 and Bratislava was the seat of the Hungarian Diet until 1848. The old parts of the city have great charm. Bratislava Castle dominates the city, massive and square but with corner towers added to relieve its heaviness. Restored in Renaissance and Baroque times, it was gutted by fire in 1811 and has been virtually rebuilt since World War II. Today it houses State offices as well as part of the National Museum and a restaurant. Traces of foundations dating back to earliest times can be seen in the grounds, and the views over three countries are splendid. The Habsburg queen Maria Theresa in particular took a fancy to the place and her presence attracted noble families whose patrician houses add much charm to the narrow streets of the old town below the castle. The Cathedral of St. Martin is the most beautiful and historically interesting church of the city, built in the 14th and 15th centuries.

Central in the Old Town is the 4th April Square (Námestie 4 Aprila) and, at one end of it, the Old Town Hall, also 14th to 15th-century, now housing part of the city and wine museums. In the fine courtyard, with its Renaissance arcades, concerts are held in the spring and summer, and in the adjoining Apony Palace you will find the Wine Museum. Close by is the neo-Classical Archbishop's Palace (Primatial Palace), 1778–80, in whose Hall of Mirrors the historic Peace of Pressburg was signed after the Battle of Austerlitz (1805) by Napoleon and the Austrian Emperor Francis I. Collections of the Municipal Gallery are housed here and in the beautifully restored Mirbach's Palace nearby. They include six magnificent tapestries depicting the legend of Hero and Leander, woven early in the 17th century in the royal workshops at Mortlake, near London.

The Old Town is the historical heart of the city and currently a good deal of restoration work is in progress. Approached from a Gothic chain bridge is October Square (Októbrove nám.). Here is Michael's Gate, with its 15th-century tower; this is the best preserved part of the town's fortifications and offers excellent views. Built into the barbican of the gate is a Baroque building now housing the Pharmaceutical Museum in what was one of the first of the city's apothecaries, once known as the Red Crayfish (U Červného Raka). Nearby is Baštova street, old world and charming, which leads into Klariská street where you'll find one of the oldest Gothic buildings in Bratislava, the Church of the Sisters of the Order of St. Clare (early 15th century). A section of the Municipal Gallery is here.

From Michael's Gate a walk down Michalská street, which leads into Jiráskova street, gives sight of some of the loveliest buildings of the city. There is the Segner House (Segnerova Kuria) with Renaissance bay win-

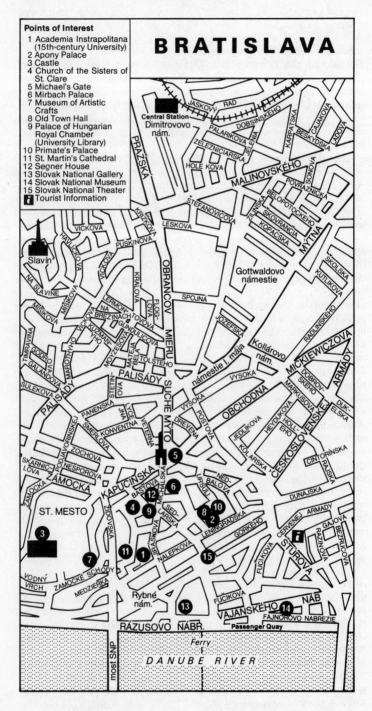

Points of Interest
1 Academia Instrapolitana (15th-century University)
2 Apony Palace
3 Castle
4 Church of the Sisters of St. Clare
5 Michael's Gate
6 Mirbach Palace
7 Museum of Artistic Crafts
8 Old Town Hall
9 Palace of Hungarian Royal Chamber (University Library)
10 Primate's Palace
11 St. Martin's Cathedral
12 Segner House
13 Slovak National Gallery
14 Slovak National Museum
15 Slovak National Theater
i Tourist Information

BRATISLAVA

dows and a finely decorated facade; and the University Library which was the former Royal Chamber (built 1753–56) and the seat of the Hungarian Diet from 1802–48. Further along in Jiráskova street are the Renaissance buildings of the 15th century University.

South of the Old Town and nearer to the Danube is the business section of the city where are also the best hotels. Here, too, are the Slovak National Theater, the National Gallery and, further down the Danube, the Slovak National Museum. In Rusovce, a few miles south of Bratislava across the Danube, the recently-opened Museum of Roman Culture displays finds from the excavations of the Roman settlement of Gerulata. The nearby 19th-century castle is the home of Sl'uk, the exceedingly talented Slovak Folk Artistic Ensemble.

West Slovakia—Little Carpathians

Just outside Bratislava, where the Little Carpathians slide down to the Danube, the majestic castle ruin of Devín stands high on a rock promontory at the confluence of the Morava and Danube rivers. The castle, destroyed by Napoleon's Army, dates from the 9th century and the days of the Great Moravian Empire. A few miles to the north, Stupava is a good starting point for walks into the southwest part of the Little Carpathians.

The southeastern slopes of these hills are vine-growing country and Jur pri-Bratislave is an early wine-producing town in this area. From here you can continue to the attractive little town of Pezinok whose Renaissance castle is now a Museum of Viticulture; there are also remains of 17th-century fortifications and, on the main square, two interesting churches. Close to Pezinok is the village of Slovenský Grob, famous for folk crafts, painted peasant cottages, and the goose feasts it holds each autumn. The latter take place in private homes. A few miles on is Modra, notable for its wines and crafts, especially ceramics.

One of the castles you should seek out in the Little Carpathians is Červený Kameň, originally a frontier fort on the old 13th-century trade route from Hungary to Bohemia. It is being restored as a museum of Renaissance and Baroque artifacts from the whole of West Slovakia. A little further north are the villages of Smolenice and Jahodnik, both typical villages of the Little Carpathians. While you are in this direction one of the richest archeological sites in Czechoslovakia is at Skalica, on the Moravian-Slovak border, with late Stone Age settlements as well as a Slav burial ground from the 8th and 9th centuries.

West Slovakia—The Váh Valley

If you head northeast from Bratislava, you will soon come to the Váh valley, on the way passing one of the oldest towns in Slovakia. This is Trnava, raised to town status in 1238 and, from 1635, a university town. After the occupation of Buda by the Turks it became the cultural and intellectual center of Hungary and for nearly three centuries the see of the Archbishop of Esztergom. The silhouette of the town bristles with towers and spires. The Gothic Church of St. Nicholas dates from 1380; the Church of St. Elizabeth is even earlier as is the hospital adjoining it. Most famous is the University Church of St. John the Baptist, the earliest Baroque structure in Slovakia.

Northwards up the broad Váh valley you will come to Piešťany, ranking in fame with the best known spas of Bohemia. The therapeutic use of its mineral waters and mud for relief of rheumatism and other disorders goes back to very early times and is well documented in the town's well-arranged Balneological Museum. Most of the spa installations are in the town's park-like island of Kúpelný Ostrov. Nearby Slňava dam lake offers boating and water sports.

The next major town is Trenčín, originally a Roman fort and, indeed, the site of the most northerly situated Roman military settlement in Central Europe. There is an inscription on the castle rock proclaiming the victory in A.D. 179 of Emperor Marcus Aurelius over the Germanic tribes then residing in these parts, but to see it you will need to visit the Hotel Tatra; here, next to the dining room, a window faces the inscription only a few feet away. An imposing castle, built over several centuries, dominates the town and is partly open after restoration. A few miles away is another very well-known spa, Trenčianske Teplice, with a natural thermal swimming pool called the Green Frog (Zelená Žaba) cut into the rock. It has a particularly attractive setting.

In due course, the Váh curves eastwards and passes through Žilina, one of the most industrialized towns in Slovakia. Nevertheless, its Dukla square goes back to medieval times and is graced with arcaded houses, mostly in Renaissance style. The most historic building is the late Romanesque St. Stephen Church with wall paintings from the 14th century. South of Žilina, you can follow the valley of the Rajčianka to the medieval town of Rajec.

East of Žilina and on the north side of the Váh, a road will take you to the lovely old village of Terchová, birthplace of the hero Janošík, a kind of Slovak Robin Hood around whom many legends are woven; this is the starting point for the Vrátna Dolina, one of the most beautiful valleys of Czechoslovakia leading into the heart of the Malá Fatra mountains. This is wonderful walking country and, in winter, there is some of the best skiing in the country.

Further east along the Váh, this great Slovak river is joined by one of its major northern tributaries, the Orava. A short drive upstream, Dolný Kubín is the starting point for climbs into the Oravska Magura range and the Chočské Pohorie. Dramatically perched on a rocky cliff above the village of Oravský Podzámok, the 13th–17th-century castle of Orava has been completely restored. Further on, Podbiel gives access to the Roháče massif. Trstená, nearer to the Polish border, is another good center. The area is notable for woodcarving and folk architecture.

The Upper Váh valley falls more naturally into the eastern half of Slovakia and we shall deal with it later.

West Slovakia—The Danube and Its Plains

The route from Bratislava to Komárno is through one enormous island, contained between the so-called Little Danube and the main river. As well as being a rich agricultural area, its considerable watery areas provide one of Europe's richest natural habitats for waterfowl and game birds. It is a veritable paradise for fishermen and naturalists, and there are a number of important reservations. In future years, however, there are likely to be many changes as major hydro-electric projects in co-operation with Hungary take shape, raising the level of the Danube and flooding considerable areas. Komárno itself lies at the confluence of the Váh and the Danube and is an important river port, as well as an official crossing point for Hungary (Komárom) to which it is linked by road bridge. The underground fortifications, first built after the Turkish occupation of Hungary, are of interest, as is the Danubian Museum with its archeological finds from the surrounding lowlands.

Among the many rivers that flow down from the Slovak mountains into the Danube basin is the Nitra. The important town of Nitra itself lies about an hour's drive north of the Danube and today is mainly a modern agricultural town despite its ancient origins. Of particular interest, however, is the Episcopal Cathedral consisting of three churches in different architectural styles, and the Baroque Bishop's Palace, which houses the Archeological Institute and a fascinating display of finds from remotest times. East of Nitra is the Mlyňany Arborétum, open to the public in the summer, and outstanding of its kind with its 2,000 different species of tree. A short drive to the northeast, Topol'čianky has a Renaissance and neo-Classical château, part of which is now a museum of period furniture and local arts and crafts. It is also known for its stud farm, breeding Lippizaners, Arab stallions and English thoroughbreds.

East Slovakia—Upper Váh Valley and the Low Tatras

Now you come to the region of soaring landscapes, of peaks that seem suspended in their own remoteness, of deep valleys ribbing their flanks: these are the mountains of the Nízke Tatry and Vysoké Tatry (the Low and the High Tatras). The Upper Váh has its source in both, for two main streams meet to form it, the Čierny (or Black) Váh from the Low Tatras, and the Biely (or White) Váh from the High Tatras.

But before you reach them, you come to industrial Ružomberok, a good starting point for the tourist centers in the Great Fatra and Low Tatras ranges to the south of the Váh, and Chočské mountains to the north. There is skiing and walking to suit all grades. A few miles east and to the north of the road is the great lake created by the Liptovská Mara dam, which is being developed as a tourist area with all kinds of water sports. After this you reach Liptovský Mikuláš, starting point for excursions into the loveliest parts of the Low Tatras. The town's excellent Peter Michal Bohúň Gallery shows the development of Slovak art. There's also a museum of Slovak karst; tickets for the latter are valid for visiting the fine caves mentioned below. Worth visiting in the vicinity is the splendid 18th-century wooden church of Paludza.

South of the town is the Demänovská Dolina, the most beautiful valley of the Low Tatras. This leads to Demänovská ice cave and the Demänovská Jaskyňa Slobody (Freedom Cave), both part of a massive cave system whose known caverns and passages cover 19 km. (12 miles) on nine levels. Liptovský Ján is a summer resort and a starting place for ascents of Dumbier, the highest peak in the Low Tatras. Another resort a little further east is Liptovský Hrádok. The nearby villages of Východná and Važec are rich in folklore; indeed the annual folklore festival at Východná in June is a highlight of the Slovak calendar.

Three particularly interesting old and now protected mining towns in the mountains of central Slovakia are Banská Bystrica, Kremnica and Banská Štiavnica. Banská Bystrica is in the upper Hron valley. This industrial and historic town has a splendid situation with hills and mountains in all directions. From the 14th century, and for 200 years, it held an important position in the copper trade, mined near the town. It has many handsome Renaissance mansions, the best being around the main square. Surviving from the old castle complex are the gate, the Gothic Royal Palace, the Praetorium, and two Gothic churches. A few miles to the south, Zvolen is another ancient town, much restored, but still with a Gothic concept. The impressive castle has part of the collection of the Slovak National Gallery.

West of Banská Bystrica is another beautifully situated Slovak town, dominated by a castle complex in the heart of the Kremnice Mountains. Kremnica's days of glory were in the 14th and 15th centuries when it minted gold ducats which became a standard of currency in Europe. The mint has been in operation ever since and a museum is devoted to its activities. The heart of the Old Town has some of the best-preserved Gothic burgher houses in Slovakia, contrasting with the miners' charming little houses with their wooden balconies. Also well worth visiting is Banská Štiavnica farther south, its castles and steep, twisting streets full of architectural interest from its medieval hey-day. About two km. (one mile) out of town, the unusual open-air and underground Mining Museum is being expanded. A few miles to the southeast, the splendid Baroque château of Antol houses a Forestry and Hunting Museum.

East Slovakia—the High Tatras

The region that most people come to see is the Vysoké Tatry, the High Tatras, Czechoslovakia's highest mountains and some of the finest in the world. The best point of entry is the road and rail junction of Poprad (it also has an airport), a major tourist and industrial town. In addition to the magnificence of the neighboring High Tatras, this area is of particular interest architecturally and ethnically. Known as Spíš, many of the towns are prefaced with the word *Spišský*. It was originally settled by Slavonic, then Saxon immigrants who came to work in the mines and act as a defense against eastern invasion in medieval times. In all, 24 towns were founded forming almost a kingdom within a kingdom.

These are predominantly Gothic towns beneath their graceful Renaissance over-lays. Their steep shingled roofs, high timberframed gables and brick-arched doorways, have survived in a remarkable state of preservation, several of them now protected urban reservations painstakingly restored or undergoing restoration. The smaller artisans' houses contrast with the grander dwellings of the rich merchants which are usually grouped round a spacious main square dominated by a church. Gothic churches with imposing separate Renaissance bell towers are other major features of the area, as are some quite stunning altar triptychs and exquisite wood carvings. The great master artist of the area was Pavol of Levoča in the 16th century, and his most famous work is the altar of the Church of St. Jacob in Levoča, said to be the largest in the world and incorporating a truly magnificent carving of *The Last Supper* in limewood; the 12 disciples are, in fact, portraits of Levoča merchants. Look out for other examples of his work in many churches in this region.

Almost any small town in this area has something of interest, but Spišská Sobota, Levoča, Kežmarok and Spišská Kapitula are places to look out for in particular. The first of these is a suburb of Poprad, itself not a very interesting town, so you could easily miss its charming satellite.

Spišská Kapitula was the religious center of Spíš and its Romanesque-Gothic cathedral is a jewel. The little town is dominated by the massive castle ruins of Spíš, Slovakia's biggest ruin, now partly restored and scheduled to be a major museum complex. Kežmarok is charming and has the oldest of the Renaissance bell towers, an impressive Renaissance castle and an 18th-century Evangelical Church built entirely of wood. But of all the Spíš towns, probably the most harmonious is Levoča, once a rich trading center on a main route from the Baltic to the Black Sea.

To the south of Levoča is another mountain area deserving attention. This is Slovenský Raj, the Slovak Paradise to the southwest, to which the inhabitants of the Spíš towns fled during the Tartar invasion of 1241–42. It is a wild and romantic region of gorges and cliffs, caves and waterfalls. The main tourist center is at Kláštorisko (745 meters/2,445 ft.), best reached from Spišská Nová Ves.

Yet another fine region lies to the north of Kežmarok: the Pieniny National Park in the Spišská Magura mountains right on the border with Poland. The villages are delightful with much typical folk architecture. At road's end lies the monastery of Červeny Kláštor, now a museum, beside the modest river Dunajec on whose opposite bank lies Poland. Raft trips are arranged on its swift waters.

And, of course, for most visitors the main magnet of this region is the magnificent scenery of the High Tatras, which remained virtually uninhabited until the first embryonic tourism began in the late 18th century, British climbers being the earliest foreigners on the scene. But it was not until after the railway through to Poprad was completed in 1871 that tourism began to develop.

The best possible way to explore these scenic splendors is on foot, remembering that these are mountains to be reckoned with and you should not embark on any major walk without proper clothing and footwear, and clear directions. Many marked trails make it quite easy to explore some of this exciting area. The highest mountain is Gerlachovský Štít (Gerlach Peak), 2,655 meters (8,710 ft.), and the whole area is the nature preserve of the Tatra National Park.

A chain of High Tatras villages and resorts is connected by the Freedom Road and an electric railway. Traveling northeast on this road, you come first to the well-equipped ski resort of Štrbské Pleso, site of many an international ski event; then the health resorts of Vyšné Hágy and Tatranská Polianka. A little way beyond is Smokovec, the largest of the tourist centers and the most important starting point for many of the mountain excursions. From here a funicular takes you to Hrebienok, 1,263 meters (5,144 ft.), from which there are many marked trails. Another excellent center for both summer or winter is Tatranská Lomnica from which there are cable railways to Skalnaté Pleso (Rock Lake), at 1,600 meters (5,250 ft.). The splendid Museum of the Tatra National Park in Tatranská Lomnica is a "must," combining both natural and human history in imaginative displays. Further north, Ždiar is an enchanting little place with its timber-built folk architecture; and it's the only farming community in these parts.

The Easternmost Corner

To the east of these grandiose mountain ranges are yet more mountains which, though of rather lesser stature provide a setting for some of the most charming folk architecture and folkloric traditions. This part of Slovakia is still relatively little known to Western visitors.

Either Poprad or Rožňava would be a good place from which to start. Rožňava is a medieval gold mining town and, as in so many other towns, the best and oldest architectural gems are concentrated round the main square, built over the former passages and shafts of the gold mines. The Cathedral, originally a Gothic church of the 13th century but enlarged and restyled, has an altar piece of scenes from the working life of miners. The town museum is devoted to the same theme. Hill-top Krásna Hôrka castle five km. (three miles) away, is one of Slovakia's best.

South and east of Rožňava is the region of Slovenský Kras (Slovak Karst) with more caves and natural limestone features. There is the Domica cavern which was inhabited by Neolithic man, where visitors can now go by boat along the aptly named river Styx. North of the road to Košice is the Zádielska valley, a long and narrow limestone gorge. Nearby is the Jasovská cave and, in the town of Jasov, a fine complex of Baroque church and monastery.

Košice is the second-largest town in Slovakia, and it was here that the Czechoslovak Socialist Republic was first proclaimed in 1945. Again the best historical features are spread around the original medieval square. The most important building is the Gothic cathedral of St. Elizabeth completed in 1508; the high altar is a monumental piece of wood carving by an unknown genius. Near the Cathedral is an old cremation tower and a chapel incorporating interesting old epitaphs. The Miklušova prison in a remnant of the old walls and its torture chamber are genuine pieces of pure medieval horror.

One of the unusual sights of the neighborhood is the Herl'any Geyser, 30 km. (20 miles) to the northeast. As it has an eruption interval of 28 to 36 hours you should first check with the Čedok office in Košice. The display, shooting up to nearly 40 meters (130 ft.), lasts for about 20 minutes.

Farther north, although now a fast-growing industrial town, the heart of Prešov has much interest. Its center is the long spindle-shaped square with ornate burgher houses and arcades. The three churches—the late-Gothic St. Nicholas, the late-Renaissance Evangelical and Baroque Greek Catholic (Uniat) churches—represent three different Christian sects and three different styles. Prešov is also of interest as a cultural center for the Ukrainians of East Slovakia.

Both the Orthodox and Uniat faiths are strong in this area, echoing the work of Byzantine missionaries over a millennium ago and evidenced by a legacy of enchanting wooden churches. The Uniat Church is particularly interesting since it acknowledges the Pope's supremacy, but retains its own organization and liturgy, and its priests may marry. A good center from which to visit a selection of these churches is Bardejov, farther north towards the Polish border, and another fascinating town in this Šariš area of Slovakia, with well-preserved medieval fortifications. Its cobbled square is a veritable outdoor museum of Gothic and Renaissance architecture, many buildings with a characteristic sign above the door. The Gothic-Renaissance town hall, currently under restoration, is of special note and the monumental late-Gothic Church of St. Egidius (St. Giles) has Gothic aisle altars, with complex decorations in their original 15th-century state. The Šariš Museum contains a valuable collection of 16th-century icons.

Only six km. (four miles) from Bardejov is Bardejovské Kúpele (Bardejov spa), a peaceful place to stay, with an open-air museum of old wooden houses and an 18th-century church.

But the great delight of this area are the old wooden churches in their original settings and still in use. About 10 km. (six miles) from Bardejov is the oldest of these at Hervatov, dating from 1480 with some remarkable 17th-century frescoes. This church is Roman Catholic, but dotted about the mountains that form the border with Poland, north of Svidník, are about a score of Uniat churches, mainly from the 17th and 18th centuries, and showing an intriguing combination of Gothic and Byzantine influences. Some recommendations are the churches of Vyšný Komárnik, Nižný Komárnik, Bodružal, Mirola and Šemetkovce (you'll need a good map).

The same road from Svidník leads in 19 km. (12 miles) to the Dukla Pass on the Polish border, scene of ferocious fighting in the winter of 1944 when Russian and Czechoslovak troops battled for many weeks to break through the pass into Slovakia. A great memorial and cemetery commemorate the struggle at the top of the pass. In Svidník itself, completely rebuilt since the battle, is a memorial and museum complex.

PRACTICAL INFORMATION FOR SLOVAKIA

TOURIST INFORMATION. Most towns and resorts have a Čedok office. The principal ones for the region are: **Banská Bystrica**, nám. V.I. Lenina 4; **Bratislava**, Štúrova 13; **Košice**, Rooseveltova 1; **Nitra**, Leninova 72; **Piešťany**, Pavlovova 38; **Starý Smokovec**, Starý Smokovec 22; **Žilina**, Hodžova 9.

WHEN TO COME. Wonderful hiking in late spring and summer, the best time for general touring and sightseeing. Winter brings the crowds to the splendid skiing grounds for the High and Low Tatras and elsewhere. Spring and fall are good for blossom or wonderful colors. As in Bohemia, spa treatment is available year round.

GETTING AROUND SLOVAKIA. Čedok arrange tours in and around Bratislava and also have a 7-day tour of Slovakia, but your own car gives the greatest freedom. Rail and bus service cover the region.

HOTELS AND RESTAURANTS. Please note the comments regarding classification in *Facts at Your Fingertips*. Hotels listed below have a restaurant and all or a good proportion of rooms have bath or shower, unless otherwise stated.

Banská Bystrica. *Lux* (M), 150 rooms. *Národný Dom* (M), 40 rooms; Interhotel. *Ulanka Motel* (M), 30 rooms, new, attractive, six km. (four miles) out of town to northwest. *Junior Hotel* (I), 50 rooms without bath, run by CKM.

Bardejov. *Dukla* (I), 37 rooms, a few (M). *Minerál* (M), 70 rooms, in Bardejov spa six km. (four miles) away.

Bratislava. *Forum Bratislava* (L), Mierove náměstí 2, due to open early 1989 in the city center, with top facilities. 219 rooms, French and Slovak restaurants, pool, gymnasium, nightclub; Interhotel. *Devín* (E), Riečna 4, modern building on Danube bank near old town, recently renovated. 93 rooms, French, Slovak and Asian restaurants, nightclub; Interhotel.

Bratislava (M), Urxova 9, modern high-rise about 5 km. (3 miles) from center. 344 rooms, nightclub; Interhotel. *Motel Zlaté piesky* (M), Senecká cesta 12, pleasant location near lake, 10 km. (6 miles) from city in recreation area. 33 rooms, swimming, windsurfing; Interhotel. *Juniorhotel Sputnik* (M), Drieňova 14, with lakeside location, 5 km. (3 miles) from center. 95 rooms, disco; run by CKM.

Restaurants. *Café Bystrica* (L), Most NSP, gives a gull's eye view of the Danube and city from its perch atop the bridge's single pylon; grill specialties. *Bajkal* (E), Bajkalská 25, has a modern section as well as rustic *Grandma's Room* (lunches only serving Slovak specialties such as *Cerveny Kamen,* sirloin in a piquant sauce. *Kláštorná vináreň* (E), Pugačevova 2, in vaulted cellars of old monastery in old town; Slovak specialties include pork fillet (*Liptovský Hradok*) coated with cheese pastry. *Rybarsky cech* (E), Žižkova 1, is in historic house of Fishermen's Guild by the Danube, below castle, complete with aquarium—a good place to try the carp. *Stará sladovňa* (E), Cintorínska 32, is a converted old malthouse with taverns serving best Czechoslovak beers; restaurant on the upper floor. *U zlatého kapra* (E), Prepoštská 6, spescializes in freshwater fish in the heart of the old town. *Vel'kí františkáni* (E), Dibrovovo náměstí 10, an old favorite set in medieval vaults in the old town, with folk music. *Slovenská reštaurácia-Luxor* (M), Štúrova ul. 3, one of best for Slovak specialties prepared by award-winning chef Gašpar Fukas; good folk-art décor.

Further afield there is a rotating cafe atop the *TV tower* on Kamzik hill; *Baba,* attractive folk-style restaurant in Little Carpathians, about a 30-minute drive; *Koliba Expo,* offers gypsy music and heady wines in a lovely setting of wooded hills; *Zochova Chata,* charming folkstyle complex near Modra, about 40 minutes' drive away, with three restaurants.

Kežmarok. *Lipa* (M), 52 rooms, new, central. *Štart* (I), 32 rooms without bath, on outskirts of old town at foot of ski slope.

Komárno. *Europa* (M), 60 rooms; Interhotel.

Košice. *Imperiál* (M), 45 rooms, some (I), central; Interhotel. *Hutník* (M), 200 rooms, modern. *Slovan* (M), over 200 rooms, central; Interhotel.

Levoča. *Biela Paní* (I), 12 rooms, on main square, modest, but good value, with wine cellar restaurant below. Restaurant and coffee house *Spišsky Dom* (I), on main square.

Liptovský Mikuláš. *Jánošík* (M), 68 rooms, some (I), Interhotel.

Nitra. *Nitra* (M), 135 rooms, pool, in new housing district; Interhotel. *Tatra* (I), 11 rooms without bath, cafe. *Zobor* (I), 50 rooms, some (M).

Piešťany. *Magnólia* (E), 120 rooms; Interhotel. *Eden* (M), 50 rooms; Interhotel. *Lipa* (I), 47 rooms without bath.

Poprad. *Europa* (M), 73 rooms without bath, near railway station, old-fashioned, over-priced; Interhotel. *Gerlach* (M), 120 rooms, some (I), modern. *Zimný Stadion* (M), 15 rooms.

Prešov. *Šariš* (M), 110 rooms, new, a short distance from main square. *Dukla* (M), 90 rooms; modern, near main square; Interhotel.
Motel Stop (I), 15 rooms, modern, five km. (three miles) from town.

Rožňava. *Kras* (M), 41 rooms; Interhotel.

Ružomberok. *Hrabovo* (M), 22 rooms, in recreation area by reservoir; Interhotel. *Kulturný Dom* (I), 40 rooms without bath.

Smokovec. Really three resorts in one, linked together on the lower slopes of the High Tatras. Main center for shops and information is **Starý Smokovec** with the plush old *Grand* (E), built in 1904: 83 rooms, some (M); Interhotel. *Úderník* (M), modern, 34 rooms without bath, snack bar.

Restaurant. *Tatranská kúria,* with attractive decor and Slovak specialties prepared by award-winning chef.

In **Nový Smokovec:** *Park* (M), 96 rooms, modern, one of the best for value, wine tavern, nightclub, mini-golf; Interhotel. *Tokajík* (M), 13 rooms, some (I); Interhotel. *Bystrina* (I), 44 rooms, snack bar.

In **Horný Smokovec:** *Bellevue* (E), 110 rooms, some (M), modern, pool, comfortable, but insufficient elevators; Interhotel. *Juniorhotel Vysoké Tatry* (M), 50 rooms, run by CKM. *Šport* (M), next to Bellevue, modern, 66 rooms without bath.

At **Hrebienok,** reached by funicular, several chalets with good, simple accommodations and restaurants.

Štrbské Pleso. Scene of many international ski championships, with ski jumps and ski lifts. *Patria* (E), 157 rooms, restaurants including folk-style *Slovenka;* the newest with attractive paved garden in foyer; Interhotel. *Fis* (M), 50 rooms, pool, sauna, faces the ski jumps. *Panoráma* (M), 80 rooms, garden restaurant; Interhotel.

Svidník. *Dukla* (M), 100 rooms.

Tatranská Lomnica. *Grandhotel Praha* (E), 90 rooms, some (M), traditional style, modernized, next to cable-car station; Interhotel. *Motel Eurocamp FICC* (M), splendid campsite with chalets for hire, shops, restaurant and fabulous view of the High Tatras. *Lomnica* (I), 16 rooms, a few (M).

Restaurant. *Zbojnícká koliba* (M), folk style, excellent food, with Slovak folk band.

Trenčianske Teplice. *Jalta* (M), over 100 rooms, recent.

Trenčín. *Laugaricio* (M), 100 rooms, half (I). *Tatra* (I), 70 rooms, some (M).

Žilina. *Polom* (M), 50 rooms. *Slovakia* (M), 140 rooms, pool, nightclub, central. *Metropol* (I), 51 rooms without bath.

Zvolen. *Polana* (M), 85 rooms; Interhotel.

TOURIST VOCABULARY

Most letters in the Czech alphabet are pronounced approximately as in English but here are the basic variations, with their corresponding English sounds italicized in brackets. All vowels are pronounced long if provided with an accent; thus á (*al*mond or b*ar*), é (*a*rea or c*a*re), í (*ea*sy or s*ee*m), ó (*o*rchestra or d*oo*r), ú or ů (*Ou*se or s*ou*p). The letter ý is pronounced like the í.

Other letters are pronounced as follows—a (*A*lbert, never as in case, share, etc.), c (Be*ts*y or tidbi*ts*), č (*ch*arter or bit*ch*), dě, tě, ně (*Di*ego, *Ti*entsin, *Nye*rere), e (s*e*t, *e*nd, etc., even at the end of a word!), g (*g*ame or bo*g*ey, never as in ginger!), ch (a Scottish lo*ch,* symbolized in our pronunciation by kh), i (*i*nk, Mapl*i*n or b*u*sy), j (*Y*ank, pa*y,* never as in jam), o (*O*scar, b*o*ss), ou (kn*ow* or *ow*n, never as in thousand or now), ř (pronounced roughly like the middle group of consonants in cou*rge*tte, it is symoblized in our pronunciation by rzh), s (*s*alt, bo*ss,* never as in easy), š (*sh*ine or cu*sh*ion), u (b*oo*k, never as in ukelele), y (pronounced like the Czech i, see above), ž (as in French bon*j*our or English vi*si*on, symbolized in our pronunciation by zh).

A final note on tonal stress—this is practically always on the *first* syllable, as in the English words *coo*ker, *Al*bert, *ba*con.

USEFUL EXPRESSIONS

Hello, how do you do	Dobrý den (dobree den)
Good morning	Dobré jitro (dobreh yitro)
Good evening	Dobrý večer (Dobree vecher)
Goodnight	Dobrou noc (dobrow nots)
Goodbye	Sbohem; Na shledanou (sbohem; Na skhledanow)
Please	Prosím (proseem)
Thank you	Děkuji (dyekuyi)
Thank you very much	Velmi děkuji (velmi dyekuyi)
Yes	Ano (ano)
No	Ne (neh)
You're welcome	Prosím (proseem)
Excuse me	S dovolením (s dovolenyeem)
Come in!	Dále! (dahle!)
I'm sorry	Lituji (lituyi)
My name is . . .	Jmenuji se . . . (menuyi se . . .)
Do you speak English?	Mluvíte anglicky? (mluveete anglitsky?)
I don't speak Czech	Nemluvím česky (nemluveem chesky)
Please speak slowly	Prosím, mluvte pomalu (proseem, mluvte pomalu)
I don't understand	Nerozumím (nerozumeem)
Please write it down	Prosím, napište to (proseem, napishte to)
Where is . . . ?	Kde je . . . ? (kde ye . . . ?)
What is this place called?	Jak se to (místo) jmenuje? (yak se to/meesto/imenuye?)
Please show me	Prosím, ukažte mně (proseem, ukazhte mnye . . .)
I would like . . .	(Já) bych chtěl; (yah bykh khtyel . . .) a woman says (Já) bych chtěla (yah bykh khtyela . . .)

How much does it cost?   Kolik to stojı? (kolik to stoyee?)

SIGNS

Entrance	Vchod (vkhod)
Exit	Východ (veekhod)
Emergency Exit	Nouzový východ (nowzovee veekhod)
Toilet	Toaleta, záchod (toaleta, zahkhod)
men, gentlemen	muži, páni (muzhi, pahnyi)
women, ladies	ženy, dámy (zheny, dahmy)
vacant	volno (volno)
occupied	obsazeno (obsazeno)
Hot	Horký (horkee)
Cold	Studený (studenee)
No smoking	Kouření zakázáno (kowrzhenyee zakahzahno)
No admittance	Vstup zakázán (vstup zakahzahn)
Stop	Stát! (staht!)
Danger	Nebezpečí, Výstraha (nebezpechee, veestraha)
Open	Otevřeno (otevrzheno)
Closed	Zavřeno (zavrzheno)
Full, no vacancy	Obsazeno (obsazeno)
Information	Informace (informatse)
Bus stop	Zastávka (zastahvka)
Taxi stand	Parkoviště taxiků (parkovishtye taxeekoo)
Pedestrians	Pěší (pyeshee)

ARRIVAL

Passport check	Pasová prohlídka (pasovah prohleedka)
your passport, please	Váš pas, prosím (vahsh pas, proseem)
I am with the group	Já jsem se skupinou (yah sem se skupinow)
Customs	Celnice (tselnitse)
Anything to declare?	Máte něco k proclení? (mahte nyetso k protslenyee?)
Nothing to declare	Nemám nic k proclení (nemahm nyits k protslenyee)
Baggage claim	Výdej zavazadel (veedey zavazadel)
This suitcase is mine	To je me zavazadlo (to ye meh zavazadlo)
A porter, baggage carrier	Nosič (nosich)

Transportation

to the bus	k autobusu (k autobusu)
to a taxi	k taxi (k taxi)
to the Hotel . . . , please	k hotelu . . . , prosím (k hotelu . . . , proseem)

MONEY

Currency exchange office	Směnárna (smnyenahrna)
Do you have change?	Máte drobné? (mahte drobneh?)

May I pay	Mohu platit (mohu platyit)
with a traveler's check?	cestovním šekem (tsestovnyeem shekem?)
with a voucher?	voucher/kuponem (voucher/kupohnem?)
with this credit card?	touto kreditni kartou (towto kreditnyee kartow?)
I would like to exchange some traveler's checks	Chtěl (a woman says chtěla) bych Vyměnit několik šeků (khtyel (khtyela) bykh vymnyenyit nyekolik shekoo)

THE HOTEL

I have a reservation	Mám zajištěn pokoj (mahm zayishtyen pokoy)
A room with a bath	Pokoj s koupelnou (pokoy s kowpelnow)
a shower	sprcha (sprkha)
a toilet	toaleta (toaleta)
hot running water	teplá voda (teplah voda)
What floor is it on?	V kterém poschodí je to? (v kterehm poskhodyee ye to?)
ground floor	přízemi (przheezemee)
first floor	první poschodí (prvnyee poskhodyee)
The elevator	Výtah (veetakh)
Have the baggage sent up, please	Dejte, prosim, poslat nahoru zavazadlo (deyte, proseem, poslat nahoru zavazadlo)
The key to number . . . , please	Klíč číslo . . . , prosím (kleech cheeslo . . . , proseem)
Please call me at seven o'clock	Prosím, vzbuďte mě v sedm hodin (proseem, vzbudte mnye v sedm hodyin)
Have the baggage brought down	Dejte snést dolů zavazadlo (deyte snehst doloo savazadlo)
The bill	Účet (oochet)
A tip	Spropitné (sropitneh)

THE RESTAURANT

Restaurant	Restaurace (restauratse)
Waiter!	Pane vrchní! (pane vrkhnyee!)
Waitress!	Slečno! (slechno!)
Menu . . . please	Jídelní lístek (yeedelnyee leestek) . . . prosim
I would like to order (this) . . .	Chtěl (a woman says, chtěla) bych si objednat . . . (khtyel (khtyela) bykh si obyednat . . .)
Some more . . . please	Ještě vic . . . prosím (yeshtye veets . . . proseem)
That's enough	Je to dost (ye to dost)
The check, please	Platit, prosím (platyit, proseem)
Breakfast	Snídaně (snyeedanye)
Lunch	Oběd (obyed)
Dinner	Večeře (vecherzhe)
Bread	Chléb (khlehb)

Butter	Máslo (mahslo)
Jam/Marmelade	Marmeláda (marmelahda)
Salt	Sůl (sool)
Pepper	Pepř (pepezh)
Mustard	Hořčice (horzhchitse)
Sauce, gravy	Omáčka (omahchka)
Vinegar	Ocet (otset)
Oil	Olej (oley)
Bottle	Láhev (lahhev)
Wine	Víno (veeno)
red, white wine	červené, bílé víno (cherveneh, beeleh veeno)
A bottle of wine	Láhev vína (lahhev veena)
beer	Pivo (pivo)
Water	Voda (voda)
Mineral water	Minerálka (minerahlka)
Milk	Mléko (mlehko)
Coffee (with milk)	Káva (bílá káva); (kahva/beelah kahva)
Tea with lemon	Čaj s citrónem (chay s tsitrohnem
Chocolate	Čokoláda (chokolahda)
Sugar (some sugar)	Cukr (tsukr)
Plum Brandy	Slivovice; (slivovitse)
Spirits	Lihoviný

MAIL

A letter	Dopis (dopis)
An envelope	Obálka (obahlka)
A postcard	Pohlednice (pohlednitse)
A mailbox	Poštovní schránka (poshtovnyee skhrahnka)
The post office	Pošta (poshta)
A stamp	Známka (znahmka)
By airmail	Letecky (letetsky)
How much does it cost	Kolik stojí (kolik stoyee)
to send a letter?	poslat dopis (poslat dopis)?
to send a postcard	poslat pohlednici (pohlednitsi)
air mail to the United States, Great Britain, Canada?	letecky do Spojených států, Velké Británie, Kanady (letetsky do Spoyeneekh stahtoo, Velkeh Britahnyye, Kanady)?
to send a telegram, cable?	Poslat telegram (poslat telegram)?

LOCATIONS

. . . Street	. . . ulice (ulitse)
. . . Avenue	. . . třída (trzheeda)
. . . Square	. . . náměstí (nahmnyestye)
The airport	Letiště (letyishtye)
A bank	Banka (banka)
Bathing place	Koupaliště (koupalishtye)
The bridge	Most (most)
The castle	Zámek (zahmek)
The cathedral	Katedrála (katedrahla)
The church	Kostel (kostel)
The coffee house, cafe	Kavárna (kavahrna)
The garden	Zahrada (zahrada)

The hospital	Nemocnice (nemotsnyitse)
The movies, cinema	Kino (kino)
a movie	film (film)
The museum	muzeum (muzeum)
A nightclub	Nocni klub (nochnyee klub)
The palace	Palác (palahts)
The park	Park (park)
The post-office	Pošta (poshta)
The station	Nádraží (nahdrazhee)
The theater	Divadlo (dyivadlo)
a play	hra (hra)
The tourist office	Cestovní kancelář (tsestovnee kantselahzh)
The university	Univerzita (univerzita)

TRAVEL

Arrival	Příjezd (przheeyezd)
Departure	Odjezd (odyezd)

The airplane

Letadlo (letadlo)

I want to reconfirm a reservation on flight number . . . for . . .

Chtěl (a woman says chtěla) bych potvrdit rezervaci na let . . . do . . . (khtyel (khtyela) bykh potvrdyit rezervatsi na let . . . to . . .)

Where is the check-in?

Kde je kontrola? (kde ye kontrola?)

I am checking in for . . .

Letím do . . . (letyeem do . . .)

Fasten your seat belt

Připoutejte se (przhipowteyte se)

The railroad

Železnice (zheleznyitse)

The train

Vlak (vlak)

From what track does the train to . . . leave?

Z kterého nástupiště odjíždí vlak do . . . ? (z kterehho nahstupishtye odyeezhdyee vlak do . . . ?)

Which way is the dining car?

Kde je jídelní vůz? (kde ye yeedelnyee vooz?)

Bus, streetcar

Autobus, tramvaj (autobus, tramvay)

Does this bus go to . . . ?

Jede tento autobus na . . . ? (yede tento autobus na . . . /do . . . /?)

trolley bus

trolejbus (troleybus)

I want to get off at . . . Street

Chtěl (chtěla) bych vystoupit na . . . ulici (khtyel/khtyela/bykh vystowpit na . . . ulitsi)

at the next stop

na příští stanici (. . . na przheeshtye stanitsi)

Taxi

Taxi (taxi)

I (we) would like to go to . . . , please

Chtěl (a woman says chtěla) bych (chtěli bychom) jet na . . . , prosim (khtyel (khtyela) khtyeli bykhom/yet na . . . , proseem)

Stop at . . .   Zastavte na . . . (zastavte na . . .)
Stop here   Zastavte zde (zastavte zde)

NUMBERS

1 jeden (yeden)	20 dvacet (dvatset)
2 dva (dva)	25 dvacet pět (dvatset pyet)
3 tři (trzhi)	30 třicet (trzhitset)
4 čtyři (chtyrzhi)	40 čtyřicet (chtyrzhitset)
5 pět (pyet)	50 padesát (padesaht)
6 šest (shest)	60 šedesát (shedesaht)
7 sedm (sedm)	70 sedmdesát (sedmdesaht)
8 osm (osm)	80 osmdesát (osmdesaht)
9 devět (devyet)	90 devadesát (devadesaht)
10 deset (deset)	100 sto (sto)
11 jedenáct (yedenahtst)	200 dvě stě (dvye stye)
12 dvanáct (dvanahtst)	300 tři sta (trzhi sta)
13 třináct (trzhinahtst)	400 čtyři sta (chtyrzhi sta)
14 čtrnáct (chtrnahtst)	500 pět set (pyet set)
15 patnáct (patnahtst)	600 šest set (shest set)
16 šestnáct (shestnahtst)	700 sedm set (sedm set)
17 sedmnáct (sedmnahtst)	800 osm set (osm set)
18 osmnáct (osmnahtst)	900 devět set (devyet set)
19 devatenáct (devatenahtst)	1,000 tisíc (tyiseehts)

DAYS OF THE WEEK

Sunday	neděle (nedyeleh)
Monday	pondělí (pondyelee)
Tuesday	úterý (ooteree)
Wednesday	středa (stzheda)
Thursday	čtvrtek (chtvertek)
Friday	pátek (pahtek)
Saturday	sobota (sobota)

EAST GERMANY (GERMAN DEMOCRATIC REPUBLIC)

EAST GERMANY—FACTS AT YOUR FINGERTIPS

HOW TO GO. Advance booking through an authorized travel agent is the easiest way to visit East Germany (officially known as the German Democratic Republic— G.D.R. for short in English, D.D.R. in German). This does not mean that it is necessary to take one of the several package tours offered; instead, the various formalities involved in arranging your trip (visas, hotel vouchers or booking, advice on currency exchange, etc), which in one way or another interlock, will be taken care of for you and you should have no (or at least fewer) hitches at the border or once in the country. Given the reluctance of the East German authorities to allow visitors to stay anywhere other than in officially designated hotels or campsites—with friends or relatives, for instance—and the consequent delays and difficulties you will encounter in arranging a visit of this type—there is little real benefit in not booking via a travel agent. Note that a visa-processing fee is charged for all visitors, however.

The authorized travel agencies are those officially accredited by the *Reisebüro der D.D.R.,* the East Germany state tourist organization and the ultimate source of all wisdom and most hotel bookings. Unfortunately they will only direct you toward those hotels, attractions and activities which the G.D.R. thinks should or might be of interest to you. There are very few alternative sources of information, but you will find the Reisebüro up-to-date and authoritative, if not quite as complete as you might wish. All of the information is available without charge, and should you contact the Reisebüro directly with a specific enquiry, you are likely to get a personal letter in return. Do, therefore, let them know of any special wishes such as visiting cities associated with music or finding the country's top art museums. In general, tourist officials are interested in making the country appealing.

If you decide to travel independently, there are two ways of obtaining the visa essential to entering the country, but unless you're willing to leave this until the last minute and get a pass at the border crossing into East from West Berlin, you must still go to one of the officially approved travel agencies which will forward your request for a visa together with your wishes for hotel reservations, to the Reisebüro. Generally you will be issued vouchers, to be paid for before you enter East Germany. This process takes six to eight weeks, longer if you wish to stay in cheaper hotels which do not belong to Interhotel. A fee of about $25 is charged for this service, $30 for "express handling." The East German consulates in the U.S. and U.K. do not have tourism offices; you will find that the consulate in the U.S. (1717 Massachusetts Ave., NW, Washington, DC 20036) will simply refer you to a travel agent in your area, and the U.K. Embassy (34 Belgrave Sq., London SW1) will head you directly toward Berolina Travel, the British branch of the Reisebüro.

Among the authorized travel agents in the U.S. are: *Kenwood Travel,* 2002 Colfax Ave. South, Minneapolis, MN 55405 (tel. 612–871–6399); *Koch,* 157 E. 86th St., New York, NY 10028 (tel. 212–369–3800); *Maupintour,* 1515 St. Andrews Dr., Lawrence, KS 66046 (tel. 800–255–4266).

In the U.K., *Berolina Travel Ltd.,* 22 Conduit St., London W1R 9TD (tel. 01–629–1664) is the British branch of the Reisebüro der D.D.R. and can make all necessary reservations, arrange visas and look after details of your trip, or alternatively will give you names of other travel agencies authorized in the U.K. to do so via Berolina.

The *Reisebüro der D.D.R.* in East Berlin is at Alexanderplatz 5 (tel. 2–215–4402).

TOURS. Several ready-made inclusive and package tours are available and specialized programs are being expanded. Your travel agent will have details. The standard packages are labeled: "B," focusing on Berlin and its attractions; "C," charm of East Germany both in the cities and the countryside; "E," East Germany's extensive railroad system, with special attention to steam motive power and the narrow-gauge lines; "K," featuring the G.D.R.'s art and culture; "L," for those who want to retrace Luther's life and working stations; and "M," the country's five cities most associated with classical music and composers. These tours run on a fixed set of dates each year throughout the year and are guaranteed to take place even if you're the only one who has booked!

There are also escorted package tours available from U.S. operators which include East Germany along with other East European countries or with West Germany. These are a few of the possibilities: *Love Holidays* offers a half-dozen tours that stop in East Germany, such as "Central & Eastern Europe," "Best of Eastern Europe," "Grand Eastern Europe," and such. All spend two to three days in East Berlin and Dresden, and follow with stops in other Eastern European countries.

Hemphill Harris offers a 24-day, in-depth excursion, "The Best of Germany." It visits Berlin, Leipzig, Dresden, and Meissen, as well as exploring a dozen West German cities. Cost is $5,980, not including airfare.

The Polish National Tourist Organization, *Orbis,* also has a program, "Poland and the Heart of Europe," which spends two nights in Berlin and one in Dresden. The 18-day tour costs $1,300 (land costs only).

"Germany's Medieval Castles & Towns" is *Travcoa's* offering, which visits Weimar, Eisenach, and Erfurt as part of its exploration of Germany's medieval past. Land costs: $3,795.

Hemphill Harris Travel Corp., 16000 Ventura Blvd., Encino, CA 91436 (tel. 818–906–8086).

Love Holidays, 15315 Magnolia Blvd., Ste. 110, Sherman Oaks, CA 91403 (tel. 818–501–6868).

Orbis, 500 Fifth Ave., New York, NY 10110 (tel. 212–391–0844).

Pecum Tours, 2002 Colfax Ave. South, Minneapolis, MN 55405 (tel. 612–871–8171).

Travcoa, 4000 MacArthur Blvd. Suite 650E, Newport Beach, CA 92660 (tel. 714–476–2800).

VISAS. A valid passport and a visa are requirements of all persons entering East Germany. The East German embassy strongly recommends using a travel agent to obtain your visa. You will need your passport, a voucher from a travel agency verifying your accommodations, and confirmation from the Reisebüro der D.D.R. in East Berlin. Visas cost approximately $9.00/£4.90 (subject to the exchange rate). Children under 16 free. You will also be given a small form to fill out. This will be stamped as you enter the country and must be surrendered when you leave, so take care not to lose or misplace it.

You can visit East Berlin from West Berlin on a daily pass card good for a 24-hour stay and this can be extended for up to a week either by an Interhotel or by the Reisebüro der D.D.R. once you are in the country. Transit visas for stays of up to 72 hours may be obtained at border crossing points provided you have a valid visa for the country subsequently to be entered (usually Poland or Czechoslovakia). Obtaining a daily pass from West into East Berlin is no major problem, but bear in mind that any of these ad hoc arrangements take officials away from their usual chores and considerable delays can be expected. The far preferable procedure is to make arrangements well in advance and have visa and other papers ready when you reach the border. If you are staying in the country, you must be registered with the police, a formality which your hotel will take care of unless you are staying with relatives.

MONEY. You are obliged to change the equivalent of West German Deutschmark 25 per day, Dm. 7.50 per day for children between six and 15. These amounts will be turned into East German Marks (M.) and must be spent in East Germany, as you are not allowed to take local money out of the country, nor can you convert back into Western currency unless you can prove that you have changed the minimum amount.

The basic monetary unit is the Mark (M.), divided the same as West German currency into 100 pfennigs. There are banknotes of 100, 50, 20, 10 and 5 marks and coins in general circulation of 10, 5, 2 and 1 mark and 50, 20, 10, 5 and 1 pfennig. Except for the copper 20 pfennig coin, all pieces are aluminum. Hang onto any 20 and 10 pfennig coins that come your way; the 20 pfennig piece is needed for a pay phone and the 10 pfennig pieces are useful for the streetcar or bus where no change is otherwise available. The exchange rate for the East German mark is the same as that for the West German deutschmark against other Western currencies. At the time of writing (mid-1988), this is M.1.72 to the U.S. dollar and M.3.10 to the pound sterling. These rates will certainly vary through 1989. However, the one-to-one relationship of the Dm. to the G.D.R. mark remains fixed.

You may bring as much foreign currency into East Germany as you wish, but you must declare it upon arrival. Officials do not seem too particular about this procedure, but in East Germany it is never possible to tell when they may decide to "go by the book." According to the law, if you fail to declare what you have brought in, none of it may be taken back out. In no case is East German currency allowed to be exported, although again controls are often lax. Nevertheless, the currency has little value outside of East Germany.

When changing currency or paying for anything in Western currency, be sure to get a receipt showing the exchange, as this is the only way you can get your G.D.R. marks changed back into something useful when you leave the country (after you have spent the minimum, of course).

Credit Cards. In all of the Interhotels, some shops and restaurants, you can use an American Express or Diners Club credit card. Visa and Eurocard/MasterCharge are to coming into wider use. These cards, as well as Hertz, Avis and Europcar (National in the U.S.) are valid for car rentals, too.

COSTS. For the most part East Germany is not an expensive country to visit by Western standards. The exception is hotel prices; both the hotels and their prices are up to best Western levels, particularly in the larger cities. Off the beaten track, prices drop back to very reasonable levels, but at the same time, accommodations are more modest.

Sample Costs. Cinema ticket M.3–4; theater ticket M.5–10; concert ticket M.5–12; opera ticket M.5–15; beer in a keller (half-liter) M.2–3; cup of coffee in a cafe M.1.50–2; vodka or schnapps M.2.50–4; scotch M.4–7; wine in a restaurant per glass M.7.50–12, half-bottles about M.20–30. Prices will vary according to the classification of the establishment—and its location. A drink in a 4- or 5-star Interhotel in Berlin will probably be double the cost shown here; prices in other East German cities will be slightly lower than these, except in Leipzig at Fair time.

MEDICAL INSURANCE. The G.D.R. has no reciprocal arrangements on medical coverage for U.K. or U.S. citizens. Should you need help, you will be asked to pay for this—in hard currency—so be sure to get receipts with which to file a claim later. Medical trip insurance is thus strongly advised.

CUSTOMS. Customs procedures vary from casual to meticulous, but it is wisest to follow the rules and not take chances. You may import any amount of tobacco, spirits or wine. Spare parts for cars may be imported only with permission. You may import gifts to the value of M.200 duty-free per person for visits of up to five days. If your visit will last longer than five days, this amount is increased to M.100 for each day of your stay in East Germany. Note that the value of goods brought in is based on their price in East Germany, not necessarily what you paid for them. Note also that some books and medicines beyond those for personal use are not allowed to be brought in. Policies regarding Western newspapers and magazines and music and video cassettes are now more liberal, but these items are subject to control and, depending on their contents, possible confiscation. The degree of enforcement of these regulations often depends on the general East-West political climate.

When you leave the country, duty may be charged on goods you take out beyond the value of M.20 per person per day's stay in East Germany for up to five days, or M.100 for a longer stay. Once again, this regulation is rarely enforced, and is designed primarily to restrict Poles from coming across the border and buying goods "on the cheap." If you buy antiques or anything else of substantial value, you will be given an official receipt (assuming you bought the goods from an authorized source) which will solve any export problems, should Customs officials ask. For regulations covering the import and export of currency, see *Money.*

CLIMATE. The main tourist season runs from late April to early October, when the weather is at its best and most important tourist events are held. The advantages of off-season travel—lower prices and fewer crowds—are slight, however, given that prices are generally low anyway, even in the high season, and crowds are few and far between, added to which the winter weather is grim at the best of times.

The summer climate is delightful and settled. Winter, as we say, is not so much fun.

Average afternoon temperatures in degrees Fahrenheit and centigrade:

Berlin	Jan.	Feb.	Mar.	Apr.	May	June	July	Aug.	Sept.	Oct.	Nov.	Dec.
F°	35	38	46	55	65	70	74	72	66	55	43	37
C°	2	3	8	13	18	21	23	22	19	13	6	3

SPECIAL EVENTS. The *Leipzig Trade Fair* takes place during the first week of **March** and **September** and is a showcase of East European and East German industrial products. Many Western firms also participate and all accommodations during the fair period are preempted for business visitors. Weimar holds a *Shakespeare Festival* in **April;** Berlin's major festival in 1987 to celebrate the city's 750th anniverary of founding was such a success that it is to be repeated annually.

In **July** the Hanseatic cities of Rostock and Stralsund host a week of festivities, the *Ostseewoche;* **September/October** is occasion for the *Berlin Music and Drama Festival.* Your travel agent will have details.

National Holidays. Jan. 1 (New Year's Day); Good Friday; May 1 (Labor Day); Whitsun Monday; Oct. 7 (Republic Day); Dec. 25, 26 (Christmas).

LANGUAGE. English is fairly widely spoken in all centers where American or English tourists are likely to be, but if you wander off the beaten path you will find that English is far less prevalent as a second language than in Western Europe. German, of course, is the national language, with Russian, English and French taught in schools.

HOTELS. East Germany classifies its hotels by a star rating, from 5-star downward. This ranking corresponds closely to our grading system in the lists that follow. The 5-star category approximates our Deluxe (L), 4-star our Expensive (E), 3-star Moderate (M) and 2- and 1-star our Inexpensive (I). The East German classification system has become somewhat confused through the opening of the new Grand Hotel in Berlin; this hotel, officials claim, is better than 5-star and assuredly the most expensive in East Germany. That argument notwithstanding, East Germany's older 5-star hotels offer virtually every amenity you could want with the exception, in a couple of cases, of complete air-conditioning, something you may want to check on when you make bookings. Public rooms and restaurants of these hotels are air-conditioned, however.

All of the 5- and 4-star hotels belong to the Interhotel group, with a few exceptions in some of the smaller cities. In the 4- and 3-star categories some hotels are run by local trade organizations ("H-O"), and the Evangelical Church operates seven hostels, open to anyone with a booking, in the 2-star category. There are a few small private hotels as well, in the 2-star category. Bookings in other than the Interhotels are difficult to arrange, first because the official state tourist office wants you to stay in the country's better facilities, and because the smaller groups and individual hotels are ill-equipped to handle the correspondence and paperwork associated with a Western guest, particularly if the stay is just for a couple of nights. Nevertheless, if you want the country's least expensive accommodations and are willing to argue for it, the H-O hotels and Evangelical hostels are clean and comfortable if modest.

This table shows approximate prices for rooms in the first three categories, with breakfast service charges included. Prices are generally steady but do increase substantially in Leipzig at the time of the twice-yearly fair when hotel prices are likely to spring over into the next higher category.

Two people in a double room with bath and continental breakfast will pay approximately:

Deluxe:	U.S.$145–200
Expensive	100–130
Moderate	75–100
Inexpensive	45–75

A single room with bath will cost about $12–25 more than half the double cost. Single rooms in the (L) and (E) categories all have baths.

Not all of the hotels in the smaller cities are as well equipped as those in the main centers, but are comfortable enough and even the (I) hotels will have hot water in the rooms.

Private Accommodations

In theory, foreign guests are not allowed to take private accommodations with other than relatives; in practise, this situation changes at the time of the Leipzig Fair, but the arrangements are made through the tourist office.

Hostels

Youth hostels are not officially open to Western visitors, although in practise campers under 30 may sometimes be allowed to use them if space is available. For a list of hostels, write *Jugendtourist,* Alexanderplatz 5, D.D.R.–1026 Berlin.

Camping

There are over 30 "Intercamp" sites in East Germany, all with electricity, water, sanitation and other facilities. Camping at other than the designated sites is not permitted. The Intercamps are open from May 1 to Sept. 30. Camps are located in Berlin, Zierow (Baltic coast), the Mecklenburg lake district, Dresden, Erfurt, Leipzig and the Hartz mountains. You must, however, book your campsite *before* arriving in East Germany. You will be issued with vouchers which you must surrender upon entering the country in exchange for marks (M. 25 for adults, M. 10 for those 6–16 years, per day of camping, those under 6, free). This scheme ensures that there will be space for you at the designated campsite and at the same time accomplishes the compulsory exchange of currency. The marks you get cover the campsite rental, food purchases and other incidentals. Travel agents will have more details.

Those traveling in a camper or with camping trailer are allowed entry to the G.D.R. only at the following border points: Lübek–Selmsdorf; Gudow–Zarrentin; Lauenburg–Horst; Helmstedt–Marienborn; Herleshausen–Wartha; Rudolphstein–Hirschberg; West Berlin–Drewitz (all crossing points from West Germany); Warnemünde, on the ferry from Denmark; Sassnitz, on the ferry from Sweden; Görlitz, for those coming from Poland; and Zinnwald, for those entering the G.D.R. from Czechoslovakia.

RESTAURANTS. The number and quality of restaurants in East Germany has increased considerably in recent years and aside from the hotel restaurants, which have always been good if a bit expensive, hungry tourists now have a good range of places and food types from which to choose. Berlin in particular now offers an excellent choice, with some restaurants of very good quality and service standards indeed, and this despite the fact that most restaurants are state-run. A few are leased to private individuals and fewer yet are in private hands, but these are sufficient to encourage a better standard all around. Many of the newer places are small and incoming guests have no qualms about asking if they can join you at a table where there are free places. Unfortunately, there are few restrictions on smoking in restaurants, and other than those in hotels, restaurants are not air-conditioned.

Alas, the once-standard menus posted outside restaurants are disappearing, leaving would-be diners to guess about both offerings and prices, although this bad habit is more evident in Berlin than elsewhere. On the other hand, head waiters seem little distressed over guests who ask to see the menu before sitting down.

Our restaurant grading system is divided into three categories. Expensive (E), M.30–45; Moderate (M), M.20–30; Inexpensive (I), M.10–20. These prices are for one person and may include a small beer in the (M) and (I) categories; wine and mixed drinks or Schnapps in East Germany are considerably more expensive.

Reservations are suggested in our listings where space is tight or where this is the accepted procedure. Some restaurants tend to be busier in the evenings, others at noon. In fact, finding a table at one of the more moderate or inexpensive restaurants at noon may be a bit of a trick; if you see a line outside a restaurant, it is probably both good and inexpensive and people are waiting for a place inside. Many of the cafes offer light dishes, particularly at lunchtime, although in East Germany the tendency is to take the larger meal at midday if eating at home.

TIPPING. Officially abolished but still widely practised. Tipping at restaurants is done by rounding up the bill by a couple of marks to the nearest even figure. For special wants or services, tip in West German deutschmarks if possible, otherwise in U.S. dollars and coins. Tips in local currency are accepted, of course, but do far less to win a table or smile or improve service from your waiter or concierge. For special attention, give the waiter or headwaiter Dm. 2 when he seats you. Taxi drivers, too, will appreciate a small tip in West German currency.

MAIL AND TELEPHONES. Letters within Europe to 20 grams, M.0.35, postcards M.0.25. Check with the post office on overseas and airmail (*Luftpost*) rates. Your hotel can also assist, but don't be surprised if you are asked to pay for the G.D.R. stamps in Western currency. The post office deals only in local currency.

Local telephone calls from a pay telephone take a 20 pfennig coin. Long distance calls are not possible from a booth but can be made either from your hotel or from a post office. Direct dialing, including to overseas destinations, is possible from all of the larger hotels. Overseas codes are in the front of the telephone book. For the U.S. and Canada, the code is 012–1 plus area code and local number. For the U.K., dial code 0644 plus city and number.

TIME. The G.D.R. is six hours ahead of Eastern Standard Time and one hour ahead of Greenwich Mean Time. From April to September, the country changes over to summer time along with most of the rest of Europe, East and West, meaning that the clocks are seven hours ahead of E.S.T. and two hours ahead of G.M.T.

CLOSING TIMES. Shops in Berlin are open weekdays from 10 to 7, Thursdays 10 to 8; outside of Berlin 9 to 6. Larger department stores and shops are open on Saturday mornings. All are closed on Sundays. Bank hours vary, but generally run from 8 to 11.30 on weekdays, closed Saturdays and Sundays. Museums are open daily from 10 to 6 except (and this varies from museum to museum) Mondays and Tuesdays. Restaurants open from 10 to midnight; closing days vary, but usually a sign on the door of a closed restaurant will indicate the next open restaurant. Bars open at 9 P.M. and stay open until 4 A.M.

SHOPPING. Handicrafts, wood carvings and textiles are typical items to buy. Sheet music is at almost give-away prices. Books are reasonable, but mostly in German. For antique editions, try the upper Friedrichstrasse in Berlin. For other antiques, the State-run shop in the lower Friedrichstrasse or on the 10th floor of the Metropol hotel. The Centrum department store on Alexanderplatz in Berlin has a huge range of goods. Government-run "Intershops" in all cities offer mainly imported goods, but only against hard currency, i.e., deutschmarks, dollars, sterling or the like.

SPAS. The country offers a number of spas, with cures for various assorted ailments at very reasonable prices, throughout the year. Travel agents can get you specific details, but be advised that the G.D.R. officials suggest that you need at least 21 days for a cure to "take."

SPORTS. The mountain areas in the south of the country offer opportunities for skiing but these areas have not been developed for tourism. The lake areas within and just outside the city of Berlin offer excellent water sports. Even more developed are the resort and beach areas on the Baltic Sea, the centers being Warnemünde and Rügen.

All of the cities have ample indoor pools and swimming pools in parks, all open to tourists. Your hotel will have details. The newer deluxe hotels also have indoor pools and saunas.

GETTING AROUND EAST GERMANY. By Train. Rail service throughout the country is good, with fast trains connecting the major cities. Trains are inexpensive as well, even if a supplement is required on the express lines. Look for the indication "EX" alongside the train number to identify the fastest; "D" trains are not so fast, and "E" somewhat slower. Complete schedules are posted at all rail stations and many hotels as well, and tell you when trains arrive at their destinations as well as departing times.

Since rail travel is the main means of inland transportation for many, trains are fairly full, so it is a good idea to reserve a seat in advance, done either through a travel agent, your hotel or at the rail station almost up to departure time. You will get a car as well as a seat number and East Germany follows the European practice of showing the makeup of the train on identifying posters at the station so you will know if your car is at the front or back. Most long- and medium-distance trains have both first class and second class cars and will have either a dining car or buffet as well. Meals are satisfactory and inexpensive, but choice is limited. Overnight trains will usually also have first and second class sleeping cars and second class couchettes.

Main lines are electrified but steam can still be found in many areas and indeed is being promoted as a tourist attraction. So are the narrow gauge lines around Leipzig, on which four-day tours are available (details from your travel agent). Happily the East German authorities have become increasingly tolerant of rail enthusiasts, but taking pictures of trains in and around rail stations is prohibited.

By Air. There is no internal air service in the G.D.R. Main international airports are *Schönefeld* (Berlin) and Leipzig.

By Car. Close to 1,600 km. (1,000 miles) of motorway and nearly 11,000 km. (7,000 miles) of secondary roads crisscross the country. Roadways and routes are well marked but detailed maps will be useful. A highway-use tax is charged, M.5 for up to 200 km. (125 miles), M.15 for up to 300 km. (186 miles), M.20 for up to 400 km. (248 miles), and M.25 for up to 500 km. (311 miles). This tax is payable in western currency only. Green cards for insurance and registration documents are required for all vehicles except those registered in Britain, which require registration documents only.

Traffic regulations are specific and strictly enforced, from parking rules to speed limits, for which radar traps have been cleverly contrived. Drivers would do well to get a copy of the rules in English before attempting to motor in East Germany, as the police levy fines (in West German currency, for foreigners) for the slightest offence. Speed limits on the Autobahn are 100 km. (63 m.p.h.), on other roads 80 km. (55 m.p.h.) and in towns 50 km. (30 m.p.h.).

Gasoline or petrol (*Benzin* in the G.D.R.) is available either at *Minol* or *Intertank* filling stations. Both chains sell regular and premium grades by the liter. Minol stations supply gas against G.D.R. marks (you may be asked to show your currency exchange receipt) or against coupons which may be bought at a discount at the border. Otherwise, the Intertank stations sell gas at reduced prices but only for West German deutschmarks. Current prices at the time of writing (mid-1988) for a liter of premium gas at Minol is M.1.65; an Intertank station by comparison charges Dm. 1.36.

Drinking and driving is strictly forbidden and fines are heavy for violators. You may even find yourself subject to an on-the-spot fine if you are sighted getting into your car after leaving a bar, regardless of whether or not you have actually been drinking. It is usually easier just to pay up rather than argue. Seat belts are required at all times, with fines for non-use. Road accidents, no matter how apparently minor, should be reported immediately at or to the nearest police station.

Car Hire. Cars can be rented at all Interhotels and some other locations as well. Cars may be returned to the starting point or dropped off elsewhere, including in Czechoslovakia. Car models range from Lada to Volvo, with rentals accordingly. Prices are generally reasonable, though the cars tend to have run up more miles than in most other countries. If you prefer a better car, best reserve well in advance. Rentals can be paid for with American Express, Diners Club, Europcar, Avis or Hertz credit cards.

INTRODUCING EAST
GERMANY

East Germany (more correctly known as the German Democratic Republic) poses a fascinating problem for the historian today: What really *is* Germany? Or more specifically, what is the G.D.R.? In fact, this country had its beginnings in postwar Europe, in effect starting from April 1945, with German surrender to the allied powers. An uneasy occupation began, with the country divided; the three Western zones under control of the French, British and U.S. forces, and the Eastern zone regulated by the Soviet occupying power. Berlin, former capital of the old Germany, was also divided into four zones.

The key problem for Germany was that the occupying powers were unable to agree over a future for the country. At the four-power conference in Yalta, leaders had called for reunification of Germany. No one knows whether Soviet leader Josef Stalin really thought this a possibility or not; certainly the Soviets were highly wary of the Germans in view of what had happened from 1939 onward.

But by 1948, Soviet plans were clear enough. In early April 1945, barely a month before the end of the war, Stalin is reported to have said, "whoever occupies a territory imposes his own social system on it, as far as his army reaches." In the case of Germany, this statement has indeed proved to be the case.

In 1948, the Soviets attempted to isolate Berlin's Western sector by blocking the land routes to the city, but Moscow leaders had not reckoned with the determination of the Western powers. The famous "Berlin airlift" was the answer, supplying the allied sector with tons of food and fuel and other essentials, keeping the city running for well over a year.

In 1949 the Western allies agreed to the establishment of a new German state, the Federal Republic of Germany, made up of the three Western zones under their occupation. The Soviets responded six months later in October 1949, by setting up the German Democratic Republic in their zone of occupation.

Thus the territory of the G.D.R. today represents mainly the Soviet zone of occupation as it stood in the postwar days of the mid-1940s. Bounded on the west mainly by an arbitrary border, and on the east by the Oder-Niesse rivers, the country cannot disassociate itself from the "old Germany" in terms of culture and history; politics and all other aspects of daily life however are quite a different thing, when one compares the two Germanys nearly 40 years later.

Back to Beginnings

In many ways East Germany today is still very much a part of that earlier Germany. Indeed, recently the country's leadership has finally felt sufficiently relaxed to concede the history which the two Germanys share. Statues out of the past of figures such as Frederick the Great are once again being restored to places of honor and the role of past leaders recognized.

But political turnaround is nothing new to Germany or the Germans. For hundreds of years the country was a fluid state made up of a host of dukedoms small and large. Central leadership came and went. In the 9th century one powerful ruler controlled the whole area, but by the 18th century an assortment of powers, including Popes, emperors, Austrians, Spaniards, Swedes, Frenchmen, Poles and Italians, had all laid claim to one piece of territory or another of what today is basically Germany, West and East.

The feeling of regionalism which thus resulted can be felt in Germany even today. While most prevalent in West Germany, regional spirit can be detected in East Germany as well, divided as it is into 15 internal districts, *Bezirke,* several roughly comparable to the old regional subdivisions.

These shifts have left their mark in other ways, too. Although the church has been suppressed under the East German regime, the G.D.R. remains staunchly Protestant, in contrast to the Catholicism of much of West Germany. In addition, even before the stronger political ties which developed from 1945 onward, the common borders with Poland and Czechoslovakia had tended to give a more "eastern" inclination to the country.

Early Influences

In their efforts to build an empire, the earliest Romans never got as far as present-day East Germany. Julius Caesar felt little-threatened by the assorted tribes to be found in the area, suggesting that his legions could sweep the territories if they wanted. Augustus and his Roman forces reached the Elbe, but their presence in the area was not long-lived; the Germans united sufficiently to trounce the Romans, sending them back to the Rhine once again. Over a period of some four centuries, as the empire crumbled, the German tribes moved out across the former Roman borders to gain pieces of France and whatever other territories were for the easy taking.

Out of this chaos sprang Charlemagne, whose diplomatic and military prowess enabled him to put together an immense empire running from the Baltic to northern Spain. After being crowned Emperor of Rome in the year 800 and being recognized by the Byzantine Empire to the East, his position was secure. His death put an end to an era of scholarship and flourishing of the arts, marked in particular by the introduction of Byzantine design into Western Europe. Charlemagne's empire split, with one section becoming what is generally Germany today. The Church played an important role in holding the pieces together, with various bishops given land to help influence their earthly allegiance. The power of Rome over the German lands increased, consolidating in 1122 when Rome, not the German emperors, won the right to nominate German bishops.

Religious Rome brought a far-reaching artistic influence with it. The Romanesque style moved northward. Vast, heavily-decorated buildings were constructed with their colonnades and arches; delicate illuminated scrolls were generated by scholars and copyists.

Interest in art and culture continued even as the political power of the German rulers was eroded in favor of Rome. Local leaders enlarged their own holdings with little interference, and in 1231 the first moves were made by the Germans which would lead to incorporation of Prussia into the German Empire.

Yet the arts flourished. Early musical tradition began with such figures as Walter von der Vogelweide (c. 1160–1230), a Minnesinger who traveled the empire singing of love and knightly deeds, and considered the father of German lyric poetry, from which sprang such classics as *Parsifal* and *Tristan,* immortalized by Richard Wagner's music. Architecture sought inspiration in the Gothic designs of northern France and the lighter, more buoyant Gothic began to replace the heavier Romanesque style. Cities and trade prospered, with merchants finding riches to be brought back from the exotic East. Europe generally, northern Germany in particular, was gaining from the development.

Enter Luther

At the end of the 15th century, one Martin Luther (1483–1546) appeared upon this relatively (by European standards) calm scene. Luther was a Roman Catholic priest at the Augustinian monastery at Wittenberg (now in East Germany), who publicly objected to the Church's selling of indulgences, whereby for an amount of cash, various sins would be forgiven. The practice was in wide use and abuse, and Luther's criticisms quickly found favor with the oppressed peasantry. For his ideas, Luther was banned from the empire by a decision of the Diet of Worms in 1521, but the Reformation was underway.

Efforts to squelch the reform movement were made, but to little avail. In 1526, the "Lutheran" landholders were given the right to practise their own religion within their own holdings. Wittenberg is close to the center of what is now East Germany; logically then, as the movement spread it attracted adherents in the immediate region, accounting for the Protestantism of East Germany today.

The development of movable type by Johann Gutenberg in Mainz and the spread of printing, contributed to the diffusion of new ideas, of which

Protestantism was only one part. A spirit of change was sweeping through Europe. A broad Renaissance ensued, embodying new concepts of art, architecture, literature and music. The new church would have done better but for the divisions among the Protestants, with one force supporting Luther's concepts, another the ideas put forth by John Calvin in Geneva.

Meanwhile Rome had launched a counter-reformation to combat the rise of Protestantism. One escalation led to another during the latter part of the 16th century, and the opposing forces found themselves locked into what was to be called the Thirty Years' War (1618–1648). This, of course, contributed much to the chaos which led to the early Protestant emigrations from Europe to America. Within Europe, when the war ended, no one had won, except possibly the Swiss and the Dutch—the independence of Switzerland and the Netherlands was confirmed by the Peace of Westphalia which ended the war. Germany, however, was a patchwork of religious enclaves, the empire again shattered.

The arts in Germany which had so prospered along with the flowering of the Reformation, collapsed during the Thirty Years' War and lay dormant for most of the rest of the century, the talented artists having fled to Italy or the Netherlands.

When prosperity began to return to the region, it was to Italy that the wealthy rulers and merchants looked for new ideas. The Baroque, so popular in lands to the south, was seized as the newest artistic movement. Of the examples which abound, few are more glorious than the (now restored) Zwinger in Dresden, designed by Matthaeus Daniel Pöppelmann (1662–1736) for the Elector of Saxony. Occasional pieces by Fischer von Erlach (1656–1723) and Johann Lucas von Hildebrandt (1668–1745) can be found in East Germany, although these masters of Italian Baroque architecture are more generally associated with Austria, Bohemia and Bavaria. Wealth also supported music, giving rise to such figures as Johann Sebastian Bach (1685–1750) who began in Weimar but is more closely associated with Leipzig. His post as cantor (choir leader, really; Bach was a staunch Protestant) and organist in the St. Thomas church shaped much of his musical outpouring, but his inventiveness and musical genius have left a permanent mark on all music to this day. In Halle, not far from Leipzig, George Friedrich Handel (1685–1759) was experimenting in a more Italianate, lighter style.

Enter the Prussians

During the 15th and 16th centuries the Prussian territories had been expanded many times over, and by the mid-17th century, the Hohenzollern dynasty was firmly in charge. The family head had progressed from Elector to self-proclaimed king. At the start of the 1700s Frederick William I reinforced the military position of his kingdom, making Berlin its center. When his son Frederick the Great took over in 1740, he inherited a powerfully armed Protestant military state lacking only further consolidation, which Frederick promptly undertook. With other European leaders preoccupied by their own affairs, Frederick launched campaigns which gained him large areas of Poland to the east; then with West Prussia secured as well, a tie was created to the state of Brandenburg.

Frederick's interests were not only military. He was tolerant of the Catholics and sought to promote German literature and music. Although his rule ended in 1786, the climate had been such as to encourage such writers as Johann Herder (1744–1803); playwright and critic Gotthold Ephraim Lessing (1729–81) was the first German to achieve European recognition in his field.

Prosperity was relatively shortlived. Prussia was defeated by Napoleon and had to submit to being carved into a collection of small pieces. But in the end the Prussians won out: Napoleon, victim of his own illusions of grandeur, lost to the Russians. The ensuing Congress of Vienna (1814–15) put both Prussia and Austria back together again. German nationalism took on a resurgence, inspired by such literary giants as Johann Wolfgang von Goethe (1749–1832) and dramatist Friedrich Schiller (1759–1805).

In 1818 Prussia established a customs union which triggered a period of both new prosperity and unity. As more German states joined the union, Prussia became the focal point of the unity movement. Bismarck rose to the premiership of Prussia in 1862 and by a succession of military moves, gained control of all Germany and election to chancellorship of the confederation's parliament. War with France only fired German nationalistic feelings even further. But weaknesses in the confederation were starting to show, and only firm measures could keep the union together. At the same time, social changes were taking place with the increase of industrialization and the formation of early trade unions. Karl Marx (1818–83) and Friedrich Engels (1820–95) had introduced new and, to Bismarck, disturbing ideas of worker power in their *Communist Manifesto* in 1848. Rather than address the social ills of the day, Bismarck turned to foreign adventures in Africa, at the same time building a powerful navy and arms industry. These were no panaceas for domestic problems. Bismarck resigned in 1890, leaving behind a strong militaristic regime and an uncertain Kaiser. Germany floundered until the assassination at Sarajevo put the spark to the powder and World War I began.

Postwar Disaster

When the allied powers met in Versailles, it was to have been a peace for all time. But the Weimar Republic was proclaimed by German politicians with no claim to national concensus or real leadership. The period after World War I was marked by one economic collapse after the other. Inflation was rampant, the government unable to achieve real reform. Fears of communism led to worker oppression. Unemployment was widespread and the middle and working classes were forced to seek any way out of their problems. The cultural scene was mad: artists such as George Grosz (1893–1969) and Max Beckmann (1884–1969) painted the world as they saw it, in a new realism which did not seek to hide the harshness; the *Bauhaus* movement flourished under the leadership of architect Walter Gropius (1883–1969), seeking relief from the chaos through simplification and coordination of design and elements in architecture, furniture and decoration.

The scene was set for the rise of Adolf Hitler, who offered a mix of nationalism, militarism, jobs and the promise of a Germany reborn into a better tomorrow. Hitler achieved election to the position of chancellor in 1933, by means mainly legal under Germany's postwar Weimar constitution. A series of tough measures succeeded in accomplishing an economic turnaround. Yet his thundering antisemitism sent vast numbers of artists and intellectuals, by no means all of them Jews, out of the country, to the gain of the nations in which they sought refuge.

Hitler had become a popular figure, a rallying point around which the German people could regain some of their lost self-respect. The rebuilt armed forces bullied their way into the Rhineland, demilitarized following the war. Austria was annexed to form the greater German empire. War was inevitable, and came as German troops marched into Poland in September 1939. The French and British moved to meet their guarantees toward Poland. World War II was underway. The Soviets had been silenced by a pact signed just a month before, conveniently kept by Hitler until his forces attacked the Soviet Union in June 1941.

Slow Recovery

When the German forces surrendered in 1945, Soviet troops were in the eastern part of the country, U.S., British and French forces in the western. This fact set the course of subsequent history. The split was a difficult one for the eastern sector: while there had been heavy concentrations of industry around such centers as Berlin, Leipzig and Dresden, most of the raw materials to support industry are found in the west. East Germany has thus become heavily dependent on the Soviet Union for its fuels, particularly gas and oil, and for ores and other raw materials. In the immediate postwar years, the Soviets carried off as war reparations nearly all industrial and transport equipment of any value whatsoever, leaving East Germany to rebuild its industrial base as best it could. It is a tribute to the people that this has been achieved at all—East Germany now ranks about eleventh among world industrial powers—but the contrast to West Germany is instantly evident when the border is crossed. Nevertheless, living standards are high by East European norms and continue to improve at a steady pace.

In June 1953, workers in East Berlin and other major cities rose up in protest over the government's policies. Soviet troops put down the disturbance. This chain of events in turn helped inspire one of the more lasting landmarks of the cold war of the '50s and '60s: the Berlin Wall. This demarcation line appeared overnight on 13 August 1961, built by the G.D.R. to prevent further migration to the West via Berlin. During the 1950s, close to four million East Germans sought refuge in the West, many of them doctors, engineers, skilled laborers and others whom East German officials were unwilling to have leave the country, then as now suffering from labor shortages.

In the 1960s, East Germany's isolation forced it to turn even more toward the Soviet Union and the other Warsaw Pact allies for economic and political support. Not until the end of 1972 did the Western powers agree to extend diplomatic recognition to the G.D.R.; up to that point, they had maintained that the G.D.R. was a zone of Germany occupied by the Soviet Union. Whether as a direct result of diplomatic acceptance to the world community or not, the policies of the G.D.R. have since undergone notable relaxation. The country is a member of the United Nations and has increased contacts with other countries, ranging from political to commercial to cultural.

The country as a whole most definitely has not been made over in a new mold by the socialist leadership. Traditions and culture have been kept, particularly in the smaller villages. Religion is still important, with close to 50 percent of the population declaring itself as Protestant, another 8 percent as Catholic. With ongoing restoration and reconstruction in such cities as Berlin, Dresden and Leipzig, the country is proclaiming its links to the past, ties of which no one today in the G.D.R. is ashamed.

EAST GERMAN
FOOD AND DRINK

Beer, Eisbein and Sauerkraut

Dishes on East German menus in the cities reflect two strong traditions: standard fare found throughout Germany, East or West (very often north German), and East European cuisine. Proximity to the eastern cultures of Poland and Czechoslovakia has made the foods of these countries familiar to most East Germans, and the pervading sense of isolation from the West and pressure toward acceptance by the Eastern bloc, has also brought about a greater—if enforced—acquaintance with the foods of the Baltic states and the rest of the Soviet Union. Only the hotels have wandered toward the more exotic, as represented by the Chinese and Japanese; even Italian is surprisingly absent. Without the "guest workers" so prevalent in West Germany, the G.D.R. has sadly missed out on the Turkish, Yugoslav and Greek influences which have so brightened food and restaurant offerings in West Germany and other parts of Europe.

While few surprises are to be expected when dining out in East Germany, many of the "standards" are excellent and will vary from restaurant to restaurant depending on the prestige of the house and the enthusiasm of the chef for mild experimentation. In the hotels and restaurants which cater particularly to tourists, explanations on menus may be in several languages including English, and waiters are always willing to attempt a translation, even in the smaller restaurants.

Soups and Salads

Main meals in East Germany usually start with a soup (*Suppe*), which can range from a clear broth (*Klare Suppe*) to a thick mixed vegetable soup (*Gebundene Gemüsesuppe*), or a thick soup based on a specific vegetable such as green peas (*Erbensuppe*), cauliflower (*Blumenkohlsuppe*), or cabbage (*Krautsuppe*). These are served with a basket of rolls or dark bread— note that in smaller restaurants you will be charged separately for the number of rolls you take.

Salads in the U.S. or British sense are not as widespread in East Germany, but a small salad is often included as part of or alongside a main dish. The concept of a salad bar is growing, at least in Berlin, where you simply help yourself to as much of whatever it is you want. Otherwise, the fare is standard: cabbage (*Krautsalat*), cucumber (*Gurkensalat*), German potato (*Kartoffelsalat*), beet (*Rote Ruben Salat*), white beans (*Bohnensalat*), to list the ones you are most likely to encounter, aside from plain lettuce (*Grünen Salat*).

Standards and Specialties

In the category of main dishes, certain standards will appear regularly. Most famous of these is *Eisbein* (knuckle of pork), usually served with *Sauerkraut* and *Knödel* (bread dumpling). But you will also find *Rindgeschabtes,* a local version of beefsteak Tartare, *Hackepeter,* a minced mixture of pork and beef, thus a form of hamburger, *Kassler Rippchen,* a cut of ham steak, and *Schlachteplatte,* a mixed grill. These traditional dishes are evident throughout the country, brightened by local specialties.

In Berlin, for example, the best fish is to be found among the restaurants in the *Spreewald,* the Spree forest surrounding a group of lakes and waterways easily reachable by the "S"-Bahn rail line (to Treptower Park, Schöneweide or Grunau stations) and if time allows by boat onward (*"Weisse Flotte";* the "White Fleet"). In addition to *Fisch in Spreewaldsosse* (freshwater fish in season with a local sauce), you will also find *Aal* (eel) dishes. In the country sausages are ubiquitous as well, and in addition to fish, in the woods around the lake area you will be offered *Spreewälder Wurstplatte mit Meerrettich,* cold cuts and cold sausages with (usually freshly-grated) horseradish, and *Quark mit Leinöl,* a rather strong cheese doused with oil. Other than herring—pickled and otherwise—fish is not so prevalent again on restaurant menus until you reach the Baltic coastal areas. In other parts of the country, head for a *Gastmahl des Meeres,* the name under which a number of fish restaurants operate throughout the country.

Various other parts of East Germany have their own local specialties. In Thuringia you will be offered game and poultry. *Röstbrätl* (pot roast), *Thüringer Sauerbraten mit Klossen* (a form of roasted corned meat with dumplings) and *Bärenschinken* (a type of cured ham) are typical. Harz mountain specialties include *Halberstädter Käsesuppe* (cheese soup) and *Harzer Köhlerteller mit Röstkartoffeln* (charcoal grilled meat, usually a form of mixed grill, with roast potatoes).

Desserts in East Germany can range from fancy cakes (*Torte*) to cheeses (*Käse*) of various sorts, the cheeses usually far more readily identifiable than the assortment of cakes. *Eis* is ice cream, and although an egg in German is an *Ei, Gemischtes Eis* is not scrambled eggs, but ice cream of mixed flavors.

What to Drink

Beer is the national drink in East Germany, and there are a number of breweries, even in Berlin itself, and they all have their loyal followers. Many restaurants have a separate *Bierstube* where you can get a glass of beer and a light salad plate or snack at very reasonable prices. Note, however, that "wine restaurants" do not serve beer. Beer prices are both subsidized and fixed by the state, so outside of the 5-star hotels, you can enjoy and enjoy with not a care for the bill. Beer is served by the glass on draft (*Fassbier*) in two basic sizes, large, or ½ liter (about a pint) and small, or ¼ liter, about a half pint. Bottled beer will either be in ½ liter or 1/3 liter containers. The Berliners in particular like to "strengthen" their beer with a healthy shot of one liquor or another, either alongside or within the beer, but all that is a matter of taste and fortitude. The beer itself is so good it seems a shame not to enjoy it in its unadulterated state.

Wines in East Germany tend to come from other East European countries, although they do have their own white wine, rather on the sweet side. For an economical and drier choice, try the Bulgarian and Hungarian wines, both red and white, many of which are excellent. West German, Austrian, French and Yugoslav wines can also be found, priced according to the fact that they have been imported for hard currency. Vodkas tend to come from Poland or the Soviet Union and are excellent. The offering on the hard side is rounded out by local *Schnapps* (brandies and liquors), distilled from anything ranging from cherries to grains. Try a *Kornbranntwein* for the East German idea of a rye whiskey.

Drinking of coffee or tea in East Germany is according to central European tradition: ample quantities with breakfast, and later in the day a small cup of coffee may end a meal or it may serve as reason for a break in a shopping or sightseeing trip, then often accompanied by a slice of cake or other similar restorative.

If you prefer to avoid wine or beer with meals, simply ask for mineral water (*Mineralwasser*); a glass of plain water may be served alongside a cup of coffee in one of the more elegant cafes but would never be offered at mealtime.

EAST BERLIN

Capital City

Much of Berlin (then with no East or West) was devastated during World War II. East Berlin, without the massive financial backing of the Western allies, has had to rebuild piecemeal as best it could. First priority was given to housing, and the results, in the form of such huge apartment complexes as those along the Leipziger Strasse, are functional if not attractive. Other areas and features of the city have taken longer to be restored, rebuilt or replaced. War ruins are still much in evidence in East Berlin, although with the major problem of providing housing generally taken care of, officials are now moving with greater speed toward sprucing up the less essential elements of the city.

Berlin celebrated the 750th anniversary of its founding in 1987. This gave East Germany reason enough to undertake a massive rebuilding of the Friedrichstrasse, the first thoroughfare Western visitors see when entering the city from West Berlin via "Checkpoint Charlie." The country's most luxurious hotel and a host of new restaurants and cafes give a very different first impression of the city as construction work is completed and scaffolding is moved to the next project.

The city itself was created when two small fishing villages were merged: Berlin, on the right bank of the Spree river, and Cölln, on an island in the river. The Fischerinsel (Fisherman's Island) of today's Berlin thus marks the core of the original city, first established in 1237 according to the earliest records. As a waterway for trade, the river gave rise to the city's growth and prominence, with the Havel and Spree rivers tying into the Elbe and onward to the sea.

In 1432 the two communities jointly took the name Berlin. The city and its merchant class prospered. Corn and grain were brought to Berlin from surrounding areas for shipment by river to the port of Hamburg; indeed, Berlin achieved sufficient importance that it was joined with Hamburg, Lübeck, Bremen and other northern cities in the Hanseatic League. This confederation of traders and merchants was set up in the Middle Ages to defend, in every sense of the word, the trade monopolies and member towns.

The character of Berlin changed rapidly when the city dropped its Hanseatic League membership and construction began on a palace for the Hohenzollern ruling elector Friedrich II. At that point Berlin became the residential seat of the Hohenzollern family, exchanging some of its coarser trappings as a trading center for the formalities and elegance of the court.

The Reformation and the Thirty Years' War left their mark on the city and it was not until the mid-1600s under the next Friedrich II that the city began to prosper again. Craftsmen and tradesmen reappeared; manufacturing began. The first Jewish community was established in 1671 and even exiled Huguenots found quarter in the city. New districts were added, including parks and the thoroughfare Unter den Linden.

As the Prussians took control, the spirit of Berlin shifted again under Friedrich Wilhelm I. The residency was upgraded to a full royal capital, but it was not until the reign of yet another Friedrich II—this one being "the Great" (reign 1740–1786)—that the city began to take on true European character. The royal opera was established in 1743 and St. Hedwig's cathedral built (reconstructed 1963).

Napoleon swept into Berlin through the Brandenburg Gate in 1806, occupying the city for three years. Once freed of the French forces, redevelopment took hold. Wilhelm von Humboldt established the university in 1810 and such architects as Schinkel, Rauch and Schadow created the Schauspielhaus (theater), the Altes (Old) Museum and the Neue Wache (New Guard House).

In the late 19th century, the city burst beyond its former core. Swept up with the industrial revolution, Berlin became one of the leading manufacturing centers of the world. This in turn led to the city's becoming a focal point for the German working class movement and its struggles which marked German politics so strongly in the 1920s and '30s. It was the city of Marx, Engels and Lenin—the German communist party was formed here in 1919. The names of early party leaders now identify major streets in East Berlin: Karl Liebknecht, Ernst Thälmann, Wilhelm Pieck and Rosa Luxemburg were all prominent in the party movement up to the takeover by the Nazis under Hitler in 1933.

When the Soviets entered Berlin in April 1945, it was a ruined city. The sectoral division followed that June, with the Eastern Sector proclaimed capital by the G.D.R. in October 1949.

Exploring East Berlin

East Berlin is a fairly easy city to see. Regular tours are available for those who want a reasonably fast, organized once-over. But by far the best way to get acquainted with East Berlin is on foot or by means of the easy and cheap public transportation system.

Those who enter via Checkpoint Charlie will find themselves at the lower end of the Friedrichstrasse, still a main north-south artery of what

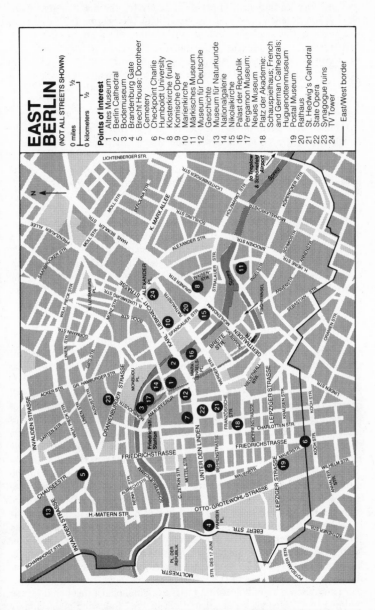

EAST BERLIN
(NOT ALL STREETS SHOWN)

0 miles   ½
0 kilometers   ½

Points of interest

1   Altes Museum
2   Berlin Cathedral
3   Bodemuseum
4   Brandenburg Gate
5   Brecht House; Dorotheer Cemetery
6   Checkpoint Charlie
7   Humboldt University
8   Klosterkirche (ruin)
9   Komische Oper
10 Marienkirche
11 Märkisches Museum
12 Museum für Deutsche Geschichte
13 Museum für Naturkunde
14 Nationalgalerie
15 Nikolaikirche
16 Palast der Republik
17 Pergamon Museum; Neues Museum
18 Platz der Akademie: Schauspielhaus; French and German Cathedrals; Huguenottenmuseum
19 Postal Museum
20 Rathaus
21 St. Hedwig's Cathedral
22 State Opera
23 Synagogue ruins
24 TV Tower

—— East/West border

was once the city center. The first main cross street is the Leipziger Strasse, with the rather dilapidated Postal Museum further to the left, and a broad thoroughfare leading east, impressive mainly for the massive apartment blocks along the south side of the street, plus the possibility of dining in Bulgarian or Czechoslovak style in one or other of the restaurants in the buildings. But pressing along up the refurbished Friedrichstrasse, turn right into the Mohrenstrasse to discover the recently-restored twin cathedrals (French to the north, German to the south), which help shape the Platz der Akademie. The neo-Classical Schauspielhaus (literally, theater, but now the leading concert hall), designed by the architect Karl Friedrich Schinkel in 1818–21, was reconstructed and reopened in 1984.

Headed west again along the Behrenstrasse, the corner of Friedrichstrasse is now graced by the new Grand Hotel, a complex which includes restaurants, cafes, bars and other service facilities—the most luxurious (and expensive) of East Germany's hotels, opened in 1987. Next to the hotel in the Behrenstrasse is the Komische Oper (Comic Opera), Berlin's main operetta and light opera theater in its modern quarters, where Walter Felsenstein established his reputation as an operatic producer.

Turning right into the Otto-Grotewohl-Strasse brings you almost immediately to Pariser Platz, with the massive Brandenburg Gate (completed in 1791) at your left, now rather definitively marking the border between east and west. The monument is on the eastern side of the line, so presumably East German officials were within their rights when they turned the chariots-and-horses sculpture (by J. G. Schadow) at the top around to face eastward a few years ago.

Along the Unter den Linden

Should you decide to approach the city from other than Checkpoint Charlie, the Brandenburg Gate at the foot of Unter den Linden is also a good point from which to begin. The boulevard leads east to the Schlossbrücke, renamed Marx-Engels Bridge, across the Spree Canal, and still reflects the elegance which typified Berlin from the 18th century onward.

Heading eastward along Unter den Linden, you will find both left and right a range of buildings, new, old and reconstructed, housing embassies, shops, restaurants, cafes and all manner of cultural attractions. Across the Friedrichstrasse, on the left, is the Interhotel Unter den Linden; directly opposite, the Linden Corso—a restaurant, cafe and dance hall. On the north side is the State Library, with a host of treasures covering the entire history of Germany. Next door, Humboldt University, a former palace (completed 1766), but since 1810 home of Berlin's first and major university. Opposite is the State Opera, built at the command of Frederick the Great in 1743, rebuilt and reopened in 1955 and again restored in 1986. Next to the opera is the Opera Cafe, housing not only a very elegant cafe, but restaurants and other public rooms. Alongside is the Baroque residence and former palace of the Prussian princes, now the official government guest house, rebuilt according to the original plans. Just behind these buildings is St. Hedwig's Cathedral, built in 1747 following plans similar to Rome's Pantheon; rebuilt in 1963. Note the old street name "Hinter der Katholiche Kirche," quite literally "behind the Catholic church."

Back on Unter den Linden, tucked in next to the university, you'll discover the Central House of German-Soviet Friendship which includes a small restaurant and occasionally has an exhibition which may be of interest. Next door, however, is the Museum für Deutsche Geschichte (Museum of German History), covering all of Germany from the beginnings onward and with occasional special exhibits of wider interest. The building itself was the former Zeughaus or arsenal, built 1695–1706; go into the courtyard to see the 22 impressive reliefs portraying facial expressions of dying soldiers.

The adjoining Schlossbrücke, the bridge over the Spree, has also been restored, including the dramatic figures created by architect-sculptor Schinkel. Cross the bridge over the canal and you will be confronted with a decision: to turn left toward the museums, or right toward the Fischerinsel (Fisherman's Island)? Whichever, the choice will be right. Assuming it is that direction as well, wander back along the canal. The huge edifice off to your left is the Palace of the Republic, a showcase affair, surely with at least one lightbulb for each of the thousands of people it can hold in the main floor rooms; location of pop concerts, shows and other popular events and containing a gallery and a variety of restaurants and cafes.

Once beyond postwar ostentation, you will soon come toward what is really the oldest part of Berlin. If you can ignore the modern party headquarters building on the west side, look ahead to the old drawbridge and concentrate more on the left, where there are some interesting if not antique buildings. Turn into the Sperlgasse or into the Scharengasse to the Breite Strasse, where you will find other older and charmingly quaint buildings (Alte Marstall, 1670, Ribbeckhaus, 1624).

Across the Gertraudenstrasse you will come to the walkway on the south side of the canal; it has been beautifully restored, including the Ermeler Haus (moved here from the Breite Strasse) with its restaurants and the Otto Nagel Haus, now a museum of proletarian-revolutionary art. Not much further along is the Märkisches Museum—the cultural museum of the city of Berlin—which has displays showing the city history from the beginning onward; in fact, it all began just about here. Alongside are the (live) Berlin bears, traditional symbol of the city.

The Museuminsel

At the north end of the area between the Spree canal and the river is the Museuminsel, or Museum Island. No matter what your feelings about art and history, there are enough treasures here alone to justify a visit to Berlin. The Pergamon Museum is the goal of thousands; allow enough time for it. The Pergamon altar, part of an ancient temple complex unearthed and brought stone by stone from Turkey to Berlin, is one of the Seven Wonders of the World, and sensational to behold—as is the partly reconstructed street of Babylon.

The other museums of the complex are less sensational, but certainly worth a visit. The Bodemuseum has an outstanding Egyptian collection, early Christian and Byzantine art, a coin collection and sculpture and painting galleries. The National Gallery shows mainly 19th and 20th century works, and has an emphasis on art from the Soviet Union and the other Eastern bloc countries. The "New Museum" to the south remains a ruin, but the neo-Classical Altes Museum (Old Museum), designed by K.F. Schinkel and originally built in 1825–30, has been rebuilt and houses an interesting collection as well as regular shows. Across from the Altes Museum is the Berlin Cathedral, something of an amalgam of architectural styles, built 1894–1905 and now restored thanks to contributions from West Germany. A small museum traces the reconstruction of the building.

From the north end of the Museuminsel, wander up the Monbijoustrasse to the Oranienburger Strasse. On the north side you will find the ruin of the former main synagogue (scheduled for restoration), designed by the architect Knoblauch, built in 1859–66 and a fascinating example of both brickwork and Moorish influence. The building was not only a victim of wartime bombing, but also of the "crystal night" in 1938 in which Jewish shops and synagogues throughout Germany were destroyed and burned by Nazis and their sympathizers.

Alexanderplatz

Wherever you may have been in Berlin, the mast of the TV tower on Alexanderplatz will have served as an easily-identifiable marker. Indeed, the 365 meter (1,190 ft.) tower, opened in 1969, serves not only as a central point for radio and TV transmissions and other communications, and home to a revolving restaurant at the 200 meter (650 ft.) level, but as symbol of East Berlin as well. The area around the tower and the surrounding park deserve exploration, whether or not your curiosity over "the best view in Berlin" requires that you take the lift to the observation levels of the tower.

To the northeast (just beyond the "S"-Bahn station) is the Centrum department store, Berlin's largest. Alongside is a plaza with the international clock, a host of specialized snack bars and cafes and the Interhotel Stadt Berlin, with several good restaurants. Across the Karl-Liebknecht-Strasse are a number of shops, several of which are national outlets run by other East European countries and featuring handiwork and specialties, often at rather good prices. For a fascinating experience, wander around back of the block into the market hall, a collection of stands and stalls offering about as wide a variety of foods, fresh and otherwise, as is to be found in East Germany.

Across the street is the restored Marienkirche (13th century), interesting not only for its construction as a brick building, but also for the triple nave design. The *Totentanz* (Dance of Death) fresco in the church dates from the 15th century. South of the church in the center of the park is the Neptune fountain. Further along Karl-Liebknecht-Strasse is the Palast Hotel, the city's very best and newest until the Grand opened, still a central point for theater tickets and some excellent restaurants. The southeast side of the plaza offers a long modern block (Rathauspassagen, or city hall passages) housing a number of shops, restaurants and snack bars on several levels. Alongside is the city hall itself (Rathaus), a block-large brick edifice in neo-Gothic style as interpreted in 1861–69, badly damaged in the war but rebuilt in 1945, with its frieze depicting famous events from the city's history. The cellar of the Rathaus contains both a wine restaurant and a Bierkeller.

Just south of the Rathaus is one of the more fascinating reconstructions in Berlin, an entire quarter which has been partially restored, partially rebuilt. The heart of the complex is the Nikolaikirche (St. Nicholas' Church), the city's oldest (begun in 1230), surrounded by a collection of small shops, restaurants and miniature parks, altogether a jewel well worth exploring. Nearby, back of the Mühlendamm, is a small park including the ruins of the Klosterkirche, an early cloister built alongside the old city wall (pieces of which are still in evidence). Not far away is the Waisenstrasse, a tiny street but known to insiders for Berlin's oldest and surely one of its quaintest restaurants, where Napoleon is said to have sat and dined in front of the impressive tile stove.

Chauseestrasse and Two Cemeteries

Given sufficient time and energy, the upper end of Friedrichstrasse and the Chauseestrasse are worth exploring. The stretch is undergoing restoration, a project which will take until 1990. Moving from Unter den Linden northward, the impressive skyscraper to the right is the International Trade Center, drawing attention away from the Metropol Hotel and the Friedrichstrasse railway station on the left. Cross under the tracks and head toward the bridge. The Schiffbauerdamm to your left just over the bridge offers several choices in restaurants as well as the Berlin Ensemble theater. There are shops for prints and old books in the upper Friedrichstrasse.

Further along into the Chauseestrasse is the one-time residence of Bertolt Brecht, now a combined museum/theater/cellar restaurant/cafe. Alongside is the Dorotheenstädtischer Friedhof (Dorotheer Cemetery), an intriguing collection of final resting places for a host of names you will by now find familiar: not only Brecht and his wife Helene Weigel, but also the architect/sculptors Schinkel and Schadow and the Berlin printer Litfass, who invented those cylindrical columns now familiar in cities throughout the continent which carry theater schedules and advertising posters.

The last stop on most tours of the city is generally to the Soviet military cemetery at Treptow, another monolithic construction, built with marble taken from Hitler's Reich Chancellery among other places. On either side of the broad avenue leading up to the massive statue of a Russian soldier that forms the heart of the complex are stone reliefs portraying episodes from World War II, lauding the heroic Soviet troops who defeated the fascist forces of the Nazis. Visitors to the cemetery will experience much more commentary in this vein from their guide.

Potsdam

Potsdam, some 30 km. (20 miles) southwest of Berlin, assumed significance in German history in 1660 when the Prince Elector of Prussia, Friedrich Wilhelm, determined to make what had until then been no more than a small settlement the site of his palace. He duly built a palace there and the town thereafter became the principal seat of the Hohenzollerns, later Kings of Prussia, and in the 18th century the dominant power in German affairs. As the influence of the Hohenzollerns grew, so they built ever more lavishly, largely in imitation of the French kings, in particular of their magnificent palace at Versailles. This French influence, in part at any rate the result of the influx of Huguenots from France at the beginning of the 18th century but owing as much to Frederick the Great's admiration for all things French, is most evident at Sans Souci, a delightful Baroque palace dating from 1745. Its Concert Room is particularly fine, but there are also a number of magnificent picture galleries, containing works by Rubens, Van Dyck and Caravaggio among others. In addition, the rooms where Voltaire lived have also been preserved. Voltaire was the most celebrated of 18th-century French philosophers and greatly admired by Frederick the Great who invited him to Potsdam. A visit to the Cecilienhof, a modern palace built in a medieval mode, also presents certain features of interest. Here Truman, Stalin and Churchill signed the Potsdam Agreement in 1945 which effectively sealed the fate of post-war Germany, enabling the Soviet forces to remain in control of those areas of Germany that their drive into Germany had won for them; in other words, East Germany. The significance and meaning of the Agreement tends, not unnaturally perhaps, to be seen in a somewhat different light by the East German authorities, as your guide will no doubt make clear.

As well as its architectural treasures, Potsdam today is also a substantial industrial center, with a population in excess of one million. Nonetheless, areas of the center and much of the surrounding countryside are generally unspoilt, the latter being densely wooded in parts.

PRACTICAL INFORMATION FOR EAST BERLIN

TOURIST INFORMATION. *Reisebüro der D.D.R.,* Alexanderplatz 5 (tel. 215–4328); special service office for foreign visitors on second floor (tel. 215–4402).

WHEN TO COME. Berlin is a year-round city with something going on all the time. But winter is a dreary season, cold and damp, and the air hangs heavy with acrid fumes generated by brown coal, the basic East German heating fuel. Unfortunately much of the cultural activity reaches its peak during winter. The city comes to life in late April or early May and is thoroughly enjoyable at least until October. Summer evenings are pleasant for strolling or dining outdoors.

GETTING AROUND EAST BERLIN. Public transportation is generally good and very inexpensive. You can save yourself the bother of separate tickets by getting a tourist ticket (*Touristenfahrkarte*) at any of the main railroad stations, "S"- or "U"-Bahn stations or at the central information center, Reisebüro der D.D.R., at Alexanderplatz. A ticket good for unlimited travel for one day costs M.1.00 for the "S"-Bahn alone, M.2.00 for all surface and underground transport. The latter ticket also covers the run out to Schönefeld Airport.

To get into town from the airport there is a shuttle bus which runs from the air terminal to the Schönefeld "S"-Bahn station (fare M.0.10 for you and M.0.10 for each large bag, tickets out of an automatic dispenser on the bus), although you still have a moderate hike within the rail station to the platform. Trains run every 20 minutes to the Friedrichstrasse station via Alexanderplatz, or change at Ostkreuz. Fare is M.0.30 to the city center, about a 40 minute ride. Tickets from a dispenser (exact change!) in the passageway under the tracks. There is also a shuttle bus service from Schönefeld to West Berlin.

By Tram, Bus and Subway. Fares on buses, streetcars and subway are a uniform M.0.20 within the main city area, allowing transfer from one line or form of transport to the other. The scheme is much on the honor system: you deposit the coin(s) into a box on the bus or tram, pull a lever several times until the machine dispenses a printed strip of paper which is your ticket, and off you go. If you transfer, you are expected to deposit the ticket from the first line into the box and dispense yourself a new one for the next leg, but as the dispensers are not altogether reliable and you are a foreigner anyway, you probably don't need to worry much about the foibles of the system's mechanics.

Maps are available showing bus and streetcar routes. The latter are somewhat more difficult to decipher than the subway routes, which are better identified. Stops on bus and streetcar routes are marked with an "H" or "HH" sign, under which you can find a listing of streets and stops on each route. Routes and stops are also identified in the buses and streetcars themselves, and other passengers are generally helpful in assisting tourists find their destinations. Subway stations are marked with a prominent "U", trains with their ultimate destinations.

By "S"-Bahn. The elevated electric rail line through the city is fast and frequent. Pasteboard tickets are dispensed from machines (exact change!) for M.0.20 (some distant destinations M.0.30 or higher; fares are posted at all stations) or can be had from the ticket offices in the larger stations. The ticket is then validated by poking it in the slot of a device at the bottom of each platform, banging a lever and extracting the stamped ticket. Take your cue from the other passengers. The "S"-Bahn comes to a halt at the Friedrichstrasse station although passenger trains cross over into West Berlin at that point. Main transfer points are Alexanderplatz (to the "U"-Bahn) and Ostkreuz, to other "S"-Bahn lines.

By Taxi. Finding a taxi in Berlin can be an adventure, although there are fixed ranks at such popular points as the Friedrichstrasse and Alexanderplatz stations. Taxis can nearly always be flagged around the major hotels. If the "TAXI" light is lit, the cab is available. To order a taxi, ask your hotel concierge, or phone 3644 if you need a cab immediately or the same day in one of the westerly districts of East Berlin, 3366 for the districts to the east of the center, including the airport. Phone 365–4471 if you want to book a taxi for any time in the coming week. Taxi fares are low, with a ride in the center of the city costing M.2–4 (M.0.70–1.10 per km.). Most taxis are metered; round up the fare to the nearest M.0.50 as a tip. You can also take a taxi sightseeing tour of the city, selecting from any of six planned routes starting and ending at Alexanderplatz. Tours last from 40 minutes to 2½ hours and cost M.16.50–55 for up to four persons, depending on the route. Call 246–2255 for details.

Car Hire. Rental cars are available at any of the Interhotels. Rental headquarters is at the Metropol Hotel (tel. 220–4695); cars can be arranged for Schönefeld Airport (tel. 672–2418) as well. Cars range from a small Lada 1300 to Volvo 264. Rates run from about Dm.200 to Dm.510 ($110–285 at writing; both rental and exchange rates may vary) per week. In Berlin there should be sufficient cars available but it pays to order in advance to be sure of getting the model you prefer.

HOTELS. The biggest problem with hotel space in Berlin is that the newer hotels built over the past few years have all been in the deluxe category. Those seeking more modest and less expensive accommodations will have a tough time, as East German travel officials prefer visitors to stay in the newer hotels of the Interhotel group, and often advise that the smaller places are booked. There is little you can do but to insist on your wants; you may even win out. The more modest hotels are filled with guests from the other socialist countries and other parts of East Germany. All Interhotels take credit cards.

The system is such that you cannot get into East Germany—other than on a 24-hour pass from West Berlin—without a hotel reservation, but should you find yourself needing a hotel room, check with the Reisebüro der D.D.R. at Alexanderplatz 5 (tel. 212–4328) and ask for the *Zimmervermittlung.*

Deluxe

Grand Hotel, Friedrichstrasse 158–164, corner Behrenstrasse (tel. 20–920). Interhotel. Berlin's newest and most expensive, opened 1987. Central. 350 rooms and suites, all with bath and color TV, minibar. Air-conditioned, atrium foyer, four restaurants, winter garden, bierstube, bars, concert cafe, swimming pool, sauna, squash courts, shopping arcade, hairdresser, theater tickets, car and yacht rental, garage, convention and meeting facilities.

Metropol, Friedrichstrasse 150–153 (tel. 22–040). Interhotel. Opposite Friedrichstrasse rail station and the International Trade Center. Excellent location, preferred by businessmen. Particularly friendly and helpful staff. 320 rooms, all with bath and color TV, minibar. Public rooms are air-conditioned. Three restaurants, two bars, nightclub, swimming pool, sauna, fitness room, solarium, antiques gallery, shops, car and yacht rental, garage, banquet rooms.

Palast, Karl-Liebknecht-Strasse 5 (tel. 2410). Interhotel. Central, close to museums, many rooms overlooking the Spree river. A favorite with tour groups. 600 rooms, all with bath and color TV, minibar, fully air-conditioned. Six restaurants, four bars, bierstube, nightclub, swimming pool, sauna, fitness room, solarium, bowling, antiques gallery, shops, travel office, theater tickets, car and yacht rental, garage, convention and meeting rooms.

Expensive

Berolina, Karl-Marx-Allee 31 (tel. 210–9541). Interhotel. Less central but quite satisfactory. Convenient to Alexanderplatz, Kongresshalle; Schillingstrasse "U"-Bahn station. 350 rooms, all with bath or shower. Three restaurants, including roof garden restaurant, cafe, bar, souvenir shop, garage.

Stadt Berlin, Alexanderplatz (tel. 2190). Interhotel. The city's largest hotel, something of a landmark for its 40-story height. Central, convenient to shops and transportation. 975 rooms, all with bath or shower. Four restaurants, including roof dining room, cafeteria, beer garden and bierstube, cafes, three bars (one on rooftop), sauna, shops (also adjacent to Centrum department store), garage, meeting facilities.

Unter den Linden, Unter den Linden 14, corner Friedrichstrasse (tel. 220–0311). Interhotel. Less class, but a splendid location, popular gathering point. 307 rooms, all with bath or shower. Restaurant, bar, souvenir shop, garage.

Moderate

Adria, Friedrichstrasse 134 (tel. 282–5451). H-O group. Fairly convenient location, but few rooms with bath. Popular and inexpensive restaurant.

Newa, Invalidenstrasse 115 (tel. 282–5461). H-O group. Ten-minute direct streetcar ride to the city center. Older hotel, few rooms with bath. Inexpensive and fairly good restaurant.

Inexpensive

Hospiz am Bahnhof Friedrichstrasse, Albrechtstrasse 8 (tel. 282–5396). Evangelical church hospice. Fairly convenient location, close to Friedrichstrasse station. 110 rooms, some with bath. Inexpensive and popular restaurant.

Hospiz Auguststrasse, Auguststrasse 82 (tel. 282–5321). Evangelical church hospice. About a ten-minute streetcar ride to city center. 66 rooms, some with bath. Friendly staff. Breakfast only.

MOTELS AND CAMPSITES. Airport-Hotel Schönefeld, Berlin-Schönefeld (tel. 672–3824). Mitropa. Shuttle bus between air terminal and Schönefeld "S"-Bahn station stops at the door.

Motel Grünau, Libboldallee (tel. 681–4198). Wooded part of Berlin, straight out from Treptower Park, in the city district of Grünau. Close to the lake, Grünau "S"-Bahn station for trains to city center.

Campsite "Am Krossinsee", Berlin-Schmockwitz. Intercamp. (See details of camping under *Facts at Your Fingertips*). Open May 1 to Sept. 30. In the southeast corner of the city, directly on a lake. Toilets and showers, hot water, tourist restaurant, food store, sports grounds.

RESTAURANTS. Dining in Berlin has improved remarkably since the days when only the hotel restaurants offered a better class of food and atmosphere. The hotel restaurants remain the more expensive, but for the most part, prices elsewhere are reasonable, quality good to excellent, portions more than adequate and service friendly and quite accommodating. Restaurants are officially classified and priced accordingly, but our listing is based on more direct experience. Note that wine restaurants generally do not offer beer. Most restaurants are open from 10 A.M. to midnight.

Expensive

Ermeler Haus, Märkisches Ufer 10–12 (tel. 279–4036). Wine restaurant upstairs, in a series of rooms reflecting the elegance of this restored patrician house which goes back at least to 1567. Superb atmosphere, excellent food, service, wines. Reservations advisable.

Forellenquintett, Friedrichstrasse, in Grand Hotel. Fish specialties done in the manner of the nearby Spree Forest.

Ganymed, Schiffbauerdamm 5 (tel. 282–9540). Particularly attractive rooms, piano in the evening. Wide choice of excellent dishes from cold plates to cordon bleu, mixed grill, even Indonesian. Closed Monday noon. Reservations advisable, particularly for evenings.

Havanna, Friedrichstrasse 150–153, in Hotel Metropol (tel. 22–040). Cuban and Mexican cuisine à la G.D.R.

Jade, Karl-Liebknecht-Strasse 5, in Palast Hotel (tel. 241–2333). Chinese/Asian specialties, from good to excellent. Reservations recommended for evenings.

Roti d'Or, Karl-Liebknecht-Strasse 5, in Palast Hotel (tel. 241–2245). French cuisine, attractive atmosphere. Hotel guests or payment in hard currency or credit cards only. Reservations essential.

Schwalbennest, Am Marstall (upstairs), Rathausstrasse at Marx-Engels-Forum (tel. 212–4569). New and extremely attractive. Outstanding service and food, with wide choice. But if having a dish flambéed note that the additional price is not on the menu and may come as a surprise. Reservations essential, at noon as well.

Zur Goldenen Gans, Friedrichstrasse, in Grand Hotel. Specialties, particularly game and venison, from the Thüringer Forest area.

Moderate

Berlin-Esprit, Alexanderplatz, in Hotel Stadt Berlin (tel. 2190). Among top choices for Berlin specialties. Reservations recommended.

Brecht-Keller, Chauseestrasse 125, in Bertolt Brecht house (tel. 282–3843). Intimate cellar restaurant serving Viennese cuisine, weekdays only from 7.30 P.M. Reservations essential.

Café Flair, Am Marstall (ground floor), Rathausstrasse at Marx-Engels-Forum (tel. 212–4569). New, excellent, and justifiably immensely popular. Slightly limited but good choice of food, fine service. Tables outside for fine days. Reservations recommended for dining hours.

Gastmahl des Meeres, Spandauer Strasse 4 (tel. 212–3300). International fish specialties.

Historische Weinstuben, Poststrasse 23 (tel. 212–4122). Intimate wine restaurant, Berlin's oldest. Limited menu. Reservations essential.

Linden-Corso, Unter den Linden 17 (tel. 220–2461). Restaurant, concert cafe, dancing evenings; Havanna bar open to 4 A.M.

Operncafé, Unter den Linden 5 (tel. 200–0256). Elegant rooms in one-time palace. Restaurant, popular cafe and wine tavern. Reservations advisable for the restaurant.

Ratskeller, Rathausstrasse 14, in basement of the huge brick City Hall (tel. 212–4464; 212–5301). Atmospheric and highly popular wine and beer cellars (entrances at opposite corners of the building). Reservations recommended.

Stammhaus Bierclub, Friedrichstrasse, in Grand Hotel. Wide range of beers and lighter dishes and snacks.

Wernesgrüner Bierstube, Karl-Liebknecht-Strasse 4 (tel. 282–4268). A pleasant beer cellar serving Berlin food. No-smoking room at noon. Reservations advisable, particularly at lunch.

Inexpensive

Alex Grill, Alexanderplatz, in Hotel Stadt Berlin (tel. 2190). Cafeteria, with no-smoking section. Highly popular at noon.

Alt-Cöllner Schankstuben, Friedrichsgracht 50 (tel. 212–5972). Friendly and charming. Cafe and beer restaurant. Tables outside overlooking canal on pleasant days.

Arkade, Französische Strasse 25 (tel. 208–0273). Cafe-restaurant in art deco style, tables outside in good weather. Grill counter in back. No reservations.

Newa, Invalidenstrasse 115, in Hotel Newa (tel. 282–5461). Short on charm but a fairly extensive menu, even a limited salad bar.

Quick, Karl-Liebknecht-Strasse 5, in Palast Hotel. Self-service cafeteria, good variety and quality. Packed at noon. Open to 8 P.M.

Raabe Diele, Märkisches Ufer 10–12, basement of Ermeler House (tel. 279–4036). Beer cellar with excellent service, good food. House was moved in 1969 to present location, so cellar is new and less atmospheric than upstairs rooms, canned music included.

Rathauspassagen, Rathausstrasse 5. An assortment of restaurants ranging from the **Bierhaus "zur Haxn"** tucked inside the complex specializing in Eisbein (knuckle of pork) from 8 A.M. to midnight, to the **Wurstchen Bar** directly on the street offering various types of frankfurters and sausages. Also includes the **Café Rendezvous** upstairs and the **Alex Treff,** a self-service restaurant and dance cafe.

Zenner, Alt-Treptow 14–17, in Treptower Park outside the center, reachable by streetcars. One of the city's oldest beer gardens, tables outside in summer on the banks of the Spree river.

Zillestube, Alexanderplatz, in Hotel Stadt Berlin (tel. 2190). Typical and popular beer cellar/restaurant serving Berlin specialties.

Zum Paddenwirt, Poststrasse 17 (tel. 212–5067). Small but charming beer restaurant. Limited variety of hot and cold foods. Live music Sundays at 10 A.M. No reservations.

Zum Trichter, Schiffbauerdamm 6–7. Interesting neighborhood establishment, privately run. Open 4 P.M.–1 A.M. daily.

Zur letzten Instanz, Waisenstrasse 14–16 ("U"-Bahn Klosterstrasse) (tel. 212–5528). Original (established 1525) and utterly charming. Limited food choice but genuine Berlin and good. Friendly service. Reservations essential, noon and night.

Zur Rippe, Poststrasse 17 (tel. 212–4932). Minuscule but delightful, specializing in spare ribs. Excellent service. Reservations advisable.

POTSDAM

Hotels and Restaurants. *Potsdam* (L), Lange Brücke (tel. 4631). Interhotel. A 17-story block overlooking the Havel river. 189 rooms, all with bath and color TV. Three restaurants, two cafes, tea salon, coffee bar and nightclub. Sauna, water sports facilities.

Hotel Cecilienhof (L), Neuer Garten (tel. 23–141). Recently rebuilt, the hotel section of this former palace now offers period rooms and suites in a beautiful, quiet garden setting. Less central, but luxury at a somewhat more affordable price.

Restaurants. *Café Rendezvous* (M), Friedrich-Ebert-Strasse 114. Pleasant concert cafe. *Havelland Grill* (E) in Hotel Potsdam. Area specialties. *Klosterkeller* (M), Friedrich-Ebert-Strasse 94, central. *Kulturhaus Hans Marchwitza* (M), Am Alten Markt. Complex includes restaurant, wine restaurant, bar with dancing. *Weinberg-terrassen* (M), Gregor-Mendel-Strasse 29. Choice of a wine pub, bar, restaurant with dancing.

MUSEUMS AND GALLERIES. Altes Museum (Old Museum), Marx-Engels-Platz, entrance Lustgarten. Works by East German artists, print room, collection of sketches and lithographs. Open Wed. to Sun. 9–6, Fri. 10–6.

Bode Museum, Am Kupfergraben, entrance by Monbijou bridge. Egyptian, early Christian and Byzantine collections. Coin collection; prehistoric and early civilization, sculpture. Open Wed. to Sun. 10–6.

Brecht House, Chauseestrasse 125. Berlin living and working quarters of author Bertolt Brecht and Helene Weigel; Brecht archive. Open Tues. and Fri. 10–12, Thurs. 5–7, Sat. 9.30–12 and 12.30–2.

Huguenottenmuseum (Huguenot Museum), Platz der Akademie, Am Französischen Dom. History and art of the Huguenots.

Kunstgewerbe Museum (Arts and Crafts Museum), Köpenck Palace. European crafts covering ten centuries. Jewel room. Contemporary East German handicrafts. Open Mon. to Sat. 9–5, Sun. 10–6.

Märkisches Museum (Cultural Museum), Am Köllnischen Park 5. City museum covering Berlin's history, art, crafts; theater from 1740–1933, art from Baroque to 1945. Open Wed. and Sun. 9–6, Thurs. and Sat. 9–5, Fri. 9–4.

Museum für Deutsche Geschichte (Museum of German History), Unter den Linden 2. Former city arsenal in magnificent Baroque building. History divided into periods for easier consumption; 1917–1945 and 1945 onward are interesting for their East German angle. Special exhibits. Open Mon. to Thurs. 9–7, Sat. and Sun. 10–5.

Museum für Naturkunde (Museum of Natural History), Invalidenstrasse 43. Paleontological, mineralogical and zoological departments. Open Tues. to Sun. 9.30–5.

Nationalgalerie (National Gallery), Bodestrasse. Masters of the 19th and early 20th century; Soviet and other socialist art; items on permanent loan from the Ludwig collection, West Germany. Open Wed. to Sun. 9–6, Fri. 10–6.

Pergamon Museum, Am Kupfergraben. Houses the Pergamon Altar, plus other items from Pergamon and Middle East. Islamic collection. East Asiatic collection. Pergamon Altar and architectural rooms open daily 9–6, Fri. 10–6. Other sections closed Mon. and Tues.

Postmuseum (Postal Museum), Leipziger Strasse/Mauerstrasse. From the postal coach to modern telecommunications. Stamp collection. Check to determine how much can be seen during the period of extensive renovations.

OPERA, CONCERTS, THEATER. Opera and concerts get particularly high ratings in Berlin, but theater is not to be scorned either. Note, however, that productions will be in German. Tickets for concerts and theater can be obtained at the separate box offices in advance or an hour before performance, from the central tourist office (Reisebüro der D.D.R.) at Alexanderplatz 5 or from your hotel service desk. There are special ticket sales offices in the Grand and Palast hotels. To find what's going on, pick up a copy of the monthly publication *Wohin in Berlin?* or check the newspapers. The daily listing also shows if events are sold out or if some tickets are still available.

Concerts generally take place either in the rebuilt Schauspielhaus on Platz der Akadamie (tel. 227–2156) or in the Palast der Republik, Marx-Engels-Platz (tel. 238–2354).

Opera, operetta, ballet and musicals are performed at the Deutsche Staatsoper, Unter den Linden 7 (tel. 20–540); Komische Oper, Behrenstrasse 55–57 (tel. 220–2761); Metropol Theater, Friedrichstrasse 101 (tel. 200–0651); and in the Palast der Republik.

Leading theaters include:

Berliner Ensemble, Bertolt-Brecht-Platz (tel. 28–880). Brecht and works of other international playwrights.

Deutsches Theater, Schumannstrasse 13–14 (tel. 287–1225). Classic and contemporary German drama.

"Distel" (cabaret), Friedrichstrasse 100, plays various locations (tel. 287–1226).

Friedrichstadtpalast, Friedrichstrasse 107 (tel. 28–360). Variety, revue, historic old-Berlin theater pieces.

Kammerspiele, Schmannstrasse 13–14 (tel. 287–1226). Studio theater with works of contemporary and classical authors; jazz concerts.

Maxim-Gorki-Theater, Am Festungsgraben (tel. 207–1843). Plays by local authors, plus some contemporary classics and sharp humor.

Puppentheater (Puppet Theater), Greifswalder Strasse 81–84 (tel. 365–0696). Marionette shows for young and old.

Theater im Palast, Palast der Republik, Marx-Engels Platz (tel. 238–2354). Studio theater with readings, literary programs.

Volksbühne, Rosa-Luxemburg-Platz (tel. 282–9607). Classical and contemporary drama.

NIGHTLIFE. Although not on a par with West Berlin in terms of extravagance, neither are the prices. There are ample diversions after hours; shows, dancing, or both. An evening of dancing, entertainment and wine at the Stadt Berlin can cost as little as Dm.20 (payable in hard currency or with credit card). The other larger hotels offer dinner-dancing as well. For nightclubs with music and atmosphere, try one of the following, bearing in mind that music in the hotels is usually live, discos in the clubs.

Club Metropol, in Hotel Metropol, Friedrichstrasse 150. Show program.

Hafenbar, Chauseestrasse 20. Pleasant ambience, disco.

Haifischer, Unter den Linden 5, in the Opern Café complex.

Panorama Bar, in Hotel Stadt Berlin, Alexanderplatz. Top of the hotel, great view of the city as well.

Sinusbar, in Palast Hotel, Karl-Liebknecht-Strasse 5.

SHOPPING. Shops along Unter den Linden offer goods ranging from porcelain to sheet music, old books, records and textiles. Along the west side of Karl-Liebknecht-Strasse are a number of shops run by other socialist governments. Locally-made jewelry can be found at *Skarabäus,* Frankfurter Allee 80. For antiques, try the state-run shop at Friedrichstrasse 180–184, but note that it is open weekdays only, 12–7, closed Saturdays. There are also antique galleries in the Palast, Metropol and Grand hotels.

For general goods, the *Centrum* department store at the north end of Alexanderplatz offers a full range. The *Intershops* sell a great variety of wares, but only against hard currency or credit cards (American Express, Diners Club). Major Intershops are in the Metropol and Palast hotels, others at various locations around the city.

SIGHTSEEING. The Reisebüro der D.D.R. runs 11 sightseeing tours of the city, ranging from a quick one-hour once-over-lightly of the city center (Tour 1) to a fairly extensive 3 ½-hour trip which includes some of the Berlin lake area as well (Tour 11). Prices range from M.3–M.12, with some of the more extensive tours including a coffee stop. English-speaking guides are available. Details from the Reisebüro (tel. 215–4328 or 215–4402) or from your hotel service desk. Be careful, however; the hotels will encourage you to take a hotel taxi or limousine tour rather than one run by the Reisebüro.

Regular taxi tours run from Alexanderplatz over six fixed routes. See details under "Getting Around East Berlin" at the beginning of this chapter or call 246–2255 for details.

USEFUL ADDRESSES. Embassies. *American,* Neustädtische Kirchstrasse 4–5 (tel. 220–2741). *British,* Unter den Linden 32–34 (tel. 220–2431). There is no Canadian Embassy in East Berlin at present but if circumstances demand, call the Canadian Embassy in Warsaw (from East Berlin, tel. 064–822/298–051; address is Ulica Matejiki 1–5, PL-00481 Warsaw). Alternatively, try the Canadian Military Mission in West Berlin (tel. 849/261–1161). If that fails, the British Embassy will help, provided they know you have made an effort to contact the other two.

Emergency Numbers. Police 110; Fire department 112; Ambulance 115; Pharmacy (apothecary) central service 160. Central motorist's assistance 524–3565, 6 A.M. to 10 P.M.

Exchange. Outside of bank hours, hotel cashiers or the State Bank windows open 24 hours daily at Friedrichstrasse "S"-Bahn station and Schönefeld Airport.

Lost Property. Wilhelm-Pieck-Strasse 164 (tel. 282–6135, 282–3472), open Tues. and Thurs. 10–1 and 2–6, Fri. 10–1. The railroad lost property office is at the rail station at Marx-Engels-Platz (tel. 492–1671), open Mon., Wed. and Fri. 10–4, Tues. 10–6.

Main Post Office. Corner of Ostbahnhof and Strasse der Pariser Kommune, open day and night for telegrams, express letters and small express parcels.

THREE SOUTHERN CITIES

Dresden, Meissen and Leipzig

Splendidly situated on the banks of the broad and impressive Elbe River, Dresden became the capital of Saxony as early as the 15th century, although the architectural masterpieces for which the city was known dated mainly from the 18th century. The famous Italian artist Canaletto (1697–1768) was court painter to Augustus the Strong, who ruled 1694–1733; many Canalettos portraying Dresden and the area can now be found in the city's justly famous picture gallery, in a section of the Zwinger Palace.

The city has long held an attraction for artists. Being in the south of the country and further away from the Prussian dictates of the north, Dresden was more susceptible to Italianate influences in art and architecture. That master of German poetry and drama, Friedrich Schiller (1759–1805) spent the years 1785–1787 in Dresden, during which time he wrote the drama *Don Carlos* (upon which Verdi based his opera of the same name) and the *Ode to Joy,* which forms the text of Beethoven's Ninth, or Choral, symphony. Composer Carl Maria von Weber (1786–1826) lived and worked here, as did Richard Wagner (1813–1883).

A Phoenix Arisen

All this glory came to a sudden end in early February 1945, barely three months before the end of the war. British and U.S. bombers literally laid waste to the city, leaving it a smouldering ruin as they returned to bases in England. The debate continues to this day as to whether the destruction of Dresden speeded the end of the war or not; one argument is that it was wanton bombing by the allies, the other holds that Hitler was shattered to find that whole armadas could sweep into the furthest point of Germany. Whichever, the glories of pre-1945 Dresden can never be revived, although East Germany has done a magnificent job of tackling some of the more difficult tasks of reconstruction.

Two features stand out in Dresden today—and draw hordes of visitors from all over the world. First, the Zwinger Palace and the portrait gallery it houses, and second, the Semper Opera.

The portrait gallery in the Semper building of the Zwinger contains one of the most highly concentrated collections of magnificence to be found anywhere. In addition to its most famous masterpiece, Raphael's *Sistine Madonna,* there are 12 Rembrandts, 16 Reubens and 5 Tintorettos, just to drop a name or two. For Italian and Dutch paintings of the 16th and 17th centuries, few museums can match the Zwinger collection.

The Zwinger itself is a masterpiece not only of Baroque architecture but of the skills involved in restoration. The building was constructed in 1710 of Saxon sandstone, following drawings of M. D. Pöppelmann. At the time, it was regarded as the most beautiful Baroque building in existence. The complex contains the Crown Gate, the Carillon Pavilion with a set of bells made of Dresden china, the Nymph's Baths and the Picture Gallery. After the near-total destruction in 1945, craftsmen took 18 years in painstaking reconstruction to return the building to its former splendor. Their skills were equal to those of the original builders some 250 years earlier. The Zwinger now forms an ensemble including a growing number of other restored buildings.

Dresden's second major attraction is the rebuilt Semper Opera, named for its architect, Gottfried Semper (1803–1879). When the building was completed in 1850, it was considered a masterpiece and brought Semper many more commissions. Wagner and von Weber conducted here. Many Richard Strauss operas were premiered in the Dresden house. But in 1945, it too lay in ruins. Miraculously, full and detailed drawings had been preserved. But much of Semper's construction used mixtures of plaster, glue and coloring to achieve the illusion of marble columns and fine wood paneling. East German artisans had to reinvent the techniques of creating and dealing with these materials. The ten-year restoration followed the plans almost to the letter; in 1985, 40 years after its destruction, the house was reopened to the applause of music enthusiasts and architects the world over and has been drawing crowds ever since.

Logically, much more of Dresden reflects the city's immediate past. Contrasted against the splendidly restored buildings and other city features such as the Brühl Terrace along the Elbe, is the stark ruin of the Frauenkirche (Church of the Madonna), a reminder of the grimness of war and its consequences, and the modern uninspired blocks.

"White Gold"

The countryside around Dresden includes Meissen, world-famous for its porcelain, and a number of other quaint small towns and cities. The Saxon kings established hunting preserves throughout the region, building splendid hunting lodges to serve as bases. The architect Pöppelmann, designer of the Zwinger, also created the Baroque palace at Pillnitz, reachable from Dresden by tram or river boat. This former country residence of Augustus the Strong was built in rather unconventional manner, with curved roofs in Chinese style and Japanese motifs painted on the facades. Pöppelmann was also responsible for the former hunting lodge at Moritzburg, which now houses a large and excellent Baroque Museum. The amount of Meissen china included in the collection will come as no surprise.

Meissen itself is easily reached by one of the river boats. Its castle and late-Gothic cathedral with an excellent Cranach are vivid reminders of the town's ancient history. Factory visits are possible to the porcelain works, where fine china has been produced since the secret of the "white gold" was discovered here in 1710. Further upstream by paddle-wheel river boat, you will discover what is known as "Saxon Switzerland," with steep hills of bare sandstone carved into bizarre shapes by natural forces. Fascinating panoramic views are to be had from the top of a group of rocks known as the "Bastei."

Leipzig—City of Bach and Books

Leipzig was known as a crossroads of both trade and information for many hundreds of years. It was a center of printing and book production as well as the European fur trade. Astride major trade routes, Leipzig became an important market town in the Middle Ages, setting the scene for what is now the twice-yearly (March and September) trade fair. This event has been bringing buyers and sellers together from all over the world for over 800 years. Today the fair is one of the most important single meeting places of East and West for commerce and industry.

Attention was focused on Leipzig when the Battle of Nations, which led to Napoleon's downfall, was fought here in 1813. The ponderous Völkerschlachtdenkmal memorial on Leninstrasse near the exhibition grounds commemorates the event. A diorama portraying the battle forces is one of the features of the nearby exhibition pavilion.

Among music lovers, Leipzig is most closely identified with Johann Sebastian Bach (1685–1750), and his statue is prominent alongside the Thomaskirche where he worked as organist and choir leader and indeed where he is buried as well. Today the church is still the center of Bach tradition in Germany and is the home of the Thomaner Choir.

The German poet and author Johann Wolfgang Goethe (1749–1832) studied in Leipzig and there are close associations with him and his works in the city.

Because of its position as an industrial center, Leipzig suffered considerably from bombing during the war. Alas, little is left of old Leipzig, although a few traces remain, such as the (partly-restored) 12th-century marketplace, with the Renaissance town hall (Altes Rathaus) now housing the city museum. A gateway in the town hall leads to the Naschmarkt, Leipzig's most famous square, formed by the facade of the 17th-century Old Trade Exchange. The Thomaskirche nearby remains from what was once a 13th century monastery, rebuilt in the 15th century.

While you may have to search for indications of old Leipzig, the Leipzig of the 20th century is very much in evidence. The buildings in the center of the city are prominent, housing offices and some exhibition halls of the twice-yearly trade fair. Fortunately the center of the city soon proved to be too small to accommodate the major exhibits of the other socialist partners, so new grounds were established outside of the center on the Strasse des 18 Oktober. Within the center of the city, bounded by the "Ring," are the new opera house and the cubistic new Gewandhaus, the city's main concert center and home to the famous Gewandhaus orchestra. As in many European cities, the main railway station forms a focal point. The station in Leipzig is huge, and with its 26 platforms, is Europe's largest.

Printing and book production still feature heavily in Leipzig industry and trade. The city has the largest German-language library and hosts the annual International Book Show. Printing of sheet music and playing cards is also concentrated in Leipzig. More recently, however, the city has developed once again as a center of heavy industry, with emphasis on electrical engineering.

Not far from the city center in what is now a park area, including the extensive city zoo, is the district of Gohlis (take the "S"-Bahn from the main railway station). There are two places of interest which might tempt you to make this excursion. First is the small house in which German poet and dramatist Friedrich Schiller (1759–1805) lived for a time and wrote his *Ode to Freedom*. The other point of pilgrimage is the adjacent Gohliser Schlösschen (Menckestrasse 23), formerly a gathering place for artists and intellectuals, today housing the Bach archive.

Excursions from Leipzig

Excursions are a fairly easy matter from Leipzig to several other East German cities. Prominent among those of interest is Lutherstadt-Wittenberg, where Luther lived and worked as a Roman Catholic priest, in the 16th-century Augustine monastery. As he developed and promoted his concepts of a reformed Church, Wittenberg became one of the centers of the reformation. Luther is buried in the cemetery of the 15th century Schlosskirche (Castle Church), which was totally destroyed in the Seven Years War (1756–63) and only rebuilt in the 19th century. The tower offers a fine view of the town and its quaint, narrow streets.

Another historic town easily visited from Leipzig is Halle, birthplace of composer George Friedrich Handel (1685–1759), whose statue graces the town's central market square. Handel's house is now a museum of musical instruments, covering five centuries.

Further side trips can be made to the medieval towns of Naumburg and Altenburg, where playing cards are produced to this day. The Castle Museum has a fascinating collection of such cards.

PRACTICAL INFORMATION FOR DRESDEN

TOURIST INFORMATION. *Reisebüro der D.D.R.,* Prager Strasse 11 (tel. 495–5025). *Information center* open Mon. to Wed. 9–6, Thurs. 9–6.30, Fri. 9–7, Sat., Sun. and holidays 9–2. Sightseeing roundtrips on foot daily; by streetcar from Postplatz on Tues. to Sun. at 9, 11 and 1.30. By bus from Dr.-Kulz-Ring on Tues., Wed. and Thurs. at 11.

WHEN TO COME. Winter is particularly dreary, but that is when the opera is in full swing. Late April through October are the best months. Music festival in May and June.

GETTING AROUND. Dresden is a city best explored on foot, although trams and buses are available for those who would rather not take the long walk over the river bridges or from the new city center around Leninplatz to the river. Taxis (812) either for that day or forward booking up to three days ahead. The "White Fleet" of river boats plys the Elbe both to the north to Meissen and southward into Czechoslovakia. Some are side paddle-wheelers of a venerable age still in service; all offer food and amenities on board.

HOTELS

Hotel Bellevue (L), Köpckestrasse (tel. 56–620). Interhotel. Across the river from the Zwinger, opera and other main museums. Opened in 1985, cleverly designed to incorporate an old restored town house. 328 rooms, all with bath, color TV and minibar. Fully air-conditioned. Four restaurants, wine cellar, cafe, bars, nightclub. Swimming pool, sauna, solarium, bowling, jogging course. Souvenir shop, jeweler, antiques, Intershop. Car rental, parking. Convention and meeting facilities.

Hotel Newa (E), Leningrader Strasse 34 (tel. 496–7112). Interhotel. Close to main railroad station. 314 rooms, all with bath or shower. Good restaurant (for hard currency or credit cards only); cafe, two bars. Sauna, souvenirs and Intershop. Garage.

Motel Dresden (E), Münzmeisterstrasse (tel. 47–5851). Three km. (two miles) from city center. 82 rooms. Restaurant, terrace cafe.

Astoria (M), Ernst-Thälmann-Platz (tel. 475–5171). Interhotel. About one km. from city center; near zoo. Simple but comfortable. Two restaurants, souvenirs, garage.

Gewandhaus (M), Ringstr. 1 (tel. 49–6286). H–O group. Central location and good cafe. Some rooms with bath.

Interhotel Prager Strasse (M), Prager Strasse (tel. 48–560). Interhotel. Consists of two hotels in tandem, **Königstein** and **Lilienstein**, each with 300 rooms with bath. Near the main railroad station. Hotel restaurants, sauna, souvenir shops, garage.

Parkhotel Weisser Hirsch (I), Bautzner Landstrasse 7 (tel. 36–851). Considerable distance from city center. 50 rooms in pleasant surroundings, although facilities are simple. Restaurant, cafe, dancing.

RESTAURANTS

Canaletto, Elbterrassen, Wackerbarth's Keller (wine restaurant) and **Buri-Buri** (Polynesian restaurant), all (E) and all located in Hotel Bellevue.

Café Pöppelmann, (M), Grosse Meissner-Gasse 15. Baroque atmosphere in a restored old city house incorporated into the Hotel Bellevue.

Café Prag (M), Altmarkt. Central location, popular; evening shows.

International (M), Prager Strasse 15. Nice atmosphere and food is good.

Luisenhof (M), Bergbahnstrasse 8. Reached by cable car, overlooking the city and the Elbe.

Meissner Weinkeller (M), Strasse der Befreiung 1. Good food, wide variety of local wines.

Sekundogenitur (M), Brühlsche Terrasse. Wine restaurant with view of the Elbe; outside terrace, weather allowing.

Äberlausitzer Töppl (I), Strasse der Befreiung 14. Regional specialties, good fish, splendid dark beer.

Kügeln Haus (I), Strasse der Befreiung 14. Complex of a grill, coffee bar, restaurant and historic beer cellar. Popular; go early or book ahead (tel. 52–791).

Pirnaisches Tor (I), Pirnaischer Platz. Near city hall. Choice of fish grill, self-service restaurant, terrace cafe or coffee bar.

WHAT TO SEE. Armeemuseum (Military Museum of the G.D.R.). Dr.-Kurtz-Fischer-Platz. Military history in fact predating the G.D.R. Open Tues. to Sun. 9–5.

Baroque Palace at Pillnitz by Pöppelmann featuring Chinese and Japanese influence. By tram or river boat from Dresden.

Buchmuseum (Book Museum). Marienallee 12. History of books running from Middle Ages to present. Open Mon. to Sat. 9–4.30

Deutsches Hygene-Museum (German Museum of Health). Lingnerplatz 1. History of medical equipment, including glass anatomical figure. Open Sat. to Thurs., 9–6.

Museum für Geschichte der Stadt Dresden (City Historical Museum), Ernst-Thälmann-Platz 2. Open Mon. to Thurs. and Sat. 10–6; Sun. 10–4.

Schloss Moritzburg, near Dresden. Designed by Pöppelmann, this former hunting lodge houses a large and excellent Baroque museum containing fine examples of Meissen china, furniture and hunting weapons.

Semper Opera House in city center. Dresden's second major attraction, reopened in 1985, named after its architect Gottfried Semper.

Technisches Museum (Technical Museum). Friedrich-Engels-Strasse 15. Open Mon. to Wed., Fri. 9–4; Thurs. 9–6.

Verkehrsmuseum (Transportation Museum). Johanneum am Neumarkt, Augustusstrasse 1. Rail, truck, air, ship and regional transportation with old streetcars, etc. Open Apr. 1 to Sept. 30, Tues. to Sun. 9–5.

Zwinger Palace and Portrait Gallery in the heart of old Dresden. An 18th-century fortress in magnificent Baroque style which houses one of the world's most famous collections of paintings. Collections of china, coins and hunting weapons. Art gallery open Tues. to Sun. 10–5, closed Mon; Porcelain collection open Mon. to Thurs. 9.30–4, Sat. and Sun. 9–4, closed Fri.; Gallery of New Masters open Fri. to Wed. 10–5, Tues. 10–6, closed Thurs.

PRACTICAL INFORMATION FOR MEISSEN

HOTELS AND RESTAURANTS

Hotel Goldener Löwe (I), Rathenauplatz 6 (tel. 3304). Modest but comfortable; a few rooms with facilities.

Restaurants. Am Tuchemachertor (M), Lorenzgasse 7; **Ratskeller** (M), Marktstrasse 1; **Vincenz Richter** (M), An der Frauenkirche. Old timbered house, definitely worth a visit. **Winkelkrug** (M), Schlossberg 13. Also recommended.

In the vicinity of Moritzburg, with its Baroque hunting lodge, the historic **Rauberhütte** and **Waldschenke** offer local specialties in a rustic setting.

PRACTICAL INFORMATION FOR LEIPZIG

TOURIST INFORMATION. *Reisebüro der D.D.R.,* Katharinenstrasse 1 (tel. 79–210), or *Leipzig Information,* Sachsenplatz 1 (tel. 79–590). Open Mon. through Fri. 9–7 (theater tickets until 6), Sat. 9.30–2. Sightseeing tours by bus daily at 10 and 1.30; from Mar. to mid-Oct. also 4 P.M., starting point Information Building in city center (tel. 795–9329). Central reservations for restaurants and nightclubs (tel. 795–9315); tickets and information on public transport (tel. 795–9331).

WHEN TO COME. Leipzig at the best of times is either an industrial or a trading city, not a major tourist goal. Winter is dreary, overcast and cold, and the air hangs even more heavily with the fumes generated by soft coal used not only for heating, but for power and industrial needs. At all costs, avoid the fair weeks (first weeks of March and September) and those immediately preceding and following. The city is overflowing, and prices are steeply increased. Between the fairs, the city is far more attractive, although autumn after the fair can be pleasant too.

GETTING AROUND. The city center can easily be tackled on foot; indeed, parts are a pedestrian zone. Otherwise, buses and trams are available, in addition to the "S"-Bahn city railway lines. Tickets for both must be obtained in advance, various prices according to the number of rides, to be validated on the bus or streetcar. For the "S"-Bahn, tickets in advance at the main railroad station (M.0.30 for up to five stations, M.0.50 for longer trips to six stops or beyond), also to be validated at the station when starting the trip. Taxis are available throughout the city (ample, because of the number needed at peak fair time); for a taxi, call 7160 or 70–171.

HOTELS

During fair time be aware that deluxe and expensive hotels will increase their prices. Likewise, hotels and restaurants in the lower categories may also increase their rates and prices putting themselves temporarily into a higher category of rating.

Hotel Astoria (L), Platz der Republik 2 (tel. 71–710). Interhotel. Central, opposite main railway station. Still preferred by many. 332 rooms, all with bath, color TV. Two restaurants, bar, dance cafe, nightclub, sauna. Souvenir shop, Intershop. Car rental, garage. Meeting rooms.

Hotel Merkur (L), Gerberstrasse (tel. 7990). Interhotel. Central, close to main rail station, the city's newest and by far most luxurious accommodation. 447 rooms, all with bath, color TV, minibar. Fully air-conditioned. Four restaurants, two bars, coffee bar, nightclub. Swimming pool, sauna, solarium, bowling, jogging course. Japanese garden. Souvenir shop, boutiques, art and antiques gallery, Intershop. Car rental, parking. Congress and meeting facilities.

Hotel am Ring (E), Karl-Marx-Platz 5–6 (tel. 79–520). Interhotel. Central, closest to opera, Gewandhaus. 278 rooms, all with bath. Two restaurants, bar, nightclub, sauna. Souvenir shop, Intershop. Car rental, garage.

Hotel Stadt Leipzig (E), Richard-Wagner-Strasse 1 (tel. 28–8814). Interhotel. Central, opposite main rail station. 340 rooms, all with bath, color TV. Three restaurants, cafe, bar, nightclub, sauna. Souvenir shop, Intershop. Car rental, garage.

International (M), Tröndlinring 8 (tel. 71–880). Interhotel. Central, near main rail station; older hotel with appropriate charm. 104 rooms, all with bath. Restaurant, beer stube, bar. Pleasant sidewalk cafe. Souvenir shop, Intershop. Car rentals, garage.

Zum Löwen (M), Rudolf-Breitscheid-Strasse (tel. 7751). Interhotel. Central, near rail station. Postwar modern, but cheerful and pleasant if not opulent. 108 rooms, all with bath or shower. Restaurant. Souvenir shop, Intershop. Car rental, garage.

Bayrischer Hof (I), Wintergartenstrasse 13 (tel. 20–9251). H-O group. Fairly central if modest.

RESTAURANTS

Sakura (E), Gerberstrasse, in Hotel Merkur (tel. 7990). In honor of the Japanese firm that designed and built the hotel. Reservations required.

Altes Kloster (M), Klostergasse 5 (tel. 28–2252). **Auerbach Keller** (M), Grimmaische Strasse 2 (tel. 20–9131). Historic restaurant in city center, immortalized in Goethe's *Faust*. Both visit and reservations are musts. **Burgkeller** (M), Naschmarkt 1–3. Includes "Doina" Romanian restaurant which you may prefer to miss in favor of the more local atmosphere. **Gastmahl des Meeres** (M), Dr.-Kurt-Fischer-Strasse 1. Specializes in seafood. **Paulaner** (M), Klostergasse 3. Attractive and quiet, good food.

Kaffeebaum (I), Fleischergasse 4. Reportedly the oldest cafe in the country, in a Burgerhaus well over 450 years old. Worth visiting. **Panorama Café** (I), Karl-Marx-Platz, atop the university building. **Regina** (I), Hainstrasse 14 (tel. 28–2052).

Cozy wine restaurant, book ahead. **Stadt Kiew (I)**, Petersstrasse, Messehaus am Markt. Ukrainian specialties.

WHAT TO SEE

Altes Rathaus, in the 12th-century marketplace. A Renaissance town hall housing the city museum. Open Tues. to Sun. 9–5.

Bach Memorial, Thomaskirchhof 16. Church where Johann Sebastian Bach worked and was buried. Open Tues. to Sun. 9–12, Mon. 2–4.

Botanischer Garten (Botanical Gardens), Linnestrasse 1. Open-air gardens. Open Mon. to Fri. 9–4, Sun. 10–4; greenhouses Sun. 10–12.30, 2–4.

Exhibition Pavilion, Leninstrasse 210. Diorama portraying battle forces of the Battle of Leipzig 1813. Open Tues. to Sun. 9–4.

Georgi Dimitrov Museum, Georgi-Dimitroff-Platz 1. Museum of fine arts, with graphic arts collection. Open Tues. to Sat. 9–12, 1–5; picture gallery open Tues. to Fri. 9–6, Sat. 9–5, Sun. 9–1.

German Language Library. Open Mon. to Sat. 9–6.

Gohliser Schlössen (Gohliser House), Menckestrasse 23. Contains the Bach archive. Open Mon. and Fri. 1–5, Tues., Thurs. and Sat. 9–1, Wed. 1–8.

Grassimuseum, Johannesplatz 5–11. Complex includes **Museum of Arts and Crafts** (open Tues. to Fri. 9.30–6, Sat. 10–4, Sun. 9–1); **Geographical Museum** (open Tues. to Fri. 10–3, Sun. 9–1); **Musical Instruments Museum** (enter from Täubchenweg 2; open Tues. to Thurs. 3–6, Fri. and Sun. 10–1, Sat. 10–3).

Naturwissenschaftliches Museum (Natural Science Museum), Friedrich-Engels-Platz. Open Tues. to Thurs. 9–6, Sat. 9–5.

Schiller's House, Menckestrasse 21. For a time, the home of the German poet and dramatist. Open Tues., Wed., Fri., and Sat. 11–5.

Schloss Dölitz, Torhaus, Schloss Dölitz, Helenstrasse 24. Contains exhibition of *zinnfiguren,* historical tin soldiers. Open Sun. 9–1.

Volkerschlachtdenkmal Memorial, on Leninstrasse near the exhibition grounds. Commemorates the Battle of Nations 1813. Open daily 9–4.

HALLE

Hotel

Hotel Stadt Halle (L), Ernst-Thälmann-Platz (tel. 38041). Interhotel. Central. 345 rooms, all with bath, color TV. Two restaurants, cafe, bar, nightclub. Souvenir shop, Intershop. Car rental, garage.

NORTHERN COAST, SOUTHERN MOUNTAINS

The Smaller Centers and Countryside
of East Germany

Above the northern lakeland district of East Germany, you come to that part of the coast known as Ostsee, or Baltic. Old Hanseatic cities alternate with well-known beach resorts. The largest of the East German ports, Rostock lies in almost the geographical center of the coastline. Its architectural unity has been broken by wartime damage, but there are still interesting sights to be seen. The town hall has seven towers, spanning the 13th to 18th centuries. Medieval Rostock can still be seen in the Stone Gate and parts of the old town wall. The Kröpelin Tor (gate) is now a museum for local history. Important examples of ecclesiastical architecture are the Kreuzkirche, Marienkirche (St. Mary's church) and the 13th-century Nikolaikirche. The busy modern harbor is also of interest. The train and car ferry to Denmark (about the cheapest in Europe, and thoroughly comfortable) leaves East Germany at Warnemünde, one of the best-known seaside resorts.

To the west is Wismar, from 1648 to 1803 a Swedish possession, with its evidence of old Hanseatic traditions. Wismar is the second-largest East German Baltic seaport, with an attractive 14th-century market square and Alte Schwede (Old Swede) burgher house. But architecturally the most enchanting town is Stralsund, with its quaint streets and venerable red-brick public buildings and churches, fine examples of northern Gothic. Further inland, Schwerin was the seat of the Dukes of Mecklenburg and is typical of the old German provincial capitals with its stately castle (lovely silk tapestries in the hall and superb gardens) and opera house. Throughout the north of Germany right down to Potsdam and with a few examples in Berlin as well, you will find the red brick architecture now so admired, but favored in the Middle Ages solely because of the lack of natural building stone.

Excursions that can be made from Rostock include a trip around the port and boat trips to Hiddensee Island and to the beach at Warnemünde; to Bad Doberan with its 14th-century Gothic cathedral and numerous art treasures; narrow gauge railway to seaside resorts of Heiligendamm (the first German bathing resort, established in 1793) and Kühlungsborn.

Neubrandenburg is another old town with many fine churches, the east gable of one, Marienkirche (St. Mary's), being in Gothic brick and in imitation of Strasbourg Cathedral. From Neubrandenburg you can make a side trip to Lake Müritz, with East Germany's largest nature reserve on the eastern shore, excellent for hiking on marked trails.

The woodlands of the Darss Peninsula represent perhaps the last example of primeval forest formations in Europe and are now a national park. To the east, the narrow island of Hiddensee was always a favorite haunt of artists and bohemians. The playwright Gerhart Hauptmann came here every year from the turn of the century and was buried on the island in 1946.

The highlight of the coast is Rügen, Germany's largest and most beautiful island, dented by hundreds of bays and creeks. The vast bay of Lietzow, protected on all sides, is ideal for sailing or windsurfing. The 400-foot-high chalk cliffs of Stubnitz drop almost vertically into the sea and are the landmark of Rügen. Of the many fishing villages and beach resorts, Binz is the best known. The Munich–Berlin–Stockholm train reaches the ferryboat at Sassnitz. Southwest of Rügen is the island of Usedom, with a string of seaside resorts, some famous, such as Heringdorf and Zinnowitz, some infamous, like Peenemünde, launching site of Hitler's V-1 and V-2 missiles which wreaked havoc on England in World War II.

Harz Mountains

Of the mountain districts in central Germany, the Harz is the best known. Delightful surroundings help enhance the medieval character of Wernigerode, dominated by a feudal castle. Nearby thousand-year-old Quedlinburg is a picturebook town with its half-timbered houses, winding lanes and outsize cathedral. It is well worth visiting, although accommodations are very limited and it may be advisable to stay at the Magdeburg Interhotel and make excursions from there. Magdeburg has Germany's first Gothic cathedral, some fine Baroque buildings and several theaters, including a puppet theater.

The distance to Halberstadt, with its half-timbered houses, is not great. Thale is best reached via Quedlinburg and the Devils' Wall. Thale's surroundings include the beautiful Bode valley, the witches' dancing place (Hexentanzplatz) and the Harz mountain theater, also accessible by cable railway. Then on to Rübeland, with its stalactite caves, and Stolberg in the southern Harz, with fine Renaissance houses, Baroque castle and museum.

Thuringia

This region in the southwesterly corner of East Germany includes some of the country's most glorious unspoiled wooded mountain slopes, forests, clear streams and rare plants. It is also the source of traditional handicrafts in the form of glass and wooden toys. Hikers will enjoy the Schwarztal, Inselberg and Rennsteig subregions; the air is the most remarkably heady in all of Germany. At the two extremities of the Thüringer Wald (Thuringia Forest) lie two historic cities: Eisenach and Saalfeld, the latter with the most beautiful stalactite caves in East Germany, really fairytale grottos. Eisenach is dominated by the 900-year-old Wartburg castle, feature of many a German legend. Here minstrels like Tannhauser, Walter von der Vogelweide and Wolfram von Eschenbach sang of noble lords and lovely ladies. During the stormy days of the Reformation, Wartburg served as a refuge for Martin Luther, who translated the New Testament into German here in 1521. Bach was born in Eisenach in 1685. The castle gives its name to the Wartburg car, one of two East German models, which is made here.

Further east lies the city of Erfurt, seemingly untouched by history. It remains one of Germany's finest cities, with its cathedral and the church of St. Severin, its matchless Gothic and German Renaissance houses, and its 600-year-old bridge with 33 houses built on it. Erfurt has long been associated with flowers and is host to an annual summer international horticultural show (the international part being played by the other socialist countries) on the grounds of the Cyriak Castle.

Only a few miles away, Weimar—famous as the city where German's ill-fated "Weimar Republic" was declared following World War I—retains the atmosphere of the old residential towns of the German princes. The artist and engraver Lucas Cranach (1472–1553) lived and worked here. The city's greatest period came at the turn of the 18th century when Goethe, Schiller, Wieland and Herder, all giants of the era of German humanism, made Weimar famous in the realms of literature and philosophy. Later, Böcklin and Lenbach founded the Weimar school of painters. Among the places to visit are Goethe's residence in Frauenplanstrasse and his summer house in the beautiful park on the Ilm; the Dower Palace of the Duchess Anna-Amalia; Schiller's house opposite the Gänsemännchen (Little Goose Boy) well; his and Goethe's burial vaults; the Franz Liszt museum; the Herder church with its Cranach altar. Weimar is a town where history can be felt, for the most part unimpeded by contemporary comment.

The same can hardly be said for Buchenwald, site of the famous Nazi concentration camp somewhat to the north on the Ettersberg. The scene is grim enough, but visitors may object to the running theme that the unfortunate victims were anti-Fascist, which they doubtless were, and that the blame for the atrocities must be laid on the West Germans.

Near Weimar are Apolda, with Germany's oldest bell foundry and bell museum, the 13th-century cathedral town of Naumburg, and Jena, with its 16th-century university. Schiller was a professor here, and here Karl Marx wrote his doctor's thesis on philosophy. Jena is known for glass and optical instruments; visit the Zeiss planetarium even if you would normally find the subject rather dull—you'll be surprised.

Gera is a beautiful patrician and Renaissance town, with much of its past still evident, in the form of the 16th-century town hall, a 17th-century chemist's shop, patrician houses spanning four centuries (16th to 20th) and fine botanical gardens and orangery. Several castles are nearby: the 600-year-old Osterburg at Weida and the 1,000-year-old Ranis Castle.

Oberhof, a year-round resort, is the tourist center of Thuringia and in winter is the scene of bobsled and toboggan runs, skating and skiing. Suhl, capital of Thuringia, has been known for four centuries for its gun manufacturing. The Suhl district is second in popularity only to the Baltic coast, as *the* East German holiday region. Fanciers of Christmas decorations should visit the glass-blowing town of Lauscha, the source of ornaments which find their way from here to all corners of the globe. A glass industry museum records the town's fascinating history.

The Erzgebirge

In the southeast corner of the country, this dramatic, mountainous landscape forms a natural border with Czechoslovakia. It was once idyllic for hikers and even motorists, delighted to find so little traffic. Alas, pollution originating on both sides of the border has taken its toll, and vast areas of leafless trees stand where healthy green once prevailed. Extensive use of soft brown coal is the culprit, particularly in the industrial areas just to the northwest.

Karl-Marx-Stadt, Chemnitz in former times, is the principal city. Badly damaged during the war, the city has long since been re-established as a center for heavy industry, turning out all manner of machinery related to the textile industry, from spinning to knitting to weaving to dyeing. The industry accounts for the textile museum (note the 250-million-year old tree trunk in front) on Theaterplatz. The Schlosskirche and Schlossberg Museum are worth a visit, likewise the Siegert House, with its carefully restored Baroque facade. Of the city's former 25 medieval towers, only the Rote Turm still stands today. There are also some fine patrician houses, but the jewel is the late-Gothic cathedral with its carved wooden statues and the Silbermann organ from 1714, the oldest of the still existing 31 instruments he built. The Golden Door of the Marienkirche, dating from the 13th century, is built into the south side of the cathedral.

Freiberg is attractive and still has the remains of its ancient fortifications as well as the tiny miner's houses which line the narrow streets. The "Erzgebirge" are literally "ore mountains," and to this day minerals are still extracted. East Germany's most elevated community is to be found in this area, Oberwiesenthal, at the foot of the Fichtelberg. Several spas are located in this area, among them Bad Brambach and Bad Elster, the latter in a charming park-like setting.

From Karl-Marx-Stadt, you can take a trip to the 800-year-old Burg Rabenstein and the Rabenstein group of rocks, a network of caves hollowed out by mining, also with the remains of a 17th-century castle. A short ten km. (six miles) distant is Pelzmühle, with its pleasure steamers.

The open-air theater at Küchwald offers drama during the summer. The Augustusburg is a formidable Renaissance building dating from 1572, originally a hunting center, now housing a museum of the various animals to be found in the area. The castle church includes an altar painting by Lucas Cranach the Younger. The 170-meter (555-ft.) deep well is impressive, but those who want sports more accessible head for the lake behind Kriebstein Dam, some 25 km. (15 miles) distant, or to Sachsenring, the international motorcycle race course.

Seiffen, deep in the mountains, is not to be missed; like mountain villages the world over, this one too is famous for its wood carvings, but its toy museum is sheer delight, as is watching the local turners and carvers in their workshops.

Close to Annaberg in the Sehma valley is the Frohnauer Hammer, an iron processing installation from the 15th century and frame house of the former owner of the forge, today a local art museum with bobbin-lace room. Musicians may know the names Klingenthal and Markneukirchen, towns which for centuries have been centers for musical instrument manufacture. A large instrument collection is in the museum at Markneukirchen. Annaberg itself is a bobbin-lace center but was formerly famous for silver mines, long since closed. Nevertheless, a few of the older houses indicate the local prosperity of the past. The church dates from 1520.

PRACTICAL INFORMATION FOR THE NORTHERN COAST, SOUTHERN MOUNTAINS

TOURIST INFORMATION. All local tourist offices are run by the *Reisebüro der D.D.R.* Area offices are in the following locations: **Eisenach,** Bahnhofstrasse 3–5 (tel. 623–5161, 5165); **Erfurt,** Angerstrasse 62 (tel. 61–5700); **Gera,** Strasse der Republik (tel. 70–23–783); **Jena,** Spitzweidenweg 22 (tel. 791–25–428); **Karl-Marx-Stadt,** Strasse der Nation 56 (tel. 71–60–331); **Potsdam,** Friedrich-Ebert-Strasse 115 (crnr. of Yorckstrasse), (tel. 33–4221); **Rostock,** Hermann-Duncker-Platz 2 (tel. 81–3800); **Schwerin,** Leninplatz 1 (tel. 84–83–635); **Suhl,** Ernst-Thälmann-Platz 1 (tel. 66–23–012); **Weimar,** Marktstrasse 4 (tel. 621–2173).

HOTELS AND RESTAURANTS

Annaberg-Buchholz. *Hotel Wilder Mann* (I), Markt 13 (tel. 2122). H-O group.

Apolda. *Hotel zur Post* (I), Bahnhofstrasse 35 (tel. 2208). H-O group.

Eisenach. *Auf der Wartburg* (M), (tel. 5111). 30 rooms in the Wartburg castle itself. Excellent view of the city. Historic restaurant. Bus service to and from rail station. Recommended. *Parkhotel Eisenach* (M), Wartburg-Allee (tel. 5291). H-O group. Some rooms with private facilities. *Stadt Eisenach* (M), Luisenstrasse 11–13 (tel. 3682). H-O group. Restaurant and gift shop. *Hospiz "Glockenhof-Sophienhof"* (I), Grimmelgasse (tel. 3562). Evangelical hostel. Timbered house at the foot of the Wartburg. 29 rooms, simple but pleasant. Restaurant.

Erfurt. *Erfurter Hof* (L), Am Bahnhofsvorplatz 1–2 (tel. 51–151). Interhotel. Attractive older house with charm. 197 rooms, all with bath, television. Two restaurants, cafe, wine cellar, bar, coffee bar, nightclub. Sauna. Souvenir shop, Intershop. Car rental, garage.
Hotel Kosmos (E), Juri-Gagarin-Ring 126–127 (tel. 5510). Interhotel. Central, but a recent intruder from space, as the name implies. 332 rooms, all with bath. Restaurant, cafe, bar. Sauna. Souvenir shop, Intershop. Car rental, garage.

Freiberg. *Hotel Freiberger Hof* (I), Am Bahnhof 9 (tel. 2029). H-O group. *Hotel Freundschaft* (I), Bahnhofstrasse 19 (tel. 2325). H-O group.

Gera. *Hotel Gera* (L), Strasse der Republik (tel. 22–991). Interhotel. Nondescript but comfortable. 330 rooms, all with bath. Three restaurants, beer stube, bar, nightclub. Sauna. Souvenir shop, Intershop. Car rental, garage.

Jena. *International* (E), Ernst-Thälmann-Ring (tel. 25–532). Interhotel. Central; typically neat but lacking charm. Some rooms with private bath. Two restaurants, bar, cafe, dancing. *Schwarzer Bär* (M), Lutherplatz 2 (tel. 22–543). H-O group. 60 rooms, some with private facilities. Excellent restaurant, good service.

Karl-Marx-Stadt. *Chemnitzer Hof* (L), Theaterplatz 4 (tel. 6840). Interhotel. Central, comfortable. Friendly service helps make up for lack of charm. 106 rooms, all with bath. Two restaurants, beer stube, bar, nightclub. Sauna. Souvenir shop, Intershop. Car rental, garage. *Kongress* (L), Karl-Marx-Allee (tel. 6830). Interhotel. Central, huge modern block but with all amenities. 309 rooms, all with bath, television. Four restaurants, leaning heavily toward Russian cuisine; cafe, snack bar, bar, nightclub. Sauna, solarium, fitness room. Souvenir shop, excellent Intershop. Car rental, garage.
Moskau (M), Strasse der Nationen (tel. 6810). Interhotel. Plainly modern. 111 rooms, some with bath. Restaurant, dance cafe, nightclub, garden. Sauna. Souvenir shop, Intershop. Car rental, garage.

Magdeburg. *International* (E), Otto-von-Guericke-Strasse (tel 3840). Interhotel. Modern, although the style enhances the nightclub. 358 rooms, many with bath. Three restaurants, cafe, bar, nightclub. Sauna. Souvenir shop, Intershop. Car rental, garage.

Neubrandenburg. *Hotel Vier Tore* (E), Ernst-Thälmann-Strasse 16 (tel. 5141). H-O group.

Oberhof. *Panorama* (L), Theodor-Neubauer-Strasse (tel. 501). Interhotel. Dramatic holiday resort hotel resembling two back-to-back ski jumps. 363 rooms, all with bath and television. Six restaurants, outdoor terrace, two bars, nightclub. Swimming pool, sauna, bowling, minigolf. Souvenir shop, Intershop. Car rental, garage.
Ernst-Thälmann-Haus (M), Tambacher Strasse 1 (tel. 255). Reisebüro group.

Rostock. *Hotel Warnow* (L), Hermann-Duncker-Platz (tel. 37–381). Interhotel. Modern block, central. 338 rooms, all with bath. Four restaurants, bar, nightclub. Sauna. Souvenir shop, Intershop. Car rental, garage. *Neptun* (E), Warnemünde/Rostock. H-O group. On the beach. All rooms with bath. Four restaurants, one self-service; cafe, beer stube, bar, dancing. Swimming pool, sauna, bowling. Souvenir shop, Intershop. Car rental, garage.
Hotel am Bahnhof (M), Gerhart-Hauptmann-Strasse 13 (tel. 36–331). Central, but no rooms with bath.
Restaurants. *Jägerhütte* (M), Barnstofer Wald (tel. 23–457). Rustic, hidden in the woods near the zoo. Game specialties in a pleasant atmosphere. Reservations essential. *Restaurant-Komplex* (M), Schillerstrasse 14 (tel. 5371). Four restaurants under one roof: Asian, Cuban, Russian and Scandinavian. Book ahead. *Teepott* (M), in the lighthouse.

Saalfeld. *Hotel Anker* (I), Markt 26 (tel. 2654). H-O group.

Sassnitz. *Rügen-Hotel* (E), Seestrasse 1 (tel. 3141). Mitropa group. Modern, directly on the beach. All rooms with bath. Three restaurants, one self-service; cafe, bar, dancing. Swimming pool, sauna. Souvenir shop, Intershop. Car rental, garage.

Schwerin. *Stadt Schwerin* (M), Grunthalplatz (tel. 5261). H-O group. Modern. All rooms with bath. Two restaurants, grill, cafe, beer stube, bar, dancing. Sauna. Boat rental. Souvenir shop, Intershop. Car rental, garage.

Suhl. *Thüringen Tourist* (E), Ernst-Thälmann-Platz 2 (tel. 5605). Interhotel. Central, if overly modern. 109 rooms, all with bath. Three restaurants, nightclub, terrace. Sauna. Souvenir shop, Intershop. Car rental, garage.

Thale/Harz. *Berghotel Rosstrappe* (M), Rosstrappe (tel. 3011). H-O group.

Weimar. *Hotel Elephant* (E), Am Markt 19 (tel. 61–471). Interhotel. Charming old house that dates to 1696, although thoroughly modernized since. Goethe, Schiller, Herder, Liszt—and Hitler—all stayed here. Recommended. 116 rooms, most with bath. Three restaurants, historic wine cellar, terrace, bar, nightclub. Sauna. Souvenir shop, Intershop. Car rental, garage.

Hospiz (I), Amalienstrasse 2 (tel. 2711). Evangelical hostel. Quiet location in the old city, only steps away from Goethe's quarters. 41 rooms, none with baths. Restaurant, music room, garden, parking.

Restaurant. *Zum Weissen Schwan* (M), Frauentorstrasse 23. Historic inn next door to Goethe's house.

Wernigerode. *Hotel zum Bär* (I), Markt 8 (tel. 2224). *Motel Quedlinburg* (I), Ebertystrasse (tel. 2855). *Weisser Hirsch* (I), Markt 5 (tel. 2434). No rooms with bath. H-O group.

Wismar. *Hotel Wismar* (I), Breite Strasse 10 (tel. 2498). No rooms with private bath. H-O group.

TOURIST VOCABULARY

The German language follows very strict rules of pronunciation which are designated by the spelling of the words. The vowel sounds are either long or short. Long vowels are indicated when they are doubled—Aal, Tee, Boot; when followed by "h"—Bahn, Sohn, Uhr; when followed by one consonant only—gut, Hof, Tal; before a single consonant followed by a vowel—Leben, Name, Rose. Thus a long "a" as in Tal (valley), "ah" as in Hahn (rooster) or "aa" as in Aal (eel) will be pronounced as in father; a long "e" as in Esel (donkey), "eh" as in mehr (more) or "ee" as in Tee (tea) will be pronounced as in fey; a long "i", "ih" as in ihr (her), "ie" as in Tier (animal) or "ieh" as in Vieh (cattle) will be pronounced as yield; a long "o" as in rot (red), "oh" as in Sohn (son) or "oo" as in Boot (boat) will be pronounced as in bone; a long "u" as in Bruder (brother) or "uh" as in Stuhl (chair) will be pronounced as in rude.

Short vowels are indicated when they are followed by more than one consonant. Thus a short "a" as in Mann (man) is pronounced as in man; a short "e" as in Welt (world) is pronounced as in pelt; a short "i" as in Kind (child) is pronounced as in lint; a short "o" as in Motte (moth) is pronounced as in knot; a short "u" as in Butter (butter) is pronounced as in foot. The "e" in words ending in -e, -el, -en and -er, is also short.

There are also modified vowels which are those qualified by umlaut ( ): "ä," "ö," "ü," and "äu." A long "ä" or "äh" as in während (during) or spät (late), is pronounced as in late; a short "ä" as in Wände (walls) is pronounced as in pet; a long "öh" or "ö" as in Söhne (sons) is more difficult as there is really no English equivalent—the nearest would perhaps be yearn, or the French "deux"; a short "ö" as in Göttlich (divine) is pronounced as in fir; a long "üh" or "ü" as in kühn (bold) is again difficult to translate in English—perhaps prune with a Scottish accent! A short "ü" (as in Müller, miller) is similar to the long sound—only shorter!

And then there are diphthongs—but there are only three! Firstly "au" as in Frau (woman) is pronounced like the "ou" in house; "eu" and "äu" as in Leute (people) and Bäume (trees) are pronounced like the "oy" in boy; and "ei," "ai," and "ay" as in Ei (egg), Kaiser (emperor) and Bayern (Bavaria) are pronounced like the "i" in flight.

The consonants are pronounced as they are in English with the following exceptions:
"b" as in English except when it is followed by another consonant or at the end of a word in which case it is pronounced as an English "p," e.g. Obst (fruit) or Grab (grave)
"ch" is pronounced like the "h" in huge
"d" as in English unless it appears at the end of a word as in Land (land) in which case it is pronounced as the English "t"
"g" always hard (as in good). If it appears at the end of a word it is pronounced as a "k" as in Ring (ring)
"j" always pronounced as the "y" in young
"r" is usually "rolled" from the back of the palate
"s" before and between vowels as in Sohn (son) and Rasen (lawn), pronounced as in wise
   before consonants and at the end of a word, as in Geist (ghost) and Gras (grass), pronounced as in son
"sp" and "st" at the beginning of a word, as in Spiel (game) and Stuhl (chair) is always pronounced "shp" or "sht"
"β" is a signal for a sharp "s" following a long vowel, as in Straße (street). It is used instead of "ss" at the end of a word, as in naβ (wet). In this book we have used "ss" throughout

"sch" as in Schiff (ship) is pronounced simply as "sh"
"th" as in Thron (throne) is pronounced as "t" alone
"v" as in Vater (father) is pronounced as "f"
"w" as in Wagen (car) is pronounced as "v"
"z" as in Zucker (sugar) and "tz" as in Katze (cat) is pronounced like the "ts" in cats

Tonal stress is practically always on the first syllable (as in the English words cooker, Albert or bacon)—there are exceptions as there are to pronunciations, but they are too complex and numerous to go into here. Nouns are always given capital letters, as are adjectives and verbs when they are used as nouns. Best get yourself a complete German Grammar or language course if you want this sort of detail.

USEFUL EXPRESSIONS

Hello, how do you do	Guten Tag (gootn tahg)
Good morning	Guten Morgen (gootn mohrgn)
Goodnight	Gute Nacht (goota nakht)
Goodbye	Auf Wiedersehen (owf veederzayn)
Please	Bitte (bitta)
Thank you	Danke (danka)
Thank you very much	Vielen Dank (feelen dank)
	Herzlichen Dank (hairtslihen dank)
Yes	Ja (ya)
No	Nein (nine)
You're welcome	Bitte (bitta)
	Gern geschehen (gairn geshayen)
	Keine Ursache (kyna oorzaha)
Excuse me	Entschuldigung Sie mir, bitte (entshooldegoong zee meer, bitta)
Come in!	Herein (hairine)
I'm sorry	Es tut mir leid (ess toot meer lite)
My name is . . .	Ich heisse . . . (ih hyssa)
Do you speak English?	Sprechen Sie Englisch? (shprehen zee English)
I don't speak German	Ich spreche kein Deutsch (ih shprehen kine doitsh)
Please speak slowly	Bitte, sprechen Sie langsam (bitta, shprehen zee langsam)
I don't understand	Ich verstehe nicht (ih fershtayer niht)
Please write it down	Bitte, schreiben Sie es auf (bitta shriben zee es owf)
Where is . . . ?	Wo ist . . . ? (vo ist)
What is this place called?	Wie heisst dieser Platz? (vee hyst deeza plats)
Please show me	Bitte, zeigen Sie mir (bitta, tsygen zee meer)
I would like	Ich möchte gern (ih merhta gairn)
How much does it cost?	Wieviel kostet es? (veefeel kostet ess)

SIGNS

Entrance	Eingang (inegang)
Exit	Ausgang (owsgang)
Emergency exit	Notausgang
Toilet	Toiletten
- men	Herren (hairen)

- women	Damen (dahmen)
- vacant	frei (fry)
- occupied	besetzt (bezetst)
Hot	Heiss (hise)
	Warm (varm)
Cold	Kalt
No smoking	Rauchen verboten (rowhen fairboten)
	Nichtraucher (niht-rowher)
No admittance	Kein Eingang (kine inegang)
	Kein Zutritt (kine tsootritt)
Stop	Halt
Danger	Gefahr (gevehr)
Open	Offen
	Geöffnet (gayerfnet)
Closed	Geschlossen (geshlossen)
Full, no vacancy	Voll (foll)
	Belegt (beleht)
	Kein Zimmer frei (kine tsimmer fry)
Information	Auskunft (owskoonft)
Bus stop	Bushaltestelle (bus-halte-stelle)
Taxi stand	Taxistand
Pedestrians	Fussgänger (foos-genger)

ARRIVAL

Passport check	Passkontrolle (passcontrolla)
Your passport, please	Ihren Pass, bitte
	(eeren pass, bitta)
I am with the group	Ich gehöre zu der Gruppe
	(ih gehera tsu dair groope)
Customs	Zoll (tsoll)
Anything to declare?	Etwas zu verzollen?
	(etvas tsu fairtsollen)
Baggage claim	Gepäckausgabe (ge-peck-ows-gahbe)
This suitcase is mine	Das ist mein Koffer
	(dass ist mine koffer)
A porter, baggage carrier	Einen Träger, Gepäckträger
	(inen trayger, gepecktrayger)

TRANSPORTATION

to the bus	zum bus (tsoom boos)
to a taxi	zu einem Taxi (tsu inem taxi)
to the Hotel . . . , please	zum Hotel . . . , bitte
	(tsoom Hotel . . . , bitta)

MONEY

Currency exchange office	Wechselstube (vehsel-stooba)
Do you have change?	Können Sie wechseln?
	(kernen zee vehseln)
May I pay with	Kann ich mit (can ih mit)
- a traveler's check	einem Reisescheck (inem rises-sheck)
- a voucher	einem Gutschein (inem gootshine)
- this credit card?	dieser Kreditkarte
	(deeza kreditkarta)
	bezahlen? (betsahlen)
I would like to change	Ich möchte gerne Reiseschecks
some traveler's checks	eintauschen (ih merhte gairn rises-shecks eintowshen)

THE HOTEL

I have a reservation	Ich habe vorbestellt (reserviert) (ih hahba forbeshtellt (reserfiert)
A room with	Ein zimmer mit (ine tsimmer mit)
- a bath	bad (baht)
- a shower	einer Dusche (ina doosha)
- a toilet	einer Toilette, w.c. (ina toiletta, vay tsay)
- hot running water	fliessend warmen Wasser (fleesent varmen vasser)
What floor is it on?	In welchem Stockwerk ist es? (in velhem shtockverk ist es)
- ground floor	Erdgeschoss (aird-geshoss)
- second floor	Zweiter Stock (tsviter shtock)
Elevator	Aufzug (owftsoog)
Have the baggage sent up, please	Lassen Sie das Gepäck nach oben bringen, bitte (lassen zee dass gepeck nah oben bringen, bitta)
The key to number . . . , please	Den Schlüssel für Nummer . . . , bitte (dayn shloosel fur noomer . . . , bitta)
Please call me at 7 o'clock	Bitte, wecken Sie mich um sieben Uhr (bitta, vaecken zee mih oom zeeben oor)
Have the baggage brought down	Lassen Sie das Gepäck herunter bringen (lassen zee dass gepeck hair-oonter bringen)
The bill	Die Rechnung (dee rehnung)
A tip	Ein Trinkgeld (ine trinkgelt)

THE RESTAURANT

Restaurant	Restaurant
	Gaststätte (Gast-shtette)
Waiter!	Herr Ober! (Hair ober)
Waitress!	Fräulein! (froiline)
Menu	Speisekarte (shpiza-karta)
I would like to order (this) . . .	Ich möchte gerne (das . . .) bestellen (ih merhte gairn (dass . . .) beshtellen)
Some more . . . , please	Noch etwas mehr . . . , bitte (noh etvass mehr, bitta)
That's enough	Das ist genug (dass ist genuht), Das genügt
The check, please	Der Scheck, bitte (dair sheck, bitta)
Breakfast	Frühstück (fruh-shtook)
Lunch	Mittagessen (mittag-essen)
Dinner	Abendessen (abent-essen)
Bread	Brot (brote)
Butter	Butter (booter)
Jam	Konfitüre (Marmalade)
Salt, pepper	Salz/pfeffer (salts)
Mustard	Senf
Sauce, gravy	Sosse
Vinegar	Essig (essih)
Oil	Öl (oel)

Bottle	Flasche (flasha)
Wine - red, white	Wein (vine) - rot, weiss (vice)
Water	Wasser (vasser)
Mineral water	Mineralwasser (minerahl-vasser)
Milk	Milch
Coffee, with milk	Kaffee, mit milch (kaffay mit milch)
Tea, with lemon	Tee, mit Zitrone (tay, mit tsitrona)
Chocolate	Schokolade, Kakao (shockolahda)
Sugar, some sugar	Zucker, etwas zucker (etvass tsooka)
Spirits	Alkoholische Getränke (alkoholisha getrenka)

MAIL

A letter	Ein Brief
An envelope	Ein Umschlag (oomshlahg)
A postcard	Ein Postkarte
A mailbox	Ein Briefkasten
The post office	Das Postamt
A stamp	Eine Briefmarke
By airmail	Mit Luftpost
How much does it cost	Wieviel kostet es (veefeel . . .)
- to send a letter?	- einen Brief?
- to send a postcard by airmail to the United States (Great Britain, Canada)?	- eine Postkarte mit Luftpost nach Amerika zu schicken (England, Kanada)?
- to send a telegram, cable?	- ein Telegramm zu schicken?

LOCATIONS

. . . Street	. . . Strasse (shtrahsa)
. . . Avenue	. . . Allee (alleh)
. . . Square	. . . Platz (plats)
The airport	Der Flughafen (flooghafn)
A bank	Eine Bank
The beach	Der Strand (shtrant)
The castle	Die Burg, das Schloss (boorg, shloss)
The cathedral	Die Kathedrale (katedrahla)
The church	Die Kirche
The coffee house, cafe	Das Café
The garden	Der Garten
The hospital	Das Krankenhaus
The movies, cinema, film	Kino, ein Film
The museum	Das Museum
A nightclub	Ein Nachtclub (nakhtkloob)
The palace	Der Palast
The park	Der Park
The station	Der Bahnhof
The theater	Das Theater (tayarta)
- a play	- ein Schauspiel, Theaterstück (showshpeel, tayartastook)
The (official) travel bureau	Das Reisebüro (rizabooro)
The university	Die Universität (ooniverzitet)

TRAVEL

Arrival	Ankunft
Departure	Abfahrt
- airport	- Abflug

The airplane

I want to reconfirm a reservation on flight no. . . . for . . .	Ich möchte mir eine Reservierung für Flug Nummer . . . für . . . bestätigen lassen (ih merhta mir ine reserfieroong fur floog noomer . . . fur . . . beshtetigen lassen)
Where is the check-in?	Wo ist die Flugscheinkontrolle? (vo ist dee floog-shine-kontrolla)
I am checking in for . . .	Ich fliege nach . . . (ih fleega nah)
Fasten your seat belt	Bitte anschnallen

The railroad

The train	Der Zug (tsoog)
From what track does the train leave?	Von welchem Bahnsteig fährt der Zug? (fon velhem bahn-shtige ferht der tsoog)
Is this seat free?	Ist diese platz frei? (ist deeza plats fry)
Which way is the dining car?	Wo geht's zum Speisewagen? (vo gate's tsoom shpise-vahgen)

Bus, streetcar

Does this bus go to . . . ?	Fährt dieser Bus nach . . . ? (ferht deeza boos nah)
- trolleybus	- O(berleitungs)bus (ober-lite-oongs-boos)
I want to get off at . . . . . . at the next stop	Ich möchte an der . . . steigen (ih merhta an der . . . shtigen) . . . an der nächsten Haltestelle (an der nehshten halte-shtella)

Taxi

I (we) would like to go to . . . street, opera, zoo, . . . , please	Ich (wir) möchte(n) nach in die . . . Strasse, zur Oper, zum Zoo . . . , bitte (ih (veer) merhte(n) nah in dee . . . shtrassa, tsoor Opper, tsoom Tsoo . . . , bitta)
Stop at . . .	Halten Sie bei . . . (halten zee by)
Stop here	Halten Sie hier (haltn zee heer)

NUMBERS

1 eins (ains)	6 sechs (zeks)
2 zwei (tsvy)	7 sieben (zeeben)
3 drei (drai)	8 acht (akht)
4 vier (fier)	9 neun (noyn)
5 fünf (foonf)	10 zehn (tsen)

11 elf	60 sechzig
12 zwölf (tsveulf)	70 siebzig
13 dreizehn (drai-tsain)	80 achtzig
14 vierzehn	90 neunzig
15 fünfzehn	100 hundert (hoondert)
16 sechzehn	200 zweihundert
17 siebzehn (zeeb-tsain)	300 dreihundert
18 achtzehn	400 vierhundert
19 neunzehn	500 fünfhundert
20 zwanzig (tsvantsig)	600 sechshundert
25 fünfundzwanzig (foonf-und-tsvantsig)	700 siebenhundert
	800 achthundert
30 dreissig (dryssih)	900 neunhundert
40 vierzig	1,000 tausend (towzent)
50 fünfzig	

DAYS OF THE WEEK

Sunday	Sontag (zontahg)
Monday	Montag (montahg)
Tuesday	Dienstag (deenstahg)
Wednesday	Mittwoch (mitvoh)
Thursday	Donnerstag
Friday	Freitag (frytahg)
Saturday	Samstag or Sonnabend (zamstahg or zonahbent)

HUNGARY

HUNGARY—FACTS AT YOUR FINGERTIPS

HOW TO GO. Most foreign travel to Hungary is handled via the offices of IBUSZ, the Hungarian national tourist office. It has many branches in Budapest, including desks in all the major hotels and in the more important towns. In Budapest, perhaps confusingly, different branches of IBUSZ deal with different aspects of travel; one with rail or air tickets, for example, another with hotel reservations and so on. However, the IBUSZ desk at your hotel will be able to help with problems of all kinds and will also exchange foreign currency.

Outside Hungary, too, IBUSZ offices can be very helpful. They can make your hotel reservations, obtain your visa, and book you on any of the numerous tours inside Hungary. They have numerous agents, such as, in the United States, American Express and Maupintour. IBUSZ offices will be able to give you a complete list of all agents accredited to them in your country.

In addition to IBUSZ, there are other official Hungarian agencies, such as Budapest Tourist, Volántourist, Cooptourist, Express, Pegazus and Lokomotiv, as well as a few semi-private agencies. There are also local tourist offices in all major centers.

The addresses of IBUSZ offices overseas are:

In the U.S.: 630 Fifth Ave., Suite 2455, New York, NY 10111 (tel. 212–582–7412).

In Canada: Hungarian Embassy, 7 Delaware Ave., Ottawa, Ontario K2P O2Z.

In the U.K.: Danube Travel Ltd., 6 Conduit St., London W1R 9TG (tel. 01–493–0263).

You can also obtain information from the offices of MALÉV, the Hungarian airline. Their offices in New York are at the same address as those of IBUSZ; in the U.K., their address is 10 Vigo St., London W1.

TOURS. IBUSZ offers a wide range of inclusive tours. Four tours covering different parts of the country—northwest Hungary, northern Hungary, southwest Hungary and the Great Plain—each lasting five days (four nights), cost around $180–210 a head for full board in a double room with bath. Also on offer is a weekend in Budapest ($150–170) and a week-long visit to Lake Balaton ($230). In addition, there are numerous hobby tours, including accompanied bicycle tours, photo safaris, anglers' tours, visits to vineyards during the fall, cookery courses, weaving courses, keep-fit courses, agricultural courses and music courses; the choice seems endless. Tours for young people (under 30) are handled by the Express Youth and Students' Bureau.

To visit Hungary on a prepaid package tour is both less expensive and less troublesome than independent travel. A sample package tour, arranged by Danube Travel ex-London, to cover a seven-night stay in Budapest in a Moderate hotel with breakfast, return flight, a half-day sightseeing tour and visa, but not transfer between the airport and your hotel, costs from around £375 in the summer.

Riders will find that there are a large number of special riding holidays. Detailed information can be obtained from travel agencies abroad and from tourist offices in Hungary. There are holidays based on a stay at a stud farm and cross-country tours on horseback. A stay in a stud farm, which includes accommodations, all meals and tuition, ranges from about $40 to $70 a day, according to season and the comfort provided. Cross-country tours, lasting 10 days, with about 6 days' riding, cost from $700 upwards, fully inclusive.

Fugazy International Travel, 770 U.S. Highway 1, North Brunswick, NJ 08902 (tel. 201–828–4488), offers perhaps the most comprehensive tours of Hungary outside of IBUSZ' own: four different 15-day summer itineraries, cost $2,159 per person (including airfare).

In the U.K. *Swan Hellenic Tours,* 77 New Oxford St., London WC1A 1PP (tel. 01–831–1616), run a 15-day "Art Treasures Tour" of Hungary in July and August. The tours are accompanied by a guide-lecturer; cost around £1,325.

The Vienna office IBUSZ (Karntnerstrasse 26, tel. 51–55–50) organizes a whole series of tours to Budapest. A two-day tour, costing around U.S.$170 per person, covers bus travel to Budapest, lunch and a three-hour sightseeing tour, dinner with gypsy music, a night in a comfortable hotel, and a free morning shopping, returning on the Danube by hydrofoil.

VISAS. In addition to a valid passport, all West Europeans (except Austrians, Finns and Swedes), Americans, Canadians and citizens of all Commonwealth countries require visas to enter Hungary. If you arrive by air or car, you can obtain visas at Ferihegy airport or on the border, otherwise you should apply to the Hungarian consulate in your own country or to an accredited travel agent before you leave. Even if you are flying or driving to Hungary it is advisable to get your visa in advance to avoid a tiresome wait as well as an additional charge. Send a valid passport and two passport-size photos to the Hungarian Consulate in New York, 8 E. 75th St., New York, NY 10021, or the Hungarian Embassy in Washington at 3910 Shoemaker St., NW, Washington DC 20008. In Canada, write to 7 Delaware Ave., Ottawa, Ontario K2P 0Z2. In the U.K., write to the Hungarian Consulate, 35b Eaton Pl., London S.W.1, or go through Danube Travel. There is a fee of about $10 (£7 in the U.K.) and your passport must be valid for nine months after the date of entry. Visas are valid for a stay of 30 days.

Visas are no longer required for groups (with valid passports) staying for under 48 hours. This helps groups visiting from, say, Vienna.

Visas can be extended for a further 30 days by buying 300-Ft. worth of stamps from the post office and applying to your local police station. *All visitors must be registered with the police.* At hotels or private accommodations booked through an agency, this will be taken care of automatically. If you are staying with friends or relatives a 10-Ft. form must be obtained from the post office, signed by your host and taken, with your passport, to the local police station.

MONEY. The unit of currency in Hungary is the Forint, which is divided into 100 fillérs (abbreviated Ft. and f.). There are coins of 10, 20 and 50 fillérs and of 1, 2, 5, 10 and 20 Ft., and notes (bills) of 10, 20, 50, 100, 500 and 1,000 Ft. The 10- and 20-Ft. notes are rarely met with.

The tourist exchange rate was about 47 Ft. to the U.S. dollar and about 85 Ft. to the pound sterling at the time of writing, but again this is almost certain to change both before and during 1989. Traveler's checks are widely accepted, as are the usual credit cards—American Express, Diners Club, Eurocard, and Access—but these should not be relied upon in less expensive establishments or outside Budapest and the main tourist centers. Holders of Eurocheque cards can cash personal checks in all banks and in many hotels and stores.

You may bring in any amount of foreign currency, but you may only import—and take out—100 Ft. in Hungarian currency. Foreign currency may only be exchanged at official exchange agencies such as those in banks, travel agencies, hotels and airports. No foreign currency may be given or sold to individuals in Hungary. There is a black market in foreign currency in Hungary, but you will be tempting fate if you try to take advantage of it. Take care not to change too many dollars or pounds because although in theory 50% of money exchanged (up to $100 worth) can be changed back into Western currency, this may prove difficult in practice.

COSTS. At press time, mid-1988, prices in Hungary were still modest by Western standards. Even in Budapest and the larger tourist resorts prices are reasonable, while in the countryside almost everything can seem a bargain. But the situation is liable to change both before and during 1989. The introduction of up to 25% VAT on all service industries in January 1988 and the relaxation of price controls with effect from April 1988 are guaranteed to result in price increases.

Sample Costs. Cinema ticket 20–60 Ft.; theater ticket 100–300 Ft.; concert and opera tickets cost from 100 to over 500 Ft. if someone famous is performing; beer from 40–60 Ft. in a bar, more in a restaurant; coffee (espresso) from 20–40 Ft.; scotch (glass) about 150 Ft. (but much more in a nightclub or hotel bar); a bottle of wine in a moderate restaurant 150–200 Ft.; a bottle of good wine in a first class restaurant 250 Ft. and up.

MEDICAL INSURANCE. There is no reciprocal agreement concerning medical treatment between Hungary and the U.S. It is advisable, therefore, to take out comprehensive medical insurance before you leave. British subjects are entitled, on showing their passports, to *essential* or *emergency* services, including treatment in a hospital and the services of a medical practitioner; a nominal charge is made for prescriptions. But in any case comprehensive medical insurance is strongly recommended. Such medicines as painkillers can be bought at any chemist's without a prescription.

CLIMATE. From May to September is the best time, though July and August are usually hot and crowded. Spring and fall are often delightful and numerous fairs and festivals are held during the season. Winters are cold and the winter sports season lasts from late November through early March.

Average maximum daily temperatures in degrees Fahrenheit and Centigrade:

Budapest	Jan.	Feb.	Mar.	Apr.	May	Jun.	Jul.	Aug.	Sep.	Oct.	Nov.	Dec.
F°	34	39	50	63	72	79	82	81	73	61	46	39
C°	1	4	10	17	22	26	28	27	23	16	8	4

SPECIAL EVENTS. The Budapest International Fairs take place in May (capital goods) and September (consumer goods). Other important events of international interest are the Formula One motor races and the Hungarian Grand Prix, held early in August at the Hungaroring, just east of Budapest. Among the many art festivals are the Beethoven Memorial Concerts at Martonvásár, southwest of Budapest, in July and August; the Haydn and Mozart Concerts in the Esterházy Palace at Fertőd, in western Hungary, in July and August; and the Open-air Opera and Drama Festival at Szeged, which runs from mid-July to mid-August. The Budapest Musical and Art Weeks are a traditional attraction of the early fall. Dates vary from year to year and details of these and other events can be obtained from IBUSZ or from its representatives abroad.

Among the many other special events are the following: **February,** Film Festival (Budapest). "Busó" masked procession on Carnival Sunday (14th) (Mohács). **March,** Spring Festival Week (Budapest); "Spring Days" (Szentendre, in the Danube Bend). **April** (4th) Liberation Day ceremonies (Budapest). **June,** Historical Pageant and Tournament (Visegrád). **June–July,** Folk-dance and Music Festival (Győr); Festival Weeks (Sopron). **July,** Summer Theater Festival (Pécs); International Equestrian Days (Hortobágy); Nyírbátor Musical Days—concerts in the historic church; "Agria" theatrical fair (Eger); Theater Festival (Szentendre). **July–August,** Helikon Chamber Music Festival in the Festetich Palace (Keszthely), Equestrian Tournaments (Nagyvázsony), "Szentendre Days of Music and Art" (Szentendre). **August,** Cultural Days (Hollókő); organ concerts in the Abbey (Tihany); Equestrian Show (Bábolna stud farm); Horse Show (Bugacpuszta); Equestrian Fair (Hortobágy); St. Stephen's and Constitution Day (20th), open-air performances, parade on the Danube, fireworks (Budapest); Baroque and Renaissance Concerts (Pécs). **September–October,** "Nyírség Autumn", cultural and gastronomic displays (Nyíregyháza). "Savaria" Festival of concerts and gastronomy (Szombathely), "Vintage Days" (Sopron).

Occasional concerts are given during the summer in the limestone caves at Aggtelek.

National Holidays. Jan. 1; Apr. 4 (Liberation Day); Easter Monday; May 1 (Labor Day); Aug. 20 (St. Stephen's and Constitution Day); Nov. 7 (Anniversary of Russian Revolution; Dec. 25 and 26.

CUSTOMS. Objects for personal use may be imported freely. If you are over 16, you may also bring in 250 cigarettes or 50 cigars or 250 grs. of tobacco, plus 2 liters of wine and 1 liter of spirits, plus 250 grs. of perfume. In addition, small gifts not exceeding a value (in Hungary) of 1,000 Ft. each, to a total value of 5,000 Ft., may also be imported duty free. A 30% customs charge is levied on gifts intended for relatives and friends that are valued at over 10,000 Ft. in Hungary.

All personal belongings that have been imported may be freely taken out of the country. So may food for the journey, 2 liters of wine, 1 liter of spirits and 250 cigarettes. Gifts of a non-commercial character may also be freely exported, provided that they have been bought with hard currency or with forints obtained by the legal exchange of hard currency. Goods to any value bought from the Intertourist or Konsumtourist stores (for hard currency) may be exported without license, provided that the bill received at the store is produced at customs. You need a permit to export non-protected works of art valued at over 1,000 Ft.

For currency regulations see *Money*.

LANGUAGE. Hungarian (Magyar) is one of the more exotic languages of Eastern Europe and at first sight looks forbidding. Generally, older people speak some German while more and more young people now speak English. Both languages are widely spoken and understood by those who come into regular contact with tourists.

HOTELS. Accommodations should be applied for as far as possible in advance, especially in the less expensive establishments. Hungarian hotels are graded from 5-stars down to 1-star. These grades correspond closely to our grading system in the lists that follow of Deluxe (L) for 5-stars, Expensive (E) for 4-stars, Moderate (M) for 3- and the better 2-stars, and Inexpensive (I) for the cheaper 2-stars and 1-star. In practice the Hungarian grading system sometimes appears rather arbitrary, especially in more modest establishments and to be decided by factors not always clear to the visitor.

5-star hotels have every comfort and luxury, including airconditioning throughout. Only two 4-star hotels (the Béke and the Forum in Budapest) have complete airconditioning, though many have this amenity in the public rooms; however, all 4-star hotels are extremely comfortable. 3- and 2-star establishments are less luxurious, though they are usually well furnished and well run. They are often crowded with package-tour groups, but this fact will rarely affect individual travelers. Single rooms with bath are scarce. 1-star hotels are generally simply furnished with few, if any, private baths; they are rarely recommended to foreign tourists, though in some provincial towns there may be no better accommodations available. The plumbing is satisfactory almost everywhere, though some remote (I) country hotels and tourist-hotels can be pretty primitive. Visitors from the West are made very welcome and service almost everywhere will be both friendly and smooth—though here, as elsewhere in Hungary, a tip can work wonders.

The table below shows approximate prices for rooms with bath and breakfast. *Balaton hotel rates include full board, which is compulsory at most hotels during the high season (June through August).* Hotel rates are considerably lower in many hotels in the low season; in Budapest, this is December through March (with the exception of the New Year holiday); in the Balaton area, where most hotels are only open from May to September, it is May and September.

During August two people in a double room with bath and continental breakfast will pay approximately:

	Budapest	Balaton	Provinces
Deluxe (L)	US$110–200	—	—
Expensive (E)	$100–145	$90–120	$60–80
Moderate (M)	$60–95	$60–80	$30–40
Inexpensive (I)	$15–55	$14–30	$10–20

For single rooms with bath count on from $20–35 and more per head per night. All singles in (L) and (E) hotels have private bath or shower.

In Budapest the (I) hotels which we have listed are in general comfortable and well-equipped; in the provinces they are sometimes less so, though they may be the only accommodations available in some of the smaller towns. There are no (L) and only a few (E) hotels outside Budapest, but the latest (M) hotels are usually very comfortable and well run.

In addition to ordinary hotels, there are also an increasing number of small guest-houses (often privately run), as well as many tourist hotels; these latter are for the less demanding and usually have at least five beds per room, with hot and cold running water in a communal bath- or shower-room on each floor.

Hungary has recently begun to turn some of its more picturesque and historic country houses into "country-house hotels." These vary in the comfort and facilities provided. Among them are those at Bük, Fertőd, Nagyvázsony, Szirák, and Pécs (Üszögpuszta).

Self-Catering

Bungalows, fully equipped for cooking, etc., can be rented in Budapest and at a large number of resorts. Full details and rates can be obtained from tourist offices in Hungary and abroad, who can also arrange bookings. A typical bungalow for two at Lake Balaton costs around U.S. $300–450 a week.

Private Accommodations

Available almost everywhere, paying-guest accommodations are an inexpensive and excellent way of getting to know the people. In Budapest and in Lake Balaton resorts, the rate per night for a double room (single or double occupancy) is round $10–15, which includes the use of a bathroom, but not breakfast. A few rooms with private bath are available at higher rates. In provincial towns, the rates are lower. Such accommodations can be booked either through local tourist offices or by travel agents abroad. Applications should be made well in advance.

Camping

There are around 100 campsites in Hungary. They are to be found in all the country's chief beauty spots. Most of the sites cater for campers bringing in their own equipment, but a few provide tents. There are four categories of site, from 4-star to 1-star, depending on the amenities provided and most are open from May through September. Caravans are permitted in all sites that have power points; a parking charge is made for such caravans, as well as for cars, motorcycles and other forms of transport. At the time of going to press, the rates for use of the site vary from approximately 80 to 210 Ft. a day, plus a charge for hot water and electricity. Young people between two and 14 years of age pay half these rates and there is no charge for children under the age of two. Members of the FICC are entitled to reductions of between 10–30%. *Camping is forbidden except in the appointed areas.*

Bookings can be made through the *Hungarian Camping and Caravanning Club,* Üllői Út 6, Budapest VIII, or through travel agencies.

Hungary has four nudist camps: at Délegyháza, some 30 km. (20 miles) south of Budapest; at Debrecen, in eastern Hungary; at Mohács, in the south of the country and at Balatonberény, on Lake Balaton.

RESTAURANTS. There are many excellent restaurants throughout the country, most, though not all, state-owned. In the large restaurants you will find an impressive bill-of-fare, often in several languages. If you want to eat really well, with famous Hungarian specialties such as goose liver, and with some excellent Hungarian wine, you should reckon on 600 to 1,000 Ft. a head at the very least in an Expensive (E) restaurant; you could pay much more. In a good Moderate (M) restaurant, with half a bottle of wine, reckon on between 350 and 500 Ft. a head. On the other hand, for those with slender means (and not too large an appetite), there is often, even in quite high-class restaurants, an Inexpensive (I) fixed-price meal, called a *menü*, of two or three courses, which can cost as little as 60 Ft.; but in famous restaurants it can reach 100 Ft. or even more. This menü tends to be tucked away at the bottom of the bill-of-fare and to be in Hungarian, or Hungarian and German, only. Needless to say, the waiter will not usually draw your attention to it, but it is worthwhile looking for and often very good value. Drink, of course, is extra. Most of the better places have music in the evening and prices are then correspondingly higher. Note that only the better restaurants and cafes have price lists in English, so make quite sure what you are ordering and, to avoid a possible unpleasant surprise, what it will cost.

There are also many inexpensive *önkiszolgáló étterem* (self-service restaurants), *bisztró* or *étel-bár* (snack bars) and *büfé* (buffets), which serve freshly-cooked meals.

Budapest is no longer a city of great coffee houses in the old Austro-Hungarian tradition, places where people met to discuss the topics of the day. In the capital, and indeed throughout Hungary, their place has been taken by a host of small *eszpresszó* (small cafes or coffee bars) and so-called *drink-bárs*. There are also numerous excellent *cukrászda* (pastry shops), where superb pastries are consumed, with or without the accompaniment of tea or coffee. For more details on Hungarian cuisine, see our chapter on *Food and Drink*.

It is usual throughout Hungary, in all the better cafes and restaurants, to leave your hat and coat in the cloakroom; the attendant will expect a tip of a few forints.

TIPPING. Hungarians have always been generous tippers and Communism hasn't affected this in the least. Although your hotel bill may contain a service charge, tips are expected. You should be generous to the *főportás* (head-porter), who in practice supervises your stay. Then there is the chambermaid (who will get laundry done for you in a day), the breakfast waiter and the liftboy. Altogether, reckon to pay out around 15% of your bill.

In restaurants give the head waiter, who presents you with the bill, at least 10%; the money is divided among the staff. If a gypsy band plays for you and your table exclusively, you can slip a 100-Ft. note under the strings of the lead violinist's instrument or leave it in a plate provided for the purpose. It is up to you to welcome or reject his advances! Gas station attendants, taxi drivers and hairdressers all expect a few forints. In fact, if you are in any doubt—tip!

MAIL AND TELEPHONES. Postcards by surface mail to Western Europe (including, of course, the U.K.) cost 8 Ft., letters 10 Ft.; by air to the United States 10 Ft.; to western Europe 9 Ft. Letters by air cost 12 Ft. to the United States, 12 Ft. to western Europe. (There is little advantage in paying the airmail supplement to western Europe.) Stamps may be bought from tobacconists as well as post offices. In Budapest, the main post office in Petőfi Sándor Utca, in the Inner City, is open till 8 P.M., Mondays through Fridays, and until 3 P.M. on Saturdays; closed on Sundays. The post offices at the East and West stations are open day and night. Telegrams and telexes may be sent and long-distance calls made from the new post office at Petőfi Sándor Utca 17–19.

Telephoning in Hungary is usually easy; the system is automatic for almost all internal and international calls.

TIME. Hungary is six hours ahead of Eastern Standard Time and one hour ahead of Greenwich Mean Time. From April to September (dates vary from year to year) the country operates on summer time, which is seven hours ahead of Eastern Standard Time and two hours ahead of Greenwich Mean Time.

CLOSING TIMES. There is now a five-day working week in Hungary, from Monday through Friday, though most shops are also open on Saturday till around midday. The usual office hours are 8 to 5, banks 8 to 1; many shops do not open until 10 A.M. and close at 6 P.M.

SPAS. Hungary is famous for its medicinal waters and some of its spas—Budapest, Balatonfüred, and Hévíz among them—have achieved wide renown. Budapest itself is a spa of the first rank, with thermal springs supplying 31 medicinal baths; arthritis, bronchial catarrh, and locomotor disorders are among the conditions for which these waters are especially beneficial. Balatonfüred caters for heart ailments, and Hévíz for rheumatic complaints. Most of the spas have comfortable hotels for those undergoing treatment.

An example of prices for a two-week treatment, from London, covering return flight, first-class accommodations in a double room with bath, medical examination, and full medical care, full board with dietary meals where necessary, and spa treatment according to a doctor's prescription, varies from £780 to £920 in Budapest and £690 to £770 at Hévíz. In all cases, accompanying adults without treatment pay less.

SHOPPING. The best things to buy in Hungary are peasant embroideries and the exquisite Herend and Zsolnay porcelain. Hand-painted pottery and handmade lace are also attractive, as is the excellent cut glass. Dolls dressed in national costume are popular and records are of good quality and inexpensive.

Government tourist shops, called *Intertourist* or *Konsumtourist,* have multilingual assistants and stock the widest choice. They sell only against hard currency, e.g. dollars or sterling.

HUNTING. With more than 700 hunting clubs and no entirely closed season, Hungary is increasingly popular with hunters of both small and big game. Much of the big game is hunted in the hilly and forested areas of Transdanubia, while the flat country is the place for small game. Deer are native to Hungary and wild boar can be hunted all year round. Mixed small game hunts are especially popular with visitors.

Accommodations for hunters range from a simple log cabin to a country mansion. *MAVAD Hunting Office,* 1014 Budapest Uri Út 39 and VADEX, 1253 Budapest, POB 40, will send you a price list and a contract specifying hunting conditions.

RIDING. Traditionally a nation of horsemen, there are now over 100 riding schools and stables throughout Hungary. These range from small holdings with two or three horses to large establishments with 50–60 horses and comfortable guest houses. Among the many options available are one-day outings, 10-day tours covering up to 250 km. (155 miles), and even courses in horse-driving. Hungary is especially well-suited to cross-country riders who have already acquired the basic skills. IBUSZ offices abroad will supply information and make reservations. In Budapest, TOURINFORM can answer any queries.

GOLF. There is a golf course at the small village of Kisoroszi, about 38 km. (23 miles) from Budapest. At present the course has nine holes, but these will eventually be increased to 18. The clubhouse has a lounge, restaurant, and sports store.

SWIMMING AND BOATING. Lake Balaton and the Danube are the main centers. Yachts, rowboats, and sailboards can be rented at lake resorts and sailing courses are organized for beginners. Sailing holidays on Lake Balaton can be arranged through IBUSZ and SIOTOUR, Budapest VII, Wesselényi Utca 26.

Budapest is dotted with swimming pools, many of them attached to the medicinal baths and mineral springs. Of the many pools, the largest and finest is the Palatinus Lido on Margaret Island.

GETTING AROUND HUNGARY. By Train. There is an extensive network of railways. Standards are higher than average in Eastern Europe with buffet car expresses linking Budapest with a number of other cities. Country services are slow and less frequent. On the fastest express trains, seat reservation is obligatory. For those who like a lot of traveling, there are cheap Run Around tickets, allowing unlimited travel for 10, 20 or 30 days. Cost, 1st and 2nd class respectively £80, £120, £161; £53, £81, £105. Details and tickets from Danube Travel, 6 Conduit St., London W1. These fares are subject to change.

The Inter Rail Card for those under 26 and the Rail Europ Senior pass for Senior Citizens are valid in Hungary; see page 18 for details.

By Air. There is no internal air service in Hungary.

By Bus. An extensive network of medium- and long-distance buses operates throughout Hungary. But buses are always crowded and speed is not their greatest asset. Tickets and full information on the services can be obtained from IBUSZ or at the VOLÁN main long-distance bus station in Engels Tér in Budapest.

By Car. Hungarians drive on the right and the usual Continental rules of the road are observed. The speed limit for private cars in built-up areas is 60 kph (40 mph), on main roads 80 kph (50 mph) and on highways (motorways) it's 120 kph (75 mph); for cars towing trailers or caravans, the speed limit is around 20 kph (12 mph) less in each case. Seat belts are compulsory and drinking is absolutely prohibited; penalties for infringement are extremely severe. Any road accidents must be reported to the police within 24 hours. Visitors from the U.S. need an International Driving License; U.K. drivers are only required to hold a British licence. Detailed information on the documents you will need if you're taking your own car into the country is given on page 20.

Gas stations are marked on most touring maps of the country. A liter of gasoline (*benzin*) costs around 21 Ft. (a gallon is around $2). Unleaded gasoline, available at about 20 stations, including five in Budapest, costs around 24 Ft. per liter. Interag-Shell and Afor stations at busy traffic centers stay open all night. Otherwise stations are open from 6 A.M.–8 P.M.

Hungary's main roads radiate from Budapest. There are four *autopálya* (motorways), three of them only partly complete. The M1 now reaches Győr on its way to the Austrian frontier (and Vienna); the M3 will, when it is finished, connect Budapest with Eastern Hungary. The M5 to southeast Hungary is now complete most of the way to Kecskemét, while the M7 leads to Lake Balaton.

In general the main roads, which have a single number, are excellent, as are many of the secondary roads. Many of the minor country roads, however, are either dusty or muddy, according to the season.

The Hungarian Automibile Club runs a 24-hour "Yellow Angels" breakdown service from Budapest XIV, Fráncia Út 38a (tel. 691–831 or 693–714). There are repair garages in all the major towns and emergency telephones on the main highways. Members of foreign automobile and touring clubs can pay any transport and repair costs by letter of credit.

INTRODUCING HUNGARY

A visit to Hungary will reward you with an experience unlike anything else in Europe. You'll feel the curious results of, on the one hand, being right in the center of the Continent, while yet seeming to be curiously out of Europe, because of the language, the food, the music and the people—all different from anything you have seen and sensed elsewhere. The language bears no resemblance to those of its neighbors, for its nearest relatives are the tongues of the Finns and the Estonians, far away in Northern Europe.

Hungary—officially the Hungarian People's Republic—is a small, mostly flat country; to the west and north there are mountains, though few reach 3,000 ft. (914 m); to the south and east stretches a great plain. Hungary covers an area of just over 93,000 sq. km. (35,000 sq. miles)—about the size of Ireland or Indiana—and has a population of about 10½ million. It is in many ways unique in Eastern Europe; it is more than the equal of its socialist neighbors in the warm welcome its kindly people give a foreign visitor; it has first-class hotels, an outstanding cuisine and excellent facilities for every kind of sport. Its capital, Budapest, with a superb situation astride the broad Danube, is not only a busy administrative and industrial city of over two million inhabitants, it is at the same time a great holiday resort and a famous spa. A splendid palace, an impressive Parliament building, great modern hotels and picturesque churches line the river; it is one of the grandest panoramic sweeps in Europe.

Then there's Lake Balaton, Europe's largest warmwater inland sea, with its charming, almost Italianate, landscape, its Baroque towns and its sunny vineyards on the hillsides. There's the Great Plain, a land of splendid horses and their riders, the *csikós,* and of fiery food and strong wine. Eger, in the north of the country, and Sopron, in the extreme west, are two of the loveliest Baroque towns in Europe.

Enormous strides have been made in recent years to improve tourist amenities and the best hotels—often built with Western help and know-how—are probably the equals of those anywhere in the world. Only a few out-of-the-way provincial places still have older establishments with lower standards. Food is excellent almost everywhere, though one may still occasionally come across slow and off-hand service. But things get better year by year and a visit to Hungary is now very far from being the "adventure" it was only a few years ago.

Romans, Huns and Magyars

Hungary's frontiers were first defined by the Romans when they created the province of Pannonia—there is still a monastery of that name near Győr, and a popular Berlin–Budapest train with the name Pannonia Express. Some important Roman sites have been excavated in Budapest and south and west of the Danube; but the Romans never controlled the wild plains and swamps to the north and east, from where (around 430 A.D.) came Attila the Hun, the "scourge of God," leader of nomadic hordes from the deserts of Mongolia. The word Hun suggests Hungary, but the etymology is disputed. Hungarians call their country Magyarország, after another Asiatic tribe, the Magyars, who moved in during the 8th and 9th centuries. A Magyar chieftain, Stephen, became Hungary's first king (1000–1038) and was converted to Christianity and canonized. Thereafter the country was embroiled in the power struggles of Popes and Holy Roman emperors.

In 1240 her knights and bowmen prepared to repel an invasion of Mongols who, ranging unchecked through Eastern Europe, settled like locusts on her grassy, well-watered plains. "There rode forth from among us," wrote a chronicler, "to offer single combat, a knight fully accoutred, mounted on an Arab horse, solid as a mountain. Then came forth from the Mongols a horseman mounted on a horse like a donkey, having in his hand a spear like a spindle, wearing neither robe nor armor, so that all who saw him were moved to laughter. Yet ere the day was done the victory was theirs and they inflicted on us a great defeat, which was the Key of Evil, and thereafter there befell us what befell us."

The Mongolian Light Cavalry almost destroyed Hungary and half Europe too—but they vanished as quickly as they had come, leaving dynastic turmoil behind them. A succession of Angevin kings (from Anjou in France) ruled Hungary; a feudal system arose—monarch, landed aristocracy and a mass of serfs; and all lived under the constant threat of Slav and Turkish invasion.

Sigismund, King of Hungary, became Holy Roman Emperor in 1410—a year of three popes and three emperors. Sigismund's son-in-law and heir was Albert of Habsburg, and he began what was to be a 500-year association between his famous imperial family and Hungary. At first, they were bright times for Hungary. The hero János Hunyadi offered stubborn resistance to the Turks. His son and elected king, Matthias Corvinus, presided over a sort of Magyar renaissance and wielded influence throughout central Europe. But the weak rulers who followed left the country a prey to domestic unrest as well as foreign incursions.

Colonial Hungary

In 1514 György Dózsa led an abortive peasant revolt—he himself was an ambitious noble, but the present regime honors his memory. In 1526 the Turks annihilated the Magyar armies at Mohács. Here and there a minaret or city fountain survives as a relic of their subsequent 150-year occupation of lands mostly south and west of the Danube. Hungarian princes held sway in the Transylvanian forests in the east, but all the rest of Hungary was ruled by Habsburg emperors from Vienna. Even when those champions of Christendom beat the Turks decisively in 1664, the emperor Leopold I allowed the sultan to keep his Hungarian possessions. And when a great battle near Vienna (1683) removed the Turkish menace for ever, he took over Hungary as a Habsburg dependency.

Oppression and a stagnating economy frequently inspired the Hungarians to rise against their masters. Prince Ferenc Rákóczi led an eight-year war of independence (1703–1711); the French Revolution (1789) stimulated more unrest; and the Year of Revolutions (1848) saw an explosion of militant nationalism led by the poet Sándor Petőfi (the Budapest cafe in which, according to legend, he planned it is now a popular restaurant hung with the old inflammatory posters and broadsheets). That explosion actually brought about a shortlived national government under the veteran freedom fighter Lajos Kossuth, but the emperor called in Russian troops and, not for the last time in her history, Hungary's resistance collapsed and harsh reprisals followed. The Austrian emperor Franz Josef shared his ancestors' almost mystical conviction of the Habsburg right to absolute domination.

Austria, however, the decaying rump of the Holy Roman empire, was struggling to survive among more enlightened great powers. In crisis, after a short war with Prussia, she had to come to terms with her embittered eastern neighbor. Under the historic "Compromise" of 1867, Hungary became mistress in her own house and a full partner in the ramshackle Austro-Hungarian empire.

Twentieth-Century Hungary

The Emperor, who now wore the iron crown of St. Stephen, ruled a conglomeration of peoples and a babel of tongues. "I am the last monarch of the old school," he told Theodore Roosevelt in 1912. A Hungarian banknote of that date is a large document: it is lettered in Magyar, German, Czech, Slovak, Polish, Romanian, Ruthenian, Slovenian, Croatian, Serbian and Italian. But Franz Josef's long reign (1848–1916), marked by increasing isolation and family tragedies—his son Rudolf's suicide, his empress's assassination, his heir Franz Ferdinand's assassination at Sarajevo—culminated in disaster. World War I broke up the Austro-Hungarian empire and scattered the lands of the Holy Crown. Hungary the vanquished, stripped of much territory, fell under the Communist rule of Béla Kun and then under the near-fascist regime of Admiral Miklós Horthy, who had been her one outstanding war hero. Tempted by dreams of recovering lost provinces, she marched with Germany in World War II. Her armies were destroyed on the Russian front and in 1945 the Red Army completed a swift and brutal occupation.

The uprising in 1956 briefly interrupted the socialization of the nation. After some years of unpleasant repression, matters improved politically and materially. Since 1957 the Party, under its popular General Secretary János Kádár, with help from both East and West, has improved agriculture and encouraged technical and commercial expansion. There are at present more "private enterprise" shopkeepers in Budapest than in any other Warsaw Pact capital city.

Hungarians are clever and ambitious people, egocentric but realistic, adept at making the best of things at least in the short term. Point out the discrepancies between their not-uncomfortable life-style and their endless complaints of penury and they will agree with you: "Yes, we wish we could live as well as we do."

A Glance at Hungarian Culture

For a small nation, Hungary has achieved remarkable fame in the world's cultural scene, particularly in the fields of music and film.

Ferenc Erkel (1810–1893) created Hungarian opera; his patriotic *Bánk Bán* is still performed on national occasions. Ferenc (Franz) Liszt (1811–1886) was not only a great composer but an even greater virtuoso. Two modern Hungarian composers have found world fame, Béla Bartók (1881–1945) and Zoltán Kodály (1882–1967); both have gone back to the deepest roots of folk music. Nor have Hungarians lacked eminence in light music; Franz Lehár was a Hungarian and the *joie de vivre* of his *Merry Widow* continues to entrance the world; Emmerich Kalman's operettas, among them *The Czardas Princess,* are widely known. An important group of Hungarian musicians lives outside Hungary; Sir Georg Solti, George Sebestyén, George Szell and Antal Doráti are all outstanding conductors. There are also many younger musicians making their mark.

Most of the cinema's "giants"—Cukor, Fox, Korda—were Hungarians, as were the film stars Peter Lorre, Tony Curtis and Leslie Howard. The theater is very popular in Hungary, but Hungarian playwrights have been less successful abroad than at home. The best known is Ferenc Molnár (1878–1952). The Hungarian cinema has latterly achieved world fame; we mention only a few names: Miklós Jancsó, Károly Makk, István Szabó (whose *Mephisto* won an Oscar) and Pál Sándor, who is making his name in the West for the beautiful films he builds around crucial historical events.

The beginnings of Hungarian literature were in Latin; the first author who wrote in Hungarian was Bálint Balassi (1554–1594), a minstrel of love and of the soldier's life. The next name of international importance is that of Imre Madách (1802–1864), who produced Hungary's first major literary work with his epic drama *The Tragedy of Man.* Other famous literary figures are Mór Jókai (1825–1904), Kálmán Mikszáth (1847–1910) and Zsigmond Móricz (1879–1942). Among Hungarians who have lived and worked abroad one name stands out, that of Arthur Koestler (1905–1983).

Poetry in Hungary has a reputation and a popularity which it has in few other countries. Mihály Vörösmarty (1800–1855) was the first great Hungarian epic poet. Sándor Petőfi (1823–1849) was perhaps the greatest poet of all; he was a burning, restless patriot, who wrote verse of lyrical beauty and whose legacy has been inexhaustible. And the third of these great poets was Janos Arany (1819–1892). Endre Ady (1877–1919) became the leader of a new renaissance in poetry. Four final names must be mentioned: Attila József (1905–1937) was known as "the poet of the proletariat"—he killed himself at the age of 32; Miklós Radnóti

(1909–1944), a learned and lyrical poet, was murdered by a Nazi guard while being marched to a concentration camp; Sándor Weöres (born 1913) is perhaps Hungary's greatest living poet; and Gyula Illyés (1902–1983), who wrote vivid prose as well as sensuously beautiful poems.

Among the writers popular today are Tibor Déry (1894–1977), an outstanding novelist, and the dramatist István Örkény (1912–1979).

As far as architecture is concerned, it is unfortunate that successive invasions, the long Turkish occupation and the many battles waged on Hungarian soil have left few ancient buildings standing, though there are some remarkable medieval churches. Among Hungarian architects of real interest we mention Ödön Lechner (1845–1914), who created a new, short-lived "Hungarian art nouveau" style, perhaps best exemplified in the Museum of Applied Arts in Budapest.

The work of Hungary's best painters can be seen in the Hungarian National Gallery; it tended to follow French models. Names to be remembered are: Munkácsy (1844–1900), Szinyei Merse (1845–1920), Rippl-Rónai (1861–1927) and the strange naïf surrealist Csontváry Kosztka (1853–1919), the best of whose work is at Pécs. A beautiful collection of ecclesiastical art is on show in the Christian Museum at Esztergom.

The folk-art of pottery was for centuries a living tradition and it still flourishes: the Hungarian potter best known abroad is Margit Kovács (1902–1977), who has a museum devoted to her bizarre but often beautiful works at Szentendre.

HUNGARIAN
FOOD AND DRINK

From Gulyás to Dobostorta

Hungarian cooking is a sophisticated and delicious anthology of color, shape, odor and taste. It has absorbed, though with suitable modifications, the best of Viennese, French, Serbian and Oriental traditions. There have been some unjust generalizations about its being too spicy or too heavy. This may be true in some parts of the country, but certainly not in Budapest or other culinary centers.

From Soup to Soup

Hungarian soups are memorable experiences. Perhaps the most fabulous is the Magyar version of *bouillabaisse*. It is called *halászlé* and is best eaten in Szeged or on Lake Balaton, though most Budapest restaurants also serve it. The Szeged version is a thick, rich soup made from giant catfish, carp or sterlet. The Balaton *halászlé* is a clear soup that contains onions, a moderate amount of paprika and is made with bream, pike-perch or shad. In many places cubed potatoes are added and sometimes small pieces of *pasta* (gnocchi-like bits of dough, kneaded with egg) are used to make the mixture richer. There is only one caveat—beware of the bones!

Goulash or *gulyás* is the Hungarian dish that is best known internationally, but in most cases when it is served outside the country, it is not goulash at all. A proper *gulyás* is a soup, though a soup that can be a meal

238

in itself. It will contain slices of green pepper, as well as paprika, tomatoes, onions, *csipetke* (little dumplings) and enough rich gravy to make it completely liquid. Of course, its main ingredient will be pieces of beef (or occasionally pork). Contrary to popular misconceptions, it is not hideously spicy, does not contain any sour cream and is never served with rice. It does sometimes number caraway seeds among its many ingredients.

Other Hungarian soups include a modified version of the Russian cabbage soup known as *káposztaleves.* Particularly good on winter days is *bableves,* made from broad beans and lightly flavored with paprika and with boiled ham, bacon or sausages floating in it. A delicious, non-spicy but tasty soup is *Ujházi tyúkhúsleves,* a chicken broth which is served together with the meat and vegetables cooked with it. Other very popular soups include potato soup, *lebbencsleves* (a broth containing pieces of pasta and red pepper and shreds of fried bacon) and *húsleves* (bouillon), with or without a raw egg. Delicious in the summer is *meggyleves,* made from morello cherries and sour cream and chilled to an agreeably cooling temperature.

Main Courses

What *we* think of as goulash—a paprika-flavoured stew in which meat predominates—is known in Hungary as *pörkölt* or *tokány.* This can contain almost any kind of meat or fowl, though mutton and lamb are on the whole rarely eaten in Budapest, though more frequently in the provinces. It consists of much the same ingredients as the *gulyás* we have referred to, but it is a solid dish and is usually served with sour cream and one of the many variants of dumplings; it is usually accompanied by a cucumber or lettuce salad. A regional variation of this theme is the so-called *székelygulyás,* which originated in Transylvania. It is a tasty combination of cabbage, sour cream, paprika and meat, usually pork. This, of course, is a main dish. As an alternative, you might try *kolozsvári rakottkáposzta* (layered cabbage); this is a very filling dish of sour cabbage, eggs, rice, smoked sausage and pork.

Among the other typical dishes you will find in Hungary are various stuffed vegetables. For instance, *töltött paprika,* green peppers filled with minced (ground) meat and served in a rich tomato sauce and *töltött káposzta,* cabbage leaves similarly prepared. There is also *serpenyős rostélyos,* which is made from sirloin steaks with onions, paprika and potatoes. Even the Hungarian versions of such international dishes as *Wiener Schnitzel*— in Hungarian, *bécsi szelet*—have a surprising and delightful taste of their own.

A favorite meat dish is the *fatányéros* (wooden platter), the Hungarian version of a mixed grill, surrounded by small helpings of salads, vegetables and crowned with bacon.

There is a great variety of excellent freshwater fish in the country—the giant catfish of the Danube, the *fogas* (pike-perch) of the Balaton, and its young, the *süllő,* one of Hungary's greatest delicacies, the sterlet of the Tisza and the mirror carp. One of the finest fish courses is the *rácponty* (devilled carp) with potatoes, peppers, tomatoes and onions, topped with sour cream.

Turkey is particularly good in Hungary, but chickens, geese and ducks are equally luscious and tasty. *Paprikás csirke* (paprika chicken) is usually served with sour cream poured over it and a side dish of cucumber salad.

Galuska (small dumplings boiled in water) adds an additional attraction to the rich, golden-red gravy. *Rántott csirke* is the Hungarian version of Southern fried chicken.

Finishing the Meal in Style

Few countries have such variety and enchanting perfection in boiled desserts and cakes. *Túrós csusza* is made of small strips of pasta spread with curd cheese, sour cream and scraps of pork crackling. *Barátfüle* (literally, friar's ears) are, in effect, jam pockets and use the same *pasta* as *túrós csusza.* For extra sophistication they are sprinkled with ground nuts.

Hungarian noodles are called *metélt* or *nudli.* They are sprinkled with ham pieces, nuts, or poppy seeds mixed with sugar. The Hungarian pancakes *(palacsinta)* are equally tasty—their fillings can be sweetened curd cheese with raisins, ground walnuts, chocolate, various kinds of jam or poppy seeds.

Hungarian pastry is one of the most varied and tempting in the world, and can be readily sampled in any *cukrászda* (pastry shop). Perhaps the most famous is the *rétes* (the Austrian strudel), a paper-thin flaky pastry, which is filled with fruits, ground nuts, poppy seeds—even sweetened curd cheese and peppered cabbage. The *dobostorta,* a layered fancy cake with a hard burnt sugar top, is widely imitated throughout the world.

Hungarian cheeses include *pálpusztai,* which is not unlike gorgonzola, a *bakony,* which resembles camembert; an unusual cream cheese is *körözött,* a mixture of ewe cheese, butter, paprika and caraway seeds.

What to Drink

After some difficult years, Hungarian vintages have returned to their former excellence. A few of the most famous include: *Tokaji aszú* (Tokay), a dessert wine almost like a sweet, but heart-warming, brandy; *Egri bikavér,* the famous Bull's Blood from Eger (a full-bodied Burgundy); other fine red wines are *Medoc Noir,* also from the Eger district, *Szekszárdi* and *Soproni kékfrankos,* from southern and western Hungary respectively. Among white wines are *Badacsonyi kéknyelű* (moderately dry) and *Badacsonyi szürkebarát* (sweet), both from the sunny slopes of the long-extinct volcano overlooking the northern shore of Lake Balaton. *Debrői hárslevelű* is an extremely popular white wine from the famous wine district of Gyöngyös. From the extreme south of Hungary come *Villányi hárslevelü* (white) and *burgundi* (red).

There are also large vineyards in the Great Plain, around the area of Kecskemét. Hungarian *barack,* the apricot brandy, is smooth and has a deceptively mild effect, with a fiery aftermath you will remember and wish to experience again. There are other Hungarian liqueurs made from plums, pears, cherries and even green walnuts.

For those who prefer not to drink wine with their meals there is an excellent choice of natural mineral waters. Then there are several popular native brands of beer, the best known probably being *Kőbányai világos.* Foreign beers, such as Pilsen, and other Czech, as well as Austrian and East and West German, beers are also freely available, while the well-known Danish *Tuborg* lager is produced in Hungary under license. Various brands of canned beer are also on sale. Both Coca Cola and Pepsi Cola are to be found everywhere. The coffee at breakfast, which was at one time

more leisurely look at this delightful part of Hungary. The east bank has only one town, Vác, and that of only moderate interest, though it also has many pleasant holiday resorts; but it cannot be compared in its appeal to the tourist with the west bank. There are numerous ferries across the Danube, though no bridges, so that it would be possible to combine a visit to both sides of the Danube if the visitor so wished—and had ample time.

Work has started on the building of a hydro-electric dam near Nagymaros, not far from Visegrád. The project was proposed by Czechoslovakia and has been reluctantly agreed to by Hungary, which feels that the water supply to both countries will be adversely affected and that an area of great natural beauty will be ruined.

The West Bank

Whether one leaves Budapest by rail (electric suburban train from Batthyány Tér) or road for Szentendre, the nearest and most picturesque town of the Danube Bend, one sees on the right Aquincum, a Roman settlement dating from the 1st century A.D. and the capital of the Roman province of Pannonia. Little remains of the military settlement, but the civilian city has been well excavated and reconstructed and provides a good example of an important Roman town. The most notable buildings are the basilica, the forum and the public baths.

The Aquincum Museum contains relics of a Roman camp, inscribed stones, mosaics, glass and jewelry. The Hercules Villa, in Meggyfa Utca, just before Aquincum, contains beautiful mosaic floors.

Just beyond Aquincum is the Római fürdő (Roman Bath), one of Budapest's two main campsites.

Szentendre, about 19 km. (12 miles) from Budapest on a good, though very busy, road, is one of the most charming small towns in Hungary, with a population of about 17,000. It was settled by refugees from Serbia and Greece fleeing from the advancing Turks. They built their own Baroque churches, many of them beautifully decorated. The Greek-Orthodox church in the main square, and the Serbian-Orthodox Cathedral on a hill just to the north, are well worth visiting. The little cobble-stoned streets, with their picturesque Baroque houses have an old-world charm. There are several museums, including one displaying the outstanding ceramic work of the late Margit Kovács; this should on no account be missed by pottery enthusiasts. Among other museums perhaps the most interesting is the Szabadtéri Néprajzi Múzeum (Open-Air Ethnographical Museum), about 5 km. (3 miles) to the northwest (direct bus from the suburban railway station); this contains a collection showing Hungarian peasant life and folk architecture; it is being constantly expanded. The town has several good restaurants, some of which serve Greek and Serbian dishes.

We continue along the west bank of the Danube, past Leányfalu,a pleasant holiday resort, with a tourist hotel and a campsite, to Visegrád (43 km./27 miles from Budapest), once the seat of the kings of Hungary. The town now has less than 3,000 inhabitants, but in the 14th century it was both large and important. It was then that the Angevin kings built a citadel here, which became the royal residence.

Later, King Matthias Corvinus (1458–1490) had a palace built on the banks of the Danube. Its entrance is in the main street (Fő Utca). It was razed to the ground by the Turks and it is only since 1934 or so that the ruins have been excavated and much of what must have been a magnificent palace has been restored. Specially worthy of a visit is the red marble well, built by a 15th-century Italian architect, and decorated with the arms of King Matthias. This is situated in a ceremonial courtyard, which has been restored in accordance with authentic contemporary records. Above the courtyard rise the various halls; that on the left has a few fine original carvings, which give an idea of how rich and beautiful the 15th-century palace must have been. Do not fail to walk or drive up to the remains of the citadel (good restaurant and hotel at the top), which provides a superb view.

Esztergom

Esztergom can be reached either by continuing along the Danube bank from Visegrád (64 km./40 miles from Budapest) or directly from the capital by a good road (bus service). In the summer a so-called "nostalgic" train, drawn by a historic steam locomotive and with a buffet car, leaves Budapest West station each Saturday and Sunday morning, returning in the late afternoon, and allowing six hours for sightseeing in Esztergom. The city, which stands on the site of a Roman fortress, is the seat of the Cardinal-Primate of Hungary and its striking cathedral (built 1822–1869) is the largest church in the country. It lies on a hill overlooking the town. Its most interesting features are the Bakócz chapel (1506–1511), named after a Primate of Hungary who only narrowly missed becoming Pope—it was part of the earlier medieval church and was incorporated in the new edifice—and the sacristy, which contains a valuable collection of medieval ecclesiastical art. According to tradition, Géza, the father of Hungary's first king, St. Stephen, was born in Esztergom and it was here that Stephen was crowned, in 1000. Below the Cathedral Hill lies the so-called Vízi-város (Water Town), with many fine Baroque buildings, and here, in the Primate's palace, is the splendid Keresztény Múzeum (Museum of Christian Art), which is the finest art gallery in Hungary after that in Budapest and is particularly rich in early Hungarian and Italian paintings and contains, among much else of value, paintings from Duccio's workshop and by Memling and Cranach. A special treasure of the museum is the so-called "Coffin of Our Lord" from Garamszentbenedek, now in Czechoslovakia; the wooden statues of the Apostles and of the Roman soldiers guarding the coffin are masterpieces of Hungarian 15th-century sculpture. There are also fine French tapestries and a French Renaissance codex among the treasures. The same building houses the Primate's Archives, whose oldest document dates from 1187; it contains 40,000 volumes, including several medieval codices and incunabula. To visit the Archives, permission must be obtained in advance. When, in the 17th century, Buda became the political capital of Hungary, Esztergom remained—and still is—the country's ecclesiastical capital.

At Esztergom, the Danube is now the frontier; across the river is Czechoslovakia. The bridge is no longer in existence, though parts of it can still be seen; there is a ferry but it may only be used by the local inhabitants.

The East Bank

The only town of importance on the east bank, Vác, is 35 km. (22 miles) from Budapest and can be reached either by road or rail. Its two chief monuments are its Cathedral, built in 1763–77 by Archbishop Migazzi to the designs of the Italian architect Canevale, and a triumphal arch, by the same architect, erected to celebrate the visit to the town of the Empress Maria Theresa.

Along the Danube north of Vác lie a whole string of pleasant summer resorts, nestling below the picturesque Börzsöny Hills and stretching as far as Szob, just before the Czechoslovak frontier.

PRACTICAL INFORMATION FOR
HUNGARY'S HEARTLAND

TOURIST INFORMATION. The following are the addresses of the local tourist offices. **Szentendre:** near the landing stage; **Visegrád:** Fő Utca (Main Street); **Esztergom:** IBUSZ office, Széchenyi Tér; **Vác:** IBUSZ, Széchenyi Utca.

WHEN TO COME. "Szentendre Days" in July include a symposium on art, concerts of Baroque and modern music, cookery competition, beauty and dancing contests, campfire programs on the Danube embankment. A revival of the traditional market-day theatrical performances takes place in the Main Square (Marx Tér). Throughout July, some newly-discovered classic of Hungarian drama and folk poetry is performed against the background of the old medieval and Baroque houses: *commedia dell'arte* productions with close contact between audience and players. The "Szentendre Spring Days," held at the end of March, provide a program of music and folklore.

GETTING AROUND. If you have enough time, you should certainly travel by boat from Budapest, a leisurely and pleasant journey, especially in summer and spring. The steamers for Esztergom start from the main Pest landing stage near Vigadó Tér. On summer Sundays and public holidays a hydrofoil service brings Visegrád within an hour, and Esztergom within under two hours of Budapest. Timetables available at your hotel. Trains run frequently to Szentendre from Batthyány Tér, in Buda. By car via Szentendre-Visegrád, follow no. 11 highway, which more or less hugs the Buda bank of the Danube. A day-long coach tour is run by IBUSZ in the season on Tuesdays, Fridays and Saturdays, visiting Szentendre, Visegrád and Esztergom; including lunch and wine tasting, it costs around $22. Strongly recommended. For special steam train at weekends in the season, see page 255.

To reach Vác, go by steamer from Budapest, Vigadó Square, by bus or train from the West Station, or by road via highway no. 2.

HOTELS AND RESTAURANTS

Esztergom. *Esztergom* (M), (tel. 81–68); on the island in the Danube. *Fürdő* (M), (tel. 292); attached to the local spa and swimming pools. *Volán* (I), (tel. 271), in the town center, near the park. *Vadvirág,* guest house. Campsite; paying-guest accommodations.
Restaurants. *Kispipa,* Kossuth Utca. Halászcsárda (fisherman's inn), on the island. *Csülök,* in the town center.

Szentendre. *Danubius* (M), (tel. 12–511); *Party* (I), (tel. 12–491); *Sziget* (I), (tel. 10–697), all attractive hotels on the Danube bank north of the town. Guest houses; tourist-hostel; campsites; paying-guest accommodations.
Restaurants. *Arany Sárkány,* near town center, warmly recommended. *Béke,* in main square, *Görög Kancsó,* on Danube bank, and many others.

Vác. No recommended hotel; guesthouse and paying-guest accommodations.

Restaurants. *Halászkert* (fish restaurant) on Danube bank; *Fehér Galamb,* Lenin Út; snack bar in Széchenyi Utca.

Visegrád. *Silvanus* (M), (tel. 136–063) on top of Mount Visegrád, with a spectacular view; highly recommended, especially for motorists. *Vár,* (tel. 28–264) in the main street, offers simple accommodations. Also bungalows, campsites and paying-guest accommodations.

Restaurants. *Vár Étterem,* in main street; *Diófa, Sirály,* both near Danube.

LAKE BALATON

The Nation's Playground

Lake Balaton is the largest lake in Central Europe. It stretches some 80 km. (50 miles) across Western Hungary, within easy reach of Budapest. The 193 km. (120 miles) of its shoreline are almost completely occupied by a continuous chain of summer resorts. The southern shore is generally flat, with long sandy beaches and only an occasional steep hill rising from the lake, as at Fonyód; the northern shore is marked by a chain of long-extinct, eroded volcanoes, of which the Badacsony is the largest and the most remarkable. The peninsula of Tihany sweeps deep into the lake and brings the two shores quite close. The water of the southern shore is very shallow and warms up to a remarkable degree; you can walk for almost a mile before it deepens, and thus it is ideal for children. On the northern shore it shelves more abruptly and the swimming is better, though the water is also pleasantly warm even in autumn and spring.

In recent years much has been done to develop the lake into a mass recreation area. Most of the private villas and hotels have been nationalized and turned into trade union and factory holiday homes. (Hungarian writers, for instance, have an attractive literary retreat at Szigliget.) At the same time, new hotels have been built and more are being planned, with tourist hostels, students' homes and large camping sites in many places. Many privately owned villas have been built, often to be let to visitors during the season. During the three summer months, the whole lakeshore is extremely crowded. The wise visitor will choose either the late spring or the often incredibly beautiful fall for his stay, when prices are somewhat lower and he will find much more elbow room.

273

The Balaton has much to offer in water sports. Swimming, sailing, and windsurfing are all catered for—you can hire boats and boards. Motorboats are forbidden, however. There are numerous cottages for anglers (though note that April 25 to May 25 is closed season for fishing). During the winter, skating, ice-sailing and ice-fishing are especially popular. There is a special sled used on the Balaton ice known as the *fakutya* (wooden dog). Among the non-aquatic sports, various ball games are the best catered for. International fencing championships are held every year near the lake.

The Balaton is extremely well provided with both road and rail communications. In the summer, frequent fast trains run from Budapest and there are through trains from most parts of Hungary. On summer Saturdays there is a through express from Vienna to Siófok and back. Long-distance bus services connect it with every part of the country. The new M7 motorway runs from Budapest to Zamárdi, west of Siófok; it bypasses some major resorts, but is connected to them by link-roads. The lake is crisscrossed by frequent ferry-boats, which provide the most leisurely and pleasant way of exploring its shores.

The Southern Shore

Along the whole of this shore, from Balatonaliga in the east to Balatonberény in the west, there is a practically unbroken chain of summer resorts. Here are the "mass," popular, crowded beaches which attract most local and foreign visitors. But there are smaller, quieter, places, too, with an unpretentious informality of their own. It is on this shore that the family hotels and the children's holiday homes have largely been developed.

The nearest resorts to Budapest are Balatonaliga and Balatonvilágos, on the easternmost corner of the lake. Like all the places on the southern shore, they are served by the Budapest-Nagykanizsa railway, while the M7 motorway approaches the lake at Balatonvilágos, which is connected to it by a link-road. There are no hotels at either place, but ample paying-guest accommodations are available, as well as a campsite; there are plenty of snack bars and cafes.

Siófok

Siófok is the largest and by far the most popular community on the southern shore. It has a well-developed tourist organization and a long row of comfortable and pleasant modern hotels, all overlooking the lake. Its history stretches back a long time; the Romans had already settled here and had built locks to regulate the level of the lake at the mouth of the river Sió. Nonetheless, there is little to see in the town itself. The József Beszédes Múzeum in Sió Utca contains displays of the history of Balaton shipping and there is a library and a large open-air theater, which seats 1,800. But the main attraction is the long, sandy beach, where most of the "action" is, and the pleasant, shady gardens with their open-air restaurants.

There is one excursion of interest to be made from Siófok; along highway 65 we can reach Ságvár (nine km./six miles), which has Roman remains, those of the fortified camp of Tricciani (284–305 A.D.). In the clay soil of the surrounding hills, traces of primitive man's occupation 17,000 years old have been found.

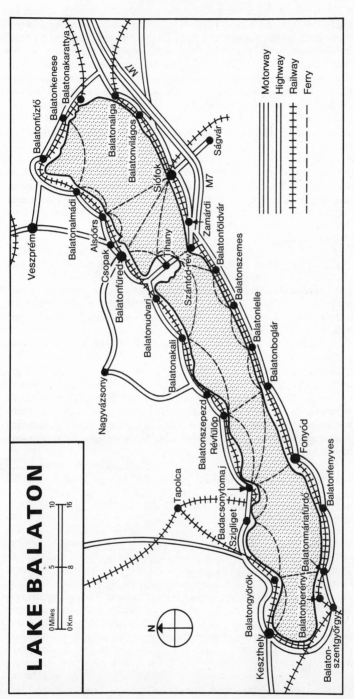

Zamárdi, a few kilometers further on, is a quiet resort. It is here that the M7 motorway reaches the lakeside, having passed just south of Siófok. The village has restaurants and cafes. To the west of it, towards the neighboring resort of Szántód-Rév, there is a campsite for motorists with its own 731-meter (800-yard) long beach, snack bar, general store and a pleasant garden-restaurant within walking distance. There are also rowing boats for hire. Zamárdi village has a few fine old peasant houses and there are ancient wine-cellars among the nearby vineyards. The baroque church dates from 1771–74. A walk of less than three hours takes us to Balatonendréd, a small village with some striking Roman remains; the community is known for its exquisite lace-making.

Szántód-Rév is at the narrowest point of Lake Balaton; the ferries to Tihany, on the northern shore, start here, taking only eight minutes. At the ferry-landing stands the old Rév (Ferry) Inn, recently and lovingly restored, with a wine room and a nearby snack bar. Close by is Szántódpuszta, with its restaurant, horseriding and trips on oxdrawn carts.

Balatonföldvár

Balatonföldvár is one of the oldest-established resorts on the southern shore of the lake. Designed and laid out around the end of the 19th century, it has a large park, promenades, many picturesque villas and excellent bathing beaches. The Fenyves (Pine) Park has an open-air theater. Three km. (two miles) or so to the south (there is a bus service) lies the village of Kőröshegy, which has a 15th-century single-naved Gothic church, restored in the 20th century but retaining many of its original features. Recitals of music by Bach, Liszt and Kodály are given in the church in the summer.

Balatonszárszó is another of the quiet, peaceful resorts, with a few charming little inns, restaurants and cafes. There is a good beach. It was here that Attila József, one of Hungary's greatest modern poets, killed himself in 1937 by throwing himself in front of a train. There is a memorial museum in the street called after him and the park contains a bronze statue of him.

Balatonszemes is another old-established lakeside resort, situated partly on the shore and partly inland. The former Hunyady mansion (built in the second half of the 18th century), the Gothic church (15th century) and the so-called Bagolyvár (Owl's Castle), which stands on the site of an old Turkish fort, are all worth visiting.

Balatonlelle is one of the busiest resorts on the southern shore. There are well-appointed beaches and much traffic at the ferry-boat pier. In the village there are one or two fine old houses. The annual meeting of Hungarian folk artists takes place here.

Balatonboglár, now administratively united with Balatonlelle under the name of Boglárlelle, was mentioned as a community as early as the 13th century. There are good beaches and much ferry traffic, with a direct line to Révfülöp on the northern shore. There is a wine research station in the village, which has a number of picturesque old houses.

Fonyód

Fonyód is the furthest from Budapest of the major resorts on the southern bank of the lake. It consists of several different settlements, stretching seven km. (over four miles). It is growing rapidly and is being developed as the most important bathing resort on the southern shore after Siófok. It is an ancient settlement; historical discoveries include late Stone Age and Bronze Age implements and there are Roman ruins. Fonyód began to be developed around 1890; since the 1930s it has been one of the most popular places on the lake's southern side; its steep wooded hills and its altogether charming situation, combined with its excellent beaches, are ensuring an ever-greater influx of visitors. An interesting excursion can be made to Buzsák, some 16 km. (about ten miles) to the south, a village famous for its colorful folk art and for its fine carvings, mostly done by shepherds.

Balatonmáriafürdő is another small, quiet resort, set among vineyards; its excellent beach stretches along ten km. (six miles) of the lake shore. There are good accommodations, as well as a restaurant and nightclub.

At Balatonberény, the last resort on the southern shore, the lake narrows and there is a fine view of the Keszthely Hills, on the opposite side. The village was settled under the Árpád dynasty and Bronze Age and Roman relics have been found here. The Roman Catholic church dates from the 15th century; its original Gothic design was remodeled into Baroque in the 18th. There is a nudist campsite here.

The Northern Shore

This is different in many ways from the southern shore of the lake. The geographical structure is less uniform and the outlying spurs of the Bakony Hills and the extinct volcanoes of the Tapolca Basin make it a romantic, often dramatic, landscape. The almost flat southern shore provides little beyond one continuous sandy beach and caters for large crowds; the northern shore, on the other hand, is more "select," more fashionable; it, too, has several fine beaches, but it has also many other attractions and many interesting objectives for excursions into the hinterland, with its ruined castles, charming valleys, forests and springs.

The water of the Balaton is just as soft and enticing as on the opposite shore, but the beaches shelve much more sharply and are, on the whole, less suitable for children, demanding swimming rather than playful splashing about. Here and there the bottom is sandy, but in places it is pebbly and stony.

Balatonakarattya and Balatonkenese are the first resorts on the northern shore to be reached by a traveler from Budapest. They lie on gentle hill slopes covered with vineyards and have campsites, bungalows, restaurants and cafes, as well as several good beaches.

Balatonfűzfő, on the northernmost corner of the lake, is surrounded on the landward side by hills and woods. Though it has a beach, it is now above all an industrial community, with paper mills and a chemical factory. However, the village has an Olympic-sized covered swimming pool, the only one of its kind in the Balaton area; it is the venue of international events.

Balatonalmádi has developed into a town of some size, with many good shops, restaurants and places of entertainment; the excellent beach is one of the best on the northern shore of the lake. Buses ply to neighboring resorts and to the picturesque town of Veszprém (see chapter on Western Hungary), and there is a boat pier.

The next resort is Alsóörs, a quiet, beautifully-situated village. It has a campsite, bungalows and an inn. At Felsőörs, a few miles to the north, is the finest Romanesque church of the Balaton uplands, as well as an 18th-century priory.

Csopak is situated on the hillside, the resort stretching down to the lake. It lies in fine wine-growing country; the beach is well supplied with all the usual holiday amenities. Paying-guest accommodations are available and there are two pleasant inns. The former Ranolder castle, dating from the middle of the 19th century, now houses the Institute for Plant Protection.

Balatonfüred

Balatonfüred is the oldest, most distinguished and most internationally famous health resort of this shore of the lake. It has every amenity of a lakeside holiday resort and is, in addition, a spa of the first class. Above the beaches and the promenade the twisting streets of the old town climb the hillsides, which are thickly planted with vines. The hills protect the town from cold northerly winds. This is one of the most celebrated wine-growing districts of Hungary and it frames an old-established spa for cardiac diseases. Great plane and poplar trees provide shade as you arrive by boat at the always-busy landing-stage.

The center of the town in Gyógy Tér (Spa Square), where the waters of the volcanic springs bubble and rise under a slim, colonnaded pavilion. The springs have a strong carbonic content. In the Square is the Cardiac Hospital, where hundreds of patients from all over the world are treated.

Balatonfüred has 11 medicinal springs and they have a stimulating and highly-beneficial effect on the heart and nerves. There is plenty of sunshine but also pleasant shade. It was here that Rabindranath Tagore, the great Indian poet and Nobel Prize winner, recovered from a heart attack. He planted a tree to commemorate his stay, a tree which still stands in a little park of its own. Another Nobel Prize winner, the Italian poet Salvatore Quasimodo, planted his own tree near Tagore's in 1961.

There is much to see in and around Balatonfüred and an excursion to Tihany (described later on) should on no account be missed. There is a classical Round church (Kerek templom), built in 1841–46, near the center of the town and there are many picturesque old houses as well as an attractive ensemble of neo-Classical villas around Gyógy Tér. There are several beaches.

The most interesting longer excursion, apart from that to Tihany, already mentioned, is to the small town of Nagyvázsony, about 19 km. (12 miles) to the northwest. Its castle was built in the 15th century and owned by Pál Kinizsi, one of the generals of King Matthias Corvinus and known for his great physical strength. In late July and early August a colorful equestrian pageant in medieval costumes is held in the grounds of the former Zichy Castle in the town (now a "country-house hotel").

Tihany

The small peninsula of Tihany, surrounded on three sides by the lake, is a rich open-air museum as well as a very popular holiday resort. There are geological and botanical rarities; the Celtic walls of the Óvár (Old Castle), the ruins of the Roman watchtower on Csúcshegy (Mount Peak), the traces of churches dating back to the Árpád dynasty, the squat Romanesque columns of the 900-year-old Abbey crypt—all bear witness to human faith and human hate.

From the ferry on the lakeside the road climbs between poplars to the range of hills which form the peninsula; these are barely 200 meters (650 ft.) high and are covered with acacia copses. Only a few hundred yards beyond the "Club Tihany" tourist complex, nature appears primitive and undisturbed. In the middle of the peninsula, framed in waving green reeds, is the smooth Belső (Inner) Lake. Around it are bare, yellowish-white rocks; volcanic cones rise against the sky. The whole area, so rich in rare flora and fauna, is a national park, where all building and agriculture are carefully controlled.

Between the Inner Lake and the eastern shore of the peninsula lies the village of Tihany, with, as its crowning glory, the famous Abbey. Its foundations were laid by King Andrew I some nine centuries ago. Only the crypt, in which the king is buried, and a priceless historical document have survived the ravages of time. This document, the Abbey charter, dating from 1055, contains in its Latin text many Hungarian words and phrases—one of the earliest surviving documents to do so. It is kept at Pannonhalma; see Western Hungary chapter. The present Abbey church is in a Baroque style and was built between 1719 and 1737; it is magnificently ornate, with silver-gilt altars and, on the large ceiling fresco, pink floating angels. The Abbey has a famous organ, on which recitals are given in the summer. It also houses a museum and is visited each year by over 100,000 people. In the village there are many beautiful old houses, the finest of which have been formed into an open-air museum. Tihany has a Biological Research Institute and an Institute of Geophysics, with an observatory.

There is no railway station at Tihany, but it is easily reached by a regular bus service from Balatonfüred or by one of the frequent ferry boats.

Going westwards along the northern shore of the lake, we come to Örvényes, a quiet resort with an 18th-century watermill, which holds an exhibition of folk art, and a Baroque Roman Catholic church. A few miles further on is Balatonudvari, with a breeding-station for Balaton fish. The beach is at Kiliántelep, about a mile to the west; here there is a large campsite with a self-service restaurant, a motel and a supermarket.

Révfülöp is a traditional crossing point of the southern basin of the lake; there are around eight ferry boats a day to and from Balatonboglár, on the southern shore, as well as ferries to most of the other lakeside resorts. There is a campsite here, and a small hotel, as well as paying-guest accommodations and a restaurant. One of the prettiest villages of the Balaton is Kővágóörs, a few miles inland. Another campsite is a few miles further along the shore, at Pálköve, near the rail station of Balatonrendes. This, together with the adjoining Ábrahámhegy, forms one of the quieter resorts of the northern Balaton. It has excellent local wines. There is a small motel and a pleasant restaurant.

The Badacsony

Along the volcanic, cone-shaped peaks of the Balaton Uplands, the broad-beamed, flat-topped Badacsony is one of the most striking. The masses of lava that coagulated here created bizarre and beautiful rock formations. At the upper edge there are 180- to 200-foot- (52- to 61-meter) high basalt columns in a huge semicircle. The land around has been lovingly tilled for centuries and everywhere there are vineyards and in every inn and tavern there is splendid wine. The Badacsony is now a protected area.

Badacsonytomaj is a holiday resort with several restaurants and cafes, as well as a well-known winetasting bar (the Borkóstoló). On the top of the mountain is the Kisfaludy House, named after the Hungarian poet Sándor Kisfaludy (1772–1844), who lived here. It has a fine view. The picturesque Baroque wine-press house belonging to the poet's wife, Róza Szegedi, is now a museum. There is also a wine museum, illustrating the history of local wines and of Hungarian wines generally.

Szigliget is a small village at the foot of the Várhegy (Castle Hill), which rises more than 183 meters (600 ft.) above the lake. The resort has a good beach, a campsite and a ferry landing-stage.

Keszthely

Keszthely is the second-largest town on the Balaton. It has a municipal charter dating from 1404; its Romanesque Roman Catholic parish church was built in 1386; and its famous agricultural college, the Georgikon, was established in 1797. The town offers the rare combination of a historical center of culture and a restful summer resort.

The magnificent Baroque Festetics Palace, begun around 1750, is one of the finest in Hungary. Concerts are held in the fine music room or, in the summer, in the courtyard. The palace is surrounded by a beautiful park. The Helikon Library, in the south wing of the palace, contains over 50,000 volumes, as well as precious incunabula, a collection of etchings and valuable paintings. The Georgikon, now the Agricultural University, has become the agricultural headquarters of southwestern Hungary. The Balaton Museum contains rich and varied exhibits of local history, ethnography, folk art and painting.

Keszthely has excellent hotel accommodations in all categories, good restaurants, cafes and pastry shops; it has several good beaches and opportunities for every kind of sport.

At Fenekpuszta, about eight km. (five miles) south of Keszthely, lie ruins of the Roman town of Valcum and an early Christian basilica. Some six km (four miles) to the northwest of Keszthely is the spa town of Hévíz. It has excellent hotels and a casino. Another popular spa is Zalakaros, southwest of Keszthely.

The Little Balaton (Kis-Balaton)

The largest river feeding the Balaton, the Zala, enters the lake at its southernmost point. On either side there is a swamp of several thousand acres, formerly part of the lake. This is now a vast protected area and the home of many rare birds. The area can be visited only by special permission, obtainable from the Országos Környezet és Természetvédelmi Hivatal (National Office for the Protection of Nature), Költő Utca 21–23, Budapest XII.

PRACTICAL INFORMATION FOR LAKE BALATON

WHEN TO COME. If you like crowds and the best of the summer sun, choose June, July and August. Spring or fall are less crowded and prices are lower. Winter is the time to go for skating, ice-sailing and ice-fishing.

Southern Shore

TOURIST INFORMATION. The following are the addresses of the local tourist offices. **Balatonboglár:** Dózsa György Utca 13; **Balatonföldvar:** Hősök Útja 9; **Balatonlelle:** Szent István Utca 1; **Fonyód:** next to the station; **Siófok:** adjoining station and in main street Fő Utca).

GETTING AROUND. All the resorts on the southern shore are either on, or just off, the M7 highway or its continuation Highway 7. By rail, they all lie on the main Budapest-Nagykanizsa line, most of the trains of which leave the South Station (Déli pályaudvar) in Budapest. Regular ferry connections link main resorts on the lake itself.

HOTELS AND RESTAURANTS

All hotels listed below have restaurants unless otherwise stated.

Balatonboglár. *Platán* (I), (tel. 561), simple. Campsite and paying-guest accommodations.
Restaurants. *Hullám, Kinizsi* (beer hall).

Balatonföldvár. *Neptun* (M), (tel. 40–388), in park near lake. *Fesztival* (I), (tel. 40–377), also near lake. *Juventus* (I), (tel. 40–379), intended for young people—self-catering villas, campsites, paying-guest accommodations.
Restaurants. *Balatongyöngye,* Szentgyörgyi Út. *Kukorica,* Budapesti Út. Self-service restaurants; wine bars.

Balatonlelle. For hotel, see Balatonboglár, above. Campsite, paying-guest accommodations. Several small restaurants, some self-service.

Balatonszárszó. Guest-house; tourist-hostel; bungalows; campsite near the rail station; paying-guest accommodations.
Restaurants. *Tóparti,* on beach; *Vén Diófa,* Kossuth Utca.

Fonyód. *Sirály* (I), in Bartók Béla Utca, above the town (tel. 60–125). Guest houses, tourist hostels; campsites; paying-guest accommodations.
Restaurants. *Présház* (wine bar), *Vadásztanya.* Several self-service restaurants.

Siófok. *Balaton* (M), (tel. 10–655); *Európa* (M), (tel. 13–411); *Hungária* (M), (tel. 10–677); *Lidó* (M), (tel. 10–633), four large and comfortable hotels on the lake shore. *Napfény* (I), (tel. 11–408), also overlooking the lake; private baths. *Vénusz* (I), (tel. 10–660), in the town.
There is a motel by the lakeside; guest house; tourist-hostel; campsites; paying-guest accommodations.
Restaurants. A large choice; we recommend *Fogas,* in the main street, with garden; *Csárdás,* also in the main street, with gypsy music in the evenings; and *Matróz,* near the pier. Among the numerous night haunts the *Pipacs,* the *Eden,* the *Maxim* and the *Delta* all offer local wines and a live show.

Northern Shore

TOURIST INFORMATION. The following are the addresses of the local tourist offices. **Badacsony:** near the landing stage; **Balatonalmádi:** Lenin Utca and at rail station in summer; **Balatonfüred:** at rail station and in town center; **Hévíz;** Rákóczi Utca; **Keszthely:** Fő Tér. **Tihany:** near the landing stage.

GETTING AROUND. Highway 71 runs the whole length of the northern shore; it branches off the M7 motorway from Budapest some miles to the east of the lake. By rail, there is a good direct service to all the resorts on the north of the lake from Budapest South. Tihany and Hévíz have no railway stations; for Tihany one must get out at Balatonfüred and for Hévíz at Keszthely; in both cases there are frequent connecting buses. Regular ferry connections link main resorts on the lake itself.

HOTELS AND RESTAURANTS

All hotels listed below have restaurants unless otherwise stated.

Badacsony. *Egri József* tourist-hostel; guest houses, campsite, paying-guest accommodations.
Restaurants. *Bormúzeum* (wine-tasting), *Halászkert* (garden restaurant specializing in fish), *Kisfaludi Ház.*

Balatonalmadi. *Auróra* (M), (tel. 38–811). *Tulipán* (I), (tel. 38–317). *Kék Balaton* tourist-hostel; motel; campsite; paying-guest accommodations.
Restaurants. *Aranyhíd, Kakascsárda, Muskátli;* self-service restaurant on the beach.

Balatonfüred. *Annabella* (tel. 42–222) and *Marina* (tel. 43–644), both (M), are two fine modern hotels on the lakeside. The *Margaréta* apartment-house (tel. 43–824), also (M), is for self-catering; its guests use the beach and other facilities of the *Marina,* which it adjoins.
Arany Csillag (I), (tel. 43–466), old-fashioned hotel in town center with no private baths. Guest houses; bungalows; splendid campsite; paying-guest accommodations.
Restaurants. *Balaton,* in the park; *Baricska, Hordó,* both near the lake. The *Kedves* pastry shop, in Blaha Lujza Utca, serves excellent tea, coffee and cakes in elegant surroundings.

Hévíz. *Aqua* (E), (tel. 11–090). Large luxurious spa hotel. *Thermál* (E), (tel. 11–190), with casino for hard currency. *Napsugár* (M), (tel. 13–208). Guest houses, paying-guest accommodations.
Restaurants. *Kulacs, Piroska, Tokaj-Hegyalja* and many others.

Keszthely. *Helikon* (M–E), (tel. 11–330), large and comfortable new hotel on the lakeside. *Phoenix* (I), (tel. 12–630), next to the Helikon, whose amenities its guests can use. *Amazon,* (tel. 12–448), simple tourist hostel in town center. Several campsites; paying-guest accommodations.
Restaurants. *Béke,* in the main street, simple but good. *Halászcsárda* (fish), on the lakeside; and many others. The *Helikon Tavern,* 8 km. (five miles) east on Highway 71, occupies a neo-Classical building built in the early 19th century by Prince Festetics; open evenings only, all the year round, with a good choice of wines and a gypsy band.

Nagyvázsony. *Kastély* (I), (tel. 31–029), a simple "country-house hotel" in the former Zichy castle; some private baths, pleasant restaurant; riding facilities. Motel; riding-school; tourist-hostel; paying-guest accommodations; several small restaurants.

Tihany. *"Club Tihany complex,"* near the landing-stage, comprising the *Tihany Hotel* (E), (tel. 48–088) and the *"Tihany Holiday Village"* (E), same telephone number, with luxury bungalows; restaurants, tennis courts, squash and minigolf. Paying-guest accommodations.
Restaurants. *Fogas, Sport,* and others. There is a good pastry shop, the *Rege,* near the Abbey.

Zalakaros. *Thermál* (I), (tel. 18–202); bungalows, campsite, paying-guest accommodations.

NORTHERN HUNGARY

Small Mountains, Great Beauty

Northern Hungary is the region which stretches from the Danube north of Budapest to the northeastern borders of the country, to Czechoslovakia and the Soviet Union. It is a clearly defined area, marked by several mountain ranges of no great height but considerable scenic beauty; these form the southernmost outcrops of the Carpathians. Most of them are limestone hills with some volcanic rocks. Few of the peaks reach 914 meters (3,000 ft.) and most of them are thickly wooded almost to their summits. Oak, beech, and hornbeam are the main forest trees, with comparatively few patches of pine and fir. Naturalists, botanists, geologists, ethnographers and folklorists find much of interest in the hills. In the state game reserves herds of deer and wild boar roam freely; the eagle and the rare red-footed falcon still survive.

Within this region most of Hungary's mineral wealth is concentrated—iron, some copper, and rich (though inferior) coal deposits.

The Northern Hills

Historically, the valleys of Northern Hungary have always been of considerable strategic importance, as they provided the only access to the north. Eger, renowned in Magyar feats of arms as one of the guardians of these strategic routes, is in this region, while many ruined castles sit picturesquely on the hilltops. The Mátra mountains, easily reached from Budapest, have been developed into an important winter sports area. Last but not least, this is one of the great wine-growing districts of Hungary,

284

with Gyöngyös and Eger contributing the "Magyar nectar" and (most famous of all) Tokaj producing the "king of wines."

We have already mentioned the Börzsöny Hills in our "Danube Bend" section; they contain many of the most delightful country resorts near Budapest, most of which can be easily reached by the Budapest-Vác-Szob railway line or by bus. Dotted throughout the region are the ruins of many old castles. Nógrád Castle was originally built under the Árpád dynasty; its ancient tower is still a landmark. In the Nógrád valley, which runs between the Nógrád and Mátra Hills are the Palóc villages, representing one of the most interesting and individual ethnic groups of Hungary. In their villages, Hungarian national costumes have been preserved and are still occasionally worn; Hollókő, recently included in UNESCO's World Heritage conservation scheme, is the most picturesque of these.

The Mátra, a volcanic mountain group, rises with dramatic suddenness above the Palóc world. The capital is Gyöngyös, famous for the excellent wine produced round about—do not miss *Debrői hárslevelű,* a magnificent white wine—and, more recently, for its new industrial importance. Early in the 1960s huge lignite deposits were discovered and the large-scale mines and power-stations established since then have changed the character of the whole region. Among the chief sights of the town are the 14th-century church of Szent Bertalan (St. Bartholomew) and the Mátra Museum, which exhibits folk art of the region. To the north of Gyöngyös lie many beautiful resorts, popular in summer for their invigorating mountain air and in winter for their skiing and other seasonable sports. The most famous is Mátrafüred (400 meters/1,312 ft.). Bus services connect the resorts with Gyöngyös and Budapest. The highest peak is Kékestető (1,015 meters/3,330 ft.), the highest point in Hungary, with a sanatorium.

About 11 km. (eight miles) west of Gyöngyös is the charming village of Gyöngyöspata, with a beautifully restored 12th–13th-century church, with frescoes and a unique altar-piece showing the Tree of Jesse. About 24 km. (15 miles) still further west, along minor roads, lies Szirák, with one of the most attractive of Hungary's "country-house hotels." It dates from the late 17th-century and is situated in a fine park.

Highway 3 (a motorway—M3—as far as the town of Gyöngyös) is the main road link between Budapest and Northern Hungary.

Eger

The famous and picturesque city of Eger lies on the line where plain and mountain meet, between the Mátra mountains and their eastern neighbor, the Bükk. It bears within its limits much of the history, the heartbreak and the glory of Hungary's past and should on no account be missed. Eger was settled very early in the Hungarian conquest of the country and one of the five bishoprics founded by King Stephen was here. Eger castle was built after the devastating Tartar invasion and the cathedral, originally Romanesque, was rebuilt in Gothic style in the 15th century, though few vestiges of this structure now remain.

In 1551 the city was attacked by the Turks, but the commander, István Dobó, held out against vastly superior forces. It fell in 1596 and was until 1687 one of the most important northern outposts of Muslim power. The main aspects of present-day Eger were developed in the 18th century and it is now a splendid example of a Baroque city. The imposing Cathedral was completely rebuilt, in Classical style, early in the 19th century; it is the second-largest church in Hungary. Opposite the Cathedral is the former Lyceum, an impressive Baroque building which is now a teachers' training college and includes an observatory.

The most picturesque street of Eger is Kossuth Lajos Utca, which consists almost entirely of Baroque and Rococo buildings. No. 4 is the Minor Canons' residence and one of the most beautiful Rococo palaces in Hungary. Further on, the County Council Hall dates from 1749–56; it has exquisite wrought-iron gates. To the north, in Dobó István Square, stands the fine Baroque Minorite Church. Continuing northwards we reach one of Eger's landmarks, the Turkish minaret. The Castle is best reached along Kossuth Lajos Street, turning to the left at the end; the original casemates survive and much excavation is being carried out. The Castle Museum is worth a visit. Eger is also a spa, with valuable therapeutic waters and bathing facilities of all kinds; the water is recommended for rheumatic ailments.

Eger wine is famous and perhaps the best known is *Bikavér* (Bull's Blood), a full-blooded red wine; *Leányka,* a delightful white wine, and the Eger version of *Medoc Noir,* a heavy, sweet dessert wine, are also outstanding.

A particularly pleasant excursion from Eger is to Szilvásvárad, a charming small resort deep in the wooded Bükk Mountains, some 28 km. (17 miles) north of Eger and easily reached by train or bus. Its streams are full of trout and there are many small waterfalls. Here is the famous Lippizaner stud; there are also facilities for horse riding.

Mezőkövesd, about 16 km. (10 miles) to the southeast, is famous for its folk art, examples of which are on display in the village museum; many of them are for sale.

Miskolc

East of the picturesque Bükk Mountains lies Miskolc, the second-largest town in Hungary and one of its chief industrial centers. A vast conurbation with a population of some 200,000, it is surrounded by beautiful country. It contains some interesting buildings, many of them Baroque, and, in a western suburb, the medieval castle of Diósgyőr. South of the city is the spa-suburb of Miskolc-Tapolca, with the town's best hotels.

Beyond Miskolc lie two objectives of the greatest interest to the visitor; the vast cave system of Aggtelek and the vineyards of Tokaj.

Aggtelek

One of the most extensive cave systems in Europe lies at the extreme northern end of Hungary, right on the Czechoslovak border. The caves are spectacular in the extreme and have been ranked with such natural monuments as the Grand Canyon or the Niagara Falls. The largest of the caves, the Baradla, is 24 km. (over 15 miles) long, with stalactite and stalagmite formations of great beauty and extraordinary size, some more than 45 meters (80 ft.) high. A full tour of the caves takes five hours, but there are shorter tours taking one to two hours, which will give the visitor a very good overall impression of the majesty of this underground marvel of nature. In one of the chambers of the cave a concert-hall has been created; it can hold 1,000 people and concerts are given here. Further caves are being discovered and opened to the public. There are two entrances, at Aggtelek and Jósvafő.

Sárospatak, some 70 km. (45 miles) to the northeast of Miskolc, is the cultural center of this part of Hungary. It is a picturesque old town, with many fine old houses. Its ancient castle was begun in the 11th century and contains a museum of old furniture. Its Calvinist College was founded in 1531 and for many years had close links with Britain. In the 18th century King George II of England took a personal interest in the college and, for about 50 years, education was conducted in both English and Hungarian. Many famous Hungarians were educated here. It is now a state school.

Tokaj

Tokaj, the home of Hungary's most famous wine, lies about 48 km. (30 miles) east of Miskolc. The countryside round it is beautiful, especially in October, when the grapes hang from the vines in thick clusters. Tokay, the "king of wines," as it has been called, is golden yellow with slightly brownish tints and it has an almost oily texture. It has been cultivated for over 700 years. Other countries—France, Germany and Russia—have tried to produce the wine from Tokaj grapes; all failed. It would seem that the secret of the wine lies in a combination of the volcanic soil and the climate. The little town of Tokaj is built on the slopes and contains many wine-cellars. In the Museum of Local History objects connected with the history of the production of the wine are on display.

PRACTICAL INFORMATION FOR
NORTHERN HUNGARY

TOURIST INFORMATION. The following are the addresses of the local tourist offices. **Aggtelek:** at the entrance to the Baradla cave. **Eger:** Bajcsy-Zsilinszky Utca and in the Castle; **Gyöngyös:** Szabadság Tér; **Miskolc:** Széchenyi Utca; **Sárospatak:** Kossuth Utca; **Tokaj:** Bem J. Utca 44.

WHEN TO COME. Spring and summer are the best seasons for the hill resorts. The traditional and extremely colorful wine festivals are held in the fall, when the weather can also be quite delightful.

GETTING AROUND. There are good rail connections from Budapest (East Station). Local trains and buses complete the network. Otherwise, traveling by car gives you the greatest freedom.

HOTELS AND RESTAURANTS

All hotels listed below have restaurants unless otherwise stated.

Aggtelek. *Cseppkő* (I), (tel. 7), very simple. At Jósvafő is the equally simple *Hotel Tengerszem* (tel. 49). Tourist-hostel; campsite; paying-guest accommodations.

Eger. *Eger* (M), in part recently constructed, and *Park* (M), close together and sharing the same telephone number (13–233); the Eger is perhaps short on charm, if up-to-date; the Park is elegant, but rather old-fashioned. Both have rooms with bath. *Unicornis* (I), (tel. 12–886). Several guest houses; motel; campsites; paying-guest accommodations.

Restaurants. *Fehér Szarvas,* adjoining Park Hotel; game. *Kazamata,* Martírok Tere. *Mecset,* Knézich Utca; and many others.

The town has many wine-tasting bars and shops.

Gyöngyös. *Mátra* (M), (tel. 12–057), in town center. Paying-guest accommodations. At Mátrafüred, in the hills some miles north of the town, is the *Avar* (tel. 13–195). Motel, two campsites; private accommodations.

Restaurants. *Kékes,* in main square. *Olimpia*; many wine bars. There are restaurants and snack bars in all the Mátra hill resorts.

Miskolc. *Pannonia* (M), (tel. 88–022). Refurbished, in town center. *Arany Csillag* (tel. 35–114) and *Avas* (tel. 37–798), both (I), and old fashioned.

In the spa suburb of **Miskolc-Tapolca,** *Juno* (tel. 64–133) and *Park* (tel. 60–811), both (M), and comfortable. Guest houses, campsites and paying-guest accommodations.

Restaurants. *Alabárdos* and *Bükk* in town center; *Kisvadász* at Tapolca.

Sárospatak. *Bodrog* (M), (tel. 11–744), new. *Borostyán* (M), (tel. 11–611); campsites; paying-guest accommodations.

Szilvásvárad. *Lipicai* (I), (tel. 55–100), simple but comfortable, some private baths; tourist-hostel, campsite, paying-guest accommodations.

Szirák. *Kastély* (M), (tel. 37); late-17th-century castle-hotel; refurbished and decorated to a high standard. All rooms with bath. Riding facilities available.

Tokaj. *Tokaj* (M), (tel. 58), doubles with private bath. First-class international campsite; paying-guest accommodations.

Restaurants. *Rákóczi, Tiszavirág Halászcsárda* (fish), and many snack bars and wine bars. The *Rákóczi Cellar,* which may be visited, contains 20,000 hectoliters (nearly 450,000 gallons) of wine.

THE GREAT PLAIN

Magyar to the Core

The Great Plain, which stretches from Budapest as far as the borders of Romania and Yugoslavia and covers an area of some 51,800 sq. km. (20,000 sq. miles), is what most people think of as the typical Hungarian landscape. Almost completely flat, it is the home of shepherds and their flocks and, above all, of splendid horses and the *csikós,* their riders. The plain has a wild, almost alien, air; its sprawling villages consist mostly of one-story houses, though there are many large farms and up-to-date market gardens. The Plain, which is divided into two almost equal parts by the River Tisza, also contains several of Hungary's most historic cities.

Three main road routes link Budapest with the Great Plain. The first leads east to Szolnok, Debrecen, Nyíregyháza and the Soviet frontierpoint of Záhony; the second southeast to Kecskemét and Szeged; the third, hugging the Danube, south to Kalocsa and Baja.

The most northerly part of the region is known as the Nyírség; it borders on the Soviet and Romanian frontiers and its chief town is Nyíregyháza. This will hardly detain the visitor, who, however, will find a famous medicinal spa, Sóstó, only six km. (four miles) away and easily reached by bus. From an architectural point of view the most interesting place in the district is Nyírbátor, 39 km. (24 miles) east of Nyíregyháza and easily reached by train or bus; it has a very fine 15th-century Gothic Protestant church; a musical festival is held in the church in July.

Debrecen and the Hortobágy

Forty-eight km. (30 miles) south of Nyíregyháza is Debrecen, one of the largest and historically most important towns of Hungary. It is the economic and cultural center of Eastern Hungary and a town with a character all its own—its inhabitants have called it "the Calvinist Rome" and most of its people are Protestants. Its University has always been famous as a center of learning and its predecessor, the Calvinist College, was founded more than 400 years ago. In its Great Church Hungarian independence from the Habsburgs was proclaimed by Kossuth in 1849. Here, too, in 1944, the anti-Nazi coalition government met, bringing the hope of peace to the war-ravaged country.

Debrecen has been inhabited since the Stone Age. It was already a sizable village by the end of the 12th century and by the 14th century it was a privileged and important market town. After the Reformation it became—and has remained—the stronghold of Hungarian Protestantism.

The street leading from the railway station to the Great Church contains many of Debrecen's most interesting buildings. The Old County Hall was built in 1912 in what is known as the "Hungarian style," with majolica ornaments. In the neo-Classical Town Hall, farther on, Kossuth lived in 1849. The Great Church, which faces a tree-lined square, is the largest Protestant place of worship in Hungary; it was built early in the 19th century in an impressive neo-Classical style. Near it are the original Calvinist College, already referred to, and one of Hungary's best-known hotels, the art nouveau Arany Bika (Golden Bull), whose cuisine is famous. In the northern part of the city lies the Nagyerdő (Great Forest), a large park with thermal establishments and every facility for water sports.

Just over 19 km. (12 miles) south of Debrecen lies Hajdúszoboszló, one of Hungary's oldest and most famous medicinal spas.

Stretching for many miles to the west of Debrecen is the Hortobágy, the most typical and most romantic part of the Great Plain, a grassy *puszta* or prairie covering over 100,000 hectares (250,000 acres). Though much of it has, in recent years, become agricultural land, there is still enough of its unique atmosphere left to attract the foreign visitor. The center of the Hortobágy is where highway 33 crosses the Hortobágy river on a famous nine-arched bridge dating from the beginning of the 19th century. Near it is the Nagycsárda (Great Inn), built in 1699; there are guest rooms, a restaurant and a cafe. "Equestrian Days" are arranged here every summer.

The road (highway 4) from Budapest to Debrecen passes just north of Cegléd and through Szolnok, two towns which are chiefly of importance as road and railway junctions and as the economic centers of important agricultural districts. Cegléd has a neo-Classical Protestant church of some interest. Szolnok lies on the River Tisza and is the geometrical center of the Great Plain. It has several fine old churches, among them the high-Baroque Franciscan church near the river bank. In addition it houses a well-known artists' colony and has good facilities for swimming and other water sports. It is now an important industrial center.

Kecskemét

Both highway 5 and motorway M5 (under construction) lead us southeast from Budapest to Kecskemét, one of the most characteristic of Hungarian towns, with a population of around 100,000; it is an important railway junction and the center of a large and rich agricultural district. Here is one of the most valuable fruit-growing areas in the country; it produces the delicious Hungarian apricots, from which the famous *barack,* the fiery yet smooth apricot-brandy, is made.

The heart of the sprawling town is formed by two vast squares which join each other: Szabadság (Liberty) and Kossuth Squares. In Szabadság Square is a remarkable double Synagogue, recently restored and housing some public collections. A fine, Hungarian-style art nouveau building called the Cifrapalota (Ornamental Palace) stands opposite; today it is the home of the local trade union council. In Kossuth Square is the Town Hall, built in 1893–96 by Ödön Lechner in the Hungarian art nouveau style which he created. There are several interesting churches in Kecskemét, including the Baroque "Old Church" (1772–1805), just north of the Town Hall; the oldest and most important building in Kossuth Square is the Szent Miklós Templom (Church of St. Nicholas), on the south side, originally built in a Gothic style in the 15th century but rebuilt in a Baroque style in the 18th. A little to the west of the town center, in Gáspár András Utca, stands the Magyar Naiv Festők Múzeuma (Museum of Hungarian Naïve Artists). Kecskemét has an artists' colony and was the birthplace of the composer Kodály. An excursion can be made to Kiskőrös, 48 km. (30 miles) to the southwest along road 54; here Sándor Petőfi, one of Hungary's most famous poets and a leading spirit of the 1848 revolution against the Habsburgs, was born. The tiny house—his father was the village butcher—is now a memorial museum. Kiskőrös can also be reached from Kalocsa on the east bank of the Danube.

About 32 km. (20 miles) south of Kecskemét and easily reached by road lies Bugac *puszta,* the center of a large sandy area, which has provided poets and artists with inexhaustible material. It has a famous inn (the Bugac csárda), with excellent food, drink and music, as well as an open-air museum. While much of the region has now been brought under cultivation, the landscape has kept its character. In the summer there are horse shows (the Hungarian version of rodeos) and festivities with gypsy music. There is also good pheasant-shooting in the woods.

Szeged

Szeged is the traditional economic and cultural center of the southern part of the Great Plain. Its great tourist attraction is its open-air festival (July–August each year), but it has many other features to interest the visitor. It was almost completely rebuilt after a great flood in 1879; and constructed on a concentric plan, not unlike that of Pest. There is an inner boulevard, now named after Lenin, and an outer ring, whose sections, named after Rome, Brussels, Paris, London, Moscow and Vienna, recall the international help given in the reconstruction of the city. Avenues connect these two boulevards like the spokes of a wheel.

The heart of the Inner City is the large Széchenyi Square, full of trees and surrounded by imposing buildings, among them the Town Hall and a large hotel, the Tisza, which has a fine concert hall. The most striking building in Szeged is the Votive Church, or Cathedral, a neo-Romanesque edifice built between 1912 and 1929 in fulfillment of a municipal promise made after the great flood. It is one of Hungary's largest churches and has a splendid organ with 12,000 pipes. The church forms the backdrop to the open-air festival, held in Dóm (Cathedral) Square. The Festival started in 1933 and has been held ever since, though with occasional gaps. The stage is huge—502 sq. meters (600 sq. yards)—and the square can hold an audience of 7,000. Outstanding performances are occasionally given of Hungary's great national drama, *The Tragedy of Man,* by Imre Madách. The program contains a rich variety of theatrical pieces, operas and concerts.

Dóm Square is impressive, with arcaded buildings, among them scientific institutes and a theological college. In the center of the Square stands an isolated Romanesque tower, which was formerly part of the 11th-century Dömötör Templom (Church of St. Demetrius). Other interesting sights are the Baroque Greek Orthodox Church, in the Inner City, built between 1743 and 1745, and the so-called Alsóvárosi Templom (Lower City Church), in the southwest part of the town. This was built in the 15th and 16th centuries, but much of it is now in a Baroque style.

Szeged is famous for its paprika, an important ingredient of Hungarian cuisine. It has two universities. Újszeged (New Szeged), on the opposite side of the river, is something of a holiday resort, with every facility for water sports and an open-air theater.

To the northeast of Szeged and near the Romanian border there are several places of interest. One of them, Gyula, has recently developed into a spa of some importance. It has an interesting medieval castle and plays are performed each summer in the castle courtyard.

There is much of this vast central part of the Great Plain that we have not touched on, but a visitor with time to spare—and, if possible, a slight knowledge of Hungarian—will find in many of its small towns things of interest which reflect, perhaps more accurately than anywhere else in Hungary, the genuine life and customs of Hungarian country people.

The East Bank of the Danube

Highway 51 leads due south from Budapest, never far from the east bank of the Danube. Apart from the town of Ráckeve, on the Danube island of Csepel, where there is a museum in the former palace of Prince Eugene of Savoy as well as an interesting Serbian Orthodox church, there is little to detain the traveler until he reaches Kalocsa. This is a town unusually rich in architectural beauty and in memorials of Hungarian cultural history. It was formerly on the Danube, but now, because of a change in the river's course, lies over six km. (four miles) away from it. Kalocsa is rich in charming Baroque buildings. The cathedral, the seat of a Roman Catholic archbishop, was built between 1735 and 1754. The archbishop's palace is another fine Baroque edifice; the archiepiscopal library is one of the most valuable in Hungary, with over 100,000 volumes and many rarities. Kalocsa is famous, too, for its richly colored embroideries, created by its "painting women," examples of whose exquisite work can be seen in a permanent exhibition in the town and can, of course, be bought. Kalocsa can also, though not without inconvenience, be reached by train; the walls of its rail station are covered with examples of this beautiful form of decoration. Kalocsa is, like Szeged, famous for its paprika.

Highway 51 brings us in another 43 km. (27 miles) to the pleasant town of Baja, built on an arm of the Danube. It contains several interesting Baroque churches. Béke (Peace) Square, on the river bank, is lined with fine old houses. A bridge from the square leads to Petőfi Island, where there is a pleasant beach and a large stadium. Baja boasts a considerable artists' colony.

PRACTICAL INFORMATION FOR
THE GREAT PLAIN

TOURIST INFORMATION. The following are the addresses of the local tourist offices. **Baja:** Béke Tér; **Cegléd:** Szabadság Tér; **Debrecen:** next to **Arany Bika** Hotel; **Gyula:** Kossuth Lajos Utca; **Hajdúszoboszló:** in spa quarter; **Hortobágy:** in the village; **Kalocsa:** in town center; **Kecskemét:** Kossuth Tér; **Nyíregyháza:** Dózsa György Út; **Szeged:** Klauzál Tér; **Szolnok:** Kossuth Lajos Utca.

WHEN TO COME. Spring, summer or fall are best, especially as the most interesting events and festivals are held in July and August.

GETTING AROUND. There are good rail connections from Budapest (East and West Stations); local trains and buses complete the network. Otherwise traveling by car gives you the greatest freedom.

HOTELS AND RESTAURANTS

All the hotels listed below have restaurants unless otherwise stated.

Baja. *Sugovica* (M), (tel. 12–988), on Petőfi Island; pool. *Duna* (I), Béke Tér. (tel. 11–765). Campsites.
Restaurant. *Halászcsárda* (fish), on Petőfi Island.

Bugac. Bungalows; paying-guest accommodations.

Cegléd. *Kossuth* (I), (tel. 10–990). Paying-guest accommodations.
Restaurants. *Alföld, Magyar, Zöld Hordó.*

Debrecen. *Arany Bika* (M), (tel. 16–777), a historic hostelry famous for its food. *Főnix* (I), (tel. 13–355). *Debrecen* (I), (tel. 16–550). Campsites and paying-guest accommodations; bungalows in Nagyerdő Park, to the north of town.
Restaurants. *Gambrinus, Hungária,* and *Szabadság* all in town center. *Újvigadó* and several others in Nagyerdő Park.

Gyula. *Park* (I), (tel. 62–622); *Komló* (I), (tel. 61–041), simple. *Aranykereszt Szálló* (I), (tel. 62–057). Motel, tourist-hostel, campsites and paying-guest accommodations.
Restaurant. *Budrió,* Béke Sugárút.

Hajdúszoboszló. *Délibáb* (M), (tel. 60–808). *Gambrinus* (I), (tel. 60–100). Campsites; paying-guest accommodations.
Restaurants. *Alföldi,* Hősök Tere, *Szigeti Halászcsárda* (fish), near the thermal baths.

Hortobágy. *Hortobágy Nagy Csárda* (I), (tel. 69–139); *Csárda Inn* (I), (tel. 69–139), both have double rooms with shower. Tourist-hostel; campsites; good restaurant.

Kalocsa. *Piros Arany* (I), (tel. 200). Paying-guest accommodations.
Restaurant. *Kalocsai Csárda,* István Utca.

Kecskemét. *Aranyhomok* (I), (tel. 20–011). Guest houses; campsites; paying-guest accommodations.
Restaurants. *Hirös,* Rákóczi Utca, *Strand,* Sport Utca, and many others.

Nyírbátor. Paying-guest accommodations.

Nyíregyháza. *Szabolcs* (M), (tel. 12–333). *Kemév* (I), (tel. 10–606). Paying-guest accommodations. (See also under **SÓSTÓ,** a spa six km. (four miles) to the north.)

Ráckeve. *Keve* (M), (tel. 85–147), new and comfortable. Campsites; paying-guest accommodations.

Sóstó. *Krúdy* (M), (tel. 12–424). *Svájci Lak* (I), (tel. 12–424). Tourist-hostel; holiday-village; campsite; paying-guest accommodations.

Szeged. *Hungária* (M), (tel. 21–210), modern, on river bank. *Royal* (M), (tel. 12–911). *Tisza* (M), (tel. 12–466), in town center, older, but comfortable. Several guest houses, bungalows, campsites; paying-guest accommodations.
Restaurants. *Alabárdos,* Oskola Utca. *Hági,* Kelemen Utca, recommended. *Gambrinus Beerhouse,* Deák Utca. *Halászcsárda* (fisherman's inn), on the river bank. *Szeged,* Széchenyi Tér. Many snack bars.

Szolnok. *Pelikán* (M), (tel. 13–356), new and comfortable. *Tisza* (M), (tel. 17–666), older, doubles with bath. *Touring* (M), (tel. 12–928), in the park. Two motels; campsites; paying-guest accommodations.
Restaurants. *Aranylakat,* in the park. *Múzeum,* Kossuth Tér. *Nemzeti,* Ságvári Körút.

WESTERN HUNGARY

Civilized and Mellow

Western Hungary—often known as "Transdanubia" (Dunántúl in Hungarian)—is that part of Hungary south and west of the Danube, stretching to the Czech and Austrian borders in the north and west and to Yugoslavia in the south. It is an undulating country, with several ranges of hills and outposts from the Alps. The part of the region around Lake Balaton we have already described in an earlier chapter.

Western Hungary's climate is rather more humid than that of the rest of the country; most of its surface is covered with farmland, vineyards and orchards. It presents a highly picturesque landscape with many attractions for the tourist.

The Romans called the region Pannonia; for centuries it was a frontier province and it is richer in Roman remains than the rest of Hungary. The towns are mostly old and have highly civilized traditions. Some industrial complexes have recently developed, the most important of them being at Dunaújváros, a large iron and steel town on the west bank of the Danube.

Győr and Pannonhalma

Entering Western Hungary at Hegyeshalom, on the Austrian border, the first important town one reaches is Győr. It lies exactly halfway between Vienna and Budapest and is both an ancient city and a modern industrial community. It was known to the Romans as Arrabona and here they built a fortress on what is now Káptalan (Chapter) Hill, in the heart of the Old Town. Most of the streets below the hill are built in a regular, checkboard pattern, dating from the 16th century, and many of them are extremely picturesque. The most beautiful Baroque church is the Carmelite church (1721–1725) in Köztársaság (Republic) Square, whose eastern side is lined with fine Baroque houses. The Castle district on Káptalan Hill contains Győr's oldest church, the Cathedral, whose foundations are believed to go back to the time of St. Stephen (11th century). It has been frequently rebuilt and is now largely Baroque, though with a neo-Classical facade. In the Héderváry chapel (15th century) is a masterpiece of medieval Hungarian goldsmith's art, the reliquary of King St. Ladislas (1040–1095).

Altogether the streets and squares of the Old Town present one of the most delightful Baroque townscapes of Hungary. They include the Bishop's Castle, opposite the Cathedral, the Diocesan Library and Museum, the house at 4 Alkotmány Street in which Napoleon stayed in 1809 (now a museum) and many other interesting buildings too numerous to mention.

About 21 km. (13 miles) southeast of Győr lies the great Benedictine Abbey of Pannonhalma, which dates back a thousand years. In the Middle Ages it was immensely powerful and, though, of course, it no longer exerts any political influence, it still pursues its tasks of religion and learning and has a large and important grammar school.

The present abbey was rebuilt in Baroque style on 13th-century foundations. Its cloisters are the sole surviving monument of monastic architecture of the Árpád dynasty. The abbey church is the only early Gothic church in Hungary, but there have been many later additions, including a 52-meter (165-ft.) high tower in a classical style built early in the 19th century. The library, which contains 300,000 volumes, is one of the most important in Hungary. The archives contain priceless 11th- and 12th-century documents, including the foundation deed of the abbey at Tihany, on Lake Balaton, dating from 1055 and the first Hungarian document to contain a large number of Hungarian words inserted into its Latin text. The abbey also contains a superb collection of ecclesiastical plate and vestments.

Tata and Tatabánya

Continuing eastwards from Győr or towards Budapest you reach Tata, another of Hungary's interesting old towns; it is also a spa and well-known equestrian center. On the shores of the large lake, which is in the middle of the town, stands the Castle, medieval in origin but rebuilt at the end of the last century. It contains a museum of local history. Most of the town is Baroque, designed by the architect Jakab Fellner on the instructions of Count József Esterházy between 1751 and 1787. The Hungarian Olympic training camp is at Tata, which is one of the country's leading sports centers. At Remeteségpuszta nearby there are opportunities for riding.

At Bábolna, on a minor road between Győr and Tata, is one of Hungary's chief horse-breeding centers, with a museum.

Tatabánya, a few miles further on, is a fast-growing industrial town, with important coal mines, factories and power-stations, but little to detain the tourist. From here it is 56 km. (35 miles) along the M1 motorway to Budapest.

Sopron, Fertőd and the Esterházy Palace

Sopron lies on the Austrian frontier, between Lake Fertő (in German *Neusiedlersee*) and the Sopron Hills and is one of the most picturesque towns in Hungary. It has many historical and cultural monuments and it enjoys a sub-alpine climate—cooler than the sultry lowlands in summer and sheltered by its hills from the harsh western winds in winter.

The chief sights of Sopron, mostly Medieval and Baroque, are to be found in the horseshoe-shaped inner town, which was formerly enclosed by the city walls. Széchenyi Square—not far from the main rail station—links the two ends of the boulevard that follows the horseshoe line of the city. The former Dominican church, on the south side of the square, is a fine example of Baroque (1719–1725). Petőfi Square lies to the west and two curving streets lead from this square to Lenin Boulevard, a long, busy shopping street and promenade, built on the site of a former moat. On the odd-numbered side of the boulevard are a whole row of interesting Baroque, Rococo and Classical houses. Near the Előkapu (Outer Gate), leading into the inner town, stands the Baroque St. Mary Column (1745).

Further on along the boulevard we find several outstanding buildings; the Patika-ház (no. 29) has been the home of the Arany Sas (Golden Eagle) pharmacy since 1724; no. 55 was formerly the Fehér Ló (White Horse) Inn, where Haydn often stayed and where Johann Strauss composed part of his *One Night in Venice*. The Előkapu (referred to above) is a short street, with medieval houses, leading to the spacious Fő Tér (Main Square) through a passage under the 56-meter (180-ft.) high Várostorony (City Tower). The tower—the symbol of the city—was begun not later than the 12th or 13th century, though it has clearly-marked Romanesque, Renaissance and Baroque additions.

The square contains many fine buildings, varying from Gothic, through Baroque, to the late 19th-century Town Hall. The Benedictine church was built between 1280 and 1300; its 43-meter (144-ft.) high steeple dates from the 14th century. In the interesting Gothic interior five national assemblies were held between 1553 and 1681 and three kings and queens were crowned. The Storno house, near the City Tower, is Sopron's most beautiful Baroque building; still in private ownership, it houses a fine collection of furniture, porcelain and paintings. The 1701 Baroque statue of the Trinity in the middle of the Square is the oldest such monument in Hungary. The Baroque Fabricius House, in the same square, contains some of the exhibits of the Ferenc Liszt Museum, the main building of which is situated just west of the inner town, in Május 1. (May 1st) Square.

Templom (Church) Street leads to the south. Here the former Esterházy Palace, part medieval, part Baroque, contains a Mining Museum. Most of the other houses in this street are officially-protected Gothic or Baroque monuments. Új (New) Street, to the east, in spite of its name one of Sopron's oldest streets, contains several interesting buildings, including a medieval synagogue, unique in Hungary, now a religious museum. The former Erdődy Palace, in Szent György (St. George) Street, close by, is the finest Rococo building in Sopron. Almost all of the narrow and picturesque streets of the inner town and those just outside it offer views of historic and picturesque buildings.

The most interesting excursion from Sopron is to Fertőd, 17 miles (27 km.) to the southeast, where the largest and most splendid Baroque palace in Hungary, the Esterházy Palace, stands. It is easily reached by bus from Sopron; it also lies only a short distance north of one of the main roads between Vienna and Budapest—and so is easily reached by motorists. The palace was built between 1760 and 1770 by Prince Miklós (Nicholas) Esterházy. Though badly damaged in World War II, it has been painstakingly and beautifully restored. It attracts over 200,000 visitors annually, partly because of the celebrated concerts held here each year and also because of the Haydn Memorial Museum. Haydn was the court conductor of the great Esterházy family from 1761 till 1790. The palace contains 126 rooms; it is horseshoe-shaped and is surrounded by splendid gardens. In the magnificent white and gold ballroom Haydn conducted the first performance of his "Farewell Symphony." The house in which Haydn lived and a contemporary Baroque inn are also fine buildings. One wing of the palace is now a simple "country-house hotel."

Another worthwhile trip is to Nagycenk, 13 km. (eight miles) southeast of Sopron. Here is the former home of the Széchenyi family, where the great Hungarian statesman, Count István Széchenyi, lived for many years and is buried. The beautiful Baroque mansion is now the Széchenyi Memorial Museum. There is also a toy railway, with a steam engine and signal equipment that are 100 years old.

Szombathely and Kőszeg

Another interesting town, also not far from the Austrian border, is Szombathely. It was the Roman Savaria and has for centuries been an important economic center. It has several sights which will appeal to the tourist. Two important squares lie in the town center—Köztársaság (Republic) Square and Berzsenyi Square. Köztársaság Square, formerly the marketplace, is still the business center of the city. In Berzsenyi Square are the Baroque cathedral and Bishops' Palace, which, with adjoining buildings, form a harmonious whole. To the south lie the remains of the Temple of Isis, which are believed to date from the 2nd century A.D. Here devotees of a cult which originated in Egypt used to worship. The Savaria Festival takes place in the grounds each summer.

Several interesting excursions can easily be made from Szombathely. Kőszeg, 16 km. (ten miles) to the north, is reached by frequent trains in about half an hour. It is one of Hungary's most fascinating small towns. It lies higher than any other town in the country (270 meters/855 ft. above sea-level), among the eastern outcrops of the Alps, and is very rich in medieval monuments; indeed, its appearance can have changed little since the Middle Ages. It is, too, important historically; the stand of a few hundred Hungarian troops here in 1532 forced the Turkish army of almost 200,000 to abandon their attempt to capture Vienna. A gate in Jurisich Square (Jurisich was the Hungarian commander) was erected in 1932 to commemorate the historic event. The square leads to the heart of the old town, in which medieval churches, houses and public buildings alike preserve their ancient appearance. The Castle contains an interesting museum.

Ják, 11 km. (seven miles) south of Szombathely, has the finest Romanesque church in Hungary, dating from the period of the Árpád Dynasty, with two fine towers, crowned with spires. The outside of the church, particularly the west door, is profusely ornamented with carvings. It is reached by road; there is a regular bus service.

Sárvár and Bük

Two other places worth a visit from Szombathely are Sárvár and Bük. Sárvár lies 27 km. (17 miles) east of Szombathely on the left bank of the Rába. Its castle, first mentioned in the 12th century, became an important cultural center during the Reformation. Its halls contain a memorial exhibition devoted to Sebestyén Tinódi Lantos (1505–1556), a famous wandering minstrel, much of whose work has survived. The first book printed in Hungary in the Hungarian language, a Latin-Hungarian grammar, was printed here in 1539, as was the first Hungarian translation of the New Testament (1541). The little town's streets are lined with old houses and the castle gardens have many rare trees. Sárvár has now become a spa of some importance.

Bük (also known as Bükfürdő; "fürdő" means "spa" or "bath") is 32 km. (20 miles) northeast of Szombathely. It too has valuable alkaline waters, mainly used for the treatment of locomotor and gynecological diseases. One of the picturesque "country-house hotels" is located here—a Baroque building, once the home of the Szapáry family.

There are frequent trains from Szombathely to both Sárvár and Bük.

Veszprém and the Bakony Hills

Veszprém is not only a picturesque center of cultural and economic life, but also unique in Hungary in that it is built on five hills and in the intervening valleys. Its traffic center is Szabadság (Liberty) Square, on which is situated the Baroque Town Hall.

The most interesting quarter of the town lies to the north and is approached along Rákóczi Road; this ends in Vöröshadsereg (Red Army) Square, at the top of the Várhegy (Castle Hill). Here is the southern entrance to the Castle, which rises on a dolomite rock 30 meters (100 ft.) above its surroundings. The Hősi kapu (Heroes' Gate), at the entrance to the Castle, contains the Castle Museum. On the left a short cul-de-sac leads to the Tűztorony (Fire Tower), which is partly medieval and partly Baroque; its gallery offers a fine panorama of the town and its environs. Continuing along Tolbuhin Street we pass the fine Baroque Bishop's Palace; the 13th-century Gizella chapel adjoining it is one of Hungary's most famous early Gothic buildings, with contemporary murals.

The road ends in a spacious square where, on the left, stands St. Michael's Cathedral, one of the most precious architectural features of Veszprém. The city has been an episcopal see since the time of King St. Stephen and the cathedral was begun in the 11th century in a Romanesque style; in the 14th century Gothic details were added. It was remodeled along Baroque lines in the 18th century, after destruction by the Turks, while in the 20th century it was recast in a neo-Romanesque style. Its Baroque and Classical altars are exceedingly fine and there is a large collection of plate and vestments in the sacristy. The new town of Veszprém is being developed in and around Rákóczi Square, east of the traditional center, while the university district lies to the south of the town.

The Bakony lies to the west of Veszprém, north of Lake Balaton. It is a hilly and forested area and one of the most attractive regions of Hungary. Its ruined castles recall the age of chivalry, its ancient cultural centers confirm long-established traditions, while new mines and industrial plants have much improved the region's standard of living. Communications are fairly good, both by rail and road.

About 16 km. (ten miles) west of Veszprém lies Herend, the Hungarian Sèvres or Nymphenburg. The porcelain works were founded in the 19th century and its products are world famous. A museum showing some of the best examples of Herend work is open to the public. Twenty-two km. (14 miles) to the north of Veszprém lies Zirc, an important tourist center with many historic buildings. In Rákóczi Square there is a large group of buildings of which the former abbey and church of the Cistercians (founded in 1182) form part. The large, ornate Baroque church was built between 1739 and 1753; its interior is particularly rich, with murals by Maulbertsch. The former abbey is now a library and museum. There are many attractive small resorts around Zirc. Bakonybél, 17 km. (some ten miles) to the west, is the site of the first Benedictine monastery in Hungary.

Pápa, still further west, is an important town lying on the railway to Pannonhalma and Győr. It is the economic and cultural center of the western Bakony. The former Esterházy Castle, built between 1773 and 1782, lies on the northern side of Szabadság (Liberty) Square. The large Baroque parish church (1774–1783) was built by Jakab Fellner and is decorated with murals by Maulbertsch. A Protestant college was established here in 1531 and two of Hungary's greatest 19th-century writers, Petőfi and Jókai, were students here.

Székesfehérvár

Székesfehérvár lies some 40 km. (25 miles) east of Veszprém and is one of the most interesting and important provincial towns of Hungary; it is also one of the country's most important traffic junctions. Known to the Romans as Herculia, its neo-Latin name of Alba Regia was bestowed on it during the Middle Ages. Under King Stephen it was already an important place and it was he who built its first cathedral and royal palace. Although the royal capital was established at Esztergom, and later transferred to Óbuda and then to Buda, Székesfehérvár long preserved its royal links—until 1527 Hungarian kings were crowned here and many were buried here. The town has played an important role throughout Hungarian history and latterly it has become a very busy industrial center.

Szabadság (Liberty) Square is the hub of the city and almost all the sights lie close by. In the square itself lies the Town Hall, a Baroque building, with beautiful gates at its eastern end, and the Bishop's Palace begun in 1790 in an Empire and Biedermeyer style. To the south of the square, in Arany János Street, stands the Baroque Cathedral, built in 1758–78 on the site of an earlier medieval church. King Bela III, who ruled from 1174 to 1196, and his consort were buried in the crypt. At the eastern end of Szabadság Square is the Garden of Ruins (Romkert) on the site of the former cathedral and royal palace, both of which have been extensively excavated. There are many fine Baroque buildings all over the old town, and pleasant cafes and restaurants, together with shady gardens, so that a stroll will prove both interesting and agreeable.

Only a few miles away and just south of the road from Székesfehérvár to Lake Balaton lie Tác and the recently-excavated ruins of the Roman city of Gorsium. A restaurant and cafe have been opened here.

Not far to the east of Székesfehérvár lies Lake Velence, with a number of popular summer resorts; part of the lake is a protected haunt of water birds. Still further to the east, on the way to Budapest, lies Martonvásár, with the picturesque Brunswick Palace, built in 1773–75 but rebuilt in an "English" Gothic style a century later. Beethoven often stayed here and Beethoven Memorial Concerts are held each year in June and July.

Pécs and Southwest Hungary

Southwest Hungary, the district lying south of Lake Balaton, is a smiling, fertile region. Its climate is much milder than elsewhere in Hungary and in the extreme south of the region there are some fair-sized hills. The chief city of the entire region is Pécs, the third-largest provincial town in Hungary. It was the Roman Sopianae, the capital of southern Pannonia, and here several Roman commercial and military roads met. Its great four-towered cathedral rests on Roman foundations. Pécs has always been a prosperous town and was an important staging-post for German and Italian merchants on their way to Byzantium. Hungary's first university was founded here in 1367. During the 143 years of Turkish rule (1543–1686), Pécs acquired a new architectural image, some of which remains to this day.

The center of the town is Széchenyi Square. This contains, among many other old buildings, one dating from the time of the Turkish occupation; the Gazi Kassim Pasha mosque, the largest Turkish monument in Hungary, is now a parish church. Built in the 16th century, it still has its mihrab, the Muslim prayer-niche facing Mecca. Along Janus Pannonius Street, to the northwest, we reach the ecclesiastical center of the city, Dóm (Cathedral) Square, itself a fine piece of architectural planning. The entire northern side of the square is taken up by the Cathedral, one of the most splendid medieval monuments in Hungary. It was begun by King Stephen, but has been rebuilt and remodeled several times. Of its four great, spire-capped towers, two date from the 11th and two from the 12th century. Both externally and internally, the cathedral is impressive and beautiful. On the west side of the square is the Bishop's Palace, whose garden facade is perhaps the finest Baroque monument in Pécs. Nearby there are some early Christian catacombs. Excavations at the southern end of the square are now open to visitors. They have brought to light some remarkable wall paintings in the catacombs, now carefully preserved behind glass.

At Janus Pannonia Utca 11 is the Csontváry Museum, which houses the chief works of the artist Tivadar Csontváry Kosztka, the importance of whose neo-surrealist *oeuvre* was not fully recognized until 50 years after his death in 1919.

Other buildings of note in the city include several Turkish monuments. One is the Jakovali Hassan mosque, in Rákóczi Street, southwest of the town center, built late in the 16th century; this is the only Turkish building in Hungary to have survived intact and it still has its minaret. It is now a museum. Another is the *türbe* (tomb) of Idris Baba, northwest of the inner city; there are also many fine Baroque churches and houses in and around Széchenyi Square.

Pécs is famous for the Zsolnay porcelain produced here since 1851. The Zsolnay Museum, in Káptalan (Chapter) Street, which links the Cathedral Square with the northern part of the town center and which is lined with fine old houses, each an "ancient monument," contains valuable examples of Zsolnay ware. The Vasarely Museum, in the same street, contains the works presented by the famous artist to his home town. Pécs is also a university city and is rapidly developing into an important industrial town.

Two towns well worth visiting from Pécs are Szigetvár and Siklós, both of which have interesting medieval castles. The castle at Szigetvár played an important role in the fight against the Turkish invaders of Hungary in 1566, when a handful of soldiers held out against the army of Sultan Soliman II. There is a Turkish mosque in the castle courtyard. At Siklós, about 32 km. (20 miles) due south of Pécs, the castle has been continuously inhabited since the Middle Ages and now houses a comfortable hotel. The town lies in the center of a rich wine-producing district at the foot of the Villany Hills.

The West Bank of the Danube

There remains to be mentioned the country along the west bank of the Danube. Mohács, 40 km. (25 miles) to the east of Pécs, lies on the river and is famous above all for the disastrous battle fought there in 1526, in which the defending Hungarians were routed by the Turkish army of Sultan Soliman II. It contains a number of pleasant Baroque churches, but nothing of special interest. The town is also noted for its Carnival procession, when many of the participants wear horror masks. It has a nudist camp. Szekszárd, 43 km. (27 miles) further north, lies some miles to the west of the present course of the Danube. The former County Hall, built in 1780 on the site of a Benedictine abbey, and a late Baroque Roman Catholic church are its chief sights. Liszt spent much of his time here and gave several concerts. Szekszárd is the center of notable vineyards, famous from Roman times; and the Gemenc forest nearby is a well-known game reserve.

Finally we must mention Dunaújváros, almost exactly halfway between Szekszárd and Budapest. It is Hungary's greatest purely industrial city. Until the Fifties, it was no more than a small village. It has no buildings of historical importance, but it will interest those—and they amount to over 100,000 visitors a year—who wish to see how a small country has, in not much over 30 years, transformed a sleepy country hamlet into an industrial complex, with vast iron and steel works. A museum illustrates the town's growth.

PRACTICAL INFORMATION FOR
WESTERN HUNGARY

TOURIST INFORMATION. The following are the addresses of the local tourist offices. **Bük:** Termál Körút 43; **Dunaújváros:** Korányi Utca; **Fertőd:** in the Castle; **Győr:** next to Hotel Rába, in town center; **Ják:** opposite the church; **Kőszeg:** Várkör; **Mohács:** Tolbuhin Utca; **Pannonhalma:** close to the Abbey; **Pápa:** Fő Tér 12; **Pécs:** Széchenyi Tér; **Sárvár:** Várkerület 33; **Siklós:** in village center; **Sopron:** Lenin Körút, near Pannonia Hotel; **Székesfehérvár:** Március 15. Utca and Ady Endre Utca, both just north of town center; also opposite Alba Regia Hotel; **Szekszárd:** Széchenyi Tér; **Szigetvár:** Zrínyi Tér; **Szombathely:** Mártírok Tere and Köztársaság Tér; **Tata:** Ady Endre Utca; **Veszprém:** Münnich Ferenc Tér.

WHEN TO COME. Spring, summer and fall are all delightful times to visit western Hungary. Most of the more interesting festivals and popular events are held in July and August.

GETTING AROUND. There are good rail connections from Budapest (South and East Stations). Traveling from Vienna it is necessary to change trains at the frontier station Hegyeshalom. Local trains and buses are adequate. Of course, a car provides you with the greatest freedom.

HOTELS AND RESTAURANTS

All the hotels listed below have restaurants unless otherwise stated.

Bük. *Thermál* (E), (tel. 13–366), modern and comfortable spa hotel. *Bük* (M), (tel. 13–363). *Kastély* (I), (tel. 205), Baroque "country-house hotel" with period furniture, a number of valuable pictures, and fine plasterwork in its great hall; some doubles have bath. Campsite; paying-guest accommodations.

Dunaújváros. *Arany Csillag* (M), (tel. 18–045). Guest house; campsite; paying-guest accommodations.
Restaurants. *Dunagyöngye, Kohász.*

Fertőd. *Kastély* (tel. 45–971); simple "country-house hotel." No private baths. Guest house, tourist hostel, paying-guest accommodations.
Restaurant. *Haydn,* in the village, recommended.

Győr. *Rába* (M), (tel. 15–533). Large, modern hotel. Guest houses, campsite, paying-guest accommodations.
Restaurants. *Hungária,* Lenin Út 23, *Vaskakas,* Köztársaság Tér 3, and many others.

Kőszeg. *Írottkő* (M), (tel. 333); *Expressz-Panoráma* (I), (tel. 280), on hills west of town; *Strucc* (I), (tel. 7281), historic hostelry dating from the 17th century. Two tourist hostels, one in the ancient castle, the other outside the town; paying-guest accommodations; snack bar in castle.

Mohács. *Csele* (M), (tel. 10–825). *Korona* (I), (tel. 10–541). Paying-guest accommodations.
Restaurants. *Béke,* in the town; *Halászcsárda* (fisherman's inn on the island).

Pápa. *Platán* (M), (tel. 24–688). Paying-guest accommodations.
Restaurant. *Béke,* Fő Tér 27.

Pécs. *Nádor* (E), (tel. 10–779), famous old house in the main square. *Főnix* (M), (tel. 11–680). Well placed near the town's main square. *Hunyor* (M), (tel. 15–677), on hills above town with lovely view; serves only breakfast but there is a restaurant close by. *Pannonia* (M), (tel. 13–322), modern, in town. Comfortable. *Fenyves* (I), (tel. 15–996), above town. Guest houses, tourist hostel, campsite; paying-guest accommodations.
Restaurants. *Elefántos Ház,* praised; *Sopiana, Minaret,* in town center; *Vadásztanya,* game specialties, in hills above town.
Kastély (M), (tel. 12–176) at Üszögpuszta, just outside the city. This, the former Batthyány castle, is now a "country-house hotel" with period furniture; double rooms have up-to-date bathrooms. Tennis and horseriding.

Sárvár. *Thermál* (E), (tel. 16–088), modern and comfortable spa hotel. *Minihotel* (I), (tel. 228); campsite, paying-guest accommodations.

Siklós. *Tenkes* (M–I), (tel. 61), in the medieval castle, some rooms with bath. Guest house, tourist-hostel; paying-guest accommodations.

Sopron. *Lövér* (M), (tel. 11–061), pleasant hotel in the wooded southern outskirts. *Palatinus* (M), (tel. 11–395), in charming town house. *Pannonia* (M), (tel.

12–180), in town center. *Sopron* (M), (tel. 14–254). Outside town, fine views, swimming pool. Several guest houses, tourist-hostels and bungalows; campsites; paying-guest accommodations.

Restaurants. *Cézár, Deák, Gambrinus,* all in town center; *Alpesi,* on hills southwest of the town. Many wine bars.

Székesfehérvár. *Alba Regia* (M), (tel. 13–484), modern and comfortable. *Velence* (I), (tel. 11–262). Old-fashioned, but with some private baths. Guest house, tourist-hostel; campsite; paying-guest accommodations.

Restaurants. *Kiskulacs; Ősféhervár,* in town center, good.

Szekszárd. *Gemenc* (M), (tel. 11–722). *Garay* (I), (tel. 12–177). Guest house; campsite; paying-guest accommodations.

Restaurants. *Halászcsárda* (fish-restaurant), *Kispipa, Szász* (beer hall).

Szigetvár. *Oroszlán* (M), (tel. 284). Tourist-hostel in the castle; paying-guest accommodations.

Szombathely. *Claudius* (E), (tel. 13–760), in park, recommended. *Isis* (M), (tel. 14–990). *Savaria* (M), (tel. 11–440), in Martírok Tere, is an art nouveau masterpiece, recently completely restored both inside and out. *Tourist* (I), (tel. 14–168), in the town. Tourist-hostel; paying-guest accommodations.

Restaurants. *Halászcsárda* (fish-restaurant), *Pannonia,* both in town center; *Tó, Pásztorok,* near lake outside town.

Tata. *Diana* (M), and *Dianatouring* (I), both (tel. 80–388), at Remeteségpuszta, five km. (three miles) out of town, are parts of an old castle converted into a hotel and near the State Riding School, with excellent opportunities for horseriding.

Malom (tel. 81–530), *Kristály* (tel. 80–577) and *Pálma* (tel. 80–577), all (I), are all in the town. Several guest houses, campsites, paying-guest accommodations.

Restaurants. *Aranyponty, Jázmin, Vár, Zsigmond* (wine bar).

Veszprém. *Veszprém* (M), (tel. 12–345), modern and comfortable. Bungalows; paying-guest accommodations; tourist-hostel for students at the University hall of residence during the summer vacation.

Restaurants. *Halle söröző* (beer hall), *Malom* (wine bar), *Vadásztanya.*

Zirc. *Bakony* (I), (tel. 168), simple. Tourist-hostel; paying-guest accommodations.

POLAND

POLAND—FACTS AT YOUR FINGERTIPS

HOW TO GO. Orbis, the official Polish Travel Bureau, though not actually able to arrange travel to Poland themselves, have a number of officially accredited travel agents overseas, of which the principal agent is Polorbis. They will organize travel to and from Poland, whether by plane, train, ship, or bus and can also book hotels and organize visas. They can also supply prepaid vouchers for hotels, campsites, gasoline and the like. For independent travelers these last can be extremely useful. However, the many other travel agents who organize travel to Poland (Thomas Cook, Maupintour and American Express among them) can also help in many of these areas.

Within Poland itself, you will find that the major hotels are owned and operated by Orbis. They have offices in all main towns and cities.

The addresses of Orbis offices overseas are:
In the U.S.: 500 Fifth Ave., New York, NY 10110, (tel. 212–391–0844).
In the U.K.: 82 Mortimer St., London W1, (tel. 01–636 2217).

TOURS. Apart from package holidays in one town or center, a number of tours of Poland are also available. For example, there is a *Panorama of Poland,* a 15-day tour of Warsaw, Toruń, Gdańsk, Posnan, Wrocław and Cracow, from $599. Orbis also organizes special-interest holidays such as biking, horseriding, mountain walks and fly-drive vacations. Among their 10-, 15- and 20-day tours, *Highlights of Poland* visits Warsaw, Cracow, Zakopane and Częstochowa for $569 for 12 days (land costs only); *Grand Heritage Tour of Poland* stops in 20 Polish cities over 22 days for $860 (land costs).

VISAS. In addition to a valid passport, visitors resident in all Western European countries, North and South America and all Commonwealth countries require a visa to enter Poland. These are available from Polish Consulates, or through Orbis offices or travel agents. To apply for a visa your passport must be valid for at least nine months from the date of application. You must submit a completed application, two passport-size photographs, copies of any prepaid services already booked and a money exchange order certifying that you have obtained the proper amount of currency. You can get these from your travel agent or Orbis. The fee for a visa is approximately £15 for British citizens and $18 for American ($14 for those under 24 or traveling on a prepaid tour). Children under 16 traveling on their parents' passports do not require visas. It is advisable to apply a few weeks in advance of your departure date. Visas are not issued at border points.

American travelers should submit materials to Orbis Polish Travel Bureau, 500 Fifth Ave., New York, NY 10110, Nationwide Services, or the Polish consulate nearest you. Orbis can provide addresses of consulates in the U.S. and Canada. Visa applications from the U.K. should be sent to the Polish Consulate General, 73 New Cavendish St., London W1.

Visitors staying in private homes must register themselves at the local police station within 48 hours of arrival in the country. To extend your stay beyond the authorized time, refer to the Passport section of the local police station.

MONEY. Travelers to Poland must exchange a minimum of $15 per day which must be done at the official exchange rate. Exempted are people under 21 years of age, students and foreign passport holders recognized by the Polish Consular Office as of Polish descent: they must pay only $8 a day. Payment can be made either before or after you arrive in Poland.

The unit of currency in Poland is the złoty which is divided into 100 groszy, though the latter are rarely seen. There are coins of 1, 2, 5, 10 and 20 zł.; bank notes are in denominations of 50, 100, 200, 500, 1,000, 2,000 and 5,000 zł.

The official rate of exchange at the time of writing (mid-1988) was about 430 zł. to the dollar and about 750 zł. to the pound. But these rates are certain to change both before and during 1989. It is important therefore to check the latest rate when planning your trip.

Foreign currency may be exchanged at all border points (ie. air, sea and road), in most hotels and at any Polorbis exchange counter. Exchange of foreign currency on the black market (though actually widely practised) is strictly forbidden and subject to penalties. Remember also that the import and export of Polish currency is not permitted. You may bring in any amount of foreign currency.

Credit Cards. Major credit cards such as American Express, Bank America, Access, Visa, Carte Blanche, Diners Club, MasterCard etc. are accepted at all principal hotels and restaurants, nightclubs, selected stores in larger towns and for Orbis services. Money can be changed at nearly all Orbis hotels.

COSTS. Despite 50% inflation and considerable rises in many basic commodities, not least food, Polish prices are still very reasonable by Western standards, though you may find some services unpredictable. The least expensive and in many ways the most convenient way of visiting Poland is on a package tour with all expenses prepaid before you leave home. But even if you travel independently with or without prepaid vouchers, you will still find costs low.

Summer, being the high season, is the most expensive time to visit, especially the seaside resorts of Gdańsk, Gdynia and Sopot. The mountain resorts, as might be expected, are most expensive in winter. You will also find that hotel prices in particular go up when special events take place, such as the Poznań International Fair in June. However, in Warsaw and Cracow hotel prices remain fixed all year long.

Sample Costs. Beer 150–400 zł.; glass vodka 200 zł.; opera ticket from 200 zł., theater or concert ticket from 200 zł.; movie 200 zł.; cup of coffee 300 zł.; cup of tea 100 zł.

MEDICAL INSURANCE. Medical insurance is strongly recommended for visitors to Poland from North America, as charges are made for all medical treatments and medicines. However, visitors to Poland from Great Britain are entitled to free treatment in emergencies upon presentation of an NHS medical card.

CLIMATE. Spring and summer, frequently very warm though the spring can be windy, are the best periods for sightseeing. Fall sees most of the major cultural events, which mostly take place in the cities. The Tatra mountains are at their best in the fall, which can be long and sunny. The winter sports season lasts from December to March.

Average afternoon temperatures in Fahrenheit and centigrade:

Warsaw	Jan.	Feb.	Mar.	Apr.	May	June	July	Aug.	Sept.	Oct.	Nov.	Dec.
F°	30	32	41	54	67	72	75	73	65	54	40	32
C°	-1	0	5	12	19	22	24	23	18	12	4	0

SPECIAL EVENTS. January, "Golden Washboard" Traditional Jazz Meeting (Warsaw). **February,** Highland carnival in the Tatra Mountains (Bukowina Tatrzańska); Festival of Modern Polish Music (Wrocław); "Jazz on the Odra" Student Festival (Wrocław); Festival of Polish Art (Wrocław). **March,** National Review of Professional Variety Theaters (Szczecin). **April,** National Student Song Festival (Cracow). **May,** International Chamber Music Festival (Łańcut, near

Rzeszów); Festival of Contemporary Polish Plays (Wrocław); International Book Fair (Warsaw); "Apple Blossom Days" folk festival (Łąck, near Sącz); "Neptunalia" Student Festival (Gdańsk and Szczecin); "Juvenalia" Student Festival (Cracow).

From **May to October,** Sunday Chopin recitals take place in Łazienki Park (Warsaw). **May–December,** Symphonic and chamber music concerts in Wawel Castle courtyard (Cracow). **June,** Folk Festival (Kazimierz Dolny); International Short Film Festival (Cracow); International Poster Biennale (even-numbered years, at Wilanów, just outside Warsaw); "Cepeliada" Folk Art Fair (Warsaw); International Trade Fair (Poznań); Chamber and Organ Music Festival (Kamień Pomorski, Szczecin Bay); Polish Song Festival (Opole, between Wrocław and Katowice); International Graphic Art Biennale (Cracow); Organ Music Festival (Frombork); Polish Days of the International Highland Folklore Festival (Żywiec in the Beskidy Mountains); International Puppet Theater Festival (Bielsko-Biała, south of Katowice); Folklore Festival (Ostrołęka, north of Warsaw and at Płock and Olsztyn); Midsummer "wianki" celebrations on June 23 throughout Poland, when small flower garlands carrying lit candles are thrown on the river, an echo of a pagan Slavonic tradition.

June–September, Chopin recitals at composer's birthplace (Żelazowa Wola just outside Warsaw). **June,** Festival of Short Films (Cracow); **July,** "Fama" Student Festival (Swinoujście), "Jazz Jantar" (Sopot, Olsztyn, Szczecin, Kołobrzeg, Koszalin). **August,** Chopin Festival (Duszniki-Zdrój, in the mountains of Lower Silesia); Dominican Fair, a commercial fair that draws on local traditions, with a good flea market (Gdańsk); Dymarki (Old Smelting Furnaces) Festival with demonstrations of 2,000-year-old smelting methods (Nowa Słupia in the Świetokrzyskie Mountains); International Song Festival (Sopot); Folk Art Fair (Cracow).

September, "Wratislavia Cantans" Oratorio and Cantata Festival (Wrocław); International Festival of Highland Folklore (Zakopane); "Warsaw Autumn" International Festival of Contemporary Music, Feature Film Festival (Warsaw); Musica Antiqua Europae Orientalis (Bydgoszcz); International Festival of Song and Dance Ensembles (Zielona Góra, west of Poznań); International Old Music Festival (Toruń). **October,** Jazz Jamboree (Warsaw). **November–December,** Presentation of year's most outstanding dramas (Warsaw); Festival of One Actor Plays (Toruń). **December,** Competition for the best Christmas Crib (Cracow); "Sylwester" New Year's Eve celebrations everywhere.

National Holidays. Jan. 1; Easter Monday; May 1 (International Labor Day); Corpus Christi; July 22 (National Day); Nov. 1 (Remembrance Day); Dec. 25 & 26.

CUSTOMS. Personal belongings may be brought in duty free, including sports equipment (but guns and ammunition require a Polish permit), musical instruments, a typewriter, radio, cassette recorder, two cameras with 24 films or ten rolls of film for each as well as ten films for one movie camera (16mm), one liter of wine and spirits, 250 cigarettes or 50 cigars or 250 grams of tobacco.

Articles not exceeding 10,000 zloty can be taken out of Poland duty free, but there are restrictions on certain items. It is not always clear which goods are liable for extra duty, so check carefully with Orbis and tourist shops. Goods bought with foreign currency are not liable for duty providing you have the sales receipts with you at the customs control. No works of art or books of any kind published before 1945 may be taken out.

For currency regulations, see *Money.*

LANGUAGE. Polish is a Slavonic language. Unlike Russian, it uses the familiar Roman alphabet, but with many additional accents. German, Russian, English and French are spoken by members of the travel industry, in hotels and are understood in the larger cities.

HOTELS. Hotels in Poland are reasonably plentiful, though quite expensive by the standards of other East European countries. All the top hotels are owned and operated by Orbis and, though other hotels exist outside the Orbis ambit, it is unlikely that Western visitors will come into contact with them. Certainly, if you have prepaid hotel vouchers or have booked your hotel in advance through Polorbis, you will stay in one of the Orbis hotels. However, non-Orbis hotels are considerably less expensive, though at the same time you may well find difficulty making reservations. You can also be sure that Orbis hotels will have the best food supplies, and, if for no other reason than this, they are definitely the best bet for Western visitors.

However, of the other hotels, the best are Municipal Hotels, run by local authorities. There are also a number of PTTK hotels (run by the Polish Tourist Association); these are frequently called *Dom Turysty*. There are also a number of inexpensive roadside inns known as *zajazdy*, but these are most likely to suffer from erratic food supplies. Information on all Polish hotels is available from Polorbis and Orbis within Poland.

Polish hotels are graded from luxury through 4- to 1-star. These categories correspond closely to our gradings of Deluxe (L), Expensive (E), Moderate (M) and Inexpensive (I). 3- and 2-star hotels are graded as Moderate in our listings. Most Orbis hotels come within our Expensive category.

Rates quoted below are for Orbis hotels. They include bed and breakfast and all taxes and service charges. A number of hotels, especially the larger ones, often have rooms in more than one category. Rates are in U.S. dollars.

A double room with a bath or shower plus breakfast will cost in U.S.$:

	Warsaw	Provincial centers
Deluxe	$100–120	—
Expensive	55–70	45–55
Moderate	40–55	40–50
Inexpensive	20–35	18–30

Youth Hostels

The Polish Youth Hostels Association operates about 1,200 hostels, which are open to all. It is best to join the Association or belong to any other similar association of the International Youth Hostels Federation, thus entitling you to reductions. A list is included in the IYHF international register.

Camping

There are over 250 campsites in Poland, nearly 75% of which are fitted with 220-volt power points and most with 24-volt points for caravans. Facilities also include washrooms, canteens and nearby restaurants and food kiosks. Polish campsites are divided into three categories, and conditions vary considerably.

RESTAURANTS. The selection of restaurants is wide, but food supplies are currently erratic so it is advisable to book meals in top-class hotel restaurants as they receive the best ingredients. A meal in an expensive (E) restaurant will cost 2,000–3,000 zł., moderate (M) 1,000–2,000 zł., inexpensive (I) from around 600 zł., but can even be less.

Roadside inns (*zajazdy*) are inexpensive and serve traditional Polish cuisine. Self-service snack and coffee bars are to be found in larger centers; *kawiarnia,* (cafes), a way of life in Poland, serve delicious pastries. The sale of alcoholic beverages other than beer is illegal before 1 P.M. except in Pewex and Baltona hard currency stores.

TIPPING. A service charge is usually added to restaurant bills, but if not, add 10%. Tipping for other services is not obligatory, but is readily accepted. Cab drivers get 10% and expect to be tipped.

MAIL AND TELEPHONES. An airmail letter to the U.S. costs 50 zł., a postcard 35 zł.; a letter to the U.K. or Europe costs 45 zł., a postcard 30 zł. A letter sent by registered mail costs 20–30 zł. extra. These rates will increase in 1989. Post offices are open from 8 A.M. to 8 P.M. and there is usually one main post office in major towns that is open 24 hours a day. Telegrams are inexpensive.

In public phone booths (for local and long-distance calls) you'll need 2, 5, 10 and 20 zł coins. Long-distance calls can also be placed from your hotel or post office. Be sure to check the surcharge if placing the call from your hotel; this can sometimes double the basic price of the call. Telephoning in Poland, especially if you are making a long-distance call—provided there is no direct-dialling connection—can be both frustrating and time consuming. For international calls it is better to phone after midnight when the service is quicker.

Emergency telephones are 997 (Police) and 998 or 999 (Ambulance) in Warsaw. Other areas have different numbers which are given in every phone booth.

TIME. Poland is six hours ahead of Eastern Standard Time and one hour ahead of Greenwich Mean Time. In the summer, clocks are put forward by one hour so that the country is seven hours ahead of Eastern Standard Time and two hours' ahead of Greenwich Mean Time.

CLOSING TIMES. Food shops are open from 6 or 7 A.M. to 7 P.M., others from 11 A.M. to 7 P.M. "Ruch" newspaper kiosks open from 6 A.M. to 9 P.M. Offices are generally open from 8 A.M. to 3 P.M. or 9 A.M. to 4 P.M., banks from 8 A.M. to 12 noon. Local tourist information centers can advise on up-to-date opening times of exhibitions etc. Museums generally close on Mondays. Most shops are open on one Saturday a month—ask the locals which.

SHOPPING. The wide range of chain stores specializing in different items makes shopping in Poland relatively easy, though not necessarily cheap. Glassware, ceramics, woodcarvings, articles of amber, silver and other metals, embroideries and pictures all make good gifts to take back home.

Some of the best souvenirs can be bought from Cepelia (Folk Arts and Crafts Cooperative) with stores all over Poland. They sell a wide range of genuine folk art from all regions. Desa stores stock tapestries, paintings, sculptures and porcelain, while branches of Orno specialize in handmade silver work. All these accept local and foreign currency. The Pewex and Baltona stores accept only hard currency. They sell local and imported items such as imported spirits (very reasonable vodka), imported chocolate, coffee and clothing.

SPAS. There are several dozen spas and health resorts scattered throughout Poland, the largest of which is Ciechocinek. Orbis takes care of all the arrangements. A high-season stay in a spa starts at $50 per person per day, in a double room with bath. This includes full board and treatment.

WINTER SPORTS. The most popular resorts are Zakopane in the Tatra Mountains and Krynica (also a well-known spa) in the Beskidy Mountains. Skiing from November through May. You'll find good Orbis hotels and boarding houses, ski-runs, restaurants, lots of après-ski, and cable railways and lifts to nearby peaks. Ski-jumping competitions are frequently staged. In Lower Silesia, holiday resorts with good skiing facilities include Karpacz, Szklarska Poręba, Szczawno, Polanica, Kudowa, and Duszniki. Beginning to rival Zakopane as Poland's winter capital is Szczyrk in the Beskid-Ślaski Mountains; good facilities, but snow cannot be guaranteed.

WATER SPORTS. Main sailing regions in Poland are the Mazurian Lakes and the nearby Suwałki and Augustów Lakes, a natural continuation of the waterways. Zegrzyńskie Lake not far from Warsaw offers splendid facilities. In winter there is ice-boating on many of Poland's frozen waterways.

No special qualifications or documents are required for tourists entering Poland with their own yachts or motor boats, but you must have life-saving equipment on board. Many Polish waters have "quiet zones" where motor-powered boats are banned; these areas include many of the Mazurian Lakes, as well as (on Sundays and holidays) Warsaw's Zegrzyńskie Lake. In some lakes you may not swim beyond certain marked buoys without a swimming proficiency certificate. Check with the lake guard and arrange a simple test if necessary.

Canoeing enthusiasts have many good river routes to choose from, but especially recommended are the Krutynia river in the Mazury region, the Dunajec Gorge (skilled canoeists only), the Pilica river, and of course, the Vistula.

There are swimming pools in most cities; sandy beaches along the Baltic coast and Mazurian Lakes. Avoid swimming in the rivers as pollution is high.

HUNTING. Poland is definitely a hunting country, but fairly expensive. After hard winters, hunting can be cut back severely for some time to allow game to recover. In a number of reserves, fallow deer, roe deer, elk, wild boar, lynx, wolf, and fox are to be found and you get a run for your money. Game birds include woodgrouse, blackcock, woodcock, pheasant, and partridge. The best hunting can be found in the Bieszczady and Carpathian Mountains, Białowieża Forest, Mazury, Augustów, and Koszalin. Full details of gun licenses and rates for organized hunting trips from Orbis.

ANGLING. The best places for quiet fishing in lovely surroundings are Western Pomerania (Białogard and Kołobrzeg), and the Mazurian Lakes in the neighborhood of Giżycko (Kamień, Stare Jabłonki, Paławki, Węgorzewo). There are over 47 kinds of fish to choose from—salmon, trout, chub, roach, sheatfish and pike. A crayfish hunt can be great fun, as can ice-hole angling in winter.

Foreign tourists will need to buy a fishing license valid for 14 days. There are also seven-day licenses for special angling grounds reserved for foreign tourists. Full details are available from Orbis.

RIDING. Poland has a stirring and ancient tradition of riding and horse-breeding (it even supplies the Arabs with Arabs) and a good way of seeing the countryside is from a saddle. It's becoming a very popular form of holiday, so riding centers tend to get booked up early. Biały Bór near Koszalin is situated in wooded, hilly country and also has indoor facilities. Racot near Poznań is set amid forests and lakes. It is one of the oldest studs in the country and has 800 Arab horses. Many riding holidays can be spent in old manor houses and palaces, as at Czerniejewo, Dłusko, Ptaszkowo, Sieraków, Iwno and Podkówka Leśna. Poland's own Hucuły ponies, known for their small size, patience, and tolerance, offer a unique opportunity for learning to ride.

GETTING AROUND POLAND. By Air. LOT, the state airline, flies into 11 cities and towns in the country, as well as into Warsaw, whose airport, Okęcie, is about six miles south of the city and handles both international and domestic traffic. There are bus services into the city (no. 175) as well as taxis. If you are intending to travel by internal flights, book well in advance.

By Train. Polish State Railways (PKP) suffered very badly during World War II and are still being rebuilt and modernized. Steam engines are widely used, but all the expresses are now either diesel or electric.

Trains are well-patronized and provide the main method of long-distance travel. Seat reservation is mandatory on all expresses, but is advisable also for fast trains, especially at the peak holiday times, the 1st, 15th and 31st July and August. Cost of reservation is 30 zł. To reserve your seat, go to the Polres office at the railway depot, or make use of any Orbis office. Remember lines are a Polish way of life—especially for rail tickets—so if you have not prebooked and reserved your seat, turn up well in advance of departure time.

There is a runabout ticket called *Polrail Pass* which costs only $72 for eight days, $84 for 15 days, $96 for 21 days, and $108 for one month, a true bargain. First-class travel is well worth the extra, due to the crowded trains. Seats have to be reserved on express trains. The Polrail Pass can be purchased at Polorbis offices, through a travel agent, or at Orbis offices in Poland.

If you are buying an international rail ticket, even if it is for travel within the Eastern Bloc, it is essential to change money specially for that purpose and receive the correct receipt.

By Bus. The state-run bus service (PKS) operates several long distance routes, but mainly as a feeder service for the railway system. It is cheap, always very crowded and probably best suited to the adventurous.

By Car. Poles drive on the right and the usual Continental rules of the road are observed. There is a speed limit of 90 kph (55 mph) on the open road and 50 kph (31 mph) in built-up areas. Drinking is absolutely prohibited and carries heavy penalties. In built-up areas, horn blowing is also prohibited.

Detailed information on the documents you will need if you're taking your own car into the country is given on page 20.

Foreign tourists can only buy gasoline in exchange for gasoline coupons bought in foreign currency at the frontier and at Orbis hotels in batches of 40 liters. Coupons are available for 94 and 78 octane, the first low, the second terrible. There is no limit on the amount of gasoline you can buy and unused coupons are refundable. Gas stations are situated in towns and along major routes, usually open from 6 to 10, but some are open 24 hours a day.

In case of accident or repair problems, contact the Polish Motoring Association, *PZM (Polski Związek Motorowy)*, ul. Krucza 14, Warsaw (tel. 29 62 52). PZM can also supply you with a list of gas stations, service centers and road maps; they have branches all over Poland. It is sensible to carry a spare parts kit with you.

A number of main European (E) routes cross Poland. They include E12 from West Germany through Prague to Wrocław, Łódź, Warsaw and Białystok; the E14 from Austria, through Czechoslovakia to Swinoujście and on to Ystad in Sweden; and the E8 from East Germany through Poznań, Warsaw and on to the U.S.S.R.

Even the main roads can often be in poor condition, and the minor roads tend to be narrow and cluttered with horse-drawn carts. Nevertheless, visitors find them acceptable and much more interesting than the main roads. The numbering system for main roads was changed in 1986 so make sure you have an up-to-date map with you.

Car Hire. Cars are available for hire from Avis or Hertz at international airports or through Orbis offices. Rates with unlimited mileage for one week range from $235 to $393, depending on season and model of car; two weeks costs $440–718. Fly-drive holidays are also available through Polorbis. Rented cars may be driven out of the country and left abroad for an extra charge.

By Taxi. Taxis are cheap and cost about 200–300 zł. for an average ride. The taxi meters are out of date, but if you multiply the figure they indicate by five, you should get approximately the right price. Fares double after 11 P.M. and on Saturdays and Sundays. Taxis operate only from special taxi ranks and you sometimes have to wait a fairly long time.

Hitchhiking. Poland is one of the few countries that does not frown on this method of travel. Hitchhikers can buy special books of coupons at border points, tourist information centers etc., and, on obtaining a lift, give drivers the appropriate coupons covering the distance they plan to ride. Drivers who collect the largest number of coupons during the year actually receive prizes. A system of inexpensive accommodations for hitchhikers has also been evolved. Directing this unusual aspect of travel is the Hitchhiking Committee (*Komitet Autstopu*), ul. Narbutta 27a, Warsaw.

INTRODUCING POLAND

Throughout their troubled history the Poles have been set down by other Europeans as strange, wild, unpredictable and given to excesses; enthusiastic eaters and drinkers, suckers for a noble cause, inclined to go over the top on slight provocation without a thought for the consequences. Yet it is precisely these characteristics that have enabled the Poles to endure even the most difficult of times and still retain their dignity and sense of humor.

Seeing the confines of the state reorganized has been a Polish experience for several centuries. Like other nations in the historically unsettled region of Central Europe, Poland has been embroiled in the power struggles of larger nation-states, fought over by warring Slav and Mongol hordes, squeezed almost out of existence by the mutually hostile great powers—Russia, Prussia, Austria-Hungary—on her borders. Yet today she remains by far the largest of the Warsaw Pact countries apart from the Soviet Union.

Poland does not easily fit one's preconceptions of a Communist state. The country's peculiarities include the fact that more than 80% of the land is under private ownership, and a population that, despite more than 40 years of atheistic Communist rule, remains profoundly Roman Catholic. Moreover, Polish culture both past and present is strongly Western oriented, and continues to flourish with or without government approval.

The People and Their Past

Poland came into existence as a separate unit in the 10th century when one of the Slavonic tribes, the Polanie, began to lord over other Slavs in the area. The first crowned king of Poland was Boleslaus "The Brave" who consolidated the power of the country's first great dynasty, the Piasts. Boleslaus was a good fighting man and under him the kingdom was enlarged, but after his death it gradually fell to pieces. Neighboring countries seized part of it while the rest, though continually ravaged by the Mongols who pushed into Europe during the Middle Ages, was divided up into petty dukedoms. The feudal landowners quarreled with each other, big chieftains swallowed little chieftains and those who survived became the ancestors of the proud Polish aristocracy. They grew rich and powerful and their estates were the size of small countries.

In the 14th century Poland was again reunited, and under Casimir the Great she became a great power. Casimir took the first sensible steps to develop the economy and make the country prosperous. It is said of Casimir that "he found a Poland of wood and left her built of stone." In due course a grand-niece succeeded Casimir, and by her marriage to the Grand Duke of Lithuania she united Poland and Lithuania thus founding the family of Jagellon, Poland's second great dynastic line. In 1410 her husband achieved an important victory at the battle of Grunwald (Tannenberg) over the league of Teutonic Knights that had long tried to dominate Poland.

The Knights returned again and again. Long wars were fought in East Prussia (was this when Hamlet's father "smote the sledded Polacks on the ice"?), but Poland at last emerged from them with a settled coastline on the Baltic. The Poles revealed an unsuspected talent for building ships and sailing them. Around 1500, as an agricultural and maritime land, she was a power to be reckoned with in European affairs. As is so often the case, power led to prosperity and the 16th century subsequently became a golden age of economic and cultural development.

When the royal Jagellons died out in 1572, Poland's nobility began electing her monarchs, not always from among themselves but sometimes from foreign stock in order to separate the crown from the domestic feuds of the court officials. Domestic or foreign, her kings knew no peace. No sooner had the threat from the west been dealt with than another sprang up in the east: the rising power of Russia and Turkey.

In 1683 King John Sobieski defeated the Turks at the gates of Vienna and rescued Christian Europe from the Ottoman onslaught. But Poland's neighbors rewarded her sacrifices by taking advantage of her exhaustion and moving in with invading armies. Piece by piece Russia, Prussia and Austria dismembered her until, a century later, scarcely anything was left of the proud kingdom but the unquenchable patriotism of her people. Exiled Poles, unable to help their native land, led freedom movements in distant countries. In the American War of Independence, for example, Pulaski died for the colonial cause and Kościuszko distinguished himself.

Into the 20th Century

Rebellions in Poland, mostly romantic and ill-conceived adventures, brought harsh reprisals from her foreign occupiers but helped to keep the national spirit alive. During this period many Poles fled poverty and repression in their country to seek a new life in America and other countries. Those that stayed had to wait, as did other European peoples, for the 1919 Versailles settlement to grant them freedom and independence.

The early interwar years were a difficult time for the Poles. An invading force from Soviet Russia was defeated, and the daunting task of national reconstruction was begun. By 1923 the Poles were building up industry, particularly coal-mining and shipbuilding, and were constructing a new naval base and commercial harbor at Gdynia.

But economic, ethnic and political problems constantly plagued the country. Party strife intensified, governments rose and fell. In 1926 her war hero Marshal Piłsudski, the man to whom she owed her freedom, marched on Warsaw and took control, establishing what was virtually a military dictatorship. He remained the arbiter of his country's destiny, with one brief interval, until his death in 1935, and then left his less competent lieutenants and nominees to carry on the work.

World War II and After

It was in Poland that World War II began. On 1st September 1939 the Germans invaded the country in pursuance of Hitler's territorial demands. An extraordinary diplomatic coup the previous month had secured the Soviet Union's approval of the invasion—at a price. With Hitler's blessing, the Red Army entered eastern Poland and in a short space of time the whole nation was split down the middle, half occupied by the Nazis and the other half by the Soviets.

No nation suffered more terror, death, and devastation in World War II than Poland. Six million Polish citizens, half of them Jews, were exterminated. Millions more were deported for forced labor. Many cities and huge areas of countryside were destroyed. Yet despite the severe repression, Polish soldiers and civilians set up the most widespread and possibly most effective of Europe's underground organizations. Thousands of Polish sailors, soldiers, and airmen also managed to find their way to Britain from where they went on to fight alongside the Allies.

The defeat of Germany in 1945 permitted the Soviet Union to "liberate" the whole country. The Polish people found themselves with no alternative but to accept Soviet-style communism. The country was thus duly turned into a People's Republic and had to endure a grim chapter of Stalinist repression.

All the enslaved nations faced enormous reconstruction problems after the war, but none so much as ruined and famine-stricken Poland. To revive her major industries and her agriculture took longer than many Poles thought reasonable; a further cause of disaffection was the increasing pressure which the government put on the Catholic Church, an institution of central importance in the spiritual and moral life of the nation. In 1956 the people's patience ran out and, following civil disturbances, the government leadership was changed in favor of a more liberal regime under Władysław Gomułka.

The Bubbling Pot

Sadly, Gomułka's promises of a better life under communism fell short of expectations, and by 1970, following riots and reprisals, he was forced to stand down. A new reformist and ostensibly liberal regime under First Secretary Edward Gierek took over. Gierek embarked on an ambitious but poorly conceived program of industrialization and modernization, which by the late 1970s disintegrated into an economic crisis. Nationwide strikes, initially against food prices, broke out in 1980 and led to the formation of Eastern Europe's first independent trades union, Solidarność (Solidarity), led by its charismatic leader, the shipyard worker Lech Wałęa. The union's popularity and enthusiasm for democratic change, however, alarmed the government, and martial law was declared in December 1981. Solidarność was subsequently banned, forcing it underground where it continues to exist today. The emotional visit made to Poland by the Pope in 1987 showed how potent support for Solidarność still was among large numbers of the population. Although martial law has been lifted, today Poland is still ruled by a soldier, General Jaruzelaski.

Poland Today

Forty years of Communist rule has failed to produce the economic miracle experienced by the democratic countries of Western Europe. Although big strides have been made in industrialization and education, standards of living in Poland remain low and life is hard. The country has been racked by a decade of economic crises. For the average Pole, this means shortages of consumer goods, inflation, poor welfare services and a waiting period of some 30 years for houses.

On top of this an oppressive government insults the political maturity of most Poles. Poland is predominantly a youthful nation (the average age of the population is 28, and is the lowest in Europe) and the hopes and expectations of this generation, which has listened to promises for so long, are far from satisfied.

Despite communism's traditional wariness of priestly involvement in politics, the majority of Poles remain practicing Catholics and community life is still focused on the church. Poland's bond with Rome in the present decade has been firmly cemented by the election of one of her archbishops to the papacy as Pope John Paul II.

The Cultural Scene

The Polish writer who is best known outside Poland is Joseph Conrad, born Josef Korzeniowski (1857–1924), author of some classic English novels of the sea. He did not learn English until he was 20, but became one of the greatest novelists in the language. Even in Poland his *Typhoon, Lord Jim* and *The Outcast of the Islands* are widely read. Of Polish authors writing in Polish, Henry Sienkiewicz (1846–1916) received the Nobel Prize for Literature on the strength of his one memorable novel *Quo Vadis?* Władysław Reymont (1868–1925) also won the Nobel Prize—in 1924 for his novel *Chłopi* (The Peasants)—but his near-contemporary Witold Gombrowicz (1904–1969) is more admired. Gombrowicz's best-known novel *Ferdydurke* had the distinction of being banned by both prewar right-wing and postwar left-wing governments. The third and most recent Polish Nobel laureate (1980) is Czeslaw Miłosz. In novels such as *The Captive Mind,* Miłosz deals outspokenly with the plight of intellectuals who are forced into compromise with a rigid political system.

Polonaise and Polka

Poland could fairly claim to have been the fountainhead of popular music in Europe, from the 18th century to the period Chopin (1810–1849) was alive. Her polonaises, polkas and mazurkas whirled their way round the continent, her stirring march tunes set feet tapping to unfamiliar rhythms.

The works of Frédéric Chopin, her greatest composer, took their roots from folk rhythms and melodies of exclusively Polish invention. Equally indebted to the national heritage of song and dance were Henryk Wieniawski (1835–1880), a celebrated violinist as well as a composer, and Karol Szymanowski, who flourished early this century. Among renowned living composers and conductors are Witold Lutosławski and Kryzysztof Penderecki, the latter an important innovator. Immortal virtuosi on violin and piano have sprung from Poland's large Jewish community. The mantle of Ignacy Paderewski settled on the shoulders of Artur Rubinstein and has now passed to Krystian Zimmerman.

A dense network of musical institutions covers the whole country. Every major city has its opera company and symphony orchestra and numerous semi-professional ensembles. Poles respond avidly to music—where but in Poland would you find a musician elected to the highest political office, as Paderewski was? A concert by the National Philharmonic of Warsaw or the Great Symphony of Katowice is a red-letter event, and audiences discuss the performances of individual musicians the way spectators in some countries discuss football players.

Art and Architecture.

The best of native architecture is seen in the old city of Cracow with its well-preserved or restored medieval and Renaissance buildings. All over the country fine manor houses and palaces have been rebuilt in their original styles. If contemporary architecture is not especially exciting, contemporary art is vigorous and imaginative and of global significance. From Toronto to Tasmania, one-man shows by living Polish painters and sculptors are a feature of gallery programs.

The works of the "constructivists," from Staweski and Kantor onwards, are brilliantly displayed in the national museums of Warsaw and Poznań and at the modern arts museum in Łódź, whose director is the much-respected Rsyzard Stanisławsky. There are sculpture galleries in Warsaw's parks and the leading sculptor, Xavery Dunikowsky, has his own Warsaw gallery, the Królikarnia.

Stage and Screen

Theater in Poland enjoys high prestige in an open-minded and artistically enlightened society. The standard of stage design is particularly high: the best artists do not disdain to compete for this kind of work. Jerzy Grotowski, impresario and director of the Laboratory Theater of Wrocław, is a household name abroad—he pioneered "essential" theater, which is serious, austere and intent on keeping the actor at the center of the drama. The Laboratory Theater has toured in France, Germany and the U.S.A.

Possibly the best-known Polish playwright living is Sławomir Mrożek, author of some *avant-garde* comedies and a favorite of the more progressive young directors. But foreign drama is extremely popular too, if it is sharp and witty or if it comes into the category of "world literature." Both in large cities and in provincial towns the broad cosmopolitan sweep of drama is covered, from Shakespeare to Albee (*Tiny Alice* and *Who's Afraid of Virginia Woolf*? played to packed houses in Warsaw and Cracow) and from adaptations of Dostoevsky to adaptations of James Joyce and Samuel Beckett.

There has been cinema in Poland since 1909, but Polish movies were almost unheard-of abroad until an eruption of outstanding films occurred in the 1950s. One of Andrzej Wajda's trilogy, *Ashes and Diamonds,* made an international star of the late Zbigniew Cybulski, dubbed the James Dean of Poland. Wajda is now the patriarch of Polish cinema, revered at home and abroad, and still capable—as his epics *Man of Iron* and *Man of Marble* showed—of keeping up the momentum of his country's movie renaissance.

POLISH FOOD AND DRINK

Fish, Mushrooms and Herbs

Poland's shifting borders and history of foreign domination have, not unnaturally, left their mark on the Polish cuisine. But though there are Austrian, French, Italian, and Russian echoes in some of their dishes, the Poles have managed to produce a specifically Polish cuisine characterized by the use of certain typical ingredients such as dill, marjoram, caraway seeds, and wild mushrooms (gathered in enormous quantities and varieties by large family contingents during the autumn months). The mushrooms (*grzyby*) are dried or pickled for winter use, used fresh as a garnish for soups and meat dishes or as a vegetable in their own right. Sour cream, which is inexpensive, is another hallmark of Polish cooking, being frequently added to soups, sauces, and braised meats.

In Poland, as in many countries, there is a sharp distinction between the food you get in a restaurant and what the ordinary people eat; the closest you'll get to the latter is in villages and market towns, where delicious *barszcz* (beetroot soup) is served, along with sausages, cabbage, potatoes, sour cream, *czarny chleb* (rye bread) and beer.

Important note: The one thing about food and drink in Poland that visitors should know is that supplies are erratic. Housewives can spend hours lining up each day for what little is available. So it is best to eat in the top-class hotel restaurants which tend to be able to produce the best food.

Starters

Polish meals start with przekąska, which, if you're in a smart restaurant might include marinated fish in sour cream, pike in aspic, stuffed carp, herrings (*śledźiki*) in various guises, pig's knuckles (*nózki*), Polish sausage (*kiełbasa*)—like the long, thin and highly spiced *kabanos* or the hunter's sausage (*myśliwska*) made with pork and game—cheese spreads garnished with chives (a good one is *bryndza,* made of ewe's milk and not unlike Greek *feta*),various kinds of pâtés (*pasztety*) and galantines, as well as tasty Polish smoked bacon and ham (*szynka*). Good hot appetizers to try are *kołduny* (beef or lamb turnovers served in hot bouillon) and *kulebiak* (a large mushroom and cabbage pasty).

To a Pole a meal without soup *(zupa)* is almost unthinkable, and a Polish soup can be an awesomely rich and filling knife-and-fork affair, thickened with sour cream or made even more substantial by the addition of pearl barley, Cracow groats, noodles *(łazanki),* dumplings *(uszka),* stuffed with mushrooms or meat, suet balls *(pulpety)* and potato dumplings of various kinds *(pyzy* and *kopytka).* Apart from the ubiquitous *barszcz* (one form of which is traditionally served during the Christmas Eve supper with mushroom-stuffed *uszka),* the soups you're most likely to come across are *kapuśniak* (sauerkraut), *kartoflanka* (potato), *grochówka* (pea soup, often served with croutons), *krupnik* (pearl barley), *grzybowa* (mushroom) and *jarzynowa* (vegetable).

Clear soups, such as *barszcz* or *rosół* (beef bouillon), are often served in cups, accompanied by small hot pasties stuffed with meat or cabbage (*paszteciki* and *kapuśniaczki).* In restaurants specializing in Old Polish cookery (currently springing up all over the place) you'll find traditional *żur* (sour rye or oat soup), *czarnina* (literally, "black soup," made with fresh blood, bones, giblets and dried prunes or cherries!), *zupa piwna* (beer soup) and *zalewajka* (onion soup). *Chłodnik,* which literally means "cooler," is a delicious cold sour-cream soup with crayfish. In summer, sorrel soup *(szczawiowa),* garnished with hard-boiled eggs, is very popular, as are the rather unusual cold summer soups made with puréed fruits such as strawberries, raspberries, apples, cherries or blueberries, and thickened with sour cream.

Meat Dishes

Pork (*wieprzowina*) and beef (*wołowina*) are used a great deal, as is game (*dziczyzna*), which the Poles are very fond of, in particular wild duck with apple *(kaczka),* hare in sour cream *(zając)* and roast venison *(sarnina).* Roast pork loin *(pieczony schab)* is a great treat, generally served with pickled plums and sauerkraut and apple salad.

Other popular Polish dishes are *zrazy zawijane* (mushroom-stuffed beefsteak rolls in sour cream served with boiled rice or *kasza*—buckwheat groats), *gołąbki* (cabbage leaves stuffed with minced beef and rice) and Polish-style *flaki,* which is tripe seasoned with ginger, nutmeg, marjoram and garnished with Parmesan cheese.

Pierogi (pockets of noodle dough stuffed with meat, cabbage or cheese and potatoes) can be a bit heavy, but are consumed in vast quantities by every Pole worth his salt.

The menu will invariably include *bigos,* which must rank as the national dish of Poland. Made with sauerkraut, fresh cabbage, onions and a variety of leftover meats (pork, game, sausage and smoked bacon) it was once traditionally served at hunt meetings and allegedly improves with each reheating (optimum flavor is supposedly reached the seventh time around).

Homegrown Vegetables

Frozen or packaged foods are not popular in Poland, so ingredients are usually fresh and not ruined by chemical additives. Typical vegetable accompaniments *(jarzyny)* and salads *(sałatki)* include sauerkraut garnished with caraway seeds *(kiszona kapusta)*, pickled dill cucumbers *(ogórki kwaszone)*, grated beets with horseradish *(ćwikła)* and sliced fresh cucumbers garnished with dill and served in sour cream or yogurt *(mizeria)*. Grated potato pancakes *(placki kartoflane)*, smothered in sour cream, are absolutely gorgeous—a meal in themselves.

The Ubiquitous Herring

Poland is a great country for fish *(ryba)*, particularly the freshwater variety, which is prepared in a way Westerners may find rather unusual. Try *karp w galarecie* (carp served in a sweet and sour jellied sauce) and *szczupak po Polsku* (poached pike with horseradish and sour cream sauce). Crayfish *(raki)*, boiled and served in a green dill and sour cream sauce, are also extremely popular. The Baltic Sea provides the Poles with cod *(dorsz)* and, of course, the herring *(śledź)*, which they serve in every way imaginable. Salted herring fillet, rolled up tight and served with pickles and onions, features as a starter on most menus, and is traditionally associated with Lent (the high point of the last carnival dance on Shrove Tuesday is marked by the bringing in of a mock herring on a stick).

Refreshing Desserts

Most full-scale Polish meals are best rounded off with a refreshing stewed fruit *kompot,* but if you're feeling adventurous (and not counting the calories) the things to try are fruit or milk *kisiel* (a very popular dessert thickened with potato starch giving it the consistency of a jelly), *knedle* (dumplings stuffed with plums or apples), *pierożki* (dumplings with blueberries, cherries or prunes), *naleśniki* (pancakes with fruit or cheese), *racuszki* (sour-milk pancakes) and *leniwe pierogi* (poached cheese dumplings, which can also appear as a light main course for lunch). *Kutia* is a traditional Christmas Eve dessert made with whole wheat grains, ground poppy seeds and honey.

A Necessary Accompaniment

The national drink of Poland is undoubtedly vodka *(wódka),* which is drunk chilled in staggering quantities before, during and after virtually every meal. *Wyborowa* is the best standard vodka, but you shouldn't leave the country without trying some of the many flavored varieties, such as *żubrówka* (bison grass), *tarniówka* (sloe-plum), *śliwowica* (prune), *jarzębiak* (rowan berry) and *pieprzówka* (vodka with ground white pepper—apparently the local cure for an upset stomach). *Krupnik,* vodka with honey and spices, and *miód* (mead) are extremely popular, as are cherry cordials, such as *wiśniówka* (sweet) and *wiśniak* (dry), which the Poles often make at home on a base of 96° spirits.

Western drinks, such as whiskey, gin or brandy, can be had in most bars, but are expensive. Wine *(wino)* is drunk, but again is imported and between 1580 and 1610 by the enterprising chancellor Jan Zamoyski in a "barren field" on his estates, which stood on the trade route connecting the Black Sea with northern and western Europe. The town was built on the plans of the Italian architect Bernardo Morando and sure enough, much of Zamość bears remarkable resemblance to Italian towns of the same epoch; hence its nickname "the Padua of the North." Dominating the market square is the impressive 16th-century town hall, with a spire that reaches 50 meters (164 ft.) high. You almost expect characters in period costume to come sweeping down its grand entrance staircase. The 16th- and 17th-century arcaded houses round the square and side streets, none of them more than two stories high, are a salutary example of human-scale architecture. The Renaissance St. Thomas Collegiate Church houses a library of manuscripts and rare books.

In Łancut, 17 km. (some 10 miles) east of Rzeszów, visit the 17th-century palace of the Lubomirski family, which has been turned into a museum and picture gallery. Built in a square around an inner courtyard, the palace contains lovely historical furniture, clocks, and Gobelins. In the park is an old coach-house converted into a coach museum; excursions in horse-drawn carriages to explore the surrounding countryside can be arranged. In May an International Festival of Chamber Music is held in the palace's interior.

Right down in the southeastern corner of Poland, in Sanok's History Museum, you'll find Poland's largest collection of icon paintings and other liturgical items. On the other side of the river is an enormous open-air Folk Museum, including among its exhibits an 18th-century Orthodox church, an old mill, and a peasant cottage from 1681. Krosno (about 50 km./31 miles from Sanok) has a Museum of Kerosene Lamps (which were invented in Poland in 1853), and just outside is Bobrka, which has its very own oil-well, dating back to 1854, which is now open to the public.

PRACTICAL INFORMATION FOR LUBLIN

TOURIST INFORMATION. There are Orbis offices in most of the main towns. The principal tourist offices for **Lublin,** who can supply information for the surrounding region, are: *Orbis,* ul. Krakowskie Przedmieście 25 (tel. 27778); *PZM,* ul. Prusa 8; *Central Tourist Information Office,* Krakowskie Przedmieście 78 (tel. 24412). In **Zamość,** go to the TIC at ul. Grodzka 18 (tel. 3001).

WHEN TO COME. Any time of year for Lublin, though summers are obviously warmer. Spring or summer for the Bieszczady Mountains in the southeast. This area is a real paradise for ramblers with miles of ancient forests and lakes.

GETTING AROUND. There is a direct air link from Warsaw to Rzeszów, but not to Lublin, which is only a short distance by road from Warsaw (route E81) or three hours by train. Lublin is included in Orbis tours from Warsaw, as is Rzeszów. Rail and bus networks cover the region.

HOTELS AND RESTAURANTS

All hotels listed below have restaurants unless otherwise stated.

Lublin. *Lublinianka* (M), ul. Krakowskie Przedmieście 56. *Orbis-Unia* (M), al. Racławickie 12. *Victoria* (M), ul. Narutowicza 58/60. *Motel,* ul. Prusa 6. *Almatur Youth Hostel* (I), ul. Langiewicza 20.

Restaurants. Best restaurants are in the Unia, Lublinianka and Victoria hotels. Recommended also are *Europa,* Krakowskie Przedmieście 29, and *Powszechna,* Krakowskie Przedmieście 56, both (M).

Łancut. *Zamkowy* (I). Set at the back of Łancut Castle, the hotel is Poland's most beautiful "English" park; single and double rooms; riding facilities.

Lesko. *Motel* (M), ul. Bieszczadzka 4. A 16th-century castle converted into a delightful 120-bed hotel.

Zamosc. *Jubilat* (M), reader-recommended. *Renaissance* (M), ul. Grecka 6.

POZNAŃ

The Fair City

Situated halfway between Warsaw and Berlin, in the middle of the monot-
onously flat Polish lowlands, Poznań has been an east-west marketplace
for over 1,000 years. During medieval times, merchants made a great point
of bringing their wares here on St. John's Day (June 24), and the annual
tradition has continued. The markets have now been superseded by the
important International Trade Fair, which has been held here since 1922
and has become a major trading point between the communist and capital-
ist worlds.

Up until the 13th century, Poznań was (on and off) the capital of Poland, and in 968 the first Polish bishopric was founded here by Miezko
I. It still remains the capital of the Wielkopolska ("Great Poland") region.
Poznań is a sedate and quiet town, very conscious of its historical role
as the cradle of the Polish state. Architecturally, there's lots to see here,
from Romanesque right through to neo-Classical and even Romantic-
Byzantine. Start your sightseeing in the Old Market Square (Rynek Stare-
go Miasta), with its superb Renaissance Italian-style town hall. Poznań
locals will proudly tell you its the most splendid building in Poland. Best
time to be here is around noon, which is when you can watch the three
famous Poznań goats appear over the town hall clock. The old pillory outside (erected from fines imposed on Poznań prostitutes for wearing exces-
sively extravagant dresses) is only a copy, but you can see the original in
the History Museum of the City of Poznań inside the town hall. The tiny
arcaded shopkeepers' houses by the town hall date back to the mid-16th
century, when they were built to replace the herring stalls that had been

erected here since the middle of the 13th century. At no. 45 is an interesting Museum of Musical Instruments, containing exhibits from all over the world.

Poznań's many historical churches and palaces had to be either rebuilt or greatly restored after the war, since 55% of the town was destroyed during the fighting. Of particular interest are: Działynski Mansion, now a Dom Turysty hotel; Przemysław Castle, former seat of the great Dukes of Poland and now a Museum of Arts and Crafts (particularly interesting is its collection of woven sashes worn by Polish noblemen in the 18th century); the Raczyński Library, built in the 19th century with the Paris Louvre as its model; Gorki Palace, a unique Renaissance structure, with a roof-garden-cum-fishpond; the state ballet school (a former 18th-century Jesuit school), with a lovely Baroque arcaded courtyard; a Baroque parish church with 17th-century stuccos and wall paintings; and Poznań's oldest brick structure, the Church of St. John, built in about 1187 by the Knights Hospitallers of St. John of Jerusalem.

Ostrów Tumski (Cathedral Island), an islet in the Warta river, is the historic cradle of the town. This is where the Polanie tribe built their first fortified settlement and their first basilica in the 10th century. The present cathedral was rebuilt after the war in 15th-century Gothic, but 10th- and 11th-century remains can be seen in a special crypt, (a baptismal font and the supposed tombs of Poland's first kings—Mieszko I and Bolesław Chrobry). The Golden Chapel, containing the sarcophagi of these two kings, is worth seeing for the sheer opulence of its Romantic-Byzantine style (1840), an extraordinary contrast with the stark bricks of the nave.

Of more recent interest is the huge monument erected in memory of the workers killed by the police during disturbances here in 1956. Situated in Plac Mickiewicza, it is one of the only officially recognized testimonies to civil unrest in Eastern Europe.

Music features large in Poznań. It is the home of the famous Poznań Boys' Choir—"Słowiki" (nightingales)—the State Philharmonic and the Henryk Wieniawski International Violin Competition, which is held here every five years.

Around Poznań

For nature lovers and the sport-minded, the Wielkopolski National Park southwest of Poznań is a marvelous place for a day trip out of town. It has 16 lakes set in pine forests full of many different types of birds and game. Lake Rusałka and Lake Strzeszynek have long beaches, tourist accommodations and water sports equipment for hire. Kiekrz is the place for sailing enthusiasts. Splendid legends abound here. At the bottom of Lake Góreckie, for example, there is supposed to be a submerged town, and on still nights if you're very lucky you can hear the faint ringing of the town bells, although it's probably nothing more eerie than water birds calling.

The old town of Kórnik, 20 km. (12 miles) southeast of Poznań, is worth visiting for its moated medieval castle housing a museum of old furniture, pictures, and hunting trophies, as well as an enormous library of incunabula and rare books (over 150,000 volumes including manuscripts by Mickiewicz and Słowacki). Watch your feet—you'll be walking on some really magnificent wooden inlaid floors. The castle, remodeled in the 19th century in English Mock Gothic, stands in Poland's largest arboretum.

In Rogalin, 12 km. (eight miles) from Kórnik, you'll find an 18th-century Rococo-Classical palace containing a folkcraft collection and paintings by French Impressionists. Some of the oaks in the park around the palace are said to be over 1,000 years old; and three hoary old giants, measuring about nine meters (30 ft.) around the middle, have been christened "Lech," "Czech" and "Rus," the three legendary founder-brothers of the Slavic nations.

Gniezno and the "Piast Route" to "Pompeii"

For a trip along Poland's folk memory lane, take the *Piast Route* from Poznań to Kruszwica, 105 km. (65 miles) away in the northeast. First stop is Gniezno, residence of the first Polish rulers and Poland's legendary birthplace. According to legend it was here that Lech, one of the three Slav brothers, decided to build his city when he found white eagles nesting on the site. The white eagle was adopted as the new nation's symbol, which it has been ever since, and the settlement was named *Gniezno,* meaning nesting site in Polish. The most important monument in Gniezno is the cathedral, restored to its basic Gothic after the war (traces of a late 10th-century, Romanesque cathedral were uncovered during rebuilding). Many of the cathedral treasures were plundered during the occupation, but luckily not the amazing Gniezno Door, an enormous pair of 12th-century Romanesque doors cast in bronze and covered with intricate bas-relief scenes from the life of St. Adalbert whose tomb is inside the cathedral (the doors are now kept in the chapel behind the presbytery). St. Adalbert—or St. Wojciech to the Poles—was the first Polish saint (actually a Czech missionary) who was martyred by pagans. It is said that his body was ransomed from its murderers by its weight in gold, which the Poles paid ungrudgingly.

On now to Biskupin (29 km./18 miles northeast of Gniezno), where you can visit the largest, best preserved, prehistoric fortified swamp settlement in Europe. This 40-hectare (100-acre), 2,500-year-old "Polish Pompeii" was discovered by archeologists at the bottom of a lake near Biskupin village. Parts of it have been reconstructed and you can take yourself back into the Stone Age by wandering along the wood-paved streets and peering into the small wooden huts.

Kruszwica, a small town on Lake Gopło, 105 km. (65 miles) from Poznań, is the final stop on the Piast Route. The place has legends galore about the Piast dynasty and the founding of the Polish state, probably reflecting the tribal battles fought by the Polans and Goplans for supremacy. The most popular centers on Mysia Wieża (Mouse Tower), the only surviving part of a brick castle built in 1320 by Casimir the Great. This is where the cruel king Popiel is said to have made his exit, pursued not by a bear but by hordes of ravenous, vengeful mice (Popiel had in a fit of pique poisoned his dinner guests, who were casting envious eyes on his throne, and thrown them in the lake; mice had emerged out of the bodies, besieging Popiel in his tower until he starved to death).

The other legend is of course about Piast, the humble cartwright, and how he became king. Piast's son was having his hair cut for the first time on his seventh birthday to mark his passage from the nursery into his father's strict care, when two beautiful strangers knocked on the door. Piast welcomed them and asked them to perform the rite of cutting the boy's hair. They did so, baptized the child and prophesied that Piast would one day found a dynasty. The Lake Gopło area is a picturesque landscape reserve.

PRACTICAL INFORMATION FOR POZNAŃ

TOURIST INFORMATION. The two main tourist offices are: *Orbis,* pl. Dąbrowskiego 1 (tel. 330–221) and *PZM,* ul. Ratajczaka 44 (tel. 59726). The Tourist Information Center is on Stary Rynek 77 (tel. 56156).

WHEN TO COME. The main event of the year is the International Trade Fair in June, which has been held annually for over 50 years. The Henryk Wieniawski International Violin Competition is held in November. Summers are warm, with water sports on the nearby lakes, set among pine forests.

GETTING AROUND. There are regular connections by air from Warsaw, which are more frequent during the Trade Fair. Fast train (3 hours) connections also exist, though traveling by car gives you more freedom. Poznań lies on two main routes, E8 and E83 and is also included in Orbis tours from Warsaw.

HOTELS AND RESTAURANTS

All hotels listed below have restaurants unless otherwise stated. During the fair, accommodations can be very hard to find. It is advisable to book well in advance if you plan to visit Poznań during this period.

Expensive

Orbis-Merkury, ul. Roosevelta 15–20 (tel. 408 01). 351 rooms, 42 suites; every comfort.
Orbis-Novotel, ul. Warszawska 64 (tel. 700 41). 154 double rooms with bath.
Orbis-Polonez, ul. Stalingradzka 54/68 (tel. 699 141). 408 rooms, most with bath.
Orbis-Poznan, ul. gen. Dąbrowskiego 1 (tel. 332 081). 425 rooms, 20 suites.

Moderate

Lech, ul. Czerwonej Armii 74 (tel. 60051).
Orbis-Bazar, al. Marcinkowskiego 10 (tel. 512 51). 89 rooms, all with bath.
Poznanski, Marcinkowskiego 10 (tel. 51251).
Wielkopolska, ul. Czerwonej Armii 67 (tel. 576 31). 106 rooms, most with bath.

Restaurants. Poznań eating places are apt to be very crowded during the fair. Apart from those in the hotels mentioned above, you can eat and dance at the following (all M–E). *Adria,* ul. Głogowska 17; *Magnolia,* ul. Głogowska 40; *Moulin Rouge,* ul. Kantaka 8/9; *Piracka,* Park Sołacki; *Pod Koziołkami,* Stary Rynek 63; *Smakosz,* ul. 27 Grudnia 8; *U Dylla,* Stary Rynek 37; *Darz Bór,* ul. Libelta 37.

Cafes. *Ewa,* ul. Dąbrowskiego 12; *Literacka,* Stary Rynek 46; *Filmowa,* ul. Gwardii Ludowej 36.

MUSEUMS. *Archeological Museum,* ul. Wodna 27; *Army Museum,* Stary Rynek 45; *Museum of Musical Instruments,* Stary Rynek 9; *National Museum,* ul. Marcinkowskiego 9.

THEATERS, ENTERTAINMENT. *Poznań State Philharmonic,* ul. Stalingradska 1; *St. Moniuszko Opera,* ul. Fredry 9; *State Theater,* ul. 22 Grudnia 8–10. The best nightclubs are in the Orbis hotels.

WROCŁAW AND THE
SOUTHWEST

Youth and Health

Situated midway between Cracow and Poznań on the Odra river, Wrocław, the capital of Lower Silesia, dates back to the 10th century when Ostrów Tumski islet on the Odra became a fortified Slav settlement. There are now some 100 bridges spanning the city's 90-km. (56-mile) network of slow-moving canals and tributaries, giving it its particular charming character. Indeed, after Venice and Leningrad, Wrocław is the city with the third-largest number of bridges in Europe. The other overwhelming impression you will get is of the extraordinary preponderance of young people—almost half of the population is under 30 years old—something which is reflected in the large number of institutions of higher learning in the city.

Having suffered tremendous losses during the last war, Wrocław has worked hard to restore its old buildings. Sightseeing should start in the market square, which is almost as grand as the one in Cracow. The dominant feature here is the Town Hall, basically Gothic with a dash of Renaissance and Baroque. There is a Historical Museum inside. Of the many old houses around the square, with their characteristic steep gables, the two little Hansel-and-Gretel houses are particularly appealing, coyly holding hands over a linking arcade.

Ostrów Tumski (Cathedral Island—though it's no longer an island) is the cradle of Wrocław and one of its most charming olde-worlde quarters.

Dominating it is the impressive Gothic cathedral, with a high altar that has been ascribed to the workshop of Wit Stwosz, the famous 15th-century master sculptor. On the other side of the river are two fine Baroque buildings. One is the University of pl. Uniwersytecki (occupying a former Jesuit Academy built in 1728–42) which has a magnificent assembly hall, the Aula Leopoldina, with some rather lush frescoes. The other, in ul. Szweska, is the Ossolineum National Institution which houses the biggest collection of manuscripts and old prints in Poland. Unfortunately, this whole area lacks cafes and other amenities for the visitor, so plan your refreshments for either before or after you venture out this way.

Wrocław buzzes with culture, which is reflected in the many artistic festivals held here each year and its flourishing experimental theater groups, particularly Henryk Tomaszewski's pantomine theater and the world-famous Jerzy Grotowski Laboratory Theater. Following in the footsteps of Stanislawski, the great Russian theoretician, Grotowski places the actor in the heart of theatrical spectacle. His austere and serious theater, often described as "bare" and "essential," places enormous demands on actor and public alike, but gives them in return a unique spiritual and artistic experience.

Surrounding Sights

The countryside around Wrocław is particularly rich in architecture, and every small town and hamlet seems to have its four-star monument. The following are all within 80 km. (50 miles) of Wrocław and worth visiting, perhaps on your way to the Karkonosze Mountains bordering Czechoslovakia. Lubiąż (famous Cistercian Abbey); Henryków (an equally fine Cistercian Abbey); Świdnica, the medieval capital of the Piast dukes (Gothic church); Bolków (13th-century castle); Bolesławiec (Baroque houses and town hall, defense walls); Legnica, the site of the famous battle against the Tartar hordes in 1241 (Baroque church with magnificent murals); Oleśnica (14th-century castle); Trzebnica (Romanesque-Gothic basilica rebuilt in the 18th century, with two surviving tympana from about 1230–40); Opole (14th-century Piast Tower); Paczków, a magnificent little town, a kind of Polish Carcassonne, completely ringed by medieval walls with towers and bastions.

Into the Valley of Health

Wrocław is a good jumping-off point for touring the holiday resorts and spas in the southwest of the country, and in the Kłodzko valley you'll find some of Poland's most famous spas. Kudowa-Zdrój (zdrój means "spa" in Polish by the way) was once visited by Winston Churchill; situated in a deep, sheltered valley it was a popular health resort as early as the 17th century. In July it plays host to the Moniuszko Festival, celebrating the creator of the Polish opera style. The ghoulish might like to visit the Skull Chapel in Czermna (two km./one mile to the north), which is lined with thousands of human skulls and bones. Behind Kudowa-Zdrój, sheltering it from the north wind, stretch the Stołowe (Table) Mountains, a labyrinth of gorges, ravines, and really extraordinary rock formations.

Of the other spas in the area—Lądek-Zdrój, Polanica-Zdrój and Duszniki-Zdrój—the last is perhaps the most famous. An annual Chopin festival (mid-August) takes place in the small spa theater in which the 16-year-old Chopin once gave two public concerts to raise money for some orphaned children while he was staying here for treatment.

Skiing Country

Further west is the Jelenia Góra valley, with its main ski resorts of Karpacz and Szklarska Poręba situated on the thickly wooded slopes of the Karkonosze, the highest range of the Sudety Mountains. The climate is fairly severe here, with heavy snowfalls, so skiing conditions are exceptionally good. Karpacz has a bob-sleigh track and a ski lift up the slopes of Mount Śniezka, (1,602 meters/5,257 ft.). While you're up here try and see the local curiosity in Bierutowice (in upper Karpacz). This is a 13th-century wooden church that originally stood on Lake Wang in Norway. In 1841 Frederick William IV of Prussia brought it over lock, stock, and altar and erected it on the present site. Even now after more than 100 years, the Romanesque-cum-Viking elements carved on the doorpost look strangely alien here.

PRACTICAL INFORMATION FOR
THE SOUTHWEST

TOURIST INFORMATION. The main tourist offices for **Wrocław** are: *Orbis,* Rynek 29 (tel. 34780) and ul. Świerczewskiego 62 (tel. 38745); *PZM,* pl. Solny 15 (tel. 38058). For **Duszniki-Zdrój,** ul. Wojska Polskiego 6 (tel. 349); **Jelenia Góra,** ul. 1 Maja 1 (tel. 26521); **Karpacz,** ul. 1 Maja 50 (tel. 547); **Kłodzko,** ul. Grottgera 1 (tel. 2775); **Kudowa-Zdrój,** ul. Zdrojowa 27 (tel. 266); **Świdnica,** Rynek 31 (tel. 22658).

WHEN TO COME. From August through September, the "Wratislavia Cantans" Festival of Oratorio and Cantata Music is held in Wrocław. A Chopin Festival of Music is held at Duszniki-Zdrój in August. From November to May, there are excellent winter sports facilities in the southwest. The spas are open year-round. The "Jazz on the Odra" Festival is held near Wrocław in May.

GETTING AROUND. There are regular connections by air from Warsaw to Wrocław; trains (6 hours) and buses complete the network. Four international road routes run through this region—E14, E22, E83, and E12.

HOTELS AND RESTAURANTS

All hotels listed below have restaurants unless otherwise stated.

Duszniki-Zdrój. *Pod Muflonem* chalet, ul. Górska 14 (tel. 337); private accommodations office is at Rynek 14 (tel. 540).

Jelenia Góra. *Cieplice* (I), ul. Cervill. *Europejski* (I), ul. 1 Maja 16; *PTTK Tourist Hostel,* ul. 1 Maja 88.
Two good **restaurants** are *Karczma Staropolska* (M), ul. 1 Maja 35, and *Pod Różami* (M), ul. Piastowska 26, which is just outside the town.

Karpacz. *Orbis Skalny* (E), ul. Obrońców Pokoju 5 (tel. 721); *Orlinek* (M), ul. Olimpijska 9; private accommodations office is at ul. 1 Maja 8.
Restaurant. *Patria,* ul. Słowackiego 9.

Kłodzko. *Astoria* (I), pl. Jedności 1 (tel. 3035) also handles all private accommodations.

An acceptable **restaurant** is *Wilcza Jama*, ul. Grottgera 5.

Kudowa-Zdrój. *Kosmos* (I), ul. Buczka 8a.
Restaurant. *Piekiełko*, ul. Moniuszki 2.

Świdnica. *Piast* (M), ul. K. Marksa 11. Two good **restaurants** (both M) are *Stylowa*, with Hungarian interior and food (try their *halasle* fish soup), and *Zagloba*, ul. Wrocławska 46, a tavern serving Old Polish dishes, specialty of spiced hot mead.

Wrocław. *Europejski* (M), ul. Świerczewskiego 88. *Grand* (M), ul. Świerczewskiego 102 (tel. 33983). *Novotel-Orbis* (E), ul. Wyścigowa 31 (tel. 675–051). 154 rooms, restaurant, outdoor swimming pool. *Orbis-Monopol* (M), ul. Modrzejewskiej 2 (tel. 37041), has good restaurant. *Orbis-Panorama* (M), pl. Dzierżyńskiego 8 (tel. 34681). *Orbis-Wrocław* (M), ul. Powstanców Śląskich 7 (tel. 654 651). Modern and centrally located with all mod cons.

Restaurants and Cafes. *Lotus*, ul. Grabiszyńska 9, *Stylowa*, pl. Kościuszki 1/4, (both E). *Bieriozka*, ul. Nowotki 13 (Russian food) and *Lajkonik*, ul. Nowowiejska 102 (both M). *Herbowa*, Rynek 19, is a tearoom-cafe with no smoking upstairs. *Polonez*, pl. Hirszfelda. The cafe in the hotel Grand is also atmospheric.

MUSEUMS. Wrocław: *Archeological Museum*, ul. Kazimierza Wielkiego 34; *Historical Museum*, Town Hall; *National Museum*, pl. Powstanców Warszawy 5.

THEATERS AND CONCERTS. Wrocław. *State Opera House*, ul. Świdnicka 35; *Wrocław Operetta*, ul. Swierczewskiego 67; *Pantomime Theater*, al. Dębowa 15; *Polish Theater*, ul. Zapolskiej 3.

THE NORTHEAST

Land of a Thousand Lakes

In the northeast of Poland—formerly part of East Prussia—lies a land of 1,000 lakes, 1,000-year-old forests; and thousands of mosquitoes. Hardly known to western tourists, the Mazurian and Augustów-Suwałki lakes form an intriguing labyrinth of interconnecting lakes, rivers, and canals, set in ancient forests teeming with birds and wild animals. Whatever you're looking for—a "back to nature" type of holiday, sailing, canoeing, hunting with a gun or camera, foraging for mushrooms (the national pastime), fishing, or even ice-sailing on the frozen Mazurian lakes in winter—you'll find it here.

The area's 90 nature reserves are a paradise for both birds and animals, some of them now extremely rare and found only in zoos elsewhere in Europe. In the Borecka Forest, 25 km. (15 miles) northeast of Giżycko, lives a wild herd of European bison, some 300 strong, while at Popielno on Lake Śniardwy there are wild tarpan ponies, the smallest forest ponies in the world, which until recently were on their way to becoming extinct. The largest herd of elk (300 head) in Europe can be spotted in the Czerwone Bagno (Red Swamp) reserve, 12 km. (eight miles) southeast of Rajgród, not far from Augustów. Other less exotic animals include lynx, roedeer, foxes, and beavers (particularly on the Pasłęka river). Shoots are organized for wild goose, duck, wood grouse, and black grouse, but you'll need a permit. Take along your camera to take shots of the area's protected eagles circling the sky, nesting grey herons on Lake Śniardwy and the largest concentration of mute swans in Europe on Lake Luknajno. Ostrów Wysoki island on Lake Mamry is the place for cormorants.

So large are some of the lakes that they're known as the "Mazurian seas;" there's no pollution as yet since the Poles very sensibly don't let motor boats into some of the waterways (good news, too, for those who don't like the constant whine of outboard motors). Fish thrive here and anglers can hook salmon, trout, miller's thumb, European whitefish, eel, pike, and many other fish characteristic of foothill and lowland regions. A special treat is hunting for crayfish by torchlight and fishing with nets for delicious bleak and lavaret on Mamry and Wigry lakes in depths of up to 40 meters (131 ft.)

This sparsely populated area also has its ethnic oddities, in the form of a sect of Russian Old Believers who settled in these parts in the 17th century. In several of their close communities people still speak an archaic form of Russian and keep to their religious practices. They intermarry and the men are not allowed to shave their beards.

The Mazurian lakes are synonymous with sailing, however. Here the wind can almost always be guaranteed, averaging 3–5 on the Beaufort scale for about 70 percent of the time. For canoeists the chains of interconnected lakes and rivers offer some of the finest routes in the country. Best are the Łyna and Krutynia rivers and the Czarna Hańcza, perhaps the prettiest and most winding river in the country. While in the Augustów area take a trip down the Augustów Canal, built in 1824–39 to link the Vistula and Niemen basins. The old canal buildings and locks have been carefully preserved.

Olsztyn is the principal city, and Giżycko, Mikołajki, Ruciane-Nida, Węgorzewo, and Augustów are among the main resorts. In addition to inexpensive hotels and boarding houses, self-catering cottages can be rented through the Mazur Tourist Enterprise, who also arrange all kinds of special interest facilities, such as boat or bicycle hire, photo-safaris, and sailing holidays. Try their "Baked Potato Holiday" in mid-September, which includes a ride on a horse-drawn farmer's wagon, ending in bonfireside tastings of the region's culinary specialties.

Copernicus Country

In this part of Poland every other town—Lidzbark Warmiński, Olsztyn, Malbork, and Frombork—seems to have some connection with the great Polish astronomer who was born in Toruń over 500 years ago. As befitted a Renaissance man Copernicus was able to turn his hand to most things and in the years 1516–21 successfully directed the defense of Olsztyn castle against the Knights of the Teutonic Order. In Frombork, where he spent 30 years of his life, Copernicus was elected canon of the cathedral. This meant lifelong financial security, enabling him to make some of his most famous discoveries. Adjoining the massive Gothic cathedral that dominates the town is the Nicolaus Copernicus Museum, where you can see a Mercator atlas of 1595 and a 1617 copy of Copernicus's *De Revolutionibus Orbium Coelestium* (On the Revolutions of the Celestial Spheres) explaining his theory of a heliocentric universe. Lidzbark Warmiński, where Copernicus was employed by the bishop of Warmia as a personal-cum-medical secretary, has a monumental Gothic castle which survived the war only because the local population refused to help the Germans demolish it. It is one of the best preserved examples of secular medieval architecture in Poland and has been turned into a museum.

The Wolf's Den

In Gierłoż Forest, about eight km. (five miles) from Kętrzyn, stand the ruins of a massive concrete bunker known as the "Wolf's Den," the headquarters of Hitler's general staff during World War II, which the Nazis themselves blew up in 1945. An unsuccessful attempt on Hitler's life was made here on 28 August 1944.

Two places worth stopping off at between Kętrzyn and Lidzbark Warmiński are Święta Lipka, a beautiful 17th-century Baroque church built with donations collected from all over Poland, and Reszel, with its Gothic parish church, Gothic bridge, and old houses and granaries. But if you're more interested in regional folk architecture, the place to go is the Olsztynek open-air folk museum, featuring a small Mazurian thatch-roofed church, inn, mill, forge, old windmills, and thatched cottages, some of which have been furnished period-style.

For a wolf of another order, take a detour to the Grunwald Battlefield several kilometers west of Olsztynek and the E81, the site of the greatest battle of the Middle Ages. Here, on 15 July 1410, Władysław Jagiełło and his Polish-Lithuanian army annihilated the Grand Master of the Teutonic Order, Ulrich von Jungingen, and thousands of his knights. A small museum on the site (open summer only, 10 to 10) graphically explains the course of the battle.

PRACTICAL INFORMATION FOR
THE NORTHEAST

TOURIST INFORMATION. There are tourist information centers at **Olsztyn**, in the pavillion at Wysoka Brama (tel. 22738), and **Suwałki**, ul. Kościuszki 37 (tel. 5961). Orbis offices can arrange anything from standard holidays to rented cottages, scuba diving to photo safaris. Their offices are located in **Augustów**, pl. Krasickiego 12 (tel. 2613); **Elbląg**, ul. Hetmańska 23 (tel. 22364); **Ełk**, ul. Mickiewicza 15 (tel. 3573); **Giżycko**, ul. Dąbrowskiego 3 (tel. 3112).

WHEN TO COME. The main season of interest is summer, but Orbis organizes winter-break holidays that include sleigh-rides, skiing, sledging, skating, and ice-hole angling.

GETTING AROUND. There are direct rail and road connections with Warsaw. Passenger steamers through the lakes operate from Giżycko and boats and canoes may be hired through Orbis. You can tour the forest by coach or private car. Orbis also organize a Copernicus sightseeing tour from Warsaw.

HOTELS AND RESTAURANTS

All hotels listed below have restaurants unless otherwise stated.

Augustów. *Stara Poczta* (I), ul. 1 Maja 73; *Motel* (I), ul. Mazurska 4 (tel. 2867); *PTTK Tourist Hostel*, ul. Sportowa 1.

Białystok. *Cristal* (I), ul. Lipowa 3; *Leśny* (I), ul. Zwycięstwa (tel. 511 641); *Turkus* (I), ul. Zwycięstwa 54.

Elbląg. *Dworcowy* (I), al. Grunwaldzka 49; *Nowina Inn* (I), on E81 highway towards Warsaw (tel. 43182); *Żuławy* (I), al. Armii Czerwonej 126.
Restaurant. *Karczma Słupska* (M), ul. Krótka 1.

Frombork. *PTTK Tourist Hostel* (I), in cathedral precincts; *Słoneczny* (I), ul. Kościelna 2 (tel. 7285).

Giżycko. *Mazurski* (I), pl. Grunwaldzki 17. *Wodnik* (I), ul. 1 Maja 7 (tel. 3872). Two good restaurants, both (M) are: *Centralna* and *Wodnik* (in the hotel of the same name).

Lidzbark Warmiński. *PTTK Tourist Hostel* (I), in the High Gate.

Mrągowo. *Mrongovia* (E), ul. PPR 6 (tel. 3222). A modern, fully equipped hotel with sporting and outdoor activity facilities and restaurant. Picturesque location.

Olsztyn. *Orbis-Novotel* (M), ul. Sielska 4 (tel. 24081). Modern hotel with 98 rooms and swimming pool. *Gromada-Kormoran* (I), ul. Kościuszki 6. *Warmiński* (I), ul. Głowackiego 8.
Restaurants. *Nowoczesna* (E); *Pod Żaglami* (M).

Suwałki. *Hańcza* (I), ul. Wojska Polskiego 1 (tel. 3281). *Motel,* ul. Mazurska 1.

MUSEUMS. Frombork: *Nicolaus Copernicus Museum,* Wzgórze Katedralne; **Lidzbark Warmiński,** *Castle Museum,* pl. Zamkowy; **Olsztynek:** *Museum of Folk Buildings (Skansen),* ul. Sportowa 5. Timber houses of many styles and periods from all over Poland. Well worth a visit.

ROMANIA

ROMANIA—FACTS AT YOUR FINGERTIPS

HOW TO GO. A note of warning is necessary. Romania's serious economic problems, whose effects are discussed where appropriate in this chapter, have resulted in some complaints from readers about the conditions they encountered while on holiday there – usually with regard to material comforts or bureaucratic frustration. Although the State imposes no restrictions on the movements of independent travelers, food shortages and strict rationing, the price of fuel and inadequate street lighting, as well as unfavorable rates of exchange, may be quite enough to deter one from undertaking what will be at best, an extraordinarily rewarding adventure and at worst, a trial. Added to this, independent travel is often twice as expensive as any prepaid arrangements. The cushioned benefits of a package tour to one of the main tourist centers – the Black Sea summer or Carpathian skiing resorts – are much more confidently recommended. Prepaid arrangements are always very moderately priced.

All foreign travel to Romania is organized by the Romanian National Tourist Office, which is run by the Ministry of Tourism. They have a number of offices overseas dispensing advice and information, but they do not book tours to Romania. This can be done through any travel agent cooperating with the National Tourist Office. There are a good many of these, however, so booking your vacation should prove no problem, and a list of some of these agents is available free from the National Tourist Office. When you apply for the list, be sure to specify special interests you may want to follow in Romania as some agents make a point of featuring activities such as motoring, walking, bird-watching, archeology and so on.

In Romania itself, there are three main offices of the National Tourist Office (O.N.T.), giving out information and handling most tourist services: O.N.T. Carpați-București, 7 Magheru Blvd., Bucharest 1; O.N.T. Litoral, București Hotel, Mamaia; and O.N.T. Carpați-Brașov, covering the city of Brașov and nearby winter sports area of Poiana Brașov. In addition, there are county tourist offices known as U.J.T. in most towns and resorts.

The addresses of Romanian National Tourist Offices overseas are:
In the U.S.: 573 Third Ave., New York, NY 10016 (tel. 212–697–6971).
In the U.K.: 29 Thurloe Place, London SW7 2HP (tel. 01–584–8090).

TOURS. From the U.S.: Romania is the legendary home of Count Dracula, which provides the basis of several tours. *Litoral Travel* offers a "Dracula Tour", two weeks through bloodsucking country from $1,299. *Victory Tours* combine a "Dracula Tour", with a Danube cruise for $1,450. On a somewhat less spectacular level, Romania is also famous for its health spas. *Health and Pleasure Tours* especially offer two to three weeks at various spas for $1,100, including airfares. Spa tours include medical examinations and treatment. Others also offer two-three weeks in Bucharest from $1,360 double occupancy. *ETS* offer three weeks' treatment and full board in a deluxe hotel in Bucharest for $2,439.

ETS Tours, Inc., 5 Penn Plaza, New York, NY 10001 (800–346–6314; in NY, 212–563–0780).

Health & Pleasure Tours, 165 W. 46th St., New York, NY 10036 (212–586–1775).

Litoral Travel, 124 E. 40th St., Suite 403, New York NY 10016 (tel. 212–986–4210).

Victory Tours, 500 Fifth Ave., New York, NY 10110 (tel. 212–840–5964).

From the U.K., two weeks at a Black Sea resort with full board and return flight is £200–400 per person according to hotel and season. There are substantial reductions for children. *Romanian Holidays* offer a variety of reasonably priced tours and will assist with the special requirements of independent travelers.

An attractive option is to take a Danube cruise from Vienna via such ports of call as Budapest and Belgrade, through the spectacular Iron Gates to Turnu Severin and Giurgiu. This is combined with a stay in Bucharest and the mountain resort of Sinaia.

Motoring holidays are also marketed ex-U.K., either using your own car or fly-drive facilities. For the latter, the cost for 14 days works out at £300–375 according to season per person (if two), covering return flight, a week with full board on the coast, half board while on tour, seven days' car hire with unlimited mileage, car insurance and visa. A system of prepaid vouchers for camping sites or hotels guarantees accommodations while on tour.

Special-interest packages from the U.K. include art treasure tours and walking holidays. Within Romania, ONT offer a range of cultural or sports vacations, though these are mostly geared to groups rather than individuals.

Romanian Holidays, 54 Pembroke Rd., London W8 6NX (01–602–7094).

VISAS. Visitors from North America and the U.K. will require a visa, which can be obtained from any Romanian Embassy or on arrival at any entry point. However, potential delays may be avoided by obtaining it in advance. At press time, the cost of a tourist visa for British subjects, available from the Consular Section of the Romanian Embassy, 4 Palace Green, London W8, was £20 (except in the case of prepaid arrangements, when it is included in the price). American citizens should write to the Romanian Consulate, 1607 23rd St. NW, Washington DC 20008 enclosing a letter requesting a tourist visa (there is no application form or photograph necessary) and stating the length of stay, plus a valid U.S. passport, a money order for $20 and a SASE. Canadians should make their applications to the Romanian Consulate, 655 Rideau St., Ottawa, Ontario KIN 8A3. Once in Romania, visas can be extended by local police authorities.

MONEY. It is important to note that visitors to Romania *must* exchange a sum of $10, or its equivalent, per adult per day for the number of days for which they have requested a visa. Children under 14 years are exempt from this. If you have booked on a prepaid tour you will already have met this requirement, but if you have no prepaid services, you will be required to exchange the minimum sum on arrival in Romania.

The unit of currency in Romania is the leu (plural lei) which is divided into 100 bani. There are coins of 15 and 25 bani and 1, 3 and 5 lei; banknotes are in denominations of 10, 25, 50 and 100 lei.

You may bring in any amount of foreign currency, including travelers' checks, and exchange them at branches of the National Bank of Romania, most border crossings and major hotels. The import and export of Romanian currency is not permitted. All exchanges, beyond the minimum daily exchange rate (see below) can be refunded in hard currency on your departure though problems have been reported. Be sure to keep all exchange receipts.

The tourist exchange rate was about 9 lei to the U.S. dollar and 15 lei to the pound sterling at the time of writing (mid-1988). There is an active blackmarket in foreign currency which you are strongly advised to avoid. Penalties for illegal currency dealing are severe. However, packets of Kent cigarettes continue to speed up service, achieve the "impossible" and, like chocolate, coffee and toiletries, are almost essential as barter when touring the remoter regions of the country.

Credit Cards. Travelers' checks and credit cards, such as American Express, Carte Blanche, Eurocard and Barclaycard may be used to exchange currency and are accepted in most major hotels, though not in restaurants.

COSTS. A holiday in Romania will seem a bargain to package tourists who benefit from reductions of up to 30%, but overpriced to the independent traveler who may encounter bad exchange rates, unreliable standards of cuisine and a shortage of inexpensive accommodations. Travel by both air and train is good value.

Sample Costs. A one-mile taxi ride will cost around 10 lei; Romanian cigarettes 7–20 lei; Metro 2 lei; a bottle of wine in a good restaurant 150 lei, 30 lei from a shop; imported beer 25 lei, 10 lei from a shop; museum entrance 5–12 lei.

INSURANCE. Both personal insurance and insurance against loss are always a wise precaution. The Romanians have many admirable qualities, but personal possessions left unattended are liable to disappear, so take extra care. A small word of warning: attempts to obtain the usual written confirmation (for insurance purposes) that a loss has been reported to the police have been known to fail. In such situations, there is little you can usefully do.

It makes sense to take out health insurance before traveling. Emergency treatment is free but otherwise medical assistance is provided by hospitals and health units all over Romania at charges comparable with average European rates.

CLIMATE. If you're a beach-and-swimming enthusiast, opt for a summer visit to the Black Sea; the resorts don't start coming alive until mid to late May. The best time for touring the interior is any time from late spring to fall; in winter, there are increasing skiing facilities in the Carpathian resorts. Bucharest is at its best in the spring, though its cultural life is year round.

Romania's climate is of the temperate-continental type, and is generally mild and free of extremes, though it can be very hot in inland areas in high summer. Beach resorts average 12 hours of summer sunshine a day.

Average maximum daily temperatures in Fahrenheit and centigrade:

	Jan.	Feb.	Mar.	Apr.	May	June	July	Aug.	Sept.	Oct.	Nov.	Dec.
Bucharest												
F°	34	39	50	64	73	81	86	86	77	64	50	39
C°	1	4	10	18	23	27	30	30	25	18	10	4

SPECIAL EVENTS. The folkloric tradition is still very much alive in Romania, not only as part of the every day life of country folks, but as represented by a number of festivals or traditional customs of a more local nature. First, there are the annual ceremonies connected with various mountains once considered holy, a few of which survive today, the best known being the Celebration of Mount Ceahlău at Durău, Moldavia, on a Sunday in August. The Fair of the Girls on Mount Găina, Transylvania, in July is another regular colorful event; as is The Hora at Prislop on the Transylvanian-Moldavian border. The "Vintage Celebration" at Odobeşti and the "Vintage Car Rally," from Bucharest to Poiana-Braşov and back, both take place in September. Some regions also go in for big winter festivals and one of the biggest is at Sighetu Marmaţiei in Maramureş over the Christmas period, when folk masks feature prominently. And there are many other folkloric song and dance festivals, parades, contests and crafts fairs worth investigating if you are in the right area at the right time. The Ministry of Tourism publish an annual calendar of such events.

Other celebrations are less specifically timed and you need luck on your side to coincide with them. Many are connected with the rhythm of the rural calendar: for example, harvest time, or the departure of the sheep to mountain pastures in spring and their return in autumn. In some regions (notably Maramureş and Bucovina), Easter brings everyone out in their finest costumes, and on the previous Sunday the custom of taking willow branches to church to be blessed is still widely maintained; but remember Easter dates are usually different according to the Orthodox calendar.

National Holidays: Jan. 1 (New Year's Day); Jan. 2; May 1 (Labor Day); May 2; Aug. 23 (Liberation Day); Aug. 24.

CUSTOMS. Personal belongings may be brought in without declaration including the following: a reasonable amount of jewelry, two cameras and 24 cassettes or 10 rolls of film, one small movie camera and 10 rolls of movie film, binoculars, tape recorder, portable radio, portable typewriter, camping and sports equipment. Some other items may need to be declared at the border so if in doubt check. You may also bring in 2 liters of liquor, 4 liters of wine or beer, 200 cigarettes, and gifts up to the value of 2,000 lei. Purchases up to 1,000 lei in value may be exported, as can items bought for foreign currency in the special Comturist shops, so keep your receipts. Antiques, rare books, etc., may only be exported with special authorization. For currency regulations, see *Money*.

LANGUAGE. Romanian is a Romance language with some Slavonic, Turkish, Magyar and French additions. German, Russian and Hungarian are also spoken in some areas. French is widely spoken and understood; English is spoken by members of the travel industry, so in major resorts at least you should have few difficulties communicating. Romanian schoolchildren are required to study two widely-spoken foreign languages, choosing between German, English, French or Russian.

HOTELS. Nearly all hotels marketed overseas and used by western visitors belong to the Ministry of Tourism. It is worth noting, however, that there are others belonging to Consumer Cooperatives or city or local councils, some of them excellent. It is highly advisable to make advance reservations, but if you have not done so, bookings can be made through local ONT or ACR (Romanian Automobile Club) offices, or direct with the hotel. In this case, should you want to pay in lei, you must have proof of official money exchange. All hotels in principle are instructed to keep a few rooms available for foreign visitors until 8 P.M.

In due course, Romania will change to the international star system of hotel classification, but for the moment you are most likely to encounter the old system of Deluxe A and B, 1st category A and B, 2nd category, etc. This is misleading for most western visitors whose expectations from 1st category will certainly not always be met, and we have therefore graded hotels in our lists with the following equivalents: Deluxe A, approximating to 5-star (L); Deluxe B, 4-star (E); 1st category A, 3-star (M); and 1st category B, 2-star (I).

Establishments may have rooms in more than one category, but those in our lists will have all or some rooms with bath or shower, unless otherwise stated. Plumbing, that long-time bane of so many East European hotels, is often erratic. Economies have also meant that hot water has only been available between certain hours (posted up at reception or in the room).

Two people in a double room can expect to pay the following prices, all of which include breakfast except in (M) and (I) hotels in Black Sea resorts.

	Bucharest	Black Sea resort	Carpathian resorts and inland cities
Deluxe (5-star)	$110–145	$88	$76
Expensive (4-star)	$ 80–100	$52–60	$64–70
Moderate (3-star)	$ 40–75	$35–44	$52–58
Inexpensive (2-star)	—	$20–30	$46–48

In addition to the above accommodations, there is a growing network of motels and inns run by the Union of Consumer Cooperatives. These are indicated on the tourist maps revised annually by ACR and will eventually be brought into the system of star classification.

Self Catering

Such accommodations are not currently available.

Private Accommodations

Romanians are not permitted to offer tourists private accommodations in their homes.

Hostels

There are a number of student hostels, usually open from July through August. The locale varies from year to year, but the rate is from $7.50 per person per night. Bookings can be made through the Carpați National Tourist Office on arrival in Bucharest, but availability is limited.

Camping

There are well over 100 campsites in Romania, and all main towns and resorts have one. Some sites also have bungalows or chalets for hire. Details from the Romanian National Tourist Office.

RESTAURANTS. Current shortages and rationing mean that the range and quality of food in Romania is generally inferior by international standards. All too often traditional Romanian cuisine has given way to chips and meat concealed under thick sauces. However, a few of the top hotels are making commendable efforts to re-introduce regional specialties. The chapter on *Food and Drink* describes a number of dishes to watch for. Outside the capital where eating places are far and few between and often pretty basic, your choice may be limited to only one dish—in which case check the price in advance. It is advisable to dine as early as possible. By around 9 P.M. many restaurants will have run out of food and you may be refused service. A packet of Kent cigarettes can often work wonders in such a situation.

In most resorts, package tour holidaymakers are given a choice of dishes from which they are asked to make their selection for the next day. Independent travelers will find that establishments are usually geared to dealing with groups and may need firm persistence to get service.

Economy measures in recent times have necessitated the closing of restaurants at 10 P.M., except on the coast where this is extended to midnight.

We have divided restaurants in our listings into three categories; Expensive (E), up to 200 lei, Moderate (M), 80–150 lei, Inexpensive (I), 40–80 lei. All these price quotes are per person, including tip and wine.

You can eat for much less at a self-service *bufet express* or *lacto vegetarian* snack bar, though these establishments cannot be recommended. Excellent cream cakes are available at the better *cofetărie* (which rarely, however, serve coffee; soft drinks are the norm).

TIPPING. A 12% service charge is added to meals at most restaurants. Elsewhere, tipping is discouraged but the practice persists, although nowhere is it obligatory. You might want to leave about 10% if service has been exceptionally good. Give porters and taxi drivers about 5 to 10 lei.

MAIL AND TELEPHONES. An airmail letter to the U.S. costs 16 lei, a postcard 13 lei; to destinations in western Europe an airmail letter is 11 lei and a postcard 8 lei. But check prices before mailing.

Though you can make calls from both post offices and hotels, the process can be frustrating and time consuming. If you do make a call from your hotel, be sure to check the hotel's service charge, which can sometimes add substantially to the basic cost of the call. International calls are prohibitively expensive—three minutes to Western Europe will cost you 98 lei, six minutes 244 lei, and 10 minutes 503 lei.

TIME. Romania is seven hours ahead of Eastern Standard Time and two hours ahead of Greenwich Mean Time. From the first Sunday of April to the last Sunday of September, the country operates on summer time, which is eight hours ahead of Eastern Standard Time and three hours ahead of Greenwich Mean Time.

CLOSING TIMES. Shops are generally open from 9 or 10 A.M. to 6 or 8 P.M., though some food shops open much earlier but close for some hours in the middle of the day. Supermarkets are open daily from 8 A.M. to 8 P.M., and on Sundays from 8.30 A.M. to 1 P.M. Opening times of museums, art galleries and other historic monuments are best checked with local tourist offices; most are closed on Mondays.

SHOPPING. As far as forms of payment are concerned, there are two kinds of shop. Those in hotels are run by Comturist in which only hard currency is accepted; in all others payment must be made in local currency. You will find Romanian handicrafts and other products available at reasonable prices in hard-currency shops, but imported items such as tobacco and liquor are quite expensive. In addition, many hotel reception desks are now carrying a selection of the most frequently required items (toothpaste, soap, chocolate, etc.) which may be purchased at any time.

Local currency shops fall into several categories: (1) State-run stores selling mass-produced consumer goods of all kinds; (2) shops belonging to cooperatives, including those dedicated to specialist or craft goods; (3) shops run by artists' unions, such as *Galerie de Artă* belonging to the Union of Plastic Artists, in which prices will be higher, but so will the quality of workmanship; (4) markets, providing the only venue for private enterprise—mainly fruit and vegetables, but including some handicrafts; (5) *Consignația,* selling secondhand and antique items of all kinds, but note that a permit from a special branch of the Ministry of Culture is needed to export items over 50 years old.

Romania's peasant art is still very much alive and includes pottery from Bucovina as well as wood carvings and woven goods from Maramureş, and ceramics, textiles and embroidery from many regions. But even in the rural areas they're not particularly cheap. Glassware is also a traditional product of parts of Transylvania. Other items to look out for are hand-painted icons (modern or copies of famous old ones), including on glass. In modern terms, there is an excellent range of cosmetic products.

SPAS. The spas and health resorts of Romania are known all over the world, particularly for their 'antiaging' compounds, *Gerovital* and *Aslavital,* and for their sapropel mudpackings, *Pell-Amar.* Treatment is available in Bucharest at the Otopeni Sanatorium and Parc and Flora hotels. Outpatient treatment is also available at the Geriatric Institute. (In fact the emphasis on the term geriatric is perhaps a little unfortunate since the treatment has been used beneficially by many who would certainly not welcome and, in many cases, not qualify for the description.) The Boicil method of treatment, which has had remarkable results with rheumatic ailments, is described in the *Transylvania* section.

Of the 160 spas in the country, the following is a selection of the most important available to overseas visitors: on the Black Sea coast at Eforie Nord, Mangalia, Neptun; inland at Călimăneşti-Căciulata, Felix, Herculane, Sovata, Covasna, Slănic Moldova, Vatra Dornei, Tuşnad. Generally Romania can claim to have one of the widest ranges of health resources in Europe and has invested a great deal in exploiting these. Over one million Romanians follow either curative or preventative treatment in spas every year and the facilities at the best of them are being widely promoted abroad.

Most spas are open year-round. An example of prices for a 14-night stay at the Flora Hotel in Bucharest, ex-London and including top-class accommodations, full board, medical examinations and Gerovital or Aslavital treatments is from £600 to £700 depending on season and accommodations. In other spas, the range for various spa treatments is about £200 less.

SPORTS. There are good facilities for water sports, tennis, mini-golf, cycle hire and horseriding at the Black Sea resorts. The Carpathians also offer marvelous hiking possibilities and some specialist tours for walkers are arranged from the U.K.

WINTER SPORTS. The Carpathians offer some splendid conditions for skiing and facilities are being developed. Main centers are Sinaia, Predeal and Poiana Braşov. Winter sports tours are marketed ex-U.K.

MONASTERIES. A major feature of Romania's historic monuments are its magnificent monasteries. The most famous are the painted monasteries of Bucovina, but many others are dotted about the country, frequently in secluded and very beautiful surroundings. Often they are prime examples of the way in which essentially Romanian folk elements have been superimposed on imported architectural styles prevalent in other lands at the time, sometimes combining influences from both east and west. The most important are described in our Regional chapters.

GETTING AROUND ROMANIA. By Air. Regular domestic services are maintained by Tarom (Romanian Airlines) between Bucharest and most main towns and resorts, including Constanţa, Arad, Bacău, Baia Mare, Cluj-Napoca, Iaşi and Craiova. Flights leave from Otopeni Airport (international and domestic flights), which is 19 km. (12 miles) from the city center, and from Băneasa Airport (domestic flights), which is seven km. (nearly five miles) from the city center, with regular bus connections to both airports. There is also an international airport at Constanţa. Fares are reasonable but expect delays. Reservations should be made through Tarom offices or ONT, or, in towns where there is no Tarom representative, though the local Agencia de Voiaj (see below).

By Train. A good rail network is operated by the *Romanian State Railways* (CFR), with first and second class service, express trains, sleepers and dining cars, between main towns and resorts. However, trains marked "personal" are painfully slow compared to "accelerat" and "rapide" trains. Romania is affiliated to the intercontinental systems *RIT* (Rail Inclusive Tour), incorporating accommodations and other services and *Inter-Rail* (youth ticket for travelers under 26). In Bucharest, reservations can be made up to six hours before departure at the Advance Reserve Office, Strada Brezoianu 10 (tel: 13.26.44), behind the Bucureşti Hotel. In other main towns, reservations can be made through the CFR travel agency (Agencia de Voiaj) or ONT office (which charges a small commission) over six hours and less than 30 days prior to travel. Since trains are frequently crowded, it is highly advisable to buy tickets in advance, with seat reservations. Tickets can only be purchased at the railway station itself up to six hours before departure; in some cases the ONT office in the railway station holds a special allotment for last minute sales.

By Bus. The Romanian Ministry of Tourism does not recommend that tourists use the network of regular buses that serve most of the country. Buses are generally very crowded and far from comfortable. In most towns the bus station (*Autogara*) is usually located near the rail station and tickets can be bought up to two hours before departure. There are four bus stations in Bucharest.

By Boat. Regular passenger services operate on various sections of the Danube. These are of particular interest from Brăila or Tulcea via the middle or southern arms of the river, through the delta, to the Black Sea. See also reference to Danube cruises under *How to Go.*
Note that the cost of most tickets is likely to be substantially less if you purchase them in Romania rather than in advance from abroad.

By Car. Your best source for all information is the *Romanian Automobile Club* (ACR), see *Useful Addresses;* it also maintains offices throughout the country (tel. 123456 in Bucharest, and 12345 elsewhere in Romania). It provides many services including technical assistance in case of breakdown, and medical and legal assistance at fixed charges in case of accident; also touring information including a useful map, *Tourist and Motor Car Map,* with every gas station marked. Your national driving license is sufficient for motoring in Romania (though not for transit through all neighboring countries) and you should be in possession of the Green Card Insurance.

ACR also handles fly-drive arrangements through agents overseas (e.g. ex-London), with fixed itineraries or go-as-you-please arrangements, using hotel vouchers, valid in any of many hotels throughout the country. It is important to remember that you must buy gasoline with coupons paid for in hard currency; these are widely available from border points, tourist offices and main hotels. Gasoline is expensive at $1 a liter.

Speed limits are 60 kph (37 mph) in built-up areas and 80–100 kph (50–62 mph) on all other roads. Drinking and driving is absolutely prohibited. Police are empowered to make spot fines of around 250 lei. Speed checks are frequent; look out for black radar cables stretched across the roads. There is a good and improving network of main roads though the great majority are only single lane in each direction and progress is often impeded by considerable processions of agricultural machinery moving from one district to another. In country areas, you will also need to take special care of pedestrians, livestock, bicycles and other non-motorized traffic, all of which tends to act unpredictably. Secondary roads are variable from good to atrocious, but they take you into magnificent and unspoilt areas, where the rewards of being a rare tourist are great. Gas stations are rather sparse and often necessitate a long wait, so keep your tank topped up—and carry a spare parts kit. Road-side refreshment facilities are also few and far between, and it's wise to carry a cooler with cold drinks in the heat of summer, though replenishing the ice may prove difficult.

Car Hire. Car hire can be arranged through *Avis, Hertz* and *Europcar* in association with ACR. Rates are $15 a day, plus 25 cents per kilometer, plus a refundable deposit of $120. Insurance is $3.30 a day; weekly rates with unlimited mileage are obtainable as well. Cars with drivers are also available for hire. Note the fly-drive arrangements already mentioned.

INTRODUCING ROMANIA

Romania's culture, most especially its peasant culture (the product of a turbulent history allied to considerable remoteness), is unique. Though you will encounter numerous industrial and urban landmarks common to any European state, away from these you will find in many regions a way of life that barely survives outside folk museums elsewhere in Europe. Additionally, both internal and external influences have endowed the country with a fine miscellany of monuments. And to all this you can add much splendid scenery.

To deal first with the vital statistics, Romania has an area of 237,500 sq. km (91,700 sq. miles), and is the twelfth-largest country in Europe, similar in size to Yugoslavia, Great Britain, West Germany and Oregon.

The "Latin island" is bounded by two seas, one actual and the other metaphorical. The first is, of course, the Black Sea, to which Romania contributes about 245 km (150 miles) of coastline. The other is the "sea" of non-Latin countries that hem in Romania on every side—Bulgaria to the south, Yugoslavia to the west, Hungary to the northwest and the U.S.S.R. to the north and northeast.

Despite countless invasions and migratory movements, the Romanians have tenaciously clung to their Latin heritage. Of a population of nearly 22 million, 88% are ethnic Romanians, 7.9% are Hungarian, 1.6% German, and the remainder are Slavs, Jews, gypsies, Tartars and Turks.

Romania's Latin connection is linguistic and cultural as well as ethnic. Modern Romanian is primarily based on the popular Latin spoken in the eastern portion of the Roman Empire. Though foreign elements are present (Magyar, Slavic, German, Turkish and Greek), the language is about three-quarters of Romance origin.

Romanians are nothing if not unique. They are the only Latin people in Eastern Europe yet, unlike other Latins, they are mostly Orthodox in religion. Paradoxically, they are the only predominantly Orthodox country to use the Latin alphabet! And irony is further heightened by the fact that many neighboring Slavs and Magyars, though lacking the Romanians' Roman heritage, are Catholic. This uniqueness has certainly contributed to the individualism Romanians have displayed over the centuries.

Early Days

Archeological finds from neolithic times (5,500–2,500 B.C.) include items showing a high degree of artistry, of which examples are the beautiful statuette *The Thinker* from the Hamangia Culture of Dobrudja and painted ceramics of the Cucuteni Culture of southeast Transylvania and southwest Moldavia. The subsequent arrival of Indo-European tribes and the gradual fusion of cultures, skills, and social structures eventually led, about 2,000 B.C., to the emergence of a compact group of Thracian tribes in the Carpathian-Danube-Balkan area. Among these were the Dacians, also known as Getae, later described by Herodotus as "the most valiant and righteous of the Thracians." Despite internal divisions, the Dacians flourished, and their inroads south of the Danube opened a long chapter of Dacian-Roman wars. They were ruled by kings whose chief advisers were high priests, and they enjoyed an advanced civilization, being well versed in the fields of music, astronomy, and medicine.

The Romans finally conquered Dacia in A.D. 106, during the reign of the Emperor Trajan. But it was no easy victory. The Dacians, who had defeated Rome in A.D. 88, fought stubbornly and didn't yield until their king, Decebal, committed suicide to avoid capture. Celebrations of the victory went on for 30 days in Rome and the event is commemorated there in the monumental Trajan's Column (you can see a replica of it in the History Museum of Romania in Bucharest). Once conquered, Dacia was subject to intense colonization. Dacians and Romans fused into a new Daco-Roman race and this prosperous region—known as Dacia Felix—became the most Romanized of the Empire's provinces. The Roman influence lingered on even after Rome's official withdrawal in A.D. 275, kept alive by soldiers and colonists remaining behind. From them emerged the Proto-Romanians, ancestors of the Romanians of today.

From the 4th to 9th centuries, barbarian invasions came so thick and fast that the main concern of the Romanians was to maintain their identity and avoid being engulfed altogether. But gradually small political units were formed (dukedoms, or voivodeships) in the 10th and 11th centuries. At about the same time, there began the gradual penetration of Transylvania by the Hungarians which eventually resulted in Hungarian, Turkish and, later, Habsburg rule (which was to last until 1918), though numerically the Romanians continued to predominate overwhelmingly. Romania had also to withstand, in the 13th century, the great Tartar invasion, despite which, to the south and east of the Carpathians (Wallachia, Moldavia, Dobrudja), Romanian society continued its feudal evolution. At times, varying degrees of Romanian unity were achieved, especially against common enemies—Hungary to the west and Turkish expansion from south of the Danube.

Turbulent Centuries

In fact, Romania's mammoth struggle against the Turkish Ottoman Empire began in the late 14th century and the seesaw conflict dragged on for the next five centuries. With considerable justification, the Romanians point out that in their own tussle for freedom, they acted as an effective buffer, delaying the Turkish advance into central Europe which, in the end, the Turks only accomplished by taking the longer route across Bulgaria and Yugoslavia into Hungary.

The period from the late 14th to the 17th century produced a number of great military leaders, and you will come across their names many times as you visit the historic sites of Romania. Among them was Iancu of Hunedoara (János Hunyadi in Hungarian history), prince of Transylvania, who halted the advance of the Turks by successfully defending Belgrade in 1456. His son Matei Corvin became the popular King Matthias Corvinus of Hungary.

One of the most colorful and controversial characters of these times was Vlad Țepeș, prince of Wallachia (1431–76). The son of Vlad Dracul, he became known as Vlad the Impaler because of his habit of impaling his foes, and waged numerous battles against the Turks. He was the subject of many legends, some of the more colorful originating from his enemies, who depicted him as a monster of depravity engaged in savage ritual practices. It was from this lurid but unsubstantiated material that the 19th-century novelist Bram Stoker created his fictional *Dracula*. Today, Romanians honor him as a "remarkable statesman and leader who defended the independence of the country," while one British historian concludes from the scanty evidence available that "Vlad was a man of diseased and abnormal tendencies, the victim of acute moral insanity."

The achievements of Stefan cel Mare (Stephen the Great, 1457–1504) were cultural as well as military. In 1475 he dealt the Turks a bloody defeat near the Moldavian town of Vaslui. Coming shortly after the fall of Constantinople, the victory was a much-needed tonic to the Christian world. Plaudits rained down on Stephen from all over Europe and the Pope styled him Atleta Cristi—"Athlete of Christ." Nevertheless, Stephen had to compromise in the end by paying tribute to the enemy in return for non-interference in Moldavia's internal affairs. But he had succeeded in creating a climate of stability in which economic and cultural development flourished. Remarkable witnesses to this are the superb painted monasteries dating from the late 15th and 16th centuries, though their defensive walls are also a measure of the times.

By a series of splendid victories against the Turks at the end of the 16th century, Mihai Viteazul (Michael the Brave, 1593–1601) regained Romania's independence for a time. His outstanding place in his country's history, however, is marked by his achievement of the first-ever union, albeit short-lived, of Wallachia, Transylvania, and Moldavia in 1600. But it was not long before the Turks re-established control.

The struggle for emancipation continued throughout the 17th century, and produced leaders such as Șerban Cantacuzino (1678–1688) and Constantin Brîncoveanu (1688–1714) in Wallachia. The latter has also left his indelible stamp on Wallachia in the form of churches and monasteries in the distinctive Brîncoveanu (Brancovan) style. In 1691, neighboring Transylvania came directly under Habsburg rule and increasingly subject to

Austrian centralism. During the course of the shuffling power politics of the 18th century, further areas were amputated from Romanian territory, notably Oltenia (Wallachia) and Bucovina (north Moldavia) which, for varying periods, came under Austrian rule.

The Turks ruled Wallachia and Moldavia until 1821 through puppets known as Phanariots since they were all from the Phanar district of Constantinople. While a few Phanariots were Romanian, the majority were Greek. Meanwhile, in Transylvania, Austrian rule provoked a massive peasant revolt in 1784. Though it failed, the rebellion served as an inspiration of sorts for the French Revolution.

In 1821 a Wallachian army officer, named Tudor Vladimirescu, led a revolt against the Phanariot regime. Through a curious and tragic irony he was killed not by Turks but by a rival commander. But a number of his goals were attained. The Romanian lands were once more governed by native-born rulers and Phanariots were removed from civil, military, and ecclesiastical offices.

Tudor Vladimirescu's revolt coincided with a war between Turkey and Russia, won by the latter. The treaty of Adrianople (1829) eliminated many of the Turks' prerogatives in Romania, but resulted in a five-year Russian occupation. During this period Wallachia and Moldavia received their first modern constitution, known as the Règlement Organique. Though aristocratic in tone (favoring landlords over peasants), the Règlement pleased many Romanian patriots because it called for a new state based on union of the Wallachian and Moldavian principalities.

In 1848, a near Europe-wide revolution was waged against established regimes. In Romania, as in other countries, liberation movements were crushed by the military might of sultan, tsar, and Habsburg emperor. After 1848, Transylvania was ruled directly from Vienna, and in 1867 it was annexed by Hungary.

A United Romania

The principalities were a Russian protectorate from 1848 until 1858, two years after Russia's defeat in the Crimean War, when they reverted to nominal Turkish rule, with the Romanians' political rights guaranteed by the great European powers. The Règlements Organiques were replaced by more democratic assemblies known as the Ad Hoc Divans. In 1859 Colonel Alexandru Ioan Cuza, head of the army, was elected ruling prince by the elective chambers of Moldavia and Wallachia and thus, at last, the two principalities were united. In 1866 he abdicated in favor of a foreign prince, in order to ensure the protection of the central European powers.

Though the new state had considerable local autonomy, it was still officially part of the Ottoman Empire. This artificial relationship ended in 1877, when Russia and Turkey again went to war and Romania entered the conflict on Russia's side. The Treaty of Berlin (1878) recognized Romania's full independence and re-established Romanian state authority over the province of Dobrudja. Only Transylvania remained outside the new state.

The 20th Century

Prince Carol, who was crowned King Carol in 1881, died in the opening months of World War I. A kinsman of the Kaiser, he had tried to bring

Romania into the war on the German side. King Ferdinand I, his nephew and successor, was less susceptible to German pressure and his wife, English-born Queen Marie, was openly against the Central Powers. Romania entered the war, but her military difficulties were complicated by the October Revolution of 1917 and Russia's withdrawal from the war. In May 1918, she was forced to sign a harsh peace. However, all this was canceled out by the Allied victory in November. Transylvania was united with Romania on December 1, 1918, marking the formation of the Romanian state within its present-day boundaries.

The years between the wars were not happy ones. Economic crises, bitter political strife, the rise of fascism—all three left scars on the fledgling nation.

In 1925, Crown Prince Carol was forced to renounce his rights to the throne for personal reasons related to his less than discreet private life. A regency was set up with his son, five-year-old Michael, recognized as heir apparent. But Carol began to have second thoughts about his decision, and launched a successful movement to return, which resulted in his being crowned as Carol II in 1930.

This period saw the rise of a rightwing terrorist organization, usually referred to as the Iron Guard. In the interwar period, however, Romania generally followed an anti-fascist foreign policy, supporting the League of Nations and opposing Italy's 1935 invasion of Ethiopia, Hitler's 1936 occupation of the Rhineland and annexation of Austria in 1938.

But the internal situation remained chaotic, and in 1938 King Carol dissolved all political parties and set up a royal dictatorship. Realizing the precariousness of Romania's position, he tried to play both sides against the middle. He first visited London and Paris in an unsuccessful attempt to obtain Franco-British aid, then went to Germany for conversations with Hitler and Goering. Though he accepted the idea of economic cooperation, he rejected Hitler's demand that he take Iron Guardists into his cabinet. Carol, far from wishing to share power with the Iron Guard, was in fact committed to its destruction. Corneliu Codreanu, the Guards' leader, was arrested in April 1938 and brought to trial. He and 12 of his top followers were executed in November.

During the war itself, Polish civilians and soldiers were granted asylum in, or free passage through, Romania after the German invasion, including help to ship the Polish treasury to England. Nor did Romania give in to the demands of the Nazis to surrender her Jews for the "final solution."

Romania's fortunes took a disastrous plunge in 1940. Suffering territorial dismemberments that wiped out a century of gains, she lost Bessarabia and northern Bucovina to the U.S.S.R., southern Dobrudja to Bulgaria, and one-third of Transylvania to Hungary. Carol was forced to abdicate in September. Pro-Nazi Marshal Antonescu, backed by the Iron Guard, effectively ruled, though Carol's son, Michael, was, nominally at least, on the throne.

In January 1941 the Iron Guard tried to oust Marshal Antonescu and seize sole power. But Antonescu rallied the army and crushed the revolt and led Romania into the war on Germany's side. On August 23, 1944, when the tide had turned against Hitler, he was overthrown by a broad coalition including King Michael and a number of anti-fascist elements, both Marxist and non-Marxist. Romania entered the war on the Allied side and Antonescu, following a trial, was executed in 1946. Transylvania, the largest lost territory, was restored to Romania.

The Modern State

King Michael abdicated at the end of 1947 and as a result of her "liberation" by the armies of the U.S.S.R. Romania became a Marxist republic. The country today is nominally an independent communist state. However, she is, along with all the other countries of Eastern Europe, an integral part of the Warsaw Pact and as such answers to Moscow in all matters affecting the alliance.

Since the end of the war, progress has been made in the fields of education, medicine, industrialization, housing and so on. By 1973, however, with the rise in world oil prices, the development of a large petro-chemical industry had proved a costly miscalculation. Romania was saddled with a massive foreign debt that is now being repaid at breakneck speed. A vast percentage of all produce is exported; the home market is therefore chronically undersupplied, which has not only resulted in shortages of everything—food, fuel, medicines, and consumer goods—but has also led to interminable lines, rationing, and a thriving black market.

Meanwhile, the State is financing massive building projects such as the re-development of Bucharest, the building of a Metro system and the canal which links the Danube with the Black Sea. After centuries of foreign oppression, the modern Romanian state is based on the principles of independence and nationalism. The Romanian Orthodox Church is tolerated, but Soviet soldiers are not, and the secrecy surrounding workings of government is excused by the need to defend Romania against foreign intervention.

Although the Western guest is granted preferential treatment, it is difficult to escape or ignore the problems, and visitors should be warned that making contact with Romanians can be difficult, especially in towns, as they are obliged by law to report all but the most basic conversations with foreigners.

Fabulously beautiful in parts, and still agreeably underexposed to tourism, today's Romania boasts additional charms in the form of exhilarating and startling clashes between the very old and the very new. Concrete housing blocks and vast industrial complexes contrast with horse-drawn carts and plows and fully functioning medieval monasteries.

The Cultural Scene

Romanians through the ages have been lovers of art and literature, but rarely creators. No notable explosion of genius has occurred; very few Romanians—compared with Czechs and Hungarians—have entered the halls of the Muses or the reference books of world poetry, drama, painting or music. In this land one is always aware of a strong sense of beauty and color in dress, in cottage ornamentation, in folklore and most spectacularly in the painted churches of the Bukovina, which are unique on earth. One is aware of a feeling for practicality, too. Art is frequently enshrined in humble, everyday, strictly utilitarian objects.

The literary groups *Junimea* (Youth) and *Contemporanul* (Here and Now) gave literature its orientation soon after the creation of the state in 1863. It tended towards an obscure symbolism—naturally, perhaps, since censorship was strict and authors and publishers were preoccupied with the question of "how far to go too far." The movement led indirectly to the international renown of the one Romanian writer well-known abroad: Eugen Ionesco (born 1909), the prophet of the absurd. One novelist whose work is available in English—indeed, in 140 languages in the case of his novel *Barefoot*—is Zaharia Stancu (1902–1974).

The Arts of Rock and Tree

The best of native architecture first took the form of rustic work with Byzantine elements, as in the royal church and mausoleum at Curtea de Argeş (1352) and the Cozia monastery (1388). Afterwards came a positive epidemic of frothy, florid palaces in the style called Bröncoveanu, from Brancovan (mentioned above). Partly Renaissance and partly Byzantine, the surviving buildings are heavily over-decorated to western eyes; but a few, such as the Hieraşti palace and the Hurez and Vacareşti monasteries are redeemed by their richly-colored murals and intricate stucco work— another case of knowing "how far to go too far."

The exotic sham-Renaissance and Rococo palaces with their heavy *alt-deutsch* furnishings which Karl von Hohenzollern made fashionable in the 19th century—such as Peleş palace at Sinaia—now look like grandiose follies, not to be taken seriously.

Ancient monuments everywhere proclaim the abundance of wood as building material. From Tîrgu Jiu on the edge of the Carpathian forests came Romania's (and for a time the world's) most distinguished sculptor: Constantin Brâncuşi (1876–1957). In the 1920s he was a cult figure in London, Paris and New York; it made headlines when his *Bird* carving, sent to New York for an exhibition, was detained by Customs who classified it "piece of metal" instead of "work of art." Strength and simplicity identifies a Brâncuşi sculpture. He was called primitive, classicist, cubist, surrealist, expressionist—a typical Romanian, he refused to be categorized. The public park at Tîrgu Jiu has his three most puzzling and idiosyncratic works: the *Kissing Gate,* the *Table of Silence* and, best-known of all, the *Pillar of Heaven,* a sort of totem pole of rhomboidal shapes on several planes, the Carpathian "endless column" motif which links earthbound humans with limitless space.

Music, Drama, and Cinema

One of Queen Marie's discoveries, around 1900, was a talented young musician, Georges Enescu (1881–1955). As violinist and composer he became famous far beyond Romania's frontiers. Since his day, others who have built up reputations the world over include Dinu Lipatti the pianist (1917–1950), Constantin Silvestri (1913–1969) and Serge Celibidache (born 1912), both conductors. Romanians at home have many opportunities to hear serious music from home-based symphony and chamber orchestras and choirs; while folksong and jazz festivals attract large audiences and sometimes important foreign participants.

The grand old man of the theatrical tradition is not Ionesco but Ion Luca Caragiale (1852–1912); but his drawing-room comedies look very trite and dated to sophisticated modern audiences. During his heyday, several actors and actresses achieved renown, among them Grigore Manolescu (1857–1892) and Aristizza Romanescu (1854–1918). The search for new theatrical expressions was consistently hampered by the conservative attitudes of governments and audiences; and under the present regime things have not changed much. But there are theaters and drama groups in all towns, and Romania's minority communities are not neglected. At the last count, there were nine Hungarian-language theaters, three German and one Yiddish.

Cinematically the country is a backwater. Film buffs will not readily call to mind the name of a Romanian star or director—unless it be Ion Popescu-Gopo, whose cartoon films have received acclaim at some foreign film festivals. Feature films since 1945 are mainly historical epics of ancient Dacia or of World War II liberation. Since 1983, when color television came to Romania, theater and cinema have lost ground and the talent which might have gone into films or onto the stage has gone to radio and television instead.

ROMANIAN FOOD AND DRINK

Fruits of the Earth

Romania's distinctive national cuisine reflects a blend of many influences, with dishes based on a wide variety of home-grown products. However, it is not easy to find places serving traditional Romanian dishes as opposed to run-of-the-mill international food. The top hotels in Bucharest and Black Sea coast resort restaurants are probably the best bet. Unfortunately current shortages and rationing mean that eating really well in Romania is almost out of the question. Once again, the package tourist is likely to fare a good deal better than the independent traveler. The former is usually offered a menu with a short selection of dishes on which to mark his choice for the following day, while the latter will often find his choice restricted to one dish of indefinable origin.

Starters

Romania's most celebrated pre-prandial or cocktail snack is the ubiquitous *mititei,* short skinless sausages hot from the grill and moderately well-spiced. Mititei are found at all levels of society from the most luxurious restaurants to humble kiosks near the market place. Also popular as pre-meal snacks are the *brinze,* or cheeses; a much sought-after variety is the Telemea from Dobrudja.

Other cold starters come in a great variety, sometimes eaten on their own or as part of a more extensive hors d'oeuvre. There are all kinds of thick vegetable purées—for example of spinach or white beans—some of them combining several ingredients such as eggplant, tomato, onions and peppers, subtly flavored with herbs. Sometimes, a vegetable is scooped out and filled with a delicious stuffing of other finely chopped mixed vegetables. Beetroot or eggplant come in for this kind of treatment. A variation on this theme is egg stuffed with spinach *(ouă umplute cu pîre de spanac)*, popular throughout Romania. Various kinds of meat roll in pastry also feature on the list. *Piftie,* which is either pork or chicken in aspic decorated with chopped pepper or other vegetable, is another tasty starter. Some of these dishes may be beautifully decorated with radishes, onions or tomatoes "sculptured" into pretty flower shapes.

Soups

These can almost be meals in themselves. They fall into two main categories, *sopa* and *ciorbă,* the latter being made with sour cream. Ingredients are practically limitless, but some popular ones are: *ciorbă de pui* (chicken), *ciorbă de perişoare* (with meatballs), *ciorbă de potroace* (giblet), *ciorbă teraneasca* (with meat and vegetables) and *bors pescaresc* (a mixed fish soup, mainly from the Danube Delta). In addition, there are many regional variations, such as *supa gulaş* (meat and potatoes) which is popular in Maramureş.

Main Dishes

Probably the best known staple is *mamaliga,* a kind of corn mush that is eaten everywhere and with almost everything. It comes in various guises ranging from the rather leaden to the really good and tasty. In a Maramureş version *(balmoş),* it is cooked in sour cream and served with ewe's milk. Potatoes also come in for interesting treatment, as in *cartofi Bucovinei* in Moldavia; these are baked and stuffed with cheese, egg and butter and served with a slice of egg and olives.

Some dishes will seem familiar if you have visited other parts of the Balkans. There is *sarmale*—rice, usually with minced meat, wrapped in cabbage leaves. In Maramureş they use corn rather than rice *(sarmale cu păsat),* and add chopped mushrooms. Another Balkan favorite is *musaka:* eggplant, minced meat, potatoes, topped with a batter, but using other vegetables according to season.

Many dishes feature meat stuffed with a variety of ingredients. *Muşchi ciobanesc* (shepherd's delight) consists of pork stuffed with ham and cheese, covered with cheese and served with mayonnaise, cucumber and herbs. In *muşchi poiana,* beef is stuffed with mushrooms, bacon, pepper and paprika and served with a delicious sauce of veal stock, tomato and vegetable purée. Chicken comes in for similar treatment, as in the case of *pui Cîmpulungean,* sampled in the Moldavian mountains; in this case, the stuffing is often of smoked bacon, sausage meat and vegetables, flavoured with garlic. Another Moldavian dish—*rasol Moldovenesc cu hrean*—features boiled chicken, pork or beef, with a sauce of sour cream and horse radish. Across the mountains in Maramureş again, you may well be introduced to *rotogol Maramureşean:* veal meat (can also be pork) and mushrooms, fried with onions, cheese, smoked bacon, then rolled and dipped in egg, breadcrumbs and cheese before frying. The result is usually delicious.

Devotees of stew will enjoy *tocana.* This is composed of small pieces of meat (usually pork) in a stock strongly flavored with garlic or onions and served with *mamaliga*. Vegetarians will be drawn to *ghiveci*, a mélange of many vegetables, cooked in oil, which can also be served cold.

Desserts and Cakes

Plăcintă cu brinza (cheese pie) and *plăcintă cu mere* (apple pie) are popular, as are pancakes with various fillings. A Maramureş variation is *mîr în foietaj*—apple stuffed with raisins, baked in pastry and served with a sprinkling of sugar. *Papanaşi*, a very superior form of doughnut, comes with cream, a touch of cheese and dusting of flour, and melts in the mouth. Indeed, cheese is a frequent ingredient of desserts, as in *ruladă rarău*, a kind of Moldavian Swiss roll with cheese. Of oriental origin are *baclava*, soaked in syrup, and *cataif cu Frisca*, crisp pastry topped with whipped cream.

The Romanians are great cake eaters and you will find many establishments called *cofetărie* entirely devoted to cream cakes, pastries and biscuits; the best of them are luscious. The Moldavians make a tasty brioche called *cozonac*, while in almost any home you are likely to be offered *gogoşi*, a kind of doughnut.

Drinking

Romania is truly Latin in her devotion to the grape. Listen to the accolade paid to a great Moldavian Cotnari by a vintner at the court of Stephen the Great, "This princely wine should not be drunk as water, to hear it gurgle down your throat, but you must receive it on your tongue like a string of beads, so that you may catch its strength and fragrance." Today's visitors will find that wines, brandy and even champagne are in far better supply than food.

Romania's best-known vineyards are at Murfatlar, near the Black Sea coast. One of the most popular excursions for Black Sea tourists is a wine tasting at Murfatlar. Murfatlar's wines, which have won gold medals in international competitions, include a Riesling, Muscat, Pinot Noir and Chardonnay. Cotnari, so beloved of Stephen the Great's vintner, produces the noted Grasa and Feteasca brands. Other popular regional selections are the Segarcea cabernet, Sadova rosé, a cabernet from Dealu Mare, Pinot Gris and Aligoté from Iaşi, Galbena from Odobesti, Furmint from Panciu and Frincuşa and Nicoreşti. Wine is not always obtainable by the glass and, when it is, it is usually white wine only.

Romania's most highly-recommended beer comes from Azuga, a town in the Carpathians between the ski resorts of Sinaia and Predeal. Good beers are also brewed in the Black Sea province of Dobrudja.

Turning to stronger spirits, Romania's national drink is *ţuica*, a fruit brandy made mainly from plums. Indeed, almost every village has its official still (ask for the *casnul de ţuica*), where you will likely be made very welcome and invited to sample the local product. Because of its distinctive flavor, *ţuica* is best taken neat, either before or after your meal. Another plum drink, even fiercer than *ţuica*, is *rachia*. This is not to be confused with *rachiu*, made from grapes.

Among soft drinks, there are some splendid locally-made fruit juices, though they are not easily obtainable in hotels which more usually serve local or imported (and expensive) versions of international soft drinks that are not nearly as good! Coffee, not always available, may be Turkish or

Romanian (reasonably priced and usually good) or "Nes" (instant, awful and expensive), or often a chicory-based substitute. Tea is normally a cup of hot water accompanied by a tea bag.

BUCHAREST

The Forest City

Some thousands of years ago, great forests covered the plains from the Carpathian mountains down to the shores of the Danube. A major trading route crossed these forests from north to south and, in due course, small settlements developed in clearings along the way. One of these became Bucharest and that old trading route is now the main artery through the city: a chain of broad boulevards—Bulevardul 1848, Blvd. N. Bălcescu, Blvd. Magheru, Blvd. Ana Ipătescu. The first Princely Court or palace was built just west of the southern stretch of these modern thoroughfares; at that time it was just one of several main centers of medieval Wallachia. Around it grew the bustling trading area that is now the Lipscani district, with narrow streets radiating from it, linking with another major street, Calea Victoriei on or near which are most of the main hotels and shops of the city.

Though there is a mention of "a citadel on the Dimbovița" (the river that flows through Bucharest) in documents as early as 1368, the name Bucharest was first used officially by Prince Vlad Țepeș, the historic Dracula, in 1459. The name itself is said to derive from a shepherd named Bucur who was attracted to the region. For two centuries Bucharest alternated with Tirgoviște as the Wallachian capital. It has been the sole capital of Wallachia, and later Romania, since 1659.

Though the most lasting visual impression of Bucharest is of broad boulevards, verdant parks, neo-Classical 19th-century and monumental 20th-century architecture, the old core of the city is around Lipscani, and to get a true perspective of the capital, this is where your tour should begin.

The Old Core

The Old Princely Court is now a museum and, as you wander through its substantial ruins, it is possible to trace its development from the 15th century onwards. You can clearly see, for example, the rounded river stones used in the earlier construction, later alternating with red brick and then, in the 17th to 18th centuries, in brick only. In due course, the lower levels of the complex became the cellars of merchants' premises and craftsmen's workshops. Even today, the cellars spread far beyond the limits of the museum itself, and you will come upon them in the form of cellar restaurants in several of the surrounding streets. Among the exhibits are the skulls of two young Boyars who were decapitated at the end of the 17th century. A number of the more famous of the Wallachian princes mentioned in our chapter on history were associated with the Old Princely Court, incidentally. Vlad Țepeș was one; another was Brîncoveanu, the last to add to the construction of the palace.

As time went on, churches were founded and inns built to accommodate the many travelers and traders who came to do business in the growing town. Curtea Veche church, founded in the 16th century, is just next door to the Old Princely Court and, should you happen to be here on a Tuesday, you will see the astonishing sight of many hundreds of worshippers—mainly women—filing into the church to pray for some favor or express thanks for one that has been granted. Opposite the Old Princely Court is Hanul Manuc, perhaps the most attractive hotel in Bucharest; it also has a good restaurant. Manuc was a rich Armenian merchant who died from poisoning in Russia: a famous French fortune-teller had forecast his death on a certain day and could not risk sullying her reputation with a failure. The building is early 19th-century, but incorporates older walls and is arranged in traditional style round an open courtyard. The Russian-Turkish Peace Treaty of 1812 was signed here.

Lipscani's traditional role as a bustling center for trade lives on. Private enterprise may be a thing of the past, but there are innumerable small shops, artisan workshops, including a glass-blower's at Șelari Str. 11–13, and open-air stalls, mostly belonging to consumer cooperatives or craft unions and all combining to create a bazaar atmosphere humming with activity. Among them is the complex of Bazarul Hanul cu tei in which boutiques and art galleries have their premises in a restored former inn. Several of the more attractive restaurants and taverns listed under *Practical Information* are also to be found in this area. Another church well worth visiting in the vicinity is that of Stavropoleos. It was built in 1724 in Brîncoveanu style combining late-Renaissance, Byzantine and Romanian folk art elements. It includes some superb wood and stone carving, not least the remarkable and richly-decorated iconostasis that separates the nave from the altar. Boxes on either side of the entrance contain candles, for the living on the left and for the "sleeping" on the right.

Calea Victoriei

You are now a stone's throw from Calea Victoriei, Bucharest's most famous street, which winds from Piața Natiunile Unite (and the Operetta Theater) in the south to Piața Victoriei in the north, passing several major monuments and buildings on the way. To the southeast of this area, the construction of a major new administrative center is in progress, though, alas, some fine historic buildings have been destroyed in the process. From it a major new highway will pass through Piaţa Naţiunile Unite, on the southern edge of our map.

Near the southern end of Calea Victoriei (and Stavropoleos Church) is one of the most important sights: the History Museum of Romania, housed in the former Post Office. Its collections are magnificent and range from prehistoric to modern times, but the most stunning of all are contained in the Treasury which you can visit (and pay for) separately. The exhibits are changed from time to time, but the emphasis is on objects of gold and precious stones and spans Romania's history from the 4th millennium B.C. to the 20th century. The result is a staggering array of ornaments, weapons, vessels, jewelry, medals, religious and royal paraphernalia. The most famous of all is the Pietroasa treasure "The Hen with Golden Chickens" (5th century), composed of 12 pieces in gold weighing about 19 kilos; but be prepared to be dazzled at every turn. The most massive item in the whole museum is a full size replica of Trajan's Column (the original is in Rome) commemorating his victory over Dacia in the 2nd century A.D. You pass the lower end of it as you enter the Treasury.

As you continue northwards along Calea Victoriei, you pass several of the older hotels, main stores and a theater or two. The next point of sightseeing interest is on the left just before you enter the wide expanses of Piaţa Gh. Gheorghiu-Dej: the pretty little red brick Creţulescu Church. It was originally built in 1722 and subsequently rather badly renovated. But it was restored more or less to its former state in the 1930s, as were some of the original frescoes.

The church overlooks a small park surrounded by very large and more modern buildings, the contrast adding to its appeal. Immediately to the north is the huge complex of the former Royal Palace, today the Palace of the Republic and which also houses the National Art Museum. The latter contains fine collections of medieval and later Romanian art as well as a good foreign section. You are now in Piaţa Gh. Gheorghiu-Dej, the east side of which, opposite the Palace, is taken up by the headquarters of the Romanian Communist Party and in front of which, incidentally, you may not walk. Just beyond it is the fine neo-Classical concert hall of the Romanian Athaeneum with its gardens.

Parisian Aspects

Bucharest has often been described as the Paris of Eastern Europe. It would be absurd to pretend that it has the *chic* of the French capital, but there are quite a few features that bear comparison. Among them are the broad boulevards that are characteristic of modern Bucharest, including the continuous chain referred to at the beginning of this chapter, which runs more or less parallel with Calea Victoriei until the two converge at Piaţa Victoriei. It is on this chain of boulevards that you find the Intercontinental Hotel (Blvd. N. Bălcescu) next to the ultra modern National Theater; some distance north of it is the main office of Carpaţi National Tourist Office (Blvd. Magheru), hub of all tourist comings and goings in the city center. Colţea Church, a pretty little early 18th-century building, is another edifice worth visiting just south of the National Theater.

Reminiscent of Paris, too, are the terrace restaurants and brasseries, which are packed on a summer's evening. The similarities become even

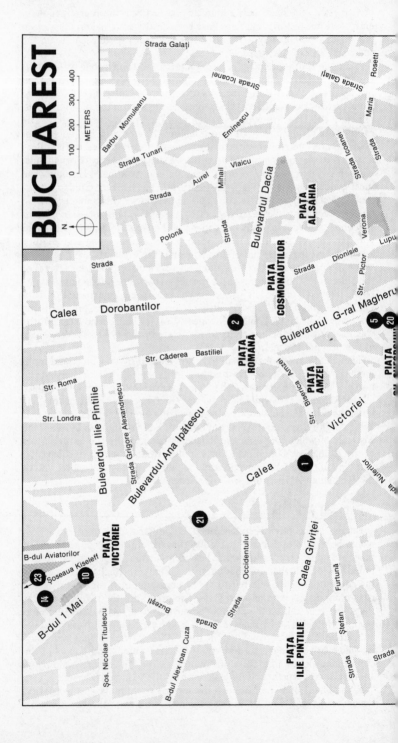

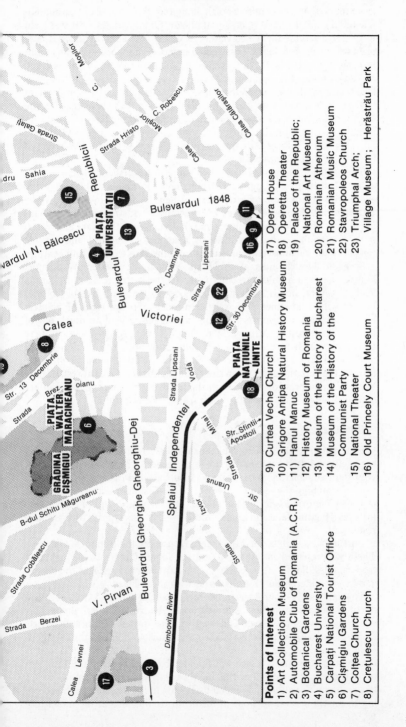

Points of Interest

1) Art Collections Museum
2) Automobile Club of Romania (A.C.R.)
3) Botanical Gardens
4) Bucharest University
5) Carpați National Tourist Office
6) Cișmigiu Gardens
7) Colțea Church
8) Crețulescu Church
9) Curtea Veche Church
10) Grigore Antipa Natural History Museum
11) Hanul Manuc
12) History Museum of Romania
13) Museum of the History of Bucharest
14) Museum of the History of the
     Communist Party
15) National Theater
16) Old Princely Court Museum
17) Opera House
18) Operetta Theater
19) Palace of the Republic;
     National Art Museum
20) Romanian Athenum
21) Romanian Music Museum
22) Stavropoleos Church
23) Triumphal Arch;
     Village Museum;   Herăstrău Park

more marked as you continue north along the wide avenue of Şoseaua Kiseleff and come to the Arc de Triomphe or Triumphal Arch. It was built in 1922 to celebrate the Allied victory in World War I and to honor Romania's war dead. Originally constructed in wood and stucco, it was rebuilt in stone in the 1930s. It was designed by the gifted Petru Antonescu and carved by some of Romania's most talented sculptors. Beyond it, the lake-laced park of Herăstrău stretches away on your right, a true playground for the city's inhabitants who come here to fish or take boat trips on the several lakes, to stroll along the extensive network of paths, to eat and drink in the several restaurants, or to visit one of the top sights of the capital. This is the Village Museum (entrance from Şoseaua Kiseleff), one of the best of its kind anywhere.

The Village Museum is truly "Romania in a nutshell." It consists of about 70 structures, brought here from all over Romania and representing every kind of folk architecture, most of them furnished in original style. The majority are peasant houses from regions as wide-ranging as the Danube Delta, Moldavia, Maramureş and the Banat, but there are also windmills, watermills, artisans' workshops, a couple of churches, and a whole range of equipment used in rural areas from the 18th to early 20th century.

Şoseaua Kiseleff ends at the Piaţa Scînteii, dominated by Scînteia House, the State publishing enterprise. To the left of it Blvd. Poligrafei leads to several hotels, including the modern Flora with its full facilities for gerovital and other anti-aging treatments. To the right of Scînteia House, Şoseaua Băneasa is the main thoroughfare leading north out of town. The interesting Minovici Museum of Feudal Art is just along here on the left, and before very long you come into another verdant area, that of Băneasa Forest (near the airport for domestic flights) and also the setting for the zoo, the main camp site and a number of pleasant restaurants. With every impression of being in the heart of the countryside, you are still only about nine km. (six miles) from the city center.

City Oases

In addition to the considerable expanses of Herăstrău Park, the heart of the city is dotted with smaller areas of greenery where you can interrupt your sightseeing and join the citizens of Bucharest in the ever-popular pastime of watching the rest of the world go by. Cişmigiu Gardens, just west of Calea Victoriei, is a favorite rendezvous for young and old alike, and features a boating lake and a small zoo, as well as the popular Monte Carlo restaurant.

Further west still, beyond the Opera House, are the Botanical Gardens. These were created in 1884 and contain some 10,000 plants, including tropical ones. South of the center is popular Liberty Park and the nearby and larger Tineretului (Youth) Park, with more lakes.

The final oasis on our list is rather further afield: about 35 km. (22 miles) north of Bucharest, in fact, but well worth the trip. This is Lake Snagov which, as well as being well endowed with campsites, restaurants, sports facilities and a lot of attractive elbow room, is also of some historical significance. One of its main features is a large lake and on an island in it is the Snagov Monastery, which was founded by Vlad Tepeş in the 15th century. Indeed, it is here that this highly controversial gentleman has his last resting place after being killed by Boyars in the nearby forest, according to one of several versions of his death. It was also at the monastery that one of Wallachia's first printing presses was established in the latter part of the 17th century.

PRACTICAL INFORMATION FOR BUCHAREST

TOURIST INFORMATION. Carpați National Tourist Office, Blvd. Magheru 7; (tel. 14.51.60).

WHEN TO COME. Like all capitals, Bucharest is a year-round city, but spring is probably the best time when the many parks and tree-lined avenues come to life again. From May to November, it is also a city of roses.

GETTING AROUND BUCHAREST. By Subway. The first two lines of the new subway system are now ready. Cost is 2 lei for any distance; you insert the coin into a machine which opens a barrier.

Tram and Bus. Trams cost 1 leu (pay as you enter); tickets for trolley buses (1.50 lei) and buses (1.75) can be bought at kiosks.

By Taxi. Taxis are scarce but reasonably priced. You can get to anywhere in the city for 20 lei.

HOTELS. Bucharest hotels are often heavily booked during the tourist season, so if you haven't a reservation, go to the Carpați Tourist Office. The list below is a selection. Note the comments regarding standards under *Facts at Your Fingertips*. All establishments have restaurants unless otherwise stated. Many hotels have rooms in more than one category.

Deluxe

Athenée Palace, Str. Episcopiei 1–3 (tel. 14.08.99). Old fashioned, gracious and comfortable, with all the facilities of a top hotel; very central; nightclub.

București, Calea Victoriei 63–81 (tel. 15.45.80). Biggest and newest, with 442 rooms and suites, indoor and open-air pools, keep-fit complex, sauna and all amenities. Central location.

Flora, Poligrafiei Blvd. 1 (tel. 18.46.40). Modern, on outskirts of center near Herăstrău Park. Top amenities, pool and full facilities for geriatric (anti-aging) treatment.

Intercontinental, Blvd. N. Bălcescu 4–6 (tel. 14.04.00). Centrally located, with top-class amenities; 423 rooms; nightclub, indoor pool, keep-fit complex.

Expensive

Ambassador, Blvd. Magheru 10 (tel. 11.04.40). Very central; all facilities; 233 rooms.

Dorobanți, Calea Dorobanți 5–9 (tel. 11.08.60). Modern, fairly central; 298 rooms.

Hanul Manuc, Str. 30 Decembrie 62, opposite the old Princely Court Museum (tel. 13.14.15). One of the most attractive hostelries in the city, dating from early 19th century and built around courtyard. Belongs to the city authorities; 30 rooms.

Lido, Blvd. Magheru 5 (tel. 14.49.39). Central, less plush but good value; 121 rooms, pool. Newly renovated.

National, 33 Republicii Blvd. (tel. 13.01.99). Good downtown location.

Nord, Valea Griviței 143 (tel. 50.60.81). Near the Nord rail station; 245 rooms.

Moderate

Capitol, Calea Victoriei 29 (tel. 14.09.26). 80 rooms. Central.

Minerva, Str. Lt. Lemnea 2–4 (tel. 50.60.10). 83 rooms. Central.

Negoiu, Str. 13 Decembrie 16 (tel. 15.52.50). 90 rooms. Central.

Parc, Blvd. Poligrafiei 3 (tel. 18.09.50). 270 rooms. Near Herăstrău Park.

Union, Str. Decembrie 11 (tel. 13.26.40). 220 rooms. Central.

RESTAURANTS. Depending on your choice of menu, you can eat moderately in most Expensive restaurants and inexpensively in most Moderate ones. Check prices before ordering if there is no menu, and note the comments under *Facts at Your Fingertips* and the chapter on *Food and Drink.*

Expensive

Beijin, in the same building as the Minerva hotel. (tel. 50.60.10). Chinese food.

Berlin, 4 C. Mille Str. (tel. 14.46.52). Excellent food.

Capşa, 34 Calea Victoriei (tel. 13.44.82). One of the best in town, plush and with *belle époque* atmosphere.

Cina, 1 C.A. Rosetti St. (tel. 14.02.17). Pleasant and next to the Athenaeum.

Hanul Manuc, 30 Decembrie St. 62 (tel. 13.14.15). Good atmosphere in the courtyard and adjoining rooms of this old inn, now hotel, opposite the Old Princely Court.

Mioriţa, Şoseaua Kiseleff (tel. 17.10.95). Attractive situation in Herăstrău Park.

Parcul Trandafirilor, Calea Dorobanţi 3 (tel. 12.17.43).

Pescaruş, on lake shore in Herăstrău Park (tel. 79.46.40). Folk show.

Moderate

Carul cu Bere, 5 Stavropoleos St. (tel. 16.37.93). Traditional late 19th-century beer house, former meeting place of the artist set; lots of atmosphere. The ground floor tavern specializes in spicey sausages and there's a cellar restaurant below.

Crama Domnească, 13 Şelari St. (tel. 14.28.68). Very attractive setting in ancient cellars adjoining those of the Old Princely Court; from the restaurant's terrace you overlook the latter.

Doina, 4 Şoseaua Kiseleff (tel. 17.67.15). With garden terrace; on way to Herăstrău Park.

La Doi Cocosi, 6 Şoseaua Strāuleşti (tel. 67.19.98). About 15 km. (9 miles) from town.

Marul de Aur, 163 Calea Victoriei (tel. 50.76.48). Reached through courtyard, a little less central.

Monte Carlo, nicely placed in Cişmigiu Gardens (tel. 13.13.44).

Rapsodia, 2 Şelari St. (tel. 15.54.13). Another attractive cellar restaurant near the Old Princely Court, decorated with old folk masks.

Establishments marked *Cofetărie* serve rich, creamy cakes and pastries, usually with soft drinks (not coffee); the best of them are delicious.

For rock bottom prices, look out for *bufet express* or *lacto vegetarian* snack bars.

MUSEUMS. Check the opening times, but Monday is the usual closing day.

Art Collections Museum, 111 Calea Victoriei. A combination of several private collections of Romanian and some foreign art treasures, including excellent examples of icons painted on glass.

Grigore Antipa Natural History Museum, 1 Şoseaua Kiseleff.

History Museum of Romania, 12 Calea Victoriei. A vast and interesting collection from neolithic to modern times. The Treasury (which can be visited separately) has a superb and changing collection of objects in gold and precious stones from pre-Dacian times to the 20th-century. Near the entrance is the base of a full-size replica of Trajan's column commemorating the Roman victory over Dacia.

Minovici Museum of Feudal Art, 3 Dr. Minovici St., near Herăstrău Park. A villa furnished mainly in 18th- and 19th-century style. Next door is the small but interesting **Minovici Folk Art Museum.**

Museum of the City of Bucharest, 2 Anul 1848 Blvd.

National Art Museum of Romania, 1 Ştirbei Voda St. Ground floor: feudal art with icons and copies of monastery frescoes from all over Romania; first floor: Romanian art; second floor: foreign art.

Old Princely Court Museum, 30 Decembrie St. 31. In the heart of the oldest part of the city.

Railway Museum, 193B, Calea Griviţei.

Romanian Music Museum, 141 Calea Victoriei. The collection is devoted to the renowned composer and musician George Enescu.

Theodor Aman Museum, 8 C.A. Rosetti St. Devoted to the well-known Romanian painter.

Village Museum, 28–30 Şoseaua Kiseleff, in Herăstrău Park. Ancient buildings of all kinds from all over Romania, furnished in original style. One of the best of its kind anywhere.

OPERA, CONCERTS, THEATER. The magnificent *Romanian Athenaeum* at Str. Franklin 1, regularly plays host to two distinguished Romanian symphony orchestras and many noted foreign performers. For opera lovers, there is the *Opera House* at Blvd. Gheorghiu-Dej 70 or the *Operetta House,* 1 Piaţa Natiunile Unite. Don't miss the fine folkloric show at the *Rapsodia Romana Artistic Ensemble Hall* at Str. Lipscani 53.

Theatrical performances range from serious drama at the *Caragiale National Theater,* Blvd. N. Bălcescu 2, to lighter entertainment at the *Comedy Theater* on Str. Mandinesti, but these of course are in Romanian. Of more international appeal are the charming shows at the *Tandarica Puppet Theater* at Calea Victoriei 50. Of ethnic and cultural interest are Yiddish-language performances offered at the *State Jewish Theater,* Str. Barasch 15.

Bucharest has many cinemas that frequently run old American and English films; they are rarely dubbed.

NIGHTLIFE. In recent times, economy measures have meant that most streets are unlit and restaurants close by 10 P.M. and nightlife tends to stop by 11 P.M. or even earlier. The garden cafe of the *Cina* restaurant and the *Gradinita* and *Casata* terrace bars along Blvd. General Magheru are well-patronized in summer. Among those with entertainment and live music for dancing are the *Melody, Bucureşti, Athenée Palace* and *Doina.* There are also folkloric shows in many restaurants.

SHOPPING. The different types of shops are outlined in *Facts at Your Fingertips.* There are Comturist branches in all main hotels.

Should you be paying in Romanian currency, the leading department stores are *Unirea,* Piaţa Unirii 1; *Cocor,* Blvd. 1848 33; *Bucur,* Şoseaua Colentina 2; *Romarta,* Calea Victoriei 60–68; *Victoria,* Calea Victoriei 17; *Bucureşti,* Baraţiei 2; *Tineretului,* Calea Dorobanţi 10. The following are some of the best shops specializing in various items. **Foreign books:** *Dacia Bookshop,* Calea Victoriei 45; *M. Sadoveanu,* Magheru 6. **Jewelry:** *Bijuteria,* Calea Victoriei 25. **Handicrafts:** *Artă Populară,* Calea Victoriei 118; *Artizanat,* Str. Academei 25; *Săteanca,* Calea Victoriei 91; *Hermes,* Şepcari 16; *Meşteri Făurari,* Strada Gabroveni 6. **Glassware:** *Stirex,* Calea Victoriei 88. **Woolens:** *Electa,* Calea Victoriei 95. **Stamps:** *Filatelia,* 13 Decembrie 25. **Records and Music:** *Muzica,* Calea Victoriei 41.

Keep an eye open, too, for *Galerie de Artă* shops run by the Union of Plastic Artists *(Fondul Plastic),* specializing in various kinds of arts and crafts of high standard, though probably at fairly high prices. *Horizont* is one of the main ones; it is almost opposite the Intercontinental Hotel. Other small specialist shops are run by consumer cooperatives.

The traditional shopping area is the Lipscani district of the old part of the city, where there are many picturesque, varied and old-style small shops within walking distance of central hotels. In this area is *Bazarul Hanul cu tei,* a complex of small shops and galleries in the courtyard of a restored early 19th century inn. Here, too, is the *Consignaţia,* a kind of vast warehouse of second hand and antique items of all kinds. The main *market* is at Piaţa Uniiri, open seven days a week, but best visited in the morning.

Finally, the Romanians do some good lines in cosmetics; you can check these out in *Parfumerie* shops.

SIGHTSEEING. The Carpaţi National Tourist Office arrange a wide variety of tours from half-day city sightseeing to 12-day packages ranging across the country. Some city sightseeing tours are of general interest, others concentrate on particular aspects such as folk, art, architectural monuments, etc. There are also day trips into the areas round the capital, or two-day arrangements to the mountains, the coast, the monasteries or the Danube Delta.

USEFUL ADDRESSES. The main embassies are all in Bucharest: *British,* Strada Jules Michelet 24 (tel. 11.16.34); *American,* Tudor Arghezi 7–9 (tel. 10.40.40); *Canadian,* Nicolae Iorga 36 (tel. 50.63.30).

Romanian Automobile Club (ACR), Strada Cihovschi 2 (tel. 11.43.65). *Tarom* (Romanian Airlines), Athenée Palace, Calea Victoriei 96, and Strada Brezoianu 10 (tel. 33.00.33). *Agencia de Voiaj* (CFR), Strada Brezoianu 10 (tel. 16.33.46). *Navrom* (Danube river boat travel), Blvd. Dinicu Goleseu 58 (tel. 16.74.54).

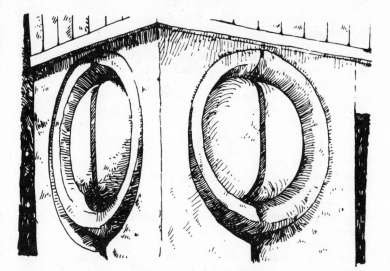

WALLACHIA

Mountains and Plains

Much of Wallachia (Valahia in Romanian) is made up of plains—those flat lands, once covered with forests, that stretch from the Carpathians down to the Danube. Today they are largely fertile farmlands; even the great marshy tracts created by the Danube and its tributaries have to a large extent been drained and replaced in due season by a sea of waving corn or the bright blaze of sunflowers. And where farmland ends, industry takes over. In the middle of the plains sits Bucharest, the focal point from which main roads radiate in all directions.

The Danube

It is a mere 64 km. (40 miles) from the capital south to Giurgiu on the Danube and the Bridge of Friendship that leads across it into Bulgaria. Romania has a 965-km. (600-mile) share in the Danube, much of it forming a border with Yugoslavia and Bulgaria until, near Calaraşi, it eases northwards to become wholly Romanian. The Wallachian Danube, however, is not particularly interesting. By far the most fascinating or dramatic stretches lie in the west (covered by the chapter on Transylvania) or to the northeast (described in conjunction with the Black Sea coast). The most likely circumstance in which you might be traveling the intervening stretches would be on a Danube cruise ship en route from Vienna to the Black Sea.

The Valleys

The most scenically and culturally rewarding regions of Wallachia lie in the southern parts of the Carpathians or the river valleys boring into them. Several of these rivers are pursued by main roads, leading eventually north into Moldavia or Transylvania, and the best plan if you intend touring the region would be to combine two of them in a circular trip beginning and ending in Bucharest. Though there are, of course, other routes, the three principal ones follow the valleys of the Prahova, the Olt and the Jiu.

Whichever route you decide to take from Bucharest into the Carpathians, it would be difficult to miss one of two major oil cities: Ploieşti and Piteşti. Neither is worth detailed investigation unless you have an interest in the oil business, but they do have their own curious appeal, especially if you happen to approach them at dusk when the massive petro-chemical works (and all their attendant paraphernalia), billowing smoke and flames into the sky, acquire a dramatic aura of their own.

The Prahova valley leads eventually to Braşov via Predeal, Romania's highest town and located on the watershed which acts as the border with Transylvania. It is one of Romania's busiest roads, but a lovely one nevertheless once you have shaken off Ploieşti and the plains, and begun the long climb into the Carpathians. But the greatest attractions lie at the upper end of the valley where a number of winter sports centers cluster beneath the towering Bucegi mountains.

The best known of these is Sinaia, so called because of the monastery of the same name built in the 17th century by Mihail Cantacuzino in memory of his visit to Mount Sinai. The monastery now has two churches, the original one from the late 17th century and to which the indefatigable Brîncoveanu added a porch, and another from the 19th century whose frescoes include a portrait of King Carol. Near the monastery are a great many villas that used to belong to the Romanian aristocracy and are now used as holiday accommodations. The other architectural sight of Sinaia is the former royal summer palace of Peleş Castle, an exotic hybrid of Renaissance, Baroque and Rococo styles from the late 19th-century. Sinaia is a lively resort with some excellent hotels and plenty of entertainment facilities, but the ski slopes are not exactly on the doorstep. For these, you take the two-stage cable car leading up into the mountains where there are fine ski runs for all levels of skier. Equally, there are excellent opportunities for summer hiking.

The Olt valley, which takes you through to Sibiu, is reached via Piteşti and joined at Rimnicu Vilcea, itself of no great interest. The Olt has been subjected to a great deal of construction of a hydro-electric nature of recent years. Scenically, it is a fine road, much of it winding through steep rocky or thickly-wooded mountains. It also links a number of popular small spas, of which the best known and perhaps the nicest is Călimaneşti Căciulata. About three miles to the north of it, you reach one of Romania's prettiest monasteries: Cozia, dating from the 14th century. The church was built by Mircea the Old and has changed little over the centuries except for the addition of an open porch by Brîncoveanu in the 18th century. The frescoes are from the late 14th to early 18th century.

The Jiu valley is the most westerly of the three and eventually leads to Deva. For much of the way, it is a steep narrow gorge with some evidence of coal mining. The main town in the valley is Tîrgu Jiu, an industrial center whose main claim to the visitor's attention is an unusual collection of sculptures. These are the works of Constantin Brăncuși (d. 1957), Romania's best-known sculptor. He was born in a nearby village. Three sculpture groups in all were created by him in the 1930s as monuments to those who fell in World War I. Two of them—the *Kissing Gate* and *Table of Silence*—are in the town park; the third—the *Endless Column*—raises its slender silhouette above the town center. The design of these works is very simple yet full of symbolism; the *Table of Silence* for example is surrounded by twelve stools representing both the continuity of the months and the traditional number of seats at a funeral feast.

Historic Centers and Folklore

The several main routes that cross the Carpathians are, in turn, linked by a network of other roads, usually of a more minor nature, that serve the communities in the southern foothills. They are usually well worth taking, for as soon as you leave the main roads you are back amongst the predominantly folk architecture that characterizes much of rural Romania. The houses quite often carry the year they were constructed, but don't be misled if some of them appear to be of recent date for in many cases they have been built in just the same style as the houses they replaced. They are charming and colorful, usually with a porch or verandah (called *prispa*) that may run the length of the building beneath the jutting eaves of the roof; at higher altitudes, this verandah will be enclosed as protection against the elements. Roofs of wooden tiles are another common feature of rural areas. In these mountain regions, land is privately owned, fragmented into small fields or orchards or grazing land. It is all very lovely and unspoilt, and a far cry from large-scale state or cooperative farms only a short drive away down in the plains. You need to drive carefully though, for the farming folk, their livestock and their nonmotorized transport are all totally unpredictable.

Such a road is the one that links the Olt and the Jiu valleys. This also provides an opportunity to visit a monastery of particular interest at Horezu. This is another of the creations of Constantin Brîncoveanu, that Prince of Wallachia who probably contributed more than any other individual to the architectural awareness of his people. The monastery was built in the late 17th century and you can pick out quite well the Renaissance, Byzantine and Romanian folk elements whose combinations were the hallmark of the Brîncoveanu style, whether in the heart of Bucharest or in the depths of the countryside. There are some beautiful examples of carved wood and stonework and plenty of frescoes. Those inside the church are rather dark for, when the Turks briefly sojourned here, it served as the quarters for their slaves who lit fires to keep warm; but elsewhere, for example in the nuns' refectory, the pure colors of the original frescoes are untarnished. Part of the church exterior is also decorated, including the usual picture of the *Last Judgement* showing the frightful things that will happen to sinners. Within the monastery is an excellent small museum whose exhibits include the oldest bible in Romanian (late 17th century).

Horezu Monastery is a delightfully peaceful place and, as is the case of some other monasteries in Romania, it has a few guest rooms, though foreigners will need special permission to stay there and this is not always easily obtained. Initial enquiries should be made through Carpați. The nearby village of Horezu is known for its pottery. There is still a strong tradition of special feasts held during the weeks following a funeral at which each guest keeps his or her plate as a kind of keepsake of the departed. Victor Vicsoreanu, who has his pottery on the outskirts of the village, is a third generation craftsman in this particular skill and is creating a small museum to display this type of ware.

Another rewarding area lies further east in the hills between the Argeş and Dîmboviţa valleys. Here you will find the charming village of Lereşti, one of the few places where private accommodations are available to foreigners.

In the Argeş valley to the east of the Olt, one of the early capitals of Wallachia, Curtea de Argeş, is another point of interest. Its most striking sight is the Episcopal Church, built in the early 16th century by Prince Neagoe Basarab, a most exotic structure combining a melange of oriental influences. The story goes that the prince was so determined no other building should be the equal of this, that when it was completed he left its skilful mason Manole trapped on the roof without any possibility of getting down. Manole jumped to his death and, according to legend, a fountain appeared where he fell.

Like every historic town in Wallachia, Curtea de Argeş had a Princely Court and its 14th-century ruins can be seen by the Princely Court Church, one of the oldest in Wallachia.

Another former capital of Wallachia lies much closer to Bucharest. This is Tîrgovişte, under two hours' drive from the capital, roughly half way between Piteşti and Ploieşti. There is quite a lot of interest to be seen here, especially round the museums associated with yet another Princely Court, in this case built in the reign of Mircea the Old, though subsequently added to by later princes, including Brîncoveanu. The Chindia Tower, though since rebuilt, also dates from the 15th century and now houses a museum dedicated to the legendary Vlad Ţepeş. The Princely Church was built a century later. Also worth visiting in the vicinity of Tîrgovişte is Dealu Monastery (late 15th century) in whose crypt is kept the head of one of Wallachia's greatest rulers, Michael the Brave, the first to achieve, albeit briefly, the union of the Romanian people. It was here also that Romania's first printing press was installed in the early 16th century, and there is a museum of Printing and Old Romanian Books in the town.

PRACTICAL INFORMATION FOR WALLACHIA

TOURIST INFORMATION. Carpaţi or ONT have offices in most towns and resorts, as does the Romanian Automobile Club (ACR). In addition there are County Tourist Offices (OJT) as follows: **Brăila,** 58 Republicii St.; **Piteşti,** 1 Muntenia St.; **Sinaia,** 19 Carpaţi Blvd.; **Slatina,** 223 August St.; **Tîrgu Jiu,** 6 Eroilor St.

WHEN TO COME. Apart from Bucharest itself, the most attractive parts of Wallachia are the southern areas of the Carpathians and the deep valleys that penetrate them, so spring, summer, and early fall are the best times for touring. The area also includes some excellently-equipped winter sports resorts.

GETTING AROUND WALLACHIA. There are organized excursions from Bucharest to some main points of interest. Otherwise travel by car gives the greatest freedom. There are regular passenger boats on the Danube. Details from Carpaţi.

HOTELS AND RESTAURANTS

All hotels listed below have restaurants unless otherwise stated. Note the comments regarding standards under *Facts at Your Fingertips.*

Brăila. *Traian* (E), 110 rooms.

Călimanesti-Căciulata. Spa attractively situated in the Olt valley. *Vîlcea* (M), 120 rooms.

Curtea De Argeş. A former capital of Wallachia. *Posada* (M), 53 rooms.

Piteşti. Major oil town. *Muntenia* (M), 275 rooms.

Ploieşti. Major oil town. *Prahova* (E), 126 rooms.

Sinaia. Winter sports town. *Montana* (E), 180 rooms. Central, modern and near cable car station. *Palas* (E), 148 rooms. *Sinaia* (E), 248 rooms. Modern, also central. *Alpin* (M), 56 rooms. Many attractive villas offer Inexpensive accommodations, though without food which is available in nearby restaurants.

Tîrgoviste. A former capital of Wallachia. *Dimbovița* (M), 107 rooms. *Turist* (M), 29 rooms.

Tîrgu Jiu. *Gorj* (M), 235 rooms.

TRANSYLVANIA

Folklore, History and High Places

Transylvania is a region of enormous beauty and variety, not the least of which is the extremely vital peasant culture surviving in many areas. Contributing to this variety are the substantial national minority groups (especially German and Hungarian) reflecting the region's long, if often reluctant, association with the Habsburg empire.

Topographically it consists of the Transylvanian Plateau, with an average altitude of 397–610 meters (1,300–2,000 ft.). This is bounded by the sickle-shaped Carpathian Mountains, the inner ranges of which also form part of Transylvania. The plateau in turn is divided by the Mureş river flowing down through the less substantial western Carpathians into the Banat before eventually joining the Tisza river in Hungary. The Banat Mountains (that part of the Carpathians lying between the Danube and the Mureş) contribute to probably the most spectacular stretch of the entire Danube on its approaches to the Iron Gates. In the far northwest of Romania, Maramureş concludes the list of regions associated with Transylvania, and in many respects it is the most enchanting of all.

Braşov and Sibiu

Two of Romania's most interesting towns are to be found on the Transylvanian plateau: Sibiu, more or less half way along its southern fringes, and Braşov, at its upper end, tucked in at the foot of the eastern Carpathians. Both are linked to Bucharest and each other by good roads, and both can boast very beautiful old districts of Gothic, Renaissance and Baroque houses reflecting in style the predominantly Germanic influence on the area of those times. Sibiu is the more attractive of the two, but Brașov has the most rapid access to Romania's best winter sports facilities.

We'll begin with Brașov, this being the nearest town to Bucharest in the area. It is reached by the Prahova valley (described in the chapter on Wallachia). You enter Transylvania at the ski resort of Predeal (Romania's highest town) straddling the heights which divide the Prahova and Timiș valleys. Its situation gives it good access to the skiing and hiking facilities of both the Bucegi and Baiu Mountains. From here it is only about 24 km. (15 miles) into Brașov.

Today, Brașov is a busy industrial center, but the old core of the town, founded back in the 13th century, still survives in many aspects despite fires and battles. The History Museum in the attractive former Town Hall is one place where you can trace local history, though of greater interest still is the Museum in Brașov Citadel and housed in the medieval Weavers Bastion, to the south of the town center. To the north of it, Cetățuia is a small fortress rebuilt in the 17th century and offering good views of the city as well as a pleasant complex of restaurants. But Brașov's most famous sight by far is the Black Church in the heart of the old city, so called because it still bears the marks of the fire caused by the Austrians in 1689. Though largely reconstructed, it is a fine Gothic building, especially noted for its collection of old oriental carpets and its massive organ (which dates from 1839). Other nearby traces of the old fortifications are the Ironsmiths' Bastion and Ecaterina's Gate. A little away from the center, look out for the charming 16th-century St. Nicolae Church—an Orthodox church built in what was at the time a predominantly Roman Catholic town; it was funded by ruling Orthodox families in Wallachia.

Only about 11 km. (seven miles) winding up through the forests is Poiana Brașov, in some ways the most appealing of Romania's winter sports resorts. Its situation on a small plateau beneath Postăvarul mountain means that you can ski from your hotel doorstep. But you can also take advantage of the cable cars, gondola lifts and other skiing facilities to reach greater altitudes. There are about a dozen hotels in all categories, several folk-style restaurants and also summer sports facilities, including a riding school. There is easy access to the town.

In complete contrast is another highly popular excursion from Brașov: Bran castle, this of Dracula fame and about 32 km. (20 miles) to the southwest along a narrowing valley. The connection with Vlad Țepeș (the original Dracula of legend) is, in fact, very tenuous, but the castle is well worth visiting anyway. It dates from 1377 when it was built by the citizens of Brașov to guard the narrowest point of the valley and its border with Wallachia (a remnant of the frontier wall is still to be seen) and though there have been many changes since then, Bran remains a most satisfying castle, both in its situation and its construction with its courtyards, galleries and narrow passages. One of its early owners was the grandfather of Vlad Țepeș, and a further connection with this enigmatic Wallachian prince is that he is said to have been imprisoned here by Matei Corvin (King Matthias Corvinus of Hungary) in 1462 on his way to Buda—though technically the castle was not on his route. The castle today is a museum and contains medieval and later furnishings and weaponry. Its last owner was Queen Marie (the English-born wife of King Ferdinand).

About 144 km. (90 miles) separate Brașov from Sibiu. It is worth pausing at Făgăraș on the way to glimpse the restored 13th-century citadel, which contains a museum as well as a hotel and restaurant. It is also worth the detour to take in the Monastery of Sîmbăta de Sus, another of Brîncoveanu's creations from the late 17th century and surrounded by orchards and beautifully-framed by the highest peaks of the south Carpathians. The monks here specialize in painting icons on glass and have a fascinating exhibition of these, some dating back to the monastery's earliest days though it was deserted for a long period after destruction by the Austrians (its reconstruction was completed in 1936). It is a splendidly peaceful place, and the countryside in these parts has an unchanging quality emphasized by the sight of horsedrawn plows and carts powered by black water buffalo.

Sibiu is a lovely town and a great deal of its medieval past survives. There are substantial sections of the old defensive walls and three of the original bastions. These date from the 14th century when the town was divided into guilds, each with its own defence system (at one time there were as many as 40). The old town is built on two levels which adds to its visual appeal, for steep stairways link the small squares and narrow streets of the two. Many of the houses are colorful and charming, a characteristic being the small windows, like sleepy eyes, peering out from the middle of their ancient roofs. The hub of the old town is Republic Square and close to it is the Brukenthal Museum, one of the best ethnographic collections in Romania. This is a must if you have any interest in the development of folk art of all kinds—pottery, textiles, furnishings and many other crafts—from different parts of the country, many also reflecting the influences of other nationalities. Brukenthal, incidentally, was Governor of Transylvania in the 18th century at the time of Empress Maria Theresa, and created the building for his collections which have since been expanded. It also features a gallery of fine Romanian paintings and a number of other European works including a couple of pictures by Rubens and a Van Dyck.

To the south of Sibiu is the fine oak forest of Pădurea Dumbrava, setting for a zoo and an open-air museum. You pass through this on your way to the delightful village of Răşinari, about 19 km. (12 miles) away—a gem of a place with colorful houses and courtyards tucked away behind high walls. It is a village of shepherds, craftsmen and artists, many of the inhabitants combining all three skills. It may be possible to arrange a visit to one of them, such as Vasile Frunzete who paints on glass while his wife and parents produce superb hand-embroidered leatherwork. At the same time you will learn a good deal about a way of life which has changed little, for transhumance (the seasonal movement of livestock) is still a governing feature of this village from which 25,000 sheep leave for the summer pastures each May and return in the fall. About 16 km. (10 miles) beyond Răşinari, the road comes to an end at the winter sports resort of Păltiniş.

About 19 km. (12 miles) west of Sibiu is another delightful place, Sibiel, where, unusually, private accommodations are available.

Along the Mureş River

About 72 km. (45 miles) to the northwest of Sibiu on the Mureş river is Alba Iulia. This was not merely a Roman town, as you might guess from the name, but was at one time the capital of Roman Dacia. Its main sights, however, are of more recent date. The present Citadel is of Italian design and dates from the early 18th century though with later restoration and additions. The Orthodox church for example was built in the 1920s and it was here that the coronation of King Ferdinand and Queen Marie took place. There are also a number of 19th-century buildings, one of which contains a particularly well-planned History Museum. Opposite the History Museum is a place of special significance in Romanian history. This is the Museum of the Union—the very spot where the Unification of Transylvania with the rest of Romania took place in 1918.

Follow the Mureş river for 77 km. (48 miles) downstream and you come to Deva, associated with an earlier attempt to unite the Romanian states by Michael the Brave. He was briefly successful in this effort at unification at the end of the 16th century, but soon afterwards, alas, the new "king of the three Romanian countries" was defeated in a battle here. You can hardly miss Deva's most significant monument—the Citadel—for its ruins crown a hill rising almost out of the city center. It's quite a slog to the top, but worth it for the view. Only a few miles south of Deva is Hunedoara which has not only one of Romania's biggest and earliest steel works but, more or less engulfed by it, an astounding castle. It was first built in the 14th century, but every subsequent century has added something to it, giving it both a massive and a flamboyant presence. Much of it is due to Iancu de Hunedoara who, in the 15th century, turned it from a stronghold into a sumptuous castle, and some of those details—such as the Renaissance loggia—you can see today. Iancu fought and beat the Turks in Belgrade in 1456 and his son Matei Corvin was to become King (Matthias Corvinus). Though there have been many alterations since those days and a major fire caused much damage in 1854, much has been restored.

The road south into the Carpathians from Deva leads eventually into the Jiu valley described in the chapter on Wallachia. On the way, a minor road leads to Densuş and one of the many delightful and more remote monuments that Romania has to offer: a remarkable little 13th-century church (with 15th-century frescoes), largely built of Roman stones and bricks excavated from Sarmizegetusa. Rather confusingly there are two major archeological sites bearing this name. The full title of the one referred to here is Ulpia Traiana Augusta Dacica Sarmizegetusa, the political and administrative center of Roman Dacia, founded by Trajan in the second century A.D. The ruins are the most extensive from that period in the country, and well worth a detour. Preceding them by up to 200 years are the remains of pre-Roman Sarmizegetusa, the fortified Dacian capital. These are to be found at Grădiştea Muncelului, a remote place in the mountains, 40 km. (25 miles) south of Orăştie, which lies east of Deva.

Nearly 161 km. (100 miles) west of Deva along the Mureş river is Arad, close to the Hungarian border. Its main points of interest are the Citadel, the St. Simion Stîlpnicul Monastery and the Chapel St. Florian, all dating from the 18th century.

Other Transylvanian Centers

Some of the most important towns in the more northern parts of Transylvania will feature on the itinerary of any motorist entering Romania from Hungary. Three of them, for example, are on the main E15 from the Hungarian border to Braşov and Bucharest, and could be incorporated into your tour should you wish.

The first, Oradea, is only a few miles from the Hungarian border. As your first stop in Romania, Oradea offers two main areas of interest. The first, a little north of the center, is a group of Baroque buildings in a park-like area including the former Palace, the largest Baroque cathedral in Romania, and the Cannons' Corridor, a passage of arches along a row of old houses. The palace now contains the district museum (Țării Crișurilor) and near it is a charming late 18th-century wooden church brought here from the countryside.

If you stroll down the pedestrian precinct of Calea Republicii and cross the river to the square of Piața Victoriei, you will see most of the other older buildings in the town center. Restoration has greatly improved this and other town centers, while carefully maintaining their original style and attractive coloring. On the Piața, main buildings include Biserica cu luna (the Church with the Moon) from the late 18th century whose tower incorporates a solid sphere indicating, by means of an ingenious mechanism, the phases of the moon. For a fine view of the city, steps near the Dacia Hotel lead up to a hill-top restaurant, also accessible by road.

Oradea, incidentally, is close to several of Romania's many spas, the best known being Baile Felix, only eight km. (five miles) away—worth considering for a peaceful overnight. Fine glass and, in Cluj-Napoca (150 km./93 miles east), porcelain are also traditional products of the area; you will find displays in some of the hotels—and be pleasantly surprised by the prices.

Cluj-Napoca, where the western Carpathians meet the Transylvanian plains, is a major educational and economic center and undoubtedly the finer of the two cities. It is also much older, for this was the Napoca of Roman times—hence its double name. Its main development, however, came in the 15th century, when it was powerfully fortified by Matei Corvin (Matthias Corvinus), King of Hungary. His equestrian statue is one of the landmarks of the city, and stands before another landmark, the great church of St. Mihail—the largest Roman Catholic church in Romania—founded in the 14th century and rebuilt following a fire in 1698. A short stroll from here is the History Museum of Transylvania which features an extensive Roman lapidarium, including an altar fragment from 104 A.D. on which the inscription Napoca is the earliest yet discovered.

The Art Museum is opposite the Cathedral in an 18th-century Baroque palace built by local Hungarian rulers. There is also a good Ethnography Museum in the Empire-style Reduta Palace, with an open-air section in Hoia forest. Of the original 15th-century defence walls, the only surviving remnant is the Tailors Bastion, a reminder of the responsibility of the various medieval craftsmen's guilds towards the protection of their city.

A further 110 km. (68 miles) southeast on the road to Brașov, you come to Tîrgu Mureș on the Mureș river, with a citadel and a late-Gothic church. More impressive though is the hill-top citadel of Sighișoara, 50 km. (31 miles) further still, its 14th-century clock tower now containing the History Museum. Not far from this, a yellow house announces itself to be the birthplace of the inescapable Vlad Țepeș.

Maramureș

Tucked away close to the Soviet border in northwest Romania is one of this area's most charming regions. Despite industrial development around one or two main towns, much of Maramureș is blessedly untouched by the more garish aspects of the 20th century. The deeprooted traditions reflected in its rural architecture, its peasant costumes, its crafts and customs have remained intact to a remarkable degree, and it is infinitely worthwhile taking the time to wander through its villages at leisure. Don't delay your visit too long. Recent years have brought inevitable signs of change as new buildings are increasingly interspersed among the old—undoubtedly more convenient to live in, but certainly less esthetic.

Baia Mare is the main town of the area. Its extensive modern districts and industrial developments seem to offer an unpromising start, but there are a number of interesting sights in or near Liberty Square, the old core of the town. One of the several ancient buildings round the square, for example, contains the Mineral Exhibition with quite stunning geological specimens in exotic shapes and colors. The History Museum, in a restored 17th-century building on the square, is interesting too, and there are also a number of surviving remnants from the medieval town such as parts of the 15th-century citadel and St. Stephen's tower. The Cathedral is 18th century, with original furnishings and stained glass. But above all this is a good place to get an introduction to the very rich folkloric traditions of the region; the place to go is the well-planned Ethnographic Museum.

The outstanding attraction of Maramureș, as we have said, is its peasant culture, and there are any number of places where you will find evidence of it. The following route, which will eventually lead you east into Moldavia, is one suggestion for getting the best from your visit. The route first heads northwest to Sighetu Marmației. Your first stop should be the village of Sat Șugatag. Maramureș is famous for its old wooden churches and this is the oldest of them all (from 1642), complete with original frescoes and altar gate. From Sighetu Marmației (good Ethnographic Museum with folk masks) follow the Soviet border westwards for a few miles to Sapința, which boasts one of Europe's strangest cemeteries, and certainly its jolliest. Indeed, it is known as the "Merry Cemetery" and was the creation of one man, Stan Pătraș, who, until his death in 1977, carved the incredible range of wooden memorials which fill the graveyard, each vividly describing in pictures and words the life or character of the person buried beneath it. His house is now a museum and the work is being continued by one of his students.

You will need now to return to Sighetu Marmației. Beyond it, take the road which follows the Iza valley southeast towards Moisei. There are two roads, so be careful to take the one that links the villages of Rozavlea and Bogdan Vodă, if possible including a short detour to Ieud. In the villages along this road you will see all that is most typical of Maramureș: the beautiful folk architecture of the houses with their open verandahs, wooden-tiled roofs, colorful decoration and, most typical of all, the ornately carved gateways leading into their courtyards. Several of the villages have beautiful examples of the old wooden churches of the region, notably the three villages already mentioned. You will see, too, to what a remarkable degree the delightful traditional costumes are still worn—especially by the women—not as a tourist attraction, but as part of every day life. Particularly striking are the woven aprons with their broad horizontal stripes of black alternating with a bright color, and the exquisitely embroidered blouses or waistcoats. Distinctive, too, are the soft moccasin-type shoes, bound round the lower leg with a long leather thong.

From Moisei you begin the steady climb into the eastern Carpathians which culminates at the Prislop Pass, the watershed which divides Maramureș from Moldavia. It is a magnificent road scenically and on the way you will pass the little mountain resort of Borșa, a good place for an overnight stop—or longer if you want to take advantage of the marked mountain trails for some rewarding exercise.

The Banat and the Iron Gates

Our final region in this section is the most southwesterly corner of Romania, the plains of the Banat and that part of the Carpathians that stretches down to the Danube.

In the plains, the town of Timişoara has some good 18th-century architecture, some of it tastefully restored to its original warm colors, especially around Piaţa Uniiri (Unity Square) which also features a Baroque Serbian Orthodox church from the mid-17th century. Not far from here is a chunk of the fortifications built in Turkish times, now housing shops and a restaurant. The hub of the city is Opera Square, with the modern Orthodox Cathedral at one end and the main theater-opera house at the other. Nearby is the hulk of Iancu de Hunedoara's castle, built in the 14th century, but much enlarged and restored since. It now contains the excellent Banat Museum.

But Timişoara has another and somewhat unusual claim to fame for this is the original center for the development of a very particular form of treatment for rheumatic afflictions, known as the Boicil method. Based on a particular herb, it has had some quite startling results on acute or chronic conditions that had not responded to other forms of treatment. No drugs are involved and there are said to be no side effects. Though now available elsewhere in Romania, the main center remains in Timişoara (Methodological Center for Rehabilitation with Boicil). The Center itself, or the local ONT office, can provide details of treatment and accommodations.

Buzias, 30 km. (20 miles) from Timişoara is a spa specializing in heart diseases. Its parks, planted nearly 150 years ago, are pleasant and motorists might find this a restful alternative to a city overnight. Treat the spa waters cautiously though—the iron content is astronomic.

Around 100 km. (62 miles) south of Timişoara is the junction of the western and southern Carpathians. A few miles off the main road, up the Cerna Valley, is the spa of Băile Herculane, which is undoubtedly the best-equipped of all Romania's inland watering spots, as well as having a superb setting and unusual historic interest. Indeed, it was the Romans who founded it and named it, for it was here, according to legend, that Hercules slew the Hydra, healing himself afterwards in the mineral springs. The spa boasts many Roman traces, the most interesting being part of the baths rediscovered during the building of the Roman Hotel and now incorporated in its ground floor. Close to the hotel are the remains of another bath from Roman times, showing traces of a bas relief of Hercules himself. Other Roman relics can be seen in the local History Museum.

The spa gained a new lease of life in the 19th century during Habsburg rule, and much of the little town center dates from that period. The emperor Franz Joseph and his wife Elisabeth stayed here several times in the Villa Elisabeth, now a library and House of Culture. Furniture from the time of Maria Theresa was brought from Vienna for their comfort and has now been transferred to a room in the Hotel Traian where it can be viewed. This Moorish-style building itself is scheduled for restoration as a first class hotel in the near future. In order to immerse themselves in the spa's health-giving waters, the Emperor and Empress crossed the little river Cerna to the Neptune baths, whose imposing imperial entrance can have changed little since those days. The surprisingly modest individual cubicles used by the royal pair are likewise preserved. In addition to its waters, Băile Herculane is famous for its beneficent air, and marked trails throughout this beautiful area encourage visitors to breathe it to the full. Some miles up the valley, a new lake has been created by the building of a dam, and a number of beauty spots can be visited on organized excursions. Among them are trips on one of the most spectacular sections on the entire length of the Danube.

It is only a short drive down the main road to Orşova, spread round a bay where the Danube enters the final stretch of the remarkable passage it has carved through the Carpathians. For several score of miles the river, which here forms the border with Yugoslavia, has created a series of deep gorges through which the Danube waters once swirled with awesome violence. In a massive collaboration between the two countries, the level of the river was considerably raised in the 1970s and its power harnessed to feed the great hydro-electric works of the Iron Gates (Porţile de Fier) a few miles before Drobeta Turnu-Severin.

Human history along these banks goes back a long way and the Romans in particular have left substantial traces of their presence. The Iron Gates Museum at Drobeta Turnu-Severin is exceptionally fine, with imaginative displays in its various sections devoted to the region's archeology, history, natural history and ethnography, and including a relief map of the whole course of the Danube. The campaigns of the Dacian wars are strongly featured, as you might expect, but rather less expected are fascinating exhibits devoted to the exploration of Outer Space, donated by the United States.

In the Roman section you will find a scale model of the astonishing bridge built across the Danube in the early 2nd century A.D., which was to play such a decisive part in the conquest of Dacia. It was carried by 25 huge pillars of which 20 were actually rooted in the river bed. Amazingly, remains of the bridge survive to this day, along with extensive foundations of the Roman castrum beside it. This archeological site is just beside the Iron Gates Museum and incorporates the traces of subsequent Byzantine occupation and, later still, a medieval fortress and church. Altogether it makes a fascinating complex. For the chunky remains of the Tower of Severin (Turnu Severin) which gave the town its name you must go into the grounds of the hospital on Republic Boulevard; in fact, this is now known to be a medieval fortification and nothing to do with the Romans as originally supposed.

Though well away from most tourist trails, Drobeta Turnu-Severin and its surroundings are scenically and historically very rich indeed, with a number of old monasteries and natural phenomena, such as the major caves of Topolniţa, to be visited. Out on the Danube, the island of Şimian bristles with the 17th-century Austrian-built fortifications transferred here from another island, Ada-Kaleh, when the latter was drowned by the raising of the Danube's waters.

PRACTICAL INFORMATION FOR TRANSYLVANIA

TOURIST INFORMATION. There is a Carpaţi or ONT Office in all towns and resorts. In addition County Tourist Offices (OJT) are maintained in the following

centers: **Alba Iulia,** 22 1 Mai Sq.; **Arad,** 72 Republicii Blvd.; **Baia Mare,** 1 Culturii
St.; **Bistriţa,** 14 Petru Rareş Sq.; **Cluj-Napoca,** 2 Gheorghe Şincai St.; **Drobeta
Turnu Severin,** 41 Decebal St.; **Deva,** 1 Unirii Sq.; **Oradea,** 1 Aleea Ştrandului; **Pre-
deal,** 74 Gh. Gheorghiu-Dej Blvd.; **Satu Mare,** 11 Libertăţii Sq.; **Sibiu,** 4 Unirii
Sq.; **Timişoara,** 3 Piatra Craiului St.; **Tîrgu Mureş,** 31 Trandafirilor Sq.

The Romanian Automobile Club (ACR) also maintains offices in many centers.

WHEN TO COME. Spring (for orchard blossom) and summer for walking and
hiking, and touring the region's many splendid historic sites and beauty spots. There
are especially colorful events in Maramureş at Easter and folkloric festivals in several mountain regions in summer. The fall is good for trips to the vineyards and the
winter for the growing sports facilities in the Carpathian resorts. Spa treatment is
available all year round.

GETTING AROUND TRANSYLVANIA. Carpaţi organize tours ranging from
one- or two-day trips concentrating on specific areas or incorporating them in more
extensive tours of Romania up to 12 days long. Traveling by car gives the greatest
freedom. Several of the main centers are linked by air with Bucharest, and rail and
bus connections complete the network.

HOTELS AND RESTAURANTS

All hotels listed below have restaurants unless otherwise stated. Note the comments regarding standards under *Facts at Your Fingertips.*

Alba Iulia. *Cetate* (M), 128 rooms. Modern, near entrance to Citadel. *Transilva-
nia* (M), 83 rooms. Central, a short walk from the Citadel. *Apullum* (I), 26 rooms.
Central.
Restaurant. *Crama Cetate,* wine tavern in walls of Citadel.

Arad. *Astoria* (E), 155 rooms. *Parc* (E), 80 rooms.
Restaurant. *Zarand* in typical Romanian style.

Baia Mare. *Mara* (E), 120 rooms. Recent and in newest part of city, near sports
hall. *Carpaţi* (M), 114 rooms. By river in the modern part of town. *Bucureşti* (M),
74 rooms. In modern center of town; has prize-winning chef and particularly good
food. *Minerul* (M), 48 rooms. Turn-of-century building on main square of old Baia
Mare.
Restaurants. *Păstrăvul* (M), with fish specialties, and *Birt "Igniş"* (M), both in
older part of town; *Maramureşul* (M), in newer district.

Băile Felix. *Belvedere* (E), 220 rooms, attractively designed by woman architect.
Sports facilities. Several (M) establishments, all recently built in wooded setting.

Băile Herculane. *Roman* (E), 180 rooms. Modern, and the best. Built into cliffs
on north side of resort, a short stroll from center, incorporating fascinating remains
of Roman bath. Thermal pool, full treatment facilities. Some older hotels in the
resort center are due for restoration. *Afrodita, Diana,* and *Minerva,* a trio of modern
(M) establishments on the south side of the resort, each with about 200 rooms and
treatment facilities.
Café Ada Kaleh, in attractive traditional Turkish style, is in the resort center.

Bistriţa. *Coroana de Aur* (E), 117 rooms.

Borşa. *Cascada* (M), 58 rooms. Lovely mountain setting on the western approach to Prislop Pass. Walking center with developing winter sports facilities.

Braşov. *Carpaţi* (L), 312 rooms. Top facilities; central. *Capitol* (E), 180 rooms.
Central. *Postăvarul* (E), 167 rooms. Restored late 19th-century building; near center. *Parc* (M), 38 rooms. Short stroll from center.

Restaurants. *Cerbul Carpatin* (E). Popular cellar restaurant in 17th-century merchant's house, with excellent folk show: a great favorite with visitors. In *Cetățuia* fortress, complex of restaurants, including in Transylvanian style, also tavern, coffee shop, disco.

Cluj-Napoca. *Belvedere* (E–M), 150 rooms. Located among 18th century fortifications on hill, linked by steps to center. Good views. *Napoca* (E–M), 160 rooms. Fairly modern, but not central. *Continental* (M), 50 rooms. Old-fashioned, but central opposite Cathedral.

Astoria (I), 100 rooms. Fairly central, below the Belvedere. *Central* (I). Old-fashioned, opposite the Cathedral. See also Băile Felix.

Restaurant. *Transilvania* (M). Folk restaurant serving Transylvanian specialties. Central.

Deva. *Cetate,* new. *Sarmis* (M), 124 rooms. Modern, central.

Drobeta Turnu-Severin. *Parc* (E), 130 rooms; near banks of Danube. *Trajan* (E), the latest.

Făgăraş. *Restaurant* in restored 16th-century Citadel, which is the town's impressive main monument.

Hunedoara. *Rusca* (M), 106 rooms.

Oradea. *Dacia* (E), 170 rooms. A short stroll from center. *Astoria* (M–I). Central. *Transylvania* (I), 70 rooms. Central.

Poiana Braşov. *Alpin* (E), 141 rooms. Best and quietest. *Piatra Mare* (E), 177 rooms. Recently rebuilt. *Teleferic* (E), 149 rooms. Closest to the cable car station. *Sport* (I), 122 rooms. Simple rooms but good value and nearest to the nursery slopes. There are several other Expensive hotels near the Alpin; all have good views to the mountains surrounding this popular resort which has excellent and growing winter sports facilities. In summer, there's swimming, tennis, horse riding.

Restaurants. Several in typical local style, with attractive decor, include *Şura Dacilor, Coliba Haiducilor* and *Vînătorul* (game specialties). *Capra Neagră* is a night bar.

Predeal. *Cioplea* (E), 162 rooms. *Orizont* (E), 157 rooms. *Bulevard* (M), 43 rooms. There is a wide choice of accommodations in all categories in this popular skiing resort and busy town.

Reşiţa. *Semenic* (lower M), 110 rooms. *Bistra* (M), 27 rooms.

Satu Mare. *Aurora* (M), 108 rooms. *Dacia* (lower M), 48 rooms.

Sibiu. *Continental* (E), 180 rooms. Modern, near old town. *Bulevard* (E), 129 rooms. Older, but comfortable, at entrance to old town. *Împăratul Romanilor* (E), 96 rooms. Attractively restored 18th-century building in heart of old town. *Pădurea Dumbrava* (lower M), 65 rooms, out of town in oak woods, near campsite.

Restaurants. *Butoiul de Aur* (Golden Barrel) (M), charming tavern in the old town. *Sibiul Vechi* (Old Sibiu) (M), tavern in the old town in Romanian folk style. *Bufnita* (M), tavern style in the old town. *Dunarea* (I), old town. *Unicum* (I), old town.

Sighişoara. *Steaua* (M), 54 rooms
Restaurant. *Vlad Dracul House,* in the citadel.

Timişoara. *Continental* (E), 160 rooms. Highrise hotel, short stroll from central Opera Square. *Timişoara* (E), 240 rooms. Very central. *Banatul* (M), 95 rooms.

Tourist Inn (M), motel, just over a mile on road to Bucharest. Good restaurant. *Nord* (I), 40 rooms. Near rail station.

At the spa of **Buzias** (30 km., 20 miles), several hotels include the *Timiş* and *Parc* (both M).

Restaurants. *Bastion* (E), in the old Turkish fortifications. Folk show. *Faleza Bega* (M), with terrace by the river. *Flora Terasa.* Cafe, pleasantly sited by the river.

MOLDAVIA

Mountains and Monasteries

Moldavia fills the northeastern corner of Romania, bounded by the Soviet Union to the north and east, rising into the Carpathians to the west and spreading southwards down the valleys of the Siret and its tributaries to merge into the Wallachian plains. It has many of the attributes of other parts of Romania, not least its fine mountain areas and its colorful peasant culture. But to these it can add the unique attraction of its painted monasteries, high on the list of the art treasures of Europe.

To reach it by road, you take one of Romania's main highways north through Buzău and Focșani (formerly on the Wallachian-Moldavian border) to Bacău. It is a tedious stretch of about 322 km. (200 miles) across the plains on which, in due season, you are likely to encounter vast armies of agricultural machinery moving from one district to another. As there is usually a lot of livestock and non-motorized traffic as well, you may need to drive with special care and patience. By the time you reach Bacău, the foothills of the Carpathians are gradually closing in to the west and you now have a choice of routes: the main highway continuing north to Suceava, and another road branching northwest up the Bistrița valley.

The Bistrița Valley

The upper reaches of the Bistrița form one of the lovely untouched regions of Romania and this route is highly recommended. First you come to the sizeable town of Piatra Neamț, a good place to pause and get your bearings. It has some Princely Court ruins from the time of Stephen the

435

Great, an Archeology Museum and the Museum of the Carpathians devoted to the natural history of the mountains. From here, carry on to Bicaz beyond which lies the great man-made Bicaz lake formed by the waters of the Bistriţa.

While you are in this area, you might consider a worthwhile detour if you have time. Southwest of Bicaz, a road brings you through the fabulous Bicaz gorges to the developing little mountain resort of Lacu Rosu. From here you could take a minor road northwards with Durău as your destination. This is another small mountain resort, with an attractive hotel as well as other accommodations, and a restored but interesting monastery almost next door (striking modern frescoes). Durău is overlooked by one of Romania's most distinctive mountains, Ceahlău. Like many, it was once considered holy and innumerable legends have been woven round its craggy presence. These holy mountains were traditionally the scene of annual celebrations when people flocked to the summit to greet the sun to the accompaniment of feasting, folkloric events and religious ceremonies. The practice still survives in several mountain areas, Ceahlău being the most celebrated on a Sunday in August.

Durău can more easily be reached by road from the northern end of Bicaz lake. It is northwest of the lake that the Bistriţa valley is at its best. It is a superb valley carved out through richly wooded mountains and peppered with farming and timber communities whose folk architecture and culture has, as yet, made few concessions to the jet age. Thatched or shingled roofs and color-washed facades, sometimes decorated with delicate floral motifs, reflect a quiet evolution that has grown out of generations of continuity. In the old days, the river was used for floating timber.

The road eventually brings you to the little town and spa of Vatra Dornei and a few miles beyond this it divides. To the left it pursues the Bistriţa still further before clambering up to the Prislop pass and on into Maramureş (see the chapter on Transylvania). To the right it brings you to Cîmpulung Moldovenesc, a center for the timber industry, nestling in the mountains. Here it is well worth seeking out the Museum of Wooden Spoons, the quite astonishing private collection of Ioan Ţugui containing 4,500 different spoons in 100 different kinds of wood from every corner of Romania and many parts of the world. Some are purely utilitarian, others are true works of art, and many combine both qualities. They range from historic spoons from the time of Maria Theresa to a modern contribution from New York inscribed "kissin' don't last, cookin' do!"

Cîmpulung Moldovensesc is on the threshold of painted monastery country centered on or near the Moldava valley. However, most visitors are likely to approach these from Suceava, so we will first turn our attention to this modern hub of Moldavia.

Suceava

The first impression of Suceava is of an extremely modern town, but you need only glance up at the high plateau to the east of it to realise its history goes back a long way. Up there are the substantial ruins of the Citadel, first mentioned in documents in 1388, subsequently strengthened, especially by Stephen the Great in the 15th century. In the following centuries, it suffered sieges by the Turks, featured in numerous battles and was occupied briefly by the Poles. At last, in 1675, the Turks ordered its destruction, a process further aided by an earthquake later in the 17th century. Today, it is a fine ruin offering panoramic views over the city.

Other points of interest in the town are the ruins of the Princely Court, the New St. George Church which is a monument to Moldavian art from the 16th century, other remnants from medieval times and several museums, of which the Regional Museum gives an excellent idea of court life in the times of Stephen the Great.

It was during his reign in particular that Moldavia prospered, both economically and culturally, despite constant battles with the Turks. Some of the superb monasteries and churches you are about to visit stand as witnesses to and evidence of his victories. Before you set off for these, though, you might go and see the fortified monastery of Dragomirna a few miles north of Suceava. Though it is not one of the painted monasteries, it is an interesting building from the early 17th century, with an ornate tower and curious interior columns. The museum of the monastery contains some exquisitely carved wooden crosses and some illuminated manuscripts.

The Painted Monasteries

All built in the 15th and 16th centuries and usually fortified, Moldavia's painted monasteries combine Byzantine and Gothic elements, but their unique and most characteristic feature are the frescoes which cover not only the interior but also the exterior walls, many of them of a vividness that is quite breathtaking. Of the 14 with external frescoes that still survive, we shall concentrate on five. There are plenty of organized excursions to these, but there is much to be said for an independent visit at a quiet time of day with leisure to stop and ponder.

If you have followed our route through to Cîmpulung Moldovenesc, you could quite easily take in three of the monasteries on the way to Suceava by taking a slightly devious route. Otherwise it is easy enough to visit one or more of them on a circular trip out of Suceava.

The first on the list is Moldoviţa, founded in this case not by Stephen the Great, but by his son Petru Rareş. The exterior frescoes on one side of the church have been destroyed by the passage of time but on the other they are in superb condition and repay careful examination—remembering that their original purpose was to bring the Bible alive to the illiterate populace who were not allowed, in any case, to go beyond the portico of the church. Most of their themes are common to several or all of the churches: scenes from the life of Christ, historic scenes such as the Siege of Constantinople, the Tree of Jesse with its branches entwined round an array of prophets, and a kind of portrait gallery of philosophers amongst which such familiar names as Aristotle and Socrates stand out (if you can decipher the Cyrillic alphabet!). The interior walls are divided into 365 squares, representing the days of the year, each depicting a saint or martyr from the Orthodox calendar. No one knows precisely the techniques of those anonymous painters of long ago, but the effect is quite startling with the rich deep blue of the background predominating against the soft purples, reds and yellows of the scenes imposed upon it.

Moldoviţa, now a convent, is still an active religious center. It also houses a museum whose exhibits include the chair of Petru Rareş, old manuscripts and icons, and remnants from an earlier 15th-century church destroyed by a landslide.

Voroneţ was founded by Stephen the Great in 1488, but the paintings date from the time of Petru Rareş and those inside the church include a portrait of Stephen himself, holding a model of the building. The outer frescoes feature a magnificent Last Judgment; note the hand protruding from the Throne of Justice, holding the scales with devils hanging on to one side and angels to the other. Against the background of an Eternal Fire there are gruesome portrayals of what can happen to sinners, while angels run their spears through vicious little black devils and the shrouded dead arise from their graves to be rescued by the angels, saints and bishops waiting by the Door of Paradise.

The monastery of Humor dates from 1530 and its church is one of the simplest in design. There is another fearsome Last Judgment scene (in the portico) and a stirring representation of the Siege of Constantinople on the south wall. The interior frescoes are well-preserved and there is also a finely carved iconostasis.

The furthest of the monasteries from Suceava, and only a few miles from the Soviet border, is Putna, another of the creations of Stephen the Great which is also his last resting place. It is revered for this reason especially, since it has no external frescoes and has suffered damage by fire, pillage and earthquake on several occasions, the present building being the result of extensive restoration in 1968.

Sucevița is the "newest" of our selection, built in the 1580s and painted in the first years of the 17th century; its defensive walls and towers are particularly well preserved. Today a convent, its frescoes include a massive composition of the Ladder of Heaven, each rung representing a mortal sin with winged devils waiting to snatch any luckless sinner who transgresses. Near Sucevița, the village of Marginea is worth visiting not only for its characteristically decorated wooden houses, but also for the black pottery produced here, achieved by smoking and polishing the pot before the clay hardens.

Last on our list is Arbor, similar in style to Humor and built by one of Stephen the Great's officers. The prevailing color here is green and the best known paintings, on the west wall, portray Genesis and scenes from the lives of saints.

Eastern Moldavia

Close to the eastern border with the Soviet Union is a town considered by some to be the most attractive in Romania: Iris Iași, the former capital of Moldavia. Its history has been turbulent from the plunderings of Tartar and Turk and attacks by the Poles to the ravages of fire and plague. But still much of great interest and beauty remains from the 15th to 19th centuries. One of the most beautiful buildings is the Trei Ierarhi Church (1639), its facade a veritable lacework of stone. Among many other churches and monasteries in the town is the Golia Monastery dating from the 17th century and surrounded by thick walls.

Iași got its start as an intellectual center in the 17th century when Prince Vasile Lupu founded the Vasilean School. Another Moldavian ruler, Dimitrie Cantemir, was a leading historian in his own right, and the town has produced Romania's national poet, Mihai Eminescu, as well as other literary greats. The Palace of Culture in attractive neo-Gothic style houses museums of history, art, science and ethnography. Among others are the Museum of Old Moldavian Literature and the Museum of Union (of Moldavia and Wallachia). A number of statues, from Stephen the Great to several literary figures, reflect Iași's glorious past as the political and cultural hub of Moldavia.

PRACTICAL INFORMATION FOR MOLDAVIA

TOURIST INFORMATION. Carpați or ONT have offices in most towns and resorts, as do the Romanian Automobile Club (ACR). In addition there are County Tourist Offices (OJT) as follows: **Bačau,** 14 N. Bălcescu; **Focşani,** 3 Inirii Sq.; **Iasi,** 12 Unirii St.; **Piatra Neamţ,** 38 Republicii St.; **Suceava,** N. Bălcescu St., Block 2A.

WHEN TO COME. Spring, summer and early fall are the best times for touring the mountain areas and visiting the magnificent monasteries.

GETTING AROUND MOLDAVIA. There are many organized tours from Bucharest or the Black Sea to the famous painted monasteries of Moldavia. Otherwise traveling by car gives the greatest freedom and possibilities to explore little known valleys not easily accessible by public transport. Peasant culture is still very much alive in some of these remoter valleys.

Hotels and Restaurants

All hotels listed below have restaurants unless otherwise stated. Note the comments regarding standards under *Facts at Your Fingertips.*

Cîmpulung-Moldovenesc. *Zimbrul* (M), 90 rooms; modern.

Durău. *Durău* (M). Modern attractive building in beautiful mountain setting, in interesting and unspoilt area.

Iaşi. *Traian* (M), 137 rooms. *Unirea* (M), 183 rooms.

Piatra Neamţ *Ceahlău* (E), 146 rooms. *Central* (E), 132 rooms.
Restaurant. *Colibele Haiducilor,* in typical Romanian style.

Suceava. *Arcaşul* (E), 100 rooms. *Bucovina* (E), 130 rooms. *Central* (M), 89 rooms.

THE DANUBE DELTA AND
THE BLACK SEA COAST

Sun and Sand—and a Watery Wilderness

The Dobrudja region of eastern Romania contains the historic port of
Constanţa, the Romanian Riviera pleasure coast, the celebrated Murfatlar
vineyards, fine Roman (and earlier) remains and the Danube Delta, one
of Europe's leading wildlife sanctuaries. From any of the coastal resorts
you can easily make excursions to all of these places, but do allow enough
time to do them full justice.

One of the newest man-made additions to the map is in this area: the
Danube–Black Sea Canal, linking Cernavodă (on the Danube) with the
busy Black Sea port of Constanţa. The canal, 64 km. (40 miles) long, has
actually shortened the route along the Danube to the Black Sea by nearly
400 km. (250 miles). As a result, the delta no longer features in many Danube cruises.

A Natural Paradise

Even faced with its impressive vital statistics, it is difficult to imagine
the vastness of the Danube Delta: 4,340 sq. km. (1,676 sq. miles) of watery
wilderness sprawling from the Soviet border to a series of lakes north of
the popular Black Sea resorts. As it approaches the delta area, the great
Danube river divides into three. The northernmost branch forms the border with the Soviet Union, the middle arm (to a large extent canalized)

leads to the busy port of Sulina, and the southernmost arm meanders with a marvelous lack of urgency to the little port of Sfîntu Gheorghe. Between these three main arms lie huge tracts of marshes, reed beds and smaller pockets of lush forest, laced with lakes and labyrinthine minor waterways in which the uninitiated could lose themselves for weeks.

The central Sulina channel is the main shipping lane for the ocean-going vessels, passenger ships and smaller craft; the latter two also ply the waters of the southern Sfîntu Gheorghe channel. Ocean-going vessels can go as far upstream as Brăila, but the main town of the Delta is Tulcea, a busy river port from which you can take a passenger boat or hydrofoil to the Black Sea and back, or join one of many excursions into remoter parts of the Delta. The sight of the big ships manoeuvring the twists in the river at Tulcea is fascinating. Here, too, is the excellent Danube Delta Museum which provides a very good introduction to the flora, fauna and way of life of the communities in this remote corner of Europe.

Many of the inhabitants of the area are Ukrainians, but there are also descendants of a Russian religious minority known as Lipovans who came here long ago to escape religious persecution in Russia. Fishing, of course, is a major occupation and it is quite common to see a long line of fishing boats strung together being towed out to their fishing grounds in some remoter part of the Delta by motor boat which will come and pick them up again at the end of the day. In several of the smaller communities, these same fishing boats can be hired by visitors to take them out on excursions—by far the best way of experiencing the region. Independenţa, formerly Murighiol, which has a big campsite, is a particularly popular center for tourists since, unlike many others, it is accessible by road. Crişan, on the Sulina channel, is another main tourist center. A certain amount of livestock is also reared in the Delta, and the reeds are harvested for cellulose, roofing and a variety of other purposes.

But the great attraction of this watery wilderness is the incredible bird life. There are over 300 species here, including several colonies of pelican and spectacular numbers of herons, egrets, glossy ibis and many kinds of wader. Mammals include wild cat, wild boar and deer, and marine life ranges from caviar-bearing sturgeon, sheatfish and catfish to the more plebian perch and carp, most of them adding to the variety of the Delta's gastronomy.

Ancient Histria

From Tulcea there are good roads to the Black Sea resorts, taking you first through the strange, eroded Macin hills to Babadag. Further south, make a point of visiting Histria, an impressive archeological site founded by Greek colonists in the 6th century B.C. Its name derives from *Istros,* the Greek word for the Danube, for these ancients thought they had reached one of the mouths of that great river. In fact, Histria was originally situated on a sea bay, long since closed off from the open sea by the huge quantities of silt carried down by the Danube to the north.

Histria remained occupied right up to the 6th century A.D., the Greeks being followed by the Romans and Byzantines. Over the centuries, it underwent many changes in size, character and importance, and suffered frequently from attacks by sundry barbarians. There are defensive walls that survive to this day, that were built by the Romans in frenzied haste using any available materials, including inscribed blocks, pillars, carved friezes and capitals from earlier times. Lack of fresh water was another disadvantage overcome in Roman times by the construction of huge pipe lines to bring water from the hills 15 km. (nine miles) and more away; sections of them are also still visible.

The site is much more extensive than it first appears, with substantial traces of all that went to make a thriving settlement in those ancient times: temples, early Christian churches, baths, residential, commercial and industrial districts, the latter producing coins, weapons and agricultural machinery. Such a jumble of successive cultures is not easy for the average visitor to sort out, but there is an excellent English-language booklet available on the spot, and the ancient stones have their own message for those content to wander among them in the sun-baked quiet, with only the innumerable birds and snakes (all harmless!) for company.

Mamaia

Histria is a popular excursion point from the Black Sea resorts, nearest and largest of which is Mamaia, only 60 km. (37 miles) away, mainly across marshes alive with birds. In addition to its varied amenities, Mamaia has the advantage of proximity to the archeological treasures of Constanţa, Romania's great port, only a few miles to the south.

The resort itself is seven km. (four miles) long, straggling along a narrow strip of land with the Black Sea and its fine beaches on one side, and the fresh waters of Mamaia lake on the other. A trolley bus service plies the full length of the resort whose facilities range from modern high rise blocks to neat villas, from garden restaurants to nightclubs and discos, and from campsites to shopping centers and beer halls.

The most recent hotels are at the northern end of the resort, and even further north major camping grounds are being developed. Mamaia and other Black Sea resorts are placing increasing emphasis on improving the quality of service and widening the range of sports, entertainment (for all ages) and excursion facilities. Wine and folklore are favorite themes. Cruises take you down the coast to Mangalia, or along Romania's newest waterway, the canal now linking the Danube with the Black Sea near Constanţa. Sea fishing trips include all the necessary equipment, but you'll need to be an early riser. Much longer excursions are also available, among others to the Danube delta, Bucharest or Bucovina's painted monasteries. For the youngsters special programs of events are planned from puppet shows to discos, and child-minding facilities are increasing.

Though you could hardly call Mamaia typically Romanian, any more than you could any of the other beach resorts, it is a completely self-contained community offering all that's necessary for a seaside holiday. And then, of course, there are the region's fabulous archeological and art treasures.

Constanţa

From Mamaia it's only a short trolley ride into Constanţa, Romania's second-largest city as well as one of its most ancient. If you like rummaging about in the distant past, you'll be in your element here, for traces of Constanţa's long history are scattered all over the city. It has, too, that polyglot flavor so characteristic of port communities.

Founded by the Greeks in the 6th century B.C., Constanţa was known as Tomis until the 4th century A.D., when it was renamed in honor of Constantine the Great. Ovid, the Roman poet, lived here in exile from A.D. 8 until his death nine years later and spent much of his time writing letters of complaint back to Rome for which he was passionately homesick. However, although he was apparently oblivious to the region's charms, the city has named a square after him, erecting in the middle of it a statue to his memory. The statue (1887) is the work of Etorre Ferrari, incidentally, the sculptor who also created Lincoln's statue in New York. Behind it, in what was formerly the Town Hall, is the really splendid National History and Archeological Museum, one of the top museums of Europe. Exhibits range from neolithic right up to modern times, but the most outstanding are from Greek, Geto-Dacian, Roman and Daco-Roman cultures. If you have time for nothing else, don't miss the Treasury whose unique exhibits include some stunning Greek statuettes from the 2nd and 4th centuries B.C., the Glykon serpent (antelope's head, serpent's body, lion's tail and some human elements) and the Goddess of Fortune, protector of the city of Tomis, both from the 2nd to the 3rd centuries A.D. Some of the treasures were found in the course of building new blocks of apartments in the area—just where they had been hidden to conceal them from the barbarians so many centuries ago. Two other items not to be missed among the neolithic finds are the exquisite statuettes of *The Thinker* and *Seated Woman* from the Hamangia culture of 4,000 to 3,000 B.C.

Near the museum is another of Constanţa's major sights: a Roman complex of warehouses and shops from the 4th century A.D., incorporating a magnificent mosaic floor over 2,000 meters square. Not far from this complex are remains of Roman Thermae from the same period. Yet another archeological site is the Open-air Archeological Museum by the new Town Hall right in the town center, and there are several other foundations or remnants of ancient buildings or walls in other parts of the city. From Turkish times there is the Mahmudiye Mosque and, close to it, the relatively modern Orthodox Cathedral.

And there is still plenty more to see: a fine aquarium on the sea wall opposite the Casino restaurant, the dolphinarium with displays by trained dolphins, a naval museum and several folk art and art exhibitions.

The Mythology Belt

South of Constanţa is a string of seaside resorts which, between them, attract a very high proportion of Romania's visitors from both east and west. Excursion programs will be similar to those referred to under Mamaia. Most of the resorts have the sandy Black Sea shore on one side and easy access to one of a string of freshwater lakes on the other. The lakes—especially that of Techirghiol—are known for their healthgiving sapropel mud, highly recommended for rheumatic ailments. A number of centers offer thermal establishments and full treatment facilities. Best-equipped is Eforie Nord which has an up-to-date treatment center dispensing a wide range of therapy to sufferers. This is the northernmost of the resorts only a short distance from Eforie Sud on the shores of lake Techirghiol. To the south of this are a series of new resorts begun in the 1960s, all bearing names echoing the coast's Graeco-Roman past: Neptun, Jupiter, Venus, Saturn. They are not so much towns as tourist complexes consisting of modern hotels, villas, camp sites, shopping centers, restaurants and various sports facilities and all set in pleasant gardens. Again, they are hardly typically Romanian, but they do offer good amenities for a relaxed holiday by the sea.

The southernmost resort is the old port of Mangalia, formerly the Greek city of Callatis as evidenced by its Archeological Museum and Graeco-Roman remains. Most of Callatis now lies under the sea, but a hefty chunk of its walls can still be seen and, near by, the remains of a Roman villa.

Inland Excursions

A popular excursion from any of the resorts is to the famous Murfatlar vineyards. There's usually plenty of opportunity to sample the products, too!

On the same or different occasion, you can continue further west to a village called Adamclisi, near which is one of Romania's most famous Roman monuments. This is Tropaeum Traiani, a massive circular triumphal monument, 31 meters (102 ft.) in diameter, 40 meters (131 ft.) high and built in A.D. 109 to celebrate Emperor Trajan's victory over the Dacians. Not only did it depict scenes of the battle, but recorded the names and origins of the 4,000 soldiers who died in it, thus providing an invaluable historical record. Over the centuries of invasions and neglect it fell into considerable disrepair, but in 1977 the most recent reconstruction took place and today the monument soars again out of the landscapes of Dobrudja. Though the present structure is modern, it follows as closely as possible the design of the original as far as it is known. The actual original pieces of carved stonework are kept in a special museum in Adamclisi itself. Traces of the Roman town of Tropaeum Trajani can also be seen only about a mile away.

PRACTICAL INFORMATION FOR THE COAST

TOURIST INFORMATION. The main body dealing with all tourist aspects of the coast is the Litoral National Tourist Office whose head office is Hotel Bucharest, **Mamaia** (branches in Constanța and most resorts). In addition there is a County Tourist Office (OJT) at 2 Garii-Faleza St., **Tulcea.**

WHEN TO COME. Though a handful of hotels stay open in winter and spa treatment is available year-round, the Black Sea resorts don't begin to come alive until the middle or end of May. By high summer, they are packed with people and buzzing with activity. The wild life that haunts the watery wilderness of the Danube Delta is best seen during spring and early fall (the times of the migrations); you'll be spared the worst of the mosquitoes then too!

GETTING AROUND THE COAST. The Litoral National Tourist Office arranges a variety of sightseeing tours of the region; also a number of packages further afield to other parts of the Balkans, Italy, Turkey and so on. There are air links between Bucharest and Constanța and Tulcea; rail and bus connections complete the network. Otherwise traveling by car gives the greatest freedom. Car hire can be prebooked or arranged on the spot. Regular passenger boats ply the central and southern arms of the Danube through the Delta and there are plenty of sightseeing boats as well. Tulcea is the main center, but fishermen will take you out from a number of small communities scattered about this vast watery labyrinth.

HOTELS AND RESTAURANTS. Below is a selection from the vast number available. All have restaurants, and most have access to a swimming pool as indicated. In some cases this facility will be shared with neighboring establishments. The frenzy of hotel building has eased off recently, and attention is being concentrated on the renovation of older hotels and the provision of greater camping, villa, sports and entertainment facilities. Note the comments regarding standards under *Facts at Your Fingertips.*

Constanța. *Palace* (E), 132 rooms. Recently renovated, near the city's historic center with terrace overlooking the sea and tourist port of Tomis. *Continental* (M), 140 rooms. Older, near open-air archeological museum in city center.

Restaurants. *Casino* (M), newly restored in ornate 20th-century style with night bar by the sea. *Casa cu Lei* (M), with rooms in Romanian, Spanish and Venetian style.

Eforie Nord. *Europa* (E), 242 rooms. High-rise building in small park near sea. There are hotels of all categories, but most of the buildings immediately overlooking the beach are villas. The *Delfin, Meduza* and *Steaua de Mare* (all (M), each with 218 rooms and indoor pool), are linked to the excellent facilities of the treatment center of this important spa for rheumatic complaints, but these hotels are also available to holidaymakers.

Restaurants. *Berbec,* folk music, cozy atmosphere. *Nunta Zamifirei,* on the outskirts. Folk architecture and decor, with Romanian specialties and folk shows. *Acapulco,* nightclub on the sea wall.

Eforie Sud. The resort is scattered along a narrow strip of land between the Black Sea and Lake Techirghiol with its health-giving mud. The *Capitol, Excelsior* and *Gloria* (all M), have about 130 rooms each and share outdoor pools. They stand in a row at the north end of the resort, close to the sea. *Flamingo* (M), 200 rooms, is a short stroll inland, also with open-air pool. *Mǎgura* (M–I), 240 rooms, is near the resort center.

Restaurants. *Haiduc Han,* bar with folk show. *Complex, Central* and *Vienez,* all with dancing. *Grota Nimfelor,* disco. On the sea wall.

Jupiter. *Capitol* (M), 220 rooms, open-air pool. By the sea. *Scoica* (M), 120 rooms, open-air pool. Elegant circular building, a short stroll from sea or lakes. *Cozia* (I), 200 rooms, open-air pool. By lake Jupiter. *Olimpic* (I), 220 rooms. Near the sea. *Tismana* (I), 260 rooms. Large complex near small lake Tisman. A little inland is the extensive holiday village *Zodiac* (M), in a natural park.

Restaurants. *Orizont,* garden restaurant with folk music in resort center. *Paradis,* nightclub, disco and swimming pool, attractively situated between the sea and small lake Tisman.

Mamaia. Largest of the resorts and has the most extensive facilities. In many cases, hotels have been built in small groups or complexes and, where this is applicable, have been listed together. *International* (E), 100 rooms, outdoor pool. One of the earliest and best, on the beach. *Ambassador* (M), *Lido* (M) and *Savoy* (M), are the newest trio, grouped in a horseshoe round open-air pools near the beach at the north end of the resort. Next to this complex and with a similar lay-out are the *Amiral* (M), 120 rooms, *Comandor* (M), 120 rooms and *Orfeu,* 100 rooms. *București* (M), 60 rooms, open-air pool, is in the resort center. *Dacia* (M), 370 rooms, near open-air pool, close to the beach at the resort's southern end. Nearby is high-rise *Parc* (M), 210 rooms, indoor pool. *Caraiman II* (I), 100 rooms, and *Caraiman I* (I), 200 rooms, have a disco and are placed near the Ambassador complex but on the shores of Mamaia lake.

Restaurants. *Insula Ovidiu,* rustic style on island on lake Mamaia. *Miorița,* Romanian food and attractive setting on lake shore. *Orient,* with nightclub, central. *Melody,* nightclub and music-hall, central. *Cherhana,* fish specialties served in Danube-delta style building on lake shore. *Satul de Vacanță* (Holiday Village). Attractive complex of traditional Romanian architecture from all over the country, featuring numerous small restaurants serving local specialties. At the south end of the resort on the shore of Tǎbǎcǎriei lake. *Vatra,* garden restaurant in resort center.

Mangalia. Romania's southernmost resort and spa. *Mangalia* (M), 290 rooms, indoor pool, disco, is the best. Situated near the museum and archeological remains.

Neptun. Many modern hotels, shops, restaurants, set in attractive gardens by Neptun Lakes. *Doina* (E), 330 rooms, pool, full balnealogical treatment facilities. Some distance from sea or lakes. *Neptun* (E), 126 rooms, pool, disco, excellent facilities. By one of the lakes, a short stroll from the beach. *Delta* (M), 94 rooms, *Dobrogea* (M), 110 rooms, and *Sulina* (M), 110 rooms, are grouped together near one of the lakes, each with indoor pool and disco. *Romanța* (M), 330 rooms.

In the adjoining resort of **Olimp,** the *Amfiteatru,* 330 rooms, *Belvedere,* 230 rooms, and *Panoramic,* 210 rooms, form an (E) complex with open-air pools and discos, terraced above the beach. *Oltenia* (M), 220 rooms, near open-air pool, is also well placed by the sea.

Restaurants. *Calul Bălan,* attractive setting in nearby Comorova forest at south end of resort; folk shows. *Crama Neptun,* next door, is in charming local style, also with folk show. *Insula,* on island in Neptun lake; fish specialties. *International,* with nightclub and beer house, in Olimp district.

Popasul Căprioarelor, garden restaurant, with folk show, in heart of Comorova forest, a little inland.

Saturn. High-rise blocks, interspersed with shopping complexes, restaurants and gardens. *Aida* (M), 328 rooms, near open-air pool and beach. *Cleopatra* (M), 328 rooms, open-air pool, near beach. *Hora* (M), 290 rooms, disco, near beach. *Sirena* (M), 290 rooms, disco, near open-air pool and beach. The *Alfa, Beta* and *Gama* form an (I) complex, each with 200 rooms, some distance from the sea.

Restaurants. *Dunărea* in open air. *Cleopatra Tavern,* music hall and folk show. *Pelican,* in unusual and attractive building serving fish and other Romanian specialties; folk music.

Tulcea. Main center of the Danube delta. *Delta* (M), 117 rooms; by the Danube. *Egreta* (M), 116 rooms.

At **Crişan,** on the Sulina channel east of Tulcea: *Lebăda* (M), 74 rooms. A good waterside base from which to explore the delta by fishing boat. Restaurant.

Venus. Modern hotels and resort facilities in gardens. *Cocurul* (M), 204 rooms, open-air pool, near small lake Venus, a short stroll from beach. *Raluca* (M), 132 rooms, attractively curved building, a short stroll from beach. *Silvia* (M), 128 rooms, open-air pool, close to sea. A neighboring trio of hotels *Carmen, Felicia* and *Lidia* (all M), each with 128 rooms, also border the sea.

To the north, the adjoining resort of Aurora rises in a series of pyramid-shaped hotels named after precious stone—such as *Agat, Coral, Cristal, Diamant, Granat, Safir*—each with 100–120 rooms, and with or near open-air pool, all close to the beach. All (M).

Restaurants. *Calipso* with music-hall show and beer house; near the sea. *Cătunul,* folk-style complex of restaurant, pastry shop and coffee house.

SPORTS. All the Black Sea resorts have facilities for tennis, mini golf, windsurfing, water skiing, boat and bicycle hire. There is a riding school at Mangalia.

TOURIST VOCABULARY

Of the five languages which appear in this book Romanian is the easiest for an English-speaking person to handle. Not that Romanian is all that easy a language, but since it is related to the Romance languages, Spanish or Italian, it is more immediately recognizable. It stems from the Latin spoken along the Danube by the Roman colonists and has survived countless conquests.

Here are a few pronunciation rules—"e" at the beginning of a word is pronounced "ye"; "e" and "i" before another vowel is "y", consonant; "i" at the beginning of a word "yi"; "i" at the end of a word "y" as in "yellow"; "o" and "u" before another vowel is "w"; consonants are much as English except that "c" is "k", except before "e" and "i" when it is "ch"; "che" and "chi" are "ke" and "ki"; "g" is hard, but pronounced as "j" before "e" and "i"; "j" is "zh" as in French; "ş" is "sh"; "ţ" is "ts"; stress is usually on the penultimate syllable, but on the last if the word ends in a consonant or a dipthong.

USEFUL EXPRESSIONS

Hello; how do you do	Bună ziua
Good morning	Bunădimineaţa
Good evening	Bună seara
Goodnight	Noapte bună
Goodbye	La revedere
Please	Vă rog
Thank you	Mulţumesc
Thank you very much	Vă mulţumesc foarte mult
Yes	Da
No	Nu
You're welcome	Cu plăcere
Excuse me	Scuzaţi-mă
Come in!	Intraţi
I'm sorry	Îmi pare rău
My name is	Mă numesc . . .
Do you speak English?	Vorbiţi engleză?
I don't speak Romanian	Nu vorbesc româneşte
I don't understand	Nu înţeleg
Please speak slowly	Vorbiţîrar, vă rog
Please write it down	Scrieţi, vă rog
Where is . . . ?	Unde este . . . ?
What is this (place) called?	Cum se numeşte acest (loc)?
Please show me	Indicaţi-mî-mî, vă rog
I would like . . .	Aş vrea. . .
How much does it cost?	Cît costă?

SIGNS

Entrance	Intrare
Exit	Ieşire
Emergency exit	Ieşire in caz de pericol
Toilet	Toaletă
men, gentlemen	domni, barbatî
women, ladies	doamne, femei
vacant	liber
occupied	ocupat
Hot	Cald

Cold	Rece
No smoking	Fumatul Oprit
No admittance	Intrarea Oprită
Stop	Stop
Danger	Pericol
Open	Deschis [deskis]
Closed	Inchis
Full, no vacancy	Complet
Information	Informații
Bus stop	Stație de Autobus
Taxi stand	Stație de taxi
Pedestrians	Pietonî

ARRIVAL

Passport check	Controlul pașapoartelor
Your passport, please	Pașaportul, vă rog
I am with the group	Sînt cu grupa
Customs	Vama
Have you anything to declare?	Aveți ceva de declarat?
Nothing to declare	Nimic de declarat
Baggage claim	Primirea Bagajelor
A porter	Un hamal

Transportation

to the bus	La autobus
to a taxi	La un taxi
to the Hotel . . . please	La Hotelul . . . , vă rog

MONEY

Currency exchange office	Banca
Do you have the change for this?	Aveți mărunțiș?
May I pay	Pot plăti [plûti]
with a traveler's check?	cu un traveler's check?
with this credit card?	cu acest credit card?
I would like to exchange some	Aș vrea sa schimb niște traveler's
traveler's checks	checks
What is the exchange rate?	Care-i cursul?

THE HOTEL

A hotel	un hotel
I have a reservation	Am o cameră rezervată
I would like a room	Aș vrea o cameră
with a double bed	cu pat dublu
with a bath	și baie
with a shower	cu duș
with a private toilet	cu toaletă separată
without a bath	fără baie
What is the rate per day?	Cît costă pe zi?
Is breakfast included?	Este micul dejun inclus?
What floor is it on?	La ce etaj este?
ground floor	parter
second floor	etajul unu
Is there an elevator?	Are ascensor?
Have the baggage sent up, please	Vă rog să trimeteți bagajul sus
The key to number . . . please	Cheia camerei numărul . . . , vă rog
Please call me at seven o'clock	Sculați-mă la șapte, vă rog

Have the baggage brought down	Vă rog sa duceți bagajul jos
The bill	plata
A tip	bacşiş

THE RESTAURANT

A restaurant	Restaurantul
café	cafeneá
Waiter!	Ospătar!
Waitress!	Domnişoară!
Menu	Meniul, lista
I would like to order this	As vrea să comand acesta
Some more . . . please	Înca puţin . . . , vă rog
That's enough	Destul
The check, please	Plata, vă rog
Breakfast	micul dejun
Lunch	dejun, prînz
Dinner	masa de seară
Bread	pîine
Butter	unt
Jam	gem
Salt	sare
Pepper	piper
Mustard	muştar
Sauce, gravy	sos
Vinegar	oţet
Oil	untdelemn
The wine list	lista vinurilor
red wine	vin roşu
white wine	vin alb
rosé wine	vin roz
Bottle	o sticlă
A carafe	o garafă
A beer	o bere
Some water	nişte apă
A bottle of mineral water	o sticklă de apă minerală
carbonated	gazosă
non-carbonated	negazosă
Some ice	nişte gheaţă
Some milk	nişte lapte
Lemonade	limonată
Coffee (with milk)	cafeá (cu lapte)
Tea (with lemon)	ceai (cu lămîie) [chai cu lûmiye]
Chocolate	cacao
Juice	suc
Sugar	zahăr

MAIL

A letter	o scrisoare
An envelope	un plic
A postcard	o carte poştală
A mailbox	o cutie de scrisori
The post-office	poşta
A stamp	un timbru
Airmail	un avion
How much does it cost to send a letter (a postcard) air mail to the United States (Great	Cît costă o scrisoare (o carte poştală) cu avionul în Statele Unite? (Marea Britanie,

Britain, Canada)?   Canada)?
to send a telegram, cable?   a trimite o telegrammă?

LOCATIONS

. . . Street	strada . . .
. . . Avenue	calea . . .
. . . Square	piaţa . . .
The airport	aeroportul
A bank	o bancă
The beach	plaja
The bridge	podul
The castle	castelul
The cathedral	catedrala
The church	biséri
The garden	grădina
The hospital	spitalul
The movies, cinema	cinema
a movie	un film
The museum	muzéul
A nightclub	un bar
The palace	palatul
The park	parcul
The post-office	posta
The station	gara
The theater	teatrul
a play	o piesă
The travel bureau	Oficiul National de Turism ONT [oneté]
The university	universitatea

TRAVEL

Arrival	Sosire
Departure	Plecare

The airplane — Avionul

I want to reconfirm a reservation on flight number . . . for . . .	Aş vrea să reconfirm o reservă, zborul numărul . . . spre . . .
Where is the check-in?	Unde se face controlul?
I am checking in for . . .	Plec la . . .
Fasten your seat belt	Puneţi centura de siguranţă

The railroad — Calea ferată

The train	trenul
From what track does the train to . . . leave?	De la ce peron pleaca trenul spre . . . ?
Which way is the dining car?	Pe unde este vagonul restaurant?

Bus, streetcar, subway — Autobus, tramvai, metro

Does this bus go to . . . ?	Acest autobus merge la . . . ?
trolley bus	troleibuz
I want to get off at . . . Street at the next stop	Doresc să cobor la . . . strada la staţia următoare

Taxi — Un taxi

I (we) would like to go to . . . please	Aş vrea să merg (Am vrea să mergem) la . . . vă rog
Stop at . . .	Opriţi la . . .

Stop here
Opriți aíci

NUMBERS

1 unu, una		20 douăzeci	
2 doi, două		25 douăzecisicinci	
3 trei		30 treizeci	
4 patru		40 patruzeci	
5 cinci		50 cincizeci	
6 șase		60 șasezeci	
7 șapte		70 șaptezeci	
8 opt		80 optzeci	
9 nouă		90 nouăzeci	
10 zece		100 o sută	
11 unsprezece		200 două sute	
12 doisprezece		300 trei sute	
13 treisprezece		400 patru sute	
14 paisprezece		500 cinci sute	
15 cincisprezece		600 șase sute	
16 șaisprezece		700 șapte sute	
17 șaptesprezece		800 opt sute	
18 optsprezece		900 nouă sute	
19 nouăsprezece		1,000 o mie	

DAYS OF THE WEEK

Sunday   duminică
Monday   luni
Tuesday   martî
Wednesday   mercurî
Thursday   joi
Friday   vinerî
Saturday   sîmbătă

Index

In this index **E** indicates Entertainment (theatre, opera, ballet & concerts), **H** indicates Hotels & other accommodations, **M** indicates Museums and art galleries, **R** indicates Restaurants

GENERAL INFORMATION

BULGARIA

CZECHOSLOVAKIA

EAST GERMANY

Practical Information

HUNGARY

POLAND

ROMANIA

Practical Information

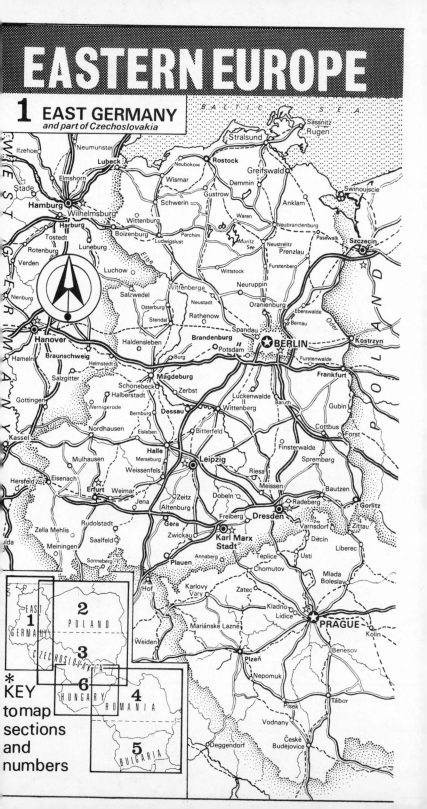

EASTERN EUROPE

1 EAST GERMANY
and part of Czechoslovakia

*KEY to map sections and numbers

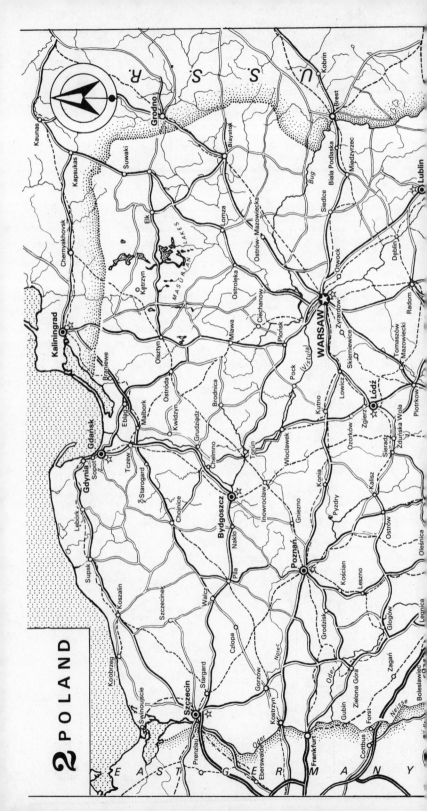

2 POLAND

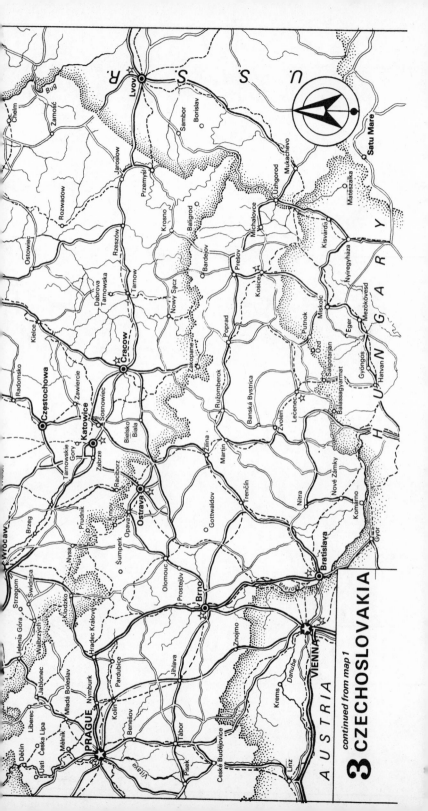

3 CZECHOSLOVAKIA

continued from map 1

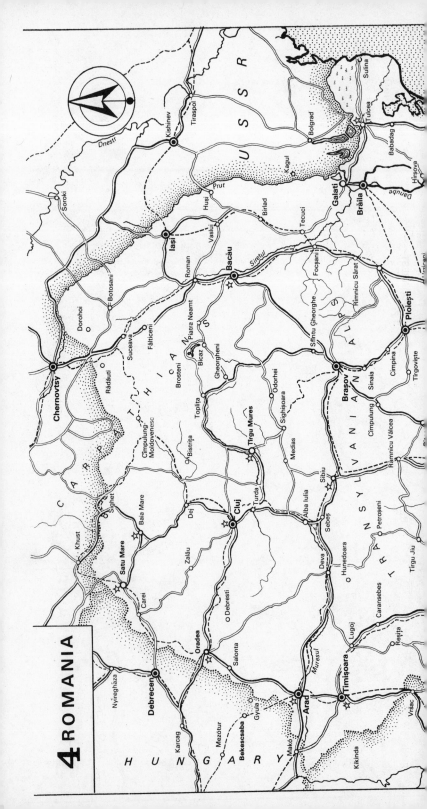

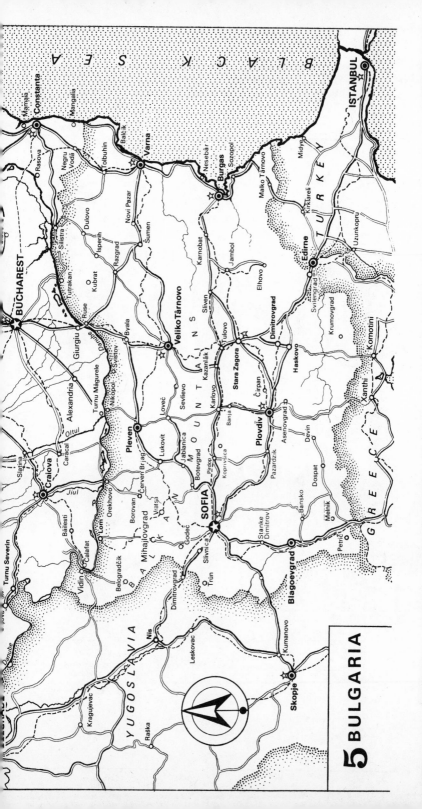

5 BULGARIA

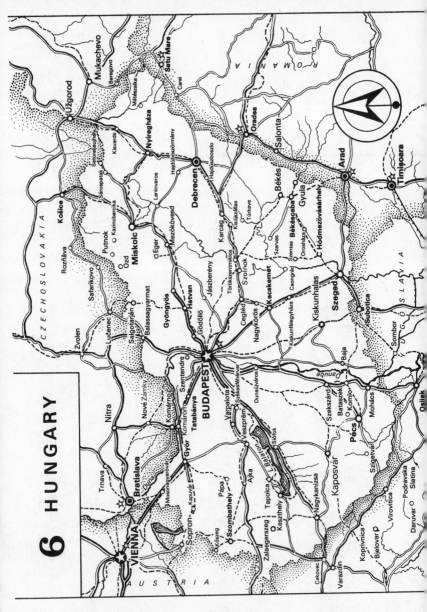

6 HUNGARY

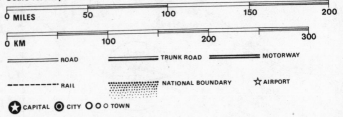

✱ *Scale for Maps 1 to 6.*

| 0 MILES | 50 | 100 | 150 | 200 |

| 0 KM | 100 | 200 | 300 |

═══════ ROAD   ═══════ TRUNK ROAD ═══════   ═══════ MOTORWAY

----------- RAIL   ⬚⬚⬚⬚ NATIONAL BOUNDARY   ☆ AIRPORT

⭐ CAPITAL   ◉ CITY   O◉O○ TOWN

Fodor's Travel Guides

U.S. Guides

Alaska
American Cities
The American South
Arizona
Atlantic City & the
  New Jersey Shore
Boston
California
Cape Cod
Carolinas & the
  Georgia Coast
Chesapeake
Chicago
Colorado
Dallas & Fort Worth
Disney World & the
  Orlando Area

The Far West
Florida
Greater Miami,
  Fort Lauderdale,
  Palm Beach
Hawaii
Hawaii (Great Travel
  Values)
Houston & Galveston
I-10: California to
  Florida
I-55: Chicago to New
  Orleans
I-75: Michigan to
  Florida
I-80: San Francisco to
  New York

I-95: Maine to Miami
Las Vegas
Los Angeles, Orange
  County, Palm Springs
Maui
New England
New Mexico
New Orleans
New Orleans (Pocket
  Guide)
New York City
New York City (Pocket
  Guide)
New York State
Pacific North Coast
Philadelphia
Puerto Rico (Fun in)

Rockies
San Diego
San Francisco
San Francisco (Pocket
  Guide)
Texas
United States of
  America
Virgin Islands
  (U.S. & British)
Virginia
Waikiki
Washington, DC
Williamsburg,
  Jamestown &
  Yorktown

Foreign Guides

Acapulco
Amsterdam
Australia, New Zealand
  & the South Pacific
Austria
The Bahamas
The Bahamas (Pocket
  Guide)
Barbados (Fun in)
Beijing, Guangzhou &
  Shanghai
Belgium & Luxembourg
Bermuda
Brazil
Britain (Great Travel
  Values)
Canada
Canada (Great Travel
  Values)
Canada's Maritime
  Provinces
Cancún, Cozumel,
  Mérida, The
  Yucatán
Caribbean
Caribbean (Great
  Travel Values)

Central America
Copenhagen,
  Stockholm, Oslo,
  Helsinki, Reykjavik
Eastern Europe
Egypt
Europe
Europe (Budget)
Florence & Venice
France
France (Great Travel
  Values)
Germany
Germany (Great Travel
  Values)
Great Britain
Greece
Holland
Hong Kong & Macau
Hungary
India
Ireland
Israel
Italy
Italy (Great Travel
  Values)
Jamaica (Fun in)

Japan
Japan (Great Travel
  Values)
Jordan & the Holy Land
Kenya
Korea
Lisbon
Loire Valley
London
London (Pocket Guide)
London (Great Travel
  Values)
Madrid
Mexico
Mexico (Great Travel
  Values)
Mexico City & Acapulco
Mexico's Baja & Puerto
  Vallarta, Mazatlán,
  Manzanillo, Copper
  Canyon
Montreal
Munich
New Zealand
North Africa
Paris
Paris (Pocket Guide)

People's Republic of
  China
Portugal
Province of Quebec
Rio de Janeiro
The Riviera (Fun on)
Rome
St. Martin/St. Maarten
Scandinavia
Scotland
Singapore
South America
South Pacific
Southeast Asia
Soviet Union
Spain
Spain (Great Travel
  Values)
Sweden
Switzerland
Sydney
Tokyo
Toronto
Turkey
Vienna
Yugoslavia

Special-Interest Guides

Bed & Breakfast
  Guide: North America
1936...On the
  Continent

Royalty Watching
Selected Hotels of
  Europe

Selected Resorts
  and Hotels of the U.S.
Ski Resorts of North
  America

Views to Dine by
  around the World